The History of Ideas and Doctrines of Canon Law in the Middle Ages

Stephan Kuttner

The History of Ideas and Doctrines of Canon Law in the Middle Ages

VARIORUM REPRINTS

London 1980

British Library CIP data   Kuttner, Stephan
                             The history of ideas and doctrines of canon
                             law in the Middle Ages. — (Collected studies
                             series; CS113).
                             1. Canon law — History   2. Europe — Church
                             history
                             I. Title   II. Series
                             262.9′094   BV760.2

                             ISBN 0-86078-058-9

Copyright © 1980   Variorum Reprints

Published in Great Britain by   Variorum Reprints
                                  20 Pembridge Mews London W11 3EQ

Printed in Great Britain by   Galliard (Printers) Ltd
                                  Great Yarmouth Norfolk

                                  VARIORUM REPRINT CS113

TABLE OF CONTENTS

This volume contains a total of 394 pages

PREFACE

The essays assembled in this volume were originally published over a span of forty years, between 1936 and 1976. Much of what I had set out to discuss when I first wrote them is concerned with problems of jurisprudence and history that do not cease to be problems by being written up and thus, in a way, have always been with me. I therefore gladly accepted the suggestion of the publishers of VARIORUM to depart from the chronological sequence of these studies. They are reproduced here in a loosely topical arrangement that proceeds from fundamental notions concerning canon law, its making and interpretation, to particular doctrines; to the interplay in canonical institutions of reality and semantics; to the tracing of specific conceits.

I wish to express my sincere thanks for permission to republish these essays to the editors of *Studi Gregoriani* and *Studia Gratiana,* of *Analecta Cracoviensia* and the *Medieval Studies presented to Aubrey Gwynn;* and to the managers of the St. Vincent Archabbey Press (Latrobe, Pennsylvania), Fordham University Press (New York), Éditions Sirey (Paris), The Catholic University of America Press (Washington D.C.), and Cambridge University Press.

I should not have been able to provide VARIORUM with the copy for this volume without the generous help of my friend Professor Stanley Chodorow, University of California, San Diego, who directed and supervised the resetting by computer of 'Harmony from Dissonance' (No. I of this volume), a process made necessary by the unusual format of the original edition; nor without the generous help of Mr. Steven Horwitz, M.Ph., of the Institute of Medieval Canon Law, and my granddaughter Ann Kuttner, B.A., who took it upon themselves to compile the index and to program the typesetting by computer, at Berkeley, of both the index and the new material after the last of the articles. Here, once more, Prof. Chodorow lent valuable assistance.

Finally, I am most grateful to Mrs. Eileen Turner of VARIORUM not only for her offer to republish these essays, but especially for her patience in letting me write the additions and corrections that appear at the end of the volume. In going over my original papers again, collecting and sifting the notes I have over the years jotted down in the margins or on slips between the pages of my personal copies, I am following in the footsteps of an incomparably greater scholar, from whom I shall borrow the title of these reconsiderations and whom I want to quote in conclusion:

> 'In multis enim offendimus omnes. Si quis in uerbo non offendit, hic perfectus est uir' (Jac. 3.2). Ego mihi hanc perfectionem nec nunc arrogo cum iam sim senex: quanto minus cum iuuenis coepi scribere...(S. Aurelii Augustini *Retractationum libri duo*, Prologus).

University of California,
Berkeley,
November 1979

STEPHAN KUTTNER

I

Harmony from Dissonance

An Interpretation of Medieval Canon Law

I

Nearly eight hundred years ago, a cleric returned from Bologna, where he had spent several years at the feet of the masters, to his native Orléans, and there he set out to write a treatise by which he intended to introduce the new learning in canon law he had acquired beyond the Alps to his fellow countrymen of France. He was Stephen, an Augustinian Canon of the house of St. Eveurt in Orléans, better known as Stephen of Tournai, from the name of the see he was to occupy in the last twenty years of his life (†1203).[1] He began his treatise by comparing his task to that of a host who has invited two men of different tastes for dinner and feels embarrassed at the thought that either man may take offense at the dishes which the other would like. This, Stephen goes on to say, is my lot: I have invited a lawyer and a theologian to this intellectual banquet; now the lawyer will wrinkle his nose in disgust at the manner in which I am going to speak here of laws; the theologian will become impatient because of my way of treating Scripture and the Fathers. So Stephen begs his guests to bear with him for a while, for his task is really difficult.[2]

I have always felt great sympathy for the quandary of my venerable namesake of the 1160's. The canonist today finds himself in an even more difficult position if he tries to make the vital importance of his field understood by others. The future bishop of Tournai could address himself to an audience for which the unity and omnipresence of the ecclesiastical order was an experience of living reality, and for which consequently the universal significance of canon law, i.e., of the legal aspects of this order, needed no explanation. No matter how violent were the recurrent conflicts between Church and State in the Middle Ages, the medieval mind had no difficulty in seeing ecclesiastical and secular society as but two aspects of a higher unity: as two estates, each with its own order of jurisdiction, and yet fused to be one, in the one city whose king is Christ. But with the birth of the modern state and the breaking asunder of Christendom at the end of the Middle Ages, canon law ceased to be a universal bond of one Christian commonwealth. Step by step it lost its once imposing place in the universities; and an ever-growing legal monism, which conceives of all law only as a function of sovereign nations or states, left to canon law at best the modest place of a set of rules which is tolerated as the internal ordinance of one among several recognized religious bodies.

Catholics, to be sure, see it differently. They know that as a perfect society the Church must possess an autonomous legal structure, independent of the State. But the general devaluation of canon law in the modern world and its gradual divorce from all other legal learning and practice have left their mark on the

---

[1] J. Warichez, *Étienne de Tournai et son temps* (Tournai-Paris 1937).

[2] The text of the preface, beg. 'Si duos ad coenam conuiuas inuitaueris,' is found in *Die Summa des Stephanus Tornacensis über das Decretum Gratiani*, ed. J. F. von Schulte (Giessen 1891) p. 1.

Catholic mind as well. To many of us, clergy or lay, the law of the Church appears as no more than a sum of dry technical rules for ecclesiastical administrators and judges, the rubrics, as it were, of ecclesiastical routine or, even worse, a stifling instrument of regimentation. But in fact canon law is something much nobler and greater: it is a living force, giving form to the social body which is the Church; a rational order encompassing her sacramental and pastoral functions; an organized mode of thinking that teaches us the right reason of ecclesiastical life, from essential principles to practical particulars—in short, a universal system of jurisprudence, composed of divine and human elements, and of no lesser intellectual dignity than the speculative disciplines of theology and philosophy.[3] The fact that in its details canon law deals with contingencies and practical necessities rather than with timeless truths must not blind us to the grandeur of its purpose, which is the ordering of those contingencies in a coherent whole.

In the millenary historical development on which the present-day Code of Canon Law is founded, perhaps no period can bring us closer to an understanding of this great conception than the period stretching from the Gregorian reform of the eleventh century to the tragedy of the Great Schism at the end of the fourteenth. It was the age in which the Christian mind first became conscious of canon law as an all-embracing, rational principle of order in the Church which is neither a mere practical adjunct of theology nor a mere accumulation of enactments, precepts, and customs; the age which discovered the properties of juristic thought as a scientific discipline in its own right; the age, finally, which shaped this system of thought into a powerful, structural element of Christian society, firmly rooted in the teachings worked out by the masters in the schools and in the rulings handed down by the Supreme Pontiffs in their responses, decisions, and legislative decrees.

It was during this age that the law of the Church became stabilized in the set of books which eventually were to be known as the *Corpus iuris canonici*[4] and as such for centuries remained the foundation of ecclesiastical jurisprudence, through all the changes, reforms and modern developments in legislation and interpretation; a set of books that gradually became obsolete in part and was superseded by countless amendments, overgrown as it were by a maze of new law, yet was never abolished until our own century, when the new Code of Canon Law drafted at the bidding of St. Pius X and promulgated by Benedict XV in 1917 fused into a modern, concise form all that was still living of the old law and brought it into line with the needs of the Church in the present age.[5] At a superficial glance, the slender volume which is the Code does not seem to have much in common with the big tomes of the old *Corpus*, but the historically-minded student will not be

---

[3] The fundamental importance of canon law for the entire life of the Church and Christian society is one of the main themes of the stimulating book by G. Le Bras, *Prolégomènes* (Histoire du droit et des institutions de l'Église en occident 1; Paris 1955).

[4] *Corpus iuris canonici* ed. A. Friedberg (2 vols.; Leipzig 1879-81). The official Roman edition was first printed in 1582. It is now generally agreed that a new critical text is desirable, to replace Friedberg's edition.

[5] *Codex iuris canonici Pii X Pont. Max. iussu digestus, Benedicti XV auctoritate promulgatus.* The date of promulgation is 28 June 1917. A collection of the historical material used by the papal commission in drafting the Code was published by P. Card. Gasparri and J. Card. Serédi, *Codicis iuris canonici fontes* (9 vols.; Rome 1923-39).

deceived: he will recognize how much of the substance of the old law is still alive here in modern garb.

II

To the historian the books of the *Corpus iuris canonici*, together with their interpretation by the great canonistic writers of the Middle Ages, are known as the classical law of the Church,[6] and we should never forget (although many modern canonists are apt to do so) that its riches of thought are as inexhaustible as are, in the fields of theology and philosophy, the classical books of the medieval school-men. The main parts of the *Corpus iuris canonici* are: (1) A collection of all the diversified authorities handed down from the first millennium of Church history—all these thousands of texts, the spurious together with the genuine, which were recompiled with the aid of a good many earlier collections about 1140 by a Camal-dolese monk at Bologna, Gratian, to whom posterity has rightly given the sobri-quet, 'Father of the Science of Canon Law,' and who inscribed his book with the title *Concordia discordantium canonum*, cited for short as the *Decreta*, or the *Decretum Gratiani*; (2) The *Decretals* of Pope Gregory IX, promulgated in 1234 as an official, authoritative collection chiefly of the rulings issued by the popes of the century since Gratian's book, upon appeals by litigants, upon consultation by bishops, or as general constitutions in councils; (3) Supplementary enactments by later Popes, especially the *Liber Sextus* promulgated by Boniface VIII in 1298, the *Constitutiones Clementinae* of Pope Clement V promulgated after his death, in 1317, and several other supplements known as *Extravagantes*.

It will be obvious that the first of these books, the one that preceded all the papal collections, has suggested to me the title of this lecture. *Concordia discordan-tium canonum* may indeed be considered a motto which sums up the signal achieve-ment of the medieval mind in organizing the law of the Church into a harmonious system out of an infinite variety of diverse, even contradictory, elements. The title was chosen by Gratian to indicate that his book was meant to be more than a con-ventional collection of *canones*: a treatise which was to make 'concord' from what

---

[6] A detailed account on the parts of the *Corpus iur. can.* and the historical problems con-nected with each of them, with references to the vast modern bibliography, is conveniently found in A. Van Hove, *Prolegomena* (Commentarium Lovaniense in Codicem iuris canonici I 1; 2nd ed. Malines-Rome 1945) 337-69; A. M. Stickler, *Historia iuris canonici latini* I (Turin 1950) 197-276. Van Hove, *op. cit.* 423-528, is also a good bibliographical guide to the history of canonistic writers of the classical age. The only detailed major treatise on the writers of this period is in vols. 1-2 of J. F. von Schulte's monumental but antiquated *Geschichte der Quellen und Literatur des canonischen Rechts von Gratian bis auf die Gegenwart* (3 vols.; Stuttgart 1875-80), superseded in its first part—Gratian to Gregory IX—by the present writer's *Repertorium der Kanonistik (1140-1234)* (Studi e testi 71; Città del Vaticano 1937). We lack a comparable *Repertorium* for the time after Gregory IX. Many specialized articles and monographs on the sources and the science of the classical canon law have appeared since 1945 (and some earlier ones were inaccessible to Van Hove). The Gratian Congress at Bologna, 1952, stimulated a new collection of papers, *Studia Gratiana* ed. J. Forchielli and A. M. Stickler (5 vols.; Bologna 1953-58). The Institute of Research and Study in Medieval Canon Law, Washington, D. C., publishes an annual bibliography in its *Bulletin*, cf. *Traditio* 12 (1956) 616-20 and subsequent volumes.

presented itself as 'discordant.' Intended or not, Gratian's phrase makes us think of the realm of music; and in doing so it stands in a venerable Christian tradition.

Of course, *concordia* is etymologically derived from *cor, cordis*, 'the heart' and stands for 'an agreement of hearts, peace, order,' but the association with *chorda*, 'string,' leading to the idea of 'a harmony of strings,' gives the word 'a poetic ambivalence which allows for a kind of metaphysical punning';[7] indeed we find an interchangeable use of 'consonance' and *concordia* in the Vulgate, in St. Augustine, in Boethius, to name only a few.[8] If we consider the importance of musical theory for St. Augustine as a key to the understanding of the divine order of creation and salvation, it is surely no idle playing with words to point out these musical implications (should we say 'overtones'?) of Gratian's thought. We are, on the contrary, directly led to such an interpretation if we turn from Gratian to the work of one of his great predecessors. The *Panormia* (*c.* 1096) of Bishop Ivo of Chartres, one of the most influential and certainly the most widely diffused canonical collection of the generation before Gratian,[9] opens with a prologue which we find also frequently copied in the twelfth century as a separate treatise, under the title 'Of the consonance of the canons,' *De consonantia canonum*.[10]

Ivo's prologue was a milestone in the history of the art of interpretation, in that it transferred certain principles of biblical and rhetorical hermeneutics to the field of the sacred canons, enriching the traditional commonplaces with new ideas which were to prove of considerable consequence both in scholastic theology and the nascent canonical science of the twelfth century. But hermeneutics—the art of reconciliation of sacred authorities—and divine harmony are closely correlated; let us give ear once more to St. Augustine, who speaks thus of the Saints at the time of the resurrection of the flesh:[11]

> Then the Saints of God will have their differences fused as in one sound (sounding together: *consonantes*), not in dissonance; that is, in consent, not dissent; even as a sweet harmony (*concentus*) is made from sounds that are diverse but not adverse.

---

[7] L. Spitzer, 'Classical and Christian Ideas of World Harmony,' *Traditio* 2 (1944) 409-64; 3 (1945) 307-64: at 3.322.

[8] The Vulgate translates συμφωνεῖν by *concordare* in Act. 15.15; cf. Rufinus, who translates ἀσύμφωνος by *discordans* in Eusebius, *Historia ecclesiastica* 3.10.1 (Eusebius Werke II i, ed. Schwartz-Mommsen [Leipzig 1903] p. 223); St. Augustine, *De trinitate* 4.2.4, who uses as synonymous the words *congruentia, conuenientia, concinentia, consonantia* (Migne, PL 42.889); and Boethius, *De musica* 1.3: 'consonantia dissimilium inter se uocum in unum redacta concordia' (PL 3.1173 D)—all quoted by Spitzer, *op. cit.* 2.451, 435, 438.

[9] The chapter, 'Yves de Chartres,' in P. Fournier and G. Le Bras, *Histoire des collections canoniques en occident depuis les Fausses Décrétales jusqu'au au Décret de Gratien* (Paris 1931-32) II 55-114 is still the standard synthesis on Ivo the canonist. Bibliography on Ivo as statesman, bishop, and a leader of the cathedral school of Chartres is cited in Van Hove, *op. cit.* 331 n.3. See also J. Leclercq, *Yves de Chartres: Correspondance* (vol. 1-; Paris 1949-).

[10] Fournier-Le Bras II 108; J. de Ghellinck, *Le mouvement théologique du XIIe siècle* (2nd ed. Bruges-Bruxelles-Paris 1948) 478, 488; Stickler, *op. cit.* 186, 191.

[11] Aug. *Enarrationes in Psalmos* 150.4 § 7: '...ut diuersitate concordissima consonent, sicut ordinantur in organo. Habebunt etiam tunc sancti differentias suas consonantes, non dissonantes, idest consentientes, non dissentientes; sicut fit suauissimus concentus ex diuersis quidem, sed non inter se aduersis sonis' (PL 37.1964); quoted by Spitzer, *op. cit.* 2.443.

Here the whole vocabulary of music, hermeneutics, and eschatological vision has indeed become interchangeable: *differentiae consonantes non dissonantes; consentientes non dissentientes; concentus ex diuersis non aduersis.*[12]

We may make bold, then, to supplement Professor Panofsky's penetrating analysis of the connections between scholastic thought and Gothic architecture[13] with the evidence of the musical connotation of the *Concordia discordantium canonum.* Indeed, in the field of canon law, symphonic rather than architectural structure presents itself much more readily as an adequate symbol.[14] Like theological and philosophical speculation, so juristic thought aims, or at least aimed in medieval conception, at a universal order. But the order of law is not the eternal, absolute order of metaphysical being nor (at least, not primarily) of the economy of salvation; for, law in its concrete detail necessarily deals, as I observed before, with the contingencies of human existence in society, with the conflicts and tensions of the social body here and now, with all its mutations in time and space. Much greater stress lies here on the elements from which harmony is to come, the *discordantiae* and dissonances, than in other universal disciplines—and it would be rash to assume that this might be less true for canon than for civil law because the former governs a society which is spiritual in its origins and its ends. Such reasoning tends to forget that the Church militant is not yet in the glory of Heaven.

For the jurists and legislators of the Church who constructed the medieval system of canon law, the problem presented itself as a challenge on three levels: (1) the quest for harmony of the sources of law, or the problem of the confusing wealth of written traditions; (2) the quest for harmony of ecclesiastical institutions, or the problem of the varieties of social forms in time and space;[15] (3) the quest for harmony of the mystical body, or the problem of perfecting in legal terms the interpenetration of spiritual and corporate elements, which is the essential mark distinguishing the Church from all other modes of social existence.

We must, of course, not think of these three planes of harmonizing thought as separate fields of the medieval canonists' inquiry but rather as different aspects of a concern which is ultimately one. A specific problem of *concordia* could appear on different levels: the value and interpretation of a given text, such as the enactment of a given particular council, or the response of a Pope, could pose problems both as to its place among the sources of law and as to its specific institutional contents. Customs as such presented fundamental problems both in the theory of law and as evidence of particular institutions existing in a given locality or region. The

---

[12] For the history of the last-mentioned concept in Christian hermeneutics, cf. de Ghellinck, *op. cit.* 517-23 and H. de Lubac, 'A propos de la formule: "diversi sed non adversi",' *Mélanges Lebreton* (Recherches de science religieuse 39-40 [1951-52]) II 27-40.

[13] E. Panofsky, *Gothic Architecture and Scholasticism* (Wimmer Lecture 1948; Latrobe, Pa. 1951).

[14] Long before Gratian, the unknown author of the so-called *Poenitentiale Gregorii III* wrote in his prologue: '...iudicia...ita diuersa et inter se discrepantia...ut uix propter dissonantiam possint discerni' (Mansi 12.287). In the late twelfth century, the anonymous *Quaestiones* of MS 53 of Oriel College, Oxford, introduced the solution of an involved problem of jurisdiction by the apostrophe: 'Audi quanta sit armonia, quantusque concentus in organis que dei spiritu insufflantur' (fol. 338vb).

[15] Le Bras, *Prolégomènes* (n. 3 *supra*) dedicates the second of the three main parts of his book to an analysis of this problem, pp. 113-77.

adjudication of a concrete issue arising in the borderland of what we moderns would call mixed jurisdiction of Church and State could lead to definitions bearing upon the fundamental relation of the spiritual and the temporal order; and the adjudication of an issue involving the validity of a given episcopal consecration would have a bearing on the relation between the flow of sacramental life and the jurisdictional functions within the spiritual order itself.

Today, we see that for many of the discrepancies and perplexities which canonical tradition presented to the experience of the medieval lawyers, the dialectical process of thought was actually ill suited as a means of solution.[16] But it would be a mistake to criticize the schoolmen for this; for they were not called upon to explain such *discordantiae* as historians, by analyzing the accidents of their historical origin, but to justify and resolve them in a conceptual framework for which all the conflicting historical data existed, simultaneously as it were, demanding a logical and practical solution then and there.

III

The first of the three levels or planes of harmonizing thought, I have said, was that of the sources. This problem, historically, stood at the very beginning of canonistic science and provided one of its most powerful motivations. To understand its urgency in the early twelfth century, one may do well to compare the situation of canon law with that faced by the nascent science of Roman law. Medieval Romanistic thought began with the rediscovery *c.* 1070 of Justinian's *Digesta*—the central monument of ancient Roman jurisprudence, which had been completely forgotten in the Latin West from the seventh to the eleventh century.[17] The early Middle Ages had possessed only relics of the imposing structure of Roman jurisprudence. The Visigothic *Breviarium* (*Lex Romana Visigothorum*, 506 A.D.), The Visigothic *Breviarium* (*Lex Romana Visigothorum*, 506 A.D.), classical jurists with pre-Justinian imperial constitutions taken from the Theodosian Code (438 A.D.), had retained currency in the Frankish kingdom, together with similar 'barbarian' adaptations; portions of Justinian's *Codex*, his elementary *Institutes*, and an abridged Latin version of his Greek *Novellae* (*Epitome Juliani*), had survived in central Italy. The rediscovered Digest presented a formidable challenge to the

---

[16] The railings of the sixteenth-century humanists against the scholastic method are familiar; but some rare voices ridiculing the use of dialectic by the canonists were heard as early as the twelfth century. Cf. Master Vacarius and others cited in S. Kuttner and E. Rathbone, 'Anglo-Norman Canonists of the Twelfth Century,' *Traditio* 7 (1949/51) 288; also Ralph Niger, *Moralia regum* c. 19, in H. Kantorowicz and B. Smalley, 'An English Theologian's View of Roman Law,' *Medieval and Renaissance Studies* 1 (1941) 252, cf. 249.

[17] For the history of Roman law in the early Middle Ages, cf. E. Genzmer, 'Die justinianische Kodifikation und die Glossatoren,' *Atti del Congresso internazionale di Diritto romano, Bologna-Roma 1933* I (Pavia 1934) 347-430, at pp. 347-68; also F. Calasso, *Medio evo del diritto* I (Milan 1954); J. Gaudemet, 'Survivances romaines dans le droit de la monarchie franque du Ve au Xe siècle,' *Tijdschrift voor Rechtsgeschiedenis* 23 (1955) 149-206. M. Conrat, *Geschichte der Quellen und Literatur des römischen Rechts im früheren Mittelalter* (Leipzig 1891) remains fundamental although superseded in many points by later research. A preliminary report on the international cooperative project of a ten-volume history, *Ius romanum medii aevi*, is found in *Seminar* 11 (1953) 89-101; cf. 13 (1955/56) 48-50.

medieval mind, which set out to reconquer in all its detail the elaborate juristic acumen of a highly technical, complete legal system. The medieval science of canon law had to start from the opposite direction; it had to devise an intrinsic, logical coherence for a maze of rules of the most heterogeneous character handed down through the early Middle Ages in an ever-changing variety of selection, accretion, and irregular growth, assembled in a great number of collections of which many enjoyed a wide circulation, while others remained of local or regional significance only, and none of which commanded universal acceptance.

The common law of the Western Church in late antiquity, as represented by the canons of the councils of the fourth and fifth centuries, and a relatively small number of authoritative *epistolae decretales* of the popes since the latter part of the fourth, had been overgrown by the enactments of later councils and synods, national, provincial, regional; by Roman imperial statute and by ordinances of the Frankish kings; by the rules of private handbooks on penance, by the inclusion of excerpts from the Mosaic law, liturgical books, and patristic texts.[18] Efforts at reforming and unifying the canonical tradition had been made time and again: in the Roman collections of the early sixth century which were inspired by the Gelasian ideas; in Visigothic Spain, and during the Carolingian renascence; in the great forgeries of the ninth century (known as the Pseudo-Isidorian decretals), and in the great manual which a German bishop, Burchard of Worms, composed for the instruction of his clergy and the practice of the diocesan *curiae* early in the eleventh century.

Each of these revisions was premised on different aims and policies, each of them added new layers of texts to the existing traditions. Most resolute of all, the canonists of the great age of Reform that takes its name from Gregory VII, tried to create a purified canon law by combining a revival of the old law, the *canones et decreta sanctorum patrum*, with a pruning of the later traditions—that is, in an intensified search for ancient texts, or what appeared to be ancient texts (including therefore the Pseudo-Isidorian material of the ninth century), and in an elimination of all that appeared un-Roman, i.e., not in material consonance with papal or universal conciliar law.[19]

The single-mindedness of the Gregorian reformers suppressed, as contradictory with papal authority, a great portion of the source material of early medieval origin represented in the tradition of Burchard. But at the same time, the criterion of contradiction or non-contradiction prepared the way for a new development, once the Investiture Contest entered into its conciliatory phase. The need for practical completeness of the canonical books dictated the re-admission of the Franco-Germanic traditions, since in the 'Gregorian' texts, with their call for a 'return to the law of the ancient Church,' the living reality of many medieval institutions had simply been bypassed. The two traditions by the end of the eleventh century

---

[18] Fournier-Le Bras, *Histoire des collections* (n. 9 *supra*); for additional bibliography and progress of research since 1932 cf. Van Hove, *Prolegomena* (n. 6 *supra*) 116-337; Stickler, *Historia* (n. 6 *supra*) 22-195. Cf. also C. Munier, *Les sources patristiques du droit de l'Église du VIIIe au XIIIe siècle* (Mulhouse 1957).

[19] S. Kuttner, 'Liber canonicus: A Note on "Dictatus Papae" c. 17,' *Studia Gregoriana* 2 (1947) 387-401; cf. also J. J. Ryan, *St. Peter Damiani and His Canonical Sources* (Toronto 1956) 139-48.

appear juxtaposed, as two layers of authorities, and it remained only to replace the policy of elimination by a policy of reconciliation. Starting from the 'Gregorian' principle that all canon law is valid which is not in contradiction with the lawmaking authority of the Roman pontiff, the next step was to devise principles of hermeneutics whereby non-contradiction can be demonstrated through interpretation.

I have mentioned before the important place of Ivo of Chartres in this development. His canonical collections retained all the colorful variety and discrepancy of the heritage of the near and the distant past. But in the preface he wrote for the last and best of these collections, he set forth the hermeneutical principles by which all contradiction could be resolved into harmony. I have to forego here a detailed analysis of this prologue *de consonantia canonum*; of its relation to biblical hermeneutics and to precepts of rhetoric in the early Middle Ages; and I can only mention here in passing its affinity to the contemporary treatise by Bernold of Constance, *De excommunicandis vitandis*, and Ivo's influence on Abelard's system of dialectics in the *Sic et non*, the standard book of authorities for theological disputation. It is, however, pertinent to our discussion to recall some categories of thought which all these co-founders of the scholastic method put at the disposal of canonical jurisprudence: the antitheses of strict law and dispensation, of precept and counsel, of justice and mercy, of immutable divine and changeable human law, of universal and limited legislative power, of the absolute and the relative rule; the criteria of relativity such as: circumstances, motive, authenticity, and the different semantic meanings of identical terms in different contexts.[20] There lies in these concepts more than merely a methodological equipment. The mutually corrective functions of justice and mercy, for instance, which in particular occupied Ivo's thought, lead us to one of the fundamental traits of canon law, the imitation of the divine judgment itself.

What had been outlined in the dialectical precepts of these early generations was finally accomplished in Gratian's *Concordia discordantium canonum*. Conceived as a universal treatise on the institutions and problems of canon law, the book used the whole of the traditional *auctoritates* handed down in the earlier collections as material from which to draw, point for point, the textual arguments for the canonical doctrines Gratian proposed. With all its obvious deficiencies, the book demonstrated that it was possible by a process of reasoning and organization to cast all the apparently unwieldy mass of canons into a system, however imperfect, of jurisprudential thought; that it was legitimate for such organized thought to find a place, as a discipline of its own, somewhere between sacred theology and the legal science which, in the wake of the restoring of the full *Corpus iuris civilis*, had just then been reborn in the city of Bologna, where Gratian's own monastery stood.[21]

---

[20] On the developments of canonistic interpretation, cf.—in addition to Fournier-Le Bras, de Ghellinck (*op. cit.* n. 10 *supra*), and the studies cited in n. 19—J. M. Salgado, 'La méthode d'interprétation du droit en usage chez les canonistes,' *Revue de l'Université d'Ottawa* 21 (1951) 201*-13*; 22 (1952) 23*-35*; R. Losada Cosme, 'La unificación interna de derecho canónico y las colecciones anteriores a Graciano,' *Revista española de derecho canónico* 10 (1955) 353-82.

[21] It is quite another question—much debated in recent years—to what extent Gratian included sources of Roman law in his work. The pioneer in this field of critical research is Professor A. Vetulani, Cracow. Cf. especially his article, 'Gratien et le droit romain,' *Revue historique de droit français et étranger* 24-25 (1946-47) 11-48; also the present writer's 'New Studies

With the *Concordia discordantium canonum*, the age of searching for a norm of harmony of the sources came to an end. The definitive *dossier* of canonical authorities of the past had become established in this book, to remain practically unchanged. The checkered variety of law-producing agencies that had vexed earlier generations faded away, since from the struggles of the Gregorian era and the ensuing clarification of thought, the papacy had emerged as the undisputed guardian and master of the law, the sole agency which henceforth in its supreme magisterial, judicial, and legislative pronouncements would make truly 'common,' general law. This new papal law appeared in the thousands of rulings that flowed from the papal Chancery since the mid-twelfth century, settling thousands of new problems and cases. In this new procedure we should, however, not expect any sharp break with the substance of the *ius antiquum* but recognize an organic development.

Life is, of course, more inventive than academic speculation, but many of the problems that were determined in the papal decisions, responses, and constitutions of the Middle Ages, had first occurred to the masters in the schools who, in their teaching and writing on the book of Gratian, probed into the concepts underlying the old texts, abstracted definitions and doctrines from them, and tested the answers that might be gotten from the old *auctoritates*, by deduction or inference, for new questions arising in the continual process of analysis and discovery. In this intellectual debate, the ground was broken and the arguments were readied which would serve the Roman Curia in making the new law. As an early commentator on Gratian observed, the *ratio recte vivendi* in the Church is composed of two parts: one *magistralis*, in the writings of the masters in the schools; and one *autentica*, in what the Roman Pontiff ordains, the two together making a consistent whole.[22]

All the new sources of canon law being now of papal origin, the problem of *concordia* of the sources was henceforth reduced chiefly to the task of selection. The canonists had to find among the new *epistolae decretales* of the Popes the ones that were not mere routine decisions, nor merely particular answers issued for one particular case; to find, in other words, the ones that contained an authoritative teaching or precedent whereby an old law was either given greater precision in the new papal interpretation, or possibly set aside in a new papal ruling. In a first stage this process of selection was carried out by the masters in the schools; it was only with Innocent III in the early thirteenth century that the Popes themselves began to issue official collections of their decretals, promulgating them as formal law books.[23] Characteristically, these were addressed not to the hierarchy but to the schools.

---

on the Roman Law in Gratian's Decretum,' *Seminar* 11 (1953) 12-50, with an additional note, *ibid.* 12 (1954) 68-74. Since then, further studies by Vetulani and by Mme. J. Rambaud-Buhot have appeared on the subject.

[22] Gloss of the *Summa Elegantius in iure diuino* (School of Cologne, after 1169): 'Moralis sapientia in libris utriusque iuris; hec diuiditur in ratiocinatiuam et amministratiuam; hec in amministratione officiorum continetur et in echonomicam politicam [et ethicam] subdiuiditur....Ratiocinatiua moralis est que metu penarum et exhortatione premiorum mores componit, duobus his modis ad rationem recte uiuendi promouens. Hec in magistralem et autenticam distinguitur, altera in traditionibus et scriptis magistrorum, altera in constitutionibus imperatorum et romanorum pontificum continetur' (Vienna MS lat. 2125, fol. 11ʳ).

[23] Pope Innocent's collection was promulgated in 1209. For a survey of the numerous private collections cf. Stickler, *op. cit.* (n. 6 *supra*) 217-32.

IV

The harmonization of the sources, welding the old *auctoritates* and the new into a balanced juristic doctrine should be respected as one of the great achievements of the medieval mind. But we must not stop here, lest in concentrating on the techniques of the intellect we lose sight of the content of juristic thought. Through the *concordia canonum* a second level of harmony was reached, the coordination of the ecclesiastical institutions themselves, a balance of the social entities from which the visible body of the Church is composed.

We have to consider here the fact that only a few essentials of the ecclesiastical order go back to the divine foundation of the Church and to the Apostolic age. The two estates of clergy and laity, the sacraments, the gradation of orders, the power to bind and to loosen, the perpetuation of the Apostolic office in the episcopate, the primacy of the Vicar of Christ—within this immutable framework all the institutional detail was to be supplied in a development which is, above all, human history. Thus every succeeding age has left its mark on the institutions of the Church, creating new devices of organization, new agencies, new procedures, for new social necessities and contingencies. And with each succeeding age, old institutions would wither away or, as the case may be, continue awhile as obsolete forms while the life of the Church went ahead and changed in all, except that which makes her one, holy, catholic, and apostolic, today as it was nearly two thousand years ago. Who thinks today of the once extremely important functions of archdeacons, or of classes of public penitents (the weeping, the prostrate, the kneeling, and the standing)? Who remembers that porters, exorcists, and lectors were in antiquity more than passing stages on the way to the priesthood; that marriages before the Council of Trent required no canonical form; that until the Code of 1917 election by the cathedral chapter was still in theory the principal element in the making of a bishop? This random list of changing institutions could be easily extended, and new institutions of canon law are continually in the making, as one may see, e.g., in this country, where the medieval office of the bishop's vicar general has lost most of the importance it still retains in European dioceses. It is the chancellor whom we know as the chief administrative official in America, but in the old countries he is only a subordinate figure in the bishop's curia.

To the canonists of the twelfth century such historical changes appeared in a very different light. Historical rationalization for us has become an intellectual *habitus*, and for the modern student it is not difficult to gain the perspective which tells him, e.g., that a world in which parochial income was mainly based on the tenth levied from the parishioners had an economic structure very different from that of the sixteenth or the twentieth century. To the mind of the schoolmen, however, history was mainly a source of edification, in which the 'once upon a time' need not be farther away in consciousness than the childhood days at the knees of one's mother. When medieval civilian jurists wished to point out that a change in an earlier Roman institution was made by the Emperor Justinian, they usually introduced the later law by the words 'hodie vero'—the sixth century for them still being 'today.' Thus to the canonists, the conflict between the rules on married priests established by the Council of Gangra in the fourth century, and the practically opposite rules proclaimed by Gregory VII in times nearer to their own, was to be resolved in a timeless debate about principles, not in a historical consideration of clerical celibacy. All the sources of the past, inasmuch as they were enshrined in the *Concordia discordantium canonum*, were equally valid tools for determining the properties and aspects of canonical institutions of their day and age.

It is by this sublime disregard of history (or, we may say, by the primacy of reason over history) that the medieval lawyers were able to make a system out of the conflicting data they found in the experience of reality. The modern historian can resolve such discrepancies only in a consideration of the various layers super-imposed one upon the other in the course of the centuries.

We know today, for instance, that there existed fundamental differences between the characteristics of a diocese in late Antiquity (i.e. the period after Constantine) and in the early Middle Ages, and that these differences are intimately connected with certain traits of Roman public law on the one hand, and 'Germanic' and feudal conceptions, on the other. In the late Roman empire, the administrative unity of the bishopric was as self-evident as (in the secular sphere) that of an imperial province or a municipality; the bishop was the head of an administration for the city and its surrounding territory, with appropriate clerical functionaries under him for the various sacramental, jurisdictional, and patrimonial functions. To this administrative unit there corresponded a property unit of ecclesiastical goods, all vested in the bishop as in a personified institution, subject to certain restrictions concerning alienation of goods, and to certain rules concerning the distribution of revenue.

In the early medieval diocese—and here again the analogy with secular institutions is striking—everything looks different. A decentralization of powers and a disintegration of diocesan property had taken place, which followed in part from the ownership by the king or the manorial lords of the churches built on their estates; another factor was the replacement of the old concept of public office by the feudal notion that official functions in the Church are mere personal prerogatives attached to the tenure of a given church as a 'benefice,' granted by the owner. Stalls in cathedral chapters, archdeaconries, deaneries, parish rectories, all being appurtenances of tenures conferred by investiture, became so many restrictions on the prerogatives of the diocesan ordinary and threatened to absorb the whole of ecclesiastical life in a quasi-feudal network, until the trend was arrested and reversed at the last minute by the Gregorian Reform.[24]

All these institutions took root in the early Middle Ages and found expression in canonical rules and practices which the canonists somehow had to fit into their *concordia*. Patronage and advowson, prerogatives of Chapters and capitular dignities, archdeacons' rights of visitation and installation of pastors, and many other 'Germanic' remainders of the pre-Gregorian decentralization had to be harmonized with the 'old' law emphasized by the Reformers. The subtlety and complexity of the law of offices and benefices, as developed by the canonists and the decretals of the classical age, bears witness to the supreme difficulty of this *concordia* between different worlds of legal thought. Not all the problems were neatly

---

[24] Modern insight into these developments is largely based on the researches of the late Ulrich Stutz (†1938); the best summary is found in H. E. Feine, *Kirchliche Rechtsgeschichte* I (2nd ed. Weimar 1954; 3rd ed. 1955) 147-240.

disentangled. Throughout the books of decretals of the later Middle Ages, there remain definite traces of the *dissonantia* between the abstract, functional conception of an ecclesiastical office and the realistic, thing-like conception of the benefice. They can be found even in our law today, which in certain cases still requires the 'taking of possession' for the valid exercise of jurisdictional rights.[25]

The foregoing is only one example among many of the challenges presented to medieval thought by the variety and historical accidents of institutional life. To see these problems in their right proportion, one would have to review one by one the entire system of the decretal law. How could (to cite only one further example) the exemption of regulars, monks, and mendicants from the normal channels of jurisdiction be fitted into the system? The historian, of course, can explain how from the privileged status of individual religious houses there grew eventually a common law of religious institutions: but to place the result of this growth into the conceptual framework of the written law was a problem of legal logic which exercised the minds of the best canonists.

V

And yet, all such problems of harmonization remained within the realm of tangible social realities, realities of a kind which all legal systems will have to face if they want to fit the historical growth of institutions into the logic of the law. But for canon law, the task of *concordia discordantium* presented itself still on a third plane, where it left all other legal orders behind, because of the unique nature of the Church among all forms of human society: a social body which is also the mystical body of Christ. In probing into the immense detail of regulations, the medieval canonists found, beyond the antinomies of the sources and the antinomies of ecclesiastical institutions, a problem of much deeper concern: the paradox, if we may call it that, of a supernatural mystery which manifests itself in the structural forms of social life.

This twofold aspect was given, of course, from the foundation of the Church as a visible society, but its implications could be fully grasped only at a time when ecclesiastical thought resolutely turned towards understanding the inner coherence of the external, legal order of the Church with her sacramental life. It became apparent to the medieval canonists, e.g., that the efficacy, exercise, and transmission of sacramental powers in holy orders follows other laws than that of jurisdictional powers, although the two are correlated to each other and coincide on principle at many points of the hierarchical pyramid.[26] But while in the early sources the term *officium* is often vaguely applied to both, the differentiation of office from orders became increasingly clear to the classical canonists, who saw that there could be degrees of jurisdiction without any corresponding gradation in orders: for the *ordo* of the metropolitan, or, for that matter, of the Pope himself, is not different from that of any bishop. They saw that there could be functions of office even contrary to the hierarchy of orders, as in the case of the archdeacon, whose

---

[25] *Codex iur. can.* c. 334 §2; c. 461.

[26] Cf. L. Saltet, *Les réordinations* (Paris 1907); D. W. Heintschel, *The Medieval Concept of an Ecclesiastical Office* (Catholic University of America, Canon Law Studies 363; Washington 1956).

jurisdiction extended over priests no less than the minor clergy. In the Roman Curia, even subdeacons often held high offices.

Again, in the power of the Church to chastise her straying sheep, the manifold interrelations between the legal and the spiritual realm became apparent to the searching thought of the canonists. Here they met with the differentiation between the external and the internal forum—the court of law and the court of conscience—and with the fact that in the latter the sacramental absolution from sin is at the same time an act of jurisdiction; or that the imposition of penance in the internal forum could have certain effects also in the external, social order. The judicial sentence of excommunication became clarified in its two aspects as separation from the sacramental graces and as exclusion from the communion of the faithful; but its efficacy in the Church was contingent upon conformity with the canonical order of procedure, while in the sight of God it could stand only if pronounced for a just cause.[27]

Another corollary of the spiritual aspect of ecclesiastical jurisdiction originated in the interpretation of the words of Christ, "If thy brother sin against thee, go and show him his fault...; but if he do not listen to thee, take with thee one or two more so that on the word of two or three witnesses every word may be confirmed. And if he refuse to hear them, appeal to the Church..." (Matt. 18.15-17). On the strength of this text, medieval canon law gradually developed the equitable procedure of *denuntiatio evangelica*, as a remedy for the correction of faults, *ratione peccati*, without the solemnities normally required in canonical trials.[28]

The mutual penetration of two modes of thought, of supernatural ends and legal means, appears wherever we open the books of the medieval canonists. The harmonization of opposites here reaches its supreme purpose, that of integrating human jurisprudence in the divine order of salvation. It is for this reason that the canonists would not hesitate to employ scriptural and patristic texts in arguing a technical point of law, nor to cite texts of Roman civil law in order to prove a point of moral or sacramental doctrine. At times such reasonings may appear naive to the modern reader, but they were not inconsistent with what the classical canonists had perceived as the ultimate end of all law in the Church: a common good which includes the natural common good of human society, and also transcends it because it is essentially connected with something most individual and personal, 'man's friendship with God, which we call Charity.' The subject of all canon law, they

---

[27] Among recent studies in the fields of penance and excommunication, cf. P. Anciaux, *La théologie du sacrement de pénitence au XIIe siècle* (Louvain 1949); F. Russo, 'Pénitence et excommunication: Étude historique...du 9e au 13e siècle,' *Recherches de science religieuse* 33 (1946) 257-79, 431-61; A. Gommenginger, 'Bedeutet die Exkommunikation Verlust der Kirchengliedschaft?' *Zeitschrift für katholische Theologie* 73 (1951) 1-71, at pp. 34ff.; P. Huizing, *Doctrina decretistarum de excommunicatione usque ad Glossam ordinariam Joannis Teutonici* (Rome 1952); id., 'The Earliest Development of Excommunication latae sententiae...' *Studia Gratiana* 3 (1955) 277-320; also the important earlier study by F. Gillmann, in *Archiv für katholisches Kirchenrecht* 104 (1924) 5-40.

[28] Ch. Lefebvre, 'Contribution à l'étude des origines et du développement de la "denunciatio evangelica" en droit canonique,' *Ephemerides iuris canonici* 6 (1950) 60-93; cf. H. Coing, 'English Equity and the Denunciatio evangelica of the Canon Law,' *Law Quarterly Review* 71 (1955) 223-41.

would say, is not simply man, but the spiritual man, a pilgrim on his way between this world and the eternal life.[29]

From these fundamental insights we can understand the attempts of the medieval writers to give canon law a place in the universal history of mankind, the history of salvation. In the prologue of many a canonistic treatise, we meet with a standard account which begins with the creation of Adam and the natural law, then rapidly passes on through the law of Moses, the Prophets, the Gospel, the Apostolic law, the councils, the decrees of the Fathers—and so on down the ages, to the particular text or compilation the writer plans to comment upon.[30] Some authors, among them so profound a theologian as Hugh of St. Victor, considered canon law even as part of the New Dispensation, and there assigned it a place corresponding to that which the hagiographical books have in St. Jerome's scheme of the Old Testament.[31] Others expanded the historical pattern by including—usually at some point before the Gospel—the secular law, composed of the law of nations and the civil law of Rome. The Church, it was sometimes said, may have borrowed her rules of judicial procedure from civil legislation, but the latter in turn rested on Biblical precedent: did not all forms of pleading take their origin in paradise when Adam urged that 'the woman whom thou gavest me' was responsible for the Fall?[32]

Such 'historical' constructions were not meant as idle rhetoric. They expressed the canonists' genuine concern for the dignity of their calling, and this dignity stemmed from the twofold nature of canon law, in which theology and legal science were blended. The great Hostiensis (Henry of Susa, cardinal-bishop of

---

[29] Nicolaus de Tudeschis (Panormitanus, †1445), *Commentaria in primum librum decretalium*, prooem. n. 16c: 'sicut ergo potissima uirtus ad quam conatur ius ciuile est ipsa legalis iustitia et ciuilis amicitia, ita potissima uirtus ad quam conatur ius canonicum est ipsa celestis amicitia quam charitatem uocamus' (*Opera*, ed. Venice 1588, I col. 7ᵃ). Before him, Johannes Andreae (†1348), had written in *Quaestiones mercuriales*, ad reg. 2 *Possessor non praescribit:* '...ius ciuile intendit conseruare iustitiam propter terminanda litigia, nam suus finis principalis est conseruare ciuilem societatem,...ius autem canonicum e conuerso intendit terminare litigia propter conseruandam iustitiam, nam suus finis principalis est ordinare in deum et in legem euangelicam, ut homo gloriam assequatur' (ed. Venice 1581, fol. 60ᵛᵇ).—Among modern writers stressing this point, cf. P. Fedele, *Discorso generale sull'ordinamento canonico* (Padova 1941); L. Motry, 'The Connotative Value of the "Sacred Canons",' *The Jurist* 1 (1941) 50-65; Le Bras, *Prolégomènes* (n. 3 *supra*) 23-25, 97-111 and *passim.*

[30] Such accounts are found as early as the *Summa decretorum* of Paucapalea (before 1148; ed. Schulte [Giessen 1890] p. 1), in Stephen of Tournai and, more developed, in Johannes Faventinus, *Summa* (c. 1171); the most influential versions were those of Tancred's prologue, *Apparatus decretalium Comp. III* (c. 1220, beg. 'Formauit deus hominem') and of Hostiensis, *Summa aurea*, prooem. nn. 5-11 (c. 1253; ed. Venice 1570, fol. 3ʳᵇ-4ʳᵃ).

[31] Hugh of St. Victor, *Didascalicon* 4.2 (ed. C. H. Buttimer [Washington 1939] p. 72.10) and *De scripturis et scriptoribus sacris* c. 6 (PL 175.15). Cf. *Seminar* 12 (1954) 69 n. 9, where the present writer pointed to some canonistic texts that are in the same vein.

[32] Thus the preface of an anonymous *Abbreviatio decretorum* in Gdańsk (Danzig) MS Mar. F. 275 (ed. A. Vetulani, *Dekret Gracjana i pierwsi dekretyści w świetle nowego źródła* [Wroclaw-Cracow 1955] p. 62), the parallel passage in Paucapalea (*loc. cit.* n. 30 *supra*), and Stephanus Tornac. (*ed. cit.* p. 2), who all use the term *placitandi forma* in this context. The same idea, differently worded, is found in the *Summa Omnis qui iuste* and the *Prologue Sapientia edificauit*, two anonymous writings of the Anglo-Norman school.

Ostia, †1271)[33] compared the unique position of the learned canonist with the exalted nobility of man, the being that shares in the nature both of angels and earthly matter, and quoted St. Paul, "Do you not know that we shall judge angels?" (I Cor. 6.3).[34] This sounds rather presumptuous, but if we read, a little further on, "Is, then, the species of mules greater and nobler than that of horses and that of asses?" we are reminded that righteous pride in one's profession need not exclude a healthy sense of humor.[35] The facetious simile carried with it a pun on the 'asinine science' of civil law, but Hostiensis was too deeply learned in civil law himself for seriously belittling its vital role in the governance of Christian society.[36] His jest about legal learning—which elsewhere he called 'a most sacred thing'[37]—must be understood against the background of his times, when bickerings and academic feuds were going on between the university faculties, and when the canonists in particular had to defend themselves against the popular prejudice which commonly taunted them as a greedy, ambitious, self-seeking lot.

Only he who is blind to the mystery of the Church could find that the bond of law and the bond of love are mutually exclusive, that justice and mercy cannot meet on the plane of law. To the mind of the classical canonists they did meet, and from the opposites of law and mercy there arose the ideal of *aequitas canonica*, which permeates their analytical thought and their solution of cases at every step.[38] All the tensions and dissonances, all the apparent incompatibilities of the spiritual and the temporal, the supernatural and the natural, could be brought into

---

[33] On Hostiensis, cf. the article by Ch. Lefebvre in *Dictionnaire de droit canonique* 5 (1953) 1211-27, with a fine characterization of his teachings on basic problems of jurisprudence. For his biography, see the articles by N. Didier, in *Studi Arangio Ruiz* (Naples 1953) II 333-51; *Revue historique de droit français et étranger* 31 (1953) 244-70, 409-29; *Studia Gratiana* 2 (1954) 595-617.

[34] *Summa aurea*, prooem. n. 12 (*ed. cit.* fol. 4rb); also *Lectura* 1.1.1 v. *quasi communem* nn. 17-19 (ed. Venice 1581, fol. 5^v). The description of the composite nature of man is taken from the profession of faith of the Fourth Lateran Council (1215), c. 1.

[35] *Summa loc. cit.:* '...sed numquid species mulina [*ed.:* maligna] maior est et dignior equina et asinina? Et planum est quod equinam theologicae scientiae, asininam ciuili sapientiae poteris comparare. Nolo concludere, sed considera quid sequatur...'; a slightly different wording in *Lectura loc. cit.* n. 19, followed by the remark: 'Sed non est decens quod omnia genera hominum puris bestiis comparemus.'

[36] A fundamental text, in which Hostiensis casts aside all dialectical artifice and with fervor expounds his belief in the dignity of theology and the two laws, is in his *Lectura* 1.14.14, tit. *de aetate et qualitate ordinandorum*, c. *Cum sit ars artium* nn. 2-7. (W. Ullmann, *Medieval Papalism* [London 1949] 30-31, who takes both the rhetorical 'nescitis quoniam angelos iudicabimus?' and the joke about the mule in the *Summa* seriously, does not mention this text.) Only a few significant passages can be quoted here: '...sed haec est ueritas quod ars artium est diuina lex, a qua non est excludenda canonica nec humana...' (n. 2); '...unde dicas quod istae duae leges unum sunt cum theologia, et omnes sunt necessariae ecclesiae sanctae Dei' (n. 5); he then explains the different functions of the three disciplines, compares them with the parts of the body, and quotes 1 Cor. 12.21: 'Non potest dicere oculus manui, opera tua non indigeo, aut iterum caput pedibus, non estis mihi necessarii' (n. 6); '...multi tamen has leges, sc. humanam et canonicam, reprobant et blasphemant, quia secundum Boetium tot sunt hostes artis quot ignorantes...' (n. 7) (*ed. cit.* fol. 110^r).

[37] *Summa*, prooem. n. 7: 'legalis sapientia...est quidem res sanctissima,' taken from *Dig.* 50.13.1.5; developed at length in *Lectura* 1.14.14 nn. 3-4.

[38] Lefebvre, 'Équité,' *Dictionnaire de droit canonique* 5.394-410, with copious bibliography.

harmony—the ultimate *concordia discordantium* which Stephen of Tournai had in mind when he invited a theologian and a lawyer to his banquet. For the skills of both of Stephen's guests were needed to make the *concordia* come true.

LIBER CANONICUS
A NOTE ON « DICTATUS PAPAE » c. 17

The first canonical collection ever to be officially pro-mulgated by the Holy See appeared in 1209-10 and contained a selection of decretals from the first twelve years of Innocent III's pontificate, approved for general use in schools and courts.[1] Prior to the thirteenth century, the very idea of a ca-nonical compilation drawing its authority from a formal act of sovereign approval seems not even to have entered the mind of popes and canonists alike — unless we have to recognize such a statement, one-hundred and twenty-five years before Innocent III, in Gregory VII's *Dictatus papae* (DP) c. 17: *Quod nullum capitulum nullusque liber canonicus habeatur absque illius* [sc. *Romani pontificis*] *auctoritate.*[2] Since *capitulum* in this context seems to refer to a disciplinary enactment or ca-non, especially the individual conciliar statute (for the im-mediately preceding DP 16 treats of the relation between pope and general council), the bracketing of *capitulum* and *liber* under the concept of canonical authority in DP 17 would ap-pear to imply the postulate that not only each conciliar rule, but also every book of such (and similar) rules needs to be vested with the *auctoritas* of the Roman Pontiff to be truly « canonical »; or even, more pointedly, that no *capitulum* and no *liber canonicus* shall be kept and observed without papal authority.[3] Indeed several modern writers point to a connection

---

[1] For the date (probably in autumn, 1209) see KUTTNER, in *Miscellanea Giovanni Mercati*, 5 (*Studi e Testi*, 125; Città del Vaticano 1946), 621.

[2] ed. E. CASPAR, *Das Register Gregors VII.* (MGH., Epp. sel. [8°], 2; Berlin 1920-23), 205.

[3] The first grammatical construction, which takes *canonicus* as the common *nomen praedicativum*, is the more likely one; *canonicus habeatur* = *pro canonico*

between DP 17 and the well-known Gregorian efforts for a reform of the canonical collections.[4]

At first sight, more than one argument would seem to speak in favor of this interpretation. To make all canonical texts contingent upon the *auctoritas* of the Holy See, would fit in with Gregory's desire, repeatedly expressed long before his pontificate, to see St. Peter Damian compile in *parvi voluminis unionem* all papal decrees and *gesta* (the latter term probably referring to the *Liber pontificalis*) which have specific reference to the authority of the Roman Church;[5] it would fit in with Gregory's promotion of an intensified search for canonical and historical texts in general, resulting in a *dossier* of fresh materials for the Reformers' new collections,[6] several of which may have been undertaken at Gregory's behest.[7] Moreover, the

---

habeatur, « no chapter and no book shall be considered canonical without... ». Still, in the very conciseness of expression proper to the DP, it is the combination *liber canonicus* which strikes the ear; and *habeatur* might as well be read to mean *recipiatur*, « shall be held, observed ». A similar, and perhaps not unintentional ambiguity follows from the laconic manner of speech, e. g., in DP 16: *Quod nulla synodus absque precepto eius debet generalis vocari*, « no synod may be called general without... » or « no general synod may be convoked without... »; cf. CASPAR's commentary, ad loc. K. HOFMANN, *Der « Dictatus Papae » Gregors VII. Eine rechtsgeschichtliche Erklärung* (Görres-Gesellschaft, Veröff. der Sektion für Rechts- und Staatswiss., 63, Paderborn 1933), 84f., accepts only the second interpretation.

[4] E. g. HOFMANN, op. cit., 85ff.; A. FLICHE, *La réforme grégorienne*, II, Louvain-Paris 1925, 200; A. VAN HOVE, *Een inleiding tot de bronne van het Kerkelijk Recht op het einde der XIe eeuw*, in *Miscellanea historica in honorem Alberti de Meyer*, Louvain 1946, I, 365.

[5] PETRUS DAMIANI, *Opusc.* 5 (PL., 145, 89). The significance of the passage for the historical background of the so-called Gregorian collections has been frequently noted, cf. e. g. P. FOURNIER and G. LE BRAS, *Histoire des collections canoniques en Occident depuis les Fausses Décrétales jusqu'au Décret de Gratien*, II, Paris 1932, 8; HOFMANN, op. cit., 16; G. B. BORINO, *Un'ipotesi sul « Dictatus Papae » di Gregorio VII*, in *Archivio della R. Deputaz. Romana di Storia patria*, N. S., 10 (1944), 240.

[6] On these researches, see FOURNIER - LE BRAS, op. cit., II, 7ff.

[7] FOURNIER - LE BRAS, II, 16 and 35f. (for the Collection in 74 titles and Anselm of Lucca). The inscription of MS Barb. lat. 535 (ol. XI. 178) of Anselm's collection reads: *Incipit autentica et compendiosa collectio ... tempore VII. Gregorii sanctissimi papae a beatissimo Anselmo Lucensi episcopo eius... discipulo, cuius iussione et precepto desiderante consummavit hoc opus* (ed. F. Thaner, Innsbruck 1906-15, p. 2). But the value of this rubric should not be overrated, since the Barberini MS represents a posthumous recension of Anselm's work, made under the pontificate of Paschal II (1099-1118) by a cleric of Lucca, cf. FOURNIER, *Observations sur les diverses récensions* etc., in *Annales de l'Univ. de Grenoble*, 13 (1901), 450-54. HOFMANN, op. cit., 17, assumes also for Bonizo's *Liber de vita christiana* composition upon papal request, quoting the epilogue (10, 79): *Cum a me exegisses, sacerdos venerande Gregori, ut... componerem* (ed. E. Perels, Berlin 1930, p. 335, 3-5). But *sacerdos* in the ancient Christian sense of « bishop » would be a

stress laid on the legislative supremacy of the pope and on cleansing the canonical tradition from all un-Roman elements is one of the most characteristic traits of the Gregorian canonists: it would indeed find its crowning achievement in a papal prerogative of approval for any compilation of canons whatsoever.

But on the other hand, if such an interpretation of DP 17 be correct, how could it happen that even the closest collaborators of Pope Gregory — an Anselm, a Deusdedit, a Bonizo — published their several collections without expressing to have received, or asked for, pontifical authorisation? To be sure, the Collection in seventy-four titles (*Sententiae diversorum patrum*, probably compiled by Cardinal Humbert in the early fifties) [8] served many a papal legate as « manual of reform » on his missions. [9] But this use did not make it an official text *ex auctoritate Romani pontificis* — not any more than the constant use by the papal chancery, centuries before, of the *Dionysiana*, or that of Gratian's *Concordia*, a century later, would entitle us to speak in these cases of official collections. If official collections had been part of the Gregorian program, should we not expect at least some attempt at its realization before the time of Innocent III?

Still, such queries might appear to be mere *argumenta ad hominem*: for a proper determination of the problem of DP 17 a broader basis must be found. Whatever the occasion and purpose of the *Dictatus papae* — and it is not the present writer's intention to add to the number of theories circulated on the subject [10] — this particular dictum should be examined

---

highly improper form of address for the pope; moreover it is certain that Bonizo finished his work c. 1089-95 under Urban II. Hence we should say with Perels (p. xxi, n. 7) that the person of the addressee, the priest Gregory, remains unknown.

[8] On the authorship see now A. MICHEL, *Die Sentenzen des Kardinals Humbert, das erste Rechtsbuch der päpstlichen Reform* (MGH., Schriften, 7), Leipzig 1943.

[9] FOURNIER - LE BRAS, op. cit., II, 16; A. VAN HOVE, *Prolegomena* (*Commentarium Lovaniense in Codicem iuris canonici*, I, 1; 2nd ed. Louvain 1945), 323; MICHEL, op. cit., 136ff.

[10] The earlier theories are reviewed at length in W. PEITZ, *Das Originalregister Gregors VII. im Vatikanischen Archiv* (*Sitzungsberichte der K. Akademie der Wiss. Wien*, phil.-hist. Kl., 165, 5; 1911), 265ff., and briefly in CASPAR's edition, 201 n. 1. Other hypotheses have been advanced by HOFMANN, op. cit.; R. KOEBNER, in *Kritische Beiträge zur Geschichte des Mittelalters: Festschrift für R. Holtzmann*, Berlin 1933, 64-92; Julia GAUSS, *Die Dictatus-Thesen Gregors VII. als Unionsforderungen*,

against the background of the Reformers' doctrines on the sources of Canon law. For the importance of these doctrines in the general framework of the Reform went far beyond their theoretical interest: they constituted the necessary instrument for the difficult task of defining the true tradition of the Church in matters canonical. Again, only by defining this tradition could the Reformers hope to see the ancient discipline of the Church (including what as unsuspecting readers of Pseudo-Isidore they took to be part of it) being restored.

Since an early age the Church had been faced with problems arising from the fact that canonical tradition consisted only in part of enactments that unequivocally carried universal obligation by their origin: a far greater number of canons originated from regional or particular sources, and their acceptance and recognition throughout the Church universal remained for centuries a matter of varying selection and irregular growth. From the fifth century onwards, time and again efforts had been made at clarifying and unifying the laws of the Church. The letters of Innocent I rejecting the authority of the Antiochene canons in the cause of St. John Chrysostom;[11] the controversy between Rome and Carthage in the affair of Apiarius;[12] the Roman collections growing out of the so-called Gelasian reform;[13] the *syntagmata* of Chalcedon and II Nicaea,[14] are well-known cases in point. On a lower, national level they were paralleled by the *Collectio Hispana* and by the literary activities of the Carolingian renaissance. But time and again such efforts had also been thwarted by decentralizing and particularistic tendencies, by the constant encroachment of secular legislation, of penitentials, of local custom.

There was no question for the Gregorian reformers where to take their stand in this antagonism between centripetal and

in *Zeitschrift der Savigny-Stift.*, Kan. Abt., 29 (1940), 1-115; BORINO, op. cit. (n. 5 supra). On the latter, see the concluding paragraphs of this paper.

[11] JK, 288 and 294 (MANSI, 3, 1096ff.); cf. VAN HOVE, *Proleg.*, 149, with bibliography in n. 2.

[12] ed. C. H. TURNER, *Ecclesiae occidentalis monumenta iuris antiquissima*, I, 1, III (Oxford 1930), 561-624.

[13] G. LE BRAS, *Un moment décisif dans l'histoire de l'Église et du Droit canon: La renaissance gélasienne*, in *Revue hist. de droit français et étr.*, 4e ser., 9 (1930), 506-18.

[14] The *syntagma* of the Trullan Synod (692), corresponding to the second part of the *Nomocanon* of the Enantiophanes, was of course never accepted in the West.

centrifugal forces. But the fact remained that in the absence of a complete body of explicitly universal rules a rational principle had to be found by which the unity of canonical tradition could be established in the variety of its sources. Rather than postulating a system of law that would be formally papal by its origin, this was a matter of defining what might be called the « Common law » [15] of the Church, i. e. of securing the validity of a body of heterogeneous rules in their material consonance, as in a common denominator, with the supreme lawmaking authority of the Roman Pontiff. This theory may be gleaned from the rubrics and lists of rubrics composed by Anselm, Deusdedit, Bonizo, for their respective compilations; and especially from such general observations as are found in the preface of Deusdedit and the writings of Bernold of Constance.[16] Some of the latter, it is true, properly belong to the post-Gregorian phase of the Reform and in their teachings on harmonizing interpretation perhaps reflect the more conciliatory policies of Urban II.[17] Still, even in these later tracts, Bernold's basic conception of the sources of Canon law merely restates the doctrine of the earlier, the strictly Gregorian generation.

The touchstone of this doctrine remains the relation of the old synodal law to papal authority. The Reformers might have simply reasserted the principle, so pointedly and frequently uttered by Pseudo-Isidore, viz. that the validity of every council is contingent upon the convocation or approval by the

[15] Common law in this context is not to be understood, in the sense of modern canonical theory, as that species of either universal or particular law which is opposed to *ius singulare* (i. e. which is to be ordinarily observed, as contrasted with an exceptional derogation of the rule, cf. VAN HOVE, *Proleg.*, 43f.), but rather in analogy to Anglo-American Common law, or to the recent Italian doctrines on the late-medieval *diritto comune*, as the sum total of valid rules (not mere customs) which form a coherent legal system without necessarily deriving their force from the positive act of a supreme legislator. On the impossibility of defining « common law » *per se* and *a priori*, see F. CALASSO, *Storia e sistema delle fonti del diritto comune*, I, Milano 1938, ch.s 2 and 3.

[16] For Bernold's theory of the sources, see now VAN HOVE, in *Misc. de Meyer* (n. 4 supra), with bibliography listed p. 371 n. 3.

[17] P. FOURNIER, *Un tournant d'histoire du droit*, in *Nouvelle Revue hist. de droit fr. et étr.*, 41 (1917), 157f. This applies in particular to BERNOLD's *De excommunicandis vitandis*; the *Apologeticus*, however, equally important for his doctrine on the sources, was written in the lifetime of Gregory VII, probably soon after 1076; cf. F. THANER, in his edition (*MGH., Lib. de lite*, 2, Hannover 1892), 59.

pope.[18] This was in fact their starting point [19] — and we should not forget that the canonists had also better and genuine authorities to rest their case on [20] — but it was not as easy as that to explain the actual situation of the canonical sources. The difficulty did not lie with the ecumenical councils (whatever the medieval computation of their number) [21] where the confirmatory effect of the Roman assent was a matter of general historical knowledge.[22] The difficulty arose with the particular councils, national, provincial, and otherwise. Nobody could pretend that all the particular synods of the East, Africa, Spain,

---

[18] Ps. Isid., praef., c. 8 (ed. Hinschius, Leipzig 1863, p. 19); Marcellus, ep. 1, 2; 2, 10 (pp. 224, 228 Hinsch.); Julius, cc. 5, 13 (459, 471 Hinsch.); Athanasius, ep. to Felix, c. 2 (479 Hinsch.); Damasus, c. 9 (503 Hinsch.); Pelagius II, ep. 1 (721 Hinsch.), etc.

[19] Cf. Ans. Luc., rubr. 1, 58; 59; 2, 7; 26-7; 40; 42; 45; 47-8; 60; 77 (pp. 29f., 77, 87, 92ff., 103, 112 Thaner); Deusd., praef. (ed. Wolf von Glanvell, Paderborn 1905, p. 1, 10-11); capitula lib. I passim (p. 7 lin. 8, 10, 12, 28); Bonizo, rubr. 4, 71 (p. 142 Perels); Bernold, Apolog., c. 3 (p. 62 Thaner); De excomm. vit., § 25 (123, 1-3 Thaner), § 32 (126, 2-9 Thaner, where the text should probably read: Nec mireris quod ipsorum conciliorum <auctoritatem> Romano pontifici ascribimus rell.).

[20] Cf. Aurelius of Carthage to Pope Innocent I (Mansi, 4,321D - 2A; Deusd., 1, 110); Bishop Lucentius, the legate of Leo the Great, at the Council of Chalcedon, act. 1: (Διόσκουρος) σύνοδον ἐτόλμησεν ποιῆσαι ἐπιτροπῆς δίχα τοῦ ἀποστολικοῦ θρόνου, ὅπερ οὐδέποτε γέγονεν οὐδὲ ἐξὸν γενέσθαι (Mansi, 6, 581 B; Schwartz, Acta conc. oec., II, 1, 1 [1933], 65, 31-2), et synodum ausus est facere sine auctoritate sedis apostolicae, quod nunquam factum est nec fieri licuit (Versio Rustici, 582B Mansi; Schwartz II, 3, i [1935], 40, 18-9; cf. Ans. Luc. 3, 91; Deusd. 1, 35); Gelasius, JK, 611 and 664 c. 3, 10 (ed. A. Thiel, Epistolae Rom. pont. genuinae, Braunsberg 1868, pp. 287f., 395; ed. O. Günther, Coll. Avellana [CSEL 35, Vienna 1895-8], 372, 10-18; cf. Ans. Luc. 1, 49; 4, 27; Deusd. 1, 165); Cassiodorus, Hist. trip., 4, 9 (PL., 69, 960); II Council of Nicaea, act. 6 (Mansi, 13, 207f.; cf. Deusd. 1, 46); Nicholas I, epp. JE 2764, I p. 355, 2784, 2691, 2796 (ed. Perels, MGH., Epp., 6, 2, 1 [1912], 296, 30-31; 380, 3; 389, 26; 450, 13-4; 473,14ff.; cf. Deusd. 1, 160). Some of these texts are mentioned by Fournier, Étude sur les Fausses décrétales, in Rev. d'hist. ecclés., 8 (1907), 26f.; in Perels' commentary on JE 2784, MGH., Epp., 6, 389 n. 8; and by Hofmann, Dict. pap., 83f. (who includes, however, Pseudo-Pelagius JK 954; cf. Ps. Isid., praef., c. 8; JL., II, p. 695).

[21] It is known that, under the influence of Gregory the Great's Synodica JE 1092 (Reg., 1, 25; ed. Ewald, MGH., Epp., 1 [1887], 36; cf. Deusd., 1, 232; Bernold, Apol., c. 3; De excomm. vit., § 38: pp. 61f., 129 Thaner), the authority of the first four councils was compared to that of the four Gospels and far exalted above the other councils. Nicaea II is not always mentioned by the canonists (cf. e. g. Bernold, De excomm. vit., § 37), and the Eighth Synod (Cp. IV) seems not to have been counted at all, from the reconciliation of Photius (880) until the second half of the eleventh century, among the ecumenical councils; cf. F. Dvornik, L'oecuménicité du VIIIᵉ concile etc., in Académie royale de Belgique, Bull. de la classe des lettres, 5ᵉ sér., 24 (1938), 445-87 (not all of Father Dvornik's conclusions, however, can be accepted).

[22] Cf. Deusd., capit. I, Quod eius auctoritate iam VIII uniuersales etc. (p. 7, 28 Wolf von Glanv.); Bernold, passim, esp. pp. 62, 126f.

Gaul, whose canons in one or the other selection formed part of the Western canonical tradition, had severally and expressly been confirmed by positive acts of the Roman Pontiffs. The canonists consequently had to demonstrate the correctness of their general assertion, *quorum tamen iudicia Romani pontifices firmaverunt*,[23] with the aid of various interpretations and constructions:

1) Papal decrees and statutes of ecumenical councils have repeatedly urged the annual (or semi-annual) celebration of provincial synods: hence follows an implicit approval of the latters' *rationabiles sententiae*;[24]

2) certain councils stand approved by the first canon of Chalcedon;[25]

3) many are included in the collection (*Dionysiana*) which Pope Hadrian I confirmed by sending it to Charlemagne; [26]

4) many were held upon the bidding of the pope and presided over by his legates: in this context Bernold refers especially to Mayence 847, the (spurious) Council of Nantes, and « innumerable others » (*et alia huiusmodi sexcenta*); [27]

5) many oriental councils, as well as Carthage 419, have been used by the popes in their statutes and decrees.[28]

But beyond such individual constructions — not all of which can escape the censure of being somewhat specious — both Deusdedit and Bernold proceeded to the formulation of a more fundamental, comprehensive principle; a principle which amounts to a sweeping admission of all canons (*quorumlibet aliorum canonum*) that were not in contradiction with

---

[23] BERNOLD, *De excomm. vit.*, § 25 (p. 123, 2-3 Thaner).

[24] Ibid., § 40; *Apol.*, c. 4 (pp. 130, 10-14; 63, 18-21, 34-6 Thaner).

[25] DEUSD., praef. (p. 3,30 - 4,7); BERN., locc. citt. (pp. 130, 15ff.; 64, 36-65, 6).

[26] BERN., *Apol.*, c. 4 (p. 65, 6-9); *De excomm. vit.*, §§ 31, 45 (pp. 125, 40; 132, 25-9). By the same token, the Latin version of Denis the Little (§ 43: p. 131, 24-5) and the *Canones apostolorum* (§ 28: p. 124, 28) are to be considered authentic.

[27] BERN., *De excomm. vit.*, § 50 (p. 135, 20-24: ...*celebrari iusserint eaque suis legationibus auctorizare consueverint*). On the spurious nature of Nantes, see SECKEL, in *Neues Archiv der Ges. für ält. deutsche Geschichtskunde*, 26 (1900), 39-72; FOURNIER - LE BRAS, *Hist. des coll. can.*, I, 259-62. DEUSD., praef., assumes express approval of Carthage 419 by the presence of papal legates (p. 3, 24-8) and inscribes Mayence 847, c. 11: *In concilio Maguntino, cui prefuit Romanus legatus Bonifatius martyr et episcopus* (DEUSD., 3, 27, p. 280; cf. FOURNIER - LE BRAS, II, 45).

[28] DEUSD., praef., p. 3, 22-4, 28-9.

papal and universal conciliar law, nor with faith and morals, and that corresponded to the needs of the Church.[29]

Based on a canon of III Toledo (589) and on the preface of Anastasius Bibliothecarius to his translation of II Nicaea,[30] this doctrine of a Common law, which is tested by its consonance [31] with the essentially universal legislation of popes and ecumenical synods, was of far greater consequence than is usually realized.[32] Without abandoning, in their verbal assertions, the rigid rule which required positive papal approval of the synodal law, the Gregorian canonists for all practical purposes substituted for it the more flexible rule of non-contradiction. Any canon, once it had been admitted by the force of this rule, was lifted beyond the sphere of particular law to which it would be limited by its origin, and became part of the Common law, i. e. universally applicable. It is an ironical turn of history that Cardinal Atto, the only canonist who was zealot enough to insist on territorial limitations of validity in the case of all Frankish and German councils,[33] later became a traitor to the

[29] Ibid., 4, 10-19 (quoting Anastasius Bibliothecarius, see n. 30): *...illas dumtaxat, que nec recte fidei nec bonis (probis orig.) moribus obuiant, set nec sedis Romane decretis ad modicum quidem (quid orig.) resultant, quin potius aduersarios (idest hereticos add. orig.) potenter impugnant.* — BERN. *De excomm. vit.,* § 50: *Hoc vero generaliter in quibuslibet provincialibus conciliis est observandum, ut illa semper capitula recipiamus quecumque apostolicis et universalibus institutis consonare et aecclesiasticae utilitati competere videamus* (p. 135, 24-6). Cf. *Apol.,* c. 4: *Sed nec reliqua concilia parvipendere debemus, in quibus multa nusquam alibi inventa, aecclesiasticae tamen dispensationi necessaria reperimus, quae quidem a superioribus autenticis sanctionibus nullomodo discrepant, cum christianae religioni apertissime conveniant...* (p. 63, 15-9). Cf. ibid., 64, 1-9.

[30] BERN., *De excomm. vit.,* § 50, continues: *Nam sancti patres sub districto anathemate illum dampnasse leguntur quicunque orthodoxorum patrum statuta non receperit quae universalibus conciliis consonare perspexerit* (p. 135, 26-7). The reference (cf. Thaner, n. 11, ad loc.) is to III Toledo, *prof. fidei,* n. 22: *Qui concilia orthodoxorum episcoporum consona conciliis Nicaeno, C.politano, primo Ephesino et Chalcedonensi non receperit, anathema sit* (MANSI, 9, 987). Anastasius Bibliothecarius, as quoted by Deusdedit (n. 29), is found in MANSI, 12, 982C; also edd. Perels and Laehr, *MGH., Epp.,* 7, 2 (1928), 417, 6-9.

[31] *Consonare* is used twice in Bernold. On « consonance » as a principle of medieval hermeneutics, see L. SPITZER, *Classical and Christian Ideas on World Harmony,* in *Traditio,* 2 (1944), 450.

[32] Some brief remarks in E. VOOSEN, *Papauté et pouvoir civil à l'époque de Grégoire VII,* Gembloux 1927, 91; VAN HOVE, *Proleg.,* 39 n. 3, in *Misc. de Meyer,* 367. See also the present writer's forthcoming paper, *Quelques observations sur l'autorité des collections canoniques dans le droit classique de l'Église* (Institut Catholique de Paris, Cinquantenaire de la fondation de la Faculté de droit canonique, *Mémorial des Journées d'Études,* 23-26, Avril 1947).

[33] *Capitulare,* ed. A. Mai (*Script. vet. nova coll.,* 6, 2, Rome 1832), p. 61: *...in locis ubi facta sunt obtinent firmitatem;* cf. HOFMANN, *Dict. pap.,* 88; VAN

Gregorian cause. As for the less fickle among the Reformers, the principle of non-contradiction not only helped them to retain such doubtful sources as the Apostolic Canons [34] and a selection of imperial laws, but even prompted a Deusdedit to include in his collection abstracts from the Photian synods of 861 and 879-80.[35]

In the light of this doctrine, too, we have to view the famous rule of interpretation which may be called its counterpart: in case of conflict among the canons, the lesser authority yields to the greater one.[36] This maxim had been expressed by St. Augustine [37] and by St. Isidore;[38] scholars have frequently noted its traditional role in early medieval hermeneutics.[39] But it might not be superfluous to point out that this rule on conflicting authorities, as quoted by the Gregorian canonists, was but complementary to the basic rule of non-contradiction; i. e., it brought into play the so-called « hierarchy of texts » only

---

Hove, in *Misc. de Meyer*, 365 n. 3; idem, *De Oorsprong van de kerkelijke Rechtswetenschap en de Scholastiek*, in *Mededeelingen van de Koninklijke Academie... van Belgi̋*, Kl. der Letteren, 6, 3 (1946), 20. A similarly rigorous opinion in Humbert of Silva-Candida, *Contra Nicetam*, c. 24: *Ceteri autem quamvis ss. patrum conventus, etsi potuerunt de utilitate et conversatione ecclesiarum suarum tractare, nullas tamen traditiones universali ecclesiae praefigere (PL., 143, 995C; C. Will, Acta et scripta quae de controv. eccl. graec. et lat. saec. undecimo composita extant*, Lipsiae 1861, p. 146a, 15-20), should be considered a polemical overstatement, caused by Niceta's reference to the Trullan Synod.

34 Cf. Deusd., praef., p. 4, 6-10; Bern., *De excomm. vit.*, § 28 (p. 124, 27-9, 40ff.).

35 Deusd., 4, 428-31; 432-37 (pp. 603ff.). This is truly amazing in the case of the first synod, which Deusdedit knew to have been quashed by Nicholas I and in which only lip-service had been paid to the rights of the Holy See. As to the Synod of St. Sophia, however, the researches of Dvornik, Grumel, Amann, and Jugie have now established the fact that John VIII definitely approved its main decision (though with one reservation, JE 3322: *mirandum valde est cur multa que nos statueramus, aut aliter habita aut mutata esse noscantur* rell.: ed. Caspar, *MGH., Epp.*, 7, 1 [1912], 228, 1-2) and that there was actually no « second schism » of Photius. For summary and bibliography see e. g. M. Jugie, *Le schisme byzantin*, Paris 1940, 120-30; 101 n. 1. On the other hand, the question raised by Wolf von Glanvell, *Deusd.*, p. XIII (cf. also Fournier - Le Bras, II, 48) as to whether the Photian texts might not be later additions to Deusdedit's work, still awaits thorough examination.

36 Deusd., praef., p. 3, 14-5; Bern., *De excomm. vit.*, § 50 (p. 135, 34-7).

37 *De bapt. contra Donat.*, 2, 3, 4 (ed. M. Petschenig, CSEL 51, 178, 20-25; cf. Bernold, loc. cit., and Deusd., 1, 296); also *De doct. christ.*, 2, 8, 12 (PL., 34, 40).

38 *Ep. ad Massonam* (PL., 83, 901). The letter has been declared spurious by Dom P. Séjourné, *St. Isidore de Séville*, Paris 1929, 75ff.; cf. also Van Hove, in *Mededeelingen* (n. 33, supra), 20 n. 1. Contra, with good reason, Le Bras, *Sur la part d'Isidore* etc., in *Revue des sciences relig.*, 10 (1930), 224f.; cf. also Michel, op. cit. (n. 8 supra), 52 n. 4.

39 Cf. J. de Ghellinck, *Le mouvement théologique du XIIᵉ siècle*, Paris 1914, 45ff. and 326ff.; Fournier - Le Bras, II, 337f.; Van Hove, in *Mededeelingen*, 20.

where the latter failed, and not everywhere as a general principle by which the inferior authority would under all circumstances be limited in force.[40] With a certain logic of development, the scholastic reasoning of post-Gregorian times was soon to demonstrate by dialectical-rhetorical devices the non-existence of contradictions in the sources, and thus all but to eliminate the practical application of the hierarchical argument.[41] No doubt this later development went far beyond, and in many regards even ran counter to, the Reformers' ideas. But among the antecedents of twelfth-century jurisprudence, the quest of the Gregorian canonists for a consistent body of canonical rules, for a Common law of the Church, should not be overlooked.

With the aid of the concepts outlined in the foregoing, the Reformers were able to fit all the sound elements of a diversified canonical tradition into the fundamental doctrine of the legislative supremacy of the pope, as both the keeper and the master of this tradition. With respect to the latter, it suffices to recall his power to alter the law « if need be »[42] — that is, to adapt by new legislation the Common law of the Church to the necessities and demands of the times.[43] As to his guardi-

---

[40] More on this point in the present writer's paper, *Quelques observations* etc. (n. 32, supra).

[41] Cf. DE GHELLINCK, op. cit., 49 (« comme solution ultime... ») and 334 (« en cas de divergence irréductible... »). See the glossators on D. 50 c. 28 (i. e. ISID., ep. cit.), or PETRUS Blesensis, *Speculum*, c. 1, § 1 (ed. T. A. Reimarus, Berlin 1837, p. 7f.).

[42] It has been shown by HOFMANN, *Dict. pap.*, 76ff., that no restriction *de iure* was meant by such clauses as *necessitate cogente* (DEUSD., *capit.*, p. 10, lin. 22), *causa exigente* (ibid., 10, lin. 26), *pro temporis necessitate* (DP 7A), *quae necessitas temporum exposcet* (ANS. LUC., 2, 33, p. 89 Thaner, overlooked by Hofmann 77), but only that prudent consideration of the needs of the times on which the Church has always insisted in making a change of the old law (cf. especially LEO the Great JK 544 pr.: MANSI, 6, 399f.). An exceptional, restrictive interpretation, based on INNOCENT I JK 303, *cessante necessitate debet utique pariter cessare quod urgebat* (MANSI, 3, 1061B concerning dispensations) is found in BONIZO, *Vit. chr.*, 1, 44 (p. 33 Perels, cf. Hofmann 77). On the whole problem see VOOSEN, *Papauté* (n. 32 supra), 121-37, who slips however in assigning (p. 123) to Gregory VII in the Roman Synod of 1074 a passage actually by BERNOLD, *Apol.*, c. 3 (p. 62, 10-14 Thaner).

[43] After the solid refutation given by E. RÖSSER, *Göttliches und menschliches, unveränderliches und veränderliches Kirchenrecht* (Görres - Ges., Sekt. Rechts - und Staatswiss., 64, Paderborn 1934), passim, esp. 163ff. and 175ff., it is hardly necessary to demonstrate once more the historical absurdity of Sohm's theory, according to which all Canon law before the « neo-Catholic » period (i. e. before the middle of the twelfth century) would have been essentially immutable, divine law. G. LADNER, *Theologie und Politik vor dem Investiturstreit* (Veröffentl. des Oesterreichischen Inst. für Geschichtsforsch., 2, Baden-Wien 1936), pp. 43, 48

anship of the old law, we find it emphasized time and again.[44] And from the emphasis laid on determining the consonance between synodal and papal law, it should be clear that not mere political expediency [45] dictated the appeal to the consistency of canonical tradition, so frequently voiced in the letters of Gregory VII.[46]

When we now return to DP 17, it will be against the background of these theoretical clarifications that we have to measure the dictum in question. For no interpretation of the *Dictatus papae* can overlook the fundamental fact that the document as a whole is in full harmony with contemporary canonical thought and does not proclaim any principles more radical or extreme than those generally held by the Gregorian canonists.[47] Once this premise is granted, an explanation which takes this particular pronouncement, *quod nullum capitulum, nullusque liber* etc., as a papal utterance on the sources of law, cannot be correct. By such an utterance the pope would indeed have been out of step with the basic canonical thought of his own group. The word *capitulum* in DP 17, to be sure, may refer to synodal or other canons — this use of the term is not unfamiliar to the writers of the period [48] — and the phrase *absque eius auctoritate* certainly can be construed in the same broad fashion in which Deusdedit and Bernold understood the papal « confirmation » of particular law, i. e. as including cases of material non-contradiction as well. But *liber*

(at § 6), 54, seems inclined to date the dichotomy, divine-human ecclesiastical law, not farther back than post-Gregorian period (late eleventh cent.) of the Reform movement. He may have been misled by the terminology of *lex dei, ius divinum,* applied to Canon law as a whole in mid-eleventh-century texts (see the quotation, p. 43). But this was merely an antonomastic figure of speech (on ancient occurrences see RÖSSER, op. cit., 108) which persisted down into scholastic times: examples given in KANTOROWICZ, *Studies in the Glossators of the Roman Law,* Cambridge 1938, 91 n. 5; VAN HOVE, *Proleg.,* 39 n. 2, could be easily increased.

44 Cf. the sources quoted in HOFMANN, op. cit. 74ff.; VOOSEN, op. cit., 121f.

45 So HOFMANN, 75.

46 References in HOFMANN, 74 nn. 1-3; cf. esp. *Reg.,* 2, 50: *concordia canonicae traditionis* (p. 191 Caspar).

47 This is one of the chief results of HOFMANN'S careful, comparative study.

48 E. g. BERN., *Apol.,* c. 4: *Huiusmodi, inquam, capitula in quibuslibet conciliis inventa...* (p. 63, 18 Thaner); *De excomm. vit.,* § 50 (n. 29, supra); HUMBERT, *Contra Nicetam,* c. 16: ... *exceptis capitulis L quae decreverunt regulis orthodoxis adiungere* (PL., 143, 990A; WILL, *Acta et scripta* [n. 33 supra], 141b, 24), concerning the Apostolic Canons; also ibid., cc. 20, 26-7 (cols. 992A, 997-8; WILL, 143a, 28; 147-8).

canonicus in this context makes little sense. We may boldly affirm that the very idea of a « canon law book » and of its possible authority is definitely outside the purview of all eleventh-century reflexion on the sources of law.

In all the assiduous collecting and compiling activities of the Gregorian canonists, it was the authority of the source material that preoccupied the mind of the Reformers. The various collections, into which this material was gathered, represented but individual vehicles of transmission; they would not and did not by this token become « sources » themselves.[49] Therefore it is not by chance that the canonists, including Gregory VII himself, when they wished to refer to the entire body of the rules of the Church, to Canon law as a whole, did not speak of any book or books, but of *canonicae traditiones, decreta sanctorum patrum, auctoritas canonum, sanctorum patrum privilegia, canonum statuta,* and the like.[50] *Liber canonicus* would not have carried the same connotation, in fact, would have been meaningless in such contexts.[51]

The dyad, *capitulum* and *liber,* however, fits precisely into another field: a field where the sovereign papal authority over « chapters and books » had been emphasized ever since antiquity; a field where books represented literary works significant in themselves and not merely compilatory tools of reference; a field, finally, where the term *canonicus* conveyed a definite meaning, too, but was not bound up with disciplinary

---

[49] A possible exception to this statement might be inferred from the passages of Bernold dealing with Pope Hadrian I's presentation of the *Dionysiana* to Charlemagne (n. 26 supra), or with the collection of « St. Isidore » (*De excomm. vit.,* § 49: p. 135, 16-9 Thaner), i. e. the *Hispana* as transmitted in Pseudo-Isidore. But it is significant that Bernold does not deduce from such examples of the past any suggestion for a similar course of action to be taken by the papacy in his own day.

[50] Examples in HOFMANN, op. cit., 74f., from Gregory's register.

[51] A parallel problem in the history of terminology exists for the expression, *ius canonicum,* as a collective noun. An epoch which still saw in « Canon law » mainly the broad stream of tradition did not use this term except for the individual « right », or rule of law (cf. *Conc. Germ.* 742, c. 3, ed. Werminghoff, *MGH., Conc.,* 2, Hannover 1906-8, p. 3; *Conc. Suesson.* 744, c. 4, ibid., 35; cf. J. B. SÄGMÜLLER, *Lehrbuch des katholischen Kirchenrechts,* 4th ed., Freiburg 1925ff., p. 12). Only with the systematic approach to « Law » as developed in the glossators' times did the concept of *ius canonicum* in the modern sense gain a substantial meaning. The terminological problem (not to be confused with a discussion of Sohm's theories) needs further study; the brief remarks in SÄGMÜLLER, loc. cit., and VAN HOVE, *Proleg.,* 39f., do not exhaust it. For the term *ius ecclesiasticum,* used as early as Berengar of Tours, see LADNER, *Theol. und Pol.* (n. 43 supra), 43.

enactments. It is the teaching power of the Roman Church, not her prerogative of law-making, to which DP 17 obviously points: the dictum has the familiar ring of the *Decretum Ge-lasianum de recipiendis libris,* summarizing, as it were, in a few words the gist of the long catalogue of *scripturae, opuscula, tractatus, libri* etc., in which the author of *Decr. Gel.* c. 4 [52] comprises the body of doctrinal tradition sanctioned by the Church of Rome. Quotations from this venerable document, in corroboration of the teaching authority of the pope, were common among the Gregorian canonists.[53] DP 17 quite appropriately adds to the mention of *libri* that of *capitula*: for Gelasian list began with the early ecumenical synods, and the Nicene decrees had been repeatedly designated as *capitula* in a pseudo-Isidorian letter fathered upon St. Athanasius and well known to the Reformers.[54]

The connection of DP 17 with the *magisterium* of the pope and with the *Decretum Gelasianum* has not passed unobserved,[55] but is rarely seen as clearly distinct from the Gregorian ideas concerning the formation and tradition of Canon law.[56] All ambiguity, however, vanishes once we realize that *canonicus* here denotes the « canon of dogmatic tradition », as exemplified in the Gelasian canon: not a customary usage of the term, to be sure, but one justified by the obvious and familiar parallel concept of the « canon » of Sacred Scripture.

[52] For the still unsettled controversy on the authorship, see the bibliographical information given in VAN HOVE, *Proleg.,* 140 n. 5; G. BARDY, in *Dictionnaire de la Bible,* suppl. 3 (1938), 579-90 s. v. *Gélase (décret de);* H. WURM, *Studien und Texte zur Dekretalensammlung des Dionysius Exiguus (Kanon. Studien und Texte* ed. Koeniger 16, Bonn 1939), 24 n. 54.

[53] ANS. LUC., 6, 187, *Qui libri sint legendi* (p. 354 Thaner); DEUSD., 1, 130 (CVI), with the *capitulatio* (p. 10, lin. 28 Wolf von Glanv.): *Quod nulla scriptura sit autentica, nisi illius iudicio sit roborata.* Also BERNOLD, *De incontinentia sacerd.*: *Nullum caput canonicae veritati contrarium pro autentico est recipiendum* (p. 24, 13 Thaner; cf. HOFMANN, op. cit., 86 n. 40, and CASPAR'S commentary to DP 17, p. 205) would seem to refer to *Decr. Gel.* rather than to the sources of Canon law.

[54] Ps. ISID.: Athanasius, *ep. ad Marcum pp.* (p. 451 f. Hinschius), in ANS. LUC., 1, 59; DEUSD., 1, 8.

[55] For *Decr. Gel.* see CASPAR'S commentary, ad loc.; FLICHE, *Réforme grég.,* II, 200; HOFMANN, 87; for papal teaching power, KOEBNER, in *Krit. Beitr.* (n. 10 supra), 77; GAUSS, *Dictatus-Thesen* (n. 10 supra), 95 f.

[56] KOEBNER, loc. cit., is an exception to this; he finds a good parallel text in HUMBERT, *Contra Nicetam,* c. 16: *Clementis librum... numeravere inter apocrypha, exceptis capitulis L quae... (PL.,* 143, 990A; WILL, *Acta et scr.,* 141b, 23ff.), but of course an application of DP 17 to the Pseudo-Clementines alone would be, too narrow.

Not that a reassertion of the principle underlying the *Decretum Gelasianum* would be a very daring proclamation.[57] But then — and at this point we have at last to touch briefly upon the moot question as to the nature and scope of the *Dictatus papae* — the general presumption that our document represents in one way or another a summary of postulates, a platform of papal policies eastern or western, a memorandum of directives, a draft for synodal proclamations or polemical treatises, and the like, has too often beclouded its sober interpretation. Misled by what appears a somewhat abruptly imperious and sybilline style in these twenty-seven statements, and influenced even by the inscription, *dictatus papae,* which in fact was nothing but a technical term of the chancery, modern scholarship has usually approached the text with an expectation of the spectacular.

Very seldom has the close kinship of its shape with the lists of rubrics (*capitula, capitulationes*) traditionally prefixed to the contemporary canonical collections been properly observed. It is amazing that the most natural, or rather the only natural explanation of the « riddle » of the *Dictatus papae* should have been missed by scholars, until a few years ago Father Borino showed [58] that Gregory's twenty-seven dicta are nothing but the usual *capitulatio* of a lost canonical collection.[59] The small collection itself, dealing exclusively with the *privilegium Romanae ecclesiae,* did not reach the registrator of the chancery, probably because the pope kept it on individual slips of vellum: [60] thus the papal *capitulatio* alone has come down to us. It would be hard to decide whether the individual *capitula* are to be considered as rubrics, covering each one

---

[57] Except for those who with Miss GAUSS (op. cit., passim) consider any assertion of the papal primacy a revolutionary innovation over against the « traditional », pentarchical constitution of the Church.

[58] *Un'ipotesi* etc. (as cited supra, n. 5).

[59] FLICHE, op. cit., II, 192, and HOFMANN, op. cit., 18 ff., closely approached this solution. But they both speak of a *capitulatio* penned by Gregory VII in view of a collection (or collections) yet to be composed; i. e. they still view the DP as a draft for something to be completed in detail (FLICHE: « ...ait voulu tracer aux auteurs de recueils futurs une sorte de canvas »; HOFMANN, 20: «..Entwurf einer Privilegiensammlung... »; p. 153: « ...eines sozusagen im Werden erstarrten Ueberrestes... »). Hofmann's thesis is quoted with approval by MICHEL, op. cit. (n. 8 supra), 7.

[60] BORINO, op. cit., 249, where the transcriptional reasons for this assumption are given.

canon of the missing collection; or rather as lemmata of an index, bracketing (in the fashion of the *Tabula collectionis Hispanae* [61] and Deusdedit) at times several scattered texts. With arguments present in favor of both possibilities,[62] judgment must be held in abeyance until the collection is reconstructed in full, as promised.[63]

Father Borino's theory is, in our opinion, one of those happy historical insights which have only to be formulated to be at once recognized as truth. As to the subject of the present paper, the private nature of the collection behind the *Dictatus papae* furnishes an additional argument against supposing any concern for official law books with Gregory VII. We suggest that DP 17 be read as the rubric which Gregory assigned to an abstract from c. 4 of the *Decretum Gelasianum,* and perhaps to a second fragment, taken from the pseudo-Athanasian letter to Pope Mark.

---

[61] SÉJOURNÉ, *St. Isidore* (n. 38 supra), 321 ff.; FOURNIER-LE BRAS, *Histoire,* I, 69 f.

[62] Individual rubrics are suggested, e. g., by DP 3 and 25, which are nearly identical; or by DP 7, which summarizes divers matter possibly contained in a single text. On the other hand, several canons seem to have furnished the material for DP 6. Cf. BORINO, op. cit., 245-7.

[63] Ibid., 243 n. 1.

III

SUR LES ORIGINES
DU TERME « DROIT POSITIF » *

Le terme « droit positif », notion fondamentale de la théorie du droit, n'est pas d'origine classique. On le chercherait en vain dans le vocabulaire des philosophes et des juristes romains, et ce ne sont que les canonistes du Moyen âge qui se servent du mot « ius positivum » pour établir une distinction entre la loi naturelle, d'une part, et d'autre part toutes les lois dont l'origine remonte à un acte législatif, comme par exemple les commandements que Dieu donna au peuple juif par la bouche de Moïse, ou les lois civiles et les « canones ». Le savant M. H. Kantorowicz, qui le premier a abordé ce problème d'histoire de terminologie juridique, a cru trouver dans le canoniste bolonais Damasus — dont les écrits ont été publiés dans les dernières années de la vie du pape Innocent III († 1216) (1) — le premier auteur qui ait parlé

* Les pages suivantes donnent un plus ample développement à quelques observations faites dans notre ouvrage *Repertorium der Kanonistik* (*1140-1234*) [*Prodromus Corporis Glossarum*, I, Città del Vaticano, 1936], p. 175 et s. On nous permettra donc de renvoyer le lecteur à ce livre et aux listes de manuscrits, à la bibliographie et aux investigations critiques qu'il contient, soit pour les écrits canonistes inconnus jusqu'à présent et que nous avons mentionnés dans l'étude suivante, soit pour la documentation de quelques résultats de critique littéraire pour lesquels nous nous trouvons en contradiction avec d'autres auteurs.

(1) La Summa titulorum de Damasus a été publiée après le 4e concile du Latran (novembre 1215). Cf. Kuttner, *Damasus als Glossator*, dans

du « ius positivum » (1). Nous pensons toutefois pouvoir démontrer que cette terminologie date en vérité déjà du xiie siècle et que d'ailleurs, pour ce qui est de l'usage du mot « positivus », elle peut selon toute apparence se réclamer d'une généalogie encore bien plus vénérable. Pour faire cette démonstration, nous allons d'abord (I) fournir ci-après quelques notices concernant la liste des auteurs médiévaux antérieurs à Damasus qui parlent de droit positif, la chronologie de ces auteurs et leur connexe littéraire. Ensuite (II), nous tâcherons de retrouver les sources probables où ces auteurs ont puisé pour le nouvel usage du mot « positivus ». Pour la première partie de ces recherches, nous avons eu la bonne fortune de pouvoir consulter un certain nombre de manuscrits jusque-là inconnus; quant à la seconde partie, qui, vu son caractère plutôt philosophique, outrepasse la compétence des historiens du droit, nous nous bornerons à quelques indications qui seraient peut-être de nature à porter un jour nouveau sur les relations entre la philosophie de l'antiquité et les premiers essais d'une méthode scientifique du droit au Moyen âge, en laissant à de plus autorisés que nous le soin des plus amples développements dont ces indications pourraient paraître susceptibles.

I

Le même Abélard, dont on n'ignore point l'influence sur le décret de Gratien et ses premiers commenta-

---

Zeitschrift der Savigny-Stiftung für Rechtsgeschichte, Kanonistische Abteilung (= ZKan), 23 (1934), p. 388. Les Quaestiones, les Gloses et les Brocarda sont probablement antérieurs à la Summa. Voir pour cette thèse (contraire à l'opinion de Schulte, Literaturgeschichte der Compilationes Antiquae, dans Sitzungsberichte der Wiener Akademie, phil.-hist. Classe [= Wiener SB] 66 [1870], p. 153) notre Repertorium, pp. 328, 420, 427.

(1) H. Kantorowicz, Das Principium decretalium des Johannes de Deo, ZKan, 12 (1922), p. 440 et s.; Damasus, ZKan 16 (1927), p. 332.

730

teurs (1), distingue dans son *Dialogue inter Philosophum, Judaeum et Christianum* entre justice positive
et justice naturelle :

« Oportet autem in his quae ad iustitiam pertinent, non
solum naturalis, verum etiam positivae iustitiae tra-
mitem non excedi. Ius quippe aliud naturale, aliud positivum dicitur. Naturale quidem ius est... Positivae
autem iustitiae illud est quod ab hominibus institutum,
ad utilitatem scil. vel honestatem tutius muniendam,
aut sola consuetudine aut scripti nititur auctoritate... » (2).

Dom O. Lottin, qui a découvert ce passage, l'appelle
une « distinction tout à fait intemporelle » (3). Il la voit
suivie uniquement par le théologien Simon de Tournai (4).
Mais, en réalité, cette distinction n'a pas échappé aux
canonistes du xii⁰ siècle.

Un des premiers qui s'en soient servis est Maître
Odon de Doura. Cet auteur, jusqu'à présent inconnu, a
écrit une somme du décret, conservée dans le Ms.
Cotton Vitell. A. III (fortement endommagé et incomplet)
du British Museum, sous le titre « Decreta minora
magistri Odonis de Doura ». Cette somme a subi l'influence de la célèbre somme écrite après 1160 par
Étienne de Tournai, qui, après avoir étudié et enseigné
à Bologne, rentra en France, où il a non seulement
achevé sa carrière ecclésiastique, mais sans doute large-
ment contribué aussi à la diffusion des études du

---

(1) Cf. De Ghellinck, *Le mouvement théologique du xii⁰ siècle*, Paris,
1914, p. 335 et s.; Fournier et Le Bras, *Histoire des collections canoniques en Occident*, II, 1932, p. 339, n. 3; Kuttner, *Zur Frage der
theologischen Vorlagen Gratians*, ZKan 23 (1934), pp. 245, n. 2,
252 et s.

(2) Migne, *Patrol. lat.*, 178, p. 1656.

(3) O. Lottin, *Le droit naturel chez saint Thomas d'Aquin et ses
prédécesseurs*, 2⁰ éd., Bruges, 1931, p. 28.

(4) Lottin, *loc. cit.*

Décret (1). On peut établir la dépendance directe d'Odon de ce maître par une comparaison des textes. Or, dans ces « decreta minora », qui sont à la fois une « summa » et une « abbreviatio » du Décret et qui constituent un des premiers documents de l'école décrétiste française (2), nous trouvons la distinction abélardienne :

« Humanum genus… lex et prophete (= Gratien, pr. D. 1). § Ex verbis Gratiani premissis perpendi potest, que sit divisio iuris. Omne enim ius aut naturale aut positivum. Ius vero naturale dicitur tribus modis… (Ms. cit., fol. 111) ».

Nous la trouvons également dans la somme « *Elegantius in iure divino vernantia* », dite Summa Coloniensis, que v. Schulte a découverte dans le Ms. Can. 39 de la Staatsbibliothek de Bamberg, mais qui est conservée sous une forme plus complète dans les Mss. 2125 de la Staatsbibliothek de Vienne et 14997 de la Bibliothèque nationale de Paris, ignorés jusqu'ici. La somme, qui appartient elle aussi à l'école française, fut publiée en 1169 par un clerc du diocèse de Cologne, qui avait fait ses études à Bologne et à Paris(3). Dom Lottin a communiqué de cette somme un texte qui commence par les mots : « Ius humanum aut est naturale… aut est positivum » etc. (4), sans toutefois en souligner le lien avec la distinction d'Abélard.

---

(1) Cf. sur la somme d'Étienne, l'introduction à l'édition partielle de Schulte, Giessen, 1891; Gillmann, *Die Notwendigkeit der Intention aufseiten des Spenders… der Sakramente*, Mainz, 1916, p. 18, n. 5, et dans *Archiv für katholisches Kirchenrecht* (= Archiv), 106 (1926), p. 499. Pour l'enseignement donné par Étienne en France, voir aussi Saltet, *Les réordinations*, Paris, 1907, p. 344.

(2) Pour la documentation exacte de ce que nous venons de dire sur Odon, voir notre *Repertorium*, p. 172 et s.

(3) Schulte, *Zur Geschichte der Literatur über das Dekret Gratians, Zweiter Beitrag*, dans Wiener SB 64 (1870), p. 93 et s.; Singer, *Beiträge zur Würdigung der Dekretistenliteratur I*, dans Archiv 69 (1893), p. 440; Saltet, *op. cit.*, p. 331 et s.; Gillmann, *Zur Lehre der Scholastik vom Spender der Firmung…*, Paderborn, 1920, p. 22.

(4) Voir le texte complet de cette distinction chez Lottin, *op. cit.*, p. 105.

Une terminologie non point identique, mais dont on ne saurait nier la parenté avec celle des auteurs précités, se trouve chez le Cardinal Laborans, qui se voua pendant les années de 1162 à 1182 à un remaniement complet du Décret de Gratien, dont le fruit, l'énorme *Compilatio decretorum* (Ms. C. 110 du chapitre de la Basilique de Saint-Pierre au Vatican), est d'ailleurs resté sans aucun succès (1). Nous y lisons le texte suivant, publié déjà par Theiner :

« Lex omnis et positionis acceptione digna constitutio ius naturale sequitur et de naturae venia sui rivuli trahit originem... » (2).

Il ne paraîtra point trop osé de ramener cette manière de s'exprimer aux études que le Cardinal, ainsi qu'il le déclare lui-même, a faites dans sa jeunesse en France (3).

Cependant, il n'y a pas de certitude sur la provenance d'une *Introduction* sommaire au Décret qui le précède dans un grand nombre de Mss. du xii° siècle et qui commence par les mots :

« In prima parte agitur de iustitia naturali et positiva, tam constituta quam inconstituta... » (4).

---

(1) Cf. sur Laborans et sa compilation, A. Theiner, *Disquisitiones criticae*, Romae, 1836, p. 399 et s.; Schulte, *Geschichte der Quellen und Literatur des Canonischen Rechts* (= QL), 1, Stuttgart, 1875, p. 148; Landgraf, *Laborantis cardinalis opuscula*, Bonnae, 1932 (*Florilegium patristicum*, fasc. 32), p. 1 et s.

(2) Laborans, *Compilatio Decretorum*, I, 1, 2, pr.; Theiner, *op. cit.*, p. 440.

(3) Cf. Laborans, *Compilatio Decr.*, IV, 5, 20, 3, où le Cardinal donne les dates de sa vie (imprimé chez Landgraf, *op. cit.*, p. 1, n. 1) : « ...de Francorum climate per Alemanniam regressum feliciter a scolis habens... ».

(4) Voir sur cette introduction, Schulte, *Zur Geschichte der Lit.*, etc., *Dritter Beitrag*, dans Wiener SB 65 (1870), p. 24 et s., qui en a fait imprimer les premières phrases. Une édition complète selon le Ms. 64 de l'abbaye de Montecassino se trouve dans la *Bibliotheca Casinensis*, II (1875), p. 171 et s.

C'est encore l'école française des décrétistes qui nous fournit deux autres témoignages de l'emploi du mot « ius positivum ». La somme, inconnue jusqu'à présent, écrite vers 1185, avec l'incipit « *Reverentia sacrorum canonum* », du Ms. Amplon. quart. 117 de la Bibliothèque d'Erfurt (1), commente l'initium du décret :

« ...dicitur et generali vocabulo mos prout nomen moris in primo cap. huius distinctionis sumitur; hoc autem apud pl'onem in thimeo ius positivum dicitur... ».

Nous aurons l'occasion de revenir plus tard sur cette citation du Timée de Platon.

La somme « *Animal est substantia animata* », dite Summa Bambergensis, découverte par v. Schulte dans le Ms. Can. 42 de Bamberg (2), distingue entre les différentes espèces de l' « ignorantia iuris » :

« Ignorantia iuris alia iuris naturalis, alia iuris positivi... Ignorantia iuris positivi excusat milites..., ignorantia autem iuris positivi canonici non excusat presbiterum... » (3).

Cette somme a été publiée en France entre 1206 et 1210 (4). Avec elle nous entrons donc dans le xiiie siècle.

Jusqu'à cette époque, ce ne sont que les maîtres décrétistes français qui aient appliqué le terme « ius positivum » (5). A partir de ce moment il entre aussi dans le

(1) Voir notre *Repertorium*, p. 194 et s.

(2) Schulte, *Dritter Beitrag*, p. 59 et suiv., QL, I, p. 226.

(3) Sum. Bamb. ad pr. D. 38 (fol. 33 v°). Cf. Kuttner, *Kanonistische Schuldlehre*, Città del Vaticano, 1935, pp. 164, n. 5, 166, n. 4, 168, n. 2.

(4) Cf. *Damasus als Glossator* (cité suprà, p. 728, n. 1), p. 381, n. 3. Pour l'origine française, voir les citations dans *Kanonistische Schuldlehre*, pp. 288, n. 1, 291, n. 1.

(5) L'importance et l'extension de cette école — qu'on nous permette de l'indiquer ici sans documentation plus détaillée — ont été beaucoup plus grandes qu'on ne l'enseigne ordinairement. Outre les sommes trouvées par Maassen, *Summa Parisiensis* ; Schulte, *Summa Coloniensis, Distinctiones Halenses, Sum. Lipsiensis, Bambergensis* ; Singer, *Summa Monacensis, Gallicana-Bambergensis*, et outre les deux ouvrages mentionnés

734

vocabulaire des Bolonais : Laurent d'Espagne, dans son apparat de gloses à la Compilatio tertia, publié entre 1210 et 1215 et retrouvé par M. Gillmann dans le Ms. Can. 19 de Bamberg (auquel je peux ajouter les Mss. 3912 et 15398 de la Bibliothèque Nationale de Paris), s'exprime ainsi qu'il suit : « Isti nec ius naturale attenderant... nec ius etiam positivum... » (1); et Vincent d'Espagne dans son apparat à la même compilation, publié à la même époque : « Nota mitius agitur cum ignorante ius positivum... » (2).

Dans la préface de la « summa titulorum » de Damasus, publiée après le IVe Concile du Latran, nous trouvons le passage suivant :

« Iuris autem species sunt duae. Est enim ius naturale quod natura omnia animalia docuit, ut Inst. de iure nat. gent. et civ. in princ. (Inst. I, I, I). Est etiam ius positivum sive expositum ab homine, ut sunt leges seculares et constitutiones ecclesiasticae... » (3).

Et, comme la somme « Animal est substantia animata », il distingue dans les Brocarda entre l'ignorance du droit naturel et celle du droit positif (4) :

« Arg. ignorantiam excusare in his que sunt iuris positivi... in his que sunt iuris naturalis... — Contra... —

pour la première fois dans le présent article, il existe encore un nombre assez grand de « summae », de « distinctiones », etc., inconnues de l'école française, que nous signalerons dans notre *Repertorium* pour combler les lacunes des manuels d'histoire du droit canon.

(1) Laurentius, Glos. ad Comp. III : I, 1, 1 ; cf. Gillmann, *Des Laurentius Hispanus Apparat zur Compilatio III auf der staatlichen Bibliothek zu Bamberg*, Mainz, 1935, p. 97, n. 1. Pour la date, voir *ibid.*, p. 123.

(2) Vincentius, Glos. ad Comp. III : V, 21, 5, v. iurisperitiam (Ms. Bamberg, Can. 20, fol. 177 v°, Leipzig Univ. 983, fol. 176). — Pour la date, voir Gillmann, dans Archiv 106 (1926), p. 161, n. 1 (163) ; Archiv 109 (1929), p. 263, n. 1 (264).

(3) Texte complet chez Laspeyres, *Bernardi Papiensis Faventini episcopi summa decretalium*, Ratisbonae, 1866, p. 353 ; cf. Kantorowicz, *loc. cit.* (*suprà*, p. 729, n. 1).

(4) Cf. Kantorowicz, *loc. cit.*

Solutio : Si ius positivum ignoretur ante promulgationem, quia pocius factum promulgantis ius illud ignoratur quam ius, non nocet... (1). Circa ignorantiam iuris positivi ponitur regula talis : iuris positivi ignorantia non prodest acquirere volentibus, suum verum conservare volentibus non nocet, ff. de iur. et fact. ign. L. Iuris ignorantia... (Dig., 22, 6, 7) ».

Les *Casus* du décret, conservés dans les Mss. oct. 26 de Berlin, 922 de Trèves (2) et Royal 11. A. II du British Museum, écrits vers la même époque, commencent :

« Tractaturus (igitur *add*. *Roy*.) Gracianus de iure canonico orditur ab altiori, scil. (videl. a *Roy*.) iure naturali, multipharie distinguens tam ipsum ius naturale quam positivum (positorium *Berl*.)... »

Citons enfin, comme dernier représentant de l'époque prégrégorienne, Tancrède, qui a composé sa « Glossa ordinaria » à la Compilatio prima entre 1210 et 1215, bien qu'il n'en ait publié la rédaction définitive qu'après 1220 (3) :

« Nota consuetudinem excusare... Solutio : consuetudo excusat a pena temporali, ut hic, accusat in eterna, ut ibi; arg. XI. q. I. Multi (c. 18) in fine. Vel in hiis que sunt illicita iure positivo tantum excusat. In hiis autem que iure naturali, nullo modo excusat, ut XXXII. q. VII. Flagicia (c. 13) τ » (4).

Comme beaucoup de gloses de Tancrède, celle-ci a été

(1) Kuttner, *Kanonistische Schuldlehre*, p. 173, n. 3.

(2) Pour ces deux Mss., cf. Seckel dans *Zentralblatt für Bibliothekswesen*, 36 (1919), p. 274, qui toutefois parle de « Decretum abbreviatum ».

(3) Ces dates résultent du fait que Tancrède publia sa Glose à la Comp. III après 1220 (cf. Gillmann, dans Archiv 113 [1933], p. 483, n. 4, et qu'il écrit dans le prologue : « ...primas et secundas decretales, prout melius potui, glosulavi...; nunc autem... et constitutiones concilii proxime celebrati et iura a domino Innocentio PP. III. post. XII. annum edita tam in apparatibus a me factis, quam in hoc quem ordinare dispono, diligentissime collocabo ». Il déclare donc vouloir publier ces trois commentaires ensemble.

(4) Tancrède, Glos. ad Comp. I : I, 6, 2, v. consuetudo (Cod. Vat. Borgh. 264, fol. 4 v°).

736

incorporée, avec de légères transformations, par Bernard
de Botone dans la « Glossa ordinaria » aux Décrétales de
Grégoire IX (1). Dès lors, on peut constater que le terme
« ius positivum » est reçu quasi officiellement.

II

Où Abélard et les canonistes français ont-ils pris le
mot « positivum » pour caractériser le contraire du droit
naturel? Il n'est pas vraisemblable qu'ils aient inventé
eux-mêmes cette nouvelle acception du terme.

La somme « *Reverentia sacrorum canonum* » nous fournit une indication précieuse par les mots : « ...hoc autem
apud platonem in thimeo ius positivum dicitur » (voir plus
haut, p. 733). On sait que le *Timée* de Platon était connu
des théologiens médiévaux dans la traduction latine de
Chalcidius (2). Il était connu de même des canonistes par
leurs études de théologie (3). Et en effet on lit, non pas
dans le texte de Timée, mais dans le commentaire que
Chalcidius y joint (4) :

« Igitur cum illis libris (les 10 livres de la République,
disputés dans la fiction de Platon le jour qui précéda le
dialogue du Timée et mentionnés par Chalcidius dans le
chapitre précédent) quaesita atque inventa videretur
esse iustitia quae versaretur in rebus humanis, superes-
set autem, ut naturalis aequitatis fieret investigatio,
huius tanti operis effectum, quod ingenio suo diceret
onerosum Socrates, Timaeo et Critiae et Hermocrati

---

(1) Glos. ord. in X : I, 11, 2, v. antiqua.

(2) Cf. Ueberweg-Geyer, *Grundriss der Geschichte der Philosophie*, II
(11e éd., 1928), p. 148 ; M. De Wulf, *Histoire de la philosophie médiévale*
(6e éd., 1934), I, pp. 70, 72.

(3) Cf. Singer, *Beiträge zur Würdigung der Dekretistenliteratur*, II,
Archiv 73 (1895), p. 71, n. 207, et dans son édition de la *Summa Magistri Rufini* (Paderborn, 1902), p. CLVII, n. 123, p. CXXIV, n. 123; Gillmann,
dans Archiv 105 (1925), p. 565.

(4) *Platonis Timaeus interprete Chalcidio cum eiusdem commen-
tario*, éd. Wrobel (Lipsiae, 1876), c. 6, p. 72.

delegandum putavit; atque illi munus iniunctum receperunt. Ex quo adparet in hoc libro principaliter id agi, contemplationem considerationemque institui non positivae, sed naturalis illius iustitiae atque aequitatis, quae inscripta instituendis legibus describendisque formulis tribuit ex genuina moderatione substantiam. Perindeque ut Socrates, cum de iustitia dissereret qua homines utuntur, induxit effigiem civilis reipublicae, ita Timaeus Locrensis ex Pythagorae magisterio astronomiae quoque disciplinae perfecte peritus, eam iustitiam qua divinum genus adversum se utitur in mundi huius sensilis veluti quadam communi urbe ac republica voluit inquiri ».

Bien entendu, à cet endroit la « non positiva sed naturalis iustitia » n'a pas un sens juridique mais métaphysique; la « iustitia positiva » signifie ici l'ordre de la vie sociale humaine, tandis que la « iustitia naturalis » comprend la manière dont Dieu gouverne le monde entier, ordonne les mouvements des corps célestes, etc. On peut trouver une reproduction très exacte de cette notion chalcidienne dans un grand commentaire anonyme bolonais du xiiiᵉ siècle (environ 1210-1215) au Décret de Gratien, commençant par les mots « Ius naturale tres habet acceptiones », et inconnu jusqu'à présent, bien qu'il soit conservé dans plusieurs Mss. (1) :

« Hec appellatio « ius naturale » quandoque proprie accipitur, et dicitur ius naturale ius quo reguntur omnes creature, sc. Deus regit mundum, de quo iure dicitur plato tractasse in timeo. Et ibi dicitur iustitia naturalis quo iure ascendunt levia, descendunt ponderosa et ex similibus similia procreantur... ».

Nous aussi nous parlons métaphoriquement des « lois » de la nature, en empruntant le mot à la langue juridique. De même, la « iustitia » chez Chalcidius n'est qu'une diction métaphorique. Mais les épithètes accessoires qu'elle

(1) Voir sur ce commentaire notre *Repertorium*, p. 67-75. Mss. : Paris, Bibl. Mazarine 1318, Bibl. nat. 3909 et 15393, Cambrai 645, Vendôme 88. Les trois derniers Mss. donnent le commentaire sous la forme de glose marginale au décret.

738

y trouve pouvaient fort bien influencer à leur tour la terminologie juridique, d'où le mot principal « iustitia » tirait son origine. Telle pouvait être chez Abélard l'association des idées lors de l'introduction de la « iustitia naturalis » et « positiva » dans une discussion philosophique du droit.

L'antithèse « naturalis-positivum », que les auteurs du XIIe siècle empruntèrent très vraisemblablement à Chalcidius, attribue déjà chez ce dernier au « positivus » un sens particulier, qui ne correspond pas à l'usage ordinaire de ce mot dans l'antiquité latine. Je dois à la bienveillance de M. Dittmann, secrétaire général de la commission du Thesaurus Linguae Latinae à Munich, une liste complète des auteurs classiques chez lesquels on trouve le mot « positivus ». Or, exception faite pour trois auteurs (dont l'un est Chalcidius), « positivus » n'est jamais autrement employé que dans le sens grammatical de la gradation des adjectifs (1). L'acception particulière d'opposition à « naturalis » lui est donnée par les seuls Chalcidius, Fortunatianus dans son *Ars rhetorica* (2) et Aulu-Gelle. Ce faisant, ils ont simplement traduit en latin l'antithèse grecque φύσει-θέσει (3), ainsi qu'il ressort

(1) La liste de M. Dittmann contient 77 citations, dont 47 tirées des *Grammatici latini* (éd. Keil); les autres se trouvent chez Sextus Pomponius Festus, *De verborum significatione* (éd. Mueller, 1839), p. 152, et plusieurs dans le commentaire des Comédies de Térence par Aelius Donatus Grammaticus, celui de l'Énéide par Maurus Servius Honoratus Grammaticus, etc., etc.

(2) C. Chirius Fortunatianus, *Ars rhetorica* (éd. Halm, *Rhet. lat. min.*, Lipsiae, 1863), II, 3 : « Locus omnis qualis est? aut naturalis, ut in mari, in campo. aut positivus, ut in civitate. positivum quot modis consideramus? octo... ».

(3) Voir l'article sur Fortunatianus, chez Pauly-Wissowa, *Realencyclopaedie der class. Altertumswissenschaft*, VII, I (1912), col. 48, lin. 30 et s., où M. Muenscher démontre la probabilité d'une source grecque de la distinction citée du « locus ». Cf. aussi le Glossaire gréco-latin du Ms. Harleian. 5792 du British Museum (éd. Goetz et Gundermann, *Corpus Glossariorum latinorum*, II, Lipsiae, 1888), p. 328, 10 : Θετικος positiuus.

clairement des *Nuits Attiques*, où Aulu-Gelle parle de l'origine des « nomina » (X, 4) :

« Quod P. Nigidius argutissime docuit nomina non positiva esse, sed naturalia. Nomina verbaque non positu fortuito, sed quadam vi et ratione naturae facta esse P. Nigidius in grammaticis commentariis docet... Quaeri enim solitum apud philosophos φύσει τὰ ὀνόματα sint ἢ θέσει... » (1).

Cela s'accorde fort bien avec tout ce que nous savons de Chalcidius : notamment que son commentaire du Timée est traduit d'après des sources grecques, qui, peut-être, dérivent à leur tour d'un commentaire perdu de Poseidonios (2). Il semble bien que, pour le moment, ce soit dans ces commentaires que se perdent les premières traces qui nous conduisent à l'origine du mot « droit positif », et nous ne voyons pas encore de ligne directe qui mènerait jusqu'à la discussion des sophistes sur la δικαιοσύνη, dont nous informent les dialogues de Platon ; en effet, cette discussion ne se déroule point autour de l'antithèse φύσει et θέσει δίκαιον, mais les termes qu'elle met en opposition sont plutôt φύσει et νόμῳ δίκαιον (3).

---

(1) La discussion mentionnée par Aulu-Gelle se déroula entre Pythagore et Démocrite, comme nous l'apprenons par Proclus : οὐκ ἄρα, φησὶ Πυθαγόρας, τοῦ τυχόντος ἐστὶ τὸ ὀνοματουργεῖν... φύσει ἄρα τὰ ὀνόματα · ὁ δὲ Δημόκριτος θέσει λέγων τὰ ὀνόματα... (Diels, *Die Fragmente der Vorsokratiker*, 4ᵉ éd., 1922, 55 B 26). Les canonistes français ont connu Aulu-Gelle : voir les citations de « Agellius » dans la *Summa Parisiensis* (environ 1170) et dans la *Summa Antiquitate et tempore* (après 1170) mentionnées par Schulte, *Zur Geschichte der Literatur*, etc., *Zweiter Beitrag* (*suprà*, p. 731, n. 3), p. 127 ; Singer, *Beiträge*, etc., II (*suprà*, p. 736, n. 3), p. 91.

(2) B. Switalski, *Des Chalcidius Kommentar zu Platos Timaeus*, Münster, 1902, p. 109 et s., dont les résultats pourtant ne sont pas définitifs ; cf. Ueberweg-Praechter, *Grundriss der Geschichte der Philosophie*, I (12ᵉ éd., 1926), p. 649 (*Bibliographie*, p. 199*) ; sur la discussion récente concernant l'existence du Commentaire de Poseidonios : *ibid.*, p. 478, n. 1, p. 151*. — De Wulf, p. 83 et s.

(3) Cf. le discours de Kalliklès : *Plat. Gorg.*, 482 E seqq. ; celui d'Hippias :

740

Plat. Protag., 337 C seqq., et le grand et important fragment d'Antiphon περὶ ᾿Αληθείας : éd. Hunt, *The Oxyrhynchos Papyri*, XI (1915), n. 1364; éd. Diels, *Vorsokr.*, II, p. 31 et s.; Archelaos (Diels, *Vorsokr.*, 47 A 1) : καὶ τὸ δίκαιον εἶναι καὶ τὸ αἰσχρὸν οὐ φύσει, ἀλλὰ νόμῳ; Iamblich, *Protrept.* (éd. Pistelli, p. 100, 15 = Diels, II, p. 332, 12) : διὰ ταύτας τοίνυν τὰς ἀνάγκας τόν τε νόμον καὶ τὸ δίκαιον ἐμβασιλεύειν τοῖς ἀνθρώποις καὶ οὐδαμῆ μεταστῆναι ἂν αὐτά · φύσει γὰρ ἰσχυρὰ ἐνδεδέσθαι ταῦτα. Voir encore pour φύσει-νόμῳ en général dans la philosophie présocratique : Hippocrate, *De victu*, I, 11 (Diels, 12 C 1 [I, p. 108, 20]); Philolaos (Diels, 32 B 9); Leukippos, Democrite, Diogenes Apollon. (Diels, 54 A 32, 55 A 1 [II, p. 13, 31]); Nausiphanes (Diels, 62 B 2 [II, p. 158, 11]).

IV

URBAN II AND THE DOCTRINE OF INTERPRETATION: A TURNING POINT?

Much has been written on the beginnings of medieval jurisprudence and its relation to the early stages of scholastic theology
and philosophy. To the student of today the insights of such
modern classics as Grabmann, Fournier, and de Ghellinck have
become almost commonplace; at the beginning of the century
they were startling discoveries. Likewise, the modern student
of constitutional history, political thought, and institutions could
not ignore the medieval jurists, after Gierke and Maitland first
showed the way. If indeed he has learned to use them as historical sources, this is largely — and beyond the borders of this
country — the doing of the scholar and friend to whom these
pages are inscribed.

With the medieval ruler's function primarily expressed in
the vocabulary of judicial processes, and with government itself,
spiritual and temporal, basically understood as *ius dicere*, many
principles of " jurisdiction " in the broadest, political sense remained a matter for jurisprudence to determine. It is for this
reason that we have to turn to the development of certain canonical teachings on the flexibility and the mutability of laws when
we look for the beginnings of what later political theory would
call the doctrine of administrative discretion proper to the making of executive decisions.

This is not a new observation; it has also been said more
than once that in the early phases of canonistic thought the boun-
dary lines remained rather fluid between interpreting the law,
dispensing from its observance, granting a privilege, and altering
the old law by legislation (1). The possibility of dispensation
from the common law of the Church continues to the present day
as a characteristic feature of canon law; and until very recently,

---

(1) A. van Hove, *De privilegiis — De dispensationibus (Commentarium Lovaniense in
Codicem iuris canonici* I 5; Malines-Rome 1939), 297ff. and earlier writers there cited.

in a direct and significant continuation of medieval teaching, it has been construed as a part of legislative power (2).

If this paper takes up once more the relation that existed between the doctrine of dispensation and the quest for principles of hermeneutics in the canonistic developments of the period preceding Gratian's *Concordia discordantium canonum*, it is not with the intention of retelling a story that has been told before (3), but with the limited objective of re-examining one particular point in this development. Ever since Paul Fournier in 1917 published his brilliant essay, " Un tournant de l'histoire du droit: 1060-1140 " (4), the early stages of the harmonizing method of interpretation have been connected with the conciliatory policies of Pope Urban II. Fournier sensed that the acts of Urban, in upholding the Gregorian principles while tempering their application with prudent lenience — especially during the early years of his pontificate — provided a convincing background for the canonists' efforts at reconciling the discrepancies in the tradition of their sources (5). But Fournier found more than this interplay between political and intellectual trends in a letter Pope Urban wrote in 1088 or 1089 to Bishop Peter of Pistoia and the Abbot of Vallombrosa (6). The case of Daim-

---

(2) See VAN HOVE, *op. cit.*, 316ff.; R. NAZ, " Dispense ", *Dictionnaire de Droit canonique* 4 (1949) 1287, and the current textbooks. The classification is tied up with the doctrine, presented for centuries as an almost axiomatic truth that only the legislator, his successor, his superior, and his delegate can dispense from the former's law: thus still the *Codex iuris canonici* of 1917, can. 80. The decree *Christus Dominus* of the Second Vatican Council (28 October 1965) no. 8 (b) has abandoned this doctrine: a bishop can now dispense in his own right from the general law of the Church except in cases reserved to the pope. Hence the nature of dispensation as an administrative act has become more evident.

(3) *Pace* the reviewer of this writer's *Harmony from Dissonance* (Latrobe 1960) in the *English Historical Review* 78 (1963), 359.

(4) *Nouvelle Revue historique de Droit français et étranger* 41 (1917), 129-80.

(5) *Ibid.*, 157ff.

(6) Urban II, JL 5383 [the initials JK, JE, JL designate the numbers in the second edition of JAFFE's *Regesta pontificum Romanorum*, by KALTENBRUNNER, EWALD, and LOEWENFELD (Leipzig 1885-88)]; P.F. KEHR, *Italia pontificia* 3 (Berlin 1908) 119 no. 2, 320 no. 6. The letter is commonly dated 1088 *s.d.*; its chronological position in the *Collectio Britannica* (Urb. no. 30) suggests a date after July 1088 (restoration of Archbishop Anselm of Milan, nos. 11/12, 23: JL 5359,5378) and before 18 April 1089 (letter to Gebhard of Constance, no. 38: JL 5393). But the matter is complicated by the mention in our letter (JL 5383) of an uncertain *synodale concilium* held earlier; see Appendix I *infra*.

bert (Daibertus) (7), whom Urban had consecrated as bishop of Pisa after first conferring, or rather reconferring, on him the order of diaconate, had caused the indignation of the *zelanti* here addressed, for Daimbert had been ordained a deacon before by the " heretic " (i.e. simonist) Archbishop Wezelo of Mainz. The concluding part of this letter was to become a crucial text in the canonical collections, from Ivo to Gratian (C. 1 q. 7 c. 24), for the long-drawn debate on reordination and the validity of orders administered by those separated from the Church. In the longer version, however, as presented by the *Collectio Britannica* (8), the letter opens with a rebuke to those who rush into recriminations before studying a doubtful matter — a mild enough rebuke, indeed, if one considers that Peter of Pistoia's own episcopal election and consecration were tainted and very much in need of papal dispensatory toleration (9). This is followed by two paragraphs containing general considerations on the flexibility and mutability of ecclesiastical discipline; and it is here, Fournier tells us, that Urban II inaugurated the principles of harmonizing interpretation of contradictory canons — principles which would then be developed in detail in the writings of two men who both were personally close to him: Ivo of Chartres and Bernold of Constance.

> Qui ne voit les facilités données par cette doctrine, non seulement au supérieur ecclésiastique pour accommoder la législation aux besoins du temps, mais encore à l'interprète du droit, invité à recourir à l'histoire pour expliquer les apparentes contradictions des canons? (10)

---

(7) The forms Daimbertus, Daibertus, Dagobertus vary in the sources for the name of the bishop of Pisa and later Patriarch of Jerusalem.

(8) British Museum, MS Addit. 8873, fol. 147r, cf. P. EWALD, *Die Papstbriefe der Brittischen Sammlung* in *Neues Archiv* 5 (1879) 360, Urb. no. 30; edited in part by S. LOEWEN-FELD, *Epistolae pontificum Romanorum ineditae* (Leipzig 1885), 61f. no. 126.

(9) Urban II, JL 5380, *It. pont.* 3.119 no. 1: *Coll. Brit.* fol. 146r, ed. EWALD, 359, Urb. no. 25: " Quamuis de electione tua et consecratione, sicut nobis relatum est, minus canonica dubitemus, te tamen pro tempore, ut et multos alios dispensatorie sufferentes, tolleramus " (dispensatorie] dispensatoris BISHOP, dispensatores EWALD).

(10) FOURNIER, *Un tournant...* (note 4 *supra*), 157. Earlier in the same paragraph he writes: " D'après la doctrine qu'y indique le pontife, à côté des canons dont il importe d'assurer l'exécution, il en est d'autres dont la rigueur peut être tempérée, selon la discrétion des supérieurs... Il faut donc distinguer, dans la législation canonique, une part immuable et une part variable... "; cf. also his " Bonizo de Sutri, Urbain II et la Comtesse Mathilde ", *Bibliotheque de l'Ecole des Chartes* 76 (1915), 289f.

This reading of Urban's letter on the Daimbert case, reaffirmed in the concluding chapter of the *Histoire des collections canoniques* (11), has been generally accepted: authors speak of Urban II as having initiated, stimulated, pointed the way, or taken the first steps towards a harmonization of the canons (12).

I should like to argue here 1) that this text, i.e. the opening paragraphs of the letter as it appears in the *Collectio Britannica*, had no influence whatever on the canonists' doctrines; 2) that it does not deal at all with rules for interpreting apparent discrepancies or diverse categories of canons but stands entirely in a traditional line of papal and other pronouncements, from Innocent I and Leo the Great to Gregory VII, on the need for tempering or relaxing in given circumstances the strict application of a rule; 3) that these sections of the text in *Coll. Brit.* are not part of Urban's original letter on the Daimbert case but an intruded gloss, based on passages lifted from Ivo of Chartres.

I.

The first of these assertions follows from the history of the text. Its composition and the transmission of its parts are not too clearly presented in Loewenfeld's printing, nor in his edition of Jaffé's *Regesta*, nor even in Kehr's *Italia pontificia* (13). Two sections only of the letter were known before Ewald published

---

(11) P. FOURNIER et G. LE BRAS, *Histoire des collections canoniques en occident* (Paris 1932), II 358; also LE BRAS, *Le Liber de misericordia et iusticia d'Alger de Liège* in *Nouvelle revue hist. de Droit fr. et étr.* 45 (1921), 80.

(12) J. DE GHELLINCK, *Le mouvement théologique du XIIe siecle* (2nd ed. Bruges-Bruxelles-Paris 1948) 433; W. ULLMANN, *The Growth of Papal Government* (2nd ed. London 1962) 371 and n. 4; C.R. CHENEY, *From Becket to Langton* (Manchester 1956) 43f. More cautiously G.B. LADNER, *Theologie und Politik vor dem Investiturstreit* (Baden-Wien 1936) 48: " ...Diese Harmonisierungsarbeit, vielleicht durch Urban II. angeregt... ".

(13) LOEWENFELD, *Epistolae*, 62, after printing the new section from *Brit. Urb.* no. 30, refers only to *Scripsistis*, MANSI XX. 644 (*leg.* 664) for continuation; without going to JAFFÉ, *Regesta* (cited in a footnote), one would not guess that more follows. In JL 5383 (JAFFÉ 4027) the initia *Debent subditi*, *Scripsistis*, and *Daibertum* are listed, but neither *Porro Daibertum* (so *Brit.*) nor the sequence of the parts are recorded. KEHR, *It. pont.* 3.119 no. 2 records *Debent subditi* for Pistoia (the full letter) with a note on the two addressees for the " pars quae de Daiberto agit "; and again *Scripsistis nobis* under Pisa, p. 320 no. 6, but without indicating what portion the collections contain which he cites. The other initia are not given here.

the first description of the *Britannica* (14): 1) the chapter " Daibertum — nil dare potuit ", on (re)ordination of Daimbert as deacon, was included in Ivo's *Panormia* 3.81, in the *Caesaraugustana* 4.40, and several other collections down to Gratian C. 1 q. 7 c. 24 — all derivatives, directly or indirectly, of Ivo's text (15). 2) The chapter " Scripsistis nobis — deposuimus ", discussing the scandal caused by the consecration of the bishop of Pisa (i.e. Daimbert), is found only once outside the *Britannica*: in a codex of St. Victor in Paris, from which Canon Jean Picard early in the seventeenth century communicated the text " cum aliis plurimis " to Severin Binius; it was handed down through the collections from the second edition of Binius's *Concilia* (1618) to Mansi (16). The Victorinus can be identified as Arsenal MS 713 in Paris (17); like Ivo for the c. *Daibertum,* it gives Peter of Pistoia and the Abbot of Vallombrosa as addressees where *Coll. Brit.* names only the first of the two. Nevertheless, before Jaffé (18) no one seems to have recognized the two fragments as part of the same letter. With the general considerations that precede *Scripsistis* never having been included in the collections of canons except the *Britannica,* any possible influence in the mainstream of canonistic thought would seem to be out of the question.

---

(14) *Loc. cit.* note 8 *supra.*

(15) F.J. GOSSMAN, *Pope Urban II and Canon Law (Canon Law Studies* 403; Washington, D.C. 1960) 27, 56, 60, 63, 79, 90, 97; cf. 160 n. 119. See also n. 17 *infra.*

(16) BINIUS, *Concilia generalia et provincialia* (2nd ed. Cologne 1618) 3.2 col. 412; in the first edition BINIUS included no letters of Urban at all (see his note, Cologne 1606, 3.1 1294). KEHR cites from a later printing (ed. 3, Paris 1636?) 7.502. See further LABBE-COSSART, *Concilia* 10 (Paris 1671) 442; MANSI, *Coll. Amplissima* 20 (Venice 1775) 664; J.B. MITTARELLI, *Annales Camaldulenses* III (Venice 1758) 48, etc. JEAN PICARD, Canon of St. Victor's, is known above all as editor of the first *Opera omnia* of St. Bernard (Paris 1609, etc.).

(17) The writer's guess, based on the description of part B of this composite MS in H. MARTIN's *Catalogue des manuscrits de la Bibliothèque de l'Arsenal* II (Paris 1886) 52f. — a canonical collection saec. xii not recorded in FOURNIER-LE BRAS — has been confirmed by Fr. G. FRANSEN, who kindly inspected the MS: fol. 117-192, collection based on Ivo's *Decretum.* Bk. 6 c. 66 *Scripsistis* (fol. 148v) is placed between two consecutive texts from Ivo (6.65, 67 = *Decr.* 14.57, 58). *Daibertum,* with the same inscription as in Ivo, *Pan.* is in 3.6 (fol. 129r). A note at the beginning of the MS says that it was used for editing papal letters, and these are marked in the margins. [Letter by G. FRANSEN, 6 December 1969].

(18) *Regesta pont. Rom.* ed. 1 (Leipzig 1851) no. 4027; *Bibliotheca rerum Germanicarum* (1866) 373.

II.

It may be best to begin the discussion of the further, more substantial points with a printing of the full text — oddly enough, for the first time — as it appears in *Coll. Brit.* I have corrected some scribal blunders and recorded the chief variants from the separate traditions of *Scripsistis* and *Daibertum.*

B.M. Add. 8873
    fol. 147r/v   .V. Petro Pistoriensi episcopo.

Debent subditi secundum beati Iob sententiam dicentis ' Rem quam nesciebam diligentissime investigabam ', dubitacionis sue nodos morosa et patienti inquisitione dissoluere, non autem in ea redargutionis aut culpationum manum extendere.   Item.

5 Multa ecclesie principes pro tenore canonum districtius iudicant, multa pro temporum necessitate patienter tolerant, multa pro personarum qualitate moderanter dissimulant. Si enim semper protracto neruo arcus extenditur, segnius ea in quae ad tempus intendendus est iaculatur. Per apostolos siquidem communi est sententia Ierosolimis confirmatum et per Paulum et
10 Barnabam fratribus per Asiam destinatum, ne quisquam ad fidem ueniens circumcisioni legis haberetur obnoxius. Ipse etiam Paulus ad Galathas: ' Si circumcidimini, inquit, Christus uobis nil proderit '.   Item.

Multa etiam a sanctis patribus pro tempore immutata scripturarum testimonio comprobantur, sicut sancte Romane ecclesie, cui Deo auctore
15 deseruimus, sanctus pontifex Leo neophitos ad summi sacerdotii gradum permisit ascendere, quos Pauli apostoli uoce palam est ab eodem officio inhiberi. [147v] Sicut etiam Arrianos legimus, postquam conuersi sunt, in suis officiis manere permissos.   Item.

19-27 Scripsistis — deposuimus *coll. cum Mansi 20.644* [= M], *inscr. tantum cum Par. cod. Ars. 713* [= V]

27-36 Porro — potuit *coll. cum Ivonis Pan. 3.81 ed. PL 161.1148* [= Pm] *et codd. Par. lat. 10742 fol. 48r* [= Pp], *Vat. lat. 1358 fol. 44r* [= Pv] *(consensus* Pmpv = P); *Grat. C. 1 q. 7 c. 24 ed. Friedb.* [= G]

inscr. Urbanus II. P. Pistoriensi et Rustico Vall.umbr. abbati V, Urbanus secundus papa Pistoriensi et Rustico vallis Umbrosae abbatibus *male* M, Urbanus II (VII.a Pv, GR. VII. Pp) Petro Pistoriensi episcopo (episc. Pistor. *tr.* Pm) et (*om.* Pv) Rustico uallis umbrose (Rustico abb. Pm) P, Unde Urbanus II scribit Petro Pistoriensi episcopo et Rustico abbati Vallis umbrose G

1-2 Iob 29.16   8-11 cf. Act. 15.22 sqq. et 15.1, 5   11-12 Gal. 5.2   15 Leo M. JK 410 (ep. 12) c. 5 = C. 1 q. 7 c. 18, sed non bene congruit (vide infra in textu)   16 *Pauli:* 1 Tim. 3.6   17-18 *Sicut — permissos:* cf. Inn. I, JK 310 (ep. 24) c. 3 = C. 1 q. 1 c. 73, sed non bene congruit (vide infra in textu)

Scripsistis nobis maximum apud uos scandalum emersisse quod Pisianum
episcopum consecrauimus qui a Guezelone heretico diaconus fuerat ordinatus.   20
Et nos profecto scimus Guezelonem hereticum fuisse Maguntinumque episcopatum simoniaco credimus facinore inuassisse, propter quem aut alium adqui-
rendum regi sub anathemate posito diu seruierat et propter adquisitum omni
uite sue tempore deseruiuit.   Eundem etiam ipsi nos pro eadem causa, et
quia ab excommunicatis consecratus est, in sinodali concilio excommunica-   25
uimus et condempnauimus et ab omni ecclesiastico officio sine spe restitu-
cionis aliqua deposuimus.   Porro Daibertum ab eo, licet simoniaco non simo-
niace eiusdem confessione comperimus in diaconum ordinatum, et beati Innocentii pape constat sententia declaratum quod Guezelo hereticus ab hereticis
ordinatus, quia nil habuit dare nil potuit ei cui manus imposuit.   Nos igitur   30
tanti pontificis auctoritate firmati, Damasi etiam pape testimonio roborati,
qui ait reiterari oportere quod male actum est, Daibertum ab hereticis et
corpore et spiritu digressum atque utilitati ecclesie pro uiribus insudantem
et ex integro necessitate ecclesie ingruente diaconem constituimus: quod non
reiteracionem estimari censemus sed tantum integram diaconii dacionem,   35
quoniam quidem, ut prediximus, qui nil habuit dare nil potuit.

III.

After the introductory *increpatio* we have here two similarly
constructed paragraphs.   Each begins with a general statement:
1) " Multa... districtius iudicant, ...patienter tolerant, ...mode-
ranter dissimulant "; 2) " Multa etiam... immutata... comprobantur "; each is concluded by authorities from scriptural or
canonical tradition.   In the first paragraph the *multa* which
may be either judged strictly, or tolerated, or overlooked, are
evidently actions and situations: the text simply does not speak
of diverse or opposed rules, of " canons dont il importe d'assurer

19 Pisanum M   24 etiam] et M   24-5 et quia ab *scripsi*: et quia *Brit.*, qui ab M
26 et¹ *om.* M   27 Porro — eo] Daibertum a Nezelone (Guezelone Pp, Negzelone G) PG
28 rep(p)erimus PpvG   29 sententia constat *tr.* PG   Nezelon Pm, aguezelon Pp, negzelon
PvG   29-30 hereticus — ordinatus] hereticus quem constat ab hereticis ordinatum PmG,
qui hereticus constat ab her. ordinatus Pp, hereticus constat ab her. ordinatus Pv   30 dare]
da *add. et cancell. Brit.* nil dare *tr.* Ppv   ei *om.* Ppv   igitur] ergo Pm   31 etiam *om.*
PmpG   32 reiterare Pv   actum] factum Pv   et *om.* PG   34 et *om.* PG   ecclesie necessitate *tr.* G   diaconum Pmp   quod] i *add. et cancell. Brit.*, eo quod Pm   35
existimari G, censemus estimari *tr.* Pv   tantum *om.* Pp   36 quoniam quidem] quandoquidem P (quam quidem, qui quidem G *var.*)

28-30 Inn. I, JK 303 (ep. 17) c. 3 § 7 = C. 1 q. 1 c. 18 § 1   31-32 Ps.-Damasus, JK †244
(Hinschius p. 514) = C. 1 q. 7 c. 25

l'exécution intégrale " as distinct from " d'autres dont la rigueur peut être tempérée selon la discrétion des supérieurs " (19). Only the second paragraph seems at first sight to suggest a historical change of rules themselves (*multa immutata*) by contrasting St. Paul's injunction against ordaining neophytes with a Leonine permission; but again, we have no more than an example of the permissive, individual suspension of a rule *pro tempore* — in other words, dispensation.

There is nothing new in the substance of these formulations. Several strands of canonical thought on refraining at times from the strict observance of a rule can be found since late Antiquity; by the ninth century ancient authorities to this effect were already being assembled in such remarkable dossiers as Pope Nicholas I's great letter of September 865 to the Emperor Michael, or in Archbishop Hincmar's memorandum to the bishops at the Council of Soissons (866) and in his treatise on predestination (20). Two of the early papal utterances in particular were destined for a great future in the history of jurisprudence. When Innocent I decided to tolerate certain ordinations made by the heretic Bonosus because of *necessitas temporis*, he expressed the limits of this remedy by the phrase (21), " cessante necessitate debet utique cessare pariter quod urgebat ", thereby setting in motion a train of thought which would eventually lead to the legal maxim, *Cessante causa legis cessat effectus* (22). And

---

(19) Thus Fournier, *loc. cit.* note 10 *supra*.

(20) Nic. I, JE 2796 (ep. 88) ed. E. Perels, MGH *Epist.* 6 (Berlin 1925, *ex* 1912), 454-87, at pp. 480f. Hincmar, *ep.* 184c ed. Perels, MGH *Epist.* 8.1 (1939), 182-5 (= *PL* 126. 55-9); *De praedest.* 2.37.11, *PL* 125.411-13. [Much of the material considered in the present section has been recently discussed at length by H.M. Klinkenberg, *Die Theorie der Veränderbarkeit des Rechtes im frühen und hohen Mittelalter* in *Lex et sacramentum* ed. P. Wilpert (*Miscellanea Mediaevalia* 6; Berlin 1969) 157-88. The volume came to my attention only after completion of this paper].

(21) Inn. I, JK 303 (ep. 17) c. 5 § 9, ed. Coustant, *Epistolae Rom. pont.* I (Paris 1721) 835; quoted already by Hincmar, *De praedest.* col. 413. See Ivo, Prologue (*PL* 161.53C) and Decr. 6.350; much shortened in Alger of Liège, *De misericordia et iustitia* 1.9 = Grat. C. 1 q. 7 c. 7, and even more condensed in Alger 3.56 (ii) = Grat. C. 1 q. 1 c. 41. For Urban II, see Council of Piacenza c. 12 (Mansi 20.806) = Grat. C. 9 q. 1 c. 5 § 3.

(22) See H. Krause, " *Cessante causa cessat lex* " in *Zeitschrift der Savigny-Stiftung für Rechtsgeschichte, Kan. Abt.* 46 (1960), 81-111; but his analysis of Gratian's share in the formulation of the maxim needs some revision, especially since he overlooks the equally important contribution of the civil law glossators. See Appendix II, *infra*.

when Leo the Great wrote to Rusticus of Narbonne (23),

> ...Sicut quaedam sunt quae nulla possunt ratione convelli, ita multa sunt quae aut pro consideratione aetatum aut pro necessitate rerum oporteat temperari, illa semper conditione servata ut in his quae vel dubia fuerint aut obscura, id noverimus sequendum quod nec praeceptis evangelicis contrarium nec decretis sanctorum patrum inveniatur adversum,

the incisive distinction between the *quaedam* which for no reason may be flouted, and the *multa* which must be tempered if compelling reasons exist, was to provide the frame for the classical doctrines on the limits of papal dispensatory power (24). Here indeed the distinction is between categories of rules — and who would not wish he could bridge the span of fifteen hundred years and hear St. Leo develop at leisure his thinking on these problems, which — as he said with regard to Rusticus's inquiries — "are better suited for conversing than for writing about them"? (25)

To return to the *Britannica* text, all its canonical terms represent no more than the traditional vocabulary of the distinction (of which the text itself falls short) between what Hincmar had called the two *formae canonum*, the "form" of indulgence and the "form" of inviolable law (26):

> hae sententiae... ad illam canonum formam pertinent qua secundum rationis et temporis qualitatem, aut propter ecclesiae utilitatem, aut propter pacis et concordiae unitatem, non praeiudicatis maiorum statutis, quaedam aliquando indulgentur, non ad illam qua pro lege irrefragibiliter tenenda constituuntur.

The Leonine inspiration here is evident, and borne out by an immediately following quotation from the letter to Rusticus. But the expression *forma canonum* — which recurs several times

---

(23) Leo M. JK 544 (*ep.* 167 ed. BALLERINI I 1419). Quoted in Hincmar, *ep.* 184c (p. 182.11), *De praedest.* 2.37.11 (col. 411D-12A), Ivo, Prologue (col. 52A-B), and other collections, down to Gratian D. 14 c. 2.

(24) Cf. A. VAN HOVE, *op. cit.* (note 1 *supra*), 356-61; some texts are discussed in KUTTNER, *Pope Lucius III and the Bigamous Archbishop of Palermo* in *Medieval Studies Presented to Aubrey Gwynn, S.J.* (Dublin 1961) at 416-7, 441-2.

(25) "...intelligo eas colloquiis aptiores esse quam scriptis" (*loc. cit.*).

(26) *De praedest.* 2.37.11, *PL* 125.411D. Hincmar's text is noted as a precedent for JL 5383 by FOURNIER, *art. cit.* (n. 4 *supra*) 156; FOURNIER-LE BRAS, *Histoire des collections* II 358.

in this section of Hincmar's treatise (27) — probably echoes the phrase " quo nec in totum formam veterum videamur excedere regularum " in the important decretal letter of Gelasius of 11 March 494 to the bishops of the Basilicata (" per Lucaniam et Brutios ") and Sicily; a letter which by its very opening sentence became a link in the solid tradition that upheld and continued Leo's criteria for flexibility and its limits. Here Gelasius writes, with his characteristic use of semantic parallelism (28):

> Necessaria rerum dispositione [*al.* dispensatione] constringimur
>   et apostolicae sedis moderamine convenimur
> sic canonum paternorum decreta librare
>   et retro praesulum decessorumque nostrorum praecepta metiri,
> ut quae presentium necessitas temporum restaurandis ecclesiis
>   [relaxanda deposcit
>   adhibita consideratione diligenti quantum fieri potest temperemus,
> quo nec in totum formam... [*ut supra*]

This remarkable formulation was appropriated by Pseudo-Isidore for his spurious sixth synod of Symmachus (29); Pope Nicolas I quoted it from Gelasius in his letter, already mentioned, to the Emperor Michael (30). Both the Gelasian text and Nicholas's own statement, a little further on, on the right of the Apostolic See to change its sentence (31), " cum... pro consideratione aetatum vel temporum seu gravium necessitatum dispensatorie quiddam ordinare decreverit ", were taken up by the canonists of the Gregorian age and their successors, down to Gratian (32).

---

(27) *PL* 125.412A 8, C (twice), 413A 3, C, etc.

(28) Gelasius I, JK 636 (c. 9 Dion.): ep. 14 ed. Thiel, *Epistolae Romanorum pontificum genuinae* (Braunsberg 1867) at 362; W. Holtzmann, *Italia pontificia* 9 (1962) 450 no. 1. For the ancient tradition of this letter, see Thiel, 30-32 and esp. H. Wurm, *Studien und Texte zur Dekretalensammlung des Dionysius Exiguus (Kanonistische Studien und Texte*, ed. A.M. Koeniger 16; Bonn 1939) 153-60, with additional variants p. 156 n. 16. — The use of " Gedankenreim " in Gelasius would deserve a special study.

(29) Ed. Hinschius, 679; JK I p. 98 ad an. 503; included in Anselm of Lucca, *Coll. can.* 2.33, rubr. " Quod papa canonum decreta ita librare debet ut quae necessitas temporum relaxanda exposcit temperet quantum fieri potest ".

(30) JE 2796 (note 20 *supra*), p. 480.17-21. Bernold of Constance, *De excommunicandis vitandis* § 58 ed. F. Thaner, MGH *Libelli* 2 (Berlin 1892), 140.28, quotes " Necessaria rerum... " from Gelasius, Nicolaus (not identified by Thaner), and Symmachus.

(31) JE 2796, p. 481.7-11.

(32) JK 636: Ivo, *Decr.* 3.141, Grat. C. 1 q. 7 c. 6; also, as quoted by Nic. I (note 30):

The teaching of Gelasius was also invoked by Nicholas's successor, Hadrian II, writing in 869 to the Emperor Basil (33). Pope John VIII's great letter to Basil and his sons, concerning the restitution of Photius, August 879, includes again a dossier of ancient *auctoritates* on papal dispensatory powers (34). By a curious twist of history, it was not the genuine text of the letter but an old Latin retranslation of its adulterated Greek version in the acts of the Synod of 879 which found its way into the Western canonical collections of Deusdedit and Ivo of Chartres (35).

Within the tradition of the Leonine principles there appear certain shifts of emphasis in the papal pronouncements. To cite only three examples: a letter of " Leo iunior " in the collection of Turin MS E.v. 44 (Pasini 903) and assigned by Ewald to Leo IV in the year 857, though not entirely beyond suspicion (36), stresses only the mutability of ecclesiastical rules:

Ans. Luc. 1.72 (at p. 45 ed. THANER), Deusdedit 4.167, *Coll. Brit.* Var. II 115 (EWALD, 590). — JE 2796: on the distribution of its parts in the collections, see E. PERELS, *Die Briefe Papst Nikolaus' I*: II. *Die kanonistische Ueberlieferung* in *Neues Archiv* 39 (1914), 43-153, *sub ep.* 88, *passim*; also Appendix III, *infra*.

(33) Hadrian II, JE 2914, ed. PERELS, MGH *Epist.* 6.755.

(34) John VIII, JE 3271, MANSI 16.482 and 17.138; ed. CASPAR, MGH *Epist.* 7 (1928, *ex* 1912), 169-70, from the Vatican Register.

(35) Deusd. 4.434; Ivo, Prologue 56C-58A. This fact has long been known — cf. G. HOFMANN, *Ivo von Chartres über Photios* in *Orientalia christ. period.* 14 (1948) 105-37; CASPAR, MGH *Epist.* 7.479 (*addendum* to p. 166 n. 3); D. LOHRMANN, *Das Register Papst Johannes VIII.* (*872-882*) (*Bibliothek des deutschen historischen Instituts in Rom* 30; Tübingen 1968) 113-14, but must be stressed once more against the misrepresentation of the evidence in P. JOANNOU's introduction to the Acts of IV Constantinople, *Conciliorum oecumenicorum decreta* ed. J. ALBERIGO *et al.* (Herder 1962) 133-4. JOANNOU claims, e.g., a lacuna in the Latin original [but see CASPAR, *ed. cit.* at p. 170 note c] and calls the charge of falsification in the Greek Acts of 879 a fable which betrays the critics' *obstinatam pervicacemque mentem.* — There is a surfeit of Latin texts of JE 3271 in MANSI: two printings of the Latin original, *Inter claras*, 16.479-86 (*ex* ed. Rom. Conciliorum 3.444ff.) and 17.136-40 (*ex* ed. Rom. Epistolarum pont.); four Latin versions of the interpolated Greek text: 17.141-6 (tr. F. Metius in BARONIUS, *Annales* ad an. 879, inc. *Puritas et splendor*); 16.487-99 (tr. ed. Rom. Concil., inc. *Sinceritas et splendor*); 17.395-407 (tr. HARDOUIN, inc. *Puritas celebritasque*); 17.527-30 (the medieval translation, as in Ivo).

(36) The judgment pronounced on this collection by J. VON PFLUGK-HARTTUNG, *Eine grosse Fälschung von Canones* in *Zeitschrift für Kirchenrecht* 19 [N.F. 4] (1883), 361-72 is certainly exaggerated; but also PERELS, *Die Briefe...* (note 32 supra), 120-5, found a number of letters with unreliable inscription or rephrasing of text. (FOURNIER-LE BRAS, *Histoire* II, 218-22 is essentially based on PFLUGK-HARTTUNG). The letter of " Leo iunior " should be

> Multa in sancta ecclesia ordinata fuerunt et adhuc ordinantur pro temporum qualitatibus, quae quidem mutantibus temporibus oportet et cum ipsis mutari... Propterea causarum sancitae sunt varietates secundum temporum vices, sed magistra providentia semper observet congruam temperantiam (37).

On the opposite side there is Alexander II: in the Roman Council of 1063 (38), he felt constrained to put mercy before justice for those ordained without simony by the simonists, since their great numbers (*tanta... multitudo*) made it impossible to observe the *rigor canonici vigoris* (39) — but then he went beyond the conventional concern for respecting, on principle, the commands of the *antiqui patres* and issued a most unconventional, solemn prohibition to future popes lest they make a rule of the exception (40):

> ita tamen ut auctoritate sanctorum apostolorum Petri et Pauli omnimodis interdicamus ne aliquis successorum nostrorum ex hac nostra permissione regulam sibi vel alicui sumat vel praefigat: quia non hanc aliquis antiquorum patrum iubendo aut concedendo promulgavit, sed temporis nimia necessitas permittendo a nobis extorsit.

Finally, Gregory VII, who was by no means an unbending doctrinaire, balances the Leonine and the Innocentian traditions in his letter of 1081 to the Legates Hugh of Die and Amatus of

---

examined within the context of Leo IV's thought on papal office, canon law, and Roman law; a fresh study of this material would prove rewarding.

(37) Leo IV, JE 2650, ed. P. Ewald, *Drei unedierte päpstliche Schreiben* in *Neues Archiv* 8 (1883), 363, with *addendum* p. 608; ep. 48 in A. von Hirsch-Gereuth's edition, MGH *Epist.* 5 (1899), 611f. (here 612.6-9, 10-12).

(38) Alexander II, JL 4501: Mansi 19.1023-6; Jaffé, *Bibl. rerum German.* 5 (1869), 48-50. As with so many other councils of the papal Reform, the textual transmission of the Roman council of 1063 is very complex: the printings in Mansi (indirectly derived from the ed. princeps by Baronius ad an. 1063, vol. 11 [Rome 1605] 337-9) and in Jaffé (from the so-called *codex Udalrici*) represent but two of at least four different traditions which cannot be discussed in the present paper.

(39) *Conc. Rom.* c. 2 (i) Mansi = c. 2 Jaffé: " ...eos qui usque modo gratis sunt a simoniacis ordinati, non tam obtentu iustitiae quam intuitu misericordiae in acceptis ordinibus manere permittimus, nisi forte alia culpa... obsistat. Tanta quippe talium multitudo est ut, dum rigorem canonici vigoris super eos seruare non possumus, necesse sit ut dispensatione ad piae condescensionis studium nostros animos inclinemus... ".

(40) Mansi 1025A. Later common doctrine held the opposite, " papa pape non potest legem imponere " (Huguccio); " non habet imperium par in parem " (Innocent III, Potthast

Oleron (41), when he first urges dispensation and forbearance,

> ut nunc pro tempore canonicum rigorem vestra sapientia temperet
> atque hac turbationis tempestate quaedam parcendo, nonnulla
> dissimulando ita studeat moderari, ut non ex severitate iustitiae
> deteriorandi occasionem sumant,

and then continues, in the vein of the maxim, *cessante necessitate
cessare debet quod urgebat*, that after the return of tranquil times,

> id quod nunc apostolicae sedis discretio patienter differt, iustitia
> dirimens ad statutum suum restauret.

It has been noted by scholars that, from the Gregorian age
on, old and recent authorities on dispensation were also seen
in close connection with the papal prerogative of making new
laws. Under the rubric, " Quod necessitate cogente nouas instituat
leges ", Deusdedit refers in the capitulatio of his collection (42)
to Leo's *Sicut quaedam sunt*, side by side with the letter in which
Gregory VII in March 1075 explained to Archbishop Anno of
Cologne the papal office of proclaiming the *antiquorum patrum
sanctiones* and the corresponding right to put forward new decrees
and remedies against new excesses (43). A third text bracketed
under Deusdedit's rubric is the Emperor Valentinian's dictum
which recognizes as general *lex* what the authority of the Apostolic
See has sanctioned (44). Cardinal Deusdedit's formula recalls
of course Gregory's own, from the set of *tituli* traditionally known
as the *Dictatus papae*, " Quod illi soli liceat pro temporis necessitate novas leges condere " — which may well have been meant

---

953; X 1.6.20). Cf. *Medieval Studies... Gwynn* (note 24 *supra*) 420f., 425f. See also *Glossa
ordinaria* on *Dig.* 36.1.13.4.

(41) Greg. VII, *Reg.* 9.5 (JL 5208), ed. E. CASPAR, MGH *Ep. selectae* 2 (1920), 580. Cf.
also *Reg.* 5.17 (JL 5067) and 9.33 (JL 5251), CASPAR, 378, 620.

(42) Deusdedit, *Cap. libri primi*, ed. WOLF VON GLANVELL (Paderborn 1905), 10.22-23.
The references are " Cap. CI, CXCVIIII, CCXXXVI "; CI = Deusd. 1.124 = Leo M. JK 544.

(43) Cap. CXCVIIII = Deusd. 1.248 = Greg. VII, *Reg.* 2.67 (JL 4949) ed. CASPAR, 223.
31-224.5. For Gregory's emphasis on the " old " law see esp. G.B. LADNER, *Two Gregorian
Letters* in *Studi Gregoriani* 5 (1956), 236f.; J. GILCHRIST, *Gregory VII and the Juristic Sources
of his Ideology* in *Studia Gratiana* 12 (1967), 10-12.

(44) Cap. CCXXXVI = Deusd. 1.311 = Nov. Valent. 17 (HAENEL 16): " ...set hoc illis
omnibus pro lege sit quicquid sanxit uel sanxerit apostolicae sedis auctoritas " (§ 3; lin. 29-30
ed. MOMMSEN-MEYER, 103). I see no reason why WOLF VON GLANVELL, 10 n. 82 calls this
citation not pertinent (" stimmt wenig ").

as a rubric for his own letter of 1075 and for an excerpt from Pope Nicholas I's letter quoted above (45). This may be true also of the corresponding *auctoritas* in the so-called *Dictatus* of Avranches (46). Bonizo of Sutri actually attributed to Nicholas I the Gregorian doctrine (47):

> Ut enim beatus Nicholaus scribens ad Michaelem imperatorem ait, licuit semper semperque licebit Romanis pontificibus novos canones cudere (48) et veteres pro consideratione temporum immutare.

But the blinded martyr of the Reform would have quoted from memory, and in his mind Nicholas's words — " in melius commutari... pro consideratione aetatum vel temporum... dispensative quiddam ordinare... " must have coalesced with Gregory's dictum in the letter to Anno (49), " quamquam huic sanctae Romanae ecclesiae semper licuit semperque licebit contra noviter increscentes excessus nova quoque decreta atque remedia procurare ". The future of this incisive formula lies beyond the scope of the

---

(45) DP 7 (a) ed. Caspar, MGH *Ep. sel.* 2.203f. with commentary (where, however, the misunderstanding is fostered as if Deusdedit had also referred to the Nicholas text in his rubric " Quod necessitate cogente... ": this covers only Deusd. 1.124, 248, 311, not 4.167-8).

(46) *Dict. Abr.* [c. 4]: " ...Omni tempore licet ei nova decreta constituere et vetera temperare " (ed. S. Löwenfeld, *Neues Archiv* 16 [1891], 199).

(47) Bonizo, *Liber de vita christiana* 1.44, ed. E. Perels (Berlin 1930), 33.16-18.

(48) The term *cudere*, where Gregory VII and others speak of *leges condere*, seems to be a preferred expression of Bonizo's, cf. *De vita chr.* 5.6: " ...imperatores non teneri legibus quas ipsi cudunt; ...semper enim licuit Romanis pontificibus semperque licebit novos canones cudere... " (Perels, 177.12-15).

(49) *Reg.* 2.67 (note 43 *supra*). Cf. Caspar's commentary *ad loc.* (p. 224 n. 2), while Perels, *Bonizo* p. 33 n. 3 cited only the passage from Nic. I JE 2796 as a source. K. Hofmann, *Der " Dictatus Papae " Gregors VII.* (Görres-Gesellschaft: *Veröffentlichungen der Sektion für Rechts- und Staatswiss.* 63; Paderborn 1933) 76, has suggested that Nic. I, JE 2764 (ep. 29) to Rudolph of Bourges, *an.* 864, should rather be considered: " ...[sedem apostolicam] iusque semper et fas habuisse de omnibus sacerdotibus iudicare, utpote cui facultas est in tota Christi ecclesia leges speciali praerogativa ponere ac decreta statuere atque sententias promulgare " (ed. Perels, MGH *Epist.* 6, 296.34-6). This is close in doctrine but not in terminology; above all there is no indication that *ep.* 29 entered any of the canonical collections of the Reform. However, it may be worth exploring the possibility that Gregory VII in *Reg.* 2.67 was influenced by this text; compare " iusque semper et fas habuisse " and " semper licuit semperque licebit "; or " decreta statuere atque sententias promulgare " and " decreta atque remedia procurare ". (Nicholas himself here echoes Gelasius I, JK 664 [*ep.* 26.2 *forma brevior*] " ...de omni ecclesia fas habeat iudicare "; cf. Grat. C. 9 q. 3 c. 17).

present investigation (50); but the fact ought to be stressed that nearly all these affirmations of papal legislative supremacy were expressed in the conventional terms of *temporis necessitas, necessitate cogente, pro consideratione temporum* (51).

IV.

No modern writer seems to have noticed that the paragraphs here under discussion in the *Britannica* text of Urban II's letter on the Daimbert case are nearly identical with a section from Ivo's great prologue on the consonance of canons. The sequence of sentences differs at one point, at which Ivo's text is also significantly longer.

Ivo, *Prologue* PL 161.51C-52A	*Britannica*, Urb. II, no. 30 (ed. *supra*, lines 8-12, 5-8, 13-18)
Spiritualis autem tunc dispositum non implet quando consultius aliquid pro salute eorum quibus prodesse vult providet.	
Per apostolos etiam communi sententia Hierosolymis confirmatum est et per Paulum et Barnabam fratribus per Asiam destinatum, ne quisquam ad fidem veniens circumcisioni legis haberetur obnoxius. Ipse etiam Apostolus ad Galatas scribens ita dicit: 'Si circumcidamini, Christus vobis nihil proderit'.	Per apostolos siquidem communi est 5 sententia Ierosolimis confirmatum et per Paulum et Barnabam fratribus per Asiam destinatum, ne quisquam ad fidem ueniens circumcisioni legis haberetur obnoxius. Ipse etiam Pau- 10 lus ad Galathas: 'Si circumcidimini, inquit, Christus uobis nil proderit'.
Et idem Paulus, cum Petro resistisset in faciem quod simulationi quorumdam Iudaeorum consensisset, qui circumcisionem saluti putabant esse necessariam, tamen necessitati temporis cedens Timotheum Lystris circumcidit, ut scandalum Iudaeorum ibi commorantium devitaret..., cuique ita cupiens subvenire quemadmodum sibi subveniri voluisset, si ita affectus esset.	15 20

(50) For a preliminary note on the line of transmission that leads from Placidus of Nonantola to Gratian (C. 25 q. 1 c. 6) see S. KUTTNER in *Traditio* 24 (1968), 504.

(51) See HOFMANN, *op. cit.* 76-9; further bibliography cited in KUTTNER, *Liber canonicus* in *Studi Gregoriani* 2 (1947), 396 n. 42.

25 Multa quoque principes ecclesiarum pro tenore canonum districtius iudicant, multa pro temporum necessitate tolerant, multa pro personarum utilitate vel strage populorum vi- 30 tanda dispensant.

Multa ecclesie principes pro tenore canonum districtius iudicant, multa pro temporum necessitate patienter tolerant, multa pro personarum qualitate moderanter dissimulant. Si enim semper protracto neruo arcus extenditur, segnius ea in quae ad tempus intendendus est iaculatur. Per apostolos siquidem... (*ut supra*).

Multa etiam a sanctis patribus im- 35 minuta scripturarum testimoniis comprobantur. Sicut sanctae Romanae ecclesiae sanctus pontifex Leo neophytos ad summum sacerdotium permisit ascendere, 40

Multa etiam a sanctis patribus pro tempore immutata scripturarum testimonio comprobantur, sicut sancte Romane ecclesie, cui Deo auctore deseruimus, sanctus pontifex Leo neophytos ad summi sacerdotii gradum permisit ascendere,

quos Paulus publica praedicatione ab eodem officio studuit removere. Sicut etiam Arrianos, postquam conversi fuerunt, legimus in suis officiis fuisse 45 susceptos.

quos Pauli apostoli uoce palam est ab eodem officio inhiberi. Sicut etiam Arrianos legimus, postquam conuersi sunt, in suis officiis manere permissos.

If we leave aside the minor verbal variants (52), the *Britannica* text exceeds Ivo's by the gnomic sentence on the overdrawn bow, by the clause in which the papal writer calls himself a servant of the Roman Church, and by a few adverbs of emphasis (*patienter tolerant, moderanter dissimulant*) (53). On the other hand Ivo cites *personarum utilitas* and *strages populorum vitanda* — the term is Augustinian — as grounds for *dispensare* where *Brit.* has *dissimulare* and gives merely one reason, *personarum qualitas* (54). St. Paul's prohibition concerning neophytes towards the end is somewhat differently worded in the two texts (55).

---

(52) Line 5 etiam] siquidem   10-11 Apostolus... scribens ita dicit] Paulus... inquit 10 circumcidamini] circumcidimini   25 quoque principes ecclesiarum] ecclesie principes 34-5 imminuta] pro tempore immutata (I would count this too among the purely verbal variants: ‘ immutata ’ is the *lectio facilior* and found also in Ivo MSS, e.g. in Vat. lat. 1358, fol. 7va; and ‘ pro tempore ’ duplicates the terminology of line 27).

(53) Lines 29-32, 37-8, 27-9.

(54) Lines 28-30. Augustine, ep. 145 no. 45, “ [ubi]... populorum strages iacent, detrahendum est aliquid severitati... ” is quoted later on in Ivo's prologue (col. 52B) and in Decr. 6.386 *fin.* = Grat. D. 50 c. 25 *fin.* = C. 23 q. 4 c. 24 § 7.   Urban II used the same text in c. 12 of the Council of Piacenza (1095), in combination with Innocent I's *cessante necessitate...* (MANSI 20.806; MGH *Const.* 1.563).

(55) Lines 41-2.

But the main point of divergence is the totally different context in which Ivo places the apostolic ruling against circumcision of the gentiles.

At the beginning of this paper I have anticipated the conclusion to which I believe a comparison of the two texts must lead. Pope Urban's letter on the Daimbert case was written not later than the spring of 1089; about 1094/95 Ivo incorporated its decisive, concluding part as a chapter (*Daibertum*) into the *Panormia*. Is it conceivable that in the prologue of this collection he would have cunningly appropriated the doctrinal part of the same letter, passing it off as his own discourse? This would be strangely out of line in the carefully balanced composition of the prologue, made up of the author's reasoning and of authorities — papal, patristic, conciliar, and scriptural — that are expressly quoted. It also would be more than awkward if Ivo had plagiarized the reigning pontiff, his friend, who had personally consecrated him a bishop at Capua in 1090 (56).

These may be arguments *ad hominem*, but the proof lies in the texts themselves: it is Ivo's prologue that served as model for " Urban " in the *Britannica*. While passages such as " Si enim semper protractu... iaculatur " and " [ecclesie] cui Deo auctore deseruimus " remain ambivalent — for they might have been inserted in the one or deleted in the other version — there can be no doubt about the section on the apostles' stand against circumcision (57): it makes sense only when it is read completely in Ivo, with its continuation on St. Paul departing, in Acts 16.3, from the ban in the case of Timothy, " necessitati temporis cedens ". This was a classical example of scriptural antinomy (58); but without the contrast between rule and accommodation, i.e. without Timothy's case, the text as it appears in the *Britannica* remains pointless. It can only be explained as an inept excision of the original; the reverse is impossible.

Thus the two paragraphs, " Multa ecclesie principes... " and " Multa etiam a sanctis... " must be considered interpolations.

---

(56) JL 5438, 5439.

(57) Lines 5-24.

(58) Cf. Nic. I, JE 2796, ed. PERELS 481.11-12: " ...quoniam et egregium apostolum Paulum quaedam fecisse dispensatorie legimus quae postea reprobasse dinoscitur ", with *Glos. ord.* C. 35 q. 9 c. 6 v. *legimus*; Alger of Liège, *De miseric. et iustitia* 1.5 (*PL* 180.860).

In the exemplar from which the *Britannica* was copied they may have been marginal glosses, but their present position, with the " Per apostolos siquidem... " truncated and shifted, and with the simile of the overdrawn bow inserted, would be the work of the interpolator himself. The source of the simile remains to be found (59); as for the other insertion, " cui Deo auctore deseruimus ", it was needed for plausibility after the reference to *sancta Romana ecclesia.* The clause is not unfrequent in the form letters of the *Liber diurnus,* two of which at least would have been known to the compiler by way of the collection of Deusdedit (60); a knowledge of individual papal charters using the same style is less likely but not to be excluded (61).

Ivo gave, and the *Britannica* text retained, two not very precise examples for the relaxation of strict rules: a permission granted by Leo the Great for neophytes to become bishops, and a permission for Arians after conversion to remain in their functions (*officia*) (62). Leo's decretal· actually spoke of the ordina-

---

(59) Compare, however, Ovid. *Epist.* 4.91·2: " Arcus... Si nunquam cesses tendere, mollis erit " and medieval derivatives, such as " Intensus nimirum vires mox deserit arcus " (H. WALTHER, *Proverbia sententiaeque latinitatis medii aevi* [Göttingen 1963ff.] no. 12581), " Redditur invalidus si semper tenditur arcus " (*ibid.* 22642, 26448); " A bow long bent at last waxeth weak " (*Oxford Dictionary of English Proverbs* 2nd ed. [1948] p. 59) and earlier forms cited by B.J. WHITING, *Proverbs, Sentences and Proverbial Phrases...* (Cambridge, Mass. 1968) *sub* B 478.

(60) *Liber diurnus* 51, 52 (ed. TH.E. VON SICKEL [Vindob. 1889], 41.14-15, 42.13-14) = Deusd. 3.145, 146 (ed. WOLF VON GLANVELL, 331.15-6, 31; also in H. FOERSTER, *Liber diurnus Romanorum pontificum: Gesamtausgabe* [Bern 1958], 434, 435). The use made of Deusdedit by *Coll. Brit.* is well known; for one example see Appendix III B *infra.* See also LD 33-36, 64, 72, 81 (SICKEL, 24.9, 25.12-13, 26.11-12, 27.2-3, 60.6-7, 69.8, 86.12-13) and, for the variant form " sancte nostre cui Deo auctore deseruimus ecclesie ", LD 32, 39, 77, 86 (SICKEL, 23.7-8, 29.15-16, 82.10, 111.17-18).

(61) A list of charters using the forms of LD is given in L. SANTIFALLER, *Die Verwendung des Liber diurnus in den Privilegien der Päpste von den Anfängen bis zum Ende des 11. Jahrhunderts* in *Mitteilungen des österreichischen Instituts für Geschichtsforschung* 49 (1935), 225-366, at 265ff. For the forms listed in the preceding note see pp. 266-8. Besides these form letters, see Gregory VII, *Reg.* 5.17 (JL 5067): " Quia consuetudo sanctae Romanae ecclesiae cui Deo auctore licet indigni deseruimus... " (ed. CASPAR, 2.378). — A study of the phrase *Deo auctore* in the imperial (see Cod. Just. 1.17.1), the papal, and the episcopal style (see Hincmar of Laon as quoted in FOURNIER-LE BRAS, *Histoire des collections canoniques* I 223-4) would be desirable.

(62) Lines 36-9, 42-5.

tion of laymen, not neophytes (63); and Innocent I's decree on the readmission of Arians specifically excluded their clerics from ministry and priesthood (64). (Perhaps Ivo had the more permissive Nicene practice with regard to the Novatian and the Meletian clergy in mind) (65).

It has been seen that the *Britannica* somewhat changed the phraseology of Ivo's central statement, " Multa quoque principes ecclesiarum... iudicant... tolerant... dispensant ". Ivo himself used the tripartite formula again in a letter written shortly after the Council of Nîmes (1096), where after discussing the exceptional permission given by Pelagius I for a married man to be ordained bishop, he stated (66):

> In hunc quoque modum, si velimus praeteriti et praesentis temporis exempla colligere, inveniemus principes ecclesiarum quaedam pro rigore canonum districtius iudicasse, multa pro temporum necessitate tolerasse, multa pro personarum utilitate dissimulasse.

Here, as in the *Britannica* text, the reference to *strages populorum* has disappeared and the last verb is *dissimulare*, not *dispensare*. We have no certainty that " dispensant " is the right reading in Ivo's prologue; since no critical edition exists; surely " dissimulant " would be more satisfactory in the context (67). This is especially true if Ivo's writing should have been influenced here in style and rhythm by a similarly tripartite passage of a sermon attributed to St. Augustine, and first used as a canonical text by Anselm of Lucca (68): " Multi corriguntur ut Petrus,

---

(63) J K 410 (ep. 12) c. 5 = C. 1 q. 7 c. 18. See however Greg. M. JE 1747 (*Reg.* 9.218) = D. 48 c. 2 on *neophytus* in the wider sense, " repente in religionis habitu plantatus ".

(64) JK 310 (ep. 24) c. 3 = C. 1 q. 1 c. 73.

(65) *Conc. Nic.* c. 8, quoted from Inn. I, J K 303 (*ep.* 17) c. 5 § 10 by Ivo (col. 53D); and Cassiodorus, *Hist. tripart.* 2.12, quoted by Hincmar of Reims, ep. 184c (ed. PERELS, MGH *Epist.* 8.184.5ff.).

(66) *Ep.* 55, *PL* 162.67A-B; also ed. J. LECLERCQ, *Yves de Chartres: Correspondance* I (*Les Classiques de l'histoire de France au M.A.* 22; Paris 1949) 224. Neither edition notes the parallel or identifies the reference to Pelagius, J K 992 (*ep.* 33 ed. GASSÓ-BATLLE [Montserrat 1956] pp. 89-92), a letter Ivo had included in the *Tripartita* 1.54.12, and which also appears elsewhere in the canonical tradition, down to Gratian D. 28 c. 13. Dispensation is a frequent topic in Ivo's letters, e.g. *epp.* 16, 171, 190, 214, 236, 250, 260.

(67) Cf. also Gregory VII, " nonnulla dissimulando ", as quoted above at n. 41. The few MSS of Ivo's Prologue I collated have " dispensant ".

(68) Aug. *Sermo* 351 no. 10 (but see E. DEKKERS, *Clavis patrum latinorum* ed. 2 [*Sacris erudiri* 3; Bruges 1961] p. 75 no. 284 for doubts on *serm.* 351): Ans. Luc. 3.67, Grat. C. 2 q. 1 c. 18 pr. — Cf. 1 Cor. 4.5.

multi tolerantur ut Iudas, multi nesciuntur donec veniat Dominus, qui illuminet abscondita tenebrarum ". The parallelism is striking; but if a connection exists, it could be investigated only in a detailed commentary on Ivo's prologue — which, notwithstanding the copious literature on his place in the history of canonical jurisprudence, still remains to be written.

V.

A few observations follow from the textual analysis here presented.

1) In Urban II's letter to Peter of Pistoia and the Abbot Rusticus as presented by the *Collectio Britannica* only the arenga, " Debent subditi — manum extendere ", and the two-part explanation of Daimbert's case, " Scripsistis nobis — dare nil potuit ", are genuine. The interpolation of a general discourse on dispensation and leniency provides new evidence against overrating the *Britannica*: not all excerpts from the papal registers in this remarkable compilation are to be trusted. The authenticity of some of its fragments ascribed to Leo IV has been challenged of late by Professor Ullmann, who also points out that others had been challenged before (69). The collection includes one notorious forgery, the Pseudo-Pascal otherwise known as *epistola Widonis* (70), and it inflates one letter of Nicholas I by passages taken from Hincmar of Laon's tract against his uncle the archbishop (71). With the evidence of our text added, a fresh examination of other material in *Brit.* seems indicated wherever doubts exist as to its reliability (72).

---

(69) W. ULLMANN, *Nos si aliquid incompetenter...* (*Some Observations on the Register Fragments of Leo IV in the Coll. Brit.*) in *Ephemerides iuris canonici* 9 (1953), 275-87, concerning JE 2646, 2613, 2615; and reference (p. 286) to R. PARISOT, *Le royaume de Lorraine sous les Carolingiens* (Paris 1899), 739, for Leo's letters to Lothar and Hincmar.

(70) JL †6613a, *Coll. Brit.* fol. 199r-v (Var. 2.109), cf. EWALD, 590, FOURNIER-LE BRAS, *Histoire* II, 162 n. 2. This is the shorter form, as in Deusd. 4.93-94.

(71) *Coll. Brit.* fol. 209f. (Var. 2.130): additions to JE 2785, ed. PERELS, MGH *Epist.* 6.683f. (*ep.* 160); cf. Addenda, *ibid.* 811; *Neues Archiv* 39.89f. and H. FUHRMANN, *Pseudoisidor in Rom* in *Zeitschrift für Kirchengeschichte* 78 (1967), 20 n. 17. Neither PERELS nor FUHRMANN seems to consider the possibility of forgery. For another example of interpolation (Var. 2.114* *Quam periculosum*) see Appendix III (B) *infra*.

(72) Thus, e.g., in the concluding sentence of Urb. no. 33 to Anselm of Milan, JL 5386,

2) What prompted the compiler to insert the fragments from Ivo in Urban's letter? Only a guess is possible. More than other instances of leniency, the pope's action in the Daimbert case seems to have caused misgivings on the part of the intransigents. Three years later, accusations and defamations directed against the bishop of Pisa still required papal intervention (73). Bonizo's criticism of Urban II in the *Liber de vita christiana* (1.44) seems to have been prompted in particular by Daimbert's case: " Scio autem nostris temporibus quosdam promotos... et quod peius est, reordinatos et reordinasse ". Even if this was done by the authority of the Roman Church, Bonizo continues (and here follow the lines from " beatus Nicholaus " on the power to make new canons and change the old), it should not have been done: " set non omne quod licet expedit ". Quoting from Leo the Great (74), Bonizo sums up: it is difficult to bring to a good end things that have been badly started. Possibly it was in reaction to such attitudes that the Daibertus decision was dressed up in the *Britannica* with the interpolation from Ivo so as to heighten the reproach of the opening sentence,

> Debent subditi... dubitacionis sue nodos morosa et patienti inquisitione dissoluere, non autem in ea redargutionis aut culpationum manum extendere (75).

3) Finally, our notions on the early stages of the doctrine on harmonizing interpretation at the end of the eleventh century (76)

Coll. Brit. fol. 148r-v, ed. EWALD, 362: " Item. Nosti enim te officio non legaliter accepto pro utilitate ecclesie restitutum, et ubi effectus cessauerit, cause quoque cessare debet (debent MS, EWALD) intuitus ". The clause " et ubi... " *rell.* is misquoted, upside down, from Innocent I's maxim in JK 303 and similar adages (see at n. 21 *supra*, Appendix II *infra*).

(73) JL 5451 = KEHR, *It. pont.* 3.321 no. 8 to the abbots Rusticus of Vallombrosa and Martin of Camaldoli. The date, Troia, 2 id. iul., is to be assigned to 1093 (not 1091 as in JL and Kehr), see H.W. KLEWITZ, *Studien über die Wiederherstellung der römischen Kirche in Süditalien...* in *Quellen und Forschungen aus ital. Archiven und Bibl.* 25 (1933-34) 123, 129 n. 3. The letter comes from the appendix of the Burchard MS, Florence B.N. Conv. soppr. 255.F.4. — For another, less well known reordination case see Appendix IV, *infra*.

(74) JK 410 (*ep.* 12) c. 1, widely transmitted; e.g. *Coll. 74 tit.* c. 120, Ans. Luc. 6.17, Bonizo 2.20, Grat. C. 1 q. 1 c. 25.

(75) Compare Ivo, *ep.* 214: " ...unde a subditis non debet reprehendi praelatorum dispensatio " (*PL* 162.218C).

(76) To say nothing of the antecedents of the ninth century (Hincmar, *De praedest.* 2.37.12, *PL* 125.411D) or the tenth (Abbo of Fleury, *Coll. can.* c. 8, *PL* 139.481C-D).

must be revised if Urban II is eliminated as having started the trend. Such a revision is badly needed for more than one reason. For instance, the studies of Fr. Nicholas Haring have pushed back the date of Alger of Liège's treatise *De misericordia et iustitia* by at least a decade, from the early twelfth century to the years preceding the collections of Ivo (77). This reverses the commonly accepted historical sequence of Ivo's prologue and the teaching of Alger on the consonance of canons (78). Or, to cite another instance: two out of the three texts in Gratian's Dist. 29 on interpretation *ex causa, ex loco, ex tempore, ex persona* are as yet unidentified (79); also, the channels by which medieval rhetoric influenced the formulating of this canonical doctrine remain largely unexplored (80). Much more work has to be done in this chapter of medieval jurisprudence before we can say with Job, as Pope Urban quoted him in his letter: " Rem quam nesciebam diligentissime investigabam ".

Appendix I
A Council of Urban II Before Melfi?

In his letter on the Daimbert case, JL 5383, Urban II says of Archbishop Wezelo of Mainz: " Eundem etiam ipsi nos... in sinodali concilio excommunicauimus et condempnauimus et... deposuimus " (lines 24-27 of the text edited above, II). If we

---

(77) N.M. HARING, *A Study in the Sacramentology of Alger of Liége* in *Mediaeval Studies* 20 (1958), 41-78, at pp. 41-2; also his article on *Alger* in *New Catholic Encyclopedia* (New York 1967) 1.315-6.

(78) Alger's use of musical metaphors (thus *De miseric. et iust.* 1.83: " ...consonare, non dissone sed concinne et concorditer " [*PL* 180.893A-B], " ut ergo misericordia cantetur et consonet cum iudicio " [893C]) should be added to the instances quoted in *Harmony from Dissonance* (Latrobe 1960) 11-14 and 55 n. 14 (where the reference to the *Poenitentiale Gregorii III* should have been given as MANSI [not *PL*] 12.287 and its source, Ebo of Reims' letter to Halitgar, *PL* 105.652D-3A, should have been cited).

(79) D. 29 c. 1 " secundum Ysidorum "; c. 2 " Gregorius ait ". The conclusion of c. 1, " ...cum ante iudicant quam intelligant, ante inculpant quam iterando lecta perquirant ", is related as a topic to the opening sentence of Urban's letter and to Ivo, *ep.* 214 (quoted n. 75 *supra*).

(80) There are only some hints in R. McKEON, *Rhetoric in the Middle Ages* in *Speculum* 17 (1942), 1-32.

assign the letter a date between July 1088 and April 1089, as we should, this leaves no alternative but to reopen the question of a synod held by Urban before the Council of Melfi, 10-15 September 1089. The great conciliar collections (e.g. Mansi 20.719 B) assumed a Roman Synod early in 1089, on the strength of Bernold's Chronicle for that year, " Domnus papa Urbanus generalem sinodum cxv episcoporum collegit et ecclesiastica statuta suorum praedecessorum apostolica auctoritate firmavit " (ed. PERTZ, MGH *Script.*, 5.449-50). But it is now agreed that Bernold's entry refers to Melfi.

Mansi also held that both the great letter to Gebhard of Constance (JL 5393) of 18 April 1089 and its epitome addressed to the German bishops (JL 5394) in the *Codex Udalrici* were of synodal origin. The letter to Gebhard he printed twice: from Sirmond's text " ex codice Atrebatensi " in Labbe-Cossart, and from Hartzheim's somewhat shorter text " ex cod. Vatic. 382 " (i.e. Vat. lat. 3832, fol. 196r-v) (1). He followed the German editor's lead in presenting the letter as " ex synodo Romana scripta ad Gebehardum... "; but there is no authority for this in the Vatican manuscript. In his printing of the " synodica " JL 5394 Mansi " emended " the opening words to read " Fratrum nostrorum communicato concilio " (MANSI, *Supplem.* 2.86 = *Amplissima* 20.719 C) where the text (2) speaks of counsel, not council, just as in JL 5393, " ...Fratrum itaque nostrorum communicato consilio diuque excommunicationis quaestione tractata " (*Ampl.* 20.666 E; 715 C *om.* nostrorum). That is, the important pair of letters had been previously discussed at length in conference with the cardinals (*fratres*); but this cannot be construed as a formal synod; at that time, Urban's precarious situation in his refuge on the island of the Tiber (late October 1088 to early July 1089) made it difficult enough for a small group of cardinals to meet with him. Likewise, the earlier meeting with cardinals and Roman nobles, mentioned in the letter to

---

(1) LABBE-COSSART, *Concilia* 10 (Paris 1671), 444-6 = MANSI 20.666-8; SCHANNAT-HARTZHEIM, *Concilia Germaniae* 3 (Cologne 1760), 210-11 = MANSI 20.715-16.

(2) J.G. ECCARDUS [Eckhart], *Corpus historicum medii aevi* (Leipzig 1723) 2.197 no. 176; PH. JAFFÉ, *Bibliotheca rerum Germanicarum* 5 (Berlin 1869), 153 no. 74. For the textual tradition of JL 5394 see also W. HAUTHALER, *Die grosse Briefhandschrift zu Hannover* in *Neues Archiv* 20 (1895), 213; K. PIVEC, *Studien und Forschungen zur Ausgabe des Codex Udalrici* in *Mitteilungen des Oesterreichischen Instituts für Geschichtsforschung* 49 (1934), 345.

78

the bishop of Aversa, July 1088 (JL 5362), could not qualify as a council (3).

Is it possible, then, that the letter on the Daimbert case was misplaced in the *Coll. Brit.* and that in chronological sequence it would belong after the Council of Melfi (*Brit.* Urb. no. 47), September 1089? But this would mean a date more than a year later than the death of Archbishop Wezelo of Mainz († 6 August 1088) (4), and even by medieval standards of slow travel it is most unlikely that news of the death of the archbishop-chancellor should not have reached the pope earlier, to prevent the gaffe of a posthumous excommunication and deposition. Besides, no such action at Melfi is recorded.

Vague references to unspecified conciliar acts occur more than once in Urban's letters, especially toward the end of his pontificate (e.g. JL 5775, 5776). In the case of our text (JL 5383), unless we postulate an unrecorded council early in Urban's first year when Wezelo of Mainz was still alive, the only solution that makes sense is to read the words " Eundem... in sinodali concilio excommunicauimus... " as referring to an action taken by Urban II before he was pope. This brings us to the council of the Gregorian bishops of Germany at Quedlinburg in Easter week 1085, where Odo, Cardinal Bishop of Ostia, presided as Gregory VII's legate. It closed with the solemn excommunication of a number of King Henry's bishops, among whom the *invasor Moguntinae sedis*, Wezelo (5).

Appendix II
Cessante necessitate — cessante causa

Innocent I, JK 303 c. 5 : 9 (col. 835 Coustant): " Sed Anysii quondam fratris nostri aliorumque consacerdotum summa deliberatio... Jam ergo quod pro remedio ac necessitate temporis

---

(3) See A. BECKER, *Papst Urban II. (1088-1099)* I (*Schriften der MGH* 19.1; Stuttgart 1964) 100-01, 149-50.

(4) For Wezelo (Wernher) of Mainz and his dates see C. WILL, *Regesten zur Geschichte der Mainzer Erzbischöfe* 1 (Innsbruck 1877), 717-23; A. HAUCK, *Kirchengeschichte Deutschlands* III (Leipzig 1896), 979.

(5) MGH *Const.* 1 ed. L. WEILAND (Hannover 1893), 653; cf. MANSI 20.608. Cf. also BECKER, *op. cit.*, 71 n. 207.

statutum est, constat primitus non fuisse; ac fuisse regulas veteres quas ab apostolis vel apostolicis viris traditas ecclesia Ro-   5
mana custodit custodiendasque mandat eis qui eam audire con-
sueverunt.   Sed necessitas temporis id fieri magnopere postulabat.
Ergo quod necessitas pro remedio invenit cessante necessitate debet utique cessare pariter quod urgebat: quia alius est ordo le-
gitimus, alia usurpatio quam tempus fieri ad praesens impellit ''.   10
    Hincmar, *De praedest.* 2.37.11 (PL 125.413 A-B): '' [Inno-
centius]... Ergo quod pro remedio ac nessitate — impellit ''.
    Ivo, *Tripartita* 1.38.27 (Par. lat. 3858, fol. 39r-v); *Decr.*
6.350, and Prologue col. 53C-D: '' Sacerdotum summa deliberatio
— impellit ''.
    In contrast to Hincmar's and Ivo's full quotations we have
Innocent's thought paraphrased and shortened in c. 12 of the
Council of Piacenza (1095): '' Quamvis autem misericordiae intuitu magnaque necessitate cogente hanc in sacris ordinibus
dispensationem constituerimus, nullum tamen praeiudicium sacris
canonibus fieri volumus: sed obtineant proprium robur.   Et cessante necessitate illud quoque cesset quod factum est pro necessitate.   Ubi enim multorum... '' etc. (cf. n. 54 *supra*) (MANSI
20.806, MGH *Const.* 1.563; Gratian C. 9 q. 1 c. 5 § 3), and at another point in Ivo's Prologue: '' ...sic aliae dispensationes salubri
deliberatione admissae cessante necessitate debent et ipsae cessare, nec est pro lege habendum quod aut utilitas suasit aut necessitas imperavit '' (col. 58 B).
    Two different abbreviations of Innocent's text were presented
by Alger of Liège in the *De misericordia et iustitia*; both were
adopted verbatim by Gratian and thus became of decisive influence.

C. 1 q. 7 c. 7 = Alger 1.9	C. 1 q. 1 c. 41 = Alger 3.56 (ii)
Quod pro remedio ac necessitate tem-	Quod pro necessitate temporis
poris statutum est constat primitus	statutum est
non fuisse. Quod ergo necessitas pro	
remedio repperit cessante utique ne-	cessante
cessitate debet cessare pariter quod	necessitate debet cessare pariter quod
urgebat: quia alius est ordo legiti-	urgebat: quia alius est ordo legitimus,
mus, aliud quod usurpatio ad prae-	alia usurpatio.
sens fieri tempus impellit (6).	

---

(6) aliud quod — impellit *Grat.*: alia usurpatio quam tempus fieri ad praesens impellit
Alg. cum orig. (Alger's texts are found in *PL* 180.862 and 957).

The important sentence on the *regulae veteres* is dropped; otherwise the contraction in the first text leaves the meaning of the original sentences intact (lines 3-4 " Jam ergo — fuisse "; 8-10 " Ergo quod necessitas — impellit " *supra*). The context is made sufficiently clear by the preceding *dictum*, " Item Innocentius papa, cum pro necessitate temporis... ordinatos a Bonoso heretico susciperet, ait in decretis suis " (Gratian *ante* c. 7; Alg. 1.9). But the radical contraction of the second text, combining two sentences in one, and leaving out the references to *pro remedio* and the ending, opened the way to an absolute construction of the *pro necessitate temporis statutum*: especially once the reference to the Bonosus case (which still preceded the text in Alg. 3.56 and Grat. ante c. 41) was left out of sight, the short text could become a general maxim on statutory law. Gratian himself applied the rule to prohibitions: " Sed sciendum est quod ecclesiasticae prohibitiones proprias habent causas, quibus cessantibus cessant et ipsae " (D. 61 *post* c. 8, § 2).

All this is not very well presented in Krause's study on *cessante causa cessat lex*, cited in note 22 *supra*. In the fact that Gratian took up the canon of Piacenza, Krause (p. 84f.) sees a deeper meaning that simply isn't there (7). On the other hand, he fails to discuss the manipulation of Innocent I's text by Gratian (Alger is not mentioned) and its significance for the history of the maxim. The next phase of the development for Krause (p. 85) is Innocent III's decretal *Etsi Christus* of 1206 (POTTH. 2722, 3 *Comp.* 2.15.13, *X* 2.24.26), with its statement " quia cessante causa cessat effectus ", repeated also in 4 *Conc. Later.* c. 36 (*X* 2.28.60). But Innocent III here quoted a *brocardicum* that was already familiar to the twelfth-century decretists (8). What

---

(7) ". Lehrreich... erlaubt einen Einblick in die Arbeitsweise Gratians... Der juristische Gehalt der Synodalbeschlüsse war gering... Bei Gratian aber wird durch Abstrahierung von der einmaligen historischen Situation aus der Verheissung... unwillkürlich eine verallgemeinerte Regel... " Gratian's rubric to the chapter in question, C. 9 q. 1 c. 5, does not even mention the rule.

(8) See for instance the *Apparatus Ordinaturus magister* on D. 61 c. 9 v. *ubi causa*: " Arg. cessante causa cessare effectum et perpetuata causa perpetuari effectum... " (Vatican, MS Ross. lat. 595, fol. 61rb). Perhaps even earlier is a *Distinctio* (beg. " Consuetudo aliquando imitatur " in the margin of a canonical collection s. xii: Oxford, Bodleian MS Barlow 37 [S.C. 6464], fol. 3ᵛ), which contains the phrase, " ...Set tunc cessante causa cessabit effectus... ".

is more, this *brocardicum* merely canonizes a dictum of the Roman law glossators, " remota ergo causa removetur et effectus ", found as early as the generation of the *quatuor doctores*, in Martinus and Jacobus (9). If we add that still earlier the strange inversion, " et ubi effectus cessauerit, cause quoque cessare debet intuitus ", appeared in the *Coll. Britannica* at the end of Urban II JL 5386 (see note 72 *supra*), it is clear that the antecedents of *cessante causa cessat lex* thus fare have not been adequately investigated.

Appendix III

On the Canonistic Transmission of Nicholas I's ep. 88 and on the Second Recension of the Polycarpus

In Nicholas I's letter to the Emperor Michael (ep. 88 PERELS, JE 2796) the section of especial interest for the history of canonistic theory and for our inquiry is the pericope " Sed his tandem omissis — retractari rennuerit " (MGH *Epist.* 6.480.15-481.14). The canonistic tradition of the parts of ep. 88 is traced in Perels' fundamental study cited note 32 *supra*, but some suppletory notes are needed in order to clarify the distribution of this particular section in the collections, since there exist some gaps in Perels' tabulation, *Neues Archiv* 39.140ff. (10).

A) A long series of excerpts, 18 consecutive pieces taken from ep. 88 and beginning, *Non ergo quales*, is contained in Anselm of Lucca 1.72 (pp. 39-48 THANER), Deusdedit 4.159-173, and in one manuscript of Bonizo's *Liber de vita christiana*, 4.86a (pp. 148-56 PERELS), all evidently based on the same epitome of the whole letter (cf. PERELS, *Neues Archiv* 39.73, 80, 92 n. 4). Our pericope is found in Ans. Luc. p. 45f. = Deusd. 4.167-8 = Bonizo p. 152.41-153.24, abridged as follows:

---

(9) See *Dissensiones Dominorum*, Vet. coll. § 38, Roger. § 9, Hugol. § 120, § 377 (pp. 26, 78, 352, 507 ed. HAENEL). Cf. E.M. MEIJERS, *Le conflit entre l'équité et la loi chez les premiers glossateurs* in *Tijdschrift voor Rechtsgeschiedenis* 17 (1941), 126 = *Études d'histoire du droit* IV (Leyden 1966), 149.

(10) The listings for nos. 25, 38, 67, 163, and 201 in the tabulation are incomplete.

Et ut cum beato Gelasio — admonemus (= MGH 6.480.16-23)
Patet profecto — iudicio (*ibid.* 26-28)
iuxta quod (29) Bonifatius papa Rufo — iudicari (31-33)
et b. Gelasius papa (cf. 34): Nec de eius — rennuerit (481.5-14).

B) A shortened cluster of excerpts is derived from A and characterized by the intrusion, after the opening excerpt, of the fragment *Lege imperatorum* from Nicholas's ep. 57 (JE 2723; MGH 6.357.21ff.), which in Deusdedit 4.158 immediately precedes the series from ep. 88, while in Ans. Luc. 12.33 it appears in a different context. The contamination and inversion (= Deusd. 4.159, 158) clearly establishes Deusdedit as the source for the shortened series. B is represented by *Coll. Brit.* Var. 2.113-115 (fol. 200r-202r) and, in an even more condensed form, by Ivo's *Tripartita* 1.62.2-9 (Paris lat. 3858, fol. 99r-100r). As for our pericope, it omits the first Gelasius quotation (" Et ut cum beato — admonemus ") but presents the A-text from " Patet profecto... " on. The relation between A and B can be tabulated as follows:

Deusd. 4	(ed.)	*Brit.* Var. 2	*Tripart.* 1.62
159 (i)	(472.23-473.2)	(113) Non quales — obaudiendum.	(2)
158 (i)	(471.19-21)	(114) Lege imperatorum — obuiare.	(3)
(iii)	(472.4-10)	Imperiali iudicio — asseramus.	(4)
—	—	*Quam periculosum — semel cessit.	—
163	(475.11-29)	(115) Quod hi qui a fratre — criminum.	—
164 (ii)	(476.8-12)	Nonne Maximus — eiecti sunt?	—
(iv)	(476.21-25)	Ubinam legistis — christianos?	—
167 (i)	(478.25-479.3)	Per principalem — inuitare.	—
168	(479.15-480.3)	Patet profecto — rennuerit.	(5)
172 (i)	(482.10-16)	Vos autem nolite — implicari.	—
(ii)	(482.16-18)	Denique hi — ignoramus.	(6)
(iv)	(482.24-423.3)	Cum ad uerum — implicatus.	(7)

173 (i)	(483.6-15)	Satis euidenter	(8)
		— tractatibus et post pauca.	
(ii)	(483.16-20)	His itaque	(9)
		— sanctionis.	

(Once more, we find *Coll. Brit.* practicing interpolation: *114 *Quam periculosum* is a fragment from St. Cyprian, ep. 73, and as such quoted in Ivo's ep. 60 [MGH *Libelli* 2.646.24-26; LECLERCQ, p. 252], in *Caesaraug.* 5.27, and in Grat. C. 7 q. 1 c. 8) (11).

C) With Ivo's *Decretum*, the cluster of excerpts is broken up, but Ivo D. 5.19 " Patet profecto — rennuerit " is still preceded in 5.18 by the first excerpt of the series = *Tripart.* 1.62.2 = Deusd. 4.159 (i). Ivo D. 5.19 is the source from which are derived:

(*a*) Ivo *Pan.* 4.11 " Patet profecto — mandarunt " (cf. MGH 6.481.7) = Grat. C. 9 q. 3 c. 10;

(*b*) Grat. C. 35 q. 9 c. 6 " Sententiam Romanae — rennuerint " (cf. MGH 6.481.9-14). Gratian omitted the clause " Ergo de iudicio Romani praesulis non retractando, quia nec mos exigit, quod dicimus comprobato " (*ibid.* 7-9), and changed the word order of the continuation, " non negamus eiusdem sedis sententiam posse... " into: " Sententiam Romanae sedis non negamus posse (in melius commutari)... ".

D) A different tradition is represented by the *Polycarpus*, second recension, 1.32 (rubr. *Qualiter iudicium Romani pontificis possit retractari*). It begins, " Beatus presul Bonifatius ait inter cetera: Comprobatum iudicium Romani pontificis non retractandum ", which is not Boniface I's text as quoted by Nicholas (p. 480.32-33: " Nemo umquam apostolico culmini, de cuius iudicio non licet retractare, manus obvias audacter intulit " = JK 365, *PL* 20.782 A-B) but rather made up from its recapitulation, shortly after, in the phrase, " Ergo de iudicio — comprobato (p. 481.7-9, as above) non negamus ": it betrays a misunderstanding of " comprobato " as if Nicholas had spoken of an " approved judgment " where he merely said: " once it has been proved what we said about the... judgment ". Then the text continues: " Sed non negamus eiusdem sedis — decreverit " (p. 481.9-11).

---

(11) This interpolation is not mentioned by EWALD nor by PERELS.

PAUL FOURNIER, " Les deux recensions de la collection canonique dite le Polycarpus ", *Mélanges d'archéologie et d'histoire* 37 (1918-19) 86, correctly identified the paraphrase from Boniface I as JK 365 but believed that " Puis l'auteur de la recension ajoute *de son cru* [italics mine] ces paroles qu'il semble attribuer à Boniface Ier: ' Sed non negamus... [etc.] ' ", and attributed it to the " préoccupations très vives à la fin du pontificat de Pascal II ", that is, to the problems created by the *pravilegium* of Sutri (1111) and its revocation. But both the paraphrase of JK 365 and the dictum on the *commutatio in melius* of the sentence of the Roman See are by Nicholas I, not by the redactor of the *Polycarpus*. Fournier's speculation about the purpose of this second redaction (repeated in *Histoire des collections* II 184) must therefore be abandoned.

Appendix IV

The Reordination of Bishop Poppo of Metz

Another case in which Urban II had the order of diaconate reconferred before episcopal consecration could take place is that of Poppo of Metz. On 1 February 1093 Urban wrote from Benevento to the bishop's electors that they could choose " a quibus potissimum catholicis debeat episcopis consecrari ". But if the elect had been simoniacally ordained a deacon " per manum Trevirensis illius dicti archiepiscopi ", i.e. by the schismatic Egilbert, he had to obtain that order from a Catholic bishop. The same reason is given as in the Daimbert case: " cum nihil habuerit, nihil dare potuit " (JL 5442, MANSI 20.705-6; for the date see KLEWITZ, *Studien...* [n. 73 *supra*] 121). Contemporary chroniclers contradict one another as regards the person of Poppo's consecrator and the date of his consecration, Hugh of Flavigny *an.* 1092 giving the Archbishop of Lyons with his suffragans Mâcon and Langres, in the first week of lent, i.e. 6-12 March 1093, style of the Annunciation (MGH *Script.* 8.473.37-47), while Bernold of Constance *an.* 1093 has Gebhard of Constance, the papal legate, perform the consecration on 27 March in mid-lent (MGH *Script.* 5.456.15-20).

Poppo's case is less well known than its exact parallel, the

Daimbert case: several modern writers on the history of reordinations have overlooked it (12). It seems to have made all the difference that JL 5442 did not enter the tradition of the canonists. It was, however, copied in the appendix of a MS of the Collection in 74 Titles (*Diuersorum patrum sententie*), discovered by G. Le Bras in a private library in Florence (13), now MS 31 of the Yale Law School. This codex will be discussed in Gilchrist's forthcoming edition (*Monumenta iur. can.* ser. B, vol. 1, Vatican City 1972). It comes from the monastery of St. Laurent at Liège, where it was probably written. The only other record of this letter is the printed text, which goes back to the edition from a single source in MARTÈNE and DURAND, *Veterum scriptorum et monumentorum amplissima collectio* (Paris 1724) 1.529-30. The learned Maurists had copied it " Ex ms. S. Laurentii Leodiensis ". It stands to reason that they found it in what is now the Yale MS of the 74 Titles — or in its *exemplar* or a sister copy at the same monastic house. What argues for the first of these alternatives is the omission of the name of the bishop-elect — while the electors are all addressed by name — in both the Yale MS and Martène's text: it is unlikely that Poppo's name, which was certainly given to the Pope by the petitioners, should have been suppressed in the original papal reply.

---

(12) Thus A. SCHEBLER, *Die Reordinationen in der « altkatholischen » Kirche* (Bonn 1936); GOSSMAN, *op. cit.* (n. 15 *supra*) 160-63; J.T. GILCHRIST, « *Simoniaca haeresis* » *and the Problem of Orders* in *Proceedings of the Second International Congress of Medieval Canon Law* (*Monumenta iur. can.* ser. C, vol. 1; Vatican City 1965) 209-35, at 223 n. 86. See however L. SALTET, *Les réordinations* (Paris 1907) 238-9; Z.N. BROOKE, in *Cambridge Medieval History* 5 (1929) 92-3; E. AMANN, « Réordinations », *Dictionnaire de Théologie catholique* 13.2 (1937) 2418-19.

(13) G. LE BRAS, *Manuscrits canoniques* in *Revue des sciences religieuses* 8 (1928) 271-2.

V

A FORGOTTEN DEFINITION OF JUSTICE

SUMMARY: I. The traditional definition of justice by Ulpian and its interpretation in the medieval schools. — II. A definition, *nature tacita conuentio in adiutorium multorum inuenta*, attributed to Gregory the Great by Paucapalea; its author is St. Martin of Braga. Traces in a few twelfth-century glosses.— III. Elaboration of "Gregory's" concept in the *Summae Elegantius in iure diuino* and *Inperatorie maiestati*. — IV. Some further traces, down to a fourteenth-century annotator who places the text side by side with St. Augustine on justice as *amor soli amato seruiens*. — V. Related "unorthodox" concepts voiced in the twelfth-century: St. Augustine on justice *in subueniendo miseris* quoted by Peter Lombard; Plato on justice *que plurimum prodest his qui minimum possunt* quoted by Placentinus and Huguccio, from Calcidius and William of Conches on the *Timaeus*. — VI. Martin of Braga's definition and its context; emendation proposed for a corrupt passage. — VII. Some parallels and possible models: (1) "Nature" in Stoic thought, especially Cicero and Augustine; (2) *tacita conuentio* and custom in Roman legal doctrine; (3) Lactantius on justice as serving God in total dedication to fellow man [S. Kuttner].

I.

Nearly all writing on justice by the learned lawyers of the Middle Ages took for its text the celebrated statement of Ulpian, "Iustitia est constans et perpetua uoluntas ius suum cuique tribuendi", which the Emperor Justinian's commission had placed in the first title of the Digest and had used again with one slight variant (*tribuens*), as the opening sentence of the Institutes (1). But the Stoic definition of justice as the virtue which "gives every one his due" reached medieval thought through grammar and rhetoric as well, especially in the formula of Cicero's *De inuentione*, as "habitus animi communi utilitate conseruata, suam cuique tribuens dignitatem" (2); in a shorter version as presented by Isidore's Ety-

---

(1) *Dig.* 1.1.10 pr.; *Inst.* 1.1 pr. — For an outstanding discussion of the medieval lawyers' teaching on *iustitia*, see the chapter "*Iustitia*" *e principio soggettivo* in E. CORTESE's *La norma giuridica* II (*Ius nostrum* 6.2; Giuffrè 1964), pp. 1-37, published previously in *Annali di storia del diritto* 3-4 (1959-60), 119-54.

(2) Cicero *de inuent.* 2.53.160; cf. 2.22.65. — O. LOTTIN, *Le concept de justice chez les théologiens du moyen âge avant l'introduction d'Aristote*, in *Revue thomiste* 44 (1938), 511-22; republished in his *Psychologie et morale aux XIIe et XIIIe siècles*, III (Louvain-Gembloux 1949), 281ff.; M. PALASSE, *Brève histoire d'un schème cicéronien au moyen âge*, in *Revue du moyen âge*, in *Revue du moyen âge latin* 1 (1945), 35-42.

mologies and Papias, who spoke of the virtue "qua recte iudicando sua cuique tribuuntur (*var.* distribuuntur)" (3); and also through the echoes of Cicero in St. Ambrose and St. Augustine (4).

In fact much of the exegesis of Ulpian's text at the hand of glossators and commentators was prompted by the verbal differences between the several formulations of the ancient authorities. Already at the beginnings of the school of Bologna, we find Irnerius setting out to bridge the conceptual opposition between *uoluntas* and *uirtus* when he writes that Ulpian's qualification of the will to justice as "constant and enduring" amounts to the description of a *habitus*, a settled disposition ("cum enim dicit 'constans' intelligit habitum") (5). This leads us directly into the traditional Boethian scheme of virtues as "habitus mentis bene constitutae" and related notions (6); the classification of justice as an "animi congrua dispositio" for the right judgment was to become the preferred one for the *Glossa ordinaria* of Accursius (7). Medieval exegesis was here perhaps not far from historical truth: as Ulpian's "constans et perpetua uoluntas" had no direct models in the Greek Stoa (8), he might indeed have tried his hand, without much con-

---

(3) Isidorus *Etym.* 2.24.6 (*...distribuuntur* ed. Arevalo; *distribuunt* ed. Lindsay), Papias, *Elementarium* (*...tribuuntur* ed. Venice 1485, fol. m viii; *tribuunt* Cortese II 18 n. 39).

(4) E.g. Augustine *de diuersis quaest. LXXXIII*, q.31 (*PL* 40.20-21); *de Trin.* 8.6.9 (*CCL* 50.282.94-5); *de ciu. Dei* 19.21 (*CCL* 48.688.26-7); Ambrosius *de officiis ministrorum* 1.24.115 (*PL* 16.57).

(5) Irnerius *Exordium Institut.* ed. H. Kantorowicz, *Studies in the Glossators of the Roman Law* (with the collaboration of W.W. Buckland) (Cambridge 1938, reprinted Aalen 1969), 240; cf. pp. 60-61 for commentary; for Irnerius on *habitus* see also texts and bibliography cited in Cortese II 8 n. 16 (=411 lin. 2) and p. 9 at nn. 18, 20.

(6) Boethius *de differ. topicis PL* 64.1188D; see P. Weimar, addition No. 87 to Kantorowicz, *Studies* (reprint p. 333) with references, correcting p. 60f. on Papias as an independent source.

(7) Accursius, *Glos. ord. Inst.* 1.1.1 and *Dig.* 1.1.10 v. *iustitia* "...animi congrua dispositio in singulis rebus recte diiudicans"; Cortese II 18, nn. 39,40; probably derived from Azo as quoted by Odofredus, *Lect. Dig.* 1.1.10 (cf. Cortese II 16 nn. 39,40). But Azo's *descriptio iustitiae* referred to the divine mind only ("congrua et diuina dispositio..."); see also his *Sum. Inst.* 1.1 ed. Lugd. 1514 fol. cclxviijvb num. 6; Lugd. 1557 (repr. Frankfurt 1968) fol. 268vb num. 2 ("Dei dispositio..."). Interestingly enough, the variants *diuina* and *Dei* for *animi* occur also in MSS and early editions of Accursius, see the *app. crit.* of Torelli, *Accursii Florentini glossa ad Institutiones Iustiniani imperatoris* (fasc. 1, Bologna [1939]) *ad loc.*

(8) F. Schulz, *Principles of Roman Law*, from a text revised and enlarged by the author, translated by M. Wolff (Oxford 1936), p. 85 n. 1. He points, however, (n. 5) to the paral-

cern for philosophical niceties, at a workable circumlocution for the Ciceronian "habitus animi" (9). He could not foresee all the speculative discourse on the fickleness of the human, and the inscrutability of the divine will by which the glossators would probe into his brief, lawyerlike (10) words; "they spoke and wrote without end" on this, said Odofredus of the generation before him (11).

They also found another difference between Ulpian's formula and the rhetorical tradition. Bulgarus apparently was the first to observe that Ulpian had narrowed justice's concern to a strictly legal object, "giving everyone his right" (*ius suum*), which made the aim of justice identical with the aim of law, while in the non-legal texts *suum* or *dignitas sua* for everyone transcended that which is merely legal (12). Hence *ius* had here to be construed more broadly, including all that is deserved (*meritum*), all that is due (*debitum*) to God, to self, and to neighbor (13).

It was to be expected that the medieval jurists' reflection on justice would reach beyond the verbal exegesis of a plain-spoken Stoic description. For the ear attuned to the language of the Vulgate, the words *iustus* and *iustitia* would evoke other semantic associations: justice as an attribute above all of the Godhead; but also justice as the state of man "justified" before God in the divine economy of salvation (14). "Diuinam uoluntatem uocamus iusti-

---

lel in *Eth. Nic.* 1105a 34, where Aristotle requires for an act of justice or of temperance not only knowledge and deliberate choice, but also that it be done from an enduring and immovable disposition: ἐὰν βεβαίως καὶ ἀμετακινήτως ἔχων πράττῃ.

(9) Seneca *ep.* 113.7 "...Haec (iustitia) enim habitus animi est et quaedam uis'" is a less likely model, as it lacks the qualifying continuation.

(10) Schulz, *op. cit.* p. 80f. and *History of Roman Legal Science* (Oxford 1946) p. 259f. on the language of the jurists.

(11) Odofredus, *Lectura super Digesto ueteri*, *Dig.* 1.1.10 num. 1 (Lugd. 1550; [repr. Bologna 1967] fol. 8va): "...hic infinita dixerunt et scripserunt"; several pertinent texts in Cortese II 12ff.; see also Odofredus's own lengthy discussion of God's change of his judgment on Niniveh, etc.

(12) See Kantorowicz *op. cit.* 61f.

(13) E.g. Bulgarus, *Materia Instit.* (in *Sum. Vindob.* ed. Palmieri, *Bibl. iurid. med. aevi* I, 2nd ed. 1914) 271 lin. 5 from bottom (for Bulgarus as author of this *Materia* see Kantorowicz, *Studies* p. 67); Rogerius, *Quaestiones super Inst.* 11.6 ed. Kantorowicz, *Studies*, p. 273; Joh. Bassianus, *Lect. Inst.* 1.1 *pr.* in Cortese II 15 (p. 14 n. 32) and p. 411 (lin. ult.); Placentinus, *Sum. Inst.* 1.1 "idest Domino et sibi et proximo", *ibid.* 17; cf. also Cortese II 26 n. 60.

(14) "Iustitia que fit per fidem in nobis (Rom. 3.22), qua iustificatur impius... hoc

ciam..." are the opening words of an early twelfth-century tract (perhaps a *Summa* on the first title of the Institutes or the Digest) (15) which includes an interesting discussion of the differences between justice from on high (*iustitia superna*) and human justice (16). We can trace a similar line of thought, concerning the conceptual differences between *iustitia* and *ius*, from the *Materia Institutionum* of Bulgarus through several generations of civilians and canonists: God, we are told, is the author of justice; the author of law is man (17). And how easily the glossators' dialectical think-

autem pertinet ad iustitiam metaphorice dictam"; thus St. Thomas Aquinas, *Summa theol.* 2.2 q.58.2 ad 1; cf. 2.1 q.113.1 *c.*

(15) *Diuinam uoluntatem* ed. H. FITTING, *Juristische Schriften des früheren Mittelalters* (Halle 1876; repr. Aalen 1954), pp. 131-4 from MS Haenel 14, fol. 5r-6r; a fuller text in MS Vienna 212 on the flyleaf of a *Digestum vetus*, ed. R. WEIGAND, *Die Naturrechtslehre der Legisten und Dekretisten von Irnerius bis Accursius und von Gratian bis Johannes Teutonicus* (*Münchener theol. Studien, Kan. Abt.* 26; München 1967), pp. 454-9. For the classification as *Summa*: P. WEIMAR, in *Handbuch der europäischen Rechtsgeschichte* ed. H. COING I (München 1973) 193.

(16) *Diuinam uoluntatem* ed. FITTING § 8 p. 132.24ff. = WEIGAND p. 455-6: "...Est autem iustitia alia superna, alia humana. Supernam dico que et prima et ultima iure dicitur que nunc euangelica dici potest... hic inchoatur ibi perficietur. Humana est quam legibus comprehensam uidemus, quam et ipsam diuinam esse diuino didicimus testimonio...". The remarkable statement on the "divine witness" for the divine nature of human justice most probably refers to Christ before Pilate, "Non haberes potestatem aduersum me ullam, nisi tibi datum set desuper" (Jo. 19.11) as WEIGAND p. 456 n. 35 suggests. His alternative, Justinian in *Inst.* 1.2.11 on "naturalia iura... diuina quadam prouidentia constituta" could not very well qualify as Word of God (*diuinum testimonium*); moreover it is not concerned with justice *legibus comprehensa* (even though later on the author of the *Summa* says that this text makes *quosdam* wonder whether not also "ciuilia iura nitantur ratione diuina": WEIGAND p. 457 near n. 48 = p. 35f. § 49). — A. ROTA, *L'idea cristiana di giustizia...*, in *Ephemerides iuris can.* 4 (1949), 269 proposes to explain the passage by a text from the *Quaestiones de iuris subtilitatibus*, where *ipsa Veritas*: "Reddite Cesari que sunt Cesaris" (Mt. 22.21) is quoted (ed. FITTING [Berlin 1894] 1.12, p. 56; ed. ZANETTI [Florence 1958] 2.12, p. 14). But what the author of the *Quaestiones* here had in mind was the traditional dualism of temporal and spiritual power, both of which flow forth *ex eodem loco* (i.e. Rome; p. 56.33-36 FITTING), not any qualification of the civil law as "divine".

(17) Bulgarus, *Materia Inst.* (*ed. cit.* n. 13) p. 271 lin. ult. - 272 top: "...auctoritas iusticie Deus est... nam auctoritas iuris est homo, ut [papa,] imperator, populus. ...differunt tamen, nam sicut dixi auctor iusticie deus est, iuris auctor homo est" (for *papa* as an interpolation peculiar to the Vienna MS 2176 see KANTOROWICZ, *Studies* p. 67; it remains to be seen whether *auctoritas* at the first occurrence of this distinction is the correct reading — there are at least six MSS to be collated, cf. *ibid.* 66 — as against *auctor* in the continuation and in all subsequent writers). A tentative list of the numerous direct and indirect derivatives follows: (1) *Materia Inst.* of MS Munich lat. 7622 fol. 52vb (discovered by R. Motzenbäcker,

ing moved back and forth between the legal and the biblical usages one can see when they opposed to Ulpian's "justice is a constant and enduring will" etc. the text from Proverbs: "A just man shall fall seven times and shall rise again..." (18). It goes without saying that the righteousness of Solomon's just man belongs to quite another sphere than that of *suum cuique*. Yet this is only one of the instances in which medieval analysis of Justinian's texts reached out into meta-juristic dimensions (19).

II.

In 1890, Schulte published his edition of what was probably the earliest comprehensive work written on Gratian, the *Summa decretorum* of Paucapalea. For the most part, it is epitomizing in

---

cf. Weimar, add. No. 94 [repr. p. 333] to Kantorowicz, *Studies*); (2) *Definitiones Taurinenses* (MS Torino D.V. 19 fol. 97v) in Fitting, *Jur. Schriften* p. 221 (note); (3) *Abbrev. Inst. Taurin.* prologue (MS *cit.* fol. 91r, ed. F. Patetta, *Bibl. iurid. M. Ae.* II [1892] p. 120a), with the interesting variant "...iusticie Deus auctor est, iuris uero Deus hominem fecit auctorem"; (4) *Sum. Divinam uoluntatem* (*cod. Vindob.* only, ed. Weigand p. 456); (5) *Gl. anon.* on Cod. 1.14 *rubr.* in MS Vat. lat. 1427 fol. 26r (beginning "Isti tres libri"; perhaps a misplaced *accessus*, called without grounds a "prologo d'Irnerio alla Lectura Codicis" by A. Rota, *La concezione irneriana della aequitas*, in *Riv. internaz. di filos. del diritto* 26 [1949], 256; the few lines transcribed there [and repeated in Weigand p. 21-22 § 19] need emendation); (6) Placentinus, *Exordium Sum. Inst.* § 23 (ed. Fitting, *Jur. Schriften* 221); (7) Azo, *Sum. Inst.* 1.1 § *Est autem ars* (ed. Lugd. 1514 fol. cclxixr*b* num. 2; 1557 fol. 259ra num. 4) — For the canonists, see infra pp. 83, 92.

(18) Prov. 24.16: "Septies enim cadet iustus et resurget"; Joh. Bassianus as quoted by Accursius *Glos. Ord. Inst.* 1.1 v. *iustitia* (cf. Cortese II 19 n. 43); Azo *gl. Dig.* 1.1.10 (cf. *ibid.* 14 n. 32 [at p. 15]), *Sum. Inst.* 1.1 (ed. Lugd. 1514 fol. cclixr*a* num. 6; 1557 fol. 268vb num. 2); Pascipoverus, *Concordia utr. iur. Dig.* 1.1.10 v. *perpetua* (cf. Cortese II 17 n. 37).

(19) Thus the *Abbrev. Inst. Taur.* (*loc. cit. supra* n. 17, also cf. Cortese II 28 n. 64) illustrates the differences of *ius* and *iustitia* by the legal problems of the resurrected Lazarus (a popular theme in the twelfth century); for another example see Odofredus (*loc. cit. supra* n. 11). — The present paper must forego discussion of further meta-juridical aspects of medieval legal thought. On Justice personified and enthroned in the prologue of the *Quaestiones de iuris subtilitatibus* see H. Kantorowicz, *Studies* pp. 184-6 (with addition No. 270 in the repr. p. 344); E. Kantorowicz, *The King's Two Bodies* (Princeton 1957), 108-14; [anon.] *Novus regnat Salomon...*, in *Festschrift Bernhard Bischoff* (Stuttgart 1971), 381. — On *Cultus iustitiae* in Frederick II's *Liber Augustalis* 1.32, H. Dilcher has recently pointed out that Isai. 32.17 "Et erit opus iustitiae pax et cultus iustitiae silentium" is the chief source, by way of Gratian C.5 q.4 c.3 and perhaps 5 *Comp.* 1.17.1, with *Dig.* 1.1.1 "iustitiam namque colimus" only a secondary parallel: *Juristisches Berufsethos nach dem sizilischen Gesetzbuch Friedrichs II. von Hohenstaufen*, in *Studien zur europäischen Rechtsgeschichte* ed. W. Wilhelm (Frankfurt 1972), 98 n. 88.

character, with exegetical and doctrinal elements inserted but sparsely: these, however, let us catch an occasional glimpse of the intellectual interests that moved the first generation of Gratian's disciples to add to the Master's work observations gleaned from Roman law, the *sacra pagina*, and the arts (20). When Paucapalea, after his workmanlike preface, turns to the celebrated opening statement of Gratian, "Humanum genus duobus regitur, naturali uidelicet iure et moribus", he first summarizes Gratian's identification of natural law with the Golden Rule as contained in the Law and the Gospel, making one slight verbal change (or is it a variant reading?) and adding one short gloss (21). This [natural] law, Paucapalea continues, St. Gregory calls 'justice' where he defines justice as "an unspoken covenant of nature, devised for the aid of many" (22). Then, returning to Gratian's text, the glossator paraphrases rubric and inscription of the first *capitulum* (D.1 c.1), from Isidore's Etymologies, but with a significant change: Gratian and Isidore state

---

(20) For Roman law see A. VETULANI, *Le Décret de Gratien et les premiers décrétistes à la lumière d'une nouvelle source* (revised translation from his earlier publication in Polish, Wroclaw-Kraków 1955), in *Stud. Grat.* 7 (1959), 273-353 at pp. 320-31: the value of these observations does not depend upon acceptance of Vetulani's thesis on the forerunners of Paucapalea. See also WEIGAND, *Naturrechtslehre* p. 141 n. 4 for Paucapalea and Martinus. Biblical concerns are represented by the numerous *historiae* spread throughout the book; for the background in the *artes*, — to cite only one example — see the paragraph on *causa* at the beginning of C.1, deftly combined from Cic. *de inuent.* 1.6.8 and Isid. *Etym.* 18.15.2-4 (no indication of sources in SCHULTE's edition p. 51). The characterization of the *Summa* in KUTTNER, *Repertorium der Kanonistik* (*Studi e testi* 71, Città del Vaticano 1937) 126f. underrates the work.

(21) *Dict. pr.*: "Primum dicit: 'Ius naturale est quo quis iubetur alii facere quod sibi' rationabiliter 'optat (uult *Grat.*) fieri' et e conuerso." The gloss *rationabiliter* tersely answers a possible objection. *Optat fieri* may or may not represent a variant reading of Gratian's dictum: we cannot say for sure since no full collation of MSS exists. However, in Gratian's scriptural models it is "quod tibi non *uis* fieri" (Tob. 4.16) and "quecumque *uultis* ut faciant uobis" (Mt. 7.12). — Of the two anonymous *Summae* derived from Paucapalea (n. 28 *infra*), one merely abridges the *lemma* and changes the word order: "Primum dicit 'humanum' etc. usque 'quod sibi optat fieri', rationabiliter et e conuerso" (MS Alençon); the other, after explaining, "...'Ius naturale est', idest ius diuinum est", writes "'quo quisque... quod sibi uult (= *Grat.*) fieri', idest rationabiliter optat fieri et e conuerso." This could be close to what Paucapalea may originally have written. SCHULTE, whose edition on the whole merely renders the now destroyed Metz MS 250 (cf. Paucapalea p.xxi; it was not the best according to A. GIETL's review in *Literarischer Handweiser* [1891], p. 381f.), reports a suprascript *uult* (at *optat*: p. 4 n. 2).

(22) "Hoc ius a beato Gregorio iustitia appellari uidetur cum ait: 'Iustitia est nature tacita conuentio in adiutorium multorum inuenta'."

that "divine laws exist by nature (*natura constant*) and human laws by convention (*moribus*)", describing as it were a mode of being; Paucapalea, however, takes *natura* and *mores* as the respective points of origin from which the divine and the human laws take their beginning (*principium habent*) (23). A few lines later on, after explaining in Isidore's own terms the concept and different kinds of etymology, he repeats this interpretation of *constare* (24).

"Iustitia est nature tacita conuentio in adiutorium multorum inuenta": Schulte did not attempt to identify the remarkable, almost enigmatic saying here attributed to 'beatus Gregorius', and modern writers apparently have not found it worthy of comment — perhaps because it never entered the mainstream of the glossators' tradition (25). Paucapalea must have read the definition under the name of Gregory the Great in some *florilegium*: actually it comes from the *Formula honestae uitae* of St. Martin of Braga (d. 579) (26), a treatise on the four virtues widely read and commonly ascribed to Seneca in the Middle Ages (27).

Two anonymous *Summae*, closely dependant upon Paucapalea, present the definition from 'Gregory' in the same context of expounding Gratian's statement on natural law (28). But the usual

---

(23) "Ab hoc iure, ut in libro etymologiarum Ysidorus dicit, diuine leges natura principium habuerunt et humane a moribus." See Weigand's comment, p. 141.

(24) D.1 c.1: "Liber etymologiarum dicitur... garrulus [pieced together from bits of Isid. *Etym.* 1.9.1-4]. In hoc inquam libro dicit Ysidorus: 'Diuine leges natura', i.e. principium a naturali iure habent, 'humane legibus constant', quia quod prius fuit in consuetudine et postea in scriptis redactum est lex uocatur." The sequence *natura-consuetudo-lex* is quite Ciceronian, cf. *De inuent.* 2.53.160.

(25) It is barely mentioned by Weigand *loc. cit.* (from Paucapalea), and by Cortese II 18 n. 38 (from Patetta's collection of *verba legalia*, n. 33 *infra*); he noted, however, in passing its conceptual affinity with a text from Placentinus, see section V below.

(26) *Formula honestae uitae* c.5.1-2, ed. C.W. Barlow, *Martini episcopi Bracarensis Opera omnia* (*American Academy in Rome, Papers and Monographs* 12; New Haven 1950) p. 246, cf. *PL* 72.27. For this identification — which was first made by the present writer in the unpublished draft (1938) of a supplement to his *Repertorium* — see now *Summa Elegantius in iure diuino seu Coloniensis* tom. 1, ed. G. Fransen and S. Kuttner (*Monumenta iur. can.* Ser. A 1; New York 1970), app. font. to 1.3 lin. 5-6 (p. 1).

(27) See Barlow's introduction (*Opp.* pp. 204ff.) for the history of the text and bibliography.

(28) *Summa Sicut uetus testamentum*, MS Florence B.N. Conv. soppr. G. IV. 1736 fol. 1vb; *Summa Quoniam in omnibus*, MS Alençon 134 fol. 163va (for these two writings see the brief notices in *Traditio* 11 [1955] 440, 12 [1956] 563; 15 [1959] 452; for passages used in Weigand, *Naturrechtslehre*, see his index s. vv.). The minor differences from Paucapalea (see

compositions and apparatus of glosses on Gratian at Bologna did not take it up. However, without an attempt at collecting a full dossier, I have found this definition of justice in marginal glosses of several early Gratian MSS from the Western schools. In Paris BN lat. 3884, Durham C.II.1, and the fragment at Oxford Bodl. Douce 218 (29), it appears as opening glóss next to Gratian's "Humanum genus", without any indication of authorship; some relation to the Paucapalea tradition is apparent in the Paris manuscript, in the next gloss but one, at D.1 c.1 v. *natura constant*: "idest a naturali equitate habent initium" (30). In Arras MS 32 [27] the gloss "Iustitia — inuenta" is signed $\overline{GG}$ (the usual compendium for *Gregorius*) and followed by two cross-references to Grat. D.50 c. *Ponderet* [14] and C.2 q.1 c. *Primo* [13] (31), both of which quote the maxim "quod tibi non uis fieri" etc. as does the opening statement of the Decretum. But it seems rather the "in adiutorium multorum" of the gloss that led to citing these two texts which speak of *misericordia* tempering strict law, and of justice paired with *karitas*.

A fragmentary copy, or perhaps *abbreviatio*, of Gratian in Oxford Trinity College MS 70 (which deserves further study) shows a number of glosses intruded into the text; the first of these gives our definition of justice, inserted after the words "ius autem est dictum quia iustum est" of D.1 c.2 (32).

---

note 21 *supra*) do not extend to the passage "Hoc ius a beato Gregorio" etc. To complete the record, let us mention that in *Sicut uetus* a gloss follows v. *hoc est enim lex et prophete*: "idest hoc docent", and that the excerpts from Isidore at D.1 c.1 (n. 24 *supra*) there are shortened; they are altogether omitted in *Sum. Quoniam*.

(29) The fragment, briefly noted in *Trad.* 7 (1949/51) 294, is actually gathered from 38 leaves with miniatures, cut out by a barbarian 19th-century collector from a Gratian MS of English provenance.

(30) Preceded by a gloss D.1 c.1 v. *Omnes*: "Lex diuina: euangelica, mosayca, ecclesiastica".

(31) I owe this information to the kindness of Dr. H. van de Wouw. — While this paper was in the press, Professor Weigand communicated by letter that he has found the gloss 'Iustitia—inuenta' also in Cologne, Cathedral MS 128 fol. 10va, at the beginning of the *Decretum*.

(32) Oxford, Trinity College MS 70 fol. 132ra. Dr. Eleanor Rathbone kindly supplied this text (cf. *Traditio* 19 [1963] 535). The fragment, fol. 132r-173vb, covers D.1-D.63 c.23 (incomplete); it is preceded by Robert of Bridlington's *Expositio* on the Pentateuch (on the author see B. SMALLEY, *The Study of the Bible in the Middle Ages* [2nd ed. Oxford 1952, paperback ed. Notre Dame 1964 etc.] pp. 51, 61, 369); it is followed by (fol. 174-189) a fragment of Placentinus, *Summa Instit.* (cf. P. LEGENDRE, *Miscellanea Britannica*, in *Traditio* 15 [1959] 492 n.) and (fol. 190r-199v) the *Apparatus* on the *De regulis iuris*, probably of Joh.

Outside the canonistic circles, a collection of *verba legalia*, of French origin, edited in 1892 by F. Patetta from the Vatican MS Reg. lat. 435, includes the definition, "Justicia nature tacita conuentio in adiutorium multorum inuenta" (33). Preceded by such rare words as *mediastinus, atrarius,* and *parabolani,* it is followed by Isidore's definition of *ethimologia*. The latter perhaps echoes the context of Paucapalea — otherwise no coherence can be detected in this strange sequence.

III.

For writers who gave the definition of "Gregory" more than a fleeting thought we have to return, however, to some of the canonists of the Western schools. One is the author of the *Summa Elegantius in iure diuino* (Geoffrey of Cologne? Bertram of Metz?) (34) who wrote in or near Cologne about the year 1169. On the opening page of his book, under the heading, "In quo [ius] a iustitia differat" (c.3), he begins with the statement (35),

> Differt a iustitia eo quod auctor iuris homo, auctor iustitie Deus. Ideoque iustitia latius patet, multa sub se continens que necdum ius suis laqueis innodauit,

which is one of the many formulations derived from the *Materia Institutionum* of Bulgarus, with its familiar distribution of the "authorship" of law and justice and with its description of the difference in scope (*subiecta, subiectorum continentia*) by an implied quotation of Justinian's colorful simile of the snares of the law in his constitu-

---

Bassianus, ed. S. CAPRIOLI in *Annali di storia del diritto* 7 (1963) 131-248 (=cod. 0). Cf. the notice in G. DOLEZALEK, *Verzeichnis der Handschriften zum römischen Recht bis 1600* (Frankfurt 1972) II *s.v.* Oxford Trinity College.

(33) *Excerpta Cod. Vatic. Reg. 435* no. 85, in *Bibl. iurid. med. aevi* II (Bologna 1892) p. 136a. Patetta misread the compendium *nᵉ* (MS cit. fol. 43vb) as *nisi* and emended into *est* ("Iustitia est tacita..."). For the French origin of the collection see E. SECKEL, *Über neuere Editionen juristischer Schriften aus dem Mittelalter,* in *ZRG Rom. Abt.* 21 (1900) 231.

(34) For tentative statements on authorship see S. KUTTNER and E. RATHBONE, *Anglo-Norman Canonists of the Twelfth Century,* in *Traditio* 7 (1949/51), at pp. 299-300 (Godfrey?); P. GERBENZON, *Bertram of Metz, the Author of 'Elegantius in iure diuino'?* in *Traditio* 21 (1965), 510-11.

(35) *Summa Elegantius* 1.3, *ed. cit.* (n. 26 *supra*) p. 1.

tion *Tanta* (§ 18 "negotia quae adhuc legum laqueis non sunt innodata...") (36).

At this point, where the Bulgarus tradition ponders upon justice doing its bidding in secret ("...quodcumque ius dicit id et iustitia, licet in occulto dictauit") (37), the canonist from Cologne introduces another source to make the same point:

> unde Gregorius "Iustitia est nature tacita conuentio in adiutorium multorum inuenta", ideo quia de his est que iam natura set nondum nostra scientia continet.

Glosses in two of the manuscripts stress this "hiddenness": one (Vienna MS 2125) by drawing a parallel between the dialectical pairs *iustitia—ius* and *natura—ars*: "In like manner, nature encompasses more than art (science). Every art is a sum (*collectio*) of precepts while nature includes what has not yet been discovered but can be turned into precepts once it becomes known" — a thought which appears also elsewhere in the Bulgarus circle (38). (And an interlinear gloss of Cod. Vindob. v. *tacita* emphasizes "necdum uerbo uel scripto expressa".) The other manuscript (Paris BN lat. 14997) adds in the margin of the text on the differences between law and justice a comment on justice and equity (39): they differ "...because justice has its place (*consistit*) in the minds of men, equity in their words and deeds; hence, properly speaking we should call

---

(36) Bulgarus, *Materia* (see n. 17 *supra*): "patet etiam iustitia ad plura subiecta quam ius..." (*ed. cit.* p. 272); Placentinus, *Exordium Instit.*: "differunt... et in subiectorum continentia. Latius enim patet iustitia quam ius..." (FITTING, *Jur. Schr.* p. 221); *Defin. Taur.*: "set etiam ad omnia subiecta iuris porrigitur iusticia, set non conuertitur" (FITTING 221 n.). The paraphrase of *Cod.* 1.17.2.18 on *legum laquei* follows everywhere. (The *app. font.* at this point of the *Summa Elegantius* could have been more precise.)

(37) Bulgarus, *Materia loc. cit.* and cf. the *Accessus Inst. Sicut et in aliis* (*Pragensis*): "...hoc autem totum commune habet cum iure, nisi quod iusticia latens est uoluntas, ius manifesta uel scriptis uel rebus et factis" (ed. FITTING, *Juristische Schriften*, p. 215 § 9); also Azo, *gll. Dig.* 1.1.10 v. *perpetua* and *Cod.* 1.14.9, quoted by CORTESE II 29 n. 66. For Sicardus see *infra* n. 69.

(38) *Gl.* MS Vindob. v. *multa*: "Sic semper natura plurium comprehensiua est quam ars. Ars enim collectio preceptorum, natura uero etiam de his que necdum comperta similiter in precepta redigi possunt si innotescunt." Cf. in addition to texts cited in the preceding notes, the implied quotation in the *Defin. Taur.* (*loc. cit.*), "cum cotidie deproperat natura nouas edere formas" — another phrase from const. *Tanta*, Cod. 1.17.2.18.

(39) *Gl.* MS Par.: "Differt etiam iusticia ab equitate, quia iusticia consistit in mentibus hominum, equitas in dictis et factis eorum, unde si proprie uelimus loqui, dicamus hominem iustum et hominis iudicium equum."

a man 'just', but his judgment 'equitable'." This is a quotation that comes ultimately from the *Summa Institutionum* of Placentinus, though by way of another work from the Franco-Rhenish school, the *Summa decretorum* of Sicardus (40).

In the course of revising his original text, however, the author of the *Summa Elegantius* attempted to improve on the definition of justice handed down to him. He replaced the "inuenta" of the original ("in adiutorium multorum inuenta") with a phrase of his own coinage, "cordibus hominum inspirata". Thus we read it in the text of the Vienna and Paris manuscripts, but also as an interlinear gloss in the Bamberg codex (41). There it may represent a first step toward the later recension or a throw-back from the latter: either explanation is possible.

The change might have been prompted by euphonic scruples (*conuentio... inuenta*); it seems more likely, however, that the author wanted to link up what seemed to him a rather vague description of the ways of justice, with the better known doctrines of man's justice as "inspired", "infused" from above, a "participation" in the justice of God. Here he felt on familiar, Stoic and Augustinian grounds (42). But then it was no longer necessary to dwell on a

---

(40) See Sicardus's lengthy text on justice (in his prologue) published from MS Vat. Pal. lat. 653 fol. 65va by C. LEFEBVRE in G. LE BRAS, J. RAMBAUD, C. LEFEBVRE, *L'âge classique* I (*Hist. du droit et des inst. de l'Eglise en Occ.* 7; Paris 1965) p. 354 n. 4, beginning "Ius dicimus (dominis *Lefebvre*) preceptum iusticie...", with very slight variations (...equitas] uero *add. Sicardus*, — uelimus proprie *tr. Sicardus*) in lines 10-12 "Differt eciam — iudicium equum". A different order of text in Placentinus, *Summa Instit.* 1.1 (Mogunt. 1535; I used ed. 1537 p. 1): "...dicitur quoque aequitas quasi aequalitas et uertitur in rebus, id est in dictis et factis hominum. Iustitia autem quiescit in mentibus iustorum, unde si proprie uelimus loqui dicimus aequum iudicium, non iustum, et hominem iustum non aequum; abutentes tamen...". The reading *quiescit* (where Sicard and the glossator of *Summa Elegantius* have *consistit*) *in mentibus* has been confirmed by a collation of 15 MSS on microfilms kindly carried out at the Max-Planck-Institut für europäische Rechtsgeschichte in Frankfurt by Dr. Gero Dolezalek (the only variants shown being *que fit in m.*, and *que fit aliter quiesit* [*sic*], both occuring once). Azo, *Summa Instit.* 1.1 repeats this text verbatim (*ed.* 1514 fol. cclxix*rb* no. 3; 1557 fol. 269ra no. 3).

(41) See *app. crit.* ad *loc.* in the edition p. 1.

(42) Cicero *de inuent.* 2.53.161: "natura ius est quod non opinio genuit sed quaedam in natura uis inseuit, ut religionem, pietatem...", quoted by Augustine *de diuersis quaest. LXXXIII* q.31 (with the variant *quaedam innata uis inseruit, PL* 40.20). Cicero *de republica* 3.22.33, "lex diffusa in omnes", in Lactantius, *Diuinae inst.* 6.8.7; references to more patristic texts in J. GAUDEMET, *La doctrine des sources du droit dans le Décret de Gratien*, in *Revue de droit canonique* 1 (1951) 25 n. 3. — *Accessus Inst. Pragensis* "(iustitia)... in nobis

contrast of *natura* and *scientia*: once 'breathed into" the human heart, justice is no longer outside "our knowing": this sentence thus could be, and indeed was, suppressed in the Vienna-Paris recension (43). The new version, to be sure, opened a wide range of associations: with the "natural law" that God had written from time immemorial in the heart of man (to use the words of Rufinus); and also with that law which a still insufficiently explored text, attributed to Pope Urban II, had called the *lex priuata* infused by the Holy Spirit (44) and which some decretalists would soon identify with [the law of] love — *amor siue karitas* (45). Indeed a gloss

---

uero per participationem" (ed. FITTING p. 215 § 9); *Summa Diuinam uoluntatem*: "...(humanam iusticiam) uero nonnullis hominum occulto (*var.* nonnullorum... occulte) nature instinctu sanciendam inseruit" (ed. WEIGAND p. 456, FITTING p. 132 § 9). Cf. CORTESE, *La norma giurid.* II 11 n. 25. The description of natural law as inspired or infused runs through the canonists of the twelfth century; see texts (from Rufinus on) in WEIGAND §§ 240, 246, 254, 265, 271, 284, 296 etc. Among these is the *Summa Elegantius* itself at 1.29: "Lex nature est que sub primo silentio... in cordibus hominum scripsit" (ed. p. 8, cf. WEIGAND § 265 and p. 365).

(43) See *app. crit. ad loc.*

(44) JL 5760, C.19 q.2 c.2: "Urbanus papa in capitulo s. Rufi, 'Due sont', inquit, 'leges, una publica, altera priuata. Publica lex est que a sanctis patribus scriptis est confirmata, que propter transgressiones est tradita... Lex uero priuata est que instinctu s. Spiritus in corde scribitur...'." Under His guidance a secular cleric may, against his bishop's will, enter a monastery (or, as Gratian adds, a *canonica regularis*): "quia lege priuata ducitur, nulla ratio exigit ut a publica lege constringatur: dignior est enim lex priuata quam publica." Both the unusual doctrine and its unusual form — a papal ruling presented in the third person (*inquit*) — have caused authors ever since the eighteenth century to question its authenticity: see C.S. BERARDI, *Gratiani canones genuint ab apocryphis distincti* [Venice 1777] II 2, pp. 368-9; F.J. GOSSMAN, *Pope Urban II and Canon Law* (Catholic Univ. Canon Law Studies 403; Wash. D.C. 1960) 33, 131; also WEIGAND, *Naturrechtslehre* 130f. The complex problem exceeds the limits of the present paper. This writer has begun a fresh investigation in the light (1) of the early transmission of the text in pre-Gratian collections; (2) of all the canonical texts from the era of reform concerning the *transitus* from one religious state to another, several of which are likewise of uncertain origin; (3) of recent research on the status of Canons regular in this period. — Outside the problems of *transitus*, very few texts apply these peculiar notions of *lex priuata — publica*; one of them is the collection of *distinctiones, definitiones, summulae* etc. of MS Vat. Pal. 678 fol. 100v-101v (cf. *Repertorium* 215) ed. J.A. C.J. VAN DE WOUW, *Twee Kleinschriften uit de vroege decretalistiek*, in *Mededelingen van het Nederlands Historisch Instituut te Rom* 34 (1969) p. 125 No. 23, with regard to property and the law of prescription (the commentary p. 120 should have referred to C.19 q.2 c.2); and see also *Summa Elegantius* 1.39 (p. 11).

(45) See e.g. texts in *Repertorium* p. 203 (*Summa De iure canonico tractaturus* and *Summa In nomine*): "...amor siue karitas quam afflat ignis diuinus... hec lex priuata appellatur (nuncupatur) ut xix.q.ii. Due...". Others were opposed to this identification: thus Simon

in the Vienna MS of the *Summa Elegantius* assures us that the terms "cordibus hominum inspirata" and "inuenta" are interchangeable (46) — but with the new text the delicate, almost intangible yet studied oracular vagueness of the original was gone.

The second canonist to place the definition of "Gregorius" in the context of a general discourse is the unknown author of the French school in the 1170's whose *summulae* and *distinctiones* have come down to us in several different arrangements as recorded by different pupils. The most polished of these versions is the *Summa Inperatorie maiestati*, written in Carinthia *c.* 1175-78 and usually called *Monacensis* because of the present location (Munich MS lat. 16084) of the codex from St. Nicholas in Passau that contains it (47). In a distinction attached to the words "ius naturale" of Gratian's opening paragraph (48), the author connects the definition of justice with natural law but, unlike Paucapalea, not with the Golden Rule of the Gospel. He begins with a somewhat elliptic statement equating natural law with natural justice, and positive justice with custom ("idem est iustitia positiua et ius consuetudinarium"), which seems to echo a passage from Hugh of St. Victor (49). Then he

---

de Bisignano, the *Summae Tractaturus magister* and *Reuerentia sacrorum canonum*: texts in WEIGAND §§ 293, 318, 330.

(46) *Summa Elegantius* p. 1 *app. crit. ad loc.* (1.3. lin. 6).

(47) The Munich *Summa* is traditionally presented as the fountainhead of all other writings from the same circle; so also *Repertorium* p. 180ff. Evidence for the different assessment given above will be discussed elsewhere.

(48) Full text in WEIGAND § 276 (p. 163).

(49) Munich lat. 16084 fol. 1va and Arras MS 271 (1064) fol. 188rb: "*Ius naturale*. idest (*om. Atr.*) iustitia naturalis." The continuation (above) is inverted in *Atr.*: "idem est ius consuetudinarium et iustitia positiua." Cf. Hugo a S. Victore, *Didascalicon* 6.5 "...in illa enim naturalis iustitia est, ex qua disciplina morum nostrorum, i.e. iustitia positiua nascitur" (*PL* 176.805B; ed. BUTTIMER [Washington D.C. 1939], p. 123). The correspondence between *ius consuetudinarium* and *disciplina morum* is evident and quite in line with the Isidorian equation of *mores* and *consuetudo* in D.1 cc.4,5. — Hugh of St. Victor on *iustitia naturalis* and *positiua* (cf. also *Didascalicon* 3.2) should have been discussed by KUTTNER, *Sur les origines du terme "droit positif"*, in *Revue historique de droit français et étranger*⁴ 15 (1936) 728-40; cf. D. VAN DEN EYNDE, *The Terms "ius positivum" and "signum positivum"*, in *Franciscan Studies* 9 (1949) 41-49 at 43f. and S. GAGNÉR, *Studien zur Ideengeschichte der Gesetzgebung* (*Studia Iuridica Uppsalensia* 1; Stockholm-Uppsala 1960) 213, 238f. The opening sentence of the widely copied *Introductio* to Gratian, "In prima parte agitur de iustitia naturali et positiua tam constituta quam inconstituta" (on which see e.g. J. RAMBAUD-BUHOT, *Les divers types d'abrégés du Décret...*, in *Recueil de travaux offert à M. Clovis Brunel* [Paris 1955] 399f.; A.M. STICKLER, *Decretistica Germanica adaucta*, in *Traditio* 12 [1956] 604; GAGNÉR pp. 218ff.), may likewise be derived from Hugo a S. Victore, *Didascalicon* 6.5.

goes on to distinguish four meanings of the term *ius naturale*. The first three are: the laws of nature as a force implanted in all things ("uis cuilibet rei insita") which governs the universe and keeps the sun on its course; the animal instinct ("uis animantibus insita") of mating and bringing up the young, which is common to beast and man; and the reason implanted in rational beings ("ratio cuilibet rationali insita") which governs their choice of action according to the Golden Rule. With these three formulations the author sums up three strands of contemporary thought: (1) the cosmological speculation of twelfth-century Platonism (50); (2) the tradition which Rufinus called *legistica*, and which stemmed from Ulpian's "quod natura omnia animalia docuit" (51); and (3) what we may call the Victorine contribution as adopted by Gratian (52), who sharpened it by going beyond the scriptural authorities for the Golden Rule of his initial statement, back to the creation of rational beings ("ab exordio rationalis creaturae": a term he borrowed from Justinian) (53).

The fourth meaning, however, of natural law in the *Summa*

---

(50) *Cod. Mon.*: "quandoque est (*om. Atr.*) uis cuilibet rei insita qua regitur, unde superiora et media dicuntur regi iure naturali, ut sol cursum perficere". For the cosmological meaning of *ius naturale* or *iustitia naturalis* (the terms are often interchangeable) in Calcidius's and William of Conches' Commentaries on the *Timaeus* see authors cited in n.49, especially GAGNÉR, *Studien* pp. 231ff.; also PH. DELHAYE, *L'enseignement de la philosophie morale au XIIᵉ siècle*, in *Mediaeval Studies* 11 (1949) at p. 95f.; T. GREGORY, *Platonismo medievale (Istituto storico italiano per il Medio Evo: Studi storici* 26-7; Rome 1948) pp. 59-73 *passim*; and above all the critical edition by E. JEAUNEAU, *Guillaume de Conches: Glosae super Platonem (Textes philosophiques du moyen âge* 13; Paris 1965), pp. 59 (with note *b*), 71-73, 83, 98, etc. — To the known echoes of this doctrine one should probably add the *Summa Institutionum "Iustiniani est in hoc opere"* of Morgan MS 903, ed. P. LEGENDRE (*Ius commune*, Sonderhefte 2, Frankfurt 1973), *prohemium* lin. 36-7 p. 20: "Omni parti philosophie subponitur: phisice ubi tractat de naturali iusticia...".

(51) *Mon.*: "quandoque est uis animantibus insita qua trahuntur ad commiscendum, ad fetuum procreationem et educationem, quod pereque brutis et rationalibus conuenit: homo enim sine ratione impetu nature ad id trahitur". Cf. D.1 c.7; the term *legistica traditio* (Ulp. *Dig.* 1.1.1) in Rufinus, D.1 pr. (p. 6 SINGER).

(52) *Mon.*: "quandoque est ratio cuilibet rationali insita qua discernit quid faciendum quid non, ut 'quod tibi non uis fieri' etc." Cf. Gratian D.1 pr. For Hugo a S. Victore *de sacramentis* 1.11.7 (*PL* 176.347, 348 quoting Tob. 4.16 and Mt. 1.12) as Gratian's model see M. VILLEY, *Le droit naturel chez Gratien*, in *Studia Gratiana* 3 (1955) 85-99 = *Revue de droit canonique* 4 (1954) 50-65 at p. 59; WEIGAND, *Naturrechtslehre* 131-33.

(53) D.5 pr. § 1 and D.6 fin. § 1; cf. Inst. 2.1.11 med., expressly cited in the *Glossa ordinaria ad loc.* The connection is generally neglected by modern writers; see S. KUTTNER, *New Studies on the Roman Law in Gratian's Decretum*, in *Seminar* 11 (1955) 42f.

Inperatorie maiestati presents some difficulty because of an ambiguous reading: its second word, abbreviated in the Munich MS, can be expanded as "d(e)mu(m)" or "diu(in)u(m)" (54). Accordingly, we have:

> Quandoque demum ius naturale dicitur quia originem trahit a naturali ratione,

or:

> Quandoque diuinum ius naturale dicitur quia originem trahit a naturali ratione.

The latter was the choice of the scribe of the compilation transmitted of the original material in the Arras MS; it is also the reading adopted in Professor Weigand's analysis of the canonists' *Naturrechtslehre* (55). In this case, we would have to understand the text as a development of Paucapalea's remark that divine laws have their beginning (*principium*) from nature; except that *natura* or *ius naturale* are here replaced by *naturalis ratio*. The implication seems to be that natural reason lies at the root of what the revealed law of God taught us in the Old and the New Covenant — thus making our author's third and fourth definitions really say the same in different words. (Huguccio would later criticize formulations of this kind as inappropriate and repetitious.) (56) The meaning is quite different if we take "demum" as the proper reading: a reading that is paleographically acceptable and fits the symmetry of the fourfold division more convincingly ("Item ius naturale quandoque est... / quandoque est... / quandoque est... / quandoque demum ius naturale dicitur..."). If this is correct, the author wanted to convey the thought that "at times, finally, we speak of law as

---

(54) Three strokes underneath a suspension mark after the initial letter *d*. They may stand for *m, ni, in, iu, ui*. A third expansion, *d(omi)niu(m)* is possible but makes no sense in the context.

(55) Arras MS 271 fol. 188rb; Weigand p. 163; he admits, however, that "diese Begründung ist sehr auffallend" (p. 164).

(56) "Et dicitur hoc ius naturale quia summa natura, idest Deus, nobis illud tradidit et docuit per legem et prophetas et euangelium, uel quia ad ea que iure diuino continentur, naturalis ratio etiam sine [in *codd. dett.*] extrinseca eruditione ducit et impellit. Unde si audacia detur uerbo, secure dico quod hoc ius impropie dicitur naturale...": Weigand p. 217 § 371; Lottin, *Le droit naturel chez St. Thomas d'Aquin et ses prédécesseurs* (2nd ed. Bruges 1931) p. 110. Both follow the reading *etiam in extrinseca* of Vat. lat. 2280 (and some other late MSS) which misses the point (*sine*: Admont 7, Vat. Arch. S. Petr. C.114, Tarazona 151 etc.).

natural because it has its origin in natural reason", that is, he wanted
the *ius gentium* of Gaius's and Justinian's Institutes ("quod... naturalis ratio inter omnes homines constituit") included among the
several meanings of *ius naturale* (57). It is at this point that he
refers to *iustitia* in the definition of "Gregory"; but unfortunately
he garbles the text of his quotation (a sign, incidentally, that a
common faulty archetype stands behind both the Munich and the
Arras versions):

> Ius autem tale gregorius nomine iustitie describere uidetur
> dicens "Justitia est multorum nature conuentio in adiuto-
> rium inuenta".

But the intention of equating natural law, natural reason, and a
natural justice of sorts can be somehow discerned behind the poorly
formulated text.

IV.

There seems to be no further instance of our definition being
used by the twelfth-century lawyers. To be sure, Martin of Braga's
Formula honestae uitae (usually under the name of Seneca) was often
copied in the twelfth century and beyond, but as we have seen this
was not the direct source from which the canonists quoted. Speculation on justice among the theologians went in other directions (58).
One should, however, mention Hildebert of Lavardin, bishop of
Le Mans (d. 1133 as archbishop of Tours), if he is indeed the author
of the didactic poem in elegiac distichs inscribed *De quatuor uirtutibus uitae honestae* (59). Strangely, most historians of medieval
Latin literature who discuss the poem (60) seem to ignore that it

---

(57) The connection of this *ius gentium* with Rom. 2.14-16 is commonplace among
decretists; and see also Alain de Lille, *Distinctiones, PL* 210.871D; for precedents in late antiquity cf. GAUDEMET, *art. cit.* (n. 42) p. 16f. etc.

(58) See authors quoted in LOTTIN, *Le concept de justice* and Palasse, *supra* n. 2.

(59) *PL* 171.1055-64. The authorship has been questioned, not without good reasons,
by A.B. SCOTT, *The Poems of Hildebert of Le Mans: A New Examination of the Canon*, in *Mediaeval and Renaissance Studies* 6 (1968) 42-83, especially at p. 76. I owe this reference, together with much other valuable information on Hildebert, to the kindness of Mme. Philippe
Grand at the Institut de Recherche et d'Histoire des Textes in Paris.

(60) Thus M. MANITIUS, *Geschichte der lateinischen Literatur des Mittelalters* III (Munich 1931), 859; J. DE GHELLINCK, *L'essor de la littérature latine au XIIᵉ siècle* (*Musæum
Lessianum, section historique* 4-5; Bruxelles-Paris 1946) II 237; PH. DELHAYE, *art. cit.* (*supra*
n. 50) 85f.

is basically nothing but an embroidered paraphrase of the *Formula* (61). But even with the great fame Hildebert enjoyed as "incomparabilis uersificator" (62), this *libellus* had no influence to speak of. What the poet made here of St. Martin's — for him, surely Seneca's — definition,

> Quid nisi naturae tacitum perpendere foedus
> Justitiae nomen nos ratioque docet? (*PL* 171.1062C)

offers only a pale reflection of the original text. The "silent compact of nature" remains barren, without an object or purpose.

About two hundred years later, an echo of the thoughts formulated by the early generations of decretist glossators can still be found in the annotations which an unknown scholar wrote in the margins of his copy of a thirteenth-century *Lectura* on Gratian. This is now MS 2121 of the Nationalbibliothek in Vienna; it contains, after the *Casus decretorum* of Bartholomew of Brescia (fol. 1-83), the *Lectura* of Percival (or Parsifal) of Milan, canon of Monza and *doctor decretorum* in Padua in the latter part of the thirteenth century. In accordance with the spelling of some MSS, he is better known as 'Princivallus' to bibliographers and historians of canon law (63); at any rate, his work on Gratian was an important fore-

---

(61) I find no mention prior to Barlow, *Martini Brac. opp.* 208 ('A metrical version was made by Hildebertus Cenomanensis'); apparently not noticed by M. Martins, *A Formula vitae honestae de S. Martino de Dume em disticos latinos*, in *Revista portuguesa de filosofia* 20 (1964) 314-21. Note that the Formula in Barlow's edition has 238 lines; 'Hildebert' presents 212 distichs.

(62) Ordericus Vitalis, *Historia ecclesiastica* 10.6 (*PL* 188.732), quoted by Delhaye, *art. cit.* 85 n. 3.

(63) Schulte, *Geschichte der Quellen und Literatur* II 135f.; van Hove, *Prolegomena*, pp. 430, 484; J. Kejř, *Les manuscrits du Décret de Gratien dans les bibliothèques tchécoslovaques*, in *Studia Gratiana* 8 (1962) 36-42, 85. Diplovatatius (p. 137 in Rabotti's edition, *SG.* 10 [1968]) gives his name as "Princivalis"; thus also the *Lectura* in MS Vienna 2101 ("Bone rei dare consultum... ideo ⟨ego⟩ magister pricinal' [*sic*] mediolanensis..."), where the title, by another hand, reads "Lectura magistri Parciualis de Mediolano super decretorum libro". It is "Perciuallus" in Paris, BN lat. 3915, 3916, while several MSS of the *Lectura* (including Vienna 2121) remain inconclusive with a mere "ego magister p. mediolanen.", or lack the preface (thus the fragment in Prague Mus. XVII.B.8, identified by Kejř p. 85; unidentified in *Repertorium*, p. 167 note). Among the MSS of Gratian with layers of glosses additional to the *Ordinaria* (see e.g. *Repertorium* 48 for Montecassino 66, and Kejř pp. 36-42 for Prague Museum XII.A.12 [Schulte's M.82, cf. *Repertorium* 115 n.1]), MS Vat. lat. 1373 repeatedly presents the siglum "perci." (misread as *para.* by F. Gillmann, *Johannes de Phintona*, in *Archiv für kath. Kirchenr.* 116 [1936] 465). Dr. Martin Bertram has called to my attention the marginal addition "per dominum parcifallum" to Pierre de Sampson's *Lectura*

runner of Guido de Baysio's *Rosarium*, adding materials both old and new to the standard interpretations of the *Glossa ordinaria* (64). The fourteenth-century owner of MS Vienna 2121 of Percival's *Lectura* was apparently a man of erudite tastes. The material he or his *amanuensis* copied in the margins of the book begins on fol. 84r with the prologue of Simon de Bisignano's *Summa* (*c.* 1177-1179) on the left hand; to the right (84rb), near Percival's exposition of D.1 c.1, we read:

> Aug. § iusticia est amor soli amato seruiens.
> § Justicia est nature tacita conuentio in adiutorium mul-
> torum inuenta. Differunt jus et iusticia in auctoritate,
> quia Deus iusticie est auctor, iuris uero apostolicus et im-
> 5 perator; in substancia, quia iusticia est uirtus, jus precep-
> tum ejus; in subiectorum continencia, quia lacius iusticia.
> Nam quidquid dicit ius, idem et iusticia, licet in oculto
> dictauit [dictarat *scr.*]. Multa [multe *scr.*] vero latent ius-
> ticie presencia uel futura negocia que non sunt laqueis
> 10 iuris innodata. Differt vero iusticia ab equitate, quia ius-
> ticia consistit in mentibus hominum, equitas autem in dic-
> tis et factis eorum.

The opening quotation one would not have expected in a legal context. It comes from St. Augustine's *De moribus ecclesiae*, and presents us with the sublime vision of justice fused in pure love, the perfect love of God, whence the right governance of all things will flow (65). In the *Summa theologica* of St. Thomas Aquinas, this

---

(on X 4.3.2) in a miscellaneous MS from Padua, Vienna 2113 fol. 67va. For a notarial instrument drawn up in 1276 in the presence of "Perciuallus de Mandello Mediolanensis, canonicus Moedecensis, doctor decretorum" see A. Gloria, *I Monumenti dell'Università di Padova* II 1 (Padova 1888) 303, and G. Catalano, *Inventario ragionato dei manoscritti giuridici della Biblioteca Palatina di Parma* (Milan 1955), p. 73 in the notice for MS Parma 1225 of Percival's *Lectura*.

(64) Kejř, *art. cit.* 39f. (Dr. Kejř, by letter, indicates his hope to return in a major study to the *Lectura* and its author).

(65) Aug. *de moribus ecclesiae et de moribus Manichaeorum* 1.15.125 (*PL* 32.1322); cf. also 1.24.44 (*ibid.* 1330). Augustine's terms for right governance are *recte dominans, bene imperans, ceteraque omnia... regat.* — See also *De musica* 6.15.50: "...quae nulli seruit nisi uni Deo... quae tandem uirtus tibi esse uidetur? D(iscipulus): Quis non intelligat hanc esse iustitiam? M(agister): Recte intelligis" (*PL* 32.1189). On Justice and Love in Augustine see J. Mausbach, *Die Ethik des heiligen Augustinus* (Freiburg Br. 1909) I 202ff., esp. pp. 210-12.

saying appears as one of the difficulties to be resolved in debating the traditional definition (*unicuique suum*) of justice (66): and it is perhaps characteristic of Thomas that here, as in several other *quaestiones*, he chose the Augustinian notion of virtues as forms of *amor* to serve as material for his dialectic objections (67). To the annotator of the Vienna MS, wherever he may have come across the dictum of Augustine (68), it must have appeared a fitting introduction to the texts he copied next, this time from his readings in the twelfth-century canonists. The "Gregorius" label here is absent from our definition of justice as "nature tacita conuentio" etc. Therefore a Gratian with early glosses appears to be a more likely source than a *Summa* such as Paucapalea or *Elegantius in iure diuino* — even though the definition is joined, as in *Elegantius*, with a version of the familiar *differentiae* between *iustitia* and *ius* from the Bulgarus tradition. But a comparison of texts shows that here the source for the annotator of the Vienna Percival was, word for word, the *Summa* of Sicard of Cremona (69). It was Sicard who in par-

---

(66) St. Thomas, *S. theol.* 2.2.58.1 obj.6.

(67) See *S. theol.* 2.2: q.47.1 obj.1 (on prudence), 123.4 obj.1 and 7 obj.3 (on fortitude), 141.2 obj.1 (on temperance).

(68) A special study would be needed to trace the ramifications of Augustine's equation *iustitia — amor* in the Middle Ages. At random: Alcuin, *de animae ratione* c.3 (*PL* 101. 640A), cited by G. DEL VECCHIO *La giustizia* § 4 n. 13 (3rd ed. Rome 1946 not seen), = *Die Gerechtigkeit* (2nd German ed. tr. F. DARMSTAEDTER, Basel 1950), p. 34 = *Justice*, with additional notes by A.G. CAMPBELL (tr. LADY GUTHRIE, Edinburgh 1952), p. 32; Alexander of Hales, *Glossa in IV libros Sententiarum* III (Quaracchi 1954) ad 3.33, p. 390-91: "specialius dicitur iustitia cum consistit in dilectione Dei et proximi" (recension AE); p. 395 "...secundum quod est ordinata ad dilectionem Dei et proximi" (rec. L); Dante, *Convivio* 4.17.6: "L'undecima (vertù) si è Giustizia, la quale ordina noi ad amare e operare dirittura in tutta cosa", cited by DEL VECCHIO § 6 n. 21 (DARMSTAEDTER p. 77, GUTHRIE p. 71). In the philosophy of G.W. Leibniz (1646-1716), *amor* or *caritas ad normam sapientis* was to become of central importance for the doctrine of justice; cf. DEL VECCHIO § 4 with nn. 23, 24 (DARMSTAEDTER pp. 26, 43f., GUTHRIE pp. 26, 40); G. GRUA, *Jurisprudence universelle et théodicee selon Leibniz* (Paris 1953); HANS-PETER SCHNEIDER, *Justitia universalis: Quellenstudien zur Geschichte des "christlichen Naturrechts" bei Gottfried Wilhelm Leibniz* (Frankfurt 1967), esp. pp. 367-401, 453-83. An investigation of patristic and medieval elements in Leibniz's thought remains desirable.

(69) For Sicard's text see LEFEBVRE, in *L'âge classique* (as cited *supra* n. 40) p. 354 n. 4. *Variants*: Differunt uero] Differunt jus et iusticia *V* (*indob. lin.*) 3   apostolicus] uero apostolicus *V* 4   lacius patet] lacius *V* 6   ius dicit idem iusticia] dicit ius idem et iusticia *V* 7   dictauit (dictauerit *codd. nonnulli, e.g. Par. lat.* 4288, *Vindob.* 2166)] dictarat *V* 7   nondum] non *V* 9   Differt eciam] Differt uero *V* 10   equitas uero] equitas autem *V* 11

ticular had substituted "pope and emperor" (*apostolicus et imperator*) in the conventional formula for Man as "auctor iuris" (70).

V.

After this late and apparently isolated reminiscence, Martin of Braga's definition disappeared from the vocabulary of jurists. Its tradition had been somewhat esoteric even in the twelfth century, but not without a certain intellectual affinity to some other 'unorthodox' notions of justice that had likewise been handed down from late antiquity and laid greater stress on its affective than its rational aspects.

Peter Lombard quoted Augustine on the function of justice as "coming to the aid of the wretched" (71). The statement occurs in the *De Trinitate*, in the chapter where St. Augustine answers Cicero's denial of any need for the four virtues once we have passed from this life to the eternal bliss of knowing and understanding Nature (72). The Blessed, said Augustine, indeed will dwell in contemplation of "that [divine] Nature than which nothing is better and more lovable, the Nature which has created and ordered all other beings (*naturas*)"; but the complement of their contemplation will be the submission to the governance of this supreme, all-lovable, all-creating Nature, that is, to the rule of God. If this belongs to justice — and here one is reminded of Augustine's earlier "amor soli amato seruiens" — then justice is indeed immortal (73).

---

(70) Except for the interpolation in MS Vienna 2176 of the Bulgarus *Materia*, "auctoritas iuris est homo, ut [papa] imperator, populus", it is always "auctor iustitie deus est, (auctor) iuris (est) homo" (or equivalents) in the texts cited *supra* n. 17.

(71) Petrus Lombardus, *Libri IV Sentent.* 3.33.1, 3; ed. 2 Quaracchi (1916) II 697f. num. 227, 229; cf. Lottin, *Psychologie et morale* (n. 2 *supra*) 283, 286ff. See also Petrus Lombardus *in Ps.* 70.1, "Justitia autem tua est ut parcas oranti, quod est et misericordia" (*PL* 191.647).

(72) Augustine, *de Trin.* 14.9.12 (*PL* 42.1064; ed. W.J. Mountain and Fr. Glorie, *CCL* 50A.439).

(73) *Ibid.*: "...bonos animos sola beatos esse cognitione et scientia, hoc est contemplatione naturae qua nihil melius et amabilius: ea est natura quae creauit omnes caeteras, instituitque naturas. Cui regenti esse subditum, si iustitia est, immortalis erit omnis iustitia nec in illa esse beatitudine desinet, sed talis ac tanta erit ut perfectior et maior esse non possit." Compare the Neoplatonic doctrine on the justice of the *animi iam purgati* in Macrobius, *Comm. in somn. Scipionis* 1.8.9: "...iustitiae est ita cum supera et diuina mente sociari ut seruet perpetuum cum ea foedus imitando."

From such ultimate perfection of justice and the other virtues in the state of *beatitudo* Augustine turned to their transitory functions here and now — to their works "that will cease where evil will be no more" (74). It was in this context that he coined, almost as an aside, the striking phrase, "nunc autem quod agit iustitia in subueniendo miseris..." — which through Peter Lombard's more pointed formulation (75), "Augustinus ait: Iustitia est in subueniendis miseris", would gain currency in the Schools.

One may find here a parallel with the Stoic classification of *beneficentia, benignitas,* and *liberalitas* as parts of justice; in fact St. Thomas was to cite Cicero's formulation in this context side by side with the words of Augustine (76). But it should be evident that beneficence and largess belong to another region of the heart than what Augustine described as reaching out for the relief of those in misery. Where such is the "work" (*quod agit*) of justice we also are no longer within the conventional dichotomy of *iustitia* and *misericordia,* which was of course familiar to Augustine too. It is not Augustine the student of Cicero but the disciple of the Gospel who wrote the passage in *De Trinitate*: its language is that of the Sermon on the Mount where St. Matthew's text designates the acts of almsgiving, prayer, and fasting as justice: "Nolite facere iustitiam uestram (τὴν δικαιοσύνην ὑμῶν) coram hominibus ut uideamini ab illis..." (Mt. 6,1) — a connotation oddly lost in the vernacular translations we use (77). If St. Augustine elsewhere could speak of justice (and even expound the verse from Matthew) in Ciceronian

---

(74) *Ibid.*: "Nunc autem quod agit iustitia in subueniendis miseris, quod prudentia in praecauendis insidiis... non ibi erit ubi nihil omnino mali erit. Ac per hoc ista uirtutum opera quae huic mortali uitae sunt nessaria... in praeteritis habebuntur...".

(75) *Sent.* 3.33.1 (num. 227 Quaracchi); Augustine's' full text is in c.3 (229).

(76) *Sum. theol.* 2.2.58.11 obj.1 (Aug. *de trin.*) and 2 (Cic. *de off.* 1.7.20). See also earlier medieval formulations such as "iusticia *clementia siue pietas* aequitas recte iudicandi" in the tract *de legibus diuinis et humanis,* cf. CONRAT, *Geschichte der römischen Rechts im Mittelalter* 316 n. 2; J. TARDIF, *Un abrégé juridique des Étymologies d'Isidore de Séville,* in *Mélanges Julien Havet* (Paris 1895) 667 and n. 2. (The definition continues "et dicta iusticia quasi iuris *idest doctorum* status *idest firmitas*"; it is pieced together from Isid. *Etym.* 2.24.6 "uirtus qua recte iudicando...", 18.15.2 "iustitia quasi iuris status", and the *Rhet. ad Herenn.* 2.2.3 "iustitia est aequitas...", with ninth-century glosses — here in italics — inserted.)

(77) E.g. "...that ye not do your alms" (King James, with the addition "*or,* righteous acts" in the Scofield Reference Bible), "your good" (Confraternity N.T.), "your acts of piety" (Knox), "eure Frömmigkeit" (Luther), with "your justice" in the Douai Bible remaining the exception.

terms as well (78), this is characteristic of an all-absorbing mind that was always seeking, not a self-enclosed system of thought or ethics, but new and ever-changing modes of expressing his vision of God, men, and things (79).

Very much akin to the passage of Augustine's *De Trinitate* in its accent on compassion is still another 'unorthodox' description of justice from late antiquity, which was brought into the twelfth-century lawyers' field of vision by Placentinus. He attributed it to Plato, and as such it is quoted by Azo, Accursius, and Odofredus (80), though without approval. Placentinus *Summa Inst.* 1.1 writes (81):

> Restat ut exponamus quid sit iustitia. Iustitia est secundum Platonem uirtus que plurimum prodest his (*al.* potest in his) qui minimum possunt, nempe in personis miserabilibus euidentius clarescit iustitia. Vel ut Tullius ait...

I am not aware that legal historians have attempted to identify the quotation. In fact, it comes from one of the foremost sources of Platonism in the twelfth century, the Commentary of Calcidius attached to his translation of the *Timaeus* (82) — a translation, incidentally, which is also the source of the hitherto unexplained reference to the City of Plato in Gratian's Decretum (83). In the

---

(78) Thus *De perfectione iustitiae hominis* 8.18 on Mt. 6.1ff. where he expounds *elemosynam* as "omnem beneuolentiam et beneficentiam uel dandi uel ignoscendi" (*PL* 44.300, *CSEL* 42.16). For *suum cuique tribuere* in Augustine see references n. 4 *supra*.

(79) I am borrowing here from the happy formulation of F. VAN DER MEER, *Augustine the Bishop* (London-New York 1961), 566.

(80) Accursius, *Gl. Inst.* 1.1.1 and *Gl. Dig.* 1.1.10 v. *iustitia*; Odofredus, *Lectura Dig. vet.* (*ed. cit.* n. 11) *Dig.* 1.1.10 num. 2, where he also quotes Azo; cf. CORTESE, *La norma giuridica* II 18 n. 39.

(81) *Ed. cit.* (n. 40) p. 1.

(82) *Timaeus a Calcidio translatus commentarioque instructus* ed. J.H. WASZINK (with the assistance of P.J. JENSEN) (*Corpus Platonicum Medii Aevi* ed. R. KLIBANSKY: *Plato latinus* 4; London-Leiden 1962). This now replaces J. WROBEL's edition, *Platonis Timaeus Chalcidio interprete* (Leipzig 1876).

(83) In D.8 pr. Gratian cites "...unde apud Platonem illa ciuitas iustissime ordinata traditur in qua quisque proprios nescit affectus" as parallel to the communal property of the first Christians (Act. 4.32). Very few glossators tried to explain what Gratian or Plato here had in mind, and modern scholars have not attempted to identify Gratian's reference (see e.g. WEIGAND, *Naturrechtslehre* p. 311). In another paper I shall return to this text and its connection with the Latin *Timaeus*.

V

A forgotten definition of justice   97

introductory pages of the *Timaeus,* Plato had Socrates recapitulate
some of the main points developed the day before in the *Republic*;
and Calcidius comments (*inter al.*) (84):

> Nam cum pridie Socrates decem libris de re publica dis-
> putasset... siquidem cum de iustitia quaeri coeptum fuis-
> set, quam definierat Thrasymachus orator eam esse quae
> huic prodesset qui plurimum posset, Socrates contra do-
> cuisset immo eam potius quae his prodesset qui minimum
> possent...

Here the well-known position taken by Thrasymachus in the earlier dialogue — justice is what benefits the more powerful — is
couched in terms that remain close to Plato's text (85). It was
more difficult to summarize the complex refutation of this strong-
man morality by Socrates who, as always, had cast his net wide.
Calcidius coined a cogent phrase in simply reversing the key word
of Thrasymachus's assertion (*plurimum — minimum*). The statement as such has no exact equivalent in the *Republic,* but freely
renders the long Socratic exposition of governance as an art exercised for the sake of the governed (86); and with his pointed formulation, "not for the benefit of the stronger but that of the weaker",
Calcidius may have merely applied to *iustitia* what Socrates had
said of ἐπιστήμη in the course of this argument (87).

The sharp contrast between the two antagonists is of course
lost in Placentinus, whose short formula omitted the context of
the dialogue (88). Instead, the passage, as it appears in the printed
edition, by a slight change of vocabulary gives the definition a new

---

(84) Calcidius *Comm.* c.5 (ed. Waszink, p. 59.3-8, Wrobel p. 71f.).

(85) Cf. Plato, *Republic* 338 C2: φημὶ γὰρ ἐγὼ εἶναι τὸ δίκαιον οὐκ ἄλλο τι ἢ
τὸ τοῦ κρείττονος ξυμφέρον....

(86) Cf. *Republic* 345D, 346A, 346E-347A, etc. (Waszink *ad loc.* refers to 346 C12-D1).

(87) *Republic* 342 C11-D1: Οὐκ ἄρα ἐπιστήμη τὸ τοῦ κρείττονος ξυμφέρον σκοπεῖ
οὐδ' ἐπιτάττει, ἀλλὰ τὸ τοῦ ἥττονός τε καὶ ἀρχομένου ὑπὸ ἑαυτῆς "Then no art
considers or enjoins the advantage of the stronger, but every art that of the weaker which is
ruled by it", ((Shorey's translation, Loeb *Classics* I p. 63). For parallels in Lactantius
see *infra*, p. 107f.

(88) The same is true for the implicit quotation in John of Salisbury's description
of the *officium principis*: "...illis qui minimum possunt plurimum prodest", *Policraticus* 4.2
(*PL* 199.515C; ed. Webb I 238), cited by Jeauneau, *Guillaume de Conches* (n. 50 *supra*), p.
58 note *b* to *Accessus* § ii. See *ibid.* p. 18 n. 1 for John as a pupil of William of Conches.

rhetorical sharpness, substituting *plurimum potest* for *prodesset* to describe the function of justice: "which can [do] most for those who can do least" (*que plurimum potest... qui minimum possunt*). But even though this reading is supported by one group of manuscripts and the quotations in Accursius and Odofredus, the equally well attested *plurimum prodest*, being closer to the literary model, is more convincing (89). The inserted *plurimum*, moreover, suggests that what Placentinus had read was perhaps not the Calcidian text itself but rather Calcidius as restated and expanded by William of Conches in the Introduction to his Glosses on the *Timaeus* (90):

> ...Trasimacus orator sic illam diffiniuit: "Iusticia est que plurimum prodest illi qui plurimum potest"... Cuius diffinitione in scolis Socratis relata, ait: "Non. Immo iusticia est que plurimum prodest illi qui minimum potest...'.

We know from Professor Gagnér's investigation of the terminological history of "positive law" that these Glosses were of major importance in transmitting the Platonism of Chartres to theologians and canonists of the twelfth century (91). Whichever the model for Placentinus and related glosses (92), William of Conches was certainly the source of Huguccio, who in his *Deriuationes* (c. 1191) s.v. *ius, iubere*, etc., after quoting "Socrates" on justice ("a Socrate sic diffinitur, iustitia est que plurimum prodest ei qui minimum potest"), goes on to say (93):

---

(89) Collations of the Placentinus MSS kindly supplied by Dr. DOLEZALEK (cf. note 40 *supra*): *potest his* (*hiis, iis*) Düsseldorf E.9a, Leipzig Haenel 10, Oxford Trinity 70, Paris lat. 4441, Vat. Chis. E.vii. 217, Vich 156; cf. Accursius *gl. Dig.* 1.1.10 (but *in hiis potest* Berkeley Robbins MS 31); *potest in hi(i)s* Admont 182, ed. Mogunt.; cf. Accursius *gl. Inst.* 1.1, Odofredus *Lect. Dig.* 1.1.10. — *prodest his* (*hiis, i[i]s*) Berlin lat. fol. 405, Frankfurt Barth. 45, Grenoble 391.1, Paris lat. 4539; *potest uel prodest hiis* Hereford D.5.vi, *potest* with gl. marg. *prodesse* Seo de Urgel 2033; with gl. marg. *uel prodest* Vienna 2126.

(90) *Glosae super Timaeum: Accessus* § ii ed. JEAUNEAU (note 50 *supra*) p. 58; for the variant text in the Venice MS S. Marco lat. Z.225 see *ibid.* p. 293. See also the glosses on the *Timaeus* which T. SCHMID edited from Uppsala MS C.620: *Ein Timaioskommentar in Sigtuna*, in *Classica et Mediaevalia* 10 (1949) 220-66 at p. 225. Dr. Schmid cautiously suggests that this may represent an early stage of William's text; *contra* JEAUNEAU p. 14f.

(91) GAGNÉR, *Studien* (note 49 *supra*) pp. 225ff.

(92) E.g. MS Paris lat. 4458A fol. 1va, quoted by CORTESE, *La norma giuridica* II 18 n. 38; cf. note 25 *supra*.

(93) Quoted from Vat. Chis. L. viii. 289 fol. 110ra by CORTESE II 31 n. 74 but without analysis of sources or parallels. (Collated: Vienna MS 2339.) The text has been overlooked

set iustitia duas habet partes, iustitiam positiuam et iustitiam naturalem. Iustitia positiua est que ab hominibus
facta est, ut suspensio latronum et similia, et hec proprie
dicitur ius a iubendo. Naturalis iustitia est que extenditur ad naturales effectus, ut dilectio matris et similia, et
hec proprie dicitur fas a faciendo, quia a summo artifice
sit facta...

This description of positive and natural justice comes almost verbatim from William's *accessus*, where it likewise follows upon the
Socratic definition (94); however, to equate the dichotomy with that
of *ius* and *fas* was an addition of Huguccio's. One might well speculate why the great canonist did not make use of this Platonic
material in his *Summa decretorum* where it would have been very
pertinent to the discussion of the opening passages of Gratian, including the text from Isidore on *ius* and *fas*. Perhaps the first part
of the *Summa* was already completed when Huguccio collected the
material on *iustitia* for the *Deriuationes* — but every explanation
here must remain guesswork.

VI.

Designed for the aid of many — benefits most those who have
least power — acts for the relief of the wretched: in three different
formulations Martin of Braga, Calcidius, and Augustine described
the same spiritual reality, and preserved it for some medieval minds
to reflect upon, outside the mainstream of more conventional notions
of justice. Were there any genetic relations between the three definitions? Scholars disagree on St. Augustine's knowledge of the work
of Calcidius, that is, on the source of the few references he made
to the *Timaeus* (95). It would be tempting to discover in the Augus-

---

in modern studies (note **49** *supra*) on *ius positiuum*. For the date of the *Deriuationes* (before the solar eclipse of **23** June 1191) see S.G. MERCATI, in *Aevum* 33 (1959) 490-94. In line 5
above a broader MS basis would be needed to determine whether *naturalis effectus* (and not
affectus as one might expect) is the correct reading.

(94) § iii ed. JEAUNEAU p. 59: "Iusticia enim alia positiua alia naturalis. Et est positiua que ab hominibus est inuenta ut suspensio latronum etc. Naturalis uero que non est
ab homine inuenta ut dilectio parentum et similia." Cf. GAGNÉR, p. 231.

(95) H.-I. MARROU, *Saint Augustin et la fin de la culture antique* (*Bibliothèque des Écoles françaises d'Athènes et de Rome* 145; Paris 1938), pp. 34,44, where he followed G. COMBÈS,

tinian "quod agit iustitia in subueniendis miseris" a reminiscence of "quae his prodesset qui minimum possent", but in any event, St. Matthew's text of the Sermon on the Mount, with its usage of *iustitia* for the works of mercy and piety, would have been more natural to remember for St. Augustine, even apart from the tradition this usage had in some early Christian writers.

As for Martin's *Formula honestae uitae*, we have no satisfactory study of his sources for the chapter on Justice (96). To assume that the striking phrase which opens it must come from a lost text of Seneca, because the treatise as a whole (97) repeats his teaching and vocabulary, is begging the question. Seneca offers disappointingly little on justice in his moral writings, and what he offers holds no clues to St. Martin's text. Parallels from Seneca have been cited for the word *adiutorium* as well as for another passage in the chapter, where Martin says that in justice there is no room for calculating what is expedient ("in hac non est quod aestimemus quid expediat") (98). But the parallels are not very close, and to speak of justice as seeking no selfish advantage but the good of others was a commonplace of moral philosophy. Also, while it is true that Seneca's vocabulary includes the term *adiutorium* (which Cicero's does not), the word occurs only in contexts very different from that of the *Formula honestae uitae* (99) — or, for that matter, from the contexts in which it is so often found in the Itala or the Vulgate (100).

Saint Augustin et la culture classique (Paris 1927), p. 14, in assuming that most of these references came from Calcidius; but he later withdrew: "il faut même retrancher de ma liste (p. 34-37) le Timée de Chalcidius": *Retractatio* (*Bibl. des Écoles...* 145 bis; 1949), p. 635 n. 17; see also J.H. Waszink, *Studien zum Timaioskommentar des Calcidius*, I (*Philosophia antiqua* 12; Leiden 1964) 77 n. 1.

(96) *Formula* c.5 (p. 246 ed. Barlow).

(97) See E. Bickel, *Die Schrift des Martinus von Bracara formula vitae honestae*, in *Rheinisches Museum für Philologie* 60 (1905) 505-51; cf. Barlow, *Martini Bracar. Opp.* 206-8.

(98) Bickel p. 530 (for *adiutorium*) and p. 533, citing *de beneficiis* 4.1.2; *ep.* 81.20 "...non quia expedit sed quia iuuat"; *ep.* 113.31," ...Doceat me quam sacra res sit iustitia alienum bonum spectans, nihil ex se petens nisi usum sui...". Cf. St. Ambrose *de offic. ministrorum* 2.24.115 "...quae unicuique quod suum est tribuit, alienum non uindicat, utilitatem propriam negligit..." (*PL* 16.57), a text which Thomas Aquinas would cite as *sed contra* to Augustine's "subuenire miseris" (*Sum. theol.* 2.2.58.11).

(99) Cf. Seneca *dialog.* 3.5.2, 3.10.1, 3.13.5, *de benef.* 2.23.3, 6.35.2, *nat. quaest.* 5.16.4, *ep.* 27.5, 31.5, all cited by Bickel p. 530.

(100) See *Thes. linguae latinae* and scriptural Concordances *s.v.*; frequently in the Psalms, e.g. 7.10 "adiutorium meum a Deo"; 34.2, 37.22; 69.1 "Deus in adiutorium meum intende"; 123.8 etc.

A meaningful interpretation of St. Martin's initial statement is made even more difficult by the poor textual shape of the next following sentence, which was meant to elucidate it. The critical edition reads:

> Iustitiae post haec uirtus est. Quid est autem iustitia nisi naturae tacita conuentio in adiutorium multorum inuenta? Et quid est iustitia nisi nostra constitutio, sed diuina lex et uinculum societatis humanae?...

The reading is that of the β family of manuscripts, accepted without reserve by Barlow, although a rhetorical question patently makes no sense (and poor syntax) if it is cancelled at once by an assertion to the contrary: "And what is justice *other than* what we establish (our enactment), *but* the law of God...?" The corrector of the ninth-century MS Munich lat. 14492, and all the MSS of the δ family, smoothed this out by substituting *seu* for *sed*, thus abolishing any contrast between human and divine ordinance; a reading adopted by Haase in 1872 for the Teubner text (101).

There have been some strained conjectural emendations of the passage by past editors (102); but the key to the proper reading is hidden in the tenth-century Escorialensis M.III.3 (=E), the only surviving representative of a separate early tradition that is not related to the β and δ families (103). An unknown descendant of E seems to have been used by Erasmus (1529), and Henrique Florez certainly employed the MS (or a copy of it) for his edition (1759; 2nd ed. 1787) (104). Unfortunately the text of E is defective in

---

(101) Cf. BARLOW, *app. crit.* ad 5.3; one MS (Avranches 58 s.xi) reads *et.* HAASE's edition (cf. BARLOW p. 230f.) is in *L. Ae. Senecae Opera* III, *Supplementum* (2nd ed. Leipzig 1872), pp. 468-75.

(102) "Et nisi nostra constitutio est sed diuina lex, certe est uinculum..." ed. A. WEIDNER, *Jahrbuch des Pädagogiums zum Kloster Unser Lieben Frauen in Magdeburg* (1872) Heft 3 pp. 3-10 [not seen], text as quoted by O. MAY, *Die früher dem Seneka zugeschriebene Abhandlung de quattuor uirtutibus cardinalibus aus einer Handschrift des Neisser Gymnasiums veröffentlicht*, in *Jahresbericht des K. katholischen Gymnasiums zu Neisse* (1892), p. 8 n. 75; May himself prints: "...nisi nostra constitutio? Si enim est diuina lex et uinculum...". On these two editions see BARLOW, p. 231.

(103) On E see BARLOW, pp. 222-4. Also A. FONTÁN, *La tradición de las obras morales de Martin de Braga*, in *Boletin de la Universidad de Granada* 23 (1951) 73-86, at 77f.

(104) BARLOW pp. 229-30 on Florez; he does not pronounce on Erasmus (p. 225) and E, but see the variants in the *app. crit.* for 2.6 *aestimes*, 2.25 *te*, 4.32 *scurrilitas*, 9.7 *durus* 10.2 *et.*

part at this crucial passage, whence Barlow did not give it the consideration he usually shows for the Escorialensis wherever β and δ disagree. The sentence, mutilated by the omission of the three words "Et quid est", reads in E: "Iustitia nisi non nostra constitutio, sed diuina lex et uinculum...".. Erasmus tried to heal the defect by cancelling *nisi,* and Florez (among others) adopted the emendation: "Iustitia non nostra constitutio sed diuina lex (est *add. Erasm.)* et uinculum..." (105). At least this produced a reading which made sense; but for a text that rested also on manuscript authority, Erasmus would have had to know the β tradition and use it to supply the missing words in E, or vice versa to correct the text of β from E, by supplying the missing *non.* The latter had been done, centuries before, by a corrector of the β manuscript Vienna 575 (Barlow's V, saec. xi), who inserted *non* between the lines above *nisi* (106). Here, finally, we have what in all likelihood Martin wrote to make his opening statement explicit:

> Et quid est iustitia nisi non nostra constitutio sed diuina lex et uinculum societatis humanae? In hac non est quod aestimemus quid expediat...

The inner structure of the first sentences of the chapter thus becomes transparent, with an almost rhythmic elegance describing the fountainhead of justice: an unspoken covenant of nature — not of our making — the law of God; and describing her function: for the relief of many — the bond of human society — not calculating what is expedient. "But that will be expedient [in the end]", St. Martin continues, "which justice bids us to do" ("Expediet quicquid illa dictauerit"). And then, as if to underscore her being grounded in *diuina lex,* he turns to the reader in solemn apostrophe: "Whoever thou art who desirest to strive after her, first fear God and love God, that thou mayest be loved by God" ("Quisquis ergo hanc sectari desideras, time prius Deum et ama Deum, ut ameris a Deo"). In these moving lines he seems to forget that at the outset, in the dedicatory letter to King Miro he had proposed to teach,

---

(105) Barlow *app. crit.* ad 5.3: non] nisi non *E,* non *Er. Fl.* ...est *post* lex *add. Er.* — The passage should have been cited in his introduction at pp. 222-3 or 230. It should also have been discussed by A.M. Kurfess, *Weitere textkritische Bemerkungen zu Martini Episcopi Bracarensis Opera,* in *Athenaeum* 33 (1955) 55-63 at p. 59f.

(106) *App. crit. loc. cit.*

not what *pauci et egregii deicolae* can achieve, but rather what can be fulfilled also without the precepts of the divine scriptures, by all lay people who live rightly and honestly according to the natural law of human insight (107). Never mind those words, he seems to imply; here in the matter of justice I speak as a Christian philosopher.

VII.

What, then, were the literary affiliations, the intellectual ancestry of the bishop of Braga's definition of justice? The answer would require a patristic and classical equipment which lies beyond the competence of one who has entered this area of studies by the back door, as it were, through a few medieval quotations of this and similar sayings from antiquity. Some parallels, however, of thought and diction gleaned at random in other ancient writers may be recorded here in aid of future research into the sources of St. Martin of Braga.

1. "Nature" is the first word that strikes eye and ear in his definition, and in nature's covenant set over against *nostra constitutio* one is at once reminded of the Greek dichotomy of φύσει δίκαιον and θέσει δίκαιον, transmitted to the Latin world above all in Stoic garb with its emphasis on nature as both the foundation and lodestar of all moral life. More concretely, Cicero's formulation of *iustitia* having its origin in nature comes to mind ("eius initium est ab natura profectum") as it appears in the *De inuentione*, in the course of a famous passage which St. Augustine fully incorporated into his *LXXXIII Diuersae quaestiones* (108), and which would later gain much currency in medieval classifications of the virtues (109). Cicero here sketches the progression of justice from inception in nature through custom (*consuetudo*) to *legum metus et religio*: this he prefaces with the definition we know, justice as "habitus animi communi utilitate conseruata suam cuique tribuens dignitatem". It is noteworthy that these words in turn are found in the Teubner

---

(107) 1.18-22 ed. Barlow (p. 327); cf. p. 206.

(108) Q.31 (*PL* 40.20-21): Cicero *de inuent.*, 2.53.160-54.162.

(109) Cf. Palasse *op. cit.* (n. 2 *supra*). The tradition is still alive in Baldus, *Comment. Dig.* 1.1.10 add. no. 2; cf. W. Ullmann, *Baldus's Conception of Law*, in *Law Quarterly Review* 58 (1942) 386ff. at p. 390-91.

text of Martin's *Formula*, where they appear after his definition inserted between brackets (110): this indicates, if I read Haase's notation aright, an interpolation in his MS (Breslau IV 39, an. 1375), which seems to have been rich in intruded glosses (111). Thus one late medieval reader at least must have felt reminded of Cicero in studying or copying his "Seneca".

2. Nature's "tacita conuentio" leads to another line of inquiry. In one of the fragments the Digest has preserved of the *Iuris epitomae* of Hermogenianus we find custom described as "ciuium tacita conuentio" (112):

> sed et ea quae longa consuetudine comprobata sunt ac per annos plurimos obseruata, uelut tacita ciuium conuentio non minus quam ea quae scripta sunt seruantur.

The *Iuris epitomae*, dating from the reign of Diocletian (*c.* 300 A.D. or later) was the latest of the writings which Justinian's commission excerpted (113). But some texts of earlier classical jurists as well advance the theory that *consuetudo* creates legal rules and abolishes written law "by tacit consent of the people" (114). Prevailing scholarly opinion today holds that these texts had been made to say so only by much postclassical editing in, or after, the beginning of the fourth century; and that the classical *iuris consulti*, while being aware of custom as a relevant fact, never considered custom as law or among the sources of law, since they left

---

(110) Connected by the word *etiam*: "Iustitia est etiam habitus... dignitatem"; BARLOW, *app. crit.* ad 5.2 inadvertently gives Seneca, *ep.* 113.7 (instead of Cicero *loc. cit.*) as reference.

(111) See BARLOW's *app. crit.* for 2.27*, 38, 45; 3.4*, 13* (from the notation it is not quite clear whether this is a duplication or a transposition of 7.8-9); 4.5, 45, 71 etc. (I have marked with an asterisk the passages where the same interpolations are found in Erasmus and Florez.)

(112) *Dig.* 1.3.35.

(113) D. LIEBS, *Hermogenians Iuris Epitomae* (*Abhand. Akad. Göttingen, Phil.-hist. Klasse*³ 57; Göttingen 1964). Cf. F. SCHULZ, *History of Roman Legal Science* (Oxford 1946), p. 222f.

(114) Especially Julian, *Dig.* 1.3.32.1; Ulpian as quoted in the post-classical *Epitome Ulpiani* 1.4, and the unknown classical model of *Inst.* 1.2.11. Cf. further *Gaius* 3.82 on the "alterius generis successiones quae... eo iure ⟨quod⟩ consensu [concessu *cod.*] receptum est introducta sunt" (resumed in Justinian, *Inst.* 3.10 pr.).

all such theorizing to philosophical and rhetorical literature (115). Whether this is a plausible reconstruction of the historical development need not concern us here; nor could the question be answered without analyzing certain general assumptions (such as that of a wall of separation between law and letters in classical times) on which this thesis is based (116). In any event, outside the professional circles Aulus Gellius, the second-century antiquarian, used the term *tacitus consensus*, speaking in his *Attic Nights* of the abolition of the Draconic laws by the Athenians, of legal usage arising in ancient Rome against the Twelve Tables, and in similar contexts (117). We read the same language concerning custom abrogating law in a surviving fragment of the *Digesta* of the near-contem-

---

(115) The basic study remains A. STEINWENTER, *Zur Lehre vom Gewohnheitsrecht*, in *Studi in onore di Pietro Bonfante* (Pavia 1929) II 421-40; see further J. GAUDEMET, *Coutume et raison en droit romain* in *Revue historique de droit français et étranger*⁴ 17 (1938) 141-71, and his *La formation du droit séculier et du droit de l'église aux IVe et Ve siècles* (Paris 1957), pp. 110-18; A.A. SCHILLER, *Custom in Classical Roman Law*, in *Virginia Law Review* 24 (1937/38) 268-82, reprinted in his *An American Experience in Roman Law* (Göttingen 1971) pp. 41-55; F. SCHULZ, *History of Roman Legal Science* pp. 24, 137 (for an unpublished paper on *Gewohnheitsrecht* read by Schulz at the *Rechtshistorikertag* of 1932 see the report in *ZRG Rom. Abt.* 53 [1933] 641-2); M. KASER, *Das römische Privatrecht* II (*Handbuch der Altertumswissenschaft* 10.3.3.2; München 1959) pp. 35-6 with bibliography; F. WIEACKER, *Allgemeine Zustände und Rechtszustände gegen Ende des weströmischen Reichs* (*Ius romanum medii aevi* I 2a; Milan 1963) pp. 26-7; the latest monograph is B. SCHMIEDEL, *Consuetudo im klassischen und nachklassischen römischen Recht* (*Forschungen zum römischen Recht* 22; Graz-Köln 1966), especially pp. 43ff. (with further bibliography p. 43 n. 2).

(116) Important methodological outlines for a critique of the *communis opinio* are found in D. NÖRR's review of the books by SCHMIEDEL (*supra*) and G. STÜHFF (*Vulgarrecht im Kaiserrecht* [*Forschungen...* 21; Graz-Köln 1966]) in *ZRG Rom. Abt.* 84 (1967) 454-66. Recently, a retreat from the prevailing opinion can be noted: see M. KASER, *Zur Glaubwürdigkeit der römischen Rechtsquellen*, in *La critica del testo* (*Atti del secondo Congresso Internazionale della Società italiana di Storia del diritto*; Firenze 1971) I 291-370, at p. 350 n. 180; B. NICHOLAS in the third edition of H.F. JOLOWICZ's *Historical Introduction to the Study of Roman Law* (Cambridge 1972) 353-5; and D. NÖRR, *Divisio und partitio* (*Münchner Universitätsschriften: Abh. zur rechtswissenschaftl. Grundlagenforschung* 4; Berlin 1972); *contra*, however, W. FLUME, *Gewohnheitsrecht und römisches Recht* (*Rheinisch-Westfälische Akademie, Vorträge* G 201; Opladen 1975).

(117) Gellius, *Noctes atticae* 11.18.4: "Eius [i.e. Draconis] igitur leges... non decreto iussoque set tacito inlitteratoque Atheniensium consensu oblitteratae sunt"; 12.13.5: "sed legum quoque ipsarum iura consensu tacito oblitterantur"; 20.10.9: "institutum est contra XII tabulas tacito consensu...". It should be remembered that Aulus Gellius, while not a "professional" lawyer, was not alien to the legal world as a sometime *iudex*.

porary jurist Salvius Julianus (118). Now, one may or may not believe that this passage was inserted by a fourth-century redactor, but it is certain that the *topos* of tacit consent or convention in Gellius, Julian, and Hermogenianus (119) has its background in the Greek theory of νόμος ἄγραφος. Parallels in the Greek rhetors for Hermogenian's *ciuium conuentio* have been noted (120); and if we consider further that in the doctrine of custom as νόμος ἄγραφος the idea of a supra-positive, natural law is never far off (121), the possibility should be kept in mind that St. Martin's "naturae tacita conuentio" was also modeled upon a Greek phrase.

3. "Time prius Deum et ama Deum": it should be evident that the God of whom Martin of Braga speaks is not the abstract deity of the philosophers but the loving God of the Christian dispensation — the God, one is tempted to add, of Abraham, Isaac, and Jacob (122). This leads us back to Augustine's "iustitia est amor soli amato seruiens" in the *De moribus ecclesiae*, the treatise in which he reduced the entire scale of virtues to the *amor Dei* (123); and it points back further, beyond St. Augustine to Lactantius, the last of the pre-Nicene apologists.

It is a matter of record that his *Diuinae institutiones* is our most important witness for some of the lost portions of Cicero's

---

(118) *Dig.* 1.3.32.1: "...quare rectissime etiam illud receptum est ut leges non solum suffragio legis latoris sed etiam tacito consensu omnium per desuetudinem abrogentur".

(119) Also, if Kübler's conjectural reconstruction of the Verona palimpsest were acceptable, *Gaius* 3.82 (n. 114 *supra*): "...sed eo iure ⟨quod tacito⟩ consensu receptum...". The whole passage is suspected as a post-classical gloss by Schulz, *Principles* (n. 8 *supra*); p. 15 n. 4; and see Schmiedel, pp. 8-9.

(120) See A. d'Ors, *Un punto de vista para la história del derecho consuetudinario en Roma*, in *Revista general de legislación y jurisprudencia*[2] 11 (1946) 495-511 at p. 507f.; Steinwenter, *Gewohnheitsrecht* 435 (cf. πόλεως συνθήκη κοινή in Marcian, *Dig.* 1.3.2), with the pointed formulation, "nicht so sehr stillschweigende lex als stillschweigender νόμος". On popular consent as *topos*, rather than a technical concept, see D. Nörr's perceptive observation (in the book review cited n. 116 *supra*) p. 459; cf. Gaudemet, *La formation* p. 116, who compares this consent to the "myth" of the transfer of sovereign power to the prince by the *lex de imperio* (*Dig.* 1.4.1 etc.). It seems unlikely that Hermogenian's *ciuium tacita conuentio* was meant as an allusion to the republican *contio* (the pre-electoral assembly), as Schmiedel, *op. cit.* 62 argues.

(121) Thus Steinwenter p. 431.

(122) Exod. 3.6; Mt. 22.32.

(123) *De moribus eccl.* 1.8.13-9.14, 12.20-21, 13.23, 15.25, 24.44-25.46 and passim; cf. *de ciuit. Dei* 15.22.

Republic: thus for the pages that contained the debate over Carneades the Skeptic's defense of injustice, his denunciation of justice as folly, and his famous case of the two shipwrecks on a single plank (124); thus also for one of Cicero's most impressive passages ("...paene diuina uoce" says Lactantius) on Natural Law (125). Still, modern writing on legal philosophy has largely neglected the abundant material on law and justice to be found in Books Five and Six of the *Divine Institutes* (126). Here let us point out only that throughout these two books (*de iustitia, de uero cultu*) Lactantius pursued two themes with passionate eloquence: there can be no true justice without one's knowing and serving the true God; and there can be no true justice unless it is altogether unselfish, disinterested, not expecting rewards (127). To his dismay, Lactantius discovered a utilitarian note even in his much revered Cicero where the latter spoke of *homines idonei* as objects of beneficience (128). Probably this was a misunderstanding on Lactantius's part (129),

---

(124) Lactantius, *Diuin. inst.* 5.14.3-5, 16.2-13; especially at 5.16.10-11 (ed. S. BRANDT, *CSEL* 19.451).

(125) Lactantius, *Diuin. inst.* 6.8.7-9 (the words quoted above are from § 6) = *de republ.* [3.22.33].

(126) There is for instance but one reference to Lactantius in Del Vecchio's otherwise almost too heavily annotated *La giustizia* (n. 68 *supra*), § 4 n. 8 (p. 32 tr. DARMSTAEDTER, pp. 30-31 tr. GUTHRIE). Much greater attention is paid to Lactantius by B. BIONDI, *Il diritto romano cristiano* (Milan 1952-54), see references in the index *s.v.* (III 605) and the concluding remarks III 526ff.

(127) *Diuin. inst.* 5.14.12: "...si ergo pietas est cognoscere Deum, cuius cognitionis haec summa est ut eum colas, ignorat utique iustitiam qui religionem Dei non tenet" (this is why the efforts of Plato and Aristotle failed although they "honesta quidem uoluntate iustitiam defendere uoluerunt", 5.17.4-5). *Ibid.* 6.11.16: "Si uirtus mercedem non exigit, si propter se ut dicis expetenda est (Cicero *de legib.* 1.18.48), ergo iustitiam matrem principemque uirtutum suo pretio, non tuo commodo aestima, potissimum tribue a quo nihil speres." A detailed analysis would be needed on all the passages dealing with *religio* or *pietas* and *aequitas* (in the sense of human brotherhood) as the two mainsprings of justice (5.14.7, 9, 15-16, 19-20); on *religio* towards God, and *misericordia uel humanitas* towards man as the twofold *officium iustitiae* (6.10.1-3) — to cite only a few. It is noteworthy that Lactantius states Romans and Greeks did not observe justice because they had class distinctions ("quia dispares multis gradibus homines habuerunt", 5.14.19).

(128) *Diuin. inst.* 6.11.12 (after quoting Cic. *de off.* 2.15.54): "Quid est idoneis? nempe iis qui restituere et referre gratiam possint. Si nunc Cicero uiueret, exclamarem profecto: hic, hic, Marce Tulli, aberrasti a uera iustitia eamque uno uerbo sustulisti, cum pietatis et humanitatis officium utilitate metitus es. (13) Non enim idoneis hominibus largiendum est, sed quantum potest non idoneis" (BRANDT p. 521).

(129) So already Gronovius's commentary *ad loc.*; see *PL* 6.672.

but it helped him formulate his conception more sharply: justice is totally directed toward the other — the homeless stranger, the prisoner, the orphaned and the widowed, the sick and the dying (130). The traditional parts of justice (*pietas, beneuolentia* etc.) thus become infused with a new Christian fervor (131). Hence the work of justice is incorrupt only in such beneficence as we bestow "upon those who can in no way be useful" ("si praestentur iis hominibus qui prodesse nullo modo possunt") (132); and good men perceive, even without knowing the word of God as we do, that it is "by nature just to protect those who lack protection" ("natura esse iustum tueri eos qui tutela carent") (133).

Such phrases seem to anticipate what Calcidius was to present not long afterwards as the Socratic definition of justice: "quae his prodesset qui minimum possent". However, more evidence would be needed to warrant an assumption of direct relationship (134). It is otherwise with Martin of Braga. Beyond the general thrust of Lactantius's reflections on justice (135), there are some striking parallels of expression:

Martin c.5	*Diu. inst.* 3.9.19
Quid est autem iustitia nisi...? et quid est iustitia nisi... diuina lex?	Ipsa ⟨autem⟩ humanitas quid est nisi iustitia? quid iustitia nisi pietas? pietas autem nihil aliud

---

(130) *Diuin. inst.* 6.12.31: "In quo autem magis iustitiae ratio consistit quam in eo ut quod praestamus nostris per adfectum, praestemus aliis per humanitatem?"; in this long chapter 6.12 see especially §§ 15-16 (*captiuorum redemptio*), 17-20 (*alieno et ignoto facere*), 21-23 (*pupillos et uiduas tueri*), 24 (*aegros suscipere*), 25-30 (*peregrinorum et pauperum sepultura*). Cf. also *ibid.* 6.10.9.

(131) Twelfth-century glosses on this fundamental chapter, *Diuin. inst.* 6.12, in Oxford MS Bodl. Canon. Patr. lat. 131, fol. 107v-108r, apparently castigate implicitly the worldly and unchristian attitudes of Becket as chancellor of Henry II: see B. Ross, *Audi Thoma... Henriciani Nota*, in *English Historical Review* 89 (1974) 333-8. (This article also sums up information and bibliography on early Lactantius MSS, supplementing BRANDT's *Prolegomena* of 1890 in *CSEL* 19).

(132) *Diuin. inst.* 6.12.8.

(133) *Ibid.* 6.12.22.

(134) Thus far we can only say that Calcidius was a Christian and knew the work of Origen, see WASZINK, *Prolegomena*, pp. xi, cii-civ.

(135) It may be mentioned in passing that only once — but never in the *Divine Institutes* — does Lactantius mention the Stoic doctrine of *suum cuique*; see his *Epitome* c.50.5; "...sed maxime Plato et Aristoteles de iustitia multa dixerunt adserentes... quod suum cuique tribuat, quod aequitatem in omnibus seruet..." (p. 729 BRANDT; c.55 in *PL* 6.1062B).

quam Dei parentis agnitio.
(*CSEL* 19.202.1-2: ⟨sed⟩ ipsa
uel ipsa ⟨autem⟩ *scribendum
esse censet Brandt*)

6.12.1

...in adiutorium multorum inuenta... et uinculum societatis humanae

Hec est illa perfecta iustitia quae
custodit humanam de qua philo-
sophi locuntur societatem (136),
...(non...sed) ad multorum salutem.
(*CSEL* 19.524.13-16)

These could be accidental; and yet, once we abandon the traditional
verdict which labels St. Martin's *Formula* as nothing but an epitome
of a lost treatise by Seneca, we should take seriously the possibility
of direct influence by Lactantius. After all, a quotation from Seneca's *Exhortationes* in the *Divine Institutes*, "philosophia nihil aliud
est quam recta ratio uiuendi uel honeste uiuendi scientia uel ars
rectae uitae agendae", may well have been the direct source for
Martin in fashioning the title of his treatise (137).

This is as far as a medievalist would dare to go. *Videant peri-
tiores.* But let us listen attentively to St. Martin of Braga's near-
forgotten definition of justice: like the sound of a tender chord waf-
ted down through the centuries, it finds an echo in our own concern today with justice to be achieved "in adiutorium multorum":
in aid of the many.

---

(136) The twelfth-century *Moralium dogma philosophorum* c.11, "Iustitia est uirtus
humanae societatis et communis utilitatis conseruatrix" (*PL* 171.1014) or "...uirtus conseruatrix humanae societatis et uitae communitatis" (ed. J. HOLMBERG [Uppsala 1929] p. 12)
may be indebted in part to this passage.

(137) Lact. *Diuin. inst.* 3.15.1 (p. 220 BRANDT) = Seneca *frag.* 17 (HAASE). Cf. BAR-
LOW, *Martini Brac. opp.* p. 206 (with the transposition *recta uiuendi ratio*).

Additional note to section V supra: On the Augustinian "coming to the aid of the wretched" and its scholstic interpretation see also E. LIO, *Il testo di S. Agostino "Justitia [est]
in subveniendo miseris" in Pier Lombardo e nei suoi glossatori fino a S. Tommaso d'Aquino*, in
Miscellanea Lombardiana (Novara 1957) 175-222, discussing 22 pre-thomistic writers.

For stoic connotations (cf. at n. 76 *supra*) compare also the third-century provincial
petitions in which δικαιοσύνη stands for imperial *benevolentia* and *misericordia*, and further
the legend *iustitia clementia indulgentia* on imperial coins; references in A. CARCATERRA, *Iustitia nelle fonti e nella storia del diritto romano* (Bari 1951) 120-21, 144, 152 [not seen] as cited
by A. BURDESE, *Sul concetto di giustizia nel diritto romano*, in *Annali di storia del diritto* 14-17
(1970-73, publ. 1974) 103-19 at p. 117.

VI

LA RÉSERVE PAPALE

DROIT DE CANONISATION

I

La canonisation des saints (1) par un acte de juridiction suprême du Souverain Pontife n'a pas toujours été
en usage dans l'Église pour élever un serviteur de Dieu

(1) Benoît XIV (Prosper Lambertini), *De servorum Dei beatifica-
tione et beatorum canonizatione*, 1ʳᵉ éd., Bologne, 1734-1738, 4 vol.;
édition définitive dans les *Opera omnia* par les soins de Emanuel de
Azevedo, Rome, 1747-1751 (nous citerons d'après la réimpression des
Opera, Prato, 1839-1842, sous l'abréviation *Bened.*, par livres, chapitres
et paragraphes); Paul Hinschius, *System des katholischen Kirchenrechts,*
vol. IV, Berlin, 1888, pp. 239 et suiv.; Fr. X. Wernz, *Ius decretalium,*
vol. III, ps. II, 2ᵉ éd., Rome, 1908, pp. 35 et suiv.; T. Ortolan, articles
Béatification et *Canonisation dans l'Église romaine*, dans le *Dictionn.
de théol. cath.*, vol. II, col. 493 et suiv. ; col. 1626 et suiv.; Margaret R.
Toynbee, *S. Louis of Toulouse and the process of canonisation in
the fourteenth century*, Manchester, 1929, pp. 133 et suiv.; Hippolyte Delehaye, S. J., *Sanctus*, Bruxelles, 1927; L. Hertling, S. J., *Materiali per
la storia del processo di canonizzazione*, dans *Gregorianum*, 16 (1935),
pp. 170 et suiv.

Nous n'entendons pas donner avec ces indications de quelques ouvrages,
cités fréquemment dans les notes suivantes, une bibliographie complète.
Quant aux recueils de documents, regestes, etc., il y a lieu de mentionner,
outre les recueils généraux comme les *Acta Sanctorum* des bollandistes

défunt aux honneurs des autels (1). La vénération des martyrs dans l'antiquité chrétienne et, à partir du ıvᵉ siècle, celle des confesseurs avaient leur origine dans la dévotion spontanée du peuple chrétien ; on célébrait la mémoire de ces saints souvent sans enquête ni jugement préalable de la part des autorités ecclésiastiques (2). Et là où on procédait à une enquête, où on estimait nécessaire un jugement ou une approbation quelconque par des actes juridictionnels ou liturgiques, le caractère local et régional de la vénération des saints n'exigeait que l'intervention de l'autorité épiscopale.

Dès le vᵉ siècle, cette intervention devient de plus en plus régulière : le culte du saint est établi par l'acte solennel de la *translatio* ou *elevatio* (3). L'évêque transfère les reliques du saint de son tombeau dans l'église pour les déposer dans un autel et y célébrer la messe en l'honneur du nouveau saint, dont la fête est instituée par cet acte de translation. Mais souvent le

(*A SS.*), les *Regesta Pontificum Romanorum* de Jaffé (2ᵉ éd., *JL.*), les *Regesta* de Potthast (*Po.*), la *Patrologia latina* de Migne, les *Monumenta Germaniae historica*, etc., le recueil spécial de J. Fontanini, *Codex constitutionum quas summi Pontifices ediderunt in solemni canonizatione Sanctorum*, Rome, 1729.

(1) Les origines et le développement de la canonisation ont été exposés par Benoît XIV (surtout 1, 2-10) d'une manière magistrale, pleine d'érudition, et qui a influencé profondément tous les manuels de droit canon, non moins que les articles de tous les dictionnaires jusqu'à nos jours. Il faut toutefois relever que l'interprétation historique, que le savant pape a donnée aux abondants matériaux qu'il avait réunis, ne doit pas être considérée comme définitive ; à la vérité, l'histoire de la vénération des saints est plus compliquée qu'il ne l'a enseigné. C'est là ce que nous démontre en général l'immense travail critique de plusieurs siècles d'hagiographie bollandiste ; en particulier, l'histoire de la canonisation a reçu des éclaircissements importants par les études récentes des PP. Delehaye et Hertling (*supra*, p. 172, n. 1), susceptibles de modifier les vues traditionnelles. Nos observations suivantes sur l'époque du vᵉ au xııᵉ siècle sont basées surtout sur l'article du P. Hertling.

(2) Delehaye, pp. 162 et suiv., p. 169.

(3) Delehaye, p. 184 ; Hertling, pp. 171 et suiv. ; cf. Bened., 1, 6, 4.

174

rôle de l'évêque doit se borner à confirmer un culte
déjà existant, une translation déjà effectuée (1), et en
813 un synode de Mayence trouve nécessaire d'inter-
dire que les translations se fassent *sine consilio principis vel episcoporum sanctaeque synodi licentia*,
canon qui sera inséré plus tard par Gratien dans son
Décret (2).

De toute façon, l'enquête sur le « titre » du saint au
culte public n'est pas encore un élément indispensable (3) : en 1078 encore, l'archevêque Lanfranc de Canterbury confirme le culte de son prédécesseur saint
Elphège, dont le martyre lui avait d'abord semblé douteux, après une simple conversation privée avec Anselme d'Aoste (son futur grand successeur) qui sut dis-
siper ses scrupules (4).

Quoi qu'il en soit, la *translatio* épiscopale reste
pendant des siècles la forme ordinaire d'établir le culte
d'un saint, nous pouvons dire de canoniser un saint : en
effet, les mots *translatio* et *canonizatio* étaient souvent
employés comme synonymes (5). Seulement, il ne faut

---

(1) Delahaye, p. 182.

(2) *Conc. Mogunt.*, c. 51 (*Mon. Germ. Conc.*, II, p. 272) = c. 37 *de cons.*,
D. 1. Hertling, p. 174. Pour d'autres répressions d'abus dans la législation de
l'époque carolingienne, voir Bened., 1, 6, 3 ; Hinschius, IV, p. 242, n. 1 ;
Delehaye, p. 183-184 ; Wernz, III, n. 370, 50.

(3) Delehaye, p. 184.

(4) *ASS., April. 19*, II, p. 630. Exemple cité par Delahaye, p. 188, et
Toynbee, p. 141. — Sur les premiers efforts des papes pour obliger les
évêques à des enquêtes approfondies sur la sainteté et les miracles, voir les
lettres d'Urbain II, JL. 5677 (concernant saint Nicolas de Trani, 1097) et
JL. 5732 (saint Gurlo de Quimperlé. 1088-99), cités par Bened., 1, 8. 12 ;
Hinschius, IV, p. 242, n. 5, 6 ; Toynbee, p. 137 (cf. les remarques de Grosjean dans *Analecta Bolland.*, 49 [1931], p. 215) ; Hertling, pp. 187 et suiv.
Sur le développement ultérieur du procès d'information, cf. Hertling,
pp. 188 et suiv. ; il faut ajouter encore la décrétale *Venerabili* de Honorius III (1225), c. 52, X, *de testib.*, II, 20.

(5) Voir les exemples cités par Hertling, p. 173 : le chroniqueur de la
canonisation de saint Gothard (par Innocent II en 1131 : JL. 7496) promet
de raconter *quo ordine translatio praedicti confessoris nostri facta*

pas oublier que, la juridiction d'un évêque ne dépassant jamais les limites de son diocèse, il ne s'agissait toujours que de canonisations à effets particuliers, tandis que les canonisations émanant du pape étaient, dès qu'elles furent pratiquées, des actes qui obligeaient l'Église entière, des canonisations universelles (1).

Les canonistes modernes ont souvent, pour souligner la différence doctrinale entre les deux genres historiques de canonisation, la particulière et l'universelle, substitué à ces expressions des notions modernes, en réservant le nom de canonisation aux seules canonisations papales et en qualifiant les canonisations particulières ou translations épiscopales de simples béatifications (2). Mais, d'après notre sentiment, il n'est pas de bonne méthode d'appliquer la terminologie développée à une époque relativement récente aux phénomènes historiques d'une époque plus reculée (3). Depuis que la *translatio* a disparu et que le pape seul est compétent pour tout jugement en matière de vénération des saints, on entend par *canonizatio* uniquement la sentence infaillible par laquelle le Souverain Pontife déclare qu'un serviteur de Dieu défunt se trouve dans la gloire des cieux, et ordonne par conséquent que son culte soit observé dans l'Église militante universelle; la *beatificatio*, par contre, est, elle aussi, une sentence du Souverain Pontife, mais à effets mineurs : elle ne fait qu'autoriser le culte — universel ou particulier — du Serviteur

fuerit (*Mon. Germ. Script.*, XII, p. 639); tandis que les chroniqueurs du xiii° siècle parlent de *canonizare corpus* à l'occasion des translations de saint Ladislas Roi (1192) et de saint Pierre de Trévi (1215) : *ASS., Jun.* 27, V, p. 319; *Aug.* 30, VI, p. 645; cf. *infra*, pp. 182, n. 3; 210, n. 1. — Le terme *corpus canonizatum* se trouve aussi chez le décrétiste Huguccio; cf. *infra*, Appendice, n° 2.

(1) Ortolan, dans *Dict. théol. cath.*, II, col. 494, col. 1635.

(2) Bened., 1, 6, 9 et 1, 39, 2-3; Wernz, III, n. 370; Ortolan, *loc. cit.*

(3) Cf. les observations de Hertling, p. 180.

de Dieu, qualifié désormais de bienheureux (*beatus*), sans prescrire ce culte, ou si elle le prescrit, c'est en le limitant à certains lieux ou à certaines communautés; il s'agit donc d'une sentence qui ne crée jamais d'obligations pour l'Église universelle. Mais cette double distinction : universel — particulier; ordonner — autoriser, ne touche pas encore le point essentiel : à la différence de la canonisation, la béatification n'est pas une sentence définitive; elle n'est qu'une étape, qu'une station sur le chemin à reprendre et qui mène à la canonisation (1).

Le haut moyen âge ne connaissait pas de différence entre les expressions Bienheureux et Saint; il ne connaissait surtout pas de différence entre des sentences non définitives et définitives. Si la *translatio* faite par l'évêque se rapproche de la béatification par la limitation locale de ses effets, cela ne suffit pas pour lui octroyer cette dénomination moderne; car — et c'est là, nous le répétons, le point essentiel — l'institution de la fête du saint était un acte absolument définitif, un point final et non pas transitoire (2); elle avait donc bien la fonction d'une canonisation, bien que particulière (3).

Si l'on cherche de vraies analogies à ce que devait être plus tard la béatification, il faut descendre jusqu'au milieu du xiie siècle, où nous trouvons le premier cas de permission provisoire d'un culte, celui de saint Bernward de Hildesheim (4). En 1149 l'archevêque de Mayence concéda, lors du synode d'Erfurt, à l'évêque de Hildesheim la vénération de Bernward *inter sanctos* avec l'office solennel, *excepta dumtaxat translatione*, c'est-à-dire

---

(1) Bened., 1, 39, 12-14; Wernz, III, n. 362; Hinschius, IV, pp. 249-250; Hertling, p. 183, p. 180.

(2) Cf. Hertling, *loc. cit.*

(3) Le mot *canonisation* est adopté sans hésitation pour les institutions des fêtes particulières par Delehaye (cf. pp. 162, 182, 184, etc.) et par Hertling, pp. 172, 174 et suiv.

(4) Hertling, pp. 181, 184. *ASS., Oct. 26*, XI, pp. 992-993.

sans canonisation. Et les moines de Hildesheim, qui
avaient sollicité de leur côté du légat pontifical Octa-
vien la translation de Bernward, n'obtenaient eux aussi
qu'une mesure provisoire : le légat déclina de *plenarie
respondere* et permit seulement pour le moment l'érec-
tion d'un autel sur le tombeau de Bernward. Les deux
princes de l'Église regardaient donc encore la *translatio*
comme le dernier acte de la procédure de canonisation ;
mais ce n'est qu'en 1193 que se déroula ce dernier acte,
et alors il ne revêtit plus la forme de la *translatio*, mais
celle d'une canonisation universelle, qui fut prononcée
par le pape Célestin III (1). Un autre exemple de sentence
non définitive, rendue cette fois par un pape, nous est
fourni après l'an 1159 par Alexandre III : l'évêque de
Grosseto lui avait demandé la canonisation de Guillaume
de Malavalle ; le pape Alexandre promit de la prononcer
tempore opportuno, et pour le moment il concéda au
diocèse un office en l'honneur de Guillaume. Cette décision provisoire fut confirmée en 1202 par Innocent III,
mais sans qu'il procédât à l'acte définitif qui aurait été
la canonisation (2). Ce sont là les premiers précurseurs
de ce qu'on appela plus tard béatification; et ils sont
d'un caractère tout différent des canonisations particulières que constituent les translations au haut moyen
âge.

II

Nous avons cru utile de tirer quelque peu au clair ces
notions historiques fondamentales avant d'approcher la
question principale dont nous avons à nous occuper et
qui consiste à rechercher à quel moment les papes se
sont réservé le droit exclusif de canonisation. Est-ce

(1) JL. 16943, Fontanini, n. 24.
(2) Fontanini, p. 644 (n. 30 *bis*) ; Kehr, *Italia pontificia*, III, p. 261,
n. *11. — Bened., 1, 9, 2 et 1, 39, 12; Hinschius, IV, p. 245, n. 5; Hertling,
p. 182.

178

bien vraiment Alexandre III qui, dans sa fameuse décrétale *Audivimus* (1) d'entre 1171 et 1180, a formulé cette
prérogative papale de tout jugement en matière de
vénération des saints ? On a longuement discuté sur la
question de savoir si cette décrétale instituait un nouveau
droit ou confirmait une coutume déjà en vigueur (2);
mais jusqu'à présent personne n'a jamais contesté que —
constitutive ou déclaratoire — l'énonciation de la réserve
se trouve dans la décrétale. Quoi qu'il en soit, une telle
loi, qui déclarait désormais illégale toute canonisation
faite par des particuliers, ne pouvait être conçue que si
tout au moins, à cette époque, l'usage des canonisations
universelles papales s'était déjà établi concurremment
avec les anciennes translations.

Il nous faut malheureusement reconnaître que les
origines de l'intervention des papes dans les causes de
canonisation sont cachées dans l'ombre. La première
notice qui ne soit pas suspecte (3) concerne la translation
du corps de saint Séverin, faite par l'évêque de Naples
vers la fin du ve siècle, avec l'autorisation du pape
Gélase Ier (4). Des cas de ce genre restent très rares
jusqu'à la fin du xe siècle (5); il ne semble pas que les
évêques aient souvent sollicité le consentement du

(1) JL. 13546. — c. 1, X *de reliq.*, III, 45.

(2) Voir, sur cette discussion, surtout Bened., 1, 10, 4 et suiv.

(3) On ne peut pas ajouter foi au récit sur la transmission à Rome des
actes du martyre de saint Vigile de Trente († 406), *A SS., Jun. 26*, V, p. 163 ;
cf. Toynbee, p. 135, n. 1 (contre Bened., 1, 4, 12 et 1. 7, 2); et la prétendue
intervention d'Innocent Ier dans la cause de saint Jean Chrysostome est très
douteuse : cf. Bened., 1, 7, 3-6 (critiqué à tort par Toynbee, p. 135, n. 2).

(4) Eugippe, c. 46; *Corp. Script. Eccl. Lat.*, IX, 2, p. 65, cité par
Hertling, p. 175.

(5) Voir les exemples donnés, non sans réserve critique, par Bened., 1, 7,
7-16. — Hertling, p. 176, se réfère encore à l'institution de la fête de
saint Celse par l'évêque Egbert de Trèves en 980 (et non 978), *A SS., Febr. 23*,
III, p. 400, où le récit contemporain dit que l'évêque *apostolica auctoritate
mandavit...* Mais nous ne saurions admettre sans hésitation que le chroniqueur ait voulu indiquer par ces mots une autorisation papale. Dans son

pontife romain. Mais la tendance à étendre le domaine
d'un saint local au delà des limites du propre diocèse et
à donner plus de splendeur à l'institution de son culte —
tendance qui se manifestait dans des invitations d'évêques
voisins à l'*elevatio*, dans l'assistance du prince séculier
ou d'un synode — devait aboutir au désir de faire partici-
per à une canonisation l'Église universelle en la personne
de son représentant (1). La première canonisation papale,
celle de saint Ulric d'Augsbourg, prononcée en 993 par
Jean XV lors d'un synode romain (2), a sans doute été
considérée en son temps moins comme l'innovation juridique qu'elle était en réalité, que comme un acte de
canonisation se distinguant uniquement par sa solennité
extraordinaire (3). Ce sentiment nous est attesté par un
récit contemporain sur la *translatio* de saint Bononius
de Verceil qui mourut en 1027 : l'évêque décida d'aller à

récit très détaillé sur les préparatifs de la *translatio* nous apprenons
(pp. 398-399) qu'elle fut décrétée lors du synode d'Ingelheim, convoqué par
l'empereur Othon II en 980 (Mansi, XIX, col. 71-74), et le chroniqueur ne
manque pas d'énumérer toutes les autorités ecclésiastiques et séculières qui
ont contribué à la glorification du saint; mais aucune allusion n'est faite à
une intervention, spontanée ou sollicitée, du pape Benoît VII. Aussi ne
doit-on pas forcer le terme *apostolica auctoritate* qui ne désignerait
dans notre cas que l'autorité du synode, qui venait d'avoir lieu, et de
l'évêque Egbert lui-même. — Cf. pour cette terminologie par exemple les
formules du synode de Limoges (1031) : *Ex auctoritate Dei patris omni-*
potentis et filii et spiritus sancti et sanctae Dei genetricis Mariae, sanc-
tique Petri apostolorum principis et beati Martialis et aliorum apo-
stolorum atque omnium sanctorum Dei, nos episcopi... (Mansi, XIX,
col. 530), ou du testament synodal de Gervais, évêque du Mans (avant 1052) :
Omnipotentis... auctoritate et ab eodem cum ceteris apostolis beato
Petro apostolo potestate tradita... (Mansi, XIX, col. 580).

(1) Hinschius, IV, p. 242; Hertling, pp. 174 et suiv.

(2) JL. 3848, Fontanini, n. 1. — Bened., 1, 8, 2.

(3) Cf. Hertling, pp. 176-177, qui s'oppose le premier aux vues traditionnelles sur la portée canonistique de cet événement. — Il importe surtout
de rejeter l'interprétation exagérée et tendancieuse que Toynbee, p. 135,
donne à la canonisation de saint Ulric, quand elle prétend que sous Jean XV
un mouvement de centralisation aurait « attiré dans ses griffes » (*drew into*
its clutches) le culte des saints et que la théorie de la réserve papale
exclusive allait désormais se transformer en pratique réelle !

180

Rome pour obtenir l'autorisation du pape, afin que sa propre sentence fût confirmée, *ut et religio esset devotior et beatissimi Bononii commemoratio celebrior* (1).

Le même sentiment nous est attesté par l'attitude des papes eux-mêmes : loin de se servir toujours de la forme juridique d'une sentence prononcée en plein concile et notifiée par une bulle, ils se contentent parfois d'autoriser par leur consentement écrit la *translatio* locale, comme jadis aux temps antérieurs à Jean XV : c'est ainsi que Benoît VIII concéda au marquis de Mantoue la faveur de construire une église et d'y transférer le corps de l'ermite Siméon († 1016), si celui-ci vraiment *ita coruscat miraculis, ut vester homo nobis asseruit* (2). Ou bien ils procèdent eux-mêmes à une translation, comme

(1) Hertling, pp. 175-176. *ASS.*, *Aug. 30*, VI, p. 629.

(2) JL. 4055, Fontanini, n. 2. Bened., 1, 8, 3; cf. Delahaye, p. 186. Plusieurs autorisations de ce genre par les papes Jean XX (XIX), Alexandre II et Grégoire VII, mais où les documents pontificaux eux-mêmes font défaut, sont référées d'après des sources chronicales et hagiographiques chez Bened., 1, 8, nn. 4, 5, 10, 11. Parmi ces cas, quelques-uns sont très douteux, comme celui de la permission qui aurait été donnée en 1032 par Jean XX (XIX) aux moines du Val di Castro d'ériger un autel sur le tombeau de saint Romuald († 1027). La seule attestation de cette lettre papale (Kehr, *Italia pontif.*, IV, p. 125) se trouve dans la vie de saint Romuald par saint Pierre Damien (Migne, PL., 144, col. 1008), c'est-à-dire dans un ouvrage qui n'est pas toujours exact (cf. *Anal. Bolland.*, 31 [1912], p. 377); et c'est évidemment le défaut de tout autre document qui aura amené Clément VIII à procéder en 1595 à une canonisation équipollente (*Bullar. Rom.*, X, p. 201). Toutefois Bened., 1, 41, 3-4, soutient l'authenticité du fait relaté par saint Pierre Damien qu'il qualifie de béatification pour le concilier avec la canonisation de 1595. — La *translatio* des corps de saint Etienne, roi de Hongrie († 1038), de son fils Emeric († 1031), de saint Gérard, évêque de Csanad († 1046), et d'autres saints hongrois par le roi Ladislas en 1083 aurait été faite par ordre du Saint-Siège (*ASS.*, *Sept. 2*, I, pp. 555, 572; *Sept. 24*, VI, p. 724; Endlicher, *Rerum Hungaricarum monum. Arpadiana*, Sankt Gallen, 1849, p. 240), c'est-à-dire sur l'ordre de Grégoire VII. Pour saint Etienne, déjà Bened., 1, 41, 14, émet des doutes sérieux ; et surtout après les déductions critiques du bollandiste Poncelet concernant saint Emeric (*ASS.*, *Nov. 4*, II, 1, pp. 485-486; cf. aussi p. 483 pour la *Vita sancti Gerardi*) la « canonisation » papale des saints hongrois n'est plus soutenable.

l'aurait pu faire l'évêque : Léon IX, de passage à Ratis-
bonne en 1052, y canonisait saint Wolfgang par une
simple *levatio de tumulo* (1), sans concile ni bulle.

Toutefois, après le premier exemple donné par
Jean XV en 993, les canonisations au moyen d'une
sentence solennelle du pape se répétèrent, et Léon IX
s'était, lui aussi, deux ans avant la translation de saint
Wolfgang, servi de cette forme plus éclatante, en dé-
crétant lors d'un synode romain (1050) la sainteté de
Gérard, feu évêque de Toul, jadis siège épiscopal du
pape Léon lui-même (2). Dans cette sentence, *ex hoc
Sanctus habeatur*, le pape se réservait la translation
pour une future visite à Toul. Nous connaissons plusieurs cas au xie siècle de ces canonisations universelles papales, pour la plupart prononcées en plein
synode (3) ; le nombre allait en augmenter au xiie siècle.

Mais, d'autre part, l'ancien usage des translations
épiscopales autonomes se maintint partout pendant
cette époque, sans trouver d'opposition de la part des

---

(1) JL., I, p. 543 (devant n. 4280) ; Ekkehard, *Mon. Germ. Script.*,
VI, p. 196 ; Bened., 1, 8, 9.

(2) JL. 4219, Fontanini, n. 4. — La prétendue canonisation de saint
Maxime de Padoue par Léon IX en 1053 (Bened., 1, 8, 9) est assez
douteuse ; cf. le bollandiste Van den Bosche, *ASS., Aug.* 2, I, pp. 110-111.

(3) 1042. Benoît IX pour saint Siméon de Trèves : JL. 4112, Fontanini,
n. 3. — 1047. Clément II pour sainte Wiborada : JL. 4142, Bened., 1, 8, 7
(Toynbee, p. 136, fait de Clément II un antipape). — 1050. Léon IX pour
saint Gérard de Toul : JL. 4219, Fontanini, n. 4. — 1066-73. Alexandre II
pour l'ermite saint Théobald : JL. 4756, Fontanini, n. 19 (sous le nom
d'Alexandre III). — 1088-99. Urbain II pour sainte Adelheid : JL. 5762,
Hinschius, IV, p. 242, n. 5. — De toutes ces canonisations, seule la JL.
4756 a été prononcée sans synode. — La prétendue canonisation du martyr
saint Arialde de Milan († 1066) par Alexandre II (Bened., 1, 8, 10) n'a
pas de fondement dans les sources authentiques (*ASS., Jun.* 27, V, pp. 281-
303). Avant tout elle ne peut avoir été prononcée *anno sequenti, cum
papa iret ad synodum quam Mantuae celebravit*, vu qu'il est désormais certain que le synode de Mantoue a eu lieu en 1064 : JL., I, p. 574
(après n. 4552) ; Hefele-Leclerq, *Histoire des Conciles*, IV, 2 (1911),
pp. 1237 et suiv.

papes. Citons comme exemples (1) la translation de saint Eugène martyr par l'évêque de Tongres en 1083, celle de saint Guibert de Gembloux lors d'un synode de Liége en 1110, celle de saint Gautier de Pontoise par l'archevêque de Rouen en 1153 avec l'assistance des évêques de Paris et de Senlis (2), enfin la translation de saint Ladislas, roi de Hongrie en 1192 (3). Il existait donc au XIe et au XIIe siècle en matière de canonisation un dualisme de sources et de procédures pareillement légitimes, un dualisme de canonisations universelles et particulières.

III

Mettre fin à ce dualisme, c'est là le but que se proposait la réserve papale. Il ne s'agissait point de réserver à la chaire de Rome la canonisation universelle — comment telle compétence aurait-elle pu appartenir à un juge particulier (4)? —, mais d'abolir

(1) D'après Bened., 1, 10, 7; Hinschius, IV, p. 242, n. 2; Hertling, p. 177.

(2) Saint Eugène : ASS., Oct. 3, II, p. 308. Saint Guibert : ASS., Maii 23, V, p. 266. Saint Gautier : ASS., Apr. 8, I, p. 767. — La translatio de saint Guthagon par l'évêque Gérard de Tournai en 1159 (ASS., Jul. 3, I, p. 670; cf. Bened., 1, 10, 7) n'est pas très bien documentée. — Pour deux autres exemples (saint Etienne de Tiers, saint Gérard de Sauve-majeure) voir infra, p. 187.

(3) La conviction générale que saint Ladislas aurait été canonisé par Célestin III (cf. tous les dictionnaires) ne se base sur aucune source historique, mais sur une simple conjecture du bollandiste Papebroch dans une note au texte de la Vita (écrite peu après 1200) : ...anno domini millesimo centesimo nonagesimo secundo sanctum corpus eius canonizatum est (ASS., Jun. 27, V, p. 319, avec note c). Or, le terme corpus canonizare n'indique que la translation (cf. p. 174, n. 5); et en effet nous lisons dans une chronique hongroise de la fin du XIIe siècle la note : MCXCII Eleuacio S. Ladyzl. IIII. non. Februarii (Steph. Katona, Epitome chronologica rerum Hungaricarum, I, Budae, 1796, p. 359). La Legenda S. Ladislai (Endlicher, Rer. Hungar. monum. Arpad., p. 243) n'ajoute qu'un mot au texte de la Vita plus ancienne : ...gloriose est canonizatum.

(4) Bened., 1, 10, 6; cf. Wernz, III, nn. 364, 371, contre Hinschius, IV, pp. 243 et suiv. — Les guillemets ironiques entre lesquels Toynbee, p. 144, renferme the « immemorial right » of the Popes to be the source of canonisation témoignent de peu de réflexion.

l'usage, jusqu'alors légitime, des translations épiscopales. Or, il est bien évident qu'une modification si pro-
fonde n'était guère possible sans des précédents historiques qui en préparaient le climat (1). En effet, on peut
constater en premier lieu qu'au cours du xii⁰ siècle les
canonisations solennellement prononcées par les papes
se multiplient d'une manière frappante (2). Callixte II en
célébrait deux, sous Innocent II il y en eut trois, et
Alexandre III atteint le nombre de cinq canonisations
dont l'une, celle de saint Anselme de Canterbury (d'Aoste),
se fit par voie de délégation : le pape en chargea en 1163
l'archevêque Thomas Becket, canonisé lui-même plus
tard par Alexandre III en raison de son martyre (3).

(1) Cf. Hertling, pp. 174 et suiv.

(2) 1109. Pascal II pour saint Pierre d'Anagni : JL. 6239, Fontanini,
n. 6. — 1120. Callixte II pour saint Hugues de Cluny : Migne, PL., 166,
col. 845, Bened., 1, 8, 14 (JL.—). — 1123 pour saint Conrad de Constance :
JL. 7028, Bened., 1, 8, 14. — 1131. Innocent II pour saint Gothard : JL.
7496, Fontanini, n. 7. — 1134-36 pour saint Hugues de Grenoble : JL.
7742, Fontanini, n. 8. — 1139 pour saint Sturme de Fulda : JL. 8007,
Fontanini, n. 9. — 1146. Eugène III pour saint Henri Empereur : JL. 8882,
Fontanini, n. 10. — 1161. Alexandre III pour saint Edouard, roi d'Angleterre :
JL. 10653, Fontanini, n. 11. — 1163 pour saint Anselme de Canterbury :
JL. 10886, Hinschius, IV, p. 245, n. 5. — 1169 pour saint Kanut Laward :
JL. 11646, Hinschius, IV, p. 244, n. 1 (cf. Bened., 1, 9, 3). — 1173 pour
saint Thomas Becket : JL. 12199, 12201, 12203-04, 12219, Fontanini,
n. 12-14. — 1174 pour saint Bernard de Clairvaux : JL. 12328-31, Fonta-
nini, n. 15-18.

(3) Nous n'avons pas l'intention de contester la conclusion théologique que
la canonisation universelle, en ce qu'elle participe de l'infaillibilité, ne peut
pas être déléguée par le pape à un prélat inférieur (cf. Bened., 1, 44, 8 sq.;
Wernz, n. 364, 31 et n. 371, 53). Mais on ne saurait nier qu'Alexandre III
ne l'ait tenue pour délégable, quand il écrit à saint Thomas Becket :
...rogasti ut illum ...canonizare vellemus. Nos vero ...duximus dif-
ferendum. Nunc autem ...negotium istud tuae curae tuaeque discre-
tioni committimus, per apostolica scripta tibi mandantes, quatenus
fratres episcopos nostros suffraganeos tuos et abbates ...convoces, et
coram eis omnibus, praedicti viri sancti vita eius (?) perlecta et
miraculorum serie publice declarata, cum consilio et assensu con-
venientium fratrum super illo canonizando, secundum quod in
consilio eorum inveneris, nostra fultus auctoritate procedas; sciens
quod nos illud, quod tu super hoc cum dictis fratribus provideris

184

En outre, la procédure de la canonisation papale subit une transformation significative : l'usage observé comme règle au XIᵉ siècle de prononcer la sentence seulement dans un synode papal fut de plus en plus abandonné (1). Quoique Eugène III et encore Alexandre III lors de sa première canonisation proclament le principe que ces causes doivent être en règle générale traitées en plein concile (2), ils n'ont jamais appliqué ce principe ; en fait, à partir d'Eugène III ils se contentent de consulter les cardinaux (3). Cette substitution du

statuendum auctore Domino, ratum et firmum habebimus (JL. 10886 ; Migne, PL., 200, col. 236). Nous pensons avec Hinschius, IV, p. 245, n. 5, qu'il n'est pas possible d'interpréter la formule *super illo canonizando, secundum quod ...inveneris, nostra fultus auctoritate procedas* dans le sens d'une canonisation décrétée par le pape lui-même, mais subordonnée à une condition, de sorte que le délégué n'aurait eu à faire que de vérifier si la condition était accomplie et de promulguer la canonisation. Une telle interprétation a été adoptée dans un autre cas par Benoît XIV (qui ne connaissait pas encore cette lettre d'Alexandre III) : pour la délégation de Clément III aux évêques de Mersebourg, d'Eichstett et à quelques autres prélats, concernant la canonisation de saint Othon de Bamberg (Bened., 1, 44, 15). Mais alors le pape écrit : *...et si non inveneritis aliquid quod obsistat, ipsum canonizatum, auctoritate freti apostolica, solemniter et publice nuntietis...* (JL. 16411, Fontanini, n. 20; cf. aussi JL. 16412, Fontanini, n. 21) ; il s'exprime donc de tout autre façon qu'Alexandre III. Et même dans le cas de Clément III l'interprétation généralement admise de Benoît XIV — *canonizatio sub conditione, purificatio* et *promulgatio* déléguées — ne nous semble pas dogmatiquement préférable à la notion d'une canonisation déléguée : une sentence infaillible, mais subordonnée à la condition d'une enquête future, n'est-ce pas là une *contradictio in adiecto* ?

(1) Bened., 1, 10, 1; Hinschius, IV, pp. 243 et suiv. — Pour les canonisations du XIIᵉ siècle, cf. *supra*, p. 181, n. 3 ; parmi celles du XIIᵉ siècle (*supra*, p. 183, n. 2) il n'y a de canonisations conciliaires que JL. 7028 (Callixte II : 1ᵉʳ concile du Latran), JL. 7496 (Innocent II : concile de Reims), JL. 8007 (Innocent II : 2ᵉ concile du Latran). — Hinschius, p. 243, nn. 1, 2. Moins exactes les données de Toynbee, p. 138.

(2) Eugène III, JL. 8882 : *...tametsi huiusmodi petitio nisi in generalibus conciliis admitti non soleat....* ; Alexandre III, JL. 10653 : *...quamvis negotium tam arduum et sublime non frequenter soleat nisi in solemnibus conciliis de more concedi...* — Hinschius, IV, p. 243, n. 2, 4.

(3) Eugène III, JL. 8882 : *...auctoritate tamen S. R. E. quae omnium*

conseil des cardinaux (nous dirions du consistoire) au concile plénier marque certainement un pas décisif vers la centralisation.

Mais plus encore que par ces changements dans les formes de la canonisation papale, la réserve papale fut préparée par un certain affaiblissement qui s'annonce dans l'ancien système de la *translatio* épiscopale autonome (1). Dès 1120, lors du synode de Beauvais, qui réunit les évêques de plusieurs provinces ecclésiastiques de la France et où devait être décrétée la *translatio* de saint Arnoul de Pamèle, feu évêque de Soissons, on peut constater deux tendances opposées (2) : l'archevêque de Reims avait proposé en 1119 de soumettre la cause au Souverain Pontife (3), tandis qu'à Beauvais l'évêque de Chartres déclara hautement que, quant à lui, si Dieu avait opéré par un de ses prédécesseurs des miracles comme ceux de saint Arnoul, il ne consulterait ni pape, ni légat, ni archevêque pour élever un tel saint aux autels. Les évêques réunis l'applaudissent, mais ils n'en décident pas moins de soumettre la sentence favorable du synode aux archevêques de Reims, de Tours et au Légat pontifical, qui n'avaient pas pris part aux délibérations synodales; et ils obtiennent que le Légat confirme la sentence dans une nouvelle réunion (4). Nous ne savons pas quels motifs ont amené le

conciliorum firmamentum est, ...fratrum nostrorum archiepiscoporum et episcorum, qui praesentes erant, communicato consilio... constituimus...; Alexandre III, JL. 10653 : *...de communi tamem fratrum nostrorum consilio... censuimus...*; JL. 11646 : *...de communi fratrum nostrorum consilio...*; JL. 12201 : *...deliberato cum fratribus nostris consilio...*; JL. 12329 : *...fratrum nostrorum communicato consilio...* — Déjà en 1120 Callixte II canonisait saint Hugues de Cluny *...in medio Cluniacensis capituli... episcopis vero et cardinalibus pariter assentientibus...* (Migne, PL., 166, col. 845).

(1) Cf. Hertling, pp. 177 et suiv., pp. 180 et suiv.
(2) Hertling, p. 178.
(3) *ASS., Aug.* 15, III, p. 254.
(4) *Ibid.,* pp. 257-258. Il n'est pas tout à fait exact de parler simplement.

synode à solliciter cette confirmation; dans le récit que
nous en possédons, des raisons juridiques et de compétence ne sont point mentionnées; et d'ailleurs la confirmation du Légat n'a pas donné à la sentence le caractère d'une canonisation papale. Mais il n'en reste pas
moins que les avis des évêques différaient sur l'oppor-
tunité d'une *translatio* à la manière ancienne et que
l'opinion négative l'a emporté. La *translatio* décrétée
fut effectuée l'année suivante par l'évêque de Tournai (1).

On voit qu'ici la *translatio* n'était plus dans la canonisation l'acte décisif, et il y a des cas semblables où
l'accent juridique passe de la *translatio* à une sentence
qui la précède (2). Mais il y a même des cas, plus signi-
ficatifs encore pour la recherche de l'origine de la prérogative papale, où la translation va perdre non seulement son caractère décisif, mais aussi sa qualité de
sentence définitive, ainsi donc sa qualité de canonisation,
par des actes subséquents et non prévus au moment de
la *translatio* (3). Au xie siècle, un tel acte subséquent,
quand bien même il émanait du pape, respectait encore
l'état créé par une *translatio*. Saint Remi, par exemple,
l'apôtre des Francs, était vénéré dans beaucoup de
provinces de l'Église occidentale depuis sa première
translatio qui avait eu lieu avant 585. Ses reliques furent

(comme Bened., 1, 8, 14; Hefele-Leclerq, *Hist. des Conc.*, V, 1, p. 592;
Hinschius, III, p. 536) d'un synode tenu sous la présidence du Légat
pontifical. Le récit d'un des membres du synode, l'évêque Lisiard de
Soissons (*ASS.*, *loc. cit.*), source unique pour la connaissance de ce concile,
démontre clairement que le synode fut célébré par quatorze évêques (indiqués
nommément), nombre d'abbés, archidiacres, etc., et que le Légat et les
deux archevêques ne furent informés qu'après le *concilium* proprement
dit. Cela se trouve exprimé aussi dans la formule de confirmation du Légat
et de l'archevêque de Reims : *Iudicium vestrae auctoritatis plene susci-
pimus et decretum vestri consensus corroboramus.*
 (1) *ASS*, *Aug. 15*, III, p. 258, p. 223.
 (2) Cf. Hertling, pp. 180-183.
 (3) *Ibid.*, p. 183.

retransférées encore plusieurs fois (1), et quand le pape
Léon IX consacra en 1049 la nouvelle église de Saint-
Remi à Reims, il ne fit que les transférer une dernière
fois et confirmer la fête ancienne du saint, sans prononcer de sa part une nouvelle canonisation (2).

Mais au XIIe siècle il y avait déjà des prélats pour
qui le caractère définitif d'une *translatio* effectuée
autrefois n'était plus aussi sûr. En 1167 l'abbé de
Grandmont avait célébré la *translatio* de saint Étienne
de Tiers, fondateur de l'ordre, et sans doute il avait
l'intention d'instituer par là définitivement sa fête, de
le canoniser. Et pourtant un de ses successeurs crut
nécessaire de demander à Urbain III la canonisation
papale; elle fut prononcée par Clément III en 1189 (3). Il
en fut de même pour saint Gérard, fondateur de Sauve-
majeure : la translation solennelle par l'abbé Pierre
(1131-35) en présence d'évêques et de princes fut suivie
d'une canonisation par le pape Célestin III en 1197 (4).
Dans ces deux cas, la canonisation papale subséquente
détruisait rétroactivement les effets définitifs de l'ancienne *translatio*; et comme ces canonisations n'étaient
pas octroyées par le pape, mais expressément sollicitées
par une nouvelle génération de prélats, on peut parler
d'un affaiblissement intérieur de la canonisation particulière, qui préparait la voie à la proclamation de la
prérogative papale.

(1) *ASS.*, *Octob. 1*, 1, pp. 113 et suiv.

(2) JL. 4185; Migne, PL., 143, col. 616. -- Un cas analogue est celui de saint
Prosper de Reggio : la *translatio* constitutive de son corps dans l'église de
Saint-Apollinaire avait été célébrée par l'évêque Thomas sous le règne de
Liutprand (712-744); au Xe siècle il fut retransféré dans la basilique de
Notre-Dame de Reggio, d'où le pape Grégoire V transféra le saint encore
une fois en 997, sans nouvelle canonisation, dans une basilique qu'il dédia à
saint Prosper lui-même. Cf. Giov. Mercati, dans *Anal. Bolland.*, 15 (1896),
pp. 161-207; surtout pp. 193 et suiv., p. 206.

(3) *ASS.*, *Febr. 8*, II, pp. 210-211; JL. 16395; Fontanini, n. 22; Hertling,
p. 181.

(4) *ASS.*, *Apr. 5*, I, p. 421; JL. 17527; Fontanini, n. 27; Hertling, p. 182.

IV

Pourtant des faits de ce genre — d'ailleurs isolés —
ne suffisent pas pour affirmer qu'un droit papal coutu-
mier de réserve exclusive aurait précédé la décrétale
Audivimus (1). Mais à en croire certains chroniqueurs
du premier tiers du xɪɪᵉ siècle, il aurait même existé depuis
longtemps des lois canoniques positives contre les
translations épiscopales. Cosme de Prague rapporte au
deuxième livre de sa *Chronica Boemorum* (écrit
environ de 1119 à 1122) (2) l'histoire suivante : En 1039
le duc Bracislav et l'évêque de Prague, au cours d'une
invasion en Pologne, enlevèrent de la cathédrale de
Gnesen le corps du saint martyr Adalbert de Prague
et le transférèrent solennellement dans la cathédrale
de Prague (3). Là-dessus ils sont dénoncés au pape
Benoît IX du chef de violation des lois sacrées canoniques et l'affaire est soumise à un concile convoqué
d'urgence. Les délégués de la Bohême arrivent plus
tard, des intrigues se nouent (4), et enfin le Pape prononce une sentence (5) dans laquelle il réprimande le
duc et l'évêque pour les actes de violence et de rapt
qu'ils avaient commis, mais où avant tout il condamne
la translation : *quod autem nulli liceat sine nostra permissione de loco ad locum sacrum transferre corpus,
testantur canones, prohibent patrum decreta, et pre-
sumptores huiscemodi rei divina jubent eloquia gladio
anathematis ut feriantur.* Pourtant, en considération
de leur ignorance et de leur bonne intention, et à

---

(1) Cette affirmation se trouve cependant chez Hertling, p. 179.
(2) Ed. Bretholz, *Mon. Germ. Script.*, Nova series (in-8°), II, 1923.
— Pour la date, voir l'introduction, pp. xx et suiv.
(3) *Ed. cit.*, pp. 84 et suiv., p. 90.
(4) *Ed. cit.*, pp. 91-92.
(5) *Ed. cit.*, pp. 92-93.

condition qu'ils construisent un monastère, le Pape
absout les coupables.

Selon le chroniqueur, ce procès aurait donc eu pour
principal objet une *translatio* faite sans la permission
nécessaire du Saint-Siège. Mais c'est là précisément ce
qui justifie le soupçon que cette histoire (et ce ne serait
pas le seul exemple dans l'œuvre de Cosme de Prague) a
été inventée en grande partie (1). Une sentence comme
Cosme la fait prononcer au pape Benoît IX aurait été
absurde; ni en 1039, ni du temps de Cosme lui-même, il
n'y a jamais eu de *canones* ou de *decreta patrum* qui
défendissent les translations épiscopales (2), et Cosme
devait n'avoir aucune connaissance de droit canonique
pour faire passer comme authentique une sentence
papale de cette teneur. Les négociations romaines dans
cette affaire — si elles ont jamais eu lieu — n'auront
certainement point eu d'autre objet que les doléances des
Polonais contre le rapt de leurs reliques. En matière de
canonisation la chronique de Cosme ne prouve qu'une
chose : c'est qu'au commencement du XIIᵉ siècle il y avait
déjà une tendance littéraire à attribuer aux papes une prérogative qu'eux-mêmes en réalité ne devaient revendi-
quer que beaucoup plus tard (3). — Un deuxième exemple

(1) Pour les défauts d'exactitude et de véracité chez Cosme en général,
voir l'introduction de Bretholz, pp. xxxii et suiv., surtout sur les discours
inventés. Grosjean, dans *Analecta Bolland.*, 49 (1931), p. 213, ajoute foi
au récit de la *Chron. Boem.*

(2) Bretholz, *ed. cit.*, p. 92, n. 5, cite le canon de Mayence (cf. *supra*,
p. 174), à tort, s'il veut indiquer une source juridique, mais probablement
avec raison s'il veut indiquer un modèle littéraire de Cosme : les mots *nulli
liceat sine nostra permissione de loco ad locum sacrum transferre
corpus...* sont peut-être une réminiscence (ou une falsification?) dudit canon :
*corpora sanctorum de loco ad locum nullus transferre presumat sine
consilio principis*, etc.

(3) La tendance littéraire de Cosme est donc beaucoup plus radicale que
celle du grand faussaire Pierre Diacre du Mont-Cassin (✝ 1159) dont Hertling, p. 177, nous donne un exemple : dans sa *Vita sancti Martini*,
Pierre Diacre fait dissuader par un évêque de Benevent au VIIIᵉ siècle la

de cette tendance litteraire nous est fourni par l'auteur anonyme de la *Translatio Godehardi episcopi Hildesheimensis*. Saint Gothard fut canonisé par Innocent II en 1131 sur les instances de l'évêque Berthold de Hildesheim (1); et le chroniqueur, à peu près contemporain, nous donne le motif suivant pour cette attitude de l'évêque (2) : ...*cum canonica censura, propter illusiones daemonorum quae frequenter in ecclesia Dei in talibus contigerunt, statutum sit. ne quis sine apostolica auctoritate et vita ipsius per viros auctorabiles approbata, canonizaretur...* Or, il n'existait pas de *canonica censura* de ce genre, mais le passage témoigne de la manière de penser de certains milieux à l'égard du droit de canonisation.

V

Nous avons vu comment le terrain fut préparé au XIIᵉ siècle pour la réserve papale par le nombre croissant de canonisations universelles sans coopération des conciles, par un affaiblissement de la valeur des translations, par des affirmations littéraires prématurées. Il nous reste à étudier l'introduction même de la réserve qui, nous le répétons, a été attribuée jusqu'à présent sans conteste à Alexandre III. — Voyons d'abord le texte de la décrétale *Audivimus* : « Nous avons appris, dit le pape Alexandre, que quelques-uns parmi vous, trompés par les artifices du diable, vénèrent à la mode des païens comme saint un homme tué en état d'ivresse, tandis que l'Église permet à peine de prier pour ceux qui meurent dans l'ébriété ; car l'apôtre dit : les ivrognes

translation sans permission du Pape (*ASS.*, Oct. 24, X, p. 837). Ce *sine consilio et licentia papae... fieri dehortabatur* nous semble cependant interprété par Hertling dans un sens trop positif, quand il affirme que *Pietro Diacono parla della necessità di un permesso papale.*

(1) JL. 7496, Fontanini, n. 7.
(2) *Mon. Germ. Script.*, XII, p. 641. — Cf. Hertling, p. 178.

ne seront point héritiers du royaume de Dieu (*I Cor.*, 6, 10). N'osez donc pas dorénavant vouer un culte à cet homme, vu que, quand bien même beaucoup de miracles seraient accomplis par lui, il ne vous serait pas permis de le vénérer en public comme saint sans l'autorité de l'Église romaine » (1).

Est-ce que cette lettre contient vraiment le principe général que tout jugement en matière de vénération des saints sera réservé désormais au Saint-Siège? ou plus exactement, est-ce qu'elle contenait un tel principe lorsqu'elle fut écrite, entre 1171 et 1180? Il n'y a pas de doute, en effet, que du moment où elle fut insérée par Grégoire IX en 1234 dans sa collection officielle de décrétales, elle n'y ait figuré comme source positive du droit de réserve. Mais cela ne prouve rien encore quant aux intentions dont s'inspirait Alexandre III soixante ans auparavant. Pour rechercher le sens primitif de sa lettre, il faut donc oublier qu'il s'agit du chapitre Ier du titre *De reliquiis et veneratione sanctorum* dans les décrétales de Grégoire IX, et s'efforcer de rétablir les conditions historiques de la lettre originale.

Comme la lettre ne porte dans les Grégoriennes que l'inscription *Alexander III*, on a ignoré pendant des siècles qui en était le destinataire et, par conséquent, à quelle occasion elle avait été écrite (2). On ne soupçonnait non plus qu'elle n'était pas complète dans cette forme de décrétale, mais ne représentait qu'un fragment

---

(1) c. 1, X, *De reliquiis et veneratione sanctorum*, III, 45. — Pour le texte latin et les variantes, cf. Appendice, n° 1.

(2) Baronius, *Annales ecclesiastici*, XII, Romae, 1607, pp. 759 et suiv. (Éd. Lucensis, XIX [1746], pp. 520 et suiv.), émet une conjecture ingénieuse en supposant comme destinataire le monastère de Grestain, sur l'état scandaleux duquel il avait retrouvé une lettre de l'évêque de Lisieux à Alexandre III. L'hypothèse de Baronius fut accueillie par Gonzalez Tellez, *Commentaria perpetua in singulos textus quinque librorum decretalium Gregorii IX*, Lugduni, 1673, III, p. 936, et, à sa suite, par les autres canonistes.

192

découpé dans la lettre authentique. Le premier à découvrir cette particularité a été Hinschius, qui nota en 1888 que la décrétale *Audivimus* faisait à l'origine partie d'une lettre assez longue, adressée par Alexandre III au roi Kanut de Suède (1). Mais ni Hinschius, ni d'autres après lui (2) n'en ont vu les conséquences pour l'appréciation historique du fragment *Audivimus*.

La lettre au roi Kanut, qui commence par les mots *Aeterna et incommutabilis*, consiste surtout en des renseignements de caractère didactique sur quelques principes fondamentaux du droit chrétien. Cette partie de la lettre contient six paragraphes : sur le suprême magistère de l'Église de Rome (3), sur l'institution du mariage chrétien et ses principaux empêchements (4), sur les privilèges du clergé et les objets sacrés (5), sur les dîmes (6), sur la portion légitime (7), et sur le convol en secondes noces en cas d'absence du premier époux (8). Dans tous ces paragraphes le Pape écrit plutôt en précepteur qu'en juge : il enseigne et ne décrète pas (9). C'est à la suite de cette partie que nous lisons le

(1) Hinschius, IV, p. 243, n. 6, en signalant l'édition de Liljegren, *Diplomatarium Suecanum*, I, Holmiae, 1829, pp. 61-63 ; cf. Migne, PL., 200, col. 1259.

(2) Le premier après Hinschius (peut-être indépendamment de lui) à noter le rapport entre les deux pièces a été Lœwenfeld dans son édition des *Regesta* de Jaffé (vol. II, 1888) : JL., 13546. — Wernz, III, n. 361, 25; Delehaye, p. 189, et tout récemment Joseph Brosch, *Der Heiligsprechungsprozess per viam cultus*, Romae (Pont. Univ. Gregoriana), 1938, p. 5. — A d'autres, comme à Ortolan, dans *Dict. théol. cath.*, II, col. 1633, à Toynbee, p. 138, n. 2 et même à Hertling, p. 179, la vraie origine de la décrétale a encore échappé.

(3) *Eterna et incommutabilis— —placere Deo* (Liljegren, p. 61).

(4) *Inter cetera uero— —similiter custoditur* (pp. 61-62).

(5) *Preterea episcopos— —attributa facultas.*

(6) *Decimas autem— —domino persoluatis.*

(7) *Ad hec nunciatum— —ecclesiis derelinquant.*

(8) *Viris autem in captiuitate ——nouerint maculantur* (pp. 62-63).

(9) Cette affirmation peut être documentée par une analyse détaillée de

passage qui devait former plus tard la décrétale
Audivimus, le seul passage de la lettre qui concerne
un cas pratique individuel, bien qu'incomplètement
précisé, et où une sentence judiciaire est rendue (1).
La lettre finit par un dernier paragraphe, abolissant le
carême précédant la fête de saint Michel qui était
d'usage en Suède (2), et par une recommandation en
faveur du porteur de la lettre (3).

Si nous considérons ce document dans son ensemble,
nous devons nous demander si le grand juriste qu'était
Alexandre III a vraiment voulu se servir de cette
occasion pour proclamer la réserve papale du droit de
canonisation. Pourquoi aurait-il inséré une innovation
canonique aussi radicale dans une épître dont le but
principal était de donner un enseignement élémentaire
sur quelques vieilles notions fondamentales du droit de
l'Église à un peuple récemment converti au christia-
nisme? Que le Pape ajoute à cette catéchèse deux décisions d'ordre pratique — sur un carême spécial (4), sur
le culte scandaleux voué à un ivrogne —, cela n'avait
rien d'extraordinaire; mais se servir de cette occasion
pour établir une loi nouvelle dans une matière d'intérêt
universel, cela nous paraîtrait trop hors de propos. Si
Alexandre avait l'intention d'établir cette loi, de supprimer une fois pour toutes les canonisations particulières,
il l'aurait fait, nous semble-t-il, à des occasions plus

la lettre que nous ne pouvons pas envisager ici. Pour donner de brefs
exemples : le § 5 *Ad hec nunciatum* explique le texte d'Augustin, *Serm.*,
355, n. 4 = c. 8, C. 13, q. 2 (cf. aussi dict. p. c. 7); le § 6 *Viris autem*
résume la C. 34 de Gratien; etc.

(1) *Denique quiddam audiuimus— —publice uenerari.* Pour les diffé-
rences entre ce texte et la décrétale, cf. Appendice, n° 1.

(2) *Sed in hiis omnibus— —attencius uenerari.*

(3) *Super uisitacione— —in Domino commendamus.*

(4) Nous voyons le style de catéchèse dans l'introduction de ce § 8 : *Sed
in hiis omnibus que prediximus et aliis, que ad salutem uestram
pertinere noscuntur, tales uos exhibere curetis, ut bona temporalia et
eterna...,* etc.

194

éclatantes, plus exemplaires que dans cette affaire obscure, mal précisée, et qui regardait exclusivement une nation de néophytes demeurant sur les confins du monde connu.

Pourquoi ne trouve-t-on pas un mot sur la réserve papale dans les bulles des cinq canonisations célébrées par Alexandre III? Parmi elles, l'une du moins aurait fourni une excellente occasion de se prononcer dans ce sens : la canonisation de Thomas Becket, l'illustre martyr de Canterbury, assassiné dans sa cathédrale le 29 décembre 1170. Car nous savons (et le Pape lui-même ne l'ignorait pas) que dans l'Église d'Angleterre l'archevêque-martyr fut immédiatement considéré comme saint, et qu'il régnait un grand mécontentement par suite des lenteurs de la procédure de canonisation (1). Jean de Salisbury écrit à l'un des deux Légats pontificaux chargés de l'instruction du procès une lettre pleine d'amertume (2) où il émet des doutes sur la nécessité d'une canonisation papale et laisse sous-entendre que l'Église d'Angleterre élèverait le saint aux autels de son propre mouvement si le Pape ne procédait pas plus vite. Quand, enfin, en 1173 Alexandre III proclama la canonisation, il l'annonce à la chrétienté par cinq bulles (3) ; après ces velléités d'indépendance du clergé anglais, quelle occasion aurait été plus appropriée pour se prononcer sur le droit exclusif du Saint-Siège, s'il voulait vraiment le décréter?

L'invraisemblance que le Pape, s'il avait eu cette intention, s'en serait tu lors du cas de Thomas Becket,

(1) Cf. Baronius, *Annales eccles.*, XII, pp. 657 et suiv. (Ed. Lucensis, XIX, pp. 400 et suiv.) ; Reuter, *Geschichte Alexanders III*, vol. III, pp. 111 et suiv., p. 523, cité par Hinschius, IV, p. 244, n. 2. Les observations de Toynbee, p. 143, sur le cas de saint Thomas Becket, méconnaissent ces faits essentiels.

(2) La lettre se trouve chez Baronius, *loc. cit.*; Migne, PL., 199, col. 361.

(3) *Supra*, p. 183, n. 2.

et l'aurait exprimée dans la lettre au roi Kanut de Suède dont nous avons montré que son but principal était tout différent, voilà le premier point qui nous frappe dans l'étude de la décrétale *Audivimus*. Mais passons à l'examen du texte même (1). Alexandre, après avoir démontré l'absurdité théologique de la vénération d'un ivrogne, s'exprime en ces termes : *hominem illum de cetero colere in periculum animarum vestrarum nullatenus presumatis, cum... non liceret vobis pro sancto absque auctoritate Romanae ecclesiae eum publice venerari* (2). Soyons bien attentifs aux paroles qu'il emploie ; il dit : *hominem illum, eum venerari* ; il ne dit pas : *aliquem*, il ne dit même pas : *talem* ! Est-ce là le style usité pour rédiger une nouvelle loi ?

Les bollandistes du xviie siècle en ont déjà fait l'observation : *haec loquendi forma decretum non facit*, mais ils en ont conclu : *sed factum et vulgo notum supponit* (3), ce qui est une interprétation grammaticalement possible, mais qui ne correspond pas aux réalités historiques. Il faut donc écarter la solution des bollandistes, et alors il est certainement plus naturel d'entendre les mots *non liceret vobis eum publice venerari* comme décision toute spéciale d'un cas singulier ; et surtout si on lit ce passage et tout le paragraphe dans le contexte de la lettre entière, c'est-à-dire d'une lettre pastorale adressée à un peuple néophyte où régnaient encore des *mores infidelium*, cette interprétation n'est pas seulement plus naturelle, mais nous semble la seule raisonnable : c'est pour ce cas, c'est envers ce peuple que le

---

(1) Voir Appendice, no 1.

(2) C'est là le texte original ; il allait être raccourci déjà dans les premières collections de décrétales ; cf. p. 196, n. 1 et Appendice, no 1. Dans les Grégoriennes, Raymond de Peñafort a changé l'arrangement des mots et remplacé *eum publice* par *ipsum*.

(3) D. Papebroch et J. Henschen, *Propylaeum, ASS. Maii*, dissert. XX, p. *173.

196

Pape revendique pour le Siège apostolique le droit de rendre un jugement.

VI

Nous avons essayé de donner sa juste valeur à la lettre *Aeterna et incommutabilis* prise dans son ensemble; cela nous mène tout naturellement à nous demander qui a bien pu découper dans cette lettre le fragment *Audivimus* pour l'insérer dans une collection de décrétales et lui donner par cette mise en évidence — soulignée par la suppression de quelques phrases d'un caractère trop pastoral (1) — la signification d'une loi générale. Parmi les nombreuses collections privées de décrétales du xıı⁰ siècle nous rencontrons la décrétale *Audivimus* pour la première fois (2) dans la *Collectio Cottoniana I*, composée en Angleterre après 1179, mais au plus tard au cours des premières années après la mort d'Alexandre III (1181). Dans cette collection primitive de caractère local anglais, et qui ne pouvait guère être connue dans les milieux canonistes de l'époque (3), la décrétale *Audivimus* se trouve encore sous une rubrique qui n'y relève que la défense du culte d'un indigne (4). De là, la décrétale a passé dans la *Collectio Cottoniana II*, composée pendant

(1) Il s'agit des mots *unde a potationibus et ebrietatibus, si regnum Dei habere desideratis, uos continere oportet*; et *in periculum animarum uestrarum*; voir Appendice, n⁰ 1.

(2) Je dois les indications qui suivent sur la décrétale *Audivimus* dans les collections de la Cotton Library et de la Bodleian Library à M. Walther Holtzmann, le meilleur connaisseur des collections du xıı⁰ siècle.

(3) Cf. sur la *Coll. Cotton. I* (British Museum, ms. Cotton Claud. A IV, fol. 189-216), provisoirement notre *Repertorium der Kanonistik*, Città del Vaticano, 1937, p. 279.

(4) c. 212 : *Non est pro sancto colendus, per quem in ebrietate occisum fiunt miracula*. La réserve n'est mentionnée que dans une note marginale, à moitié illisible sur la photographie :

Non est pro sancto/////
qui non est a sede (?)/////
na auctoritate/////

le pontificat de Clément III (1187-1191), et dont l'arrangement répond déjà à un type anglais plus développé (1). Mais c'est en vain qu'on chercherait notre pièce dans toutes les autres collections du XIIᵉ siècle; elle ne se trouve notamment point dans les familles importantes de collections qui ont, tantôt l'une, tantôt l'autre, servi de livres de référence aux écoles canonistes de Bologne et de France (l'*Appendix Concilii Lateranensis*, le groupe autour de la *Collectio Bambergensis*, la *Francofortana*, la *Brugensis*, etc.) : elle se trouve avant tout aussi peu dans la *Compilatio I*, ce « Bréviaire des extravagantes » de Bernard de Pavie, qui dès sa publication entre 1188 et 1192 fut adopté par toutes les écoles, et d'où la science décrétaliste prend sa véritable origine.

Une décrétale du grand juriste Alexandre III, si elle avait en réalité bouleversé les fondements juridiques de la canonisation, aurait-elle pu échapper à ces canonistes collectionneurs du XIIᵉ siècle, qui étaient les vrais promoteurs du *novum ius decretalium*?

Au cours des premières années d'Innocent III (1198-1216), la décrétale *Audivimus* fut reprise par un autre groupe de collections : la *Sangermanensis* et les deux collections apparentées, l'*Abrincensis* et la *Bodleiana* (2).

_____

(1) *Coll. Cotton. II* (British Museum, ms. Cotton Vitell. E XIII, fol. 209-283) : V, 32. — Cf. sur cette collection les indications bibliographiques dans notre *Repertorium*, p. 297, et tout récemment W. Holtzmann, dans *Zeitschrift der Savigny-Stiftung für Rechtsgeschichte, Kan. Abt.*, 27 (1938), pp. 300 et suiv., avec des précisions importantes. Dans ce type anglais développé, il ne s'agit pas encore d'une collection « systématique », où les décrétales souvent sont coupées en morceaux pour les regrouper sous les titres respectifs (comme dans l'*Appendix*, la *Bambergensis*, etc.), mais du premier grossier arrangement en *libri* ou *partes*, sans démembrement des décrétales (comme dans la *Wigorniensis*); Holtzmann, p. 303.

(2) *Coll. Sangermanensis* (Paris, Bibl. Nat., ms. lat. 12459, fol. 1-106ᵛᵒ; cf. les indications bibliographiques dans notre *Repertorium*, p. 298) : VII, 147. — *Coll. Abrincensis* (Bibl. d'Avranches, ms. 149, fol. 79-109 ; *Repertorium*, p. 299) : VII, 15, 2. — *Coll. Bodleiana* (Oxford, Bodleian Library, ms. Tanner 8, pp. 593-712 ; *Repertorium*, p. 294) : VI, 9, 2. — Dans

Dans toutes les trois la décrétale est placée à la suite de la bulle *Redolet Anglia* qui notifia la canonisation de saint Thomas de Canterbury (1), et dans l'*Abrincensis* et la *Bodleiana* les deux pièces sont même réunies sous un nouveau titre programmatique : *Quod necessaria sit auctoritas Romani pontificis ad hoc, quod aliquis pro sancto habeatur* (2). Mais ce groupe de collections, appartenant lui aussi aux milieux anglais (3), est resté sans succès hors de ces milieux : la plupart des matériaux de la *Sangermanensis* et de la *Bodleiana* étaient déjà répandus sous la forme mieux ordonnée et généralement reconnue de la *Compilatio I* (4). Ainsi donc, jusqu'au commencement du XIII⁰ siècle, une réserve papale n'était connue que par quelques collectionneurs anglais de décrétales.

Ce n'est qu'en 1206 — vingt-cinq années après la mort d'Alexandre III — que la décrétale *Audivimus* trouva accès dans une collection jouissant d'un certain renom dans les écoles; la Collection du Maître Alain, professeur bolonais d'origine anglaise (5). De la collection

notre *Repertorium* la *Bodleiana* figure provisoirement comme membre du groupe autour de la *Bambergensis*; cependant M. Holtzmann a pu établir par un examen plus détaillé sa parenté avec la *Sangermanensis*; cf. *loc. cit.*, p. 303, n. 1.

(1) *Sangerm.*, VII, 146; *Abrinc.*, VII, 15, 1; *Bodl.*, VI, 9, 1; JL. 12203, *supra*, p. 183, n. 2.

(2) Cf. Appendice, n⁰ 1.

(3) Cf. H. Singer, *Neue Beiträge über die Dekretalensammlungen...*, dans *Sitzungsberichte der Kais. Akademie der Wissensch. in Wien*, 171, I (1913), pp. 113-115.

(4) Cf. pour la *Sangerm.*, Singer, *op. cit.*, p. 81.

(5) *Alanus*, recension plus longue (Fulda, Landesbibl., ms. D. 14, fol. 32 sqq.) : VI, 3, 2 = recension plus courte (Fulda, ms. D. 5, fol. 140 sqq.) : app. c. 12. — Sur la *Collectio Alani*, nous devons corriger nos indications dans le *Repertorium*, p. 316, basées sur les investigations de Schulte relatives aux deux recensions et sur celles de Schulte et de Gillmann concernant la date. Depuis, R. von Heckel a pu établir dans *Historisches Jahrbuch der Görres-Gesellschaft*, 57 (1937), p. 86, n. 3 et p. 259, que la collection plus longue (Fulda, D. 14), que Schulte, dans

d'Alain, le chapitre *Audivimus* passa dans la collection de Jean de Galles (1210) qui, bien que collection privée elle aussi, fut adoptée par l'école de Bologne comme *Compilatio II* (1). Et l'on sait que les cinq *Compilationes* (plus tard dénommées *antiquae*) formaient le matériel qui a servi à saint Raymond de Peñafort pour composer la Compilation officielle grégorienne de 1234.

VII

A l'attitude des collectionneurs correspond celle des glossateurs (2) : jusqu'à la première décade du XIIIᵉ siècle

Sitzungsber. der Kais. Akad. der Wiss. in Wien, 65 (1870), p. 605, avait prise pour la deuxième recension augmentée (*collectio aucta*), est à la vérité la collection originale d'Alain, tandis que la recension plus courte (D. 5), la *Collectio Alani* de Schulte, représente un extrait postérieur et abrégé (cas analogue à celui des deux recensions de la *Collectio Gilberti* dont Schulte avait pareillement interverti l'ordre historique; cf. notre *Repertorium*, p. 312). Quant à la date, von Heckel, p. 89, n. 9, fait remonter les pièces plus récentes d'Innocent III dans Alain à 1206, et il démontre que la date 1208, adoptée par Schulte, p. 619, n'a de fondement que dans une seule décrétale (*Alan. abbrev.*, app. c. 13; Po. 3503), intercalée par Schulte lui-même!

Toutefois, von Heckel ne s'explique pas sur la date 1209, indiquée par Gillmann (*Archiv für kath. Kirchenrecht*, 116 [1936], pp. 127, 151; cf. notre *Repertorium*, p. 316), à cause de la décrétale *Officii tui* (dans *Alan.*, app. c. 14 = *Alan. abbrev.*, app. c. 16) qui est datée de 1209 febr. 1-21 dans le *Regesta* de Potthast, n. 3660. Or, cet argument est facile à réfuter par le fait connu déjà de Baluze (négligé par Gillmann et moi-même) que les numéros Po. 3658-3673, bien qu'ils figurent dans le registre du Vatican à la fin de la XIᵉ année d'Innocent III (Reg. Vat., 7 A, fol. 90-94), ne sont pas des lettres chronologiquement disposées de cette année (1208 febr. 22 - 1209 febr. 21), mais « des fragments de décrétales sans dates ou des lettres qui appartiennent à d'autres livres que le XIᵉ » (A. Luchaire, *Les registres d'Innocent III et les Regesta de Potthast*, Paris, 1904, p. 18; cf. aussi H. Singer, dans *Sitzungsberichte der Kais. Akad. der Wiss. in Wien*, 171, II [1914], p. 24). La décrétale *Officii tui* n'empêche donc pas de dater la collection d'Alain de 1206. — Notons encore que von Heckel devrait rectifier son attribution de la décrétale *Accepimus*, Po. 5036 (*Comp. IV* : I, 8, 3 = X : I, 14, 13). aux années 1214-16 (*Histor. Jahrb.*, 55 [1935], p. 289, n. 35), puisqu'il l'a trouvée déjà dans *Alanus*, I, 8, 2 (Schulte, p. 676).

(1) *Comp. II* : V, 21, un.

(2) Pour les textes complets des auteurs cités dans les notes suivantes,

ni décrétiste ni décrétaliste ne fait allusion à un droit exclusif papal de canonisation qui aurait été réservé par Alexandre III. Et cependant, les décrétistes n'auraient pas manqué de l'occasion d'en parler : en effet, Gratien avait inséré dans la dernière partie de son ouvrage le canon du synode de Mayence de 813 qui, s'occupant de l'ancienne forme de la canonisation, la *translatio*, statuait qu'elle ne se ferait pas *sine consilio principis vel episcoporum sanctaeque synodi licentia* (1). Or, comme le canon mentionnait bien le prince séculier et l'évêque avec son synode, mais non le Pape, on déclarait souvent que le mot *principis* ne désignait pas seulement le prince local, mais aussi le Pape (2) : *prin-*

voir Appendice, n⁰ˢ 2-4. En matière de gloses du xiiᵉ siècle au Décret de Gratien, nous nous sommes borné aux manuscrits de la Vaticane (notre *Repertorium*, pp. 53-58) et de l'Angelica à Rome (*Repertorium*, p. 49). Parmi les apparats au Décret du xiiiᵉ siècle, seule la glossa *Ius naturale* (*Repertorium*, pp. 67-75) n'a pu être consultée. — Quant aux *summae*, il ne faut pas oublier qu'un grand nombre des ouvrages énumérés dans notre *Repertorium*, pp. 123-207, n'englobent point le *tractatus de consecratione* où se trouvent les canons qui nous intéressent. Et parmi ceux qui restent, quelques-uns ne commentent pas ces canons (par exemple, Paucapalea, Simon de Bisignano); tous les autres ont pu être consultés, à l'exception de la summa *De iure canonico tractaturus* (*Repertorium*, p. 198).

(1) c. 37 *de cons.*, D. 1. — Cf. *supra*, p. 174.

(2) On peut remarquer trois étapes dans l'interprétation du mot *principis* :

I. Les premiers glossateurs emploient ce terme comme expression métaphorique pour l'évêque et le synode. Ainsi, Rufin (1157-59) : « *principis* » : *hoc localiter est intelligendum*. « *uel* » : *pro* « *idest* » *episcoporum*. Jean de Faenza (après 1171) fait de cette interprétation du moins une alternative : « *principis* » : *hoc localiter est intelligendum. aut accipiatur uel* » *pro* « *idest* » *episcoporum*.

II. A la fin du xiiᵉ siècle, on admet une double interprétation du mot *principis* : c'est ou bien un prince séculier, ou le Pape. Glose anonyme (Vatic., lat. 2494 et 2495) : « *principis* » : *idest romani pontificis uel imperatoris*. Une autre glose anonyme (Rome, Bibl. Angelica, ms. 1270) ajoute : *et tunc localiter intelligitur*. Huguccio (vers 1188) : « *principis* » : *idest romani pontificis. si uero dicatur* « *principis* », *idest regis uel imperatoris, localiter intelligitur, sc. ubi non posset hoc esse sine scandalo, si fieret sine consilio principis, et specialiter de ecclesiis quarum est patronus*. La summa *Omnis qui iuste* (vers 1186) tend déjà vers la

cipis, idest romani pontificis; interprétation d'après
laquelle le canon aurait exigé ou bien la permission du
Pape, ou bien celle de l'évêque et du synode. Mais pou-
vait-on se contenter de cette interprétation du chapitre
sans mentionner que le Pape aurait tout récemment dérogé
au droit des évêques et des synodes? Et pourtant tous
s'en contentent. Il y a même beaucoup d'auteurs — parmi
eux le grand Huguccio — qui n'aperçoivent pas le véritable objet du canon de Mayence, vu qu'ils l'interprètent
comme s'appliquant à la seule translation secondaire des
reliques d'une église à une autre, et surtout au déplace-
ment des églises elles-mêmes (1). D'autres s'attachent
surtout à découvrir des dispositions analogues sur le

suppression du sens primitif : « *principis* » : *idest romani pontificis. si
autem uis intelligere de principe seculari, tunc dicetur huic cap.
derogatum, licet quidam dicant, sine consilio principis secularis non
debet fieri, quod hic dicitur.*

III. Au XIIIᵉ siècle on admet seulement l'interprétation prince = pape; cf.
Benencasa (*infra*, p. 202, n. 2). Laurent d'Espagne (1210-15) dit : « *principis* » : *idest pape*; du reste, il réfère encore l'opinion de Huguccio : *dicit
tamen h. hoc esse locale*; référence que Jean le Teutonique supprime lors
de la réception de la glose de Laurent dans sa *Glossa ordinaria* (1215-17).

(1) Rufin : *Ne uero aliquis sanctorum loca sua auctoritate mutare
presumeret, subiungit corpora sanctorum, in quorum translatione
solent mutari ecclesie, a nullo transferenda sine episcoporum consilio.* (Glose répétée par Etienne de Tournai [d'après l'édition de Schulte,
Giessen, 1891, p. 267], Jean de Faenza et la summa *Omnis qui iuste*).
Dans des mss. du Décret avec gloses du XIIᵉ on trouve à la rubrique du
canon de Mayence le *Notabile* : *Cuius auctoritate ecclesie sint mutande.*
Ce *Notabile* est repris par Huguccio (avec les mots : *unde hec notula
hic habetur...*) et par Laurent. — Sicard de Crémone (1179-81) : *Nota
quoque, quod nec ecclesie nec reliquie sunt de loco ad locum mutande
sine causa et episcoporum licentia...* Huguccio : *Ne forte quis ecclesias
sua auctoritate presumeret mutare..., ideo subiungit corpora sanctorum — intelligit mutationem ecclesiarum — a nullo esse transferenda sine consensu pape uel episcoporum, unde hec notula hic habetur : « cuius auctoritate ecclesie sint mutande, in c. ostendit ».* Corpora : *canonizata et alicui ecclesie deputata. non dicit quod reliquie
alique non possunt concedi sine consensu pape uel episcopi ; set si
corpus alicuius sancti iacet in aliqua ecclesia canonizatum, non
debet inde ferri ad alium locum sine consensu talis persone...*

deuxième ensevelissement dans le droit civil romain (1).
Je n'ai trouvé que deux auteurs qui aient reconnu que
dans le canon de Mayence il n'est pas question d'une
translation quelconque, mais de la translation constitutive pour le culte d'un saint, c'est-à-dire de l'*elevatio*
formelle. Benencasa d'Arezzo, qui écrit vers la fin du
XIIᵉ ou au commencement du XIIIᵉ siècle, déclare bien
que pour l'*elevatio* il faut la permission du Pape, mais
sans se référer à la décrétale *Audivimus*, ni à aucune
autre loi canonique (2); tandis que l'autre glose, qui se
trouve, elle, dans l'apparat *Ecce vicit leo* — ouvrage
anonyme français fort répandu des premières années du
XIIIᵉ siècle —, soutient la thèse opposée, notamment
qu'un évêque *potest reputare aliquem sanctum et
dicere esse sanctum* (3). La même thèse, parfaitement
inconsciente d'une prérogative papale, avait été déjà
professée par Bazianus (pas après 1192) qui dit, dans sa
glose à un capitulaire carolingien chez Gratien concernant l'année liturgique (4), *quod episcopus cum suis*

(1) Benencasa d'Arezzo, dans ses *Casus decretorum* (cf. sur lui notre *Repertorium*, pp. 229-230), se réfère *secundum legem humanam* à Cod.
3, 44, 14 et 1; Dig. 47, 12, 3, 4; Laurent et Jean le Teutonique allèguent
Dig. 11, 7, 8, *pr.*; Cod. 3, 44, 14 et 1 et 10. L'apparat *Ecce vicit leo* allègue le titre Cod. 3, 44 en général, la summa *Omnis qui iuste* Cod.
1, 2, 3.

(2) Benencasa : « *principis* » : *idest pape, sine cuius licentia corpora
sanctorum non leuantur de sepultura ; set ex quo sunt leuata,
possint transferri ex causa.* — Le *Casus* du maître aretin a passé dans
une composition hétérogène de gloses au Décret : Bibl. Vaticana, ms. Ross.
595.

(3) Cf. sur cet apparat notre *Repertorium*, pp. 59 et suiv. — Glose (au mot
sine consilio) : *Et hoc intellige de consensu episcopi. arg. potest
reputare aliquem sanctum et dicere esse sanctum...*

(4) c. 1 *de cons.*, D. 3; cf. *Haitonis episcopi Basileensis capitula
ecclesiastica*, c. 8 (*Mon. Germ. Capitularia*, I, p. 363). Précisément les
mots du canon qui nous intéressent : *et illae festivitates quas singuli episcopi in suis episcopiis cum populo collaudarerint* ne se trouvent pas
dans l'original, mais seulement dans la recension que Burch., II, 77, et
d'après lui Ivo, *Decr.*, IV, 14, *Coll. trium partium*, III, 4, 2 et Gratien
nous fournissent avec l'inscription faussée *Ex concilio Lugdunensi*.

quantum ad suam diocesim potest sanctum canonizare (1).

Il n'y a pas de doute : les écoles canonistes n'ont pas connu la décrétale *Audivimus* avant son insertion dans une collection de quelque importance. Et même après qu'elle eut été « reçue » à Bologne grâce à la *Compilatio secunda*, les décrétistes longtemps encore n'en prenaient pas acte (2), tandis que les premiers glossateurs décrétalistes la considéraient surtout comme réprobation du culte voué à un indigne et ne glosaient que sur cette partie de la décrétale (3).

Ce n'est que dans la deuxième rédaction (après 1217) de son apparat à la *Compilatio II* que Tancrède dédia une glose au sujet de la réserve papale. Mais cette glose renvoie le lecteur avant tout à une constitution du

---

(1) Cf. Appendice, nᵒ 3. — Le *terminus ad quem* pour Bazianus est établi par le fait qu'il n'allègue pas encore la *Compilatio I*; cf. Schulte, *Die Glosse zum Decret...*, dans *Denkschriften der kais. Akademie der Wiss. in Wien*, 21 (1872), II, pp. 57, 58, 62, et *Geschichte der Quellen und Literatur...*, I, Stuttgart, 1875, p. 155.

(2) Laurent et Jean le Teutonique la passent sous silence dans leurs gloses au canon de Mayence et même dans les gloses où ils combattent l'opinion de Bazianus au c. 1 *de cons.*, D. 3. Notamment Laurent écrit : *...b(azianus) intelligit de non canonizatis, quia dicit, quod episcopus ...potest sanctum canonizare. quod non credo, set exaudio de canonizatis, qui non habent uigilias.* Jean a recueilli cette glose textuellement dans sa *Ordinaria*, et Barthélemy de Brescia l'a laissée intacte lors de la deuxième rédaction. L'interpolation *extra de reliq. et uener. sanctorum c. i. in fine*, qu'on trouve après les mots *quod non credo* dans les éditions imprimées, est encore postérieure à la recension de Barthélemy. — Cf. Appendice, nᵒ 3.

(3) Cf. les gloses d'Albert et celles de Tancrède dans la première rédaction de son apparat (notre Appendice, nᵒ 4). — Sur les deux rédactions que Tancrède déclare avoir faites des apparats aux compilations I et II, cf. notre *Repertorium*, pp. 327-328 et p. 346. Depuis, nous avons pu vérifier pour la première fois l'existence de la première rédaction dans quelques mss., notamment les mss. de la Vaticane, lat. 2509, Urb. 178 et (partiellement) Borgh. 264; monastère d'Admont (Styrie), ms. 22. Nous devons nous borner pour le moment à ces indications, sans en fournir les preuves. — Parmi les summistes, Damase (1215 environ) passe sous silence le titre *De veneratione sanctorum*; pour Ambrosius, cf. *infra*, p. 207, n. 1.

204

IVᵉ concile du Latran (dont nous aurons encore à nous occuper) sur la vénération des saints (1) : c'était donc plutôt le concile général que la décrétale d'Alexandre III qui l'avait déterminé à se prononcer sur la réserve. Et le premier à tirer directement de la décrétale l'axiome que personne ne doit être vénéré comme saint *nisi canonizetur ab ecclesia romana* fut le maître Paul de Hongrie (avant 1221) (2), suivi après 1222 dans cette attitude par son ancien collègue bolonais, désormais confrère dominicain, saint Raymond de Peñafort, le futur compilateur des décrétales grégoriennes (3).

VIII

Cette esquisse historique de la réception du fragment *Audivimus* confirme notre thèse : ce n'est pas Alexandre III qui a pu formuler la réserve générale du droit de canonisation; sinon la décrétale découpée dans sa lettre au roi de Suède aurait eu un écho plus prompt dans les milieux canonistes. Et nous allons trouver un dernier appui du résultat de nos recherches dans l'attitude des papes eux-mêmes à cet égard. Nous avons déjà souligné que le silence sur les droits du Saint-Siège, observé par Alexandre III dans la cause de saint Thomas Becket, s'accorderait mal avec une réserve for-

---

(1) Tancrède, deuxième rédaction, gl. ad v. *venerari* : *Nullus debet publice uenerari corpora sanctorum uel reliquias de nouo inuentas, nisi prius fuerint per romanum pontificem approbate, ut in constit. innoc. iii. Cum ex eo* (Conc. Lat., c. 62). Quant à la manière d'alléguer les constitutions conciliaires de 1215 par les mots *constitutio Innocentii*, voir notre *Repertorium*, pp. 358, 461.

(2) Sur Paul de Hongrie et ses *Notabilia*, cf. *Repertorium*, pp. 411-413. — Texte dans notre Appendice, nᵒ 4.

(3) Saint Raymond, *Summa de casibus*, I, 12, § 2 (ed. Romae, 1603, p. 108), où il a incorporé dans son texte le c. 1 *de cons.*, D. 3 (*supra*, p. 202, n. 4), et le commente en relevant que l'évêque *non posset per se aliquem sanctum canonizare, ext. de relig. et vener. sanct. c. i.* — Cf. Appendice, nᵒ 3. — Pour la date de la *Summa*, cf. *Repertorium*, pp. 443-445.

mulée par le même Pape. Et nous ne trouvons aucune allusion à une telle réserve chez ses premiers successeurs, parmi lesquels certainement Clément III (1187-1191) a prononcé trois canonisations et Célestin III (1191-1198) cinq (1). Si déjà de leur temps le Saint-Siège avait revendiqué cette réserve, auraient-ils manqué de s'y référer, l'un lors de la canonisation de saint Étienne de Tiers, et l'autre lors de celle de saint Gérard de Sauve-majeure, qui étaient toutes deux des canonisations venant après une translation particulière déjà effectuée (2)?

Il est très instructif d'étudier le formulaire dont Clément III se servit pour deux de ses trois canonisations, celle de saint Étienne de Tiers et celle de saint Malachie d'Irlande, d'ailleurs le premier exemple d'un formulaire composé pour des sentences dans les causes des saints. Le Pape s'y prononce sur la juridiction et le magistère du Saint-Siège sur quatre chefs : le règlement des actions des croyants, la correction des erreurs, le conseil dans les questions douteuses, l'inviolabilité de ses décisions. Et le Pape ajoute les raisons préventives pour lesquelles Notre-Seigneur a revêtu l'Église

---

(1) 1189, Clément III pour saint Étienne de Tiers : JL. 16395, Fontanini, n. 22 ; cf. *supra*, p. 187. — 1189 pour saint Othon de Bamberg : JL. 16411-12, Fontanini, n. 20-21 ; cf. *supra*, p. 183, n. 3. — 1190 pour saint Malachie d'Irlande : JL. 16514, Fontanini, p. 642 (n. 23 *bis*). — 1191. Célestin III pour saint Pierre de Tarantaise : JL. 16690, Hinschius, IV, p. 245, n. 2. — 1192 pour saint Ubald de Gubbio : JL. 16830, Fontanini, n. 23. — 1193 pour saint Bernward de Hildesheim : JL. 16943, Fontanini, n. 24 ; cf. *supra*, p. 177. — 1193 pour saint Jean Gualbert : JL. 17035-37, 17107, Fontanini, n. 25-26. — 1197 pour saint Gérard de Sauve-majeure : JL. 17527, Fontanini, n. 27 ; cf. *supra*, p. 187. — A ces canonisations on peut en ajouter une autre : 1183 (?), Lucius III pour saint Bruno de Segni (cf. Bened., 1, 9, 5 ; JL. après n. 14912), moins certaine faute d'un document authentique ; pour les contradictions dans les sources secondaires, cf. le bollandiste Du Sollier, *ASS.*, *Jul. 18*, IV, pp. 475 et suiv. ; Kehr, *Italia pontificia*, II, p. 132, n. 5. — Quant à la prétendue canonisation de saint Ladislas de Hongrie par Célestin III, cf. *supra*, p. 182, n. 3.

(2) Cf. *supra*, p. 187.

de Rome de cette primauté : s'il y avait une licence indistincte pour chacun d'agir à son gré, cette liberté confuse, déterminée par l'individualisme, finirait souvent par supprimer le bien et par exalter les actions moins dignes sans juste mesure et de manière à scandaliser autrui (1). Après quoi, le Pape déclare avoir, sur les instances de tel et tel et après examen des faits, inscrit au catalogue des saints tel et tel serviteur de Dieu.

Ce formulaire commence donc par une définition raisonnée de la primauté de Pierre, et qui impliquerait peut-être, en ce qu'elle affirme la suprématie doctrinale du Pape et rejette la liberté confuse individuelle qui *minus digna laudibus celebraret*, en quelque sorte aussi la prérogative pour la canonisation. Nous disons : en quelque sorte ; car la formule implique ce droit sans le nommer et seulement d'une manière très vague, très voilée ; à la vérité, la formule pourrait servir d'introduction aussi bien à toute autre espèce de sentence papale. Est-ce que Clément III aurait parlé de cette manière indistincte de la primauté de l'Église de Rome si un de ses prédécesseurs avait déjà déclaré en termes exprès que la canonisation est réservée au Souverain Pontife, à l'exclusion de toute procédure particulière ? Nous ne le croyons pas, et surtout nous estimons inadmissible que dans ce cas Clément III aurait rédigé sa formule, comme il l'a fait, précisément à propos de la canonisation de saint Étienne de Tiers, qui avait été précédée d'une procédure particulière.

Mais la réserve papale était désormais préparée par ce formulaire de Clément III, venant s'ajouter aux précédents historiques dont nous avons parlé plus haut. Un dernier acte préparatoire fut accompli par le deuxième successeur de Clément, le grand Innocent III

(1) JL. 16395, 16514. Le texte latin se trouve dans l'Appendice, n° 5.

VI

(1198-1216). C'est à lui que revient le mérite d'avoir fixé
trois points importants en matière de vénération des
saints : en 1199 il a déterminé beaucoup plus distinc-
tement qu'aucun de ses prédécesseurs l'indispensa-
bilité des conditions d'ordre matériel pour la canonisation : les vertus et les miracles (1); il a défini le
premier, en 1200, la notion de la canonisation universelle et le juge compétent pour la déclarer; il a réglé
enfin, dans le concile du Latran (1215), le régime des
reliques. Nous avons à nous occuper ici avant tout de
la deuxième de ces manifestations. Dans sa bulle de
canonisation de l'impératrice Cunégonde (✝ 1039)
promulguée le 3 avril 1200, Innocent III exprima, en
parlant des prélats qui avaient sollicité la canonisation,
les considérations fondamentales et précises qui suivent (2) :

« Ils nous ont humblement suppliés, Nous et Nos frères
(les cardinaux), en vertu de la plénitude des pouvoirs
que Jésus-Christ a concédée à saint Pierre, de daigner
inscrire ladite impératrice au catalogue des saints,
et de décréter que sa mémoire parmi les saints soit
célébrée désormais par tous les croyants, parce que
ce jugement sublime appartient à celui-là seul qui
est le successeur de saint Pierre et le vicaire de Jésus-

(1) Canonisation de saint Homebone : Po. 573; Fontanini, n. 28. — Cette
formule sur les vertus et les miracles a eu sa petite histoire littéraire à
elle : Innocent III la modifia légèrement lors de la canonisation de sainte
Cunégonde en 1200 (Po. 1000; Fontanini, n. 29) et se servit de cette deuxième
formule encore une fois pour saint Wulstan en 1203 (Po. 1900; Fontanini,
n. 30). En 1208, le canoniste Bernard de Compostelle (cf. sur lui notre *Repertorium*, pp. 317-319) détacha la formule de la bulle Po. 1000 pour l'insérer
comme décrétale dans sa *Collectio Romana* sous le titre *De canonizatione
sanctorum* (III, 30, un.). Et enfin le décrétaliste Ambrosius (cf. sur lui
Repertorium, pp. 392-393) la reproduisit en grande partie dans le titre *De
sanctorum reliquiis uenerandis* de sa *Summa super titulis decretalium*, en se référant à la collection de Bernard : *ut extra. In. eod. tit.
c. uno in compil. ber.* — Nous donnerons tous ces textes dans l'Appendice, n° 6.

(2) Po. 1000; Fontanini, n. 29. — Texte latin dans l'Appendice, n° 7.

C hrist (*cum hoc sublime iudicium ad eum tantum pertineat qui est beati Petri successor et vicarius Jesu Christi)...* ».

C'est là en termes précis la première définition de la canonisation universelle qui a été donnée. Définition des éléments constitutifs : la sentence rendue *ex plenitudine potestatis* et l'ordre formel que le culte du nouveau saint soit observé *ab universis fidelibus*. Définition du seul juge compétent : le vicaire du Christ. Mais qu'on y prenne bien garde, les paroles d'Innocent III contiennent une définition et non pas une réserve papale. Il ne parle que de la canonisation universelle (1), et en proclamant qu'elle relève de la compétence exclusive du Pape il ne fait qu'énoncer un axiome d'ordre logique, parce qu'il est dans la nature d'un acte de juridiction universelle qu'aucun juge particulier n'est qualifié pour l'accomplir (2). Pour faire valoir cette prérogative naturelle, il était superflu de se la réserver; mais il était important d'en donner une fois la définition.

IX

C'est donc à un autre moment encore qu'il faut placer la création de la réserve papale, c'est-à-dire l'abolition des canonisations particulières autonomes, jusque-là légitimes. Pratiquement la question était résolue, nous paraît-il, en novembre 1215 par Innocent III lors du IVᵉ concile général du Latran. Le concile ne s'est pas

---

(1) C'est donc à tort qu'Ortolan, dans *Dict. théol. cath.*, II, col. 1634, compte cette bulle parmi les documents pontificaux renouvelant et confirmant la défense de la décrétale *Audivimus*.

(2) Cf. déjà le commentaire d'Innocent IV (vers 1251) au c. *Audivimus* (éd. Venet. 1578, fol. 188) : *Solus autem papa potest sanctos canonizare, quod ex eo apparet, quia cum constituatur omnibus fidelibus adorandus et nullus omnibus presit nisi papa...* Voir aussi *supra*, p. 182, n. 4.

occupé du droit de canonisation, mais il eut à se prononcer en matière de vénération des reliques où certains
abus s'étaient introduits. Or, parmi les résolutions du
concile à cet égard, il se trouve celle-ci : *Inventas autem*
(*sc. reliquias sanctorum*) *de novo nemo publice venerari praesumat, nisi prius auctoritate Romani pontificis fuerint approbate* (1) ; cette interdiction, qui,
prise à la lettre, ne visait que la vénération non auto-
risée des reliques des saints, devait s'appliquer à plus
forte raison aux reliques des serviteurs de Dieu non
canonisés et, par conséquent, aux translations épiscopales. En effet, c'est dans ce sens que le canon fut interprété par les glossateurs (2). Mais ce n'était là toujours

(1) *Conc. Lat. IV* : c. 62 *Cum ex eo* = *Comp. IV* : III, 17, 2 = X :
III, 45, 2.

(2) Nous ne trouvons pas encore d'annotations à cette partie du c. *Cum
ex eo* chez les trois principaux glossateurs des constitutions du concile :
Vincent d'Espagne, Damase et Jean le Teutonique (cf. sur eux *Repertorium*,
pp. 369-371. Pour Vincent, ajouter encore les ff. 255-268 du ms. 706 de Rouen,
confondus dans *Repertorium*, pp. 374, 378, avec la *Comp. IV*, ff. 269-297.
Damase et Jean ont en effet glosé sur les constitutions du Latran : quant au
premier, l'examen du ms. S. Croce III sin. 6 de la Laurenziana a confirmé
notre pressentiment exprimé dans le *Repertorium*; pour ce qui est du
second, nous pensons pouvoir démontrer dans un autre travail le bien-fondé
de notre thèse, récemment contestée par Mgr Gillmann dans *Archiv für
kath. Kirchenrecht*, 117 [1937], pp. 453-466). — Mais outre la glose de Tancrède au c. *Audivimus* (*supra*, p. 204, n. 1), on peut citer l'allégation
extra. iiii. de emunitate eccles. Cum ex eo, écrite dans le ms. Vatic.
lat. 1367 du Décret de la main *b* en marge de la *Glos. ord.* au c. 1 *de cons.*
D. 3 (cf. Appendice, n° 3), et la glose de Bernard de Botone, *Glossa ordinaria* au c. *Cum ex eo* dans les décrétales grégoriennes (III, 45, 2), v.
auctoritate : ut supra eod. c. prox. (III, 45, 1), *receptis testibus super
vita et miraculis illius, supra de testib. c. Venerabili* (II, 20, 52). Le
glossateur ne pense donc pas à une simple approbation des reliques, mais à
« l'approbation » du saint même, réservée au Pape (allégation de la décrétale *Audivimus*), et à une procédure régulière de canonisation (allégation
de la décrétale *Venerabili* de Honorius III; cf. p. 174, n. 4). Voir aussi
les commentaires de Bernard de Montmirat (Abbas antiquus), du Hostiensis,
etc., au titre *De reliq.* Depuis le concile de Trente, cette application du
c. *Cum ex eo* aux non-canonisés est devenue la seule possible ; cf. Hinschius, IV, p. 266, n. 1 ; Wernz, III, n. 384.

qu' une conséquence implicite, ce n'était pas encore une
ré serve formelle du droit de canonisation.

Cette réserve formelle, c'est l'histoire de la réception
de la décrétale *Audivimus* qui nous révèle où il faut la
trouver. Nous croyons avoir démontré qu'Alexandre III
dans sa lettre au roi de Suède, d'où cette décrétale a été
détachée plus tard, n'avait pas encore eu l'intention de
formuler une loi générale à l'égard des canonisations
particulières à supprimer. Mais l'école canoniste du
xiii⁰ siècle a attribué à ce fragment détaché ce sens de
réserve en l'accueillant dans les collections de décrétales
en usage à Bologne : d'abord en 1206 dans la collection
de l'Anglais Alain, et de là dans la *Compilatio II* (1210).
Toutefois, cette réception de la décrétale ne pouvait sup-
pléer à une intention qui avait manqué à son auteur ; car
la *Compilatio II*, bien que reconnue par l'école, n'en
restait pas moins une collection privée, qui ne pouvait
rien ajouter à l'effet légal immanent de par leur origine
aux documents qui y étaient insérés. Par conséquent,
la décrétale *Audivimus*, bien que loi dans l'opinion de
l'école, n'était en réalité à cette époque qu'un *argument
canoniste* en faveur d'une réserve papale, et non pas une
loi canonique générale. Quand un chroniqueur de la fin
du xiii⁰ siècle, qui nous décrit la *translatio* de saint
Pierre de Trévi faite par l'évêque d'Anagni encore en
octobre 1215, nous dit que l'évêque avait canonisé *ante
tempus concilii domini Innocentii* le corps de ce saint,
prout poterat, cette manière de s'exprimer correspond
exactement à la situation canonique d'alors; peut-être
plus que le chroniqueur ne le savait lui-même (1).

---

(1) *ASS., Aug. 30*, VI, p. 645 : en 1260 le cardinal Hugues de Saint-Cher,
qui se trouvait à Anagni avec Alexandre IV, fit ses dévotions aux reliques
de ce saint Pierre, les porta en procession solennelle, etc., *scito quod
bo. mem. episcopus Anagn. loci dioecesanus cum aliis episcopis
Campanis ante tempus concilii dni. Innocentii papae III prout
poterat ipsius corpus B. Petri sollempniter canonizasset.* Nous

Pour transformer la décrétale *Audivimus* d'un simple argument canoniste en une véritable loi canonique, il fallait un acte législatif. Cet acte ne fut accompli que par la réception de notre pièce dans le titre *De reliquiis et veneratione sanctorum* des décrétales de Grégoire IX en 1234. Puisqu'il s'agissait là d'une collection officielle dont la promulgation garantissait à toutes les décrétales qui y étaient recueillies, et à l'exclusion de toutes les autres, le caractère de lois universelles, la volonté du législateur Grégoire IX suppléait désormais dans la décrétale *Audivimus* à l'intention législative qui avait fait défaut chez son auteur Alexandre III. A partir de ce moment, les mots *cum non liceret vobis ipsum pro sancto absque auctoritate Romanae ecclesiae venerari* ne sont plus la décision d'un cas spécial survenu dans un pays lointain, mais une règle générale qui lie l'Église universelle (1).

En conclusion : la réserve pour le Saint-Siège du droit exclusif de canonisation est le produit d'un processus historique assez compliqué et dont les étapes principales dans l'ordre chronologique sont, *primo* : le formulaire de Clément III, qui souligne la primauté générale de l'Église romaine en présence de velléités particularistes ;

n'oserions pas affirmer que le chroniqueur, avec les mots *ante tempus*, etc , ait voulu donner plus qu'une indication chronologique ; autrement, il aurait probablement dit *prout poterat ante tempus*, etc. — Hertling, p. 185, n. 68, donne à ce récit une interprétation insoutenable en déclarant : *Certo il vescovo di Anagni... aveva ritenuto che egli fosse competente di fare... almeno una traslazione col permesso del culto. Dopo il Concilio del Laterano (1215) questa sua opinione non gli parve più ammissibile.* Evidemment Hertling voit dans le subjonctif *canonizasset* une proposition irréelle elliptique qu'il veut compléter. Mais le subjonctif dans cette période n'est que la conséquence grammaticalement correcte du discours *scito quod.* — L'hypothèse du bollandiste J. Pien, *ASS., loc. cit.,* p. 646, note *s*, qu'Innocent III aurait autorisé l'évêque à cette canonisation, est dénuée de fondement.

(1) Pour les cas d'infraction à cette loi, qui se produisent jusqu'aux temps d'Urbain VIII (constitution *Coelestis Hierusalem*, 5 juillet 1634), cf. Bened., 1, 10, 8 ; Hinschius, IV, p. 247, n. 3.

secondo : les nouvelles canonisations faites par Clément III et Célestin III dans les causes déjà terminées par une translation épiscopale; *tertio* : la définition de la canonisation universelle par Innocent III ; *quarto* : la réception de la décrétale *Audivimus* par l'école bolonaise; *quinto* : la constitution d'Innocent III, lors du concile du Latran, sur les reliques nouvelles ; et enfin l'insertion de la décrétale *Audivimus* dans la collection officielle de Grégoire IX.

Ainsi donc, à notre avis, contrairement à ce qu'on a enseigné jusqu'à présent, ce n'est pas Alexandre III, ce n'est que son huitième successeur, Grégoire IX, qui a expressément réservé au Saint-Siège le droit exclusif de canonisation.

APPENDICE

Avant de reproduire les documents réunis dans cet Appendice, je tiens à remercier MM. Émile A. Van Moé, Walther Holtzmann et Rolf Most, qui ont eu la grande obligeance de me communiquer les textes de plusieurs manuscrits que je ne pouvais pas consulter moi-même : *Paris,* Bibl. nat., 3932, 15398, 15994; *London*, Brit. Mus., Cotton Claud. A. IV, Cotton Vitell. E. XIII; *Fulda*, Landesbibl. D. 14; *Leipzig*, Univ. 986.

Dans la reproduction des textes, j'ai marqué les passages qu'un auteur a empruntés littéralement à un autre texte par des caractères plus petits.

1.

Cap. Audivimus collatum cum Alexandri III epistula originali.

Alexander III, epistula ad Kanutum regem Suecorum (*JL. 13546, ed. Joh. Gust. Liljegren, Diplomatarium Suecanum I, Holmiae 1829 p. 61-63*).

Collectio decretalium Cottoniana I : c. 212 (*Cod. Londin.
Musaei Britannici Cotton Claud. A. IV, fol. 215*ᵛ [= *Cl*]).
Coll. Cottoniana II : V, 32 (*Cod. Londin. Mus. Brit. Cotton
Vitell. E. XIII, fol. 258*ʳ [= *Cv*]).
Coll. Sangermanensis VII, 147 (*descripsit, inscriptionem,
init. et fin. ed. H. Singer, Neue Beiträge über die Dekre-
talensammlungen..., in Sitzungsberichte der Kais.
Akad. der Wiss. in Wien 171 I* [*1913*] *p. 311* [= *S*]).
Coll. Abrincensis VII, 15, 2 (*descr. et rubricam ed. H. Singer,
op. cit. p. 385* [= *Abr*]).
Coll. Bodleiana VI, 9, 2 (*Cod. Oxon. Bibl. Bodleianae
Tanner 8, pag. 690, col. 688* [= *B*]).
Coll. Alani VI, 3, 2 (*Cod. Fuldensis D. 14, fol. 99*ʳ [= *Af*]).
Compilatio secunda V, 21, un. (*Codd. Vatic. lat. 2509,
fol. 139*ʳ [= *II v₁*], *lat. 1377, fol. 144*ᵛ*-145*ʳ [= *II v₂*],
*Borgh. 264, fol. 106*ᵛ [= *IIb*], *Chis. E. VII. 207, fol. 134*ʳ
[= *II c*], *Urb. 178, fol. 116*ᵛ [= *IIu*], *Parisien. Bibl.
nat. 3932, fol. 102*ᵛ [= *IIp*]).
Decretales Gregorii IX : III, 45, 1 (*ed. Friedberg, Corp. iur.
can. II, Lipsiae 1881 col. 650* [= *F*]).

(Ex epistula originali)   (Ex decretalibus Gregorii IX)

De . reliquiis et ueneratione
sanctorum.

Alexander episcopus seruus   Alexander III.
seruorum Dei karissimo in
Christo filio K. illustri sweo- 5
rum et gothorum regi et ue-
nerabilibus fratribus episcopis et dilectis filiis, nobili uiro
duci, uniuerso clero et populo
per Gothiam constitutis salu- 10
tem et apostolicam benedic-
tionem. Eterna et incommutabilis...

Denique quiddam audiui-   Audiuimus, quod magno nobis fuit 15 mus,
horrori, quod quidam inter   quod quidam inter

uos sunt, qui dyabolica fraude
decepti hominem quendam in
potatione et ebrietate occisum
quasi sanctum more infide- 20
lium uenerantur, cum uix
etiam pro talibus in suis ebrietatibus interemptis orare permittat ecclesia. dicit enim
apostolus, quoniam 'ebriosi 25
regnumDei non possidebunt[a]'.
unde a potationibus et ebrietatibus, si regnum Dei habere
desideratis, uos continere
oportet, et hominem illum de 30
cetero colere in periculum
animarum uestrarum nulla-
tenus presumatis, cum etiam
si signa et miracula per eum
plurima fierent, non liceret 35
uobis   pro sancto
absque auctoritate romane
ecclesie eum publice uenerari.

uos   diabolica fraude
decepti hominem quendam in
potatione et ebrietate occisum
quasi sanctum more infidelium uenerantur, cum uix
pro talibus in   ebrietatibus peremptis ecclesia permittat orare.   dicit enim
apostolus :   'ebriosi
regnum Dei non possidebunt'.

illum
ergo non presumatis
de
cetero colere, cum etiam
si   per eum miracula
fierent, non liceret
uobis ipsum pro sancto
absque auctoritate romane
ecclesie   uenerari.

[a] cf. I. Cor. 6, 10.

1-2 Non est pro sancto colendus per quem in ebrietate occisum fiunt miracula Cl, absque
rubrica CvS, Quod necessaria sit
auctoritas romani pontificis ad hoc quod aliquis pro sancto habeatur
Abr B (ante cap. praeced.), An in omnibus apostolorum uigiliis
sit ieiunandum Af (ante c. praeced.), De ueneratione sanctorum II.
-- **3** Idem regi francorum (!) et clero et populo. ccxii. Cl, Idem
S Abr BIIv,u. — **14** Audiuimus] Uidimus IIc. — **17** uos] sunt qui add.
Cl B IIvu (= orig.), sint qui add. Af IIpc F, sunt add. IIb. —
18 quendam om. Cv. — **20** sanctum more] secundum morem IIv,,
sanctum morte (!) IIc. — **21** cum uix] cum uix etiam Cv (= orig.),
cum etiam uix Cl, cum uix et B. — **22** pro talibus transp. post in
ebr. IIb. — in ebrietatibus] in suis ebrietatibus Cl B (= orig.),
in sua ebrietate Cv, in ebrietate IIvbu, codd. Friedbergiani
(= Corp. iur.can. II col. LXIX) Bbh. — **23** peremptis] perceptis Cl.
— **23-24** ecclesia permittat orare] orare permittat (permittit BIIv,u)

ecclesia *Cv BAfII* (= *orig.*), perm. or. eccl. *Cl.* — **25** ebriosi] quoniam ebriosi *Cl Cv B* (= *orig.*), quod ebriosi homines *AfII.* — **30-33** illum - - colere] hominem ergo (igitur *Cl*) illum (*om. Cv*) de cetero colere (col. de cet. *IIv₁u*) non presumatis *Cl Cv BAfII* (*cf. ordinem orig.*; *male supplevit F*). — **33-35** etiam si- - fierent] etiam si signa (etiam insignia *B!*) et miracula per eum plurima fierent *Cl Cv B* (= *orig.*); *Cv legitur usque ad* signa, *duae lin. seqq. deletae per scissuram.* etiam si per (super *IIpu!*) eum miracula plurima fierent *IIv₂b*, ...mir. fi. plur. *AfIIpc*, ...multa fi. mir. *IIv₁u.* — **35** liceret] licet *Cl BIIv₂b.* — **36** ipsum *om. Cl Cv*(?) *BAfII* (= *orig.*). — pro sancto] profecto *Cl, om. IIp*, pro < sancto eum > p (= publice?) *Cv?* — **37** absque] sine *IIp.* — **38** ecclesie] eum publice *add. Cl S Abr BAfll* (= *orig., male supplevit F*).

2.

Ad c. 37 de cons. D. 1 commenta.

Rufinus, Summa (*ed. Singer, Paderborn 1902 p. 546; collat. Cod. Vatic. lat. 2585, fol. 111ʳᵇ*).

Corpora : Ne uero aliquis sanctorum loca sua auctoritate mutare presumeret, subiungit corpora sanctorum, in quorum translatione solent mutari ecclesie, a nullo transferenda sine episcoporum consilio. principis : hoc localiter est intelli-
5 gendum. uel : pro ' idest ' episcoporum.

> 5 idest] et *Singer ex nimium arbitraria coniectura contra codicum consensum.*

Johannes Faventinus, Summa (*Cod. Vatic. Borgh. 162, fol. 91ʳᵃ*).

Corpora: Ne uero - - presumeret mutare - - consilio episcoporum. principis : hoc localiter est intelligendum, aut accipiatur uel : pro ' idest ' episcoporum.

Glossae anonymae (*Codd. Vatic. lat. 2494, fol. 281ᵛᵃ et lat. 2495, fol. 212ʳᵃ*).

< Corpora: > B. iii. Notandum ᵃ. C. de relig. et sumpt. funerum ᵇ. < principis: > idest romani pontificis, uel imperatoris.

ᵃ*Burch. III, 91*   ᵇ*Cod. 3, 44.*

216

(*Cod. Romanus Bibl. Angelicae 1270, fol. 281*[va-b]).

Quomodo[a] : Cuius auctoritate ecclesie sint mutande. principis : idest romani pontificis, uel imperatoris, et tunc localiter intelligitur, B'. l. iii. Notandum[b].

> 2 idest - - imperatoris] *cf. Glos. codd. Vat.* — 3 localiter intelligitur] *cf. Rufinum.*
> [a]*Rubrica capituli; de diversis lectionibus cf. Friedberg, Corp. iur. can. I col. 1303 n. 382* [b]*Burch. III, 91.*

Sicardus, Summa (*Cod. Vatic. Pal. 653, fol. 108*[rb]).

De altaris erectione : ...§ Nota quoque, quod nec ecclesie nec reliquie sunt de loco ad locum mutande sine causa et episcoporum licentia, ut Tribus[a] et Corpora[b].

> [a]*de cons. D. 1 c. 36* [b]*c. 37.*

Summa anonyma ' Omnis qui iuste ' (*Cod. Lipsiensis Univ. 986, fol. 273*[rb]).

Corpora : Ne aliquis loca sanctorum sua presumeret auctoritate mutare, subiungit corpora sanctorum, in quorum translatione solent ecclesie mutari, a nullo transferenda esse sine consensu episcoporum. transferre : nec distrahere nec mercari, ut C. de sacrosanctis eccl. 5 l. Nemo[a]. principis : idest romani pontificis. si autem uis intelligere de principe seculari, tunc dicetur huic cap. derogatum, licet quidam dicant : sine concilio principis secularis non debet fieri, quod hic dicitur.

> 1-3 Ne aliquis - - episcoporum] *cf. Ruf. et Joh. Favent.* —
> 5 idest rom. pont.] *cf. Glossas anonymas.*
> [a]*Cod. 1, 2, 3.*

Summa anonyma' Tractaturus magister '(*Cod. Parisien. Bibl. nat. 15994, fol. 87*[vb]).

Corpora. sine consilio principis : in quem populus totum ius suum transfudit, cum hec sint comunia tam cleri quam populi secundum quosdam. uel potius locale est et forte temporale. uel : pro ' et '.

> 3 locale] *cf. Ruf.* — 4 uel : pro et] *cf. coniecturam Singer in Ruf. lin. 5.*

Huguccio, Summa (*Codd. Vatic. lat. 2280, fol. 331*[ra] [=*V*] *et Borgh. 272, fol. 187*[vb] [= *B*]).

Corpora: Ne forte quis ecclesias sua auctoritate presumeret mutare, quia dictum est illas quandoque esse mutandas. ideo subiungit corpora sanctorum — intelligit mutationem ecclesiarum — a nullo esse transferenda sine consensu pape uel episcoporum. unde
5 hec notula hic habetur : 'cuius auctoritate ecclesie sint mutande, in c. ostendit'. Corpora : canonizata et alicui ecclesie deputata. non dicit quod reliquie alique non possunt concedi sine consensu pape uel episcopi ; set si corpus alicuius sancti iacet in aliqua ecclesia canonizatum, non debet inde ferri ad alium
10 locum sine consensu talis persone. per quod intelligitur mutationem ecclesiarum non esse faciendam sine consensu pape uel episcopi, quia in mutatione ecclesiarum corpora solent transferri. in mutatione episcopalis ecclesie et illarum, que subsunt pape nullo medio, exigitur consensus pape ; in muta-
15 tione cuiuslibet alterius exigitur consensus episcopi. principis : idest romani pontificis. si uero dicatur principis, idest regis uel imperatoris, localiter intelligitur, sc. ubi non posset hoc esse sine scandalo, si fieret sine consilio principis, et specialiter de ecclesiis quarum est patronus. sinodi : sinodum
20 appellat collegium clericorum matricis, idest episcopalis ecclesie, ut. xii. q. ii. Placuit ut[a]. Episcopus qui[b]. et talia non debet episcopus facere sine consensu illorum, ut.xii.q. ii. Sine exceptione[c]. et nota quod in mutatione ecclesie, si fieri potest, prima non destruatur, set remaneat ibi presbiter prop-
25 ter diuina officia ibi celebranda, ut. xvi. q.ult. Si quis uult[d].

1-4 Ne forte quis - - episcoporum] cf. Ruf., Joh. et. Sum. ' Omnis qui iuste'. —   1 ecclesia V. — auctoritate sua B. — 2 est om. B. —   5 nota B. —   cuius auctoritate rell.] cf. Glos. Cod. Angel. —   sint mutande om. B. — 9 canonicatum B. —   10 quod om. V. —   12 quia in mutatione rell.] cf. Ruf. etc. quorum verba invertitur Hug. — 16-19 idest romani - - patronus] idest regis - - patronus, vel principis, idest romani pontificis B, ordine interpretationum converso. — 16-17 idest romani - - intelligitur] cf. Glos. Cod. Angel. —
[a]c. 51   [b]c. 58   [c]c. 52   [d]q. 7 c. 41.

Benencasa, Casus decretorum (Cod. Romanus Bibl. Casanatensis 1910, fol. 165[va] [= C] collat. cum glossa Cod. Vatic. Ross. 595, fol. 284[ra] [= R]).

218

Corpora. principis : idest pape, sine cuius licentia corpora sanctorum non leuantur de sepultura; set ex quo sunt leuata, possint transferri ex causa. secundum legem humanam corpora condam perpetue sepulture tradita sine iussu 5 principis non debent transferri, ut C. de relig. l. ult[a]., ff. de sepulcro viol. l. iii. § < non > perpetue[b]. ex iusta tamen causa transferri possunt de licentia rectoris, ut C. eod. l. i .

> **2** set] si *C.* — **3** transferri possunt *R.* — **4** condam]
> $\overline{9}$ *scr. C; om. R.* — sine] sint *R*, sunt *C.* — **5** relig.]
> leg. *C. — Allegatur hic tit. Cod. iam in glossa anon.
> Codd. Vat. 2494 et 2495. —* **6** sepulcro] sepulturis *C.*
> *— non om. C R, correxi ex Dig. —* tamen *om. C. —*
> **7** transferre *R.* — l. i.] l. ult. *C.*
> [a]*Cod. 3, 44, 14 (paenult., sed l. 15 graeca est)* [b]*Dig. 47,
> 12, 3, 4* [c]*Cod. 3, 44, 1.*

Apparatus glossarum anonymus ' Ecce vicit leo ' (*Cod. monast. S. Floriani XI. 605, fol. 119*[rb]).

Tribus ex causis[a] : Ecce quod propter has causas. < Corpora. sine consilio : > Et hoc intellige de consensu episcopi. arg. potest reputare aliquem sanctum et dicere esse sanctum. reliquie autem alique, et non corpus, possunt trans-5 ferri. similiter secundum leges non possunt reliquie transferri sine consensu principum, ut C. de religiosis[b].

> **2** *Uncis inclusa supplevi ex sensu obvio. —* **4** reliquie
> rell.] *cf. Huguccionem lin. 7-8. —* possunt] p[t] =
> potest *scr. —* **5** similiter *rell]* cf. Benencasam.
> [a]*c. 36* [b]*Cod. 3, 44.*

Laurentius in Glossa Palatina (*Codd. Vatic. Pal. 658, fol. 96*[vb] [== *P*] *et Reg. 977, fol. 277*[va] [= *R*]).	**Johannes Teutonicus,** Glossa ordinaria (*Codd. Vatic. Pal. 624, fol. 305*[va] [=*P*₄], *Pal. 625, fol. 224*[vb] [=*P*₂], *Vat. lat. 1367, fol. 293*[rb] [= *V*]).
Corpora sanctorum etc. : Cuius auctoritate ecclesie sint mutande, ostendit. sine consilio : ff. de relig. Ossa[a]. principis : idest pape. xviii.	Corpora. sine consilio : ff. de relig. Ossa[a]. 5 principis : idest pape. xviii.

q. ii. Diffiniuit[b]. et hoc uerum est, cum corpus traditum est iam perpetue sepulture, C. de relig. l. ult[c].; nisi necessitas immineat : tunc sufficit auctoritas presidis prouincie, C. t. eod. l. i[d]. si autem nondum est traditum perpetue, bene potest transferri sine auctoritate alicuius ad alium locum. C. eod. t. Si necdum[e]. dicit tamen h. hoc esse locale. — Quid dicemus de eo qui furatur reliquias? dicerem...

q. ii. Diffiniuit[b]. et hoc uerum est, cum corpus traditum est perpetue sepulture. C. de relig. l. ult[c].; nisi necessitas immineat; tunc sufficit auctoritas presidis prouincie, C. e. t. l. i[d]. si autem non est traditum perpetue, bene potest transferri sine auctoritate alicuius ad alium locum. C. e. t. Si necdum[e].

Hanc Glossam Laurentio esse attribuendam suadet Gúidonis de Baysio Rosarium, cum reproducit ad hoc cap. (ed. Venet. 1577, fol. 389ra) *quaestionem* Quid dicemus *rell.* (= lin. 18) *respondetque* ad hoc dicit Lauren. : dicerem... *et seqq. sicut in Glos. Pal.*

2 Cuius *rell*] *cf. Hug. et Glos. Cod. Angel. —* 5 idest pape] *cf. Benencasam. —* 7 cum corpus *rell.*] *cf. eundem. —* 9 nisi necessitas *rell.*] *cf. eund. —* 16 eod. t.] de relig. et sumpt. fun. *R.* — dicit tamen *rell.*] *cf. Hug. lin.* 17.

4 Ossa] Jo. *add.* P_1. — 6 et *om.* P_1. — 7 est$_2$ *om.* P_1. — 9 relig.] do < mibus? > *add.* P_2. — 10 sufficiat P_2. — 12 nondum P_1. — 13 perpetue] sepulture *add. manus recentiores* P_1 V. — 14 transferre V. — 16 necdum] Jo. *add.* P_1.

[a]*Dig.* 11, 7, 8 *pr.* [b]*c.* 21 Diffinimus? *Sed nec littera nec sensus huius cap. congruit allegationi. Forsan c.* 5 Quam sit necessarium, *ubi habentur verba* B. Petri apostolorum principis? [c]*Cod.* 3, 44, 14 [d]*ibid.,* 1 [e]*ibid.,* 10.

220

3.

Ad c. 1 de cons. D. 3 commenta.

Glossa anonyma (*Cod. Angel. fol. 291*[va]).

< episcopi in suis episcopiis > : di xi. Catholica[a] di. xii. Illa autem[b]. — arg. quod prouincialia decreta metropolitani, particularia episcopi possunt condere et leges et canones constituere et consuetudines inducere seruandas in 5 parochiis suis in subiectos suos consensu eorumdem, sine presentia pape uel eius legati.

    2 metropoli *scr.*   5 eorumde *scr.*
    [a]*c. 8*   [b]*c. 11.*

Huguccio, Summa (*Codd. V fol. 350*[va], *B fol. 202*[vb]).

episcopi in suis episcopiis : Arg. quod episcopi specialia et particularia decreta siue statuta possunt condere et consuetudines inducere seruandas in suis parochiis consensu subiectorum, sine presentia pape uel eius legati. arg. di. xi. Catholica[a] et di. xii. Illa[b] 5 et di. xvii. Multis[c]. set hoc inuenies distinctum supra plenius di. iii. § Porro[d].

    cf. Glos. cod. Angel. —   2 consuetudine *V.* —   5 supra
    om. B.
    [a]*c. 8*   [b]*c. 11*   [c]*c. 5*   [d]*p. c. 2.*

Apparatus ' Ecce vicit leo ' (*Cod. Flor. fol. 122*[ra]).

singuli episcopi in suis episcopiis : Hic ergo patet quod episcopi festa specialia et consuetudines in suis episcopatibus possunt indicere, immo etiam canones possunt facere particulares quoad suos subditos, arg. supra. xvii. di. per 5 totum, arg. xi. di. Catholica[a].

    cf. Hug. —   1 episcopiis] epistulis *scr.*   5 di.] de
    scr.
    [a]*c. 8.*

Laurentius in Glossa Palatina (*Codd. P fol. 100*[ra], *R fol. 285*[rb]).

Johannes Teutonicus, Glossa ordinaria (*Codd. P₁ fol. 316*[va], *P₂ fol. 231*[va], *V fol. 304*[ra]).

festiuitates : Set de quibus festiuitatibus hoc intelligis,

quia sancti aùt sunt canonizati aut non? b. intelligit de non canonizatis, quia dicit quod episcopus cum suis quantum ad suam diocesim potest sanctum canonizare. quod non credo, 5 set exaudio de canonizatis qui non habent uigilias.

> *Hanc Glossam Laurentio esse attribuendam suadet traditio illorum codd. Glossae ord. Bartholomaei Brixiensis, qui recensiti sunt in* ' *Repertorium der Kanonistik* ' *p. 116 sqq.* (*Laurentiustypus*). — **1** intelligis] intelligas P_1. — **2** b.] *significat Bazianum.* — non$_2$ *om.* $P_1 R$. — **4** diocesis P. — credo] *extra de reliq. et uener. sancto-rum c. i. in fine ins. edd. impressae, non autem codd. Bartholomaei Brixiensis redactionem praebentes.* — **5** uigi-lias]. Jo. *add.* P

Additio anonyma ad Johannis Glossam (*Cod. V, manus b* [*cf. Repertorium p. 53*]).

...quod non credo] extra. iiii. de emuni. eccl. Cum ex eo. Comp. IV : III, 17, 2 = Conc. Lat. IV c. 62.

S. Raymundus de Pennaforti, Summa de casibus (*ed. Romae* [*Tallini*] *1603, p. 108*).

De feriis et festis et diebus ieiuniorum (*I, 12*) ... § 2. Feriarum... non generaliter omnibus. Hoc autem intel-lige de Sanctis canonizatis auctoritate Ecclesiae Romanae; quia episcopus non posset per se aliquem sanctum canonizare, 5 ext. de reliq. et vener. sanct. c. iª.

> **2** omnibus] *Hucusque textum Raymundi pro maxima parte repetere verba c. 1 de cons. D. 3 adnotavit iam Guilelmus Redonensis in glossa (perperam Johanni Friburgensi attri-buta in ed.) ad Summam.* — **5** ext.] *Raymundum ab origine extra. ii. scripsisse non ambigas; cf. Repertorium p. 445.*
> ªX : III, 45, 1.

4.

Ad. c. Audivimus in Compilatione secunda (V, 21, un.) et in Decretalibus Gregorii IX (III, 45, 1) commenta.

Albertus, Apparatus Glossarum Comp. II (*Codd. Parisien. Bibl. nat. 3932, fol. 102* [= *P*], *15398, fol. 105*ʳᵃ [= *S*]).

222

Audivimus. cum uix : Quasi dicat : non in omni casu, quia non tunc orat pro eo, cum ebrietas fuit mortale peccatum in eo, utputa assidua, ut de con. di. v. Nullus[a]. xxv. di. § Alias[b]. xxxv. di. Episcopus[c]. secus si casualis, ut ead. di. § Alias,
5 uersu quotiens[d]. in ebrietatibus : cum nec demereri poterat, ut. xv. q. i. Sane[e], igitur nec mereri, ut hic et. xxii. q. iiii. Unusquisque[f]. apostolus : supra. xxxvii. di. in illa palea Uino inebriantur [g]. supra di. xxv. § Alias contra, uersu 'quotiens aliquis in cibo aut potu plus accipit ' etc.
10 miracula : i. q. i. Uides[h]. publice : ergo a sensu contrario secrete potest.

  2 mortale peccatum ebrietas fuit S. — **3-4** xxv. di. - - Episcopus] di. xxxv. Eps. xxv. di. § Alias S. — **5-7** cum nec - - unusquisque] *glos. om.* S. — **6** mereri ut] meruit *scr.?* **7.** xxxvii.] .xxxv. S. — **8** contra *om.* P. — **9** aut] et P. — **10** q. i.] que S.

 [a]*c. 35* [b]*p. c. 3, § 5* [c]*c. 1* [d]*D. 25 p. c. 3, § 7* [e]*c. 7* [f]*c. 8* [g] *c. 4, sed palea non est. Forsan intelligit paleam* Vinolentum *D. 35 c. 6; cf. lectionem.* xxxv. *cod.* S [h]*c. 65.*

Tancredus, Apparatus glossarum Comp. II *(Codd. primae recensionis : Vatic. lat. 2509, fol. 139*[rb] *[= V₁], Borgh. 264, fol. 106*[vb] *[= B], Urb. 178, fol. 116*[va·b] *[= U]; secundae recensionis : Vatic. lat. 1377, fol. 145*[ra] *[= V₂], Chis. E. VII. 207, fol. 134*[rb]*[= C]).*

Audiuimus. cum uix : Quasi dicat : non in omni casu, quia non tunc orat pro eo, cum ebrietas fuit mortale peccatum, utputa assidua, ut de con. di. v. Nullus[a]. xxv. di. § Alias ea demum[b]. xxxv. di. Episcopus[c], secus si ueniale, ut e. di. § Alias, uersu quotiens[d]. a. in ebrieta-
5 tibus : in ebrietate enim non potuit demereri, ut. xv. q. i. Sane. Si concupiscentiam[e], ita nec meritum augere, arg. hic et. xxii. q. iiii. Unusquisque[f]. a.   miracula : quoniam miracula sepe fiunt per malos, ut supra. i. q. i. Teneamus[g], ideo non est uenerandus pro sancto quisquis miracula facit. a. romane
10 ecclesie : eo quia quem ipsa reprobat, reprobandus est, et quem approbat, approbandus est, ut. xxiiii. q. i. Hec fides. Quoniam uetus[h], et q. ii. Sane profertur[i]. t. uenerari : nullus debet publice uenerari corpora sanctorum uel reliquias de nouo inuentas, nisi prius fuerint per romanum pontificem
15 approbate, ut in constit. innoc. iii. Cum ex eo[k]. t.

1 Quasi dicat *rell*] cf. *Albertum.* — **4** .a.] *siglum Alberti*
$V_{12}CU$, .tan. *B.* — **5** in ebrietate] in ebrietatibus V_2C.
Lectio ipsius decretalis habetur in ebrietate $V_{12}UB$. —
enim] est V_1. — **6** hic] contra V_2C. — **7** .a.] *siglum
Alberti* $V_{12}CU$, .ta'. *B.* — **9** .a.] *siglum Alani, ut
videtur (certe non Alberti)* V_2BC, .t. V_1, *sigl. om. U.,*
propter .t. *add. B.* — **12** .t.] *siglum Tancredi* $V_{12}BCU$.
— uenerari : nullus *rell.*] *glos. om.* V_1BU (= *codd.
primae recensionis*).
[a]*c. 35* [b]*p. c. 3, § 5* [c]*c. 1* [d]*D. 25 p. c. 3, § 7*
[e]*cc. 7, 8* [f]*c. 8* [g]*c. 56* [h]*cc. 14, 25* [i]*c. 6*
[k]*Conc. Lat. IV const. 62.*

Bernardus de Botone Parmensis, Glossa Ordinaria in Decretales Gregorii IX (*ed. Romae 1582, col. 1395*).

Audiuimus. cum uix : Quasi dicat - - quotiens. in ebrietatibus : In ebrietate - - unusquisque. miracula : quoniam - - miracula facit, nisi ab ecclesia Romana prius fuerit per testes legi-
timos approbatus, ut hic dicit et infra c. prox.[a] et supra de
5 testi. Venerabili[b], ubi testes super vita et miraculis reci-
piuntur : quia quem ipsa reprobat - - Sane profertur.

> Maior pars glossarum ex Tancredo, siglis suppressis, desumpta
> est; gl. ad v. miracula ex duabus contexta, quas dividit
> verbis propriis. — Omisimus lectiones differentes.
> [a]X : III, 45, 2 (= Conc. Lat. IV c. 62) [b]II, 20, 52(= Comp.
> V : II, 12, 5).

Paulus Ungarus, Notabilia ad Comp. secundam (*Cod.
Vatic. Borgh. 261, fol. 80*[rb]).

Audiuimus etc. : Nota quod interfecti in tabernis uel
mortui in ebrietatibus uix uel nunquam saluantur. item
non debet uenerari aliquis publice sanctus, nisi canonizetur
ab ecclesia romana.

Johannes Hispanus de Petesella, Summa super titulis decretalium Gregorii IX (*Cod. Vatic. lat. 2343, fol. 206*[ra]).

(*post rubricam* de baptismo *III, 42*) : Secuntur hic tres :
prima est de presbitero non babtizato[a], secunda de custodia
eucharistie, crismatis et aliorum sacramentorum[b], tertia de
reliquiis et ueneratione sanctorum[c], in quibus ipsa littera
pro summa sufficiat.
[a]*III, 43* [b]*III, 44* [c]*III, 45.*

224

Bernardus de Botone Parmensis, Summa super titulis decretalium Gregorii IX (*Cod. Roman. Bibl. Casanatensis 1094, fol. 51*^{vb}).

(*post rubricam* de presbit. non bapt. *III, 43*) : In duobus tit. sequentibus littera sit pro summa, scil. de custodia eucar^a. et de reliq. sanctorum^b.

^a*III, 44*   ^b*III, 45.*

5.

Clemens III, Arenga decretorum canonizationis pro S. Stephano Grandimontensi (*JL. 16395; ed. I. Bollandus, ASS. febr. 8, II p. 204* [= S_1], *E. Martène, Veterum scriptorum ...amplissima Collectio VI col. 119* [= S_2], *col. 1092* [= S_3]) et S. Malachia Hibernensi (*JL. 16514 ; ed. Mabillon, Sancti Bernardi abbatis primi Claraevallensis vol. I, Par. 1719 col. 697 ' ex ms. Cistercii '* [= *M*]).

Ideo sacrosanctam Romanam ecclesiam Redemptor noster caput omnium esse uoluit et magistram, ut ad eius dispositionem et nutum, diuina gratia praeeunte, quae ubicumque a fidelibus gerenda sunt, ordinentur et errata in melius corri-
5 gantur, et ad eius consilium in ambiguis recurratur, et quod ipsa statuerit nemini, quantumcumque de suis meritis glorietur, liceat immutare; ne — si forte promiscua daretur uniuersis licentia, quaecumque sibi secundum uoluntatem propriam occurrerent perpetrandi — confusa libertas, cum
10 secundum personarum diuersitatem uota dissentiant, in aliorum aliquando scandalum, sine iusti discretione libraminis, commendanda supprimeret et minus digna laudibus indebitis celebraret.

> **2** omnium] fidelium *add. M. —*   **3** ubicumque] ubique S_2M, *om.*S_3. —   **5** et$_2$] ut S_2, *om.* S_1. —   **7** ne] nam S_3. —
> **9** occurrerint *M. —* et confusa S_3. —   **10** personarum
> diuersitatem] uoluntatem personarum *M.*

6.

Innocentius III de requisitis ad canonizationem virtutibus et miraculis.

Ex decreto canonizationis
S. Homoboni (*Po. 573, Regi-*
strum Vaticanum 4, fol. 135
[= *R*], *collata ed. Baluzii,*
Epist. Innocentii III Rom.
Pont. libri undecim, Paris.
1682 I p. 300-301 [= *B*]).

Ex decreto canonizationis
S. Kunegundae (*Po. 1000,*
ed. J. Gretser, Divi Bamber-
genses, Ingolstadii 1611 p.
421-425, ex ' codice quodam
Bibliothecae Bavaricae qui
Annales Bambergenses con-
tinet ', scripto a Hartmanno
Schedel [*cf. p. 375*] *i. e. ex*
Cod. Monac. lat. 46 [= *G*];
iterum G. Henschenius ASS.
mart. 3, I p. 281, ex colla-
tione ' cum Ms. Bamber-
gensi Fratrum Minorum '
[= *H*]).

Quia pietas promissionem...

Cum secundum evangeli-
cam...

Licet autem iuxta testimonium ueritatis sola finalis
perseuerantia exigatur ad
sanctitatem anime in ecclesia
triumphanti, quoniam ' qui
perseuerauerit usque in finem, hic saluus erit '[a];

Licet enim ad hoc, ut aliquis sanctus sit apud Deum
5 in ecclesia triumphante, sola sufficiat finalis perseuerantia, testante
ueritate, quae dicit, quoniam ' qui
perseuerauerit usque in finem, hic
saluus erit '[a], et iterum : ' esto
10 fidelis usque ad mortem, et
dabo tibi coronam uitae '[b];

duo tamen, uirtus
uidelicet morum et uirtus signorum, opera scil. pietatis
in uita et miraculorum signa
post mortem, ut quis repute-
tur sanctus in militanti ecclesia, requiruntur.

ad hoc tamen, ut ipse sanctus
apud homines habeatur in ecclesia militante, duo sunt neces-
15 saria : uirtus morum et uirtus signorum, uidel. merita et miracula,

ut et haec et illa sibi
inuicem contestentur. non
20 enim aut merita sine miraculis, aut miracula sine meritis
plene sufficiunt ad perhiben-
dum inter homines testimo-

nam quia frequenter ange-
lus sathane se in lucis angelum transfigurat, et quidam
faciunt opera sua bona, ut
uideantur ab hominibus, quidam etiam coruscant miraculis, quorum tamen uita merito
reprobatur, sicut de magis
legitur pharaonis[c],   et
etiam antichristus, qui elec-
tos etiam, si fieri potest, indu-
cet suis miraculis in errorem[d],
ad id nec opera sufficiunt sola
nec signa. sed cum illis pre-
cedentibus ista succedunt,

uerum nobis prebent indi-
cium sanctitatis, nec immerito nos ad ipsius ueneratio-
nem inducunt, quem domi-
nus suus

                    ostendit
miraculis uenerandum. hec
autem duo ex uerbis euange-
liste plenius colliguntur, ubi
de apostolis loquens ait : ' illi
autem profecti predicauerunt
ubique, domino cooperante et
sermonem confirmante se-
quentibus signis '[e].

nium sanctitati, cum inter-
25 dum angelus satanae transfiguret se in angelum lucis et quidam
opera sua faciant,   ut ab hominibus
uideantur.

30

                    sed et magi
pharaonis olim signa fecerunt[c],
et antichristus tandem prodigia
operabitur, ut, si fieri posset,
35 in errores etiam inducantur electi[d].

uerum cum et merita sana prae-
cedunt et clara succedunt
miracula, certum praebent indi-
40 cium sanctitatis, ut

          nos ad ipsius ueneratio-
nem inducant, quem deus et meritis praecedentibus et miraculis subsequentibus exhibet
45 uenerandum.   quae
     duo ex uerbis euange-
listae plenius colliguntur, qui
de apostolis loquens aiebat : ' illi
autem profecti praedicauerunt
50 ubique, domino cooperante et
sermonem confirmante se-
quentibus signis '[e].

35 miraculis suis B. —
49 predicaverunt] praedi-
cabant B, pre. u. d. co.
et ser. con. se. signis R;
supplevi ex Vulg.

22 sufficiunt] proficiunt G.
— 37-38 procedunt G.

[a]Mt. 10, 22   [b]Apoc. 2, 10   [c]cf. Exod. 7, 11   [d]Mt. 24,
24   [e]Marc. 16, 20.

Bernardus Compostellanus sen., Collectio Romana decretalium Innocentii III (descripsit, rubricam, inscript., init.

et fin. ed. H. Singer, in Sitzungsberichte der kais. Akademie der Wissenschaften in Wien 171 II [1914] p. 83-84).

De canonizatione sanctorum (*III, 30*). (*c. un.* :) Idem episc. et capitulo Panbergen. : Cum secundum euangelicam ...sequentibus signis.

Excisa ex decreto canonizationis S. Kunegundae (Po. 1000), ab initio usque ad verba ultima in praecedentibus relata.

Ambrosius, Summa super titulis decretalium (*Cod. Romanus Bibl. Casanatensis 1910, fol. 72*rb).

De sanctorum reliquiis uenerandis. Dictum est supra de consecratione ecclesie uel altaris, set quia sancti sunt in ecclesia uenerandi, de eorum ueneratione et canonizatione, idest ut uenerentur ab hominibus, adnectamus. uidea-
5 mus ergo que sunt inquirenda in sancto canonizando. § Et quidem merita et miracula. licet enim ut aliquis sanctus sit - - ueritate testante, que dicit, quoniam qui perseuerauerit, etc., et iterum - - ad mortem etc. ; ad hoc tamen, ut apud homines sanctus habeatur - - scil. uirtus morum et signorum, merita uidel. et miracula, ut hec - - non enim alterum
10 sine altero sufficit - - testimonium ueritati - - se transfiguret - - sua faciunt ut uideantur ab hominibus. quibus per se ipsam ueritas dicit ' recepistis mercedem 'ᵃetc. nam et magi faraonis olim signa fecerunt similia moysi, et antichristus - - in errorem - - sana procedunt - - indicium sanctitatis iuxta illud euangelicum : ' illi autem profecti ' etc.,
15 ut extra. in. eod tit. c. uno in compil. ber. ᵇ et infra eod. c. i. ᶜ et. i. q. i. Teneamus ᵈ et q. iiii. Item peccato ciuium ᵉ, de con. di i. Placuit ut altaria que passim per agros ᶠ. § Ut autem sciatur, qualiter sanctus canonizatus sit uenerandus, notandum quod due sunt species adorationis siue seruitutis,
20 scil. latria et dulia. latria est seruitus que debetur creatori : adoramus ergo deum latria, diligendo ipsum super omnia, credendo in eum, sacrificia illi exhibendo et super omnia reuerentiam. dulia et seruitus que debetur creature sancte. adoramus ergo crucem et ymagines sanctas dulia, scil. reue-
25 rentiam exhibendo, set non in eas credendo, uel super omnia diligendo, uel sacrificia inpendendo. hoc enim esset ydolatrium exercere, ut de con. di. iii. Perlatum et c. Uenerabiles ymaginesᵍ.

228

3 canonicatione *scr.* — **6-14** licet enim *rell.*] *ex decretali Po. 1000.* — **6** sit *om.* — **10** ueritati] sanctitati *legas*; *aberravit amanuensis ad verba* ueritate testante *lin 6-7.* — **13** procedunt] *cf. lectionem G orig.* — **15** in.] *scil. Innocentii.* — **16** Teteamus *scr.* — **17** altaria] altilia *scr.* — **25** exihibendo *scr.*

ᵃ*cf. Mt. 6, 2 et 5 et 16*   ᵇ*Bern. Compost. III, 30, un.*   ᶜ*Comp. II : V, 21, un.*   ᵈ*c. 56*   ᵉ*p. c. 11*   ᶠ*c. 26.*   ᵍ*cc. 27, 28.*

7.

Innocentius III, definitio canonizationis universalis.

Ex decreto canonizationis S. Kunegundae (*cf. num. 6; G p. 423-424, H p. 281*).

...Venientes igitur ad apostolicam sedem ex parte uestra dilecti filii D. abbas Michelueldensis, Gundelus decanus, Cunradus custos, Marcus archidiaconus, Hermannus subdiaconus maioris ecclesiae uestrae, Lupoldus diaconus S. Ste-
5 phani, Burchardus diaconus S. Mariae, Heinricus presbyter S. Michaëlis, Heinricus subdiaconus S. Mariae, nobis et fratribus nostris humiliter supplicarunt, ut ex plenitudine potestatis quam Jesus Christus beato Petro concessit, praenominatam imperatricem sanctorum catalogo dignaremur adscribere,
10 decernentes eius memoriam inter sanctos ab uniuersis fidelibus de cetero celebrandam, cum hoc sublime iudicium ad eum tantum pertineat, qui est beati Petri successor et uicarius Jesu Christi. nos itaque cognoscentes, quod hoc reuera iudicium sublimius est inter cetera iudicia iudicandum...

2 D.] N. *G.* —   **5-6** Henricus *H.*

VII

POPE LUCIUS III AND THE BIGAMOUS ARCHBISHOP OF PALERMO

THE teachings of the canonists on the power of dispensing from the common law of the Church[1] are of great interest for the history of medieval thought, because they are so closely bound up with the general theory of law and legislation, and in particular with the doctrine of legislative supremacy of the pope. Already Gratian—without distinguishing much between the acts of dispensing or granting a privilege—had related all dispensatory power to the papal prerogative of making a new law and of interpreting or abolishing the old. The crucial problem was how to define the limits set to this sovereign power of the *dominus decretorum*:[2] and thus the canonists were led to discuss the pope's position with regard to divine law, natural or revealed; to law established by the apostles, by the first four ecumenical councils—which a famous dictum of Gregory the Great had likened to the Four Gospels[3]—or, for that matter, to any law affecting the general *status* of the Church. It was more often the practical question of whether the pope can interfere in a given case with such laws by dispensation, rather than the abstract extent of his legislative power, which stirred up controversy among the canonists. Like so many of their fundamental doctrines, the theory of dispensation owes much to the exegesis of individual texts and the debate on individual propositions; papal practice and papal pronouncements embodied in the decretals frequently reflected academic argument and, in turn, constantly provided fresh material for it.

The canonists found a wide field for discussion on the power of dispensing from 'apostolic' law in the age-old discipline concerning the personal fitness for the reception of holy orders. The various kinds of impediments which constitute a permanent bar to ordination, and to the exercise of the functions inherent in the orders received, were for the greater part derived, directly or indirectly, from the so-called *regula apostoli*, i.e., the catalogue of the qualifications which St. Paul had required of a bishop, priest, or deacon in his letters to Timothy and Titus. The Apostle's 'rule' had a central place in the canon

---

1. For an excellent general study see J. Brys, *De dispensatione in iure canonico, praesertim apud decretistas et decretalistas. . . .* (Bruges, 1925); A. van Hove, *De privilegiis—De dispensationibus* (Commentarium Lovaniense in Codicem iuris canonici, i.v; Malines-Rome, 1939), pp. 293ff.

2. The term is Gratian's, in C.25 q.i p.c.16, §1.

3. Gregory I, *ep.* i.24 (JE 1092), quoted in D.15 c.2. [The letters JK, JE, JL designate the numbers in the second edition of Jaffé's *Regesta pontificum romanorum* by Kaltenbrunner, Ewald, and Loewenfeld (1885-88).]

law of ordination from the early days of the Church,[4] although the technical term *irregularitas* for the impediments based on it originated only in the twelfth century.[5]

It may seem strange to us today that the medieval writers should have found so much difficulty in the problem of dispensation from one particular irregularity, the impediment of 'bigamy.' Whoever has been married more than once in life has always been, and is still under present law, excluded from ordination,[6] according to the Apostle's word, ' oportet episcopum esse unius uxoris virum ' (1 Tim. iii. 2), an injunction repeated by St. Paul for priests and deacons as well (1 Tim. iii. 12; Tit. i. 5-6).[7] *Bigamia* in this sense is in the first place the status of the remarried widower, and it is therefore well to remember that in canon law and sacramental theology the word does not necessarily carry the connotation of moral taint which we associate with it in modern parlance, where the use of the term has long become restricted to the crime of leading two married lives at once. To be sure, this *bigamia simultanea* is known as a crime in canon law, too,[8] but in respect of ordination the notion of bigamy is more subtle: it is based on the idea that in Christian marriage the union of the flesh represents the union of Christ with His Church. Patristic exegesis, especially in the West, found the primary reason for the Pauline rule in the thought that this full sacramental meaning is lacking in any second marriage: the remarried man has ' divided ' his flesh, and his marital union can no longer represent the mystical Union.[9] Because of

4. It has often been observed that the first part of Gratian's *Decretum* is in large measure, from D.25 p.c.3 on, an extended commentary on the *regula apostoli*.

5. Cf. F. Gillmann, ' Zur Geschichte des Gebrauchs der Ausdrücke " irregularis " und " irregularitas," ' *Archiv für katholisches Kirchenrecht,* xci (1911), 49-86; also W. Johl, *Die Irregularitas ex defectu nach katholischem Kirchenrechte* (Diss. Leipzig, 1909) (not seen, but cf. the review by Gillmann, *Archiv* . . . xcii (1912), 371-8). Already St. Augustine speaks of *integritas personae regularis* (*ep.* 60 (*C.S.E.L.* xxxiv. 221), cf. C.16 q.1 c.36), but the word *irregularitas* was coined by Rufinus, *Summa,* D.25 p.c.3 (ed. Singer, p. 60), cf. Gillmann, *ut supra,* xci, 54-5. Pope Innocent IV in his commentary on X i.9.10, no. 7 (ed. Venet. 1560, p. 114a) wrongly denied the derivation of the term from the *regula apostoli* (cf. Gillmann, p. 81).

6. *Codex iuris canonici,* c. 984, no. 4. For history and bibliography, see J. Vergier-Boimond, ' Bigamie (irrégularité de),' *Dictionnaire de droit canonique,* ii (1937), 853-88; also F. X. Wernz, *Jus decretalium,* ii (3rd ed. Rome, 1915), no. 120.

7. The extension to orders below the episcopate was not due to the medieval canonists, as W. Ullmann assumes, *Medieval Papalism* (London, 1949), p. 66.

8. *Cod. iur. can.* c. 2356.

9. The classical text is St. Augustine, *De bono coniugali,* c. 18 (21): '. . . uisum est eum qui excessit uxorum numerum singularem non peccatum aliquod commisisse, sed normam quamdam sacramenti amisisse; non ad uitae bonae meritum sed ad ordinationis signaculum necessariam. . . . ita noster antistes unius uxoris uir significat ex omnibus gentibus unitatem uni uiro subditam Christo ' (*P.L.* xl. 387-8); shortened and paraphrased in *Glossa ord.* on Tit. i, and so quoted in Gratian,

this *defectus sacramenti*[10] he is not fit to stand in the place of Christ and to minister to His spouse.

This conception soon led to an extensive interpretation, to the effect that the impediment would also arise from marriage to a widow, from concubinage before or after marriage, from failure to dismiss an adulterous wife, and other situations implying a *divisio carnis*. Cases of this kind were dealt with as early as the fourth century in councils and papal letters, at first perhaps in analogy to the marriage restrictions of the Mosaic law for the Jewish priesthood;[11] in the language of the classical canonists they were termed *bigamia interpretativa*.

I.

In the Roman Church, bigamy was understood, at least from the time of Pope Siricius, as a bar also to minor orders,[12] a practice which is paralleled by the precepts of the pseudo-Apostolic Canons[13] and was wrongly considered as Nicene by St. Ambrose.[14] A milder practice, however, which did

D.26 c.2. The Greek Fathers, on the other hand, gave emphasis to moral and pastoral reasons: cf. also St. Ambrose, *De officiis*, i.50. 247: ' quomodo autem potest hortator esse uiduitatis qui ipse coniugia frequentauerit?' (*P.L.* xvi. 97), in Gratian, D.26 c.4. As a practical result, marriage before baptism did not count towards διγαμία in the Eastern Church; so also St. Jerome, *ep.* 69 (83) *ad Oceanum* (*P.L.* xxii. 653-64), quoted from *Glossa ord.* on 1 Tim. iii in D.26 c.1. This interpretation was refuted at length by Pope Innocent I, *ep. ad Victricium Rothomag.* c.6 (*a.* 404, JK 286), *ep. ad Rufum Thessalon.* (*a.* 414, JK 303); cf. Gratian, D.34 c.13, D.26 c.3.

10. The term became official in Innocent III's decretal *Nuper*, Po. 700 (*a.* 1199), 3 Comp. i.14.1, X i.21.4. [The abbreviation Po. indicates the number in Potthast's *Regesta*.]

11. E.g. Council of Neocaesarea, c.8 (C.H. Turner, *Ecclesiae occidentalis Monumenta iuris antiquissima*, II.i (Oxford, 1907), pp. 30, 128-9; in Gratian, D.34 c.11); Pope Siricius, *ep. ad Himerium Tarrac.* (*a.* 385, JK 255), c.8 §12, citing Ezech. xliv. 22, Lev. xxi. 13-14 (*P.L.* xiii. 1151); *ep. ad episcopos Africanos* (Roman Council of 6 January 386; JK 258), cc. 4-5.

12. Siricius, JK 255 cc. 11, 15 (§§15, 19; in Gratian, D.84 c. 5, D.50 c.56); JK 258 cc. 4-5; Innocent I, JK 286, c.6 §9; JK 303, c.1 §2.

13. *Can. apost.* c.17: ' Si quis post baptismum secundis fuerit nuptiis copulatus aut concubinam habuerit, non potest esse episcopus, non presbyter aut diaconus aut prorsus ex numero eorum qui ministerio sacro deseruiunt ' (Turner, *Monum.* I. i.1 (1899), 15-16); c.18: ' Si quis uiduam aut eiectam acceperit, aut meretricem aut ancillam uel aliquam de his quae publicis spectaculis mancipantur, non potest esse episcopus aut presbyter aut diaconus aut ex numero eorum qui ministerio sacro deseruiunt ' (*ibid.*); in Gratian, D.33 c.1, D.34 c.15.

14. *Ep.* 63 (82) *ad Vercellenses*: '. . . patres in concilio Nicaeni tractatus addidisse neque clericum quemquam debere esse qui secunda coniugia sit sortitus ' (*P.L.* xvi. 1206=ed. *Maur.* ii. 1037; in Gratian, D.34 c.14). The text—let alone the variants ' in concilii Nicaeni tractatu ', etc.—has always been a *crux interpretum*, cf. the Maurists' note v. *patres*; their conclusion that St. Ambrose probably read a non-Nicene text in a canonical collection where it appeared as Nicene still holds

412

not go beyond the ' Pauline ' degrees and envisioned only episcopate, priest-hood, and diaconate, prevailed in Spain and Gaul as late as the fifth and sixth centuries.[15] It was therefore without any thought of dispensation when the First Council of Toledo, *c.* 400 A.D., allowed the lector who married a widow to remain in his grade or even to become a subdeacon:

> (c. 3) Item constituit sancta synodus ut lector fidelis, si uiduam alterius uxorem acceperit, amplius nihil sit, sed semper lector habeatur aut forte subdiaconus,

while the subdeacon who remarried after ordination was to be removed from his office (for incontinence?) but could continue in the lower orders as lector or porter (c.4).[16]

Both the pseudo-apostolic and the Spanish tradition appear side by side

good. (For a parallel case, St. Ambrose quoting Neocaesarea under the name of Nicaea, cf. Turner, ' Chapters in the History of Latin MSS of Canons,' *Journal of Theological Studies*, xxx (1929), 236.) This text was probably an early Latin version of the *Canones apostolorum* if we accept Turner's date, *c.* 360-380, for both the *Constitutiones* and the *Canones apost.* (' Notes on the Apostolic Constitutions,' *J.T.S.* xvi (1915), 54, 523ff.) The existence of at least one such version in the late fourth century is borne out by the *fragmentum Veronense*, MS Capit. LI (49) (saec. vi), ed. A. Spagnolo in Turner's *Monum.* I. ii.1 (1913), pp. 32*a-nn* (for the date of its model see Turner, *ibid.*, p. xv); and while the verbal differences of its cc. 14-15 (p. 32*q*=cc. 17-18 *vulg.*) from Ambrose's text seem to rule out this particular version as his source, the fact remains noteworthy that the Verona fragment was sub-scribed in its day ' a quodam bibliothecario ' (Turner, p. xv): CANON(ES) NICAENORVM.

15. Councils of Orange (*a.*441), c.25; Angers (453), c.11; Arles (524), c.3 (=D.55 c.2); Orléans (541) c.10 (Bruns, *Canones apostolorum et conciliorum. . . .* (Berlin, 1839), ii. 125-6, 138; Maassen, *Concilia aevi merovingici* (*M.G.H. Conc.* i; Hannover, 1893), pp. 37, 89). See also the fifth-century collection mislabelled as second Council of Arles, c.45 (Bruns, ii.135=Orange, c.25), and X i.21.1 ' ex concilio Aurelianensi,' which is a summary of Arles 524, c.3.—Only Tours (460), c.4, ' Ut clericus cui nubendi datur licentia internuptam non accipiat uxorem : quod si fecerit ultimum in officio teneat locum ' (Bruns, ii.140), penalizes ' bigamous ' subdeacons and clerics in minor orders (' cui datur licentia. . . .': celibacy is pre-scribed in cc.1 and 2 for *sacerdos uel leuita* only, p. 139f.). But this demotion *ad ultimum locum in officio* is still milder than, e.g., Siricius, JK 255, c.11, ' Quisquis sane clericus aut uiduam aut certe secundam coniugem duxerit, omni ecclesiasticae dignitatis priuilegio mox nudetur, laica tantum sibi communione concessa,' or Innocent I, JK 303, c.1, '. . . nec ad ultimum ecclesiastici ordinis assumere. . . '.

16. Bruns, *Canones*, i.204; c.4 reads: ' Subdiaconus autem defuncta uxore si aliam duxerit, et ab officio in quo ordinatus fuerat remoueatur et habeatur inter ostiarios uel inter lectores, ita ut euangelium et apostolum non legat, propterea ne qui ecclesiae seruierit publicis officiis seruire uideatur; qui uero tertiam, quod nec dicendum aut audiendum est, acceperit, abstentus biennio postea inter laicos recon-ciliatus per poenitentiam communicet.' The interpretation of this text presents difficulties : cc.3 and 4 appear almost contradictory, the one allowing promotion to, the other prescribing demotion from the subdiaconate. Neither the explanation that the fathers of Toledo wished to differentiate between interpretative (c.3) and true

in the *Capitula* of St. Martin of Braga (*c.* 572-579 A.D.).[17] He coupled an abbreviation of *Can. apost.* c.18 with a paraphrase of Ancyra c.21 (on homicide); he abridged I Toledo c.4, expanded I Toledo c.3 to include also bigamy proper, and inserted a qualifying clause, ' si forte necessitas sit,' for the lector's promotion to subdeaconship:[18]

> (Mart. Brac. c. 26) Si quis uiduam aut ab alio dimissam duxerit, non admittatur ad clerum, aut si obrepsit deiciatur. Similiter si homicidii aut facto aut praecepto aut consilio aut adsensione post baptismum conscius fuerit et per aliquam subreptionem ad clericatum uenerit, deiciatur et in fine uitae suae communionem recipiat.

> (c. 44) Si subdiaconus secundam uxorem duxerit, inter lectores uel ostiarios habeatur, ita ut Apostolum non legat.

> (c.43) Lector si uiduam alterius uxorem acceperit, in lectoratu permaneat, aut si forte necessitas sit, subdiaconus fiat, nihil autem supra. Similiter et si bigamus fuerit.

The *Capitula Martini* reached later generations through the Hispana and

(c.4) bigamy, nor the assumption that they wished to extend the irregularity to subdeacons (thus meeting the Roman practice halfways) seems plausible, since bigamy by remarriage before ordination is not included in c.4. The wording of the canon rather seems to indicate a beginning trend to extend celibacy (as understood in the West, i.e. the obligation of continence) to the order of subdiaconate. This would explain why the legislative reason cited is not the *regula apostoli* but ' ne qui ecclesiae seruierit publicis (='secular,' 'worldly ') officiis seruire uideatur '; it would also explain the greater severity in the case of third marriages after ordination. But the fact remains awkward that first marriages after ordination are not mentioned at all. However, if the suggested interpretation is correct (and for what it is worth, we may mention that Gratian understood the canon in this sense, D.31 p.c. 14 *Illud quoque*), the First Council of Toledo would mark a first step towards the law of celibacy for subdeacons, as we find it in the so-called *Codex ecclesiae Africanae* of 419, c.25 (Bruns, i. 163; cf. D.32 c.13) and in Leo I, *ep. ad Anastasium* (*c.* 446, JK 411; D.32 c.1).

17. On the date, see C.W. Barlow, *Martini episcopi Bracarensis opera omnia* (New Haven, 1950), p. 86. The *Capitula* are edited pp. 123-44, with the running head, ' Canones ex orientalium patrum synodis,' and Barlow insists on calling them ' canons of St. Martin '; cf. pp. 84, 103 n.43: ' there is no evidence that he [Martin] used any other word than *canones*....' Barlow seems to have in mind the use of the word *canones* (for the Greek sources) in Martin's prologue, e.g., p. 123, lines 4, 10; but cf. p. 124, 15-6 ' ut de quo *capitulo* aliquis scire uoluerit, possit celerius inuenire.' It is difficult to see why the editor should have rejected the conclusive evidence of the title given in the MSS, ' Capitula ex orientalium patrum synodis a Martino episcopo ordinata atque collecta ' (p. 123).

18. Ed. Barlow, pp. 131 (c.26), 135 (cc.43-44). St. Martin's sources were first identified by Jean Doujat (1609-1688), in the Appendix of G. Voell and H. Justel, *Bibliotheca iuris canonici veteris* (Paris, 1661), i, pp. vii-xxxii; cf. the title page, also Doujat's *Praenotationes canonicae* (1687), iii.17 (Venice, 1735, p. 327), but Barlow gives no source for c.26 (p. 131, cf. also p. 100, n. 16: '... no known source elsewhere '). For the text of *Can. apost.* c.18 see note 13 *supra*; for the various Latin versions of Ancyra c.21 (*al.* 22, 41), Turner, *Monum.* II. i, pp. 108-9.

414

Pseudo-Isidore, but became mislabelled in the collections of the eleventh century as canons ' ex concilio Martini papae ' or ' ex decretis Martini papae.'[19] This was of far-reaching consequence, because the three canons on bigamy eventually entered Gratian's Decretum with the false attribution to Pope Martin I (D.50, c.8 *Si quis uiduam*, D.34, cc.17 *Si subdiaconus* and 18 *Lector*).[20] Faced with the discrepancy of the latter two from the many texts which applied the *regula apostoli* to all clerical orders, Gratian saw no other solution but to construe the less severe canons as instances of papal dispensation: by way of dispensing with the general rule, he explained, Pope Martin had allowed that a bigamous subdeacon may officiate in minor orders; and that a bigamous lector may advance, if need be, to the subdiaconate.[21]

Thus it was really by an accident of textual transmission that the canon *Lector* would become the starting point for the long-drawn controversy of the glossators on dispensation *contra apostolum* and on the relative powers of pope and bishops in this matter. The question, ' an cum bigamo liceat dispensare,' with all its array of canonistic arguments, was soon taken up by the scholastic theologians. On some of its aspects, the debate continued down into the seventeenth and eighteenth centuries.[22]

19. Thus in Burchard's *Decretum* (e.g. ii.35 ' ex decretis Martini papae '), or the series of 84 chapters ' ex concilio Martini papae ' in the *Collectio Tripartita*; cf. the Ballerini in their dissertation (1757) *De antiquis . . . collectionibus et collectoribus canonum* (*S. Leonis Magni Opera*, iii) *P.L.* lvi. 261-2; P. Fournier, ' Les collections canoniques attribuées à Yves de Chartres,' *Bibliothèque de l'Ecole des Chartes*, lvii (1896), 673 (also published in book form, Paris, 1897; p. 29).

20. Gratian's variants: Mart. c.26 *lin.* 1 dimissam] relictam   2 aut si obrepsit] quodsi irrepserit   3 adsensione] defensione (cf. Barlow, *var. lect.*)   5 recipiat] accipiat.—Mart. c.43 *lin.* 1 uxorem alterius *tr.*   2 forte *om.*   sit] fuerit

21. Gratian, dict. a.c. 17 : ' Sed postea temporum defectui condescendens papa Martinus in minoribus ordinibus eos constitui permisit dicens: (c.17) Si subdiaconus. . . .'; dict. a.c. 18: ' Necessitate tamen exigente bigami usque ad subdiaconatum possunt promoueri. Unde Martinus papa ait: (c.18) Lector. . . .' See also the interpolated dictum, probably an early gloss, in D.84 p.c. 4 (*Conc. V Carth.* c.3): ' Contra Martinus papa " Si lector uiduam duxerit," ut supra legitur: sed illud ubi necessitas, hoc ubi nulla necessitas urget ' (cf. the *Nota Correctorum* and Friedberg, *Corpus iuris canonici*, i (1879), note 70 *ad loc.*; Mme Rambaud-Buhot has found this in at least ten MSS in French libraries).

22. To cite only a few: F. Suarez, *De censuris* (1603), disp. 49 s.6 (*Opera*, xxiii*bis* (Paris, 1861), 538-42); N. Garcias, *De beneficiis* (1609), vii. 6 no. 3ff. (Venice, 1618-19, ii. 52-3); A. Barbosa, *De officio et potestate episcopi* (1632), ii. 49 no. 20ff. (Lyons, 1656, p. 474); P. Fagnanus, *Commentaria . . . decretalium* i.21.2 (Rome, 1661, I. ii.358-64; Venice, 1709, i. 496-501); A. Reiffenstuel, *Ius canonicum universum* (1700-14), i.21 no. 28ff. (Paris, 1864, i. 517-9); L. Ferraris, *Prompta bibliotheca canonica . . .* (1746), *s.v.* ' Bigamia,' art. iii (Rome, 1885, i. 670-5); F.E. von Boenninghausen, *Tractatus iuridico-canonicus de irregularitatibus*, ii (Munster, 1863), 206-13.

II.

This paper is concerned only with the early phases of the discussion.[23] In historical retrospect it is easy for us to discard the textual basis furnished by the canon *Lector* as imaginary because the original canon had nothing to do with either pope or dispensation.[24] Still, the problems which arose in its interpretation were very real. Was Pope Martin's decree contrary to the law of the Apostle? Did it authorize dispensation from the irregularity only by the pope or also by bishops, at least in minor orders? Could the pope himself go beyond the order of subdiaconate in dispensing? And could the bigamous person, if major orders were conferred, receive the sacramental character? In the debate of all these issues, the arguments involved were not always clearly kept apart, and tempers must have grown hot if at certain points of dissent we find the masters abusing each other as madmen, fools, and dumb beasts; if some ridiculed the ordination of bigamous clerks by comparing it to that of a jackass, and called the author of the canon *Lector* contemptuously ' Martin the Goat.'[25]

1. That Martin's canon, especially as regards promotion to the subdiaconate, ran counter to other canonical rules, among which his own canon *Si quis uiduam*, was universally admitted and had to be explained by the distinction between strict law and dispensation.[26] The first generations of glossators did not consider this a dispensation *contra apostolum*. It could easily be seen that St. Paul's rule spoke only of bishops, priests, and deacons ;

23. Most of the *summae* and *apparatus* of the early glossators (before the Decretals of Gregory IX) and a few representative texts of the mid-thirteenth century have been examined, but I have not scanned the vast literature of collected *quaestiones* nor the great mass of mixed gloss compositions. Some of our texts are quoted (not always correctly) and discussed in Brys, *De dispensatione* (n. 1 *supra*), esp. pp. 133-4, 199-200, 221-3. The short paragraph on c. *Lector* and its medieval interpretation in Ullmann, *Medieval Papalism* (London, 1949), pp. 65-6, is based on an unfortunate misunderstanding of the sources.—For the full text of passages excerpted from the manuscript (and some printed) sources in the notes hereafter, see the Appendix below, pp. 439-53; in the footnotes, references to MS and folio (or edition and page) will be given only for short texts not included in the Appendix.

24. So already Suarez, *De censuris*, 49.6 no. 5 (p. 539), the Ballerini *loc. cit.* (n. 19 *supra*), and others. Cf. Wernz, *loc. cit.* (n. 6 *supra*).

25. See *infra*, pp. 428-9, 431.

26. Cf. Stephanus Tornacensis, *Summa*, D.34 c.17 (ed. J.F. von Schulte, Giessen, 1891, p. 52); Huguccio, *Summa*, D.34 c.18, v. *in lectoratu* : 'Alibi contra dicit idem Martinus, ut infra di. l. Si quis uiduam . . . set ibi ponit ius commune, hic loquitur dispensatiue'; Alanus, *Apparatus Ius naturale*, D.34, c.18, v. *necessitas* : ' puta inopia clericorum. Necessitas enim dispensationem inducit. . . .'; *Apparatus Ecce uicit leo*, eod. v. *in lectoratu* : 'l. di. Si quis contra, ubi idem Martinus infra (?) contradicit. Set illud loquitur de iure, hoc de dispensatione '; Johannes Teutonicus, *Glossa ordinaria*, eod. v. *fiat*: '. . . Innocentius tamen dicit quod non licet dispensari cum bigamo . . . et idem Martinus hoc dicit, l. di. Si quis uiduam. . . .'

416

the subdiaconate is ' quodam modo ' not a sacred order,[27] and Martin's canon merely dispenses from positive law.[28] The only difficult point was that St. Ambrose had cited the Council of Nicaea as source for the extension of the Pauline rule to the clergy at large, and on principle the first four ecumenical councils should be as immutable as the Gospels.[29] Still, there was a difference between scriptural authority and any human, ecclesiastical legislation (*institutiones ecclesiasticae*), even though it be of the highest order : Rufinus, the first glossator to discuss this problem (*c.* 1157-1159), taught that the four councils are inviolable except where they enacted ' disciplinary statutes of great severity ' (*rigore magno aliquid statuunt in personas*) ; he cited Pope Martin's dispensation as a case in point.[30] This distinction was

27. Simon de Bisignano, *Summa*, D.34 p.c. 17 v. *ad subdiaconatum*: ' Hic queritur quare bigamus nulla causa faciente possit diaconus fieri uel sacerdos, cum subdiaconus possit fieri necessitate instante. Ratio est . . . uel quia subdiaconatus quodam modo sacer ordo non est. . . .'; *Summa Reuerentia sacrorum canonum*, D.34 c.18, v. *nichil autem supra*; ' Vnde apparet subdiaconatum ceteris longe esse inferiorem et ex institutione noua sacris esse ordinibus adnumeratum, ut infra di. lx. c. ult.' (Erfurt, MS Amplon. q. 117, fo. 123vb); *Summa Omnis qui iuste*, D.34 c.14, v. *in niceno concilio*: '. . . Item queritur quare dispensauit Martinus tantum cum bigamis usque ad subdiaconatum. Forte ideo quia regula apostolica tantum de episcopo et presbitero et diacono data fuit, non de subdiacono, quia tunc temporis ordo ille inter sacros ordines non computabatur. . . .'; *Summa De iure canonico tractaturus*, D.34 c.18, v. *nichil autem supra*: '. . . Set numquid poterit dispensare usque ad diaconum? Resp. forte non, quia apostolus de hiis gradibus cogitauit qui tunc erant: soli presbiteri et diacones tunc erant. . . .' (Later on the author expresses the strange thought that St. Paul *could* have chosen to include by visionary foresight the not yet existing subdiaconate, cf. n. 32 *infra*); Huguccio, *Summa* eod.: '. . . regula enim apostoli non uidetur loqui nisi de episcopo et presbitero et diacono, et ideo dispensatio usque ad subdiaconatum non uidetur contra regulam apostoli. . . .'; Ricardus Anglicus, *App.* 1 Comp. i. 13.3, v. *priuari*: '. . . idest dispensando cum bigamo usque ad subdiaconatum, quod non est contra apostolum; usque ad diaconatum non posset. . . .'

28. Rufinus, *Summa*, C.1 q.7 p.c. 5 (after stating that there is no dispensation in those laws ' quorum mandata uel interdicta ex lege moralium uel euangelica et apostolica institutione principaliter pendent . . . quia omnia hec statuta partes sunt iuris naturalis '): '. . . Dispensabilia uero sunt cetera statuta canonum, que sola sanctorum posteriorumque patrum auctoritate promulgata sunt et firmata, ut: ne monachi publice missam celebrent, ne publice penitentes uel bigami ad clerum promoueantur, et similia ' (ed. Singer, Paderborn, 1902, p. 234); *Appar. Animal est substantia*, D.34 c.18, v. *fiat*: '. . . Nota quod in his que sunt de iure naturali, ut in adulterio, furto, papa non potest dispensare, set in illis tantum que ab inpositione sorciuntur effectum, ut in bigami promotione. . . .' The frequent identification of Biblical and natural law in Gratian and the early glossators is well known.

29. Cf. St. Gregory, n. 3 *supra*. On Ambrose see n. 14 *supra*.

30. Rufinus, *Summa*, D.14 c.2 : ' Non solum de scriptura noui testamenti hoc intelligendum est, que ex nulla dispensatione potest conuelli, sed etiam de quibusdam institutionibus ecclesiasticis. Institutionum namque ecclesiasticarum . . . alie sunt concilia patrum, uel illa [*leg*. iiii?] scil. maiora . . . uel cetera minora; alie sunt canones apostolorum ; alie decreta. . . . Illa igitur quattuor maiora concilia et canones apostolorum in nullo casu mutilari possunt, nisi quando rigore magno aliquid statuunt in personas, sicut concilium Nicenum statuit nullum bigamum fieri clericum iuxta

repeated by many : the pope's power is limited by the four councils in all that pertains to the articles of faith or eternal salvation or—as the Anglo-Norman *Summa Omnis qui iuste* (*c.* 1186) put it—to the general welfare of the Church (*statuta de statu generali ecclesie*), but not in regard to statutes of a disciplinary nature (*statuta in animaduersionem personarum*)[31]. This disposed of the Nicene argument.[32] Again, occasionally we find the canon *Lector*

illud "Cognoscamus" dist. xxxiv (c. 14) : hodie autem bigamus etiam in subdiaconatum ordinari potest, unde illud "Lector" in eadem dist....' (ed. Singer, p. 34).

31. Stephanus Torn. *Summa*, D.14 c.2 : '...Quod continetur in iv. euangeliis et apostolorum uerbis quatuorque generalibus conciliis, uel que ad articulos fidei spectant uel sine quibus homo non potest saluari, non possunt mutari, cetera ex cognitione cause [*om. ed.*] possunt. Quedam tamen in conciliis illis generalibus tradita sunt que postea immutantur, ut est illud Niceni concilii, scil. ne bigamus fiat clericus et si qua [quae *ed.*] sunt similia, cum tamen hodie etiam usque ad subdiaconatum possit bigamus promoueri. Illa ergo que quandoque immutantur ea sunt que in personas aliquid seuerius exercent. . . .' (ed. Schulte, pp. 23-4, emended). Repeated *verbatim* by Johannes Faventinus, *Summa*, eod. (Salamanca, MS 2075, fo. 15rb-15va). *Summa Omnis qui iuste*, eod.: ' Notandum quod ea que in lege et euangelio, in apostolis et iiii. conciliis generalibus continentur, indispensabilia sunt, dum tamen sint statuta de statu generali ecclesie uel de articulis fidei, ut xxv. Q.i. Sunt qui (c.6). Set tantum ea que rigorem continent et statuta sunt in animaduersionem personarum mutari possunt . . ., item illud Niceni concilii ne bigamus promoueatur, mutatur in xxxiiii. di. Lector. . . .'; *Summa De iure can. tract.* eod. v. *quedam* : ' uetus et nouum testamentum et iiii. concilia.' *conuelli* : ' in articulo fidei nec in statu ecclesie uniuersalis. Secus in aliis, puta que in personas aliquid seuerius exercent, ut plenius habes di. xxxiiii. Lector.' The important concept of ' general welfare ' (*status generalis*) of the Church still needs a full investigation, but see Brys, *De dispensatione*, pp. 133, 195-8, and the excellent observations of B. Tierney, *Foundations of the Conciliar Theory* (Cambridge, 1955), pp. 50-3, ' Pope and Council,' *Mediaeval Studies*, xix (1957), 201-2, texts pp. 210-12 ; for the parallel problem of *status regni* in constitutional theory, G. Post, ' The Theory of Public Law and the State in the Thirteenth Century,' *Seminar*, vi (1948), 42-59.

32. *Summa Omnis qui iuste*, D.34 c.14, v. *in Niceno concilio* : ' Si ita statuit concilium Nicenum, quomodo potuit Martinus dispensare contra ut bigamus promoueatur in subdiaconatum, cum contra Nicenum concilium non ualeat dispensari...? Quod tamen de hiis intellige que ad articulos fidei pertinent: hec autem in animaduersionem personarum sunt introducta.' It is noteworthy that the closely related *Summa De iure canonico tractaturus* takes the ' Nicene ' rule to be a matter of *status universalis ecclesiae* and yet dispensable, D.34 c.18 : '... Set cum Nicenum concilium, ut supra, Cognoscamus (c.14), statuerit etiam non debere esse clericum bigamum et super uniuersali statu hoc statuerit, num Martino liceat contra dispensare ? Resp. sic, quia quod Nicenum concilium adiecit statuto apostolico, quod ius commune fuit, rigor erat. Nam de iure communi futurum apostolus forte non omisisset, quia in spiritu uidit, ut creditur, futuros subdiaconos. Rigori ergo personarum licite detrahitur per papam.'—For the few authors of the early thirteenth century who still mention the Nicene Council in connection with bigamy, the dispensation is no longer a problem. Alanus, *Apparatus*, D.34 c.18, v. *necessitas* : '. . . hec autem dispensatio non est contra apostolum set contra Nicenam sinodum ...'; *Glossae Valentianenses* 1 *Comp.* i.13.3, v. *priuari* : '. . . dico quod reuera solus papa potest dispensare quod bigamus sit subdiaconus, nec est contra apostolum set contra Nicenum consilium [*sic*]. . . .'

described as contrary to the *Canones apostolorum*.[33]   But the glossators knew that these were not texts of absolute, and certainly not of scriptural authority.[34]

However, the more conservative side of the argument drew support from recent papal decretals. In a response given to the bishop of Spalato, Alexander III stated (*c.* 1168-1170) that bigamous persons who were promoted *ad sacros ordines* must be deposed, because ' in bigamis contra apostolum dispensare non licet.'[35] This shift in terminology was significant. Ever since the Gregorian Reform had revived and reinforced the ancient law of celibacy, the term *sacer ordo* had come to include, at least in this respect, the subdiaconate with diaconate and priesthood. It had been so used by the reform popes Alexander II and Urban II, and by the twelfth-century canonists;[36] and although for many centuries the theological nature of subdeacons' orders was to remain a matter of controversy,[37] any doubt about their being ' sacred ' at canon law was officially settled by a decretal of Innocent III in 1207.[38] In the meantime, Alexander's letter to Spalato became widely known through the *Compilatio prima*, where the relevant portion—wrongly attributed to his successor,

33. Ricardus Anglicus, *Summa questionum*, q.5, *De decretalibus epistulis*: '. . . In canonibus apostolorum precipitur ut si quis uiduam uxorem duxerit, non promoueatur, di. xxxiiii. Si quis uiduam (c.15; cf. n. 13 *supra*). Tamen contra id capitulum loquitur Martinus papa ead. di. Lector, contrarium ibi statuens. . . .' (Zwettl, MS 162, fo. 147va).

34. Cf. Rufinus, *loc. cit. supra*, n. 30, and quite generally, Gratian, D.16, cc.1-4.

35. Alexander III, *Super eo* (*P.L.* cc. 627), JL 11690; for the identity with this letter of the fragmentary tradition in the decretal collections (separately recorded in JL 14100) see W. Holtzmann, ' Die Register Alexanders III. in den Händen der Kanonisten,' *Quellen und Forschungen aus italienischen Archiven und Bibliotheken*, xxx (1940), 58.

36. Alexander II, JL 4575 (*a.* 1065); Urban II, Synod of Melfi, c.3 (1089). Both appear under Urban's name in Gratian, D.32 cc.11-12 (cf. also c.10=Melfi c.12). Rufinus, *Summa*, D.32 c.11 (Singer, p. 75), etc.

37. Cf. S. Many, *De sacra ordinatione* (Paris, 1905), pp. 40-43; A. Michel, *s.v.* ' Ordre,' *Dictionnaire de théologie catholique*, xi.2 (1932), 1381. It is now settled doctrine that the subdiaconate is not a sacrament.

38. Innocent III, *A multis*, Po. 3233 : 3 Comp. i.9.6, X i.14.9, quoting ' Urban II ' from D.32 cc.11, 12 and Gregory the Great, *ep.* i.42 (JE 1112), from D.31 c.1. A puzzling textual problem remains: the crucial word of Gregory's phrase, '. . . ut nullum facere subdiaconum praesumant, nisi qui se uicturum caste promiserit ' (*M.G.H. Epp.* i.67, line 25) appears in D.31 c.1, according to Friedberg's best MSS (cf. note 10 *ad loc.*), as ' diaconum '; Innocent III, however, must have read 'subdiaconum ' as in the original and as it was also read, e.g., by Rufinus (D.31 pr., ed. Singer, p. 71) and Huguccio *ad loc.* but not by all glossators (the *Casus* on D.31 c.1 in the printed editions of the *Glossa ordinaria* obviously contemplates both alternatives).—A second decretal on the same subject, *Miramur non modicum*, ascribed to Innocent III (Collection of Alanus, i.14. un.; X i.18.7), is apocryphal, cf. the latest discussion in C.R. Cheney, ' Three Decretal Collections. . . ,' *Traditio*, xv (1959), 480-3.

Lucius III—appears as cap. *Super eo* in the title *De bigamis non ordinandis*.[39] The canonists could not fail to notice the contrast between ' Pope ' Martin's having allowed dispensation up to the subdiaconate and a modern pope's having forbidden any dispensation *ad sacros ordines* as contrary to the Apostle.[40] ' Sic ergo papa dispensat contra apostolum '—with these succinct words Johannes Teutonicus begins his comments on c. *Lector* in the *Glossa ordinaria*;[41] and Innocent III himself instructed the bishop of Limoges in the case of a subdeacon, saying that dispensation would be ' contra doctrinam apostoli.'[42]

All this explains why in the exegesis of c. *Lector* some glossators used an historical argument: the term *sacri ordines*, they pointed out, had not meant at all times what it means today, and Pope Martin's dispensation must be understood according to the tenets of the early Church, when the subdiaconate was not yet reckoned among the sacred orders.[43] (Consequently, Hostiensis held, the pope would not easily grant such a dispensation today.[44])

39. 1 Comp. i.13.3=X i.21.2. Bernard of Pavia's source, *Coll. Bambergensis*, xi. 13*b* (Deeters's numbering; *Coll. Cass.* xxi.20), still gave the correct name and address. Other portions of JL 11690 (14100) appear in 1 Comp. iv.14.1 and v.2.18 (X v.3.22).

40. All glossators on *Super eo* cite c. *Lector* as *contrarium*.

41. Cf. also *Glossa ord.* C.25 q.1 c.6 *Sunt quidam*, v. *apostoli* : ' Hic uidetur quod papa non possit . . ., qualiter ergo Martinus dispensat contra apostolum, ut xxxiiii. di. Lector? . . .'; also Laurentius as cited in the stratum of additions to the *Apparatus* of Alanus (Paris, MS 15393), vv. ' non est contra apostolum set contra Nicenam sinodum ' (n. 32 *supra*) : ' immo est contra apostolum ut dicit lau.'

42. X i.21.7 *A nobis fuit* (not in Potthast; Friedberg *ad loc.* note 1 wrongly doubts the authenticity). Address and full text only in Alanus, *Coll.* i.16.1 (printed from the Weingarten text (appendix, c.43) by Heckel, *Zeitschrift der Savigny-Stiftung*, Kan. Abt. xxix (1940), 316-7).

43. So, already before Comp. 1, the *Summae Omnis qui iuste* and *De iure canonico tractaturus* (n. 27 *supra*, cf. also Simon and *Reuerentia sacr. can.*, eod.). After Comp. 1: *Apparatus Materia auctoris*, i.13.3, v. *priuari* : ' . . . uel tempore apostolorum subdiaconatus inter sacros ordines non computabatur '; Damasus, *Summa*, tit. *de bigamis* : ' . . . dispensatiue tamen usque ad subdiaconatum potest promoueri, xxxiiii. di. Lector, et non est contra decretalis in isto titulo, Super eo, quia antiquitus subdiaconalis ordo non erat sacer ordo. lxi. di. Nullus ' (D.60 c.4; MS Vat. Pal. 656, fo. 160 rb); *Appar. Ecce uicit leo*, D.34 c.18 v. *bigamus fuerit* : ' . . . quod non est contra preceptum si fiat subdiaconus, quia in tempore apostoli non erat subdiaconatus sacer ordo. . . .'; Bernardus Parmensis, *Glossa ord.* X i.21.2, v. *dispensare* : ' . . . R. dixit quod Marcellus [*sic ed. Rom.*] papa retulit se ad statum primitiuae ecclesiae, in quo subdiaconatus non erat sacer ordo . . .' (concerning the doubtful interpretation of the siglum *R.* see notes on the text, Appendix, *infra*); Goffredus de Trano, *Summa*, tit. *de rescriptis*, i.3 n. 8; tit. *de bigamis*, i.21 n. 11; Johannes de Deo, *Libellus dispensationum* (2nd ed.): ' . . . nec obstat xxxiiii. di. Lector, quia in antiqua ecclesia (*al.* tempore Martini) non fuit subdiaconatus sacer ordo, set a tempore Gregorii, xxxi. di. c.i. et ii.'

44. Hostiensis, *Summa*, tit. *de bigamis*, §*Et an cum bigamo ualeat dispensari* : ' . . . Puto quod c. Lector intelligatur secundum statum primitiue ecclesie . . . non erat sacer ordo (citing X i. 18.7). Unde papa hodie de facili cum subdiacono non dispensaret. . . .'

420

Had the glossators known the true origin of the canon, their 'historical' reasoning would not have been far from the mark.[45]

2. Behind the question of theoretical classification there were, however, issues of greater practical interest. It seems that the glossator Simon of Bisignano was the first to formulate (c. 1177-1179) the problem whether on the strength of Pope Martin's dispensatory canon every bishop can, by his own authority, promote bigamous clerks to the subdiaconate. His answer was an unqualified *No*.[46] But ten years later, c. 1188-1190, Huguccio reported that certain authors held the opposite. Their argument was based on Martin's words, '... subdiaconus fiat, nihil autem supra': a pope cannot impose a binding law on his successors, only on his subjects, but for the subjects the limitation (*nihil supra*) would be meaningless if they could not dispense at all; therefore, etc.[47] Huguccio rejected this syllogism by a different interpretation of *nihil supra*: with these words Martin did not mean indeed to make a law for later popes—but then, he did not mean to make a law at all; he merely intended to show what is fitting and what he considered permissible for himself, so that other popes might follow the same good counsel: thus the terms of the opposite argument do not apply.[48]

Huguccio's refutation of episcopal authority in this matter was accepted by many[49] but not by all. The view that Pope Martin had intended his

45. The First Council of Toledo (400) antedated Leo I, JK 411 (c. 446; D.32 c.1), and Martin of Braga's *Capitula* antedated at least Gregory I, JE 1112 (a. 591; D.31 c.1) and JE 1306 (ep. iv. 34; C.27 q.2 c.20). But on the glossators' own premises the 'historical' argument could not hold water, especially if Gregory the Great was expressly referred to, as by Johannes de Deo (cf. n. 43): Pope Martin I (649-55) reigned after Leo and Gregory.

46. Simon, *Summa*, D.34 p.c.17, v. *ad subdiaconatum*: '... Set queritur an ratione huius dispensationis quilibet episcopus possit sua auctoritate bigamos ad subdiaconatum promouere et an bigamus hoc uelut de iure sibi debitum petere possit. Nos neutrum concedimus.' *Summa Omnis qui iuste*, D.34 c.14, v. *in Niceno conc.*: '... Episcopus tamen ad instar Martini non posset dispensare ut bigamus promoueatur in subdiaconum'; *Summa De iure can. tract.* D.34 c.18, v. *nichil autem supra*: '... Set numquid episcopus <cum> bigamo potest dispensare ut faciat subdiaconum? Resp. Non credo. ...'

47. Huguccio, *Summa*, D.34 c.18, v. *nichil autem supra*: '... Set numquid episcopi possunt dispensare in bigamo uel uidue marito? Credo quod non, arg. di.l. Non confidat (c.59). Quare ergo Martinus dicit 'nichil supra'? Cum pape non possit legem imponere, subditis frustra talis lex imponeretur nisi et ipsi possent in tali casu dispensare. Ideo dicunt quidam quod episcopi in hoc casu possunt dispensare. ...'

48. Huguccio (continued): 'Set potest dici quod Martinus non imponit legem apostolicis, set ostendit quid deceat et quid ipse sibi licere uult et consulit ut et alii idem obseruent, set non cogit. ...'

49. Alanus, *Apparatus*, D.34 c.18, v. *necessitas*: '... set in hoc casu soli pape licet dispensare, arg. di. xxxii. De illo (c.4), di. l. Non confidat (c.59)....'; *Appar. Ecce uicit leo*, eod. v. *si bigamus fuerit*: 'Ecce cum bigamo hic papa dispensat. Set numquid posset hoc simplex episcopus? Quamuis quidam concesserint, dicimus

canon as a guide for bishops found defenders in Richard de Mores (Ricardus Anglicus) and Bernard of Compostella.[50] The leading decretalist of the early thirteenth century, Tancred, sought to strengthen it by the observation that bishops are expressly allowed to dispense from other precepts of the Pauline rule, to wit, in irregularities arising from minor crimes. Such dispensations, he said, are only *praeter*, not *contra apostolum*;[51] or, as others put it more bluntly, the Apostle has only forbidden to ordain, not to dispense from his prohibition.[52] But against all these arguments the dominant, stricter view

quod non, ut l. di. Non confidat. . . .'; *Glossa Valentian.* 1 *Comp.* i.13.3, v. *priuari*: '. . . dico quod reuera solus papa potest dispensare . ., episcopus simplex non potest dispensare ut fiat subdiaconus. . . .' For *Apparatus Materia auctoris* see n. 50; for Raymond of Peñafort and later authors, nn. 52ff.

50. Ricardus Anglicus, *Appar.* 1 *Comp.* i. 13.3, v. *priuari*: 'infra xxxiiii. di. Lector contra. Solutio: ibi ostendit Martinus quid liceat pape aut quid aliis episcopis, idest dispensando cum bigamo ad subdiaconatum, quod non est contra apostolum; usque ad diaconatum non posset ut michi per hoc capitulum uidetur, scil. ut statuat: sic dispensandum est. . . .'; incorporated in Tancred's *Glossa ord.* 1 *Comp.* eod. v. *dispensari* ('supra xxxiiii.—sicut michi uidetur'), with siglum ' R.', and from there in the *Apparatus* of Vincentius, X i. 21.2 v. *dispensare* ('contra d. xxxiiii.—uidetur'), with siglum ' t.' Uneasiness about Richard's opinion can be seen in the fact that the scribe of his *Apparatus* in the Avranches MS 149 wrote '. . . quid liceat pape, *non* quid aliis episcopis. . . .', and that the *Apparatus Materia auctoris*, which reproduces Richard up to the words '. . . dispensando cum bigamo,' continues (1 *Comp.* i.13.3, v. *priuari*): ' quod contra apostolum non posset, ut uidetur ex hoc capitulo. Pape ergo licet, alii non licet; uel tempore . . . (see n. 43 *supra*). Bernardus Compostellanus in *Glossa Palatina*, D.34 c.18, v. *autem supra*: ' Hic non ponit regulam successoribus iste Martinus, quia nec posset . . ., set episcopis datur hic forma dispensandi cum bigamis. *b.*'

51. Tancred *loc. cit.*, after repeating Richard's gloss, continues: ' Video enim quod apostolus prohibuit criminosum ordinari, ut xxv. di. § Nunc autem (p.c.3), et quod episcopis liceat dispensare cum criminosis, scil. cum adulteris et minoribus criminibus implicatis, infra de iudiciis, At si clerici (1 *Comp.* ii.1.6; X ii.1.4), et non est contra apostolum set preter apostolum. Quidam tamen dicunt quod episcopis nullo modo dispensare licet cum bigamo. . . .' Vincentius, *Appar.* X i. 21.2, incorporates (after Richard's gloss, n. 50 *supra*) the first part of this gloss, ' Video— preter apostolum ' without siglum, and adds: ' et dico quod Martinus non potuit legem imponere successoribus: expressit enim quid liceat [*leg.* deceat?].'

52. Raymond of Peñafort, *Summa iuris canonici*, ii.5 *de bigamis*: '. . . Set quis poterit dispensare? Dicunt quidam quod episcopus, et hoc per illud uerbum ' nichil autem supra ' positum in predicto cap. Lector. Non enim illud posset intelligi de papa, quia Martinus non poterat imponere legem successoribus. . . . Si obicias quod non licet contra apostolum episcopis dispensare, respondent quod non obstat, nam et apostolus dixit ' oportet ordinandos esse sine crimine,' et tamen episcopi dispensant in adulterio et in minoribus criminibus, ex.i. de iudic. At si [this refers to Tancred]. Item apostolus non prohibet dispensationem set de iure communi ostendit tales non esse promouendos. Alii dicunt, et forte uerius. . . .' (see n. 54); repeated almost *verbatim* in his *Summa de casibus*, iii.3 *de big.* §4. The argument, ' nec est contra apostolum, quia etsi prohibuit bigamum ordinari, non tamen cum eo prohibuit dispensari,' was later used by Goffredus de Trano for papal dispensation, *Summa*, tit. *de big.* i.21, n. 11.

could always invoke the new decretals of the contemporary popes:[53] however one might construe the canon *Lector* for the past, ' today ' positive law clearly denied bishops the power of dispensing *in sacris*.[54] There were further intrinsic reasons, as Bernard of Parma pointed out in the *Glossa ordinaria* on Gregory IX's Decretals, why Tancred's argument from the analogy of delicts could not apply to the *defectus sacramenti*.[55]

53. In addition to the old canon D.50 c.59 *Non confidat* (Gelasius I, JK 636, c.4; see Huguccio, Alanus, etc. nn. 47, 49 *supra*), the decretals cited are chiefly: *Super eo* (cf. n. 39); Celestine III, *De bigamis autem*, JL 17612, 2 Comp. i.11.2 (X i.21.3); concerning the uncertain address see W. Holtzmann, ' Kanonistische Ergänzungen zur Italia Pontificia,' *Quellen und Forschungen aus ital. Archiven* . . . xxxviii (1958), No. 125); Innocent III, *Nuper* (n. 10 *supra*; the text in X i.21.4 should read: '. . . quod cum huiuscemodi clericis . . . tamquam cum bigamis non liceat dispensari '; Friedberg's '. . . quod, quum huiuscemodi . . .' *(Corp. iur. can.* ii.147) makes no sense, for *cum* is preposition, not conjunction—let alone the deplorable, ' classical ' spelling ' quum ' in a medieval text, against the MSS), and *A nobis fuit* (n. 42 *supra*).

54. *Appar. Ecce uicit leo*, D.34 c.18 (continued from n. 49) : '. . . immo si dispensat debet deponi et ordinans et ordinatus, ut ex. de bigamis non ord. Super eo '; Albertus, *Appar.* 2 *Comp.* i.11.2, v. *admitti*: ' nec etiam ex dispensatione episcopi, secus pape, ut supra xxxiiii. di. Lector ' (F. Gillmann, ' Magister Albertus Glossator der Comp. II,' *Archiv für kath. Kirchenrecht*, cv (1925), 142, quoting from Leipzig MS 983, fo. 64va); incorporated in Tancred, *Glossa ord.* 2 *Comp.* eod.: ' nec etiam per dispensationem episcopi, ut ex. iii. eod. tit. Nuper, secus per dispensationem domini pape, ut di. xxxiiii. Lector. *a.*' (cf. Gillmann, *loc. cit.*), and from there in Vincentius, *Apparatus* X i.21.3, with his own siglum ' Vinc.' (This gloss is rather incongruous: Celestine's decretal deals with bigamous priests, but Albert, citing D.34 c.18, obviously has subdeacons in mind.) Laurentius, objecting to Bernard of Compostella's opinion, *Glossa Palatina loc. cit.* (n. 50 *supra*): 'contra l. di. Non confidat: quod tamen hodie nouo iure eis interdictum est, ut ex. de big. c. ult. (1 Comp. i.13.3) '; also in the additions to Alanus of the Paris MS (cf. n. 41 *supra*), eod.: '. . . set nunquid alii, scil. episcopus, potest *[sic]* dispensare usque ad subdiaconatum ut hic dicitur ? Non, quia prohibitum est, de big. c. ult. *la.*'; St. Raymond (continued from n. 52) : 'Alii dicunt, et forte uerius, quod hodie non licet episcopis cum bigamo dispensare, quia ius expressum est quod eis prohibet dispensationem, ex. iii. de biga. Nuper. Ad idem facit ex. i. de biga. c. ult. et di. l. Si quis uiduam. . . .'; Ambrosius, *Summa* tit. *de bigamis*: '. . . Set numquid hic episcopus dispensabit ? Nequaquam: non illa ratione quia apostolus prohibuit bigamum ordinari, licet id pro ratione assignetur infra eod. tit. Super eo, libro eodem. . . . Quod tamen aperte falsum est, dispensat enim in omnibus minoribus criminibus . . .; set alia ratione, quia id expresse episcopis prohibitum est, ut ex. iii. eod. tit. Nuper a nobis '; Johannes de Petesella, *Summa* tit. *de bigamis* (X i.2.1): '. . . dicunt tamen quidam, et male, quod episcopi possunt usque ad subdiaconatum dispensare cum bigamo per cap. xxxiiii. di. Lector, quia dispensationem talium sibi Romanus pontifex reseruat, ut infra eod. Super eo '; Bernardus Parmensis, *Glossa ordinaria*, X i. 21. 2 v. *dispensare*: '. . . Quidam dicebant quod episcopi olim poterant dispensare cum bigamis . . ., quorum opinio reprobatur infra eod. Nuper et c. A nobis. . . .'

55. Bernardus Parm. *loc. cit.* (after reporting Tancred's opinion as ' quidam dicebant '): '. . . licet dispensetur cum criminosis, non tamen sequitur quod cum bigamo, et illa est ratio quia criminosus post peractam penitentiam restitutus uidetur in pristinum statum et incipit esse quod non fuit . . . sed bigamus non prohibetur

On the other hand, since the new decretals envisaged the sacred (major) orders alone, Johannes Teutonicus proposed a compromise solution which left to the bishops the authority of dispensing in all minor orders.[56] This view found for a time wide acceptance: it was adopted by St. Raymond of Peñafort, Hostiensis, and St. Thomas Aquinas.[57] Many theologians defended the bishop's rights in minor orders long after that position had been abandoned by most canonists.[58] The issue was to occupy the Roman Congregation of the Council as late as the seventeenth century.[59] But all these later developments lie beyond the scope of this paper.

3. For the subdiaconate, in any event, only the papal prerogative of dispensation remained. In an age when the order of subdeacon was not yet a mere stage of transition and subdeacons frequently manned important curial offices at Rome as well as in the dioceses at large,[60] this was by no means a purely academic proposition. But the true test case came with the question whether the pope can go further and dispense a man from bigamy to become deacon, or priest, or bishop. To the glossators, this was an exciting question indeed: for it meant setting directly aside the Apostolic Rule,[61] and here the written law gave no answer nor precedent. Normally, such a dispensation would appear contrary to the christological symbolism of the

promoueri propter crimen sed propter sacramenti defectum, quia carnem suam diuisit in plures ab unitate recedendo. Sed illud sacramentum amplius restitui non potest per aliquam satisfactionem cum non sit crimen. . . .'

56. Johannes Teutonicus, *Apparatus* 3 Comp. i.14.1 *Nuper*, v. *dispensari*: 'nisi in minoribus ordinibus, ut l. di. Quicumque penitens (c.56) et c. Placuit (c.68), xxxiiii. di. Lector' (MS Vat. Chis. E. vii. 207).

57. St. Raymond *loc. cit.* (continued from n. 54): ' Secundum hoc non tenet illud c. Lector, nisi forte quoad minores ordines ut in illis possit episcopus dispensare . . .' (instead of ' ut . . . dispensare,' the *Summa de casibus*, iii. 3 §4 reads: ' in quibus credo quod potest episcopus propter necessitatem dispensare '); Hostiensis, *Summa*, tit. *de bigamis* § fin.: '. . . Episcopi uero dispensare possunt cum bigamis usque ad minores ordines, l. dist. Quicumque ii. (c.56), quia tales non sunt ministri nec rectores nec habent officium predicandi, unde de diuisione carnis non est timendum in talibus, secus de sacris. . . .' St. Thomas Aquinas, *In IV Sententiarum* . . ., iv. d.27 q.3 art. 3 (*Opera*, ed. Parma, 1852-73; vii pt. 2, p. 956), etc.

58. For a detailed survey of *canonistae* and *theologi* on this issue, see Fagnanus, *Commentaria* (n. 22 *supra*) i.21.2, no. 19ff.; Ferraris, *loc. cit.* art. iii, no. 4ff.

59. S.C. Conc. 30 Jan. 1589 (confirmed by Sixtus V *in consistorio*), 13 Apr. 1630, etc.: cf. Garcias, *loc. cit.* n. 22 *supra*, no. 3; Barbosa, *loc. cit.* no. 25, Fagnanus, no. 46; Reiffenstuel, no. 32; Boenninghausen, pp. 212-3; also the Ballerini, *op. cit.* n. 19 *supra*, *P.L.* lvi. 262.

60. Geoffrey of Trani, e.g., was subdeacon and *auditor litterarum contradictarum* before being raised to the cardinalate.

61. Huguccio, *Summa*, D.34 c.18, v. *nichil autem supra*: '. . . dispensatio usque ad subdiaconatum non uidetur contra regulam apostoli, set si fiat ad diaconatum uel presbiteratum aperte uidetur contra regulam apostoli. . . .'

major orders,[62] and it is perhaps characteristic of the deep respect for this symbolism that the first glossator to ask the question, Simon of Bisignano, shied away from answering it: ' Let him inquire who is harassed by the worries of the world.'[63]

But only a few years later, the Anglo-Norman author of the *Summa Omnis qui iuste* asserted without hesitation that the pope could dispense beyond the subdiaconate, ' although we do not read that he ever did so ' (*licet factum non legatur*),[64] whereas another writer of the same school had his misgivings because the apostolic rule concerned the general *status* of the Church; he admitted, however, that he had heard of such a dispensation.[65] Huguccio, taking up the problem, began by saying cautiously that the pope could dispense *de facto* and that in his day it had been done . . .: ' but perhaps this was more of a fact than a matter of law,' considering the *regula apostoli*. Therefore the pope should not go beyond what Martin I had allowed.[66] But then, taking courage as if by an afterthought, Huguccio added that the pope is not bound by Martin's prohibition; that he does and can dispense; and

> lest we should appear to belittle the power of the pope, let us say that he can do so *de iure*. Also against the Apostle? Yes: because by reason of jurisdiction (*praelatio*) every *apostolicus* is greater than the *apostolus*

62. Simon de Bisignano, *Summa*, D.34 p.c.17 (continued from n. 27 *supra*): '. . . Ratio est quod cum cuiuslibet ordinis gestaret officium Christus, sacerdotis tamen sic gessit officium quod se ipsum optulit; diaconi officium ita habuit quod idem fuit corpus tradens discipulis et oblatum . . .'; Alanus, *Appar.* D.34 c.18, v. *nichil*: ' Ecce dispensationi certus imponitur terminus ut hic . . .: hec dispensatio usque ad ordinem episcopi uel presbiteri excedere non debet, repugnante apostoli prohibitione et sacramenti significatione. Episcopus enim significat de omnibus gentibus unitatem uni uiro, idest Christo, subiectam, di. xxvi. Acutius (c.2). Set hec significatio non est in bigamo. . . .'

63. Simon *loc. cit.*: '. . . An uero summus pontifex posset bigamum ad sacerdotium promouere, uel utrum esset sacerdos si eum ordinaret de facto, hoc is inquirat quem mundi labor exagitat.'

64. Summa *Omnis qui iuste*, D.34 c.14, v. *in niceno concilio* (continued from n. 27): '. . . Posset tamen apostolicus cum talibus dispensare ulterius, licet factum non legatur. . . .'

65. *Summa De iure can. tract.* D.34 c.18 (continued from n. 27): '. . . unde contra prohibitionem apostoli super uniuersali statu ecclesie non posset papa dispensare [*i.e.* usque ad diaconatum]: audiui tamen dispensatum . . .' (For the preoccupation of this *Summa* with the *universalis status ecclesiae* see nn. 31, 32 *supra*).

66. Huguccio *loc. cit.*: '. . . Set nonne papa potest dispensare cum bigamo usque ad diaconatum? Potest quidem de facto, nostris etiam temporibus Lucius tertius dispensauit . . . (see *infra*, III), set forte plus fuit ibi facti quam iuris. Regula enim apostoli non uidetur loqui nisi de episcopo et presbitero et diacono, et ideo dispensatio usque . . . (see n. 61) . . . uidetur contra regulam apostoli, et hec est causa quare Martinus noluit dispensare nec papa debet ultra dispensare. . . .'

(the pun on the papal title defies translation), and he can dispense in all the Apostle has said, save in matters of faith or salvation.[67]

Here, nearly everything was said that need to be said. Later writers had only to elaborate on Huguccio's argument, the principle of which they found easily corroborated in certain pronouncements of his great disciple, Innocent III. 'Non habet imperium par in parem,' the pope wrote in the decretal *Innotuit*[68] (which Professor Cheney has called a 'classic discussion' of the problems of dispensation and common law);[69] and again, to the Chapter of Cambrai: 'secundum plenitudinem potestatis possumus de iure supra ius dispensare.'[70] Only few authors avoided taking a clear stand on the issue;[71] nearly all repeated that the limitation in Pope Martin's canon was not binding upon his successors, only a piece of grave counsel;[72] that the pope could set

67. Huguccio (continued): '...licet Martini prohibitione non ligetur. Dispensat tamen et potest dispensare ultra, saltem de facto, et ne uideamur diminuere potentiam pape, dicamus quod de iure potest. Set numquid contra apostolum? Dico quod sic, quia ratione prelationis quilibet apostolicus est maior quam fuerit apostolus: unde et in omnibus que dixit apostolus potest papa dispensare, nisi in his que pertinent ad fidem uel ad salutem.' This opinion is quoted in excerpt by Bernardus Parmensis, *Glossa ord.* X i. 21.2, v. *dispensare* ('...et licet ipse H. dubitet, uidetur tamen consentire, ne uideatur diminui potentia pape, quod possit dispensare cum bigamo') and Guido de Baysio, *Rosarium*, D.34 c.18 ('...secundum H.... Vnde dicebat Hug. ne uideamur,...' etc.).

68. Po. 953 (*a.* 1200), 3 Comp. i.6.5, X i.6.20.

69. C.R. Cheney, *From Becket to Langton* (Manchester, 1956), p. 44 n. 1.

70. Po. 126 (*a.* 1198), 3 Comp. iii. 8.1, X iii. 8.4.

71. Ricardus Anglicus, *Appar.* 1 *Comp.* i.13.3 (continued from n. 50 *supra*): '... sic dispensandum est [*i.e.* usque ad subdiaconatum], alias autem petentibus nichil est diffinitiue positum, ut in aut. de referendariis' (*Auth.* ii.5=*Nov.* x). This part of his gloss was not taken over by Tancred. It appears to be formulated with studied ambiguity; at first sight, Richard seems to say: 'For those who petition otherwise, nothing is stated definitively,' but one could also read: 'For those . . ., it is definitively stated: *nichil* [*autem supra*].' In *Nov.* x, Justinian rebukes petitioners who press for an excessive increase in the number of *referendarii palatii*: they will no longer be heard. This would favour the second interpretation, but the words to which Richard alludes, 'nihil enim petentibus factum est finitum [*al.* finituum]' (*Auth.* ii.5.1, *lin.* 22-3 ed. Schoell), are malapropos: in their context, they express the emperor's complaint that 'petitioners never take anything as final.'—We are also left without a definite answer, although a preference for the affirmative seems to be implied, in the question asked by the *Appar. Animal est substantia*, D.34 c.18,v. *supra*: 'Set quomodo potuit successoribus suis legem imponere? Nonne in tantum posset extendi dispensatio ut bigamus presbiter fieret?' (The Liège MS adds: 'Quidam enim dispensauit cum bigamo ut archiepiscopus fieret; see *infra*, III).

72. Alanus (see n. 74 *infra*); *Appar. Ecce uicit leo*, D.34 c.18, v. *nichil autem supra*: '... Set numquid astringit hic papa Martinus successores? Dicimus quod non, quia non posset, set quid facere debeant ostendit . . .'; Bernardus Compostellanus, in *Glossa Palatina* eod.: 'Hic non ponit regulam successoribus iste Martinus, quia nec posset, ut ex.iii. de elect. Innotuit (3 Comp. i.6.5) . . .'; Laurentius, in the additions to Alanus of the Paris MS (vv. 'certus imponitur terminus . . .,' n. 62 *supra*): 'Non tamen pape imponit necessitati [*sic*] quin possit dispensare si uelit,

426

aside in this matter the rule of St. Paul; and so forth.[73] Alanus was the first
to invoke expressly the *plenitudo potestatis* in support of the pope's unfettered
dispensatory power,[74] and the Spanish decretalist Johannes de Petesella
stated that a denial of such power amounts to denying that St. Peter has received the Keys.[75] As Peter's successor, the pope has more jurisdiction than
Paul; and even if Peter had issued the Apostolic Rule (we read in Hostiensis),

quia non habet imperium par in parem, ex.iii. de elect. Innotuit . . .'; St. Raymond,
Summa iur. can. ii.5 (after citing c. *Lector*) : 'Non enim illud posset intelligi de papa,
quia Martinus non poterat imponere legem suis successoribus, cum non habeat
imperium par in parem, ex.iii. de elect. Innotuit . . .'; Vincentius, *Appar.* X i.21.2
(see n. 51 *supra*); Hostiensis (see n. 76 *infra*).

73. *Appar. Ecce uicit leo,* D.34 c.18, v. *si bigamus fuerit* : '. . . Set numquid
posset dispensare papa ut esset bigamus sacerdos? Dicunt quidam quod non. . . .
Posset tamen dici quod posset ex ista [*leg.* iusta] causa contra preceptum dispensare
quod non pertinet ad articulos fidei'; Tancred, *Glossa ord.* 1 *Comp.* i. 13.3 v. *priuari* :
'. . . Videtur quibusdam et michi quod dominus papa directe contra apostolum dispensare posset, quoniam maior est in amministratione quam fuerit Paulus . . .':
repeated by Vincentius, *Appar.* X i.21.2. v. *contra apostolum* : 'Et dico quod dominus
—Paulus . . .,' signed 'Vinc.' Goffredus de Trano, *Summa,* tit. *de big.* no. 11 :
'. . . uel dic, proprie non obstat prohibitio Pauli, quia papa maior est in administratione Paulo . . . papa enim est loco Petri, qui maior fuit Paulo. . . .' Guido de
Baysio, *Rosarium* (*c.* 1300), D.34 c.18 cites this as being also the opinion of Laurentius : '. . . Vnde dicebat Lau. quod papa potest cum bigamo dispensare contra apostolum, quia ipse est maior potestate apostolo . . .,' but this is not what Laurentius
had to say, cf. n. 72 *supra*. Johannes de Deo, *Libellus dispensationum,* tit. *de dispensatione domini pape* : ' Super hoc diuersi doctores diuersa senciunt. Quidam dicunt
quod papa possit dispensare in omni casu, etiam contra apostolum, cum teneat locum
beati Petri et sit uicarius Iesu Christi . . .,' but he rejects this opinion, see note 90
infra. Innocent IV, *Comment.* X i.21.2 : '. . . Sed contra uidetur quod nec etiam
pape liceat, quia est contra apostolum. . . . Sed dicendum est quod non dispensat
papa contra apostolum in his quae pertinent ad articulos fidei et forte in his quae
pertinent ad generalem statum ecclesiae, sed in aliis dispensat. . . . Item maior est
papa quam Paulus in administratione.' (Ullmann, *Medieval Papalism,* pp. 65-6),
without citing the ' Sed dicendum est,' takes the ' Sed contra uidetur ' for Innocent's
own opinion.)

74. Alanus, *Appar.* D.34 c.18, v. *necessitas* : '. . . Posset tamen papa in hoc articulo contra apostolum dispensare . . .'; v. *nichil* : '. . . Posset tamen ex plenitudine
potestatis sue usque ad supremum gradum dispensare. Quare ergo dicit Martinus,
' nichil autem supra '? Resp. non ut suis successoribus prescribat, set ut quid seruare
debeant ostendat.' Both passages are found only in the second recension (*c.* 1202);
the problem of extending the papal prerogative beyond c. *Lector* is not even raised
in the first (*c.* 1192): this confirms Father Stickler's recent observations on the
development of Alanus from a moderate into an outspoken advocate of papal sovereignty in the period between the two recensions of the *Apparatus* ; 'Alanus Anglicus
als Verteidiger des monarchischen Papsttums,' *Salesianum,* xxi (1959), 346-406
(for the dates as given above, see pp. 371-3).

75. Johannes de Petesella, *Summa,* tit. *de big.* i.21 : '. . . Cum bigamo dico dominum papam dispensare posse plenarie, licet quidam negent,' which he finds absurd,
' quia negant potestatem ecclesie Romane et claues fuisse traditas Petro et per ipsum
suis successoribus . . . et expresse confunduntur l. di. Quicumque penitens ' (c.56).

the pope as his equal would not be bound by it.[76] It is another matter that it would not be fitting for the pope always to make use of the fulness of his power: in this, and only in this sense may we say he ' cannot ' dispense.[77]

4. There were, however, dissenters. What we know of their views comes almost entirely from the adverse criticism they met with in the writings of the dominant school; very little has been found of their own presentation of the case. The starting point of this doctrine was not the dispensatory power of popes and bishops but the nature of bigamy in relation to the sacraments. Whether the bigamous is a capable subject at all for receiving the sacramental character, if *de facto* ordained to the priesthood, was one of the delicate questions Simon of Bisignano had declined to investigate.[78] But the *Summa Omnis qui iuste* and Huguccio expressly stated that the order is truly received.[79] If they felt it necessary to stress the point, this seems to indicate that doubts had been raised in some quarters, as a problem distinct from, but prejudicial for that of the right to dispense. A few years later, the issue came out into the open. Alanus reports (*c.* 1192) that, on the strength of the traditional doctrine of *defectus sacramenti* in a bigamous cleric, *quidam* have come

76. Hostiensis, *Summa,* eod. § fin.: '... Solutio: dispensare potest papa, qui loco Petri successit et ideo est maior Paulo in administratione... Nam etsi Petrus hoc prohibuisset, tamen par in parem non habuit imperium, supra de elect. Innotuit §i. Alii dicunt contrarium.... Set ubi de dispensatione agitur et queritur utrum ualeat quantum ad ecclesiam militantem, quis dubitabit de plenitudine potestatis, secundum quam papa potest de iure supra ius <dispensare> ...?' Cf. also *Lectura,* X i. 21.2, n. 4: ' Potest ergo dispensare cum bigamo, quamuis beatus Paulus prohibeat ipsum ordinari, quia nedum beatus Paulus sed nec beatus Petrus apostolorum princeps in talibus possit ipsum astringere, etsi hoc expressisset ...,' etc.

77. *Summa loc. cit.*: '... Hoc tamen "non potest," idest non congruit potentiae suae. Sic exponitur infra de statu monach. Cum ad monasterium...'; *Lectura loc. cit.* no. 5: '... Licet autem hoc posset facere, non tamen decet eum quod semper utatur plenitudine potestatis, et sic potentiae suae non congruit, et hac congruentia seu decentia considerata dicimus quod "non potest." Simile infra de statu mon. Cum ad monasterium, in fine....' This stems from the standard commentaries on the decretal *Cum ad monasterium* (3 Comp. iii. 27.2, X iii. 35.6), where Innocent III had written that the pope cannot (*non potest*) dispense from the essence of vows of poverty; Johannes Teutonicus interpreted: '...quod dicit hic quod non potest, expone: idest, non congruit eius potentie ... Jo.' (thus in Tancred, *Glossa ord.* 3 Comp. *ad loc.*; cf. Bernardus Parmensis, *Glossa ord.* X *ad loc.*).

78. See note 63 *supra*.

79. *Summa Omnis qui iuste,* D.34 c.14 (continued from n. 64): '... et si bigamus sacerdos fieret, in ueritate ordinem haberet, ut di.l. Quicumque (c.56) ...'; *Summa De iure can. tract.* D.34 c.18 (continued from n. 65): ' Et num si bigamus ordinetur in presbiterum presbiter erit? Resp. sic.' Huguccio, *Summa,* eod. (continued from n. 48): ' Set illud nota quod bigamus, in quocumque ordine ordinetur, ordinem recipit, etiam episcopalem si in eo ordinetur, arg. di. l. Quicumque penitens.' The argument from this canon, D.50 c.56, lies in that here Pope Siricius (*ep. ad Himerium,* JK 255, c.15) allows the *bigamus* who was *indebite et incompetenter* ordained to remain by special *venia* in his order, though without *spes promotionis*.

428

to the conclusion that no bigamist can lawfully or unlawfully become bishop, for he is barred by an *impossibilitas iuris*. But, Alanus adds curtly, this is not true.[80]

Early in the thirteenth century, the view he rejected reappeared in the French school. An anonymous gloss on the *Compilatio prima* held that a bigamous person, if he were *de facto* promoted by papal dispensation to the priesthood, ' non reciperet characterem.'[81] And the author of the *Apparatus Ecce uicit leo* on the Decretum, who himself was inclined to recognize papal dispensation *contra apostolum* except in the articles of faith, related that others denied this power because they considered the bigamous clerk to be as incapable as a woman of the reception of priestly orders. Despairing of a solution, our author exclaimed: ' Only God knows whether the order is received or not.'[82]

In Bologna, the extreme ' sacramentalist ' view found an even more biting expression. As much as we can learn from its opponents, this view rejected both episcopal and papal powers of dispensation in major orders, and the phrase was coined of the ordained bigamist who receives as little sacramental character as an ass. According to Tancred, who was the first to mention (and to reject) this piece of irreverence, its proponents also tried to discredit the canon *Lector* by saying that ' Martinus non fuit papa set capra.'[83] Laurentius in the *Glossa Palatina* named as author of the ' sicut nec asinus ' doctrine

80. Alanus, *Apparatus* (continued from n. 62): '... Vnde dicunt quidam quod bigamus nec iuste nec iniuste potest fieri episcopus impossibilitate iuris impediente, quod uerum non est. Nec Augustinus dicit [in D.26 c.2] simpliciter episcopum hoc significare, set " unius uxoris uirum episcopum...." ' It is at this point that he added in the second recension the statement on *plenitudo potestatis*, n. 74, *supra*.

81. *Glossae Valentianenses* I *Comp.* i. 13.3, v. *priuari* (cf. n. 49): '... ut fieret sacerdos papa non posset dispensare, et hoc si faceret esset contra apostolum, et si de facto promoueretur non reciperet caracterem....' (I owe this text and the information on the French origin of the glosses of Valenciennes MS 274 to the kindness of Msgr. Charles Lefebvre.) Cf. also the marginal addition (early 13th cent.) to Honorius's *Summa questionum* in Douai MS 640, fo. 20ra: ' Item queritur an bigamus suscipiat caracterem. Non uidetur quia propter defectum sacramenti non promouetur: non ergo, cum in ipsum [*sic*] deficiat sacramentum, potest recipere sacramentum ...'; but the writer rejects this view: ' Set contra, ordinati ab hereticis uel excommunicatis ordinem recipiunt ..., item in sacramentis dum modo fiant in forma ecclesie et ab eo qui potest, uerum est quod cumferuntur [*sic*]: ergo et hic karacter.' Honorius himself does not discuss dispensation in the title *de bigamia* (ii. 9).

82. *Apparatus Ecce uicit leo* (continued from n. 73 *supra*): ' Set numquid, si de facto episcopus bigamum in sacerdotem ordinauit [*i.e.* after papal dispensation], est ordinatus? Ita uidetur.... Solutio: dicunt quidam, sicut nec femina esset ordinata quia non est apta ad accipiendum sacerdotium, non posset etiam hic papa dispensare. Quicquid dicatur, utrum recipiat ordinem uel non, solus deus scit.'

83. Tancred, *Glossa ord.* I *Comp.* i.13.3 v. *dispensari*: '... Quidam tamen dicunt quod episcopis nullo modo dispensare licet cum bigamo, et si ordinaretur non reciperet caracterem sicut nec asinus, et Martinus non fuit papa set capra. Videtur quibusdam et michi ...' (n. 73 *supra*).

the legist Nicolaus Furiosus,[84] who is elsewhere known as the *reportator* of Johannes Bassianus. When and where he made this gross remark we do not know, but it gave him a lasting if dubious fame.[85] His surname offered too obvious an occasion for punning to be resisted by later glossators: they delighted in speaking of him as Nicolaus Furiosus ' et sui sequaces, qui similiter sunt furiosi ' or who ' scripsit non sine furore.'[86]

At any rate, his ' mad ' opinion was commonly rejected. Bernard of Parma in the *Glossa ordinaria* on the Decretals and the Portuguese master Johannes de Deo in the second edition of his *Libellus dispensationum*[87] seem to have been the only decretalists of the mid-thirteenth century to disagree with the common teaching and to deny on sacramental grounds the pope's

84. *Glossa Palat.* D.34 c.18, v. *nichil autem supra*: '. . . Fuerunt tamen quidam qui dixerunt cum bigamo dispensari non posse ultra, ut hic docetur, nec reciperet caracterem sicut nec asinus: hoc dixit Nicholaus Furiosus, set confunditur ex illo cap. di.l. Quicumque '; also in the additions to Alanus of the Paris MS (v. ' unde dicunt quidam,' n. 80): ' scilicet Nich. Furiosus.' The text of *Glossa Palat.* is quoted, ' secundum L.,' in Guido de Baysio, *Rosarium*, D.34 c.18.

85. Both M. Sarti, *De claris archigymnasii Bononiensis professoribus*, i (Bologna, 1769), p. 82, and C.F. von Savigny, *Geschichte des römischen Rechts im Mittelalter*, v (2nd ed. Heidelberg, 1850), p. 71 note *f*, cite this opinion of his from Hostiensis (cf. n. 86). For MSS of Nicholas's *reportatio* see E.M. Meijers, ' Sommes, lectures et commentaires,' *Atti del Congresso internazionale di Diritto romano*, i (Pavia, 1934), at pp. 466-7 (reprinted in his *Etudes d'histoire du droit*, edd. R. Feenstra and H. Fischer, iii (Leyden, 1959), 237-8). Nicholas's own commentary on portions of the Digest (Paris MS lat. 4601, cf. Meijers ut supra, p. 471 (242)) may contain the gloss in question.

86. Johannes de Petesella, *Summa*, i.21 (cf. n. 75) '. . . licet quidam negent, ut Nicholaus Furiosus et sui sequaces, qui similiter sunt furiosi in hac parte, quia negant potestatem ecclesie . . .'; Goffredus de Trano, *Summa*, tit. *de rescriptis* (i.3), n. 8: '. . . Sed Nicholaus Furiosus scripsit non sine furore quod . . . non reciperet caracterem sicut nec asinus. Sed hoc non approbo . . .'; Hostiensis, *Summa*, tit. *de big.* §fin.: '. . . Alii dicunt contrarium, unde dicunt: Martinus papa, qui dispensauit in dicto cap. Lector, non fuit Martinus papa sed Martinus capra. Ideo Nicolaus Furiosus scripsit non sine furore quod . . . sicut nec asinus, et est ratio quia sicut oculum amissum non potest tibi papa reddere, sic nec defectum sacramenti. . . . Sed ubi de dispensatione agitur . . . (cf. n. 76 *supra*), quis dubitabit de plenitudine potestatis . . .?'; cf. also *Lectura* X i.21.2, v. *dispensare non licet*, n. 5: '. . . quamuis Nic. Furiosus non sine furore scripserit quod non possit bigamus plus quam asinus ordinari . . .'; v. *remanere*: '. . . sic ergo furor Nicolai taceat Furiosi . . .'; Vincentius, *Appar.* eod. v. *contra apostolum*: '. . . et fatui sunt qui dicunt bigamos non posse recipere caracterem. *Vinc.*'

87. A.D. de Sousa Costa, *Um mestre português em Bolonha no século XIII, João de Deus: Vida e obras* (Braga, 1957), pp. 101-3, has found internal criteria of two recensions (one written before, one during the pontificate of Innocent IV), but no manuscript evidence. I came across the first recension in Milan, MS Ambros. M 64 *sup.*, fo. lxxxxvra-ciiva, with the title, *Summula de irregularitatibus et dispensationibus*; it lacks *inter al.* the passages quoted in n. 90, 96 *infra*. Further details must be discussed elsewhere. Much of Johannes de Deo's *Libellus* was later incorporated by Willielmus Durantis (Durandi) in the *Speculum iudiciale*, i.1, tit. *de dispensationibus*.

plenary powers of dispensation for the bigamous. But they both refrained from citing the obnoxious civilian. Bernard's is only a half-hearted denial; it concludes a long, rambling discussion in which the various issues have become rather confused[88] and which seems to have convinced no one.[89] As for Johannes de Deo, he thought it wise to add, at the end of the chapter, an apologetic apostrophe to the reigning pontiff: 'And this we say saving the respect and the power of the Roman Church and thy honour, worshipful Innocent IV.'[90]

III.

In all these discussions the authors often spoke of the conferment of higher orders as something that might happen *de facto*,[91] and indeed one such papal

---

88. *Glossa ord.* X i.21.2, v. *dispensare.* A tentative analysis of the lengthy gloss as it appears in the Roman edition of 1582 (*et seqq.*) is found below, Appendix. The printed text is obviously defective; a final interpretation must await collation of MSS of the various recensions of the *Gl. ord.* (on which see Kuttner and B. Smalley, *E.H.R.*, lx (1945), 97-103). Bernard starts at one point: 'H. dixit quod episcopi dispensare non poterant...; Jo. uoluit dicere quod papa non posset' (referring to Johannes de Deo?); he then turns to the sacramentological argument against Tancred's opinion on episcopal powers (cf. n. 55 *supra*) and continues, 'propter quod uidetur quod papa non possit dispensare cum bigamo propter eandem rationem, quia propter dispensationem papae non restituitur sacramentum unitatis, cum nec posset...'; after further discussion (including a report on Huguccio, cf. n. 67 *supra*), he concludes: 'Tamen hoc quod dicitur, bigamus in quocumque ordine ordinetur recipit ordinem, arg. 50.di. Quicumque penitens: per quod capitulum uidetur quod cum bigamo dispensare possit. Sed illud tantum intelligitur in minoribus ordinibus.' (Note that the sentence 'Tamen hoc' *rell.* is incomplete and that in the end he seems to exclude papal dispensation even for the subdiaconate.)

89. Hostiensis, *Lectura*, eod. no. 5 recommends his own opinion (n. 76, 77 *supra*) with the words: '... et hoc teneas remota prolixa glossa quae hic antiquitus est signata, quam si times amittere inuenies eam in summa eod. tit. § fin. [where some of Bernard's observations are incorporated] et infra de concess. preb. Proposuit [*Lect.* iii.8.4, no. 12: ed. Venice, 1581, iii, fo. 35r] plenius prosecutam.'

90. Johannes de Deo, *Libellus dispensationum*, tit. 1, de disp. domini pape (the bracketed portions are not in the first recension): '.... Contra apostolum non potest dispensare nec debet quod bigamus promoueatur in diaconem uel sacerdotem uel episcopum ..., et hoc patres attestantur [scilicet propter significatum et consignificatum incarnationis filii dei in uterum (*sic*) uirginis et propter unionem Christi et ecclesie militantis et triumphantis. Quod autem hoc uerum sit probant patenter tam apostolici quam alii expositores noui et ueteris testamenti ..., et probat Urbanus ... et Lucius ... et Celestinus ... et Innocentius iii. ex. eod. c. Nuper. Nec obstat xxxiiii.di. Lector ... (cf. n. 43 *supra*). Nec obstat ... (cf. n. 96 *infra*)] ... Et si de facto possit quicquid uelit, tamen non debet: qui licet sine comparacione aliorum hominum sit magnus factus, debet tamen timere.... In aliis autem ratione duce bene dispensat... Et hec sufficiant causa breuitatis de dispensatione pape, qui tenet et tenere debet mundi monarchiam ... [et hoc dicimus salua honorificencia et potencia romane ecclesie tuique honoris, uenerande Innoc. iiij.]'

91. Cf. Simon (n. 63 *supra*), *Summa Omnis qui iuste* (n. 64), Huguccio (n. 66, 67), *Gloss. Valent.* (n. 81), *Appar. Ecce uicit leo* (n. 82), Johannes de Deo (n. 90).

factum[92] was constantly cited to clinch the proof of the pope's powers in this matter. It was chiefly through the *Glossa ordinaria* on the *Decretum*—although Johannes Teutonicus was not the first writer who mentioned the case—that the report of a dispensation granted by Pope Lucius III (1181-1185) to the bigamous archbishop of Palermo became universally known:[93]

> Lucius tamen dispensauit cum panormitano archiepiscopo qui fuit bigamus . . .

Some admitted that they knew it only from hearsay: 'fertur, set scriptum non uidi' had been Tancred's words when he referred to the case a few years before Johannes Teutonicus.[94] They were echoed later by Johannes de Petesella;[95] and Johannes de Deo, whose entire position would indeed have been shattered by such a precedent, boldly added that Pope Lucius' rescript of dispensation, if it were to be found, must be a forgery, 'and whoever thinks otherwise is a muttonhead' (*pecus est*).[96]

But nearly everyone else accepted it as a fact that a bigamist had become archbishop of Palermo through a dispensation given by Lucius III; the same Lucius III, ironically, to whom the Book of Decretals attributed the letter *Super eo* (actually written by Alexander III) which prescribed severe punishment for all who violated the Apostle's prohibition.[97] Without noticing how odd it was that Lucius the legislator should have been disavowed by Lucius

---

92. A similar discussion existed among the Anglo-Norman canonists on papal dispensation for a priest deposed as a murderer, cf. *Traditio*, vii (1949-51), 310. The *Summa De iure canonico tractaturus* writes, citing two decretals of Alexander III (*App. Conc. Lat.* xxvi.13-14): '. . . Alexander tamen circa promotum . . . et circa promouendum . . . dispensauit: de cuius facto non est disputandum'; Honorius, *Summa questionum*, ii.8.4: '. . . non uidetur eos qui semel post baptismum occiderunt . . . ex aliqua dispensatione posse promoueri, licet secus factum ab Alexandro reperiatur, de cuius facto non est disputandum.' For the non-permissible *disputatio de factis regum* in Bracton (fo. 34), the Assizes of Norman Sicily, and Frederick II's *Liber augustalis*, i.4, see the excellent observations of E.H. Kantorowicz, *The King's Two Bodies* (Princeton, 1957), p. 158, n. 209; the connection of these texts with the canonistic parallels remains to be examined.

93. *Glossa ord.* D.34 c.18, v. *fiat*. For Johannes's source, Bernard of Compostella, see below, at n. 105.

94. Tancred, *Glossa ord.* 1 *Comp.* i.13.3, v. *dispensari*: '. . . et fertur, set scriptum non uidi, quod Lucius papa dispensauit cum bigamo usque ad sacerdotium. *t.*'

95. Joh. de Petesella, *Summa*, i.21: '. . . et dicitur, set non inueni in aliqua scriptura autentica, quod Lucius papa dispensauit cum panormitano archiepiscopo . . .'; cf. also William of Rennes, *Glossa* on St. Raymond's *Summa de casibus*, ii.3.3 § 4, v. *Lucius papa*: 'non legitur hoc in aliquo libro quo utuntur scholares' (ed. Rom. 1603, p. 262b).

96. *Libellus disp.* (2nd ed., cf. n. 90 *supra*): '. . . Nec obstat quod dicunt quidam quod Lucius dispensauit cum bigamo, quia non inuenitur; quod si inueniretur apocriphum esset, et qui secus sentit pecus est.'

97. *Supra*, at n. 39.

the administrator, canonists and theologians alike went on to cite the Palermo case.[98] It appears for instance as a central argument in St. Thomas's discussion of dispensatory powers[99]—which goes a long way to show that in concrete issues the Angelic Doctor did not always treat canonistic reasoning with the disdain he elsewhere proclaims for it.[100] The authority of St. Thomas, in turn, may have much to do with the fact that the story of Lucius III and the archbishop of Palermo was handed down through later generations, until our own age.[101]

And yet, if we trace its origin, we find that it is at least in part an apocryphal story. During the pontificate of Lucius III, no vacancy was to be filled in the see of Palermo, and the incumbent, Archbishop Walter, whose election

98. Laurentius, as cited in the additions to Alanus of the Paris MS, D.34 c.18, v. *nichil autem supra* (before Joh. Teutonicus); St. Raymond, *Summa iuris can.* ii.5 and *Summa de casibus*, iii. 3 § 4; Goffredus de Trano, *Summa*, i.21, n. 11 and i.3, n. 8; Hostiensis, *Summa*, tit. *de big.* § fin. and *Lectura*, X i. 21, n. 5. See the stemma of texts, below, p. 434. For theologians (13th and 14th cent.) see the major commentaries on Peter Lombard's *Sententiae*, e.g. Albert the Great, iv. dist. 27 (O), art. 22 (*Opera*, ed. Borgnet, xxx (1894), p. 183); St. Thomas (note 99 *infra*), Durand de Saint-Pourçain, iv. dist. 27, q.4, giving 'Gaufredus in summa' as his source (Venice, 1571, fo. 369vb-370ra); Richard of Mediavilla, iv. 27 art.4 q.4 (Brixiae, 1591, p. 423); Duns Scotus, *Opus Oxoniense* iv.33 q.2 n. 7, etc.

99. St. Thomas Aquinas, *in Sent.* iv. 27 q.3 art.3: '... sed in contrarium est quod Lucius papa dispensauit cum Panormitano episcopo qui erat bigamus' (*Opera*, Parma, 1852-73, vii pt. 2, p. 956=*Summa theol.* Suppl. iii q.66 art.5). The addition 'ut refert glossa' (i.e. *Gl. ord.* D.34 c.18), which appears here in a footnote, is found as part of the text in other editions; clarification may be expected from the *ed. Leonina*.

100. Anti-canonistic utterances of St. Thomas Aquinas (and St. Albert) have been recently collected and discussed by I.T. Eschmann, O.P., 'St. Thomas Aquinas on the Two Powers,' *Mediaeval Studies*, xx (1958), 177-205, at pp. 183ff., but the problem of St. Thomas's relations to canon law and the canonists still awaits a thorough historical and textual investigation, to be conducted without that bias for which Domingo Soto's remark on the *interpretes canonum*, '... quia de iure diuino censere non est eorum munus' (*In quartum Sent.* ad loc.: ii (Venice, 1589), p. 148a) remains the classical expression.

101. Cf., e.g., to cite only post-Tridentine authors, Simon Maiolus, *De irregularitatibus et aliis canonicis impedimentis*... (Rome, 1575) i.33 n. 14 (p. 104b); Fagnanus, *Commentaria*, i.21.2, n. 11 (Rome, 1661, I. ii. 359); Ferraris, *Prompta bibliotheca*... (1746), *s.v.* 'Bigamia,' art. iii n. 1 (Rome, 1885, i. 670); Vergier-Boimond, *s.v.* 'Bigamie,' *Dictionn. de droit can.* ii (1937), 874 (from Durand de Saint-Pourçain), and, in a garbled form, P.M.J. Rock, *s.v.* 'Bigamy,' *Catholic Encyclopaedia*, ii (1907), 563b, who has Lucius III issue the dispensation to Nicholas de Tudeschis, the fifteenth-century canonist known as (*Abbas*) *Panormitanus*. By a curious coincidence, I find a warning against this very blunder written, in a seventeenth-century hand, in the margin of the Catholic University of America's copy of Henricus Bohic, *Commentaria in decretales*, i.21.1 (Venice, 1576, p. 92a): 'Archiepiscopus, non credas abbas.'

had been confirmed by Alexander III in 1169,[102] was certainly not in need of any dispensation to continue in office. Actually, there is no mention of an *archiepiscopus Panormitanus* in the ultimate source to which we can trace back, directly or indirectly, all later accounts of the extraordinary case: the *Summa* of Huguccio. Writing *c.* 1188-1190, a few years after the pontificate of Lucius III, the great decretist merely stated that in his own day this pope had granted a dispensation for ' a certain bigamous person in Sicily ' to be promoted to the priesthood—no more:[103]

> . . . nostris etiam temporibus Lucius tertius dispensauit cum quodam bigamo in Sicilia usque ad presbyteratum.

We can easily see how this *quidam bigamus in Sicilia* fired the imagination of some glossators. When Richard de Mores a few years later (*c.* 1196-1198) presented in his *Distinctiones* a stemma of various kinds of dispensations, he put down, under the heading ' contra apostolum,' the terse statement:[104]

> Oportet episcopum esse monogamum : contra in archiepiscopo panormitano.

These almost cryptic words had only to be conflated with Huguccio's own report to produce the standard version which was first formulated, as far as we know, by Bernard of Compostella and quoted in the *Glossa Palatina*, *c.* 1210-1215:[105]

> . . . unde papa Lucius dispensauit cum panormitano archiepiscopo qui bigamus fuerat.

102. JL 11628 (28 June, 1169). Archbishop Walter died before the end of 1190, cf. Evelyn Jamison, *Admiral Eugenius of Sicily : His Life and Work* (Oxford, 1957), p. 93, also p. 232 n. 1.

103. *Summa*, D.34 c.18, v. *nichil autem supra* (cf. the context in n. 66 *supra*).

104. *Distinctiones decretorum*, C.1 q. 7 § *Multorum* (p.c.5): 'Nota dispensationem factam : contra apostolum, oportet . . .; contra ius naturale . . .' etc. (MS Vat. lat. 2691, fo. 5v). More of this lengthy *distinctio* is printed in J.F. von Schulte, ' Literaturgeschichte der Compilationes antiquae,' *Sitzungsberichte . . . Akademie*, lxvi (Vienna, 1870), 81. Did Richard take a wrong cue from Huguccio's remark, at the end of his comments on c. *Lector*, that the bigamous cleric will receive every order, ' etiam episcopalem si in eo ordinetur' (cf. n. 79 *supra*)? It should also be noted that in Richard's *Apparatus* 1 *Comp.* (i.13.3, cf. *supra* nn. 50, 71) the Palermo case is not mentioned and that there he avoids the whole issue of dispensation beyond the subdiaconate. Perhaps one could infer that the *Distinctiones* were completed after the *Apparatus* (on the difficult chronology of Richard's works cf. Kuttner and Rathbone, *Traditio*, vii. 332).

105. *Gl. Pal.* D.34 c.18, v. *autem supra*. Bernard may of course have written this gloss long before 1210. For an earlier occurrence one would have to examine the mixed gloss compositions of the 1190's, especially the quasi-*apparatus*, beg. ' Ordinaturus magister' (on which cf. Kuttner, *Traditio*, i (1943), 285 n. 33; Stickler, *Traditio*, xii (1956), 596-7). The vague statement, made *c.* 1206-10 in the French *Apparatus Animal est substantia,* ' quidam enim dispensauit cum bigamo ut archiepiscopus fieret ' (n. 71 *supra*), could be based on a knowledge of Bernard's gloss, but was more probably derived from a reading of Richard's *Distinctiones*.

THE TEXTUAL TRANSMISSION OF THE PALERMO CASE

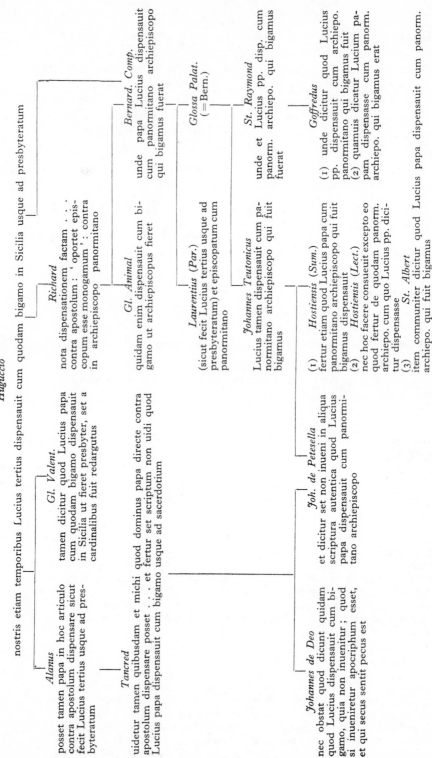

Huguccio
nostris etiam temporibus Lucius tertius dispensauit cum quodam bigamo in Sicilia usque ad presbyteratum

Alanus
posset tamen papa in hoc articulo contra apostolum dispensare sicut fecit Lucius tertius usque ad presbyteratum

Gl. Valent.
tamen dicitur quod Lucius papa cum quodam bigamo dispensauit in Sicilia ut fieret presbyter, set a cardinalibus fuit redargutus

Richard
nota dispensationem factam .:. contra apostolum: ' oportet episcopum esse monogamum '; contra in archiepiscopo panormitano

Bernard. Comp.
unde papa Lucius dispensauit cum panormitano archiepiscopo qui bigamus fuerat

Tancred
uidetur tamen quibusdam et michi quod dominus papa directe contra apostolum dispensare posset ... et fertur set scriptum non uidi quod Lucius papa dispensauit cum bigamo usque ad sacerdotium

Gl. Animal
quidam enim dispensauit cum bigamo ut archiepiscopus fieret

Laurentius (Par.)
(sicut fecit Lucius tertius usque ad presbyteratum) et episcopatum cum panormitano

Glossa Palat.
(=Bern.)

St. Raymond
unde et Lucius pp. disp. cum panorm. archiepo. qui bigamus fuerat

Johannes Teutonicus
Lucius tamen dispensauit cum panormitano archiepiscopo qui fuit bigamus

Goffredus
(1) unde dicitur quod Lucius pp. dispensauit cum archiepo. panormitano qui bigamus fuit
(2) quamuis dicatur Lucium papam dispensasse cum panorm. archiepo. qui bigamus erat

Johannes de Deo
nec obstat quod dicunt quidam quod Lucius dispensauit cum bigamo, quia non inuenitur; quod si inueniretur apocriphum esset, et qui secus sentit pecus est

Joh. de Petesella
et dicitur set non inueni in aliqua scriptura autentica quod Lucius papa dispensauit cum panormitano archiepiscopo

Hostiensis (Sum.)
(1) fertur etiam quod Lucius papa cum panormitano archiepiscopo qui fuit bigamo dispensauit

Hostiensis (Lect.)
(2) nec hoc facere consueuit excepto eo quod fertur de quodam panorm. archiepo. cum quo Lucius pp. dicitur dispensasse

St. Albert
(3) item communiter dicitur quod Lucius papa dispensauit cum panorm. archiepo. qui fuit bigamus

St. Thomas
(4) sed in contrarium est quod Lucius papa dispensauit cum panormitano

This became the immediate model for Johannes Teutonicus's *Glossa ordinaria* and the fountainhead of the whole tradition we have mentioned above.[106]

Another line of writers, however, remained closer to the terms of Huguccio's statement and merely spoke of someone's ordination to the priesthood in citing Pope Lucius's precedent. In this form we read it *c.* 1202 in the second redaction of the *Apparatus decretorum* of Alanus; he was followed by Tancred and others.[107] Even so, the case remained sensational enough; an anonymous glossator of the French school dramatized it further by adding that Lucius on this occasion was contradicted by his cardinals.[108] This author can hardly have come by such a piece of independent information in the early thirteenth century;[109] one may safely say that the added detail reflects only his own conservative persuasion, for he belonged to the group that denied all papal prerogative in this matter.

IV.

The story of the bigamous archbishop of Palermo thus turns out to be a canonistic legend which grew out of Huguccio's report on the case of *quidam bigamus in Sicilia.* Of this case no documentary evidence exists; we can only repeat with the thirteenth-century glossator: ' fertur, set scriptum non uidi.' And yet, the time and the tenor of Huguccio's statement make it unlikely that he should have brought mere gossip into the discussion of so important an issue. He speaks of a fact,[110] not a rumour, and it happened, he says, ' in our own time.'

I am indebted to Professor Walther Holtzmann for a valuable literary clue which in all probability leads us to the man whom Huguccio could not or

---

106. Note 98. In the stemma on the opposite page I have assumed that Raymond of Peñafort's text is directly derived from *Glossa Palat.* The argument is furnished by the common readings which differ from *Glossa ord.*: Lucius tamen] unde papa Lucius *Bern.*, unde et Lucius papa *Raym.*—qui fuit bigamus] qui bigamus fuerat *Bern. Raym.*

107. Alanus, *Appar.* D.34 c.18, v. *necessitas* (cf. n. 74 *supra*): 'Posset tamen ... contra apostolum dispensare, sicut fecit Lucius tertius usque ad presbyteratum '; Tancred, *Glossa ord.* 1 *Comp.* (n. 94 *supra*); *Glossae Valentian.* (n. 108 *infra*), and the *quidam* spoken of by Johannes de Deo (n. 96 *supra*).

108. *Glossae Valentian.* 1 *Comp.* (continued from n. 81): '... non reciperet caracterem; tamen dicitur quod Lucius papa cum quodam bigamo dispensauit in Sicilia ut fieret presbiter, set a cardinalibus fuit redargutus.'

109. I know only of one text which might be an allusion to the Sicilian case but is not derived from Huguccio, the Anglo-Norman *Summa De iure canonico tractaturus*, written *c.* 1186-92, D.34 c.18, v. *nichil autem supra* (n. 65 *supra*): '... non posset papa dispensare: audiui tamen dispensatum....'

110. Cf. Brys, *De dispensatione*, pp. 133-4; Van Hove, *op. cit.* n. 1 *supra*, remains doubtful, p. 358, n. 3.

436

would not identify. The *Liber ad honorem Augusti* by Peter of Eboli, a panegyric of the Emperor Henry VI in elegiac distichs, written *c.* 1195-1196, is an important source for the history of Henry's conquest of Sicily, and in particular for the brief reign of King Tancred (1190-1194), the Emperor's courageous opponent whom the poet despises and ridicules.[111] The leader of the party which had brought Tancred to the throne was Matthew of Salerno (also known as Matthew of Ajello), vice-chancellor of the late King William II from 1169 to 1189, a skilful statesman of long experience and standing in the royal chancery.[112] Tancred raised him to the chancellorship soon after his accession, and Matthew held the office, which had not been filled for many years before, until his own death in the summer of 1193.[113]

In the poem, Peter of Eboli reserves his most venomous railings for the chancellor. We need not dwell here on the more conventional terms of poetical wrath, ' pest of Sodom and progeny of Gomorrha ' (v. 969), ' vessel of fraud ' (v. 971), ' temple of Lucifer ' (v. 973), and the like; and even when the poet has Matthew seek relief from the gout in foot-baths of human blood,[114] this may be only a device for kindling the reader's hatred. But what arrests our attention is the characterisation of the chancellor as *bigamus* or *bigamus sacerdos*, which repeatedly occurs in the poem as well as in the headings of its original illuminations, executed under Peter's own direction

111. *Liber ad honorem Augusti di Pietro da Eboli*, ed. G.B. Siragusa (Fonti per la storia d'Italia, xxxix (vol. 1, text; vol. 2, plates); Rome 1906); also under the title *Petri Ansolini de Ebulo de rebus Siculis carmen*, ed. E. Rota (Rerum italicarum scriptores [Muratori], nuova ediz. xxxi, pt. 1; Città di Castello, 1904). Rota's arguments, p. xxviii, against the traditional title, attested by the MS colophon, are unconvincing. On Peter of Eboli, see M. Manitius, *Geschichte der lateinischen Literatur des Mittelalter*, iii (Munich, 1931), 703-7; F.J.E. Raby, *A History of Secular Latin Poetry* (2nd ed. Oxford, 1957), ii. 166-70 (where only Rota's edition is cited; Manitius confuses the two editions).

112. On Matthew ('der bedeutendste Kanzlist der normannischen Epoche überhaupt'), cf. K.A. Kehr, *Die Urkunden der normannisch-sizilischen Könige* (Innsbruck, 1902), pp. 54-58, 62-3, 89-92; Evelyn Jamison, *Admiral Eugenius* (n. 102 *supra*), pp. 46-7, 80, 94, 101, 222 and *passim*; see index *s.v.*; also Demus, *op. cit.* n. 115 *infra*, pp. 96, 153, n. 64. Miss Jamison has established (p. 94 n. 1) that Matthew is never called *de Agello* in contemporary sources; it was only his son Richard whom King Tancred made count of the newly created county of Ajello.

113. Kehr, *op. cit.* pp. 62-3; the date of death was 21 July 1193, cf. Siragusa, in *Bollettino dell'Istituto storico italiano*, xxx (1909), 48; Jamison, *op. cit.* p. 94, n. 1; *Necrologio del Liber confratrum di S. Matteo di Salerno*, ed. C.A. Garufi (Fonti per la storia d'Italia, lvi; Rome, 1922), p. 100: 'Dominus Matheus domini regis illustris cancellarius.' Richard of Ajello succeeded his father in the direction of Tancred's chancery, but only as acting head, cf. Kehr, p. 93; Jamison, p. 103, n. 1.

114. *Liber ad hon. Augusti*, verses 164-5, 668-70, 995-6, and the drawing of Berne MS 120, fo. 127r (see plate). Rota, *ed. cit.* p. 28, *ad* v. 164, considers this gruesome accusation as possibly true.

in the single surviving manuscript.[115] In lines 989-94 Peter of Eboli says
explicitly:[116]

> The Church against her laws received thee in her bosom :
> God's altar ill befits the sinful bigamist.
> By pray'r or price he led astray thee, Holy Pope.
> How could so much be ever granted to this man ?
> The bigamist, with evil hand, should on the altar touch
> The Everlasting, to whom God as equal gave himself ?

Matthew was indeed twice married and twice widowed: his first wife, Sica,
died before 1171 and his second, Judith, in 1180.[117] This made him bigamous
in the technical sense of the law of ordinations; but the poet's language
(*peccati bigamum, bigami scelerata manus*), especially in a context replete with
all manner of vituperation, deftly evokes the image of a criminal bigamist,
the man with two wives at the same time, and the image takes full shape in
the illustration Peter caused to be drawn on the opposite page of the original
codex (see plate). Of course, the picture may be interpreted differently, as a
symbolic representation of two successive wives, and the words *peccati* and
scelerata manus could also be construed *ex effectu* (i.e., by functioning in orders
at the altar the *bigamus* falls into sin and his hands become wicked). But the
ambiguity—if ambiguity there is—was probably intended in both verse and
picture. We cannot know for sure whether Peter, blinded as he was by
partisan hatred, misrepresented on purpose canonical *bigamia* or merely

115. Verse 140; rubric before v. 939; captions of plates vi, vii, viii, xxxii, xxxiii.
On MS Berne 120 as the dedication copy for the Emperor, produced under Peter's
direction, see Manitius, *Geschichte*, iii. 706; O. Demus, *The Mosaics of Norman
Sicily* (New York, 1950), p. 411.

116. Verses 989-94: ' Te sinus ecclesie contra decreta recepit:
>   Peccati bigamum non decet ara dei.
>   Te prece uel precio, sanctissime pape, fefellit:
>   Nescio quo pacto tanta licere uiro,
>   Ut bigami scelerata manus tractaret in ara
>   Cui deus eterno se dedit esse parem.'

On the difficult expression ' peccati bigamum ' Rota aptly remarks (p. 134, *ad
v.* 990); 'chi è bigamo di peccato—è una *constructio ad sensum*,' but his note *ad
v.* 993, *ara*: 'sottintendi *Christi*' misses the mark. The elliptic construction requires a direct object: ' ut . . . tractaret in ara [Christum, *or* corpus Christi] cui . . .
deus se dedit. . . .'

117. Siragusa, *ed. cit.*, p. 137, n. 1. Cf. Matthew's charter for the monastery
S. Maria dei Latini in Palermo, May 1171, in which there is a special benefaction
'pro domina Sica uxore nostra bone memorie,' in C. A. Garufi, *I documenti inediti
dell'epoca normanna in Sicilia* (Documenti per servire alla storia di Sicilia . . ., xviii;
Palermo, 1899), pp. 137-46, at pp. 141, 142; and the entry in the *Necrologio* of
Salerno (n. 113 *supra*) for 25 June 1180, p. 86: ' Iudicta uxor domini Mathei
uicecancellarii ' (the entries ' Domina Judecta uxor Mathei de Agello ' for 10 May
sine anno and ' Dominus Matheus de Agello ' for 20 Jan. *s.a.* in a fragmentary
calendar *saec.* xiii (*ibid.*, pp. 221, 218) must refer to members of a later generation
of the family).

438

mistook it for bigamy in the popular sense; in any event, the canonical meaning of the term has escaped his modern commentators.[118]

Verse 991 alludes to a papal dispensation.[119] Since the pontificate of Lucius III began in 1181, a year after the death of Matthew's second wife, it stands to reason that he was the pope from whom the widowed vice-chancellor obtained this favour, *prece uel precio* as Peter of Eboli says with a malicious pun. Verses 990 and 993-4, speaking of the altar and the handling of the Blessed Sacrament, leave no doubt that the poet means a dispensation for priestly orders; moreover, Matthew is explicitly called *falsus sacerdos* in verse 999 and *bigamus sacerdos* in the captions of several drawings.[120]

We know from documentary sources that Matthew of Salerno, the accomplished politician, was also a devout and generous founder of churches, monasteries, and hospitals both in Palermo and his native city;[121] that he was an oblate of the Basilians of Messina ever since 1177;[122] and that Lucius III wrote of the vice-chancellor in terms of warm praise, as Alexander III had done before him.[123] The documents, however, give no hint of Matthew's

118. Thus Siragusa, *ed. cit.*, p. 137, n. 3 ('. . . il poeta traduce in bigamia i due matrimoni legittimi . . .'); Rota, *ed. cit.*, p. 27 *ad* v. 140 ('. . . una testimonianza di quella corruzione di Corte . . . e di quella corruzione ecclesiastica . . .'); also Kehr, *op. cit.*, p. 92, n. 4.

119. This was correctly seen by Rota, p. 134 *ad* v. 991; but his notions on the nature of this dispensation (cf. p. 27 *ad* v. 140; p. 134 *ad* v. 989) are as hazy as those on bigamy.

120. Verses 999-1000: 'Urbs ita Lernina [*i.e.* Salerno] tibi credens, false sacerdos,/Mortis in obprobrium per tua facta ruet'; and see the captions of the drawings on plates vi (twice), viii, xxxii (but only *bigamus* on pl. vii, xxxiii).

121. Cf. F. Ughelli, *Italia sacra* (1642-62), vii. 578ff.=Ughelli-Coleti, *Italia sacra* (Venice, 1717), vii. 408ff.; G. Paesano, *Memorie per servire alla storia della Chiesa Salernitana*, ii (Salerno, 1852), 216ff. (not seen); Garufi, *Documenti inediti* (n. 117), pp. 137ff.; *id.*, *Necrologio* (n. 113), p. lv; R. Pirri, *Sicilia sacra*, iii [iv] (Palermo, 1637), 16=Pirri-Mongitori, *Sicilia sacra* (Naples, 1733), ii. 580; Kehr, *op. cit.*, pp. 57, 89 n. 5; Rota, *ed. cit.*, p. 133 *ad* v. 970; Demus, *The Mosaics* (n. 115 *supra*), pp. 153 n. 64, 409, 413 n. 37, 453.

122. Pirri *loc. cit.*; cf. Siragusa, *ed. cit.*, p. 137 n. 3, p. xxxix.

123. Alexander III, in the privilege confirming Matthew's foundation of S. Maria dei Latini in Palermo (cf. n. 117), 30 December 1174: '. . . a dilecto filio nostro Mattheo regio uicecancellario pia consideratione constructum et propriis dotatum redditibus . . . monasterium . . . tanto puriori debemus caritate diligere quanto deuotionem eiusdem uicecancellarii circa opera pietatis feruentiorem esse nouimus et circa nos et Romanam ecclesiam inspirante domino puriorem . . .' (ed. Garufi, *Documenti inediti*, pp. 155-61); Lucius III, for All Saints' Hospital in Palermo, 13 May 1182: 'Cum dilectus filius noster Matheus regius uicecancellarius domum Omnium Sanctorum . . . pia consideratione construxerit, nos domum ipsam tanto propensius manutenere uolumus et fouere, quanto predictum uicecancellarium abundantiori charitate diligimus . . .' (ed. Paul F. Kehr, *Göttinger Nachrichten*, 1899, p. 324); both quoted by K. A. Kehr, *Urkunden*, p. 91 n. 1. Not in Jaffé.

having become a priest late in life;[124] and his own official style remained to the end *Matheus regius (uice-) cancellarius*.[125] But on diplomatic grounds one could not expect it otherwise: the silence of the archival sources need not discredit the *Liber ad Augustum* on this point.

Whatever misgivings one might have on account of Peter of Eboli's bias, the fact remains that several years before he composed his poem, Huguccio in his lectures at Bologna had mentioned, with no political axe to grind, the ordination to the priesthood of *quidam bigamus in Sicilia*. The great canonist, and generations after him, cited Pope Lucius's grant of this dispensation as a unique precedent. It would be more than improbable that the *quidam* should have been anyone else but Matthew of Salerno, the last chancellor of the Norman kings of Sicily.

APPENDIX

In printing the texts which follow, I do not pretend to give critical editions; but where several MSS were collated, variant readings are recorded in the notes. Concerning the canonical sources cited by the medieval authors, the following key will serve for verification in modern editions of the Decretum, the *Compilationes antiquae* (=1 Comp., 2 Comp., etc.) and the Gregorian Decretals (=X).

Dist. xii. Nos consuetudinem c.18
xv. Sicut c.2
xvi. Sancta c.8
xxii. Sacrosancta c.2
    penult. et ult. cc.6, 7
xxv. § Nunc autem d.p. c.3
xxvi. Acutius c.2
    Deinde c.3
    Una tantum c.4
xxxii. De illo c.4
    Erubescant c.11
xxxiiii. Cognoscamus c.14
    Fraternitas c.7
    Lector c.18
    Si quis uiduam c.15
    Si subdiaconus c.17

xl. Homo c.5
    Si papa c.6
xlv. Episcopum c.7
l. Considerandum c.53
    Domino sancto c.28
    Ex penitentibus c.55
    Fidelior c.54
    Non confidat c.59
    Placuit c.68
    Ponderet c.14
    Quicumque penitens c.56
    Si ille c.58
    Si quis uiduam c.8
lvi. Quia simpliciter c.14
lx. Nullus (ult.) c.4
lxiii. Obeuntibus c.35

124. We do not know Matthew's age at his death (1193) but have to consider that he was *notarius* of the royal court as early as 1156, *familiaris curie* in 1162 (K. A. Kehr, p. 54), and that his son Nicholas became archbishop of Salerno in 1181; the vice-chancellor must at that time have been at least in his fifties.

125. See e.g. the royal charters in K. A. Kehr, *op. cit.*, pp. 455 (a. 1186), 457 (1188), 465 (1193).

440

lxix. ult. c.2

lxxiiii. Ubi ista c.7

lxxxi. Apostolus c.1

lxxxii. Presbiter c.5

lxxxiiii. Quisquis c.5

xcv. Olim c.5

Causa i. q.i. Quod propter (pro) c.41

i. q.vii. Saluberrimum c.21

ii. q.i. Multi c.18

ii. q.vii. Oues c.13

vi. q.i. Oues c.9

ix. q.i. Ordinationes c.5

ix. q.iii. Aliorum c.14

Conquestus c.8

Cuncta c.17

Ipsi sunt c.16

Patet c.10

xii. q.ii. Non liceat c.20

xviii. q.ii. Hoc tantum c.1

xxiiii. q.ii. Sane quod super Ric. c.3

xxv. q.i. Sunt qui dicunt c.6

De pen. di.ii. Principium inquit c.45

xxxvi. q.ii. Si autem c.10

De cons. di.i. Sicut c.11

di.ii. Accesserunt c.92

ex. de bigamis non ord. A nobis X i.21.7 (Alan. i.16.1)

ex. (ii.) de big. De bigamis (ult.) 2 Comp. i.11.2 (X i.21.3)

ex. (iii.) de big. Nuper a nobis 3 Comp. i.14.1 (X i.21.4)

ex. (i.) de big. Super eo (ult.) 1 Comp. i.13.3 (X i.21.2)

ex. (i.) de clerico percuss. c.ii   1 Comp. v.21.2 (X v.25.2)

ex. (iii.) de elect. Innotuit   3 Comp. i.6.5 (X i.6.20)

ex. (i.) de excess. priuilegiat. Cum et plantare   1 Comp. v.28.3 (X v.33.3)

ex. (i.) de iudic. At si clerici   1 Comp. ii.1.6 (X ii.1.4)

ex. de maiorit. et obedient. Solite X i.33.6 (3 Comp. i.21.2)

ex. de priuil. et excess: *vide* ex. de excess.

ex. de renunt. Nisi cum pridem X i.9.10 (3 Comp. i.8.4)

ex. de tempor. ordin. Litteras X i.11.13 (3 Comp. i.9.5)

ex. de translat. prelati (episc.) Inter corporalia X i.7.2 (3 Comp. i.5.2)

ex. ut eccl. benef. Ut nostrum X iii.12 un. (3 Comp. iii.10 un.)

Simon de Bisignano, *Summa decretorum* (Bologna, *c.* 1177-1179)

(D.34 p.c.17) § *Necessitate tamen* etc. usque *bigami usque ad subdiaconatum*: Hic queritur quare bigamus nulla causa faciente possit diaconus fieri uel[1] sacerdos, cum subdiaconus possit fieri necessitate instante. Ratio est quod cum cuiuslibet ordinis gestaret officium Christus, sacerdotis tamen sic gessit officium quod se ipsum optulit; diaconi officium ita habuit quod idem fuit corpus tradens discipulis et oblatum, ut infra de con. di.ii. Accesserunt. Vel quia subdiaconatus quodam modo sacer ordo non est, ut infra di.lx.[2] Nullus.

Set queritur an ratione huius dispensationis quilibet episcopus possit sua auctoritate bigamos ad subdiaconatum promouere et an bigamus hoc uelut de iure sibi debitum petere possit. Nos neutrum concedimus. An uero summus pontifex posset bigamum ad sacerdotium promouere, uel utrum esset sacerdos si eum ordinaret de facto, hoc is[3] inquirat quem mundi labor exagitat.

London, B.M. MS Addit. 24659, fo. 5vb.—[1]*add. marg.* L.   [2]lxi. L.
[3]his L.

Summa Omnis qui iuste (Anglo-Norman School, *c.* 1186)

(D.14 c.2) *Sicut quedam*: Notandum est quod ea que in lege et[1] euangelio, in apostolis et iiii. conciliis generalibus continentur indispensabilia sunt, dumtamen[2] sint statuta de statu generali ecclesie uel de articulis fidei, ut xxv. Q.i. Sunt qui, set tantum ea que rigorem continent et statuta sunt in animaduersionem personarum mutari possunt. Nam quamuis apostoli statuerint presbyterum deponendum esse[3] si fornicationem fecerit, tamen Siluester dispensat, ut di. lxxxii. Presbyter. Item illud Niceni concilii, ne[4] bigamus promoueatur, mutatur[5] in xxxiiii.[6] di. Lector. Item illud quod dictum est de electione, ut clerici matricis ecclesie sufficerent, mutatum est, ut di.lxiii. Obeuntibus. Nec mirum si ista uarientur, cum non[7] sint de statu uniuersalis ecclesie. *pro necessitate*: Nota contra[8] ius commune posse dispensari[9] instante necessitate, ut hic et i. Q.i. Quod propter, infra de con. di.[10]i. Sicut.

Leipzig, Univ. MS 986, fo. 10va; Rouen MS 743 (E.74), fo. 5vb.— [1]in *add*. R. [2]dummodo R. [3]*om*. L. [4]ut (?) R. [5]uel *praem*. R. [6]xxxii. LR. [7]*om*. R. [8]*om*. L. [9]dispensare R. [10]q. R.

(D.34 c.14) *Cognoscamus* usque *clericum*: in sacris ordinibus. Ex hoc capitulo habes quod regula illa[1] qua dicitur, 'oportet episcopum esse[2] unius uxoris uirum,' non solum de episcopo set etiam de presbytero debet intelligi, ut hic dicitur. Olim enim idem presbyter quod episcopus, ut di.xcv. Olim. Immo idem uidetur dicendum de diacono, ut di.lxxxi. Apostolus. *in Niceno concilio*: Si ita statuit Nicenum concilium, quomodo potuit Martinus dispensare contra ut bigamus promoueretur in subdiaconum, cum contra Nicenum concilium non ualeat dispensari, ut di.xv. Sicut et di.xvi. Sancta et di.i. Si ille? Quod tamen de hiis intellige que ad articulos fidei pertinent: hec autem in animaduersionem personarum sunt introducta.

Item queritur quare dispensauit Martinus tantum cum bigamis usque ad subdiaconatum.[3] Forte ideo quia regula apostolica tantum de episcopo et prebytero et diacono data fuit, non de[4] subdiacono, quia tunc temporis ordo ille inter sacros ordines non computabatur, ut infra di. proxima c.i. et di.lx. Nullus. Posset tamen apostolicus cum talibus dispensare ulterius, licet factum non legatur, et si bigamus sacerdos fieret, in ueritate ordinem haberet, ut di.l. Quicumque. Episcopus tamen ad instar Martini non posset dispensare ut bigamus promoueretur in subdiaconum.

L fo. 28rb, R fo. 16ra.—[1]*om*. R. [2]*om*. L. [3]*corr*. *ex* archidiaconatum L, diaconatum R. [4]*om*. L.

Summa De iure canonico tractaturus (Anglo-Norman School, after 1186)

(D.14 c.2) *Sicut quedam*: uetus et nouum testamentum et iiii. concilia. *conuelli*: in articulo fidei, nec in statu ecclesie uniuersalis. Secus in aliis, puta que in personas aliquid seuerius exercent, ut plenius habes di. xxxiiii. Lector.

(D.34 c.18) *Lector. nichil autem supra*[1]: Hinc argumentum dispensationem fines suos excedere non debere. Set numquid potuit dispensare usque ad

442

diaconatum[2]? Resp. forte non, quia apostolus de hiis gradibus cogitauit qui tunc erant, non de hiis qui non erant: soli presbyteri et diacones tunc erant. Vnde contra prohibitionem apostoli super uniuersali statu ecclesie non posset papa dispensare: audiui tamen dispensatum. Et num si bigamus ordinetur in presbyterum, presbyter erit? Resp. sic. Set numquid episcopus cum[3] bigamo potest dispensare ut faciat subdiaconum? Resp. non credo. Set cum Nicenum concilium, ut supra, Cognoscamus, statuerit etiam non debere esse clericum bigamum et super uniuersali statu hoc statuerit, num Martino liceat contra dispensare? Resp. sic, quia quod Nicenum concilium adiecit[4] statuto apostolico, quod ius commune fuit, rigor erat. Nam de iure communi futurum[5] apostolus forte non omisisset, quia in spiritu uidit, ut creditur, futuros subdiaconos. Rigori ergo personarum licite detrahitur per[6] papam.

Laon MS 371*bis*, fos. 86va, 93ra.—[1]*sac* L.   [2]diacoñ L.   [3]*om.* L.   [4]adicit L.   [5]esset *add.* L (*forsan legendum* nam quod de . . . futurum esset ?).   [6]p̄p̄ L.

Anonymous addition to Honorius, *Summa questionum* (Anglo-Norman School, *c.* 1180-1190; addition of early 13th cent.)

(ii.9 *de bigamia*) Item queritur an bigamus suscipiat caracterem. Non uidetur quia propter defectum sacramenti non promouetur: non ergo, cum in ipso[1] deficiat sacramentum, potest recipere sacramentum. Item in bigamo perpetua est prohibitio quia nec permittitur ordinari[2] nec si ordinatur[3] de facto habet caracterem. Vnde cum perpetua sit prohibitio[4] contrahere cum cognata et nunquam possit cum ea esse matrimonium, a simili cum bigamo non est caracteris collatio. Set contra, ordinati ab hereticis uel excommunicatis ordinem suscipiunt, supra ix. q.i. Ordinationes:[5] quare ergo isti non suscipiunt caracterem? Item in sacramentis, dum modo fiant in forma ecclesie et ab eo qui potest, uerum est quod conferuntur,[6] ergo et hic karacter.

Douai MS 640, fo. 20ra *marg. inf.*—[1]ipsum D.   [2]ordiari D.   [3]ordiatur D.   [4]cum *add.* D.   [5]Ordinatos D.   [6]cum feruntur D.

Huguccio, *Summa decretorum* (Bologna, *c.* 1188-1190)

(D.34 c.18) *Lector si duxerit uiduam,* olim *uxorem alterius,* uel *si duxerit uiduam alterius uxorem:*[1] idest in uxorem. *in lectoratu:* Alibi contra dicit idem Martinus, ut infra di.l. *Si quis uiduam:* ibi enim dicit quod talis non debet promoueri et promotus debet deponi. Set ibi ponit ius commune, hic loquitur dispensatiue. *nichil autem supra:* Arg. quod quando alicui aliquid conceditur uel permittitur, non debet se extendere ad alia, arg. viiii. q.iii. Conquestus et xviii. q.ii. Hoc tantum; et[2] contrario, quando aliquid alicui prohibetur, nisi expressim et nominatim exprimatur in contrarium, bene potest se ad alia extendere, set ex eo quod specialiter additur determinatio, uidetur quod ubi non additur licita sit ad alia extensio, et est argumentum quod dispensatio debet esse contenta suis finibus, arg. di.xii. Nos consuetudinem et di.l. Quicumque penitens et i.q.v. c.i. et q.vii. Saluberrimum et xxxvi. q.ii. Si autem.

Set ecce bigamus uel uidue maritus in necessitate permittitur promoueri usque ad subdiaconatum: set si ordine illo dignus est, nonne ad ulteriorem poterit promoueri propter eandem causam? Non, nisi noua dispensatio interuenerit. Set nec deberet dispensatio plus extendi, dispensationes enim certis finibus limitantur, ut in preallegatis capitulis.

Set[3] nonne papa potest dispensare cum bigamo usque ad diaconatum? Potest quidem de facto: nostris etiam temporibus Lucius tertius[4] dispensauit cum quodam bigamo in Sicilia usque ad presbiteratum. Set forte plus fuit ibi facti quam iuris. Regula enim apostoli non uidetur loqui nisi de episcopo et presbitero et diacono, et ideo dispensatio usque ad subdiaconatum non uidetur contra regulam apostoli: set si fiat ad diaconatum uel presbiteratum aperte uidetur contra regulam apostoli. Et hec est causa quare Martinus noluit ultra dispensare nec papa debet ultra dispensare, licet Martini prohibitione non ligetur. Dispensat tamen et potest dispensare ultra, saltem de facto, et ne uideamur diminuere potentiam pape, dicamus quod de iure potest. Set numquid contra apostolum? Dico quod sic, quia ratione prelationis quilibet apostolicus est maior quam fuerit apostolus: unde et in omnibus que dixit apostolus potest papa dispensare, nisi in his que pertinent ad fidem uel ad salutem.

Set numquid episcopi possunt dispensare in bigamo uel uidue marito? Credo quod non, arg. di.l. Non confidat. Quare ergo Martinus dicit 'nichil supra'? Cum pape non possit legem imponere, subditis frustra tàlis lex imponeretur nisi et ipsi possent in tali casu dispensare. Ideo dicunt quidam quod episcopi in hoc casu possunt dispensare. Set potest dici quod Martinus non imponit legem apostolicis, set ostendit quid deceat et quid ipse sibi licere uult, et consulit ut et alii idem obseruent, set non cogit.

Set illud nota quod bigamus, in quocumque ordine ordinetur, ordinem recipit, etiam episcopalem si in eo ordinetur, arg. di.l. Quicumque penitens.

Vatican, MS Borgh. 272, fo. 24rb-va (with some emendations based on MS Arch. S. Petri C. 114, fo. 44r).—[1]cf. var. lect. Gratiani ap. Friedb. ad loc. n. 132.   [2]om. B.   [3]se B.   [4]titius B.

Alanus, *Apparatus Ius naturale* (Bologna, c. 1192, revised c. 1202)

(Passages not found in the first recension are printed here within square brackets; the asterisk denotes the places in Paris MS 15393 where glosses from the *Apparatus* of Laurentius are added in a later stratum : see below, p. 445).

D.34 c.18 [*Lector*: Si quis constitutus in minoribus ordinibus ducat uiduam uel si quis bigamus dispensatiue potest promoueri in subdiaconum, supra autem non.][1] *Lector*: infra di.l. Si quis uiduam, et est casus[2] eiusdem Martini in quo rigor continetur. *necessitas*: puta inopia clericorum. Necessitas enim dispensationem[3] inducit,[4] arg. supra eadem, c. Fraternitatis. Set in hoc casu soli pape[5] licet dispensare, arg. di.[6] xxxii. De illo, di.[7]l. Non confidat.[8]

Hec autem dispensatio non est contra apostolum, set contra Nicenam sinodum,* supra[9] eadem, Cognoscamus. [Posset tamen papa in hoc articulo
contra apostolum dispensare, sicut fecit Lucius tertius usque ad presbyteratum.*][10]

nichil: Ecce dispensationi certus imponitur terminus, ut hic et di.[11]xii.
Nos consuetudinem, i.[12] Q.v. c.i.* Hec[13] dispensatio usque ad ordinem
episcopi uel presbiteri excedere[14] non debet, repugnante [apostoli prohibitione et][15] sacramenti significatione. Episcopus enim significat[16] de omnibus
gentibus unitatem uni uiro, idest Christo, subiectam, di.[17]xxvi. Acutius.
Set hec significatio non est in bigamo. Vnde dicunt quidam* quod bigamus
nec iuste nec iniuste[18] potest fieri[19] episcopus, impossibilitate[20] iuris impediente, quod uerum non est. Nec Augustinus dicit simpliciter episcopum
hoc significare,[21] set 'unius uxoris uirum episcopum.'[22] [Posset tamen ex
plenitudine potestatis sue usque ad supremum gradum dispensare. Quare
ergo dicit Martinus, 'nichil autem supra'? Resp. non ut suis successoribus
prescribat, set ut quid seruare debeant ostendat.][23]

Paris, B.N. MS lat. 3909 (=Pr), fo. 7rb; MS lat. 15393 (=Ps), fo. 27ra;
Bibl. Mazarine 1318 (=M), fo. 37va; Seo de Urgel, Cathedral Chapter
MS 113 (=U), not foliated.—PrU: first recension; PsM: second recension.
[1]Ps: *om.* PrUM. [2]et—casus *om.* Pr. [3]*om.* PsM. [4]ducit Pr. [5]soli
pape *om.* Ps. [6]supra di. PrU. [7]infra di. PrU. [8]consideret Ps,
considerat M. [9]ut supra PrU. [10]PsM: *om.* PrU. [11]supra di. PrU.
[12]infra i. PrU. [13]enim *add.* PrU. [14]procedere PrU. [15]PsM: *om.*
PrU. [16]signat M. [17]ut di. Pr, ut supra di. U. [18]nec iniuste *om.*
U, *suppl.* U[2]. [19]fieri potest *tr.* PrU. [20]uel possibilitate PsM. [21]hoc
sign. epm. *tr.* Ps. [22](. . .) p (. . .) rl'm *add.* Pr. [23]PsM: *om.* PrU.

Apparatus Ecce uicit leo (French School, after 1202)

(D.34 c.18) *Lector. in lectoratu*[1]: l.[2] di. Si quis contra, ubi idem Martinus
infra[3] contradicit. Set illud loquitur de iure, hoc de dispensatione. *nichil
autem supra*: Arg. quod dispensatio non est extendenda, arg. i. q.ult. Saluberrimum et xii.di. Nos consuetudinem. Item nec priuilegium, ut ex. de
excessibus priuil. Cum et plantare. Set numquid astringit hic papa Martinus
successores? Dicimus quod non, quia non posset, set quid facere debeant[4]
ostendit. Simile xii. Q.ii. Non liceat.[5] *similiter si bigamus fuerit*: Ecce cum
bigamo hic papa dispensat. Set numquid posset hoc simplex episcopus?
Quamuis quidam concesserint, dicimus quod non, ut l.di. Confidat. Immo
si dispensat debet deponi et ordinans et ordinatus, ut ex. de bigamis non ordi.
Super eo.[6]

Set numquid posset dispensare papa ut esset bigamus sacerdos? Dicunt
quidam quod non, quia non potest contra preceptum facere apostoli, xxv.
Q.i. Sunt qui dicunt, et dicunt[7] quod non est contra preceptum si fiat subdiaconus, quia in tempore apostoli non erat subdiaconatus sacer ordo. Posset
tamen dici quod posset ex iusta[8] causa contra preceptum dispensare quod
non pertinet ad articulos fidei. Set numquid,[9] si de facto episcopus bigamum

in sacerdotem ordinauit, est ordinatus? Ita uidetur implicite,[10] quia deponitur, ut l.di. Quicumque. Solutio: dicunt quidam, sicut nec femina esset ordinata quia non est apta ad accipiendum sacerdotium, non posset etiam hic papa dispensare. Quicquid dicatur, utrum recipiat ordinem uel non, solus deus scit.

St. Florian MS XI. 605, fo. 15vb.—[1]*in lectura puta*: F. [2]ibi F. [3]ita F?. [4]debeat F. [5]xii. Vt secunda non iaceat F. [6]eos F. [7]et dicunt *scripsi*: *om.* F (*homoiotel.*). [8]ista F. [9]non quam F. [10]i[ce] F (?).

Apparatus Animal est substantia (French School, after 1206)
(Passages not found in the Bamberg MS are printed within square brackets).
(D.34 c.18) *Lector. fiat*:[1] ex dispensatione. Nota quod[2] in his que sunt de iure naturali, ut in adulterio, furto, papa non potest dispensare, set in illis tantum que ab inpositione sorciuntur effectum, ut in bigami promotione. Vnde[3] admittitur eius dispensatio. *supra*:[4] Set quomodo potuit successoribus suis legem inponere? [De hoc dictum est xii.q.ii. Non liceat.] Nonne in tantum posset extendi dispensatio ut bigamus presbiter fieret?[5] [Quidam enim dispensauit cum bigamo ut archiepiscopus fieret.]

Bamberg MS Can. 42 (P.11.15), fo. 32va; Liège MS 127 E, fo. 28ra. — [1]*ad dict. ante c.*18 *v. bigami* L. [2]ex—quod *om.* L. [3]bene L. [4]*ibid. v. subdiaconatum* L. [5]fiat L.

Laurentius, *Apparatus decretorum* (Bologna, c. 1210-1215)
(as presented in the additions made, probably by a French disciple, to the *Apparatus* of Alanus in the Paris MS).
(D.34 c.18) *permaneat*:[1] Et est dispensatio quia ex quo contrahit cum[2] uidua, priuatur omni priuilegio, lxxxiiii. Quisquis. la.
(Alanus: . . . *contra Nicenam sinodum*): Immo est contra apostolum, ut dicit lau. (Alanus: . . . *usque ad presbyteratum*): et episcopatum cum[2] panormitano. (Alanus: . . . *i.Q.v. c.i*): Non tamen pape imponit necessitatem[3] quin possit dispensare si uelit, quia non habet imperium par in parem, ex.iii. de elect. Innotuit. Set nunquid alii, scilicet episcopus potest dispensare usque ad subdiaconatum ut hic dicitur? Non, quia prohibitum est,[4] de big. c.ult. la. (Alanus: . . . *Vnde dicunt quidam*): scilicet Nich' Furiosus.

Paris, B.N. MS lat. 15393, fo. 27ra.—[1]*gl. interlin.* [2]con P. [3]necessitati P. [4]*vel* prohibetur L (*lect. incerta*).

Glossa Palatina (Bologna, c. 1210-1215)
(D.34 c.18) *Lector. autem supra*: Hic non ponit regulam[1] successoribus iste Martinus, quia nec posset, ut ex.iii.[2] de elect. Innotuit. Vnde papa[3] Lucius dispensauit cum panormitano archiepiscopo qui bigamus fuerat. Set[4] episcopis datur hic forma dispensandi cum bigamis. b.[5]
Contra l.di. Non confidat. Quod tamen[6] hodie nouo iure eis interdictum est, ut ex.[7] de big. c.ult. Fuerunt tamen[8] quidam qui dixerunt cum bigamo dispensari non posse ultra, ut hic docetur, nec reciperet caracterem sicut nec

446

asinus: hoc dixit[9] Nicholaus[10] Furiosus, set confunditur ex illo cap. di.l. Quicumque.[11]

> Vatican, MS Pal. lat. 658, fo. 9rb, MS Reg. lat. 977, fo. 24va.—[1]*om*. R. [2]*om*. P. [3]et papa R. [4]nec R. [5]h. P (*sed agitur de opinione Bernardi Compostellani, dum Huguccio aliter sentit*). [6]bene P [7]ex. iii R (*sed agitur de* I *Comp.* 1.13.3). [8]Fuerunt tamen] cum R. [9]dicit R. [10]nichil P. [11]Contra—Quicumque: *est opinio Laurentii, cf. verba Guidonis de Baysio*.

Johannes Teutonicus, *Glossa ordinaria* (Bologna, *c.* 1216)

(D.34 c.18) *Lector. fiat*: Sic ergo papa dispensat contra apostolum, ut hic et lxxxii. Presbiter. Innocentius tamen dicit quod non licet dispensari cum bigamo, ut ex.iii. de bigam. Nuper, et idem Martinus hoc dicit, l.di. Si quis uiduam. Lucius tamen dispensauit cum panormitano archiepiscopo qui fuit bigamus. Item habes hic. . . .[1]

> Vatican, MS Vat. lat. 1367, fo. 25ra.—[1]*seqq. ut in edd.; ad rem non pertinent.*

Guido de Baysio, *Rosarium* (Bologna, *c.* 1300)

(D.34 c.18): . . . In glossa i. ibi, 'dispensauit,'[1] adde: scilicet usque ad presbyteratum. Temporibus nostris facta fuit haec dispensatio, sed forte ibi fuit plus facti quam iuris, secundum H.[2] Et ideo dicebat Nicolaus Furiosus . . . sicut nec asinus. Sed ipsius opinio confunditur 50. dist. Quicumque, secundum L.[3] Vnde dicebat Hug. ne videamur diminuere potentiam papae, dicamus quod de iure potest vltra dispensare. Vnde dicebat Lau. quod papa potest dispensare cum bigamo contra apostolum: quia ipse est maior potestate apostolo, 22. dist. Sacrosancta.[4] Item . . .

> Ed. Venice 1577, fo. 46rb.—[1]*i.e. verba Jo. Teutonici, supra*: ' Lucius tamen dispensauit ' *rell.* [2]*Huguccio ad loc.* § ' Set nonne papa potest. . . .' [3]*Laurentius, cf. Gloss. Pal. ad loc. in fine.* [4]*est opinio Huguccionis, non tamen Laurentii.*

Ricardus de Mores Anglicus, *Apparatus Compilationis primae* (Bologna, after 1196)

(*De bigamis*, i.13.3) *Super eo. priuari*: Infra xxxiiii. di. Lector contra. Solutio: ibi ostendit Martinus[1] quid liceat pape aut[2] quid aliis episcopis, idest[3] dispensando cum bigamo ad subdiaconatum, quod non est contra apostolum; usque ad diaconatum[4] non posset, ut michi[5] per hoc capitulum uidetur, scilicet ut[6] statuat: sic dispensandum est,[7] alias autem petentibus[8] nichil est diffinitiue positum, ut in aut.[9] de referendariis.[10]

> Avranches MS 149, Bamberg MS Can. 20, Halle MS Ye. 80, London, Lambeth MS 105, Munich MS lat. 6352, Vatican, MS Pal. 696, fo. 11rb. (I owe the collations of ABHM to the kindness of Msgr. Charles Lefebvre; cf. also the text published by F. Gillmann, *Archiv für katholisches Kirchenrecht*, cvii (1927), 596 n.2.)—[1]papa *add. al. m.* V. [2]*om.* V, non A. [3]scilicet BHLM, de *add.* ABHL. [4]subdiaconatum V, quod non—diaconatum *om.* L (*homoiotel.*), *suppl.* L[2]. [5]non posse (*corr.* posset) michi V. [6]*om.* BM. [7]*om.* A, *exp. V.* [8]penitentibus B. [9]in aut.] infra A. [10]*Auth.ii.*5 = *Nov. x* (*vide n.* 71 *supra*).

VII

Apparatus Materia auctoris ad Comp. I (after Ricardus)

(*De big.* i.13.3) *Super eo. priuari*: Contra xxxiiii. . . . scilicet dispensando cum bigamo,[1] quod contra apostolum non posset, ut uidetur ex hoc capitulo. Pape ergo licet, set alii non licet. Vel tempore apostolorum subdiaconatus inter sacros ordines non computabatur. *bigamus*: l.di. Ex penitentibus. Nam in aliis potest episcopus contra apostolum dispensare, quia illud[2] 'oportet episcopum esse sine crimine' est preceptum, vi. Q.i. c.i. et ut patet xlv.di. Episcopum et de clerico percussore c.ii.

Zwettl MS 162, fo. 6va-b.—[1]*vide Ric. Angl. ad loc.* [2]apostoli *add. marg.*

Glossae Valentianenses Comp. I (French School, early 13th cent.)

(*De big.* i.13.3) *Super eo*: Dicitur quod non potest dispensari cum bigamo ut ascendat ad sacros ordines, quia contra apostolum fieret, et si talem quis ordinet deponendus est, tamen ex dispensatione potest tolerari.

priuari: Hoc uidetur falsum, quia possunt fieri subdiaconi, ut xxxiiii. Lector, et subdiaconatus sacer est ordo, ut xxxii.di. Erubescant. Dico quod reuera solus papa potest dispensare quod bigamus sit subdiaconus, nec est contra apostolum set contra Nicenum concilium,[1] ut xxxiiii. Cognoscamus. Episcopus simplex non potest dispensare ut fiat subdiaconus, ut l. Non confidat ; ut fieret sacerdos, papa non posset dispensare, et si hoc faceret esset contra apostolum, et si de facto promoueretur non reciperet caracterem. Tamen dicitur quod Lucius papa cum quodam bigamo dispensauit in Sicilia[2] ut fieret presbiter, set a cardinalibus fuit redargutus.

Valenciennes MS 274, fo. 27r (communicated by Msgr. Lefebvre).—[1]consilium V. [2]Sicilia *scripsi: lacuna in* V.

Tancred, *Glossa ordinaria Comp. I* (Bologna, first recension *c.* 1210–1215; second recension *c.* 1220)

(*De big.* i.13.3) *Super eo. dispensari*: Supra xxxiiii. Lector contra. Solutio: ibi ostendit Martinus quid liceat pape aut[1] quid aliis episcopis, scilicet dispensare cum bigamis[2] usque ad subdiaconatum, quod non est contra apostolum, set usque ad diaconatum[3] non licet[4] per istud[5] capitulum, sicut michi uidetur. R.

Video enim quod apostolus prohibuit criminosum ordinari, ut xxv.di. § Nunc autem, et quod episcopis[6] licet dispensare cum criminosis, scilicet cum adulteris[7] et minoribus criminibus implicatis,[8] infra de iudiciis, At si clerici: et non est contra apostolum set preter apostolum.[9] Quidam tamen dicunt quod episcopis nullo modo dispensare licet cum bigamo, et si ordinaretur non reciperet caracterem sicut nec asinus, et Martinus non fuit papa set capra. Videtur quibusdam et michi quod dominus papa[10] directe contra apostolum dispensare posset, quoniam maior est in amministratione[11] quam fuerit[12] Paulus. Et fertur, set scriptum non uidi, quod Lucius papa dispensauit cum bigamo usque ad sacerdotium. t.

Vatican, MS Vat. lat. 2509 (rec. 1),fo. 9vb; MS Chis. E. vii. 207, fo. 10rb (rec. 2).—[1]et C. [2]bigamo C. [3]subdiaconatum C. [4]posset C.

448

⁵hoc C.   ⁶episcopi V.   ⁷adulteriis C.   ⁸implicati V.   ⁹set preter ap. *om.* C, *suppl.* C². ¹⁰set capra—papa *om.* C (*homoiotel.*), *suppl.* C². ¹¹in ammin.] amministrationem C.   ¹²fuit V.

Vincentius Hispanus, *Apparatus Decretalium Gregorii IX* (School of Bologna; after 1235 in Portugal)

(*De big.* i.21.2) *Super eo.* de bigamis: ordinatis scilicet.¹ *ordinandi*: idest conferendi consimiles ordines. Hec est enim hodie pena statuta contra,² supra de temp. ord. Litteras. Vinc. *dispensare*: Contra di.xxxiiii. Lector. Solutio : ibi ostendit... michi uidetur. t.³ Video enim... set preter apostolum.⁴ Et dico quod Martinus papa non potuit legem imponere successoribus: expressit enim quid liceat.⁵ *contra apostolum*:⁶ Et dico quod dominus papa directe contra apostolum posset dispensare, quia maior est in administratione quam fuerit Paulus,⁷ et fatui sunt qui dicunt bigamos non posse recipere caracterem. Vinc.

(ibid. c.3) *De bigamis. uiduarum*:... *admitti*: nec etiam per dispensationem episcopi, ut eod. tit. Nuper a nobis. Secus per dispensationem domini pape, ut xxxiiii. Lector. Vinc.⁸

Paris, B.N. MS lat. 3967, fo. 39rb.—¹scilicet (=s.) *scripsi*: c. P.   ²*suppleas* tales *vel aliquid simile*.   ³*vide glossam Ricardi ap. Tancredum ad loc. Comp. I.*   ⁴*vide Tancredum ibid.*   ⁵*leg.* deceat? (*cf. Huguccionis verba*). ⁶quid liceat contra apostolum *absque distinctione lemmatis scr.* P.   ⁷*vide Tancr.*   ⁸*vide glossam Alberti ap. Tancredum ad loc. Comp. II* (*in n.* 54 *supra*).

Ambrosius, *Summa titulorum decretalium* (Bologna, after 1215)

De bigamis non ordinandis. ... Dispensatiue tamen potest usque ad subdiaconatum promoueri, ut xxxiiii.di. Lector. Set numquid hic episcopus dispensabit? Nequaquam: non illa ratione quia apostolus prohibuit bigamum ordinari, licet id pro ratione assignetur infra eod. tit. Super eo, libro eod. Nam eadem ratione nec cum criminoso aliquo dispensare posset, cum apostolus in regula sua prohibeat criminosum ordinari, ut xxv.di. Nunc autem. Quod tamen aperte falsum est: dispensat enim in omnibus minoribus criminibus, etiam in adulterio, ut ex. i. de iudic. At si clerici. Set alia ratione, quia id¹ expresse episcopis prohibitum est, ut ex. iii. eod. tit. Nuper a nobis. Duo uero sunt species bigamie. ...

Rome, Bibl. Casanatense MS 1910, fo. 42ra.—¹idem R.

St. Raymond of Peñafort, *Summa iuris canonici* (Bologna, *c.* 1218-1221)

(*De big.* ii.5) ... Item bigamus exigente necessitate potest promoueri usque ad subdiaconatum dispensatiue, xxxiiii.di. Lector.¹ Set quis poterit dispensare? Dicunt quidam quod episcopus, et hoc per illud uerbum 'nichil autem supra' positum in predicto cap. Lector. Non enim illud posset² intelligi de papa, quia Martinus³ non poterat inponere legem suis successoribus, cum non habeat imperium par in parem, ex. iii.⁴ de elect. Innotuit. Vnde et⁵ Lucius papa dispensauit cum panormitano archiepiscopo qui bigamus fuerat.⁶ Si obicias quod non licet contra apostolum episcopis⁷ dispensare, respondent⁸ quod non obstat: nam et[9] apostolus dixit 'oportet ordinandos esse sine crimine,'[10] et tamen episcopi dispensant in adulterio et in[11] minoribus criminibus, ex. i. de iudic. At si.[12] Item[13] apostolus non prohibet dispensationem set de iure communi ostendit tales non esse promouendos.

Alii dicunt, et forte uerius, quod hodie non licet episcopis cum bigamo dispensare, quia ius expressum est quod eis prohibet[14] dispensationem, ex.iii.[15] de biga. Nuper. At idem[16] facit ex.i. de biga. c.ult.[17] et di.l. Si quis uiduam. Secundum hoc non tenet illud c. Lector, nisi forte quoad minores ordines ut in illis possit episcopus dispensare,[18] arg. xxxiiii. Si subdiaconus, et in eodem c. Lector, et di.l. Placuit, in principio.[19]

Item quid si aliquis . . .

Vatican, MS Borgh. 261, fo. 94rb (and cf. the ed. by J. Rius Serra, Barcelona, 1945), collated with the *Summa de casibus poenitentiae* (=S) iii.3 §4 (ed. Rome, 1603, pp. 261-3; =§2 ed. Verona, 1744, p. 238).—[1]Item numquid bigamus dispensatiue saltem poterit promoueri? Dico quod sic, usque ad subdiaconatum, exigente necessitate, Dist. 34 c. Lector S. [2]posset illud *tr.* S. [3]cuius est cap. *add.* S. [4]iii. *om.* S. [5]*om.* S. [6]fuerat big. *tr.* S. [7]liceat episcopo contra apost. *tr.* S. [8]Respondeo (R' *ed. Rom.*) S. [9]*om.* S. [10]ordinandum sine crim. esse *tr.* S. [11]*om.* S. [12]ex. de iud. At si clerici § fin. S. [13]Preterea S. [14]proh. eis *tr.* S. [15]iii. *om.* S. [16]id S. [17]ex. eod. Super eo S. [18]ut in—dispensare]in quibus credo quod potest episcopus propter necessitatem dispensare S. [19]*seqr. additio* Si tamen clericus in sacris . . . S.

Johannes de Petesella, *Summa titulorum Decretalium Greg. IX* (Bologna, after 1234)

(*De big.* i.21) . . . Cum bigamo dico dominum papam dispensare posse plenarie, licet quidam negent, ut Nicholaus Furiosus et sui sequaces, qui similiter sunt furiosi in hac parte, quia negant potestatem ecclesie Romane et claues fuisse[1] traditas Petro et per ipsum suis successoribus. Concedunt tamen quod usque ad subdiaconatum possit cum talibus dispensari, ut xxxiiii.di. Lector, et expresse confunduntur l.di. Quicumque penitens. Et dicitur, set non inueni[2] in aliqua scriptura autentica quod Lucius papa dispensauit cum panormitano archiepiscopo, nec est contra supra eod. Super eo, quia non denegatur in eo summo pontifici dispensatio set aliis episcopis. Dicunt tamen quidam et male quod episcopi possunt usque ad subdiaconatum dispensare cum bigamo per cap. xxxiiii. di. Lector, quia dispensationem talium sibi Romanus pontifex reseruat, ut infra eod. Super eo.

Vatican, MS Vat. lat. 2343, fo. 150ra.—[1]fuisset V. [2]inuenit V.

Johannes de Deo, *Libellus dispensationum* (Bologna, before 1243, revised after 1243, cf. n.87 *supra*).

(Owing to the deficiencies of the three MSS consulted, only a tentative text is given here. Passages not found in the first recension are printed within square brackets.)

[DE DISPENSATIONE DOMINI PAPE.][1] Super hoc diuersi[2] doctores diuersa sentiunt. Quidam dicunt quod papa[3] possit dispensare in omni casu, etiam[4]

contra apostolum, cum teneat locum beati Petri et sit[5] uicarius Ihesu Christi,
ex. ut eccles. benef. Vt nostrum, xxii.di. c.i. ex. de translat. prelat.[6] Inter
corporalia. Item dicunt quidam alii[7] quod in omni casu possit[8] dispensare,
scilicet cum non ligetur[9] legibus, ix. q.iii. Ipsi [sunt et c. Patet et c.] Cuncta,[10]
presertim cum non habeat imperium par in parem, ex. de elect. Innotuit.
Nichil ergo excipe[11] nisi articulos fidei tantum. Vnde uersus. . . .[12] Si
autem[13] peccat papa[14] in fide, possit puniri, xl.di. Si papa; alias non, ii. q.vii.
Oues et vi. q.i. Oues et xl.di.[15] c.i et ix. q.iii. Aliorum et lxix.di. c.ult.

Item[16] alii dicunt contra, scilicet quod[17] non potest dispensare contra apostolum, nec contra ius diuinum nec contra euangelium nec contra iiii. concilia, et inducunt pro se multa iura. . . .[18] Item alii[19] dicunt quod in eis que
spectant ad ipsum solum possit indefinite dispensare secum[20] sine offensa
iuris, que sunt hec: Solus restituit. . . .[21]

[IN QUIBUS PAPA DISPENSARE NON POTEST.][22]   Restat ergo uidere[23] in
quibus de iure non possit dispensare[24] etsi de facto possit. Contra apostolum
non potest[25] dispensare nec debet quod[26] bigamus promoueatur in diaconem
uel sacerdotem uel episcopum, ut dicit[27] apostolus in epistula ad Timo-
theum[28] et Titum:[29] 'Oportet esse episcopum unius uxoris uirum,' idest non
plurium, et hoc patres attestantur, [scilicet[30] propter significatum et consignificatum incarnationis filii dei in utero[31] uirginis et propter unionem
Christi et ecclesie militantis et triumphantis. Quod autem hoc uerum sit
probant patenter tam[32] apostolici[33] quam alii expositores noui et ueteris
testamenti: Augustinus, xxvi.di. Acutius, et Innocentius, xxvi.di. Deinde,
Ambrosius, xxvi.dⁱ. Vna tantum; et probat Vrbanus, xxv. q.i. Sunt qui
dicunt, et Lucius, ex. de bigamis, Super eo, ubi dicitur quod nullo modo
possit dispensare; et Celestinus probat illud idem ex. de big. c.[34] De bigamis,
et Innocentius iii. ex. eod. c. Nuper. Nec obstat xxxiiii.di. Lector, quia in
antiqua ecclesia[35] non fuit subdiaconatus[36] sacer ordo, set a tempore Gregorii, xxxi.di. c.i. et ii. Nec obstat quod dicunt quidam quod Lucius dispensauit cum bigamo,[37] quia non inuenitur; quodsi[38] inueniretur apocriphum
esset, et qui secus sentit pecus est.]

Item non potest dispensare contra euangelium. . . .[39]

Item in hiis[40] casibus non dispensat, etsi forte posset[41]: in symoniaco. . . .[42]

Et si de facto possit quicquid uelit, non tamen debet: qui licet sine comparacione aliorum hominum sit magnus factus,[43] debet tamen timere, de
pen. di.ii. Principium inquid [et ix. q.iii. Aliorum, xl.di. Si papa. In quibus
dicitur, si peccat artius[44] punitur quam alius, xl. di. Homo.][45] In aliis autem
ratione duce bene dispensat et debet, l.di. Domino sancto [et c.Ponderet et
c.Considerandum et c.Fidelior et lvi.di. Quia simpliciter,[46] ex. de renunt.
Nisi cum pridem[47]], et hec de expressis et de tacitis[48] dispensationibus.

Tacite enim semper dispensat, cum non possit omnia uindicare.[49] Vnde
dicit ipse quod non uult exagerare aliquod factum[50] ne cogatur iudicare[51]
quod iustum est, lxxiiii.di. Vbi ista, xxiiii. q.ii. Sane quod super Ricardo,[52]
ii. q.i. Multi. Et hec sufficiant causa breuitatis de dispensatione pape, qui
tenet et tenere debet mundi monarchiam,[53] ex. de maior. et obed. Solite,

xxii.di. c.i. ii. iii. et iiii.[54] [Et hoc dicimus salua honorificencia et potencia Romane ecclesie tuique honoris, uenerande Innocenti iiii.][55]

Vatican, MS Vat. lat. 5066, fos. 2v-5v (=V); Rome, Bibl. Casanatense 108, fos. 290rb-291ra (=C); Milan, Bibl. Ambrosiana M.64 sup., fo. a. lxxxxvra-vb (=A).—A: first recension; VC: second recension (but many readings common to AC suggest the existence of several stages in rec. 2). I have abstained from recording many readings, especially of C, which are corruptions rather than variants. [1]*bis scr.* V, IN QUIBUS DISPENSAT SOLUS PAPA A. [2]De dispensatione domini pape diuersi A. [3]*om.* A. [4]et etiam A. [5]sicut V, sic C. [6]prel. *om.* C, episcopi uel clerici A. [7]Et ideo dicunt AC. [8]potest A. [9]non legatur C, ligetur A. [10]VC: Ipsi et Cuncta A. [11]Nolunt ergo excipere AC. [12]*sqq. ita sunt corrupta ut emendari nequeant ex tribus codd. Deinde aliam paragraphum* Circa humanum genus cum ytalicis . . . *add.* V. [13]Set dicunt si autem V, et si autem C, et si A. [14]*om.* AC. [15]Si papa—xl.di. *om.* V (*homoiotel.*), ii.q.vii.—c.i. *om.* A. [16]*om.* A. [17]quia C. [18]*sqq. omisi.* [19]Item tercii C, Tercii A. [20]*om.* C. [21]*sequuntur* 24 *casus papales.* [22]VC: *om.* A. [23]Restat uidere A, Ergo uidere potes C. [24]de iure disp. non potest *tr.* C, non potest disp. de iure *tr.* A. [25]posset A. [26]scil. *praem.* A, nec debet. Quod VC. [27]ut dicit] ut C, unde A. [28]ad corinth. xi. C. [29]et Tit. *om.* A. [30]scilicet—pecus est VC: *om.* A. [31]uterum VC. [32]pat. tam *om.* C. [33]apostoli V. [34]de big. c.] eodem C. [35]in ant. eccl.] tempore Martini C. [36]subd. non erat *tr.* C. [37]cum silico (*leg.* siculo?) bigamo C. [38]et si C. [39]*sqqr. quinque genera dispensationum ubi 'non potest.'* [40]In istis A. [41]forte non posset V, forsan possit C, forte *om.* A. [42]*sqqr. quinque genera ubi 'non dispensat.'* [43]factus sit (est A) magnus *tr.* AC. [44]acrius V. [45]VC: *om.* A. [46]simplicem V, plus sui C. [47]ex. de re iud. Pridem V, ut ex. de renunt. Nisi cum C, et c. Ponderet—pridem *om.* A. [48]et de tac. *om.* V, de *om.* A. [49]de omnibus iudicare A. [50]aliquod factum] quod actum est AC (quod gestum est *can. cit.* D.74 *c.*7). [51]ne cog. iud. *om.* A. [52]lxxiiii.— Ricardo] et A *perperam.* [53]machinam V. [54]et penult. et ult. *add.* AC. [55]VC: *om.* A (*var. lect.* C *sunt corruptissimae*).

Bernardus Parmensis, *Glossa ordinaria Decretalium Greg. IX*
(Bologna, first recension before 1241, last recension after 1263)
(Reproduced from the standard edition, Rome 1582. I have numbered the sections and inserted some comments.)
(*De big.* i.21.2) *Super eo. dispensare*: Sed contra 34. dist. Lector. Ibi dispensatur ut bigamus subdiaconus fiat.
(I. Bernard reports four opinions.)
(1) Sed ibi ostendit M. quod liceat papae aut aliis episcopis, scilicet dispensare cum bigamo usque ad subdiaconatum et non supra, quod non est contra apostolum per hoc capitulum. Prohibitio apostoli est de diacono, presbytero et episcopo, et non de aliis, quia subdiaconatus non erat adhuc sacer ordo.

(' Sed ibi—capitulum ': Ricardus Anglicus and Tancred. The explanatory addition ' Prohibitio—ordo ' resembles the wording in *Summa Omnis qui iudicat.* The beginning should read: '. . . ostendit Martinus quid liceat.')

452

(2)   R. dixit quod Marcellus papa retulit se ad statum primitiuae ecclesiae, in quo subdiaconatus non erat sacer ordo, 60. dist. Nullus.

(R. is not Ricardus Anglicus nor St. Raymond, but the opinion here quoted was held by others, see note 43 *supra*. Gillmann, in *Archiv für katholisches Kirchenrecht*, cvii (1927), 596 n.2, following Johannes Andreae, *Addit. ad Speculum*, prooem., suggests R(ufinus), but admits that no such text is found in the latter's *Summa*. Panormitanus, however, read ' Rogerius ' (*Comm. Decretal.* i.21.2); yet no decretalist glossator of that name is known, cf. Kuttner, *Repertorium*, p. 373 n.6.—' Marcellus papa ' is obviously a corruption.)

(3)   Quidam dicebant quod episcopi olim poterant dispensare cum bigamis in ordinibus maioribus, hac ratione quia episcopi dispensant cum criminosis, infra de iud. At si clerici, et tamen apostolus prohibuit criminosum ordinari, 25. dist. § Nunc autem, nec tunc dicuntur facere contra apostolum: et sic eadem ratione cum bigamo.   Quorum opinio reprobatur infra eod. Nuper et c.A nobis.

(' Quidam ': Tancred's opinion is reported, but with exageration. He did not extend the bishop's dispensatory power to all major orders, *App. Comp. I*, ad loc.)

(4)   (a) H. dixit quod episcopi dispensare non poterant cum bigamo uel uiduarum marito, arg. 50. dist. Non confidat. Cuius opinio confirmatur per illa capitula Nuper et A nobis.

(b) Jo. uoluit dicere quod papa non posset.

(Huguccio's opinion on bishops is correctly rendered, but the identity of Jo. remains doubtful: neither Johannes Teutonicus nor Johannes Galensis (who was a staunch curialist, cf. Gillmann, *Arch. kath. Kirchenr.* cxviii (1938), 207, 219) held such an opinion on papal power. But Johannes de Deo did: if he were meant, the gloss must have been written or enlarged after Bernard read the *Libellus dispensationum*. Only a collation of MSS can tell.)

(II.   Bernard's own opinion (1) on bishops, (2) on the pope, (3) on validity of orders.)

(1)   Quod dicit R. et H. uerissimum uidetur: quia licet dispensetur cum criminosis, tamen non sequitur quod cum bigamo.   Et illa est ratio quia criminosus post peractam poenitentiam restitutus uidetur in pristinum statum et incipit esse quod non fuit ... sed bigamus non prohibetur promoueri propter crimen sed propter sacramenti defectum, quia carnem suam diuisit in plures ab unitate recedendo.   Sed illud sacramentum amplius restitui non potest per aliquam satisfactionem, cum non sit crimen. ...

(Bernard here develops the ' sacramental ' reason for rejecting the analogy between *bigamus* and *criminosus* (I 3, above), i.e. Tancred's doctrine on episcopal powers, although Bernard does not expressly speak of bishops.— The opening statement remains puzzling: he now associates ' R.' with Huguccio's opinion (' quod episcopi dispensare non poterant,' I 4a) although no such statement is ascribed to R. in I 2, above.)

(2)   Propter quod uidetur quod papa non possit dispensare cum bigamo propter eandem rationem, quia propter dispensationem papae non restituitur sacramentum unitatis, cum nec posset.   Nam cum Deus cetera possit, uirginem tamen post ruinam suscitare non potest . . . multo minus uidetur [papa] dispensare posse cum bigamo.   Unde opinio R. bona est.   Et licet ipse H. dubitet, uidetur tamen consentire—ne uideatur diminui potentia papae— quod possit dispensare cum bigamo.

> (The denial of papal power, attributed above (I 4b) to ' Jo.', is now cited with approval as opinion of ' R.': the siglum thus covers three different opinions—all at variance with that of Richard de Mores! As for Huguccio, he actually stated the opposite, pro-papal position much less hesitantly than Bernard (. . . *dubitet, uidetur*) makes it appear.)

(3)   Tamen hoc quod dicitur, bigamus in quocumque ordine ordinetur, recipit ordinem, arg. 50. dist. Quicumque poenitens: per quod capitulum uidetur quod cum bigamo dispensare possit. Sed illud tantum intelligitur in minoribus ordinibus.

> (The doctrine on the validity of orders received by a *bigamus* (Huguccio and others, see notes 79ff. *supra*) is whittled down to apply in minor orders only.—The sentence ' Tamen hoc quod dicitur . . .' lacks a finite verb: here again, MS evidence would be needed.)

ADDENDUM ON LAURENTIUS

By oversight I failed to copy two glosses from *Glossa Palatina*, D. 34 c. *Lector*, preceding the gl. v. *autem supra* (p. 445 *supra*)

> *fiat* : Potest ergo papa dispensare cum bigamo contra apostolum, quia ipse potestate maior est quolibet apostolo nisi Petro, nisi in articulis fidei. *nichil* : Ideo hic dicit quia apostolus non uidetur expresse prohibuisse nisi de episcopo, presbitero, diacono, et ideo hic dispensandum dicit [MS P : dispensandum. Item dicit] tantum usque ad diaconatum.   h.

The second of these glosses comes from Huguccio (cf. his *Summa*, p. 443 *supra*, lin. 4-6) ; the first is evidently the gloss of Laurentius to which Guido de Baysio refers, ' Vnde dicebat Lau. quod papa . . .' (p. 446 *supra*).   My observations on Guido's text, pp. 446 n. 4 and 426 n. 73, are to be corrected accordingly.

From Peter of Eboli, *Liber ad honorem Augusti*, Berne MS. 120, fo. 127r.

Top illustration: the bigamous chancellor with his two wives.
Lower illustration: the chancellor is depicted as seeking relief from gout in foot-baths of human blood.

VIII

ST. JÓN OF HÓLAR: CANON LAW AND HAGIOGRAPHY IN MEDIEVAL ICELAND *

In the mid-eleventh century, 1056 A.D., Archbishop Adalbert of Hamburg-Bremen consecrated Isleifr Gizurrsson as the first resident bishop of Iceland [1]. Thus, after a long period of difficult and erratic missionary beginnings, the bleak, majestic island just south of the Arctic circle became incorporated into the hierarchical structure of the Church. Only

---

* General bibliography for the early medieval history of the Church in Iceland will be found, e. g., in H. Jedin's *Handbuch der Kirchengeschichte*, III 1: *Die mittelalterliche Kirche...*, by F. Kempf *et al.* (Freiburg—Basel—Wien 1966) ch. 30, pp. 261—2 (= pp. 521—2 of the English translation by A. Briggs, *The Church in the age of feudalism;* London—New York 1969), and in the entries for Iceland by W. Göbell, *Lexikon für Theologie und Kirche*, 2nd ed. 5 (1960) 801, or by M. P. Jakobson, *New Catholic Encyclopedia* 7 (1967) 322. K. Maurer's posthumous work *Über Altnordische Kirchenverfassung und Eherecht (Vorlesungen über Altnordische Rechtsgeschichte* II; Leipzig 1908) still remains worthwhile. — The present writer, not being sufficiently familiar with Scandinavian languages, has not consulted articles and major treatises in any of them. As for the corpus of the Old Norse sources and sagas, he must rely on the English version of the bilingual edition by G. Vigfusson and F. Y. Powell, *Origines Islandicae*, I (Oxford 1905), „in spite of all its shortcomings ...a monumental work": cf. H. Hermansson, *Old Icelandic Literature (Islandica* 24; Ithaca, N. Y. 1935) p. 28. For more recent editions and bibliography of the texts chiefly used in this paper see the entries in *Kulturhistorisk Leksikon for nordisk middelalder* 7 (Copenhagen 1962) s. vv. *Hungrvaka*, by M. M. Lárusson (col. 88—9): *Íslendigabók* by B. Sigfusson (494—5), *Ións saga helge*, by Lárusson (617—18); also G. Turville-Petre, *Origins of Icelandic Literature* (Oxford 1952). — I wish to thank Mr. George Davis of the Documents Department, General Library of the University of California, Berkeley, for his kind assistance in translating some Old Norse passages where a closer scrutiny of the text in *Origines Islandicae* seemed indicated. Finally, in quoting from the sagas, I have not retained all the studied English archaisms of that text.

[1] Adam of Bremen, *Gesta Hammaburgensis ecclesiae pontificum* 4. 36, ed. B. Schmeidler (*Scriptores rerum German. in usum scholarum*, 3rd ed. 1917) p. 273; I have not seen the new edition by W. Trillmich (Darmstadt 1961). *Hungrvaka* c. 2, in *Biskupa sögür* I (Copenhagen 1858) pp. 61—2; c. . 3 in *Orig. Island.* I p. 428; I have not seen the new edition by J. Helgason, in *Byskupa sögür* I (Copenhagen 1938).

a few years earlier, Pope Leo IX had confirmed to Adalbert his prerogatives as apostolic vicar and legate, after the model of St. Boniface, for the peoples of the north and the east, beyond the confines of his own metropolitan province [2]. In those years, Adalbert could indeed proudly style himself „legate of the holy Roman and Apostolic see, unworthy minister of the church of Hamburg, and archbishop of all the nations of the North" [3].

Isleifr established his see, rather precariously, at his ancestral homestead and church of Skálholt: it was only his son and successor Gizurr (1082—1118) who had it enacted as law that the bishop's see should always be at Skálholt [4]. He built a cathedral church and dedicated it to St. Peter [5]. The creation of the second bishopric took place in a quite different setting early in the twelfth century. When Gizurr had been bishop for twenty years or so, the men from the „Northland" area of the isle asked him for a second see in the country so that Iceland would never be without a bishop. After much deliberation and consultation the choice fell upon the priest Jón Ögmundsson, who had been educated from his boyhood by Bishop Isleifr, traveled as a young deacon on the European continent in pursuit of his studies, and was admired for his gifts by all. „And he went abroad with letters from Gizurr the bishop and then went to see Pope Paschalis. And he was consecrated bishop by Archbishop Asser of Lund in Skane, two nights before the mass of Philip and James [29 April]. Then Jón went to Iceland and set up his bishop's chair at Hólar..." [6]

Thus far the anonymus author of the *Hungrvaka,* i. e. the Lives of the early bishops of Skálholt. From the synchronisms which Ari Thorgilsson (Ari Fródi), the father of Icelandic historiography, presents in the *Islendigabók* (c. 1122—1132), the year of St. Jón's consecration can be fixed at 1106 when he was fifty-four years old [7]. It was a new era for the churches of the North. The hold of Hamburg and the German

---

[2] Leo IX, JL 4290; new edition in *Diplomatarium Danicum* I 2: 1053—1169, ed. L. Weibull and N. Skyum Nielsen (Copenhagen 1963) No. 1, pp. 1—5; for the reference to St. Boniface see the text p. 4 lin. 4—7. On Adalbert's canonical position and ambitions see especially H. Fuhrmann, *Studien zur Geschichte mittelalterlicher Patriarchate (III),* in *Zeitschrift der Savigny-Stiftung für Rechtsgeschichte, Kan. Abt.* 41 (1955) 95—183, at 120—70 (p. 147 n. 154 on the authenticity of JL 4290, established by Kehr).

[3] *Diplomatarium Danicum* I 2, No. 8 (= Adam, *Gesta* 3. 76 p. 222).

[4] Ari Thorgilsson, *Íslendigabók* 10. 4 in *Orig. Island.* I p. 302.

[5] *Hungrvaka* 2. 6, *ibid.* p. 435 (= *Biskupa sögur* I p. 67 c. 6). It is chiefly on the strength of these texts that Maurer, *Altnordische Kirchenverfassung* (note * supra) pp. 53ff. argued for considering Isleifr the last of the missionary bishops rather than the first residential bishop of Iceland.

[6] *Hungrvaka* 2. 9 in *Orig. Island.* I p. 43 (= *Biskupa sögur* I p. 68—9 c. 6); shortened in *Diplom. Dan.* I 2, No. 36 col. 1.

[7] *Islendigabók* 10. 11 ed. *cit.* p. 304; cf. *Diplom. Dan. loc. cit.,* editors' comments p. 81.

Reichskirche over the Scandinavian lands had been broken in the course of a complex historical development; it culminated in the action of Paschal II, who elevated the see of Lund to become an archbishopric with metropolitan rights for all the northern kingdoms and islands [8]. Apparently the bishop of Skálholt in faraway Iceland was already aware of the news when he sent the bishop-elect abroad with his letters.

Much more detail on the first bishop of Hólar is found in the *Jóns Saga*, which exists in several Old Norse recensions [9]. Like the lost Latin *vita* it renders, *Jóns Saga* was written by Gunnlaugr Leifsson, monk of Thingeyrar Abbey (d. 1218), soon after St. Jón's canonization [10]; that is, after the solemn *translatio* of his body from the tomb to an altar in the cathedral which his third successor, Bishop Brandr Saemundarson, performed on 3 March 1200, almost eighty years after the Saint's death (23 April 1121) [11].

This is what Gunnlaugr tells us of St. Jón's voyage after his election [12]: That summer the bishop-elect took ship with his retinue and friends and with Bishop Gizurr's letter and seal to bear witness of his errand. They arrived in Denmark after a good voyage and went at once to the place where Archbishop Asser was. It was rather late in the day and the archbishop was in church et evensong. (There follows a poetic story how Jón and his clerks stayed in the nave outside the choir and joined in the singing of vespers, and how because of the beauty of Jón's voice the archbishop forgot his own command not to turn around and look out of the choir). After the two had met and the archbishop had read Gizurr's letter, the matter of the new bishopric was discussed for several days.

---

[8] Paschal II, JL 5994 (lost; reconstructed from a late tradition in the 14th-century Chronicle of the Archbishops of Lund), JL 6335, *ante* 8 May 1104. Cf. *Diplom. Dan.* I 2 p. 64 (comments to No. 28) and No. 30; for recent discussion (since 1966) see W. Seegrün, *Das Papsttum und Skandinavien bis zur Vollendung der nordischen Kirchenorganisation (Quellen und Forschungen zur Geschichte Schleswig-Holsteins*; Neumünster 1967) pp. 108—29, and the review by F. Kempf in *Archivum historiae pontificiae* 6 (1968) 446—52; N. Skyum-Nielsen, *Das dänische Erzbistum vor 1250*, in *Acta Visbyensia III: Visby-symposiet för historiska vetenskaper* 1967 (Göteborg 1969) 113—38.

[9] Two of these in *Biskupa sögur* I, only the first in *Orig. Island.* I pp. 534—67.

[10] O. Widding, H. Bekker-Nielsen, L. K. Shook, *The Lives of Saints in Old Norse prose*, in *Mediaeval Studies* 25 (1963) 294—337, at p. 317f.; and see the entries on St. Jón and his saga by Bekker-Nielsen and Widding in *Bibliotheca Sanctorum* 6 (Rome 1965) 1045f.; D. C. C. Pochin Mould, in *New Catholic Encyclopedia* 7. 1092; M. M. Lárusson, in *Kulturhistorisk Leksikon* (note * *supra*) 7. 608—12, 617—18. Not seen: J. Helgason, *Ión Ögmundsson den hellige*, in *Norvegia sacra* 5 (1925) 1—34.

[11] H. Bekker-Nielsen, *A note on two Icelandic saints*, in *Germanic Review* 36 (1961) 108—9, dispels the widespread anachronistic notion of any national disregard for papal prerogatives being shown in the episcopal „canonizations" of Sts. Thorlák and Ión: the right to canonize was not formally reserved to the pope until considerably later.

[12] *Jóns Saga* 7. 2—4 in *Orig. Island.* I pp. 546—8 (= *Biskupa sögur* I pp. 159—61), shortened in *Diplom. Dan.* I 2, Nos. 36 col. 2 and 37 col. 1.

„Then the archbishop spoke thus to the bishop-elect: 'My very dear brother, I perceive that you have nearly all the qualities that befit a bishop... but on account of one matter that you have told me, that you have had two wives, I dare not consecrate you without the knowledge and permission of the pope himself. Now it is my counsel that you hasten to the pope, and I shall write a letter with my seal to acquaint the pope with your case. And if it goes as we hope and he allows you to take consecration, and me to perform it, then return here quickly and I shall joyfully bring to an end your errand' ". (In another recension [13], Jón presents letters from Bishop Gizurr „and other chieftains of Iceland"; the archbishop speaks of the need for permission „of the apostolic see", and uses a Latinizing term: „If he [the lord pope] has granted you dispensation [hann dispenseri med thér]".)

Next we read [14] of the bishop-elect's visit in Rome (to the lord pope in the curia, i kuriam, as the other recension has it), where „holy Paschal the second of that name" was pope. St. Jón presented all his errand and showed the archbishop's letter and seal, which acquainted the pope with the whole state of the case. When the pope had seen the writings, „he granted the grace that had been humbly requested" and directed the bishop-elect to go and see Archbishop Asser, to whom he wrote under his seal, „giving him leave to consecrate the holy Jón bishop". (The other recension stresses that Pope Paschal acted supported by God's guidance, and again uses Latinizing terminology: Paschalis pape; „from his curia postulig... a letter with his bulla"; „dispenserir with blessed Jón electo", etc.)

There follows, after the pope's blessing, Jón's return to Archbishop Asser, with a further joyful sojourn, both before and after the consecration on the third of the Kalends of May.

It seems that the account of the bishop of Hólar's consecration as told in the Jóns Saga has never been critically examined by Church historians. Matters might be different, had not the Bollandists excluded St. Jón from the Acta Sanctorum at the time the first volume for March (1668) was in preparation. The brief remark we read there (3 mart.) is certainly unworthy of their own standards of hagiographic scholarship: Jonas Ogmundus episcopus Holanus, they say, will not be included

---

[13] In Biskupa sögur I p. 232f. c. 20, shortened in Diplom. Dan. I 37 col. 2.
[14] Jóns Saga 7. 5—6 in Orig. Island. I p. 548f. (= Biskupa sögur I p. 161 c. 9); the other recension in Biskupa sögur I p. 233f. c. 21; Diplom. Dan. I 2, Nos. 37, 38 cols. 1 and 2 (both shortened).

because the only available source for him is Arngrim — this means Arngrímur Jónsson the Learned (1568—1648) — and „homini a Catholica fide averso fidere non licet"; he is to be set aside „dum certiora monumenta proferentur" [15]. (As an interesting Lutheran counterpart of this piece of bigotry, we read in Finnur Jónsson's Ecclesiastical History of Iceland [16]: „Jonas Oegmundinus ... in sanctorum numerum annis post mortem 77 *puritate religionis deficiente* a nostratibus relatus...". Nothing seems to have come of the Latin translation of *Jóns Saga* which the great collector of Icelandic antiquities, Árni Magnússon (1663—1730), prepared at the beginning of the eighteenth century for the Bollandists from one of Gunnlaugr's Old Norse recensions. Magnússon's autograph and a copy exist in Copenhagen [17]; there is no mention of either in the *Bibliotheca hagiographica latina*. Thus the second national saint of Iceland—in fact the oldest, even though the *translatio* of St. Thorlák Thórhallsson of Skálholt (1133—1193), preceded that of St. Jón by two years [18] — has remained largely unknown to western students of hagiography and, we should add, to historians of canon law, for whom the tale of Pope Paschal II's writ of dispensation ought to be of considerable interest.

It is an undisputed fact of Iceland's church history that well into the thirteenth century nearly all its bishops were married, as were of course deacons, priests, and other clergy [19]. Efforts at introducing canonical legislation on celibacy, such as those made in 1153 by Cardinal Nicholas Breakspear when he was legate to Norway and Sweden [20], are not found in Iceland until much later. Against this background of insular custom, the few comments that have been made in passing on St. Jón's case merely point out that it differed from the normal situation of married bishops because there was a second marriage, and this „seemed" to be contrary to a scriptural command or „recommendation" [21].

This comfortable explanation is wide of the mark. From the early days of Christianity the injunction of the Pastoral Epistles that a bishop, deacon, of priest be *unius uxoris vir* (1 Tim. 3.2, 12, Tit. 1. 5—6)

---

[15] *Acta Sanctorum, Martii* I p. 109 in the Paris printing (1865).

[16] Finni Johannaei *Historia ecclesiastica Islandiae*, I (Hafniae 1772) 327.

[17] See Widding, Bekker-Nielsen, Shook, *op. cit.* (note 10 *supra*) 317.

[18] *De sancto Thorlaco*, in *Biskupa sögür* I p. 403: „Haec translatio corporis s. Thorlaci anno quinto ab obitu ipsius facta est ..."; cf. Bekker-Nielsen s. v. *Thorlák Thórhallsson*, in *New Catholic Encycl.* 14. 140.

[19] Maurer, *Altnordische Kirchenverfassung* p. 317; S. Kalifa, *Usages insolites dans les coutumiers ecclésiastiques et les premiers „droits chrétiens" d'Islande et de Norvège*, in *Études offertes à Jean Macqueron* (Aix-en-Provence 1970), pp. 385—98.

[20] See Seegrün, *op. cit.* (note 8 *supra*) pp. 151f., 168f.

[21] Maurer *loc. cit.*: „ ... weil dem ein bestimmtes Gebot der Schrift entgegenzustehen schien"; Kalifa, *op. cit.* p. 393: Archbishop Asser „ne contestait pas, en l'occurrence, le droit au mariage de Jon, mais sa seconde union légitime qui transgressait une recommandation paulinienne". Both authors cite 1 Tim. 3. 2.

was taken as one of the strictest among the requirements which the catalogue of the *regula apostoli* had set up for holy orders [22]. The remarried widower was barred from ordination as *digamus* or *bigamus*, not because of any moral taint (we must forget modern usage, where „bigamy" always means two simultaneous married lives), but because the full sacramental meaning is lacking in any second marriage: the remarried man has „divided" his flesh and his marital union can no longer represent the mystical union of Christ with his Church [23]. As early as the fourth century, we therefore find an extension of the impediment — the *irregularitas* as it would later be called in the schools — to other cases that imply a *divisio carnis:* marriage to a widow, concubinage before marriage, and the like. At the same time we find an extension to minor orders of the clergy, but here the disciplinary practice remained variable: as a result, the canonical tradition of the early middle ages came to include texts of different intent. One among these, from the *capitula* of St. Martin of Braga (d. 579), would even allow lectors who had remarried, or married a widow, to be promoted to the subdiaconate „if need be, but not beyond" (*si forte necessitas sit, subdiaconus fiat, nihil autem supra*) [24].

In an earlier paper [25] I have shown how many problems of interpretation would arise from this text for the canonists of the twelfth century, especially since it had, long before, been mislabelled as a decree of Pope Martin I (649—655), and also since in the meantime the subdiaconate had become canonically assimilated to the major orders. The exegesis of „Pope Martin's" text led to long-drawn and often sharp controversies over the limits of papal and episcopal powers of dispensation. For the modern mind it may be difficult to appreciate, but our texts bear witness that the debate here grew as hot-tempered as in the more famous quarrels over dispensations from the vow of poverty or over papal interpretations of the Franciscan Rule.

Until we reach the last quarter of the twelfth century, the possibility of extending dispensation from bigamy to the higher orders — diaconate, priesthood, episcopacy — was not even contemplated from afar. Simon de Bisignano (c. 1177—79), the first canonist to ask the question [26], *an uero summus pontifex posset bigamum ad sacerdotium promouere, uel*

---

[22] For history and bibliography see J. Vergier-Boimond, *Bigamie (irrégularité de)*, in *Dictionnaire de droit canonique* 2 (1947) 853—88. The early sources are assembled by Gratian, mainly in Dist. 26—28, 33—34, and discussed in the article cited *infra* (note 25), especially pp. 410—14.

[23] The *locus classicus* is St. Augustine, *De bono coniugali* c. 18 (21), in PL 40. 387—8, abridged in *Glossa ord.* on Tit. 1 and so quoted by Gratian D. 26 c. 2.

[24] Mart. Bracar. *Capitula* c. 43 (*Opera* ed. Barlow; New Haven 1950, p. 135), in Gratian D. 34 c. 18.

[25] S. Kuttner, *Pope Lucius III and the bigamous archbishop of Palermo*, in *Medieval Studies presented to Aubrey Gwynn, S. J.* (Dublin 1961), pp. 409—54.

[26] See Kuttner, *Pope Lucius...* p. 424; full text p. 440.

utrum esset sacerdos, si eum ordinaret de facto, shied away from answering it; after all, this meant for the pope openly to set aside the apostolic rule. A few years later, some author said the pope could grant such a dispensation but it was not known that he ever had done so; another held that he could not, „although I have heard of such a dispensation" [27]. The first concrete case was reported by Huguccio (*c.* 1188—90): „In our day", he wrote, „Lucius III gave a dispensation for the priesthood to some *bigamus* in Sicily" [28]. It was also Huguccio who lined up, not without hesitation, the main arguments from the doctrine of Peter's primacy for this extension of papal prerogative. His train of thought, including the caveat that it would not be fitting for the pope always to make use of his power, became the foundation for the predominant teaching [29], although a line of dissenters can be cited down to the mid-thirteenth century [30].

Pope Lucius' precedent most probably was a dispensation given for Matthew of Salerno (d. 1193), the last chancellor of the Norman kings of Sicily [31]. In the tradition of the schools, however, Huguccio's report soon was embellished, and before the end of the twelfth century, the *quidam bigamus in Sicilia* had become the bigamous archbishop of Palermo. This legendary case remained throughout the Middle Ages, and beyond, the stock example for exceptional dispensatory powers of the papacy [32].

If we now return to Gunnlaugr's Life of St. Jón of Hólar, there can be little doubt that the story he tells of the dispensation granted by Pope Paschal II was modeled upon the contemporary canonistic discussions of the archbishop of Palermo's case. A hundred years earlier, in 1105/6, it was literally unthinkable, given the state of development of doctrine, that Paschal should have written „under his seal" to the archbishop of Lund, instructing him to consecrate a *bigamus*. When even later in the thirteenth century some authors refused to believe the report

----

[27] *Ibid.* pp. 424, 441—2.
[28] *Ibid.* p. 433; Huguccio, *Summa* D. 34 c. 18 v.*nihil autem supra*: „ ... nostris etiam temporibus Lucius tertius dispensauit cum quodam bigamo in Sicilia usque ad presbyteratum".
[29] *Pope Lucius...* pp. 424—7, texts pp. 442ff.
[30] *Ibid.* pp. 427—30, 443ff.
[31] *Ibid.* 435—9. The evidence comes from Peter of Eboli, *Liber ad honorem Augusti* (*c.* 1195—6), a poem in praise of the Emperor Henry VI and full of venom against King Tancred and his chancellor; of the latter he writes:
    Te sinus ecclesie contra decreta recepit:
      Peccati bigamum non decet ara dei:
    Te prece uel precio, sanctissime pape, fefellit ...
                                    (vv. 989—91)
[32] *Pope Lucius...*, pp. 431—5.

of Pope Lucius' dispensation, or denied that holy orders so conferred could give the sacramental character, we can imagine what the reaction would have been a century before: Paschal's act would have been considered almost a deviation from the faith and probably caused an uproar similar to that which greeted his request in 1111 that the German bishops give up their *regalia* or, shortly afterwards, his grant of the „pravilegium" to King Henry V.

But one can guess why Gunnlaugr found it necessary in his day to insert this circumstantial story of the papal dispensation. Among the many archaic traits of the early Icelandic Church, with its *Eigenkirchen* and its married bishops, we must also reckon the fact that the irregularity of the *bigamus* and the *viduae maritus* was obviously unknown. We read in the Life of St. Thorlák (1133—93) that his kinsmen urged him to take a wife and that he planned to marry a certain widow. „It was not at that time greatly censured by the superiors if a priest took a widow to wife, *though it is now forbidden*". Thus the author of the *Thorláks Saga* tells us early in the thirteenth century, and apparently he considers this a quite recent restriction [33]. Thorlák was visiting at the manor of the widow with his kinsmen, ready to ask for her hand, when „a man of noble countenance" appeared to him in a dream and told him not to do so; „there is another bride much higher in store for you and you shall take none other but her". This was, of course, a prophecy of his future elevation to the bishopric of Skálholt. St. Thorlák never married at all, but the point was not that the marriage to a widowed lady would have barred him from orders.

In the case of St. Jón, his *Saga* simply tells us that he was twice married, that his first wife lived but a short while, and that from neither marriage children were known to have survived [34]. This short report follows immediately upon a section that speaks of Jón's exemplary service as a priest in the church of his ancestral estate: at this point, apparently no one was aware that by right he could not have been ordained to, or remained in, the priesthood. But after the canonization of 1200 the irregular status of the sainted bishop had somehow to be corrected. The *Hungrvaka* had mentioned his traveling south to Pope Paschal before his consecration by Archbishop Asser in Lund [35]: such travel to Rome may or may not have been merely a *topos*, a literary borrowing from the lives of the first two Icelandic bishops, Isleifr and Gizurr, both of whom had

---

[33] *Thorláks Saga* 4. 7 in *Orig. Island.* I p. 464—6 (= *Biskupa sögur* I p. 93 c. 5). Maurer, *Altnordische Kirchenverfassung* p. 367 refers to this case, citing Lev. 21. 13—14, but apparently again unaware of the whole canonical tradition (cf. notes 19, 21 *supra*).

[34] *Jóns Saga* 5. 2 in *Orig. Island.* I p. 544 (= *Biskupa sögur* I p. 93 c. 5).

[35] *Supra* at note 6.

gone to see the pope — Leo IX and Gregory VII respectively — before their consecration [36]. In any event, here was a cue for Gunnlaugr the monk of Thingeyrar to insert the story of a papal dispensation in the *Jóns Saga.*

If our conjectural interpretation of the *Saga* is correct, it presupposes that a certain amount of canonical learning had been carried to the remote North by the beginning of the thirteenth century. To verify such an assumption, however, requires a greater knowledge of Icelandic cultural history than a canonist from an altogether different background could claim.

---

[36] *Hungrvaka* 1. 3 in *Orig. Island.* I p. 428 and c. 2. 4, *ibid.* p. 434 (= *Biskupa sögur* I pp. 61 c. 2 and 67 c. 5).

IX

CARDINALIS: THE HISTORY OF A CANONICAL CONCEPT

I. Introduction*

It is commonly known that in the canonical sources of ancient and early medieval times many bishops, priests and deacons throughout the Latin Church

* In addition to the conventional sigla, abridged references will be used for the following publications: AKKR = *Archiv für katholisches Kirchenrecht.*—M. Andrieu, *Les Ordines romani du haut moyen-âge* I (Spicilegium sacrum Lovaniense 11, Louvain 1931).—Ans. Luc. = *Anselmi episcopi Lucensis collectio canonum* ed. F. Thaner (Innsbruck 1906–15).— Bonizo, *Liber de vita christiana* ed. E. Perels (Texte zur Geschichte des römischen und kanonischen Rechts im Mittelalter 1, Berlin 1930).—H. Bresslau, *Handbuch der Urkundenlehre* (2nd ed. Leipzig-Berlin 1912–31; vol. II, 2 ed. H. W. Klewitz).—H. Th. Bruns, *Canones apostolorum et conciliorum saeculorum IV.V.VI.VII.* (Berlin 1839).—J. J. Christ, 'The Origin and Development of the Term "Title",' *The Jurist* 4 (1944) 101–23.—Deusd. = *Die Kanonessammlung des Kardinals Deusdedit* ed. V. Wolf von Glanvell (Paderborn 1905).— Duchesne, LP: see LP.—V. Fuchs, *Der Ordinationstitel von seiner Entstehung bis auf Innozenz III.* (Kanonistische Studien und Texte ed. M. Koeniger 4, Bonn 1930).—*Gallia christiana in provincias divisa* edd. D. de Sainte-Marthe, B. Hauréau, P. Piolin et al. (Paris 1715–1877).—A. Gaudenzi, 'Il monastero di Nonantola, il ducato di Persiceta e la Chiesa di Bologna,' *Bulletino dell'Istituto storico italiano* 36–7 (1916).—Gothofr. = *Codex Theodosianus cum perpetuis commentariis Iacobi Gothofredi* (Lyons 1665; Leipzig 1736).—Greg. Reg. = *Gregorii I papae Registrum epistolarum* edd. P. Ewald [bks. 1–4] and L. Hartmann [5–14] (MGH *Epistolae* 1–2, Berlin 1887–99).—P. Hinschius, *Das Kirchenrecht der Katholiken und Protestanten* (Berlin 1869–95).—Kehr, IP = *Italia pontificia sive repertorium privilegiorum et litterarum* . . . ed. P. F. Kehr (Berlin 1906–35).—H. W. Klewitz, 'Die Entstehung des Kardinalkollegiums,' ZRG Kan. Abt. 25 (1936) 115–221.—B. Kurtscheid, *Historia iuris canonici* I (Rome 1941).—LD = *Liber diurnus Romanorum pontificum ex unico codice Vaticano* ed. Th. Sickel (Vienna 1889); *Liber diurnus ou recueil des formules usitées par la chancellerie pontificale* . . . ed. E. de Rozière (Paris 1869).—LP = *Le Liber pontificalis: texte, introduction et commentaire* ed. L. Duchesne (Paris 1886–92).—(Charles) Le Cointe, 'Institution et rang des cardinaux,' memorandum written by the Oratorian priest (1611–81) for Colbert and printed (from MS Paris, Bibl. nat. *Collection des cinq-cents de Colbert* vol. 172, fols. 52–159) in *Analecta iuris pontificii* 18 (1879) 28–55; 257–77.—J. Mabillon, *Museum italicum* (Paris 1687–9; 2nd ed. 1724).—E. Martène, *De antiquis ecclesiae ritibus* (Rouen 1700–2; 2nd ed. Antwerp 1736–8 [the best according to Andrieu]; 3rd ed. Venice 1783: cited according to the numbers of books, chapters, articles, *ordines*).—L. A. Muratori, *Antiquitates italicae medii aevi* (Milan 1738–42); id. *Rerum italicarum scriptores* (Milan 1723–51).— NA = *Neues Archiv der Gesellschaft für ältere deutsche Geschichtskunde.*—Onofrio Panvini, 'De origine cardinalium liber unicus' ed. A. Mai, *Spicilegium Romanum* 9 (1843) 469–511.— W. Peitz, 'Liber Diurnus: Beiträge zur Kenntnis der ältesten päpstlichen Kanzlei,' *Sitzungsberichte der kais. Akademie der Wissenschaften in Wien*, phil. hist. Kl. 185, 4 (1918).—G. Phillips, *Kirchenrecht* (Regensburg 1845–72; vols. 1–2: 3rd ed. 1855–7).—J. B. Sägmüller, *Die Thätigkeit und Stellung der Cardinäle bis Papst Bonifaz VIII.* (Freiburg Br. 1896).—E. Schwartz, *Acta conciliorum oecumenicorum* (Berlin-Leipzig 1914–38).—M. Giuseppe Tamagna, *Origini e prerogative de'cardinali della S.R.C.* (Rome 1790).—Thaner, *Ans. Luc.*: see Ans. Luc.—A. Thiel, *Epistolae Romanorum pontificum genuinae* (Braunsberg 1868).—L. Thomassin, *Vetus et nova ecclesiae disciplina circa beneficia et beneficiarios* (Paris 1688 [as translated from the French original, *Ancienne et nouvelle discipline* etc. Lyons 1676–9]; used ed. Mayence 1787: cited according to the numbers of parts, books, chapters, paragraphs).—

130

were called *cardinales*, long before that term came to be used exclusively, or even primarily, for a specific group of dignitaries in the Church of Rome. Historians do not agree, however, as to the original meaning of the word in the language of the ancient Church. Nor do they, as a rule, explain with sufficient clearness in what sense it was first applied to those members of the Roman clergy—the priests of the ancient *tituli* or quasi-parishes; the deacons both of the papal palace and the city's *diaconiae;* and seven bishops of the metropolitan province—who eventually rose to the unique position of becoming the 'senators' and sole electors of the Pope.

The complex subject has been amply, and at times hotly, discussed. Authors of the sixteenth, seventeenth, and eighteenth centuries explained the term, *cardinalis*, in various ways.[1] Many construed it as originally meaning *principalis* —like the pivot (*cardo*) which governs the revolving door—and referred it to the chief incumbent, the titular and proper superior of a church, such as the bishop, the first among several priests serving the same place, and the first deacon.[2] Other writers held that *cardinalis* was a synonym of *intitulatus, fixus,* or *incardinatus*, in the general sense of a cleric permanently and firmly attached, as a hinge, to the service of a church.[3] Others again, reversing the image of hinge and door, insisted that the term implied attachment to a *cardo* or main church (*ecclesia cardinalis*), such as a parish church, a cathedral, or, in an eminent

---

C. H. Turner, *Ecclesiae occidentalis monumenta iuris antiquissima* (Oxford 1899–1930).—F. Ughelli, *Italia sacra sive de episcopis Italiae . . .* (2nd ed. by N. Coleti, Venice 1717–22).— Wolf von Glanvell, *Deusd.*: see Deusd.—ZRG = *Zeitschrift der Savigny-Stiftung für Rechtsgeschichte.*

[1] Already Jacques Godefroy complained, *Comm. Cod. Th.* 12, 6, 7 (V, 541 Lugd.; IV, 573 Lips.): '. . . ubi cardinale quid sit, non magis quam quid cardinales presbyteri, diaconi, ad hanc diem scitur.' Muratori begins his dissertation, 'De cardinalium institutione,' *Antiq.* 5, 155 with the words: 'Multi multa de cardinalibus eorumque origine atque institutione commentati sunt; . . . actum agere non est mihi animus.' Select bibliographies of the period are found in Hinschius, *Kirchenr.* I, 309 and Kehr, IP 1, 1f.

[2] Onofrio Panvini, 'De episcopatibus, titulis et diaconiis cardinalium liber,' in *Romani Pontifices et Cardinales S.R.E. ab eisdem . . . creati* (Venice 1557) Appendix p. 51; id. *De origine cardinalium* 481; H. Plati, *De cardinalis dignitate* (Rome 1602; 6th ed. 1836) 2, 3, 23; J. Cohellius, *Notitia cardinalatus* (Rome 1653) 3; J. B. Card. de Luca, 'Relatio romanae curiae forensis' 4, 2, in *Theatrum veritatis et iustitiae* (Rome 1671) 7, 2, 17; M. Gonzalez Tellez, *Commentaria perpetua in singulos textus quinque librorum decretalium Gregorii IX* (Lyons 1673) 1, 24, 2 ad v. *sacerdotum cardinalium*; 3, 4, 2; P. de Goussainville, note to *epp.* 1, 15 and 12, 2 in his edition (Paris 1675) of the letters of Gregory the Great (reprinted in the Maurist edition, to *epp.* 1, 15 and 14, 7; cf. PL 77, 461 note *e*; 1310 note *g*); L. Thomassin, *Vetus et nova Ecclesiae disciplina* 1, 2, 115, 2; J. Kleiner, *De origine et antiquitate Eṁorum S.R.E. Cardinalium* (Heidelberg 1767; ed. A. Schmidt, *Thesaurus iuris ecclesiastici*, Heidelberg-Bamberg-Würzburg 1773: II, 443–66) §13, and many others. The doctrine goes back as far as the glossators; cf. *Glossa ordinaria* on C. 21 q. 1 c. 5 ad v. *cardinalem*; on X. 1, 24, 2 ad v. *cardinalium.*

[3] C. Fleury, *Institutiones iuris ecclesiastici* (= *Institution au droit ecclésiastique*, Paris 1676; 3rd latin ed. Venice 1779) 1, 19, 2; Gothofredus *loc. cit.*; Muratori, *Antiq.* 5, 156f.; Z. B. van Espen, *Ius ecclesiasticum universum* (Louvain 1753–68) 1, 22, 1, 1; J. Devoti, *Institutionum canonicarum libri IV* (Rome 1785–9; used ed. 1830) 1, 3, 2, 22 note 4. Also De Luca and Goussainville *locc. citt.* offer this explanation, in combination with the first theory.

sense, the Church of Rome.[4] Behind these etymological wranglings there was an issue even more passionately disputed: the 'parochialist' theory, especially dear to Gallican writers, which contended that in olden times *cardinalis* had been more or less a name for parish rectors.[5]

A few authors, finally, were struck by the fact that in the letters of St. Gregory the Great the word, *cardinalis*, appears always to be used in connection with bishops, priests, or deacons appointed to a church different from that of their first ordination. In other words, according to these authors the term was always correlated, at least in the language of St. Gregory, with *incardinare* or *cardinare* in the sense of transferring a cleric.[6] The heralds of this interpretation, in particular Tamagna (1790) and Nardi (1830), found it a useful instrument in combating the claims of the *parrochisti*. They did not attempt, however, to explain the obvious discrepancy between the Gregorian and the medieval usage nor to connect the former in any way with the origins of the Roman Cardinalate.[7]

After the middle of the nineteenth century, only George Phillips (1864) and Paul Hinschius (1869) continued to give consideration, in their respective monumental treatises of Canon law, to the peculiar use of *cardinalis* and *incardinare* in St. Gregory's correspondence.[8] But they, too, treated it rather as an isolated phenomenon of no consequence for the general institution of the cardinalate.[9] The majority of modern canonists preferred to make no further mention of the problems of interpretation created by the Gregorian texts. It became usual instead to avoid all historical difficulties by a more or less hazy juxtaposition of the several common etymologies at hand: it now was held that the various connotations of *cardinalis* and *incardinatus*—such as permanently attached to a church;

[4] St. Robert Bellarmine, *Controversiae* 2: 'De membris Ecclesiae militantis' 1, 16 (Venice 1596; *Opera omnia* ed. Naples 1872: II, 174); Cohellius, *op. cit.* 4D; L. Nardi, *Dei parrochi* (Pesaro 1829–30) II, 403–21 (but see note 6 *infra*).

[5] Thus Thomassin, *op. cit.* 1, 2, 116, 1; Muratori, *Antiq.* 1, 552; 5, 155; 162B; 163C; 164f.; the anonymous author of the pamphlet, *Cosa è un cardinale ?* reprinted and refuted by Tamagna, *Origini*; and several Gallicanists cited by Nardi, *loc. cit.* But see also Panvini, *De orig. card.* 482f.; Kleiner, *op. cit.* §21 (455 Schmidt).

[6] The *Correctores Romani* in their note on Gratian D. 71 c. 5 (Rome 1582, col. 465–6; ed. Friedberg, *Corpus iuris canonici* I, Leipzig 1879, col. 258) ad v. *cardinandum*: '. . . Cardinare vero, seu cardinalem constituere (quod est in fine huius capitis), ita videtur B. Gregorius accepisse, ut canonicam translationem significet . . .'; Panvini, *De orig. card.* 472–8; F. Florent, *Tractatus IX in IX priores titulos libri I decretalium Gregorii IX* (Paris 1641) 266–8; Cohellius, *op. cit.* 3; 4D; Le Cointe, *Instit. et rang* 29f. 33; J. Garnier, note to LD 11 ad v. *incardinari* in his edition (Paris 1680) of the *Liber diurnus* (reprinted in ed. Rozière 32); Tamagna, *Origini* I, 99–1C9; Nardi, *Dei parrochi* II, 3S6–103.

[7] Le Cointe 30–2 and Tamagna I, 109f. at least point correctly to some later instances of *cardinalis* in the Gregorian sense. Panvini 479f. and Garnier *loc. cit.* do not even admit it in all of St. Gregory's letters. A typical example for the disconnected parallelism of the different interpretations is found in Cohellius *loc. cit.*

[8] Phillips, *Kirchenr.* VI, 50–9; Hinschius, *Kirchenr.* I, 313f.

[9] Phillips VI, 53f. holds that the other meaning of *cardinalis*, i.e. cleric of a main church or *cardo* (cf. pp. 43–50; 54f.), runs parallel to the Gregorian usage since the sixth century. Hinschius arbitrarily grafts the derivation from *cardo* (I, 314–7) and the identification with *principalis* (319f.) on his discussion of the Gregorian terminology.

belonging to a main church or *cardo;* first ranking or *principalis* among the clerics of a church—had somehow been merged in forming name and dignity of the cardinals.

This syncretism[10] is still today the prevailing approach of textbooks and reference works. Several recent findings concerning the origins of the Roman cardinalate[11] have not as yet shaken this attitude.[12] The present study does not purport to present many new documents bearing on the question at issue—in fact, the majority of the pertinent texts was already known by writers of the seventeenth and eighteenth centuries. But a critical re-examination and integration of the materials will yield, it is hoped, new results as to both the history of a canonical term and the beginnings of the Sacred College.

II. The 'Gregorian' Cardinals

The canonical usage of the Ancient Church in speaking of cardinal bishops, priests, and deacons, must be studied from the authentic papal documents: a fragment of Gelasius I (492–6), two letters of Pelagius I (555–60), and the numerous pertinent letters of Gregory the Great (590–604), preserved in his *Registrum epistolarum.* The so-called *Constitutum Silvestri,* a notorious forgery of the sixth century, has to be left aside for later consideration.[1] Our principal source, then, is St. Gregory's Register. Only with the help of its abundant evidence,[2] will a correct interpretation of the few earlier but isolated papal texts be possible.

1. *Episcopus cardinalis*

It has been held that St. Gregory used this expression and its equivalents, *pontifex cardinalis, cardinalis sacerdos,* simply as synonymous with *episcopus*

---

[10] To cite a few representative names only: R. von Scherer, *Handbuch des Kirchenrechts* I (Graz 1886) 473f.; Sägmüiler, *Cardinäle* 6f.; id. *Lehrbuch des katholischen Kirchenrechts* I, 4 (4th ed. Freiburg 1934) 516; id. 'Cardinal,' *Catholic Encyclopedia* 3 (1908) 333; C. Wenck 'Das Cardinalscollegium,' *Preussische Jahrbücher* 53 (1884) 431; id. 'Kardinalat,' *Die Religion in Geschichte und Gegenwart* 3 (1st ed. 1912) 925; F. M. Cappello, *De Curia Romana* I (Rome 1911) 18; J. Forget, 'Cardinaux,' DThC 2 (1905) 1717f.; V. Martin, *Les cardinaux et la curie* (Bibliothèque catholique des sciences religieuses 36, Paris 1930) 20; A. Molien, 'Cardinal,' *Dictionnaire de droit canonique* 2 (1937) 1313–5; A. Dumas, in Fliche-Martin, *Histoire de l'Église depuis les origines à nos jours* 7 (Paris 1940) 154f.

[11] Especially by Duchesne and by Dr. Klewitz.

[12] See e.g. the most recent discussion in J. T. McBride, *Incardination and Excardination of Seculars* (The Catholic University of America Canon Law Studies 145, Washington, D. C. 1941) 1–13; these pages also separately under the title 'The Terms Incardination and Excardination,' *The Jurist* 2 (1942) 292–304.

[1] Cf. ch. V sec. 3 *infra.*

[2] Many of the letters were already studied by Panvini, *De orig. card.*, and almost all of them, by Thomassin. The latter included in his list (*Vet. et nova discipl.* 1, 2, 115, 6) also Greg. *Reg.* 4, 13 (JE 1284) of which one sentence reads in Goussainville's edition (*ep.* 3, 13): '. . . in alia quacumque ecclesia eum volumus cardinari.' But since the correct reading is: '. . . in aliam quamcumque ecclesiam . . . ordinari' (cf. MGH *Epp.* 1, 247 notes *e, f*), this text must be dropped for our purposes.

proprius, to denote the ordinary pastor of a diocese.[3] This opinion overlooks the fact that the great pope never calls a bishop *cardinalis* when writing of him, or addressing him, with reference to his original diocese, that is, to the church of his episcopal ordination. On the contrary, the term is only applied in connection with granting or not granting a bishop ordinary jurisdiction in a foreign diocese.

Greg. *Reg.* 1, 77 (JE 1146): Gregory appoints Bishop Martin of Tainate in Corsica as *cardinalis sacerdos (pontifex)* to the Church of Aleria: '. . . quoniam ecclesia Tainatis ita est . . . occupata atque diruta, ut illuc ulterius spes remeandi nulla remanserit, in ecclesiam te Alirensem, quae iam diu pontificis est auxilio destituta, cardinalem . . . hac auctoritate constituimus sine dubio sacerdotem. Ita ergo . . . cuncta dispone vel ordina, ut . . . ecclesia Dei alterno gaudio repleatur cardinalem te suscepisse pontificem' (96, 25–97, 6 Ewald). Cf. also *Reg.* 1, 79 (JE 1147).

Reg. 2, 37 (JE 1191): Gregory appoints Bishop John of Alessio on the Dalmatian coast as *cardinalis sacerdos* to the Church of Squillace in Calabria: '. . . Propterea te Johannem ab hostibus captivatae Lissitanae civitatis episcopum in Squillacina ecclesia cardinalem necesse duximus constituere sacerdotem. . . . Et licet a tua hoste imminente depulsus sis, aliam quae a pastore vacat debeas ecclesiam gubernare, ita tamen, ut si civitatem illam ab hostibus liberam effici et Domino protegente ad priorem statum contigerit revocari, in eam in qua es prius ordinatus ecclesiam revertaris. Sin autem praedicta civitas continua captivitatis calamitate premitur, in hac in qua et a nobis incardinatus es debeas permanere' (132, 30–133, 8 Ewald).[4]

Reg. 3, 13 (JE 1217): Gregory appoints Bishop Agnellus of Fondi as *cardinalis sacerdos* to the Church of Terracina: '. . . Et quia defuncto Petro pontifice suo te sibi cardinalem postulant constitui sacerdotem. . . . Quia igitur ob cladem hostilitatis nec in civitate nec in ecclesia tua est cuiquam habitandi licentia, ideoque hac te auctoritate Terracinensi ecclesiae cardinalem constituimus sacerdotem' (172, 3–9 Ewald). . . . Illud quoque fraternitatem tuam scire necesse est, quoniam sic te praedictae Terracinensi ecclesiae cardinalem esse constituimus sacerdotem, ut et Fundensis ecclesiae pontifex esse non desinas; . . . ut ante dictae Fundensi ecclesiae tibi iura potestatemve nullo modo subtrahamus' (172, 26–173, 4 Ewald).[5] Cf. also *Reg.* 3, 14 (JE 1218).

Reg. 2, 12 (JE 1162): Gregory denies the petition of the clergy and people of Naples who want Bishop Paul of Nepi as their *episcopus cardinalis* ('ut eum cardinalem habere desideretis episcopum . . .' 110, 16 Ewald), but entrusts to the latter the temporary admin-

---

[3] *Glossa ordinaria* on C. 21 q. 1 c. 5 (= Greg. *Reg.* 3, 13) ad v. *cardinalem*: 'idest proprium episcopum.' *Glos. ord.* on X. 1, 24, 2 (cf. on this doubtful canon ch. IV nn. 37, 75 *infra*) ad v. *cardinalium*: 'idest principalium. Simile vii. q. i. Pastoralis (c. 42 = Greg. *Reg.* 2, 37); et dicuntur cardinales a cardine . . . simile xxiiii. dist. Presbiter (c. 3 = Gelasius JK 677) et lxxi. dist. Fraternitatem (c. 5 = Greg. *Reg.* 6, 11). Ibi exponitur cardinalis, idest proprius, et xxi. q. i. Relatio (c. 5 = *Reg.* 3, 13).' See further Thomassin, *op. cit.* 1, 2, 115, 3–6, and, above all, Ewald in MGH *Epp.* 1, 97 note 3 to Greg. *Reg.* 1, 77; also Mommsen, 'Ostgothische Studien,' NA 14 (1888–9) 472; J. F. O'Donnell, *The Vocabulary of the Letters of St. Gregory the Great* (The Catholic University of America Studies in Medieval and Renaissance Latin 2, Washington, D. C. 1934) 136; McBride, *op. cit.* 5–7 (*Jurist* 2, 296–8).— As to the theory, *cardinalis* = *principalis*, it had always difficulties with the term, cardinal bishop. Bellarmine (*Controv.* 2, 1, 16) easily observed: '. . . nam non sunt in una dioecesi plures episcopi' (*Opp.* II, 174).

[4] This letter passed on into Gratian: C. 7 q. 1 c. 42.

[5] Gratian: C. 21 q. 1 cc. 5–6.—Phillips, *Kirchenr.* V, 462 and Ewald 173 n. 4 wrongly interpret this text as treating of a union of the two bishoprics.

istration of the vacant see with the rank of *visitator* (*Reg.* 2, 13; 18; 26: JE 1163, 1170, 1179; *Reg.* 3, 35: JE 1240).[6]

Reg. 14, 7 (JE 1920): the bishop of Euria, dispossessed of his see, has taken refuge with his clergy at Cassiope on the island of Corcyra and usurped jurisdiction over the village; Gregory upholds the rights of the bishop of Corcyra but allows the refugees to stay, provided that the bishop of Euria give a *cautio*, 'per quam promittat, nullam sibi in eo potestatem, nullum privilegium, nullam iurisdictionem, nullam tamquam cardinalis episcopus ulterius auctoritatem defendere...' (2, 426, 19–21 Hartmann); they are to remain as *hospites* (line 25) only, until they can return to Euria.

To understand these cases, we have to remember that the ancient Church abhorred the transfer of a bishop to another see, which appeared to the early Canon law as an adulterous violation of the spiritual marriage between the bishop and his Church.[7] Consequently, whenever St. Gregory found that in an orphaned bishopric an episcopal election was not possible or feasible, three ways were open to him.[8] (1) He could send another bishop and commit to him the temporary administration of the diocese until a proper election would take place; for these administrators, the term *visitator*[9] is used.[10] (2) He could temporarily

---

[6] Cf. Johannes Diaconus, *Vita s. Gregorii* 3, 18 (PL 75, 141); Phillips, *Kirchenr.* V, 459f.

[7] For the prohibition of transfers see the Councils of Nicaea c. 15; Antioch c. 21; Serdica cc. 1, 2; Chalcedon cc. 5, 20. Cf. Johannes Scholasticus, *Synagoga L titulorum* 12 (ed. V. Beneševič, *Abhandlungen der Bayerischen Akademie der Wissenschaften*, phil.-hist. Abt. Neue Folge 14 [1937] 13f. 52–5); for a Greek illustration of these rules in the tenth century see J. Compernass, 'Zwei Schriften des Arethas von Kaisareia gegen die Vertauschung der Bischofssitze,' *Studi Bizantini e Neoellenici* 4 (1935) 87–125, in particular p. 111f. The comparison with adultery is first found in a Roman synod under Pope Siricius c. 13 (Bruns 2, 280). An excellent exposé was given in the ninth century by Hincmar of Reims, *ep. de translatione episcoporum contra Actardum* (PL 126, 210–30; see also nn. 16, 27–8 *infra*).—Cf. Phillips, *Kirchenr.* V, 424–31 and note 59; L. Ober, 'Die Translation der Bischöfe im Altertum,' AKKR 88 (1908) 209–29; 441–65; 625–48; 89 (1909) 3–33; Fuchs, *Ordinationstitel* 78–85; Kurtscheid, *Hist. iur. can.* 112–6.

[8] Phillips, *Kirchenr.* V, 458–63.

[9] The visitor-administrator of a foreign diocese is not to be confused with a bishop visiting in his own diocese. On the latter see the Synods of Tarragona 516 c. 8 and II Braga 572 c. 1 (Bruns 2, 17; 39); Gelasius I JK 710; Pelagius I JK 984, 991. Cf. Thiel, *Epp. Rom. pont.* 495 n. 2 (on JK 710); Sdralek, 'Visitationen,' in F. X. Kraus, *Real-Encyklopädie der christlichen Alterthümer* 2 (Freiburg 1886) 958–60. Two instances are found in St. Gregory's letters. *Reg.* 2, 19 (JE 1172): Bishop Paulinus of Taurianum, near Reggio Calabria, who had been temporarily dispossessed of his see and given various interimistic assignments (cf. *Reg.* 1, 38–9; 2, 51: JE 1108–9; 1171), is told to visit his own church 'quotiens oportunum tempus credideris' (116, 6–7 Ewald); in fact, we find him later again at Taurianum, cf. *Reg.* 9, 134; 13, 21 (JE 1656, 1886). In *Reg.* 9, 71 (JE 1596), Gregory enjoins upon Bishop Passivus of Fermo to consecrate an oratory at Teramo, 'si in tuae dioceseos, in qua visitationis impendis officium, memorata constructio iure consistit' (2, 90, 14–5 Hartmann). Cf. n. 43 *infra*. The Teramo case has been misunderstood by most authors as treating of the visitation of a foreign diocese, see Appendix A, *infra*.

[10] Greg. *Reg.* 1, 15; 76; 79 (JE 1083, 1145, 1147); 2, 13; 18; *25–6; *39–40 (JE 1163, 1170, 1178–9, 1192–3); 3, 24–5; 35 (JE 1228–9, 1240); 4, *39 (JE 1311); 5, *12–4; *21–2 (JE 1327–9, 1336–7); 6, *21; 38 (JE 1400, 1420); 7, *16 (JE 1462); 9, 60; *80–1; *99–100; *140; *184–5; (JE 1585, 1605–6, 1624–5, 1665, 1712–3); 13, *16–7; *20–1 (JE 1880–1, 1885–6). The letters marked by an asterisk were made out according to a formulary of the chancery. *Reg.* 5, 13 and 13, 16 passed on into Gratian: D. 61 cc. 19 and 16.—Cf. Phillips, *Kirchenr.* V, 459f.; Hinschius,

unite the vacant see to a neighboring diocese: 'ecclesia . . . quam tuae ecclesiae adgregari unirique necesse est.'[11] (3) He could appoint another bishop, whose own diocese had been destroyed or temporarily invaded, as the proper ordinary of the vacant diocese. Gregory termed this latter provision *incardinare* or *cardinare*, and the incardinated bishop, hence, *cardinalis*.[12]

Such an incardination[13] was the only type of transfer which did not run counter to the canonical rules, because it did not disrupt the bond between the *cardinalis episcopus* and his original bishopric.[14] If this bishopric had been utterly destroyed, the incardination became permanent, comparable to a second marriage after the death of the first spouse. But if the former see could be recovered, the bishop would be obliged to return and the bond with the diocese of incardination would be dissolved,[15] comparable to the dissolution of a second marriage in the case of presumptive death, if the first spouse survives.[16] At any rate, the *episcopus cardinalis* did not lose his original title by the transfer,[17] yet he did become the true bishop—be it permanently or upon condition—of his new diocese.[18] In this, and only in this, sense is it correct to say that every *episcopus cardinalis* was also an *episcopus proprius*. But the converse is not true, because the fact that a cardinal bishop was always made by incardination distinguishes him from every *episcopus proprius* who acquired his see by election and ordination.

Nevertheless, the modern editor of St. Gregory's Register maintained that the two terms, *cardinalis* and *proprius*, were interchangeably employed by Gregory

Kirchenr. II, 229–32. For *visitatores* before St. Gregory see Gelasius I JK 677–8 (n. 22 *infra*); John II JK 886–8; Agapitus I JK 890.

[11] Greg. *Reg.* 1, 8 (JE 1075: Formio-Minturno); 2, 44 (JE 1197: Miseno-Cumae = C. 16 q. 1 c. 50); 2, 48 (JE 1202: Velletri-Tre Taverne); 3, 20 (JE 1224: Nomentum-Cures); 6, 9 (JE 1389: Reggio-Carina). Cf. the form-letter LD 9 (discussed by Peitz, *Lib. diurn.* 64f.); Joh. Diaconus, *Vita* 3, 14; Phillips, *Kirchenr.* V, 351f.

[12] Thus correctly Joh. Diaconus, *Vita* 3, 15–6, the *Correctores Romani*, and the other writers cited ch. I n. 6 *supra*; also Phillips VI, 52f. and Hinschius, *Kirchenr.* I, 313. The assertion by Ewald (97 n. 3 to *Reg.* 1, 77): 'incardinatus in ecclesia autem dicitur primo loco ordinatus' (repeated by Bannier, ThLL 3, 442 s.v. *cardino*) is entirely gratuitous.

[13] Hinschius I, 314 n. 3 wrongly refers in this context also to Greg. *Reg.* 2, 8 (JE 1159; *ep.* 2, 7 ed. Maur.), a letter which in fact treats of the appointment of an Apostolic Vicar for Sicily, not of an incardination.

[14] Cf. *Reg.* 3, 13 *supra*.

[15] Cf. *Reg.* 2, 37 *supra*.

[16] The analogy between incardination and second marriage in cases of uncertain death was already drawn by Hincmar, *ep. cit.* (note 7 *supra*: PL 126, 225f.); cf. also Phillips V, 464; Hinschius I, 314.

[17] Cf. *Reg.* 2, 37; 3, 13.

[18] The permanent, if conditional, nature of the incardination was rightly stressed by Phillips V, 457f. and Hinschius I, 314 n. 4 against Florent, *op. cit.* (ch. I n. 6 *supra*) 266f. who classified the institute as a mere *commendatio ad tempus*. The incardinated bishop signs, and is addressed, with the name of the new bishopric: we find e.g. Agnellus of Fondi (*Reg.* 3, 13) after his incardination styled as *episcopus civitatis Terracinensis* (Roman synod of 595: Greg. *Reg.* 5, 57a [1, 366, 3 Hartmann]), *episcopus de Terracina* (*Reg.* 7, 16: JE 1462), *episcopus Terracinensis* (*Reg.* 8, 19; 9, 45: JE 1507, 1569).

and by Gelasius I.[19] But even apart from the fact that Ewald cannot cite one instance of a bishop who is called *cardinalis* in his original diocese, his reasoning is futile. An examination of the pretended arguments from St. Gregory reveals only that in some letters certain bishops who are vested with jurisdiction in foreign dioceses—be it by virtue of visitation, incardination, or union—are allowed to act with the same authority as a proper bishop (in one case: as a cardinal and proper bishop);[20] and that in some letters certain bishops are appointed as *cardinales*. It cannot be seen how the two premises, 'Some foreign bishops may act like *episcopi proprii*' and 'Some foreign bishops are called cardinals,' should yield any valid syllogism. On the contrary, the one letter which gives to a visiting bishop powers *tamquam cardinalis et proprius sacerdos*[21] clearly distinguishes between the two qualifications.

The argument from St. Gelasius is equally fallacious. In one case the Pope asks a bishop to ordain priests in a foreign diocese, 'sciturus visitatoris nomine te, non cardinalis creasse pontificis,' and another time he gives a similar injunction, 'visitatoris officio, non potestate proprii sacerdotis.'[22] In other words, Gelasius states that a *visitator* is neither a cardinal nor a proper bishop.[23] As long as the axiom stands, *ex mere negativis nihil sequitur*, it is impossible to conclude from these two texts that *cardinalis* means *proprius*. What can be seen however, from the fragments of St. Gelasius is the fact that a hundred years before Gregory

[19] Ewald, MGH *Epp.* 1, 97 n. 3 (to *Reg.* 1, 77): 'Cardinalem sacerdotem aut pontificem idem significare ac proprium pontificem probant epistolae . . . ubi proprius, et epistolae . . . ubi cardinalis eodem modo dicitur,' referring, besides the Gregorian texts, to Gelasius JE 679, 680 (mistakenly for JE 677, 678).—See also note 3 *supra*.

[20] Greg. *Reg.* 1, 76 (JE 1145) to a *visitator*: '. . . cunctis igitur te rebus superscriptae ecclesiae ut proprium volumus uti pontificem' (96, 15–6 Ewald); 3, 25 (JE 1229) in a case of visitation: '. . . ut omnia quae ad curam utilitatemque ecclesiae pertinent tamquam proprius episcopus debeat ordinare' (183, 6–7 Ewald), cf. 3, 24 (JE 1228): '. . . Et praeter ordinationes clericorum cetera omnia in praedicta ecclesia tamquam cardinalem et proprium te volumus agere sacerdotem' (182, 14–5 Ewald); 2, 48 (JE 1202) in a case of union: '. . . quaeque tibi de eius patrimonio, vel cleri ordinatione, seu promotione, vigilanti ac canonica visa fuerint cura disponere, quippe ut pontifex proprius liberam habebis ex nostra praesenti permissione licentiam' (149, 23–5 Ewald); the same formula in other cases of union: 3, 20 (JE 1224; 178, 15–7 Ewald) and 6, 9 (JE 1389: '. . . quippe ut proprius sacerdos': 1, 388, 10–2 Hartmann); 2, 44 (JE 1197) in the case of consumptive union: '. . . quaeque tibi de earum patrimonio, vel cleri ordinatione, sive promotione, iuxta canonum statuta visa fuerint ordinare atque disponere, habebis ut proprius revera sacerdos liberam ex nostrae auctoritatis consensu atque permissione licentiam' (143, 12–5 Ewald); 3, 13 (JE 1217) to a cardinal bishop: '. . . quicquid vero de praedictae rebus ecclesiae, vel de eius patrimonio, seu cleri ordinatione promotioneve et omnibus generaliter ad eam pertinentibus sollerter atque canonice ordinare facereque provideris, liberam habebis quippe ut sacerdos proprius modis omnibus facultatem' (172, 22–5 Ewald). Note the terms, *ut, quippe ut, tamquam*.

[21] *Reg.* 3, 24.

[22] Gelasius JK 677, 678 (485 f. Thiel). The first fragment passed on into Gratian: D. 24 c. 3.

[23] Cf. Phillips, *Kirchenr.* V, 460; VI, 51; Hinschius, Kirchenr. I, 313.—In Greg. *Reg.* 3, 24 (note 20 *supra*) the cumulative formula, 'tamquam cardinalem et proprium te volumus agere sacerdotem,' was evidently used in order to make clear that both rulings of Pope Gelasius did not apply to this particular case of visitation.

the Great the canonical distinction between foreign bishops as visitors and foreign bishops as cardinals was already in existence. And obviously the term, *cardinalis pontifex* was used by Gelasius in the same sense as later by Gregory, i.e. as denoting a bishop licitly transferred to another see. In this very sense we meet the expression again, after Gregory the Great, in the *Liber diurnus*,[24] and during the ninth century in letters of Pope Hadrian II (867–72) concerning the transfer of Bishop Actard of Nantes to the metropolitan see of Tours,[25] as well as in letters of John VIII (872–82) concerning the transfer of Frothar of Bordeaux to the archbishopric of Bourges.[26] Hincmar of Reims, perhaps the foremost canonist of the Carolingian age, was still perfectly conscious of this ancient canonical usage of *incardinare*[27] and *cardinalis*.[28]

[24] LD 8. Cf. Tamagna, *Origini* I, 109; Hinschius I, 314.—Peitz, *Lib. diurn.* 67f. tries to demonstrate a pre-Gregorian origin of that formula. But it appears rather to be modeled upon a combination of various Gregorian cases.

[25] JE 2903: '. . . decernimus hunc sanctissimum crebro dictum fratrem nostrum et co-episcopum Hactardum ecclesiae, quae forte suo fuerit viduata rectore, penitus incardinari' (ed. E. Perels, MGH *Epp.* 6, 2, ii, Berlin 1925, p. 708 lines 6–8; cf. lines 31–3); JE 2904: '. . . sciens a nobis eidem ut stabiliter incardinatum' (709, 26 Perels; cf. 710, 14–5); JE 2945: '. . . constituimus cardinalem metropolitanum et archiepiscopum Turonicae ecclesiae' (738, 29–30 Perels). See also JE 2902, 2946, 2951 (706, 18–9; 742, 8; 744, 27 Perels).—Cf. Tamagna *loc. cit.*; Phillips V, 465f.; Hinschius *loc. cit.*

[26] JE 3049: '. . . fratrem scil. nostrum Frotharium in Bituricensem ecclesiam cardinalem fieri decernentes' (ed. E. Caspar, MGH *Epp.* 7, 1, Berlin 1912, p. 8 line 37–9, 1); JE 3054: '. . . in ipsa eum incardinandum necessario esse censemus' (12, 15 Caspar). See also JE 3055, 3083 (13, 13 and 20; 37, 27 Caspar).—Cf. Le Cointe, *Instit. et rang* 30–2; Tamagna *loc. cit.*; Phillips V, 467f.; Hinschius *loc. cit.*

[27] Hincmar violently opposed in his *ep. de translat.* (note 7 *supra*) the transfer of Actard. But he recalls in this letter (c. 7) various cases of incardination by earlier popes, to wit, that of St. Augustine of England: '. . . ab eodem beato Gregorio in civitate regia eiusdem gentis accepto pallio archiepiscopus est incardinatus' (PL 126, 213D–214A), and of St. Boniface: 'Winfrit cognomento Bonifacius a tertio (!) papa Gregorio Romae fuit ordinatus episcopus . . . , aliquamdiu in civitate Agrippinensi Colonia sedit et emergente necessitate atque utilitate ad Moguntinam ecclesiam translatus, ibi est archiepiscopus regulariter incardinatus' (214A), and quotes in c. 10 the letters Greg. *Reg.* 2, 37 and 3, 13. See also his letter (A.D. 866) on the case of Ebo of Reims, c. 3: '. . . Sed neque necessitate cogente, propria amissa provintia secundum Calchedonenses canones, civitate in qua ordinatus fuerat captivata, pulsus ab hostibus extitit (*scil.* Ebo), ut alibi incardinari valeret, sicut in decretis beati Gregorii et aliorum sedis Romanae pontificum invenimus' (ed. E. Perels, MGH *Epp.* 8, 1, Berlin 1939, p. 180 lines 4–7 = PL 126, 52); the new fragment discovered by Perels, 'Eine Denkschrift Hinkmars von Reims im Prozess Rothads von Soissons,' NA 44 (1922) 43–100: '. . . ordinato praefato Wintfrid cognomento Bonefacio a Gregorio praedecessore Zachariae et incardinato illo ab eodem Zacharia in metropoli ecclesia Mogontina' (77 NA = 125, 20–1 MGH); and the *Capitula synodica Rhemen.* (874) c. 1: '. . . qui vacantes ecclesiis vacantibus incardinantur' (Mansi 15, 493 B; cf. Tamagna, *Origini* I, 110 and Phillips VI, 56 n. 73).

[28] See his quotations from Greg. *Reg.* (previous note) and his tract *De iure metropolitanorum* c. 20: '. . . cui (*scil.* Bonifacio) per annos XXV in eadem praedicatione sine cardinali sede laboranti praefatorum successor Zacharias papa inter cetera in privilegio sibi directo scripsit atque firmavit ad locum' (PL 126, 201). Evidently, *sedis cardinalis* is not to be understood here as 'a cathedral' (thus Hinschius, *Kirchenr.* I, 315 n. 1) but as 'a see of incardination': for Hincmar was wont to cite the case of St. Boniface (missionary bishop

2. *Presbyter cardinalis*

In Christian Antiquity, the ordination of a cleric was essentially bound up, as we know, with his attachment not only to a diocese but also to a particular church, which was and remained, from his first orders up to the priesthood, his *titulus*.[29] The *intitulatio* created a bond between the cleric and the church of his ordination,[30] even though this bond was not as strictly indissoluble as that between a bishop and his see, because the *intitulatio* lacked the connotation of a spiritual marriage.[31] We therefore find in the ancient canons that the reception of a minor cleric, deacon, or priest in another diocese was not absolutely forbidden, but forbidden only without the proper bishop's consent.[32] Still, it follows from the permanent nature of the *intitulatio* that, like the admission of a cleric into another diocese, any change of title in his own diocese was not a matter of course, for it involved the relaxation of a canonical bond:[33] we may term it incardination

in 722, archbishop in 732, assigned to the see of Mayence in 748, cf. Gregory II JE 2160–1; Gregory III JE 2239; Zachary JE 2286) as an example of incardination, cf. note 27.—On the use made by Hincmar (in *ep. de translat.* 7, *ep. de iure metrop.* 20, and in Perels' fragment) of the spurious letter JE 2292, see M. Tangl, *Die Briefe des heiligen Bonifatius und Lullus* (MGH *Epp. sel.* 1, Berlin 1916) 202 n. 1; id. 'Studien zur Neuausgabe der Bonifatius-Briefe,' NA 41, 1 (1917) 72f., 75f.; Perels, NA 44, 60 n. 1; NA 48 (1929) 156f.

[29] Cf. the Councils of Arles 314 cc. 2, 21 (2, 107; 110 Bruns); Chalcedon cc. 6, 10, 20 (ed. E. Schwartz, *Acta concil. oecumen.* 2, 2, ii: pp. 34, 36, 39; 55–6, 59; 88–9, 91); Mileve 402 c. 4 (1, 178 c. 90 Bruns); II Arles 443 (452?) c. 13 (2, 132 Bruns); Angers 453 c. 1 (2, 137 Bruns); I Tours 461 c. 11 (2, 141 Bruns). The ancient law was stressed again in Carolingian times, cf. ch. IV note 2 *infra*.

[30] Cf. Hinschius, *Kirchenr.* I, 63; Imbart de la Tour, *Les paroisses rurales du IV* au *XI* siècle (Paris 1900) 63f.; M. Hofmann, 'Die Excardination einst und jetzt,' *Zeitschrift für katholische Theologie* 24 (1900) 100f.; C. V. Bastnagel, *The Appointment of Parochial Adjutants and Assistants* (The Catholic University of America Canon Law Studies 58, Washington, D. C. 1930) 17, 23f.; Kurtscheid, *Hist. iur. can.* 152; McBride, *Incardination and Excardination* (ch. I n. 12 *supra*) 66–8, 72, 99f.; J. Christ, *Title* 120 n. 79.—*Contra*: Fuchs, *Ordinationstitel* 95f. The dissertation by J. Weier, *Der kanonische Weihetitel rechtshistorisch und rechtsdogmatisch gewürdigt* (Cologne 1936) is not available to this writer.

[31] The indissolubility has been exaggerated by R. Sohm, *Das altkatholische Kirchenrecht und das Dekret Gratians* (Leipzig 1918) 229–31; thus far the criticism of Fuchs 99f. is justified.

[32] Cf. the canons cited (n. 29) of Chalcedon, II Arles, Angers, Tours; also Innocent I JK 286 (c. 7 = D. 71 c. 2); Leo I JK 409 (c. 4), 411 (c. 9 = C. 19 q. 2 c. 1). In Greg. *Reg.* 1, 55; 81; 5, 20; 6, 20; 14, 11 (JE 1125, 1150, 1339, 1399, 1924) the technical term for this consent is *cessio*. See also sec. 3 at n. 57 *infra*.

[33] Against the consensus of canons and authors, Fuchs, *Ordinationstitel* 95f. maintains that a change of place in the diocese was nothing extraordinary. But contrary to his contention (cf. 92 n. 11) the canons of Arles (314) leave no doubt; c. 2: 'De his qui in quibuscumque locis ordinati fuerint ministri, in ipsis locis perseverent' (2, 107 Bruns), and c. 21: 'De presbyteris aut diaconibus qui solent dimittere loca sua in quibus ordinati sunt et ad alia loca se transferunt . . .' (110 Bruns). And the Council of Merida 666 c. 12 (2, 89f. Bruns) requires the bishop's permission for the transfer of *parochitani presbyteri atque diacones* to the cathedral, not because the early medieval parish was 'a sort of bishopric in itself' (Fuchs 96), but because of the principle stated above. Otherwise there would be little sense in the precept of the Council of Vaison 529 c. 1 (ed. F. Maassen, MGH *Conc.* 1, Hannover 1893, p. 56), that the junior parish clergy be educated for ordination in the

on a minor scale.   This fact is not sufficiently realized by those writers who take pains to explain the *presbyteri cardinales* in St. Gregory's letters as archpriests of the cathedral or as rectors of a parish.

And yet the texts, if carefully studied, show with perfect clearness that in ancient times no priest was *presbyter cardinalis* in his original title.   The critical term occurs for the first time in a letter of Pelagius I: The bishop of Nola had proposed to sell the liturgical equipment (*sacra ministeria*) of a rural parish in his diocese,[34] because this church was so impoverished that it could not maintain its clergy.   Whereupon the Pope, rebuking the bishop, ordered him to reorganize the place as an auxiliary station (*titulus*) of his cathedral and to have it served 'per deputatos cardinales, ecclesiae presbyteros'[35]: obviously these priests were to become *cardinales* because detailed to the service of a new title distinct from, though depending upon, the cathedral—not in their capacity as priests of the cathedral itself.

In another case, Gregory the Great wrote to the bishop of Syracuse that a subdeacon of the cathedral, who had been promoted to the priesthood in order to serve a rural parish, be allowed to return to the city as *presbyter cardinalis*.[36] Again, this has nothing to do with an alleged quality of the cathedral as the bishopric's *cardo*[37]—the metaphor is entirely alien to St. Gregory—but indicates only that this particular rural pastor has to be re-incardinated.

A third group of cases is represented by a series of letters—one by Pelagius I and five by Gregory the Great—concerning the dedication of new oratories on

---

parishes themselves.   Finally, if certain canons required an oath from every cleric that he remain at the place of his ordination, this does not mean (as Fuchs 86f. seems to believe) that without the oath the change of title would have been licit.—See also the criticism by D. Lindner, book review, ZRG *Kan. Abt.* 21 (1932) 398.

[34] JK 976: '. . . ob necessitatem aecclesiae Sessulanae, quae Nolanae aecclesiae esse videtur parroechia, vendendi sibi (*sic*) sacra ministeria concedi . . . postulasti' (ed. S. Loewenfeld, *Epistolae pontificum romanorum ineditae*, Leipzig 1885, p. 13).   For *sacra ministeria* as denoting church goods, in particular sacred vessels, see St. Gelasius JK 688: 'Ecclesiastica ministeria, que unicuique basilice fidelium deuotio deputauit. . . .   Et ideo . . . calicem . . . restitue sine intermissione' in the collection of Deusdedit 3, 117 (320 Wolf von Glanvell).

[35] JK 976: '. . . Si tanta est aecclesiae Sessulanae penuria, ut parroechia esse non possit, eam potius in titulum Nolanae aecclesiae constitue, ut . . . per deputatos cardinales, aecclesiae presbyteros, ministeria (*leg.* misteria?) celebrentur.' (The last two commas are inserted by the present writer).   For *titulus* in the sense of an auxiliary church (*Nebenkirche, Aussenstation*), see Fuchs, *Ordinationstitel* 9; J. Christ, *Title* 118.

[36] Greg. *Reg.* 13, 32 (JE 1513): '. . . magnae benignitatis est si eum in ecclesia ubi subdiaconi est functus officio, sanctitas vestra reducere atque illic presbyterum voluerit constituere cardinalem' (2, 396 Hartmann).   The letter passed on into Gratian: D. 74 c. 6.— Johannes Diaconus, *Vita* 3, 11 is not correct if he speaks of this case as if the bishop had forcibly promoted the subdeacon and as if Gregory had commanded his return: 'Item cardinales violenter in parochiis ordinatos forensibus in pristinum cardinem Gregorius revocabat . . .' (PL 75, 135; interpretation accepted by Phillips, *Kirchenr.* V, 53 n. 64).   Correctly Tamagna, *Origini* I, 102.

[37] As suggested by Joh. Diac. *loc. cit.*

the estates of lay founders.[38] In accordance with a formulary of the papal chancery, which eventually came to be included in the *Liber diurnus*,[39] both popes authorized, on the condition that a sufficient endowment of the new foundation be shown, its consecration by the local bishop, but usually forbade the erection of a baptismal font (*baptisterium*) and the installation of a *presbyter cardinalis* at the place. If the founder wished Masses to be said at the oratory, he was to apply every time to the bishop for a priest.[40]

This formulary was designed to safeguard, at least in the Roman metropolitan province, the parochial rights of the established public *ecclesiae baptismales* against the ambitions of wealthy private founders. Prevention of the growth of lay prerogatives in any form was the keynote of the 'Gelasian' program for churches of private foundation[41]—at a time when the emperors in the East as well as the bishops of Visigothic Spain already felt obliged to make certain concessions to lay founders, and when in Gaul the independence of private churches and their clergy from the parochial-baptismal organization was already well advanced.[42] With the first clause of prohibition, therefore, the several papal

[38] Pelagius JK 959; Greg. *Reg.* 2, 15 (JE 1167); 9, 58; 71; 165; 180 (JE 1583, 1596, 1692, 1707). Note that *Reg.* 9, 165 does not regard an oratory but a monastic church of private foundation. For other letters closely related to this group see nn. 40, 43a *infra.*—The entire complex of problems connected with the 'Dedication of Sacred Places in the Early Sources and in the Letters of Gregory the Great' has been recently studied by J. A. Eidenschink, *The Jurist* 5 (1945) 181–215; 323–58.

[39] LD 11 (38 Rozière; 10 Sickel). Cf. Garnier's note ad v. *petitorii*, reprinted in Rozière's edition; Goetz, 'Das Alter der Kirchweihformeln X–XXXI des Liber diurnus,' *Deutsche Zeitschrift für Kirchenrecht* 5 (1895) 14–21; Peitz, *Lib. diurn.* 76; Eidenschink, *op. cit.* 325ff. We cannot enter here the lively discussion caused by Peitz' remarkable, but generally rejected theory which makes the LD, at least in its chief portions, an official collection of pre-Gregorian origin. But there can be no doubt that form 11 belongs to those few items in the LD which existed as individual form letters in the papal chancery already before the accession of St. Gregory, cf. Rozière p. xxviif.; Goetz, *op. cit. passim*; Bresslau, *Urkundenlehre* II, 243; M. Tangl, 'Gregor-Register und Liber Diurnus,' NA 41, 3 (1919) 752; Eidenschink *loc. cit.* The wording of the very first letter of our group, Pelagius JK 959, shows the use of a formulary, cf. Hinschius, *Kirchenr.* I, 316 n. 2; Goetz 14ff.

[40] JK 959: '. . . Ita tamen ut in eodem loco nec futuris temporibus baptisterium construatur, nec presbiterum constituas cardinalem. Set quotiens missas sibi fieri forte maluerit, a dilectione tua presbiterum nouerit postulandum . . .' in Deusd. 3, 128 (323 Wolf von Glanvell). Repeated almost verbatim in Greg. *Reg. cit.* (except for 9, 71: see note 43 *infra*). In three other letters—*Reg.* 8, 5; 9, 233; 13, 18 (JE 1492, 1760, 1882)—the pertinent part of the formula is abridged: '. . . et cetera secundum morem.' In Pelagius JK 958 (Deusd. 3, 129: oratory founded by an abbot in his monastery) and Greg. *Reg.* 2, 9 (JE 1158: basilica founded by a deacon) the entire clause 'Ita tamen . . . cardinalem' of LD 11 is omitted, see note 43a *infra.*

[41] Gelasius I JK 630, 636 (cc. 4, 25), 643, 679–81, 704, 709 etc.; LD 10. Cf. U. Stutz, *Geschichte des kirchlichen Benefizialwesens* I (Berlin 1895) 56–64; Imbart de la Tour, *op. cit.* (note 30 *supra*) 181 n. 1; A. Galante, *La condizione giuridica delle cose sacre* I (Turin 1903) 57ff. 121ff.; M. Torres, 'El origen del sistema de las "iglesias propias",' *Anuario de historia del derecho español* 5 (1928) 169–73; Fuchs, *Ordinationstitel* 142, 160, 193; Eidenschink, *op. cit.* 330.

[42] For the East see Justinian's *Nov.* 57, 2; 123, 18, and other sources cited by A. Steinwenter, 'Die Rechtsstellung der Kirchen und Klöster nach den Papyri,' ZRG *Kan. Abt.* 19

letters sought to prevent that a private oratory be raised to a baptismal church. This results quite logically in the second prohibition: for if the oratory were to be vested with baptismal, i.e. parochial functions, it would of necessity require the service of a permanently installed priest. And indeed, in the one instance in which St. Gregory positively contemplated the concession of parochial rights, he omitted the prohibitive clause relative to the *baptisterium* and ordered expressly that the oratory should obtain a *presbyter cardinalis* for saying Mass and taking care of the faithful.[43]   On the other hand, where no infringements from the founder's side were to be feared at all, the twofold prohibition of the formu lary might be left out altogether.[43a]

But from this connection between permitting (or forbidding, for that matter) parochial functions in oratories and the installation of a cardinal priest, it does not follow that the crucial term denotes the rector of a parish.[44]   The priest is called a cardinal in these particular cases simply because the oratory always had, as a new foundation, so far no clergy of its own, and thus he would needs have to

(1930) 3f.   For Spain: the Councils II Braga 572 cc. 5–6; IX Toledo 655 c. 2 (2, 41 and 1, 292 Bruns).   For Gaul: Councils of Agde 506 c. 21 (2, 150 Bruns); I Orléans 511 c. 25 (ed. Maassen, MGH *Conc.* 1, 8); Clermont 535 cc. 4, 15 (67 and 69 Maassen); IV Orléans 546 cc. 7, 33 (89 and 94 Maassen).—The moot question, passionately discussed ever since the appearance of Stutz' *Benefizialwesen*, whether these phenomena belong to the sphere of 'proprietary church' law (which in the case of an affirmative answer would no longer be a specifically Germanic institution, as Stutz maintained) lies outside the scope of the present inquiry. As to the East, Stutz later acknowledged (*Sitzungsberichte der Preussischen Akademie der Wissenschaften*, phil.-hist. Klasse 1930, p. 213) the existence of an autochthonous Byzantine proprietary church system.   It has now been studied in detail by S. Troickij, *Ktitorsko pravo u Vizantiji i u Nemanjićkoj Srbiji* (Belgrade 1935); cf. the review by F. X. Schmid, ZRG *Kan. Abt.* 28 (1939) 624–9.

[43] *Reg.* 9, 71 to Bishop Passivus of Fermo: '. . . Et ideo, frater carissime, . . . praedictum oratorium solemniter consecrabis.   Presbyterum quoque te illic (i.e. at Teramo) constituere volumus cardinalem, ut quotiens praefatus conditor fieri sibi missas fortasse voluerit vel fidelium concursus exegerit, nihil sit quod ad sacra missarum sollemnia exhibenda valeat impedire' (2, 90, 14–23 Hartmann).   Cf. Hinschius, *Kirchenr.* I, 316f. Stutz, *Benefizialwesen* 62 n. 98; id. *Göttingische gelehrte Anzeigen* 1904, p. 24 n. 1; Eidenschink, *op. cit.* 341.—The next step in such a case would have been the permission to erect a *baptisterium* (cf. the forms LD 29, 30), but the Pope's first mandate was not successful and no appropriate priest was found.   Therefore St. Gregory abandoned, three years later, the idea of a *presbyter cardinalis* for Teramo and directed that a certain Oportunus be first ordained subdeacon and subsequently promoted to *pastoralis cura* (*Reg.* 12, 4 [JE 1855]; for further discussion of the Teramo case see Appendix A *infra*).

[43a] This reason at least seems the most plausible explanation of the abridgment made of LD 11 in JK 958 and Greg. *Reg.* 2, 9 (note 40 *supra*).   In two other authorizations for the dedication of monastic oratories (*Reg.* 3, 58; 5, 50: JE 1264, 1365) St. Gregory did not use LD 11 at all but was satisfied with merely advising the bishop: '. . . ut quotiens necesse fuerit, a presbiteris ecclesiae tuae in superscripto (*al.* sancto) loco deservientibus celebrentur sacrificia veneranda missarum' (218, 7f. Ewald).   Cf. LD 15; Goetz, *op. cit.* (n. 39 *supra*.) 22f.; Eidenschink, *op. cit.* 344f.

[44] As was assumed by Panvini, *De orig. card.* 481f.; Thomassin, *Vet. et nova discipl.* 1, 2, 115, 6; Mabillon, *Museum ital.* II, xix; Hinschius, *Kirchenr.* I, 317; Goetz, *op. cit.* 16, 20f.; H. Schäfer, *Pfarrkirche und Stift im deutschen Mittelalter* (Kirchenrechtliche Abhandlungen ed. Stutz 3, Stuttgart 1903) 8 n. 3.

142

be incardinated from another *titulus* of the diocese.[45] But whenever a private church or oratory had already its own lower clergy and was to be provided with a priest, the latter could be ordained within the title:[46] in these cases, consequently, the term, *presbyter cardinalis*, was not applied.[47]

In the Register of Gregory the Great there is but one letter the facts of which are less evident. When the Church of Populonia was entirely without *sacerdotale officium*, i.e. destitute of its bishop and of any priest, the Pope appointed a *visitator* and directed him to ordain at the cathedral one cardinal priest and two deacons, also in the (rural) parishes, three priests.[48] Here the critical term, *unum cardinalem presbyterum*, seems at first sight to contain no other connotation than that of a cathedral priest[49]—unless the added injunction to ordain also two deacons can be interpreted as indicating not merely that the cathedral was somewhat short of deacons, but rather that it had no deacons left at all. In small bishoprics, as a rule, not more than two or three deacons were required,[50] and if for Populonia the Pope found it necessary, instead of simply granting the usual

---

[45] A somewhat similar explanation in Tamagna, *Origini* I, 106f.; less appropriate are the interpretations given by L. Nardi, *Dei parrochi* II (Pesaro 1830) 398 and Phillips, *Kirchenr*. VI, 58. The latter assumes that the formulary had in mind the incardination of priests from other, devastated dioceses. As Hinschius I, 316 rightly observes, this hypothesis has no foundation in the sources.

[46] This was required, for fiscal reasons, also by imperial legislation, cf. the much discussed statute of Emperor Honorius (398) in *Cod. Th.* 16, 2, 33 = *Cod. Iust.* 1, 3, 11: 'Ecclesiis quae in possessionibus ut adsolet diversorum, vicis etiam vel quibuslibet locis sunt constructae, clerici non ex alia possessione vel vico, sed ex eo ubi ecclesiam esse constiterit, eatenus (*om. Iust.*) ordinentur, ut propriae capitationis onus ad sarcinam recognoscant . . .'; cf. Imbart de la Tour, *op. cit.* 63 n. 2; F. Thaner, book review, *Gött. gel Anz.* 1898, p. 302; Stutz, *ibid.* 1904, p. 44 note.—For a description of the clergy serving in churches of private estates see also St. John Chrysostom, *Hom.* 18 *in Act.* (PG 60, 147-9); the terms of this homily should however not be pressed (as is done, e.g., by A. Pöschl, *Bischofsgut und Mensa episcopalis* I, Bonn 1908, p. 33f. and Fuchs, *Ordinationstitel* 154f. 158) as if they were intended to convey authoritative and definite legal-canonical statements.

[47] Cf. the final mandate, Greg. *Reg.* 12, 4, in the Teramo case (note 43 *supra*): the subdeacon Oportunus '. . . ad pastoralem curam debeat promoveri' (2, 350, 16-7 Hartmann). For a similar situation in a private basilica, 'quae in possessione filii et consiliarii nostri, viri magnifici Theodori fundata est,' see Pelagius I JK 995: the bishop of Sabina is told to ordain one Rufinus, presented by the founder, as subdeacon and the Pope voices his intention to promote him later to the priesthood (*presbyterum faciemus*), in order that next Easter 'sacra mysteria in memorata basilica a persona competenti valeant adimpleri' (454 Thiel). Cf. further LD 41, ordination of a *presbyter* in a previously established oratory: 'Filius noster ille postulavit in oratorio instantia (*al.* in substantia) sua conservato debere sibi ordinari presbyterum . . .' (30 Sickel; 70 Rozière; see also Stutz, *Benefizialwesen* 62 nn. 99-101). Baluze's note ad v. *presbyterum*: 'cardinalem videlicet . . .' (reprinted in Rozière) misses the point of difference between LD 41 and LD 11.

[48] Greg. *Reg.* 1, 15 (JE 1083): '. . . memoratae ecclesiae visitator accedas et unum cardinalem illic presbiterum et duos debeas diacones ordinare. In parroechiis vero praefatae ecclesiae tres similiter presbiteros . . .' (16, 10-2 Ewald).

[49] Thus the common interpretation, from Panvini, *De orig. card.* 480 down to Hinschius, *Kirchenr*. I, 315 and McBride, *Incard. and Excard.* 4; 7.

[50] Cf. J. Forget, 'Diacre,' DThC 4 (1911) 711; Kurtscheid, *Hist. iur. can.* 53. See e.g. the fragment of Gelasius JK 673: '. . . diaconos in ecclesia sua secundum possibilitatem vel loci ipsius paupertatem secundum dispositam traditionem apostolorum aut tres aut V aut VII . . .' (509 Thiel).

faculty of ordination,[51] to issue a peremptory mandate to ordain two deacons (*debeas ordinare*), it seems most plausible that a complete lack of cathedral deacons was the situation with which the visiting bishop had to cope. It would explain, too, the need for a *presbyter cardinalis*, for it would mean that at the cathedral—any *promotio per saltum* not being contemplated in the text[52]—there was nobody eligible to the priesthood.

If we consider the high improbability of St. Gregory's having arbitrarily deviated from his own concept of *cardinalis*, this conjecture seems not too daring. And it becomes fully justified if we compare the text in question with that of another letter, written by St. Gregory when a similar lack of priests befell the bishopric of Nicotera. This time, the Pope stated expressly that a priest be chosen *e clero eiusdem ecclesiae*, and in significant contrast with the Populonia case, no mandate to ordain deacons is given to the visitor, nor is the prospective priest called *cardinalis*.[53] Thus we may safely assume that the difference of expression had a sound canonical reason: in Populonia, a priest could not be ordained *e clero eiusdem ecclesiae* but only by way of incardination—whether the candidate be selected among the deacons of other churches in the diocese[54] or

---

[51] As he did in other cases; cf. e.g. Greg. *Reg.* 1, 76 (JE 1145): '. . . in qua etiam ecclesia vel eius parroechiis diacones atque presbyteros tibi concedimus ordinandi licentiam' (93, 10–1 Ewald); 4, 39 (JE 1311): '. . . ei ordinandi presbyteros ac diacones, si necesse fuerit . . ., dedimus licentiam' (276, 2–4 Ewald).

[52] The exceptional character of promotions *per saltum*—somewhat underestimated by J. Tixeront, *L'ordre et les ordinations* (Paris 1925) 230–3—makes it imperative to exclude such a possibility whenever it is not expressly mentioned in a given text. Even in such instances as Greg. *Reg.* 12, 4 or Pelagius JK 995, where nothing is said about intermediate ordination to the diaconate of subdeacons who are prospective candidates for the priesthood (notes 43, 47 *supra*), we have no right to assume that *promotio per saltum* was contemplated. Similarly in Gelasius JK 668: '. . . si quos habes vel in acolythis vel in subdiaconibus maturioris aetatis et quorum sit vita probabilis, in presbyteratum studeas promovere' (489 Thiel), observation of the regular scale of promotion is evidently presupposed though not expressed. Cf. the Council of Serdica c. 8 (c. 12 in *Coll. I Dionysiana*; c. 13 in *Coll. Hispana* and *Dion. II*: ed. C. H. Turner, *Monum.* 1, 2, iii, pp. 472–3; Gratian D. 61 c. 10); Pope Siricius JK 255 (cc. 9, 10), Innocent I JK 314 (c. 5), Zosimus JK 339; also the notice on Pope Sylvester in LP I, 171 (with Duchesne's note 25 p. 190). But for a possible abbreviation of the interstices see Gelasius JK 636 (cc. 2, 3). Cf. Hinschius, *Kirchenr.* I, 111f.; Kurtscheid, *Hist. iur. can.* 158.

[53] Greg. *Reg.* 6, 38 (JE 1420): '. . . adhortamur ut de clero eiusdem ecclesiae requirere debeatis, cuius vita et mores ad hoc possit convenire et eum illic presbyterum festinetis auxiliante Domino consecrare' (1, 415, 7–9 Hartmann).—A further analogous case, *Reg.* 1 51 (JE 1121), concerning the diocese of Canosa (today united with Bari), is not helpful because the text of the pertinent letter is defective at the crucial passage: '. . . memoratae ecclesiae visitator accedas et * vel duos parroechiales presbyteros debeas ordinare' (77, 12–3 Ewald). Ewald's conjecture: '. . . accedas et ⟨unum cardinalem illic presbyterum et duos diacones⟩ vel duos parroechiales . . .' *rell.* (77 n. 2) is unwarranted and does not make good sense. The facts of the case must have been different from those at Populonia.

[54] This possibility is indicated by the mention of other *parroechiae* in the bishopric. Whether deacons were available in these baptismal churches depends upon the construction of the passage, 'in parroechiis vero praefatae ecclesiae tres similiter presbyteros . . .': the adverb, *similiter*, may stand for *etiam cardinales* (then no deacons were on hand), or simply for *ordinabis quoque* (in this case, there were deacons present for promotion). See also Phillips, *Kirchenr.* VI, 52 n. 60.

144

from the visitor's own bishopric. His functions and position would not be different from those of the priest at Nicotera, as both of them were destined to be the sole *presbyter* each of the respective cathedral. But only the priest of Populonia, as not promoted within his title, would be a cardinal priest.

3. *Diaconus cardinalis*

It needs no further explanation, then, that for St. Gregory a cardinal deacon was a deacon incardinated from another diocese or *titulus*.

Greg. *Reg.* 1, 81 (JE 1150): Gregory advises Bishop Ianuarius of Cagliari, who had told him of a certain Liberatus serving as deacon in his church, that '. . . si a decessore tuo non factus est cardinalis, ordinatis a te diaconibus nulla debet ratione praeponi' (99, 26–8 Ewald), but that '. . . si . . . eum post haec facere cardinalem volueris, nisi pontificis sui cessionem sollemni more meruerit, abstinendum ab eius incardinatione memineris' (100, 3–5 Ewald).

Reg. 4, 14 (JE 1285): Gregory recommends to Bishop Maximianus of Syracuse the deacon Felix who had left his proper diocese during certain troubles but had obtained forgiveness from the Pope. Wishing to provide for the deacon's sustenance, Gregory writes: '. . . in tua Syracusana ecclesia eum praevidimus cardinandum' (247, 19 Ewald); the bishop may decide whether to employ Felix as deacon or to give him only a pension.

Reg. 6, 11 (JE 1390): Bishop Fortunatus of Naples had asked Gregory, 'ut Gratianum ecclesiae Benefranae diaconem tuae cederemus ecclesiae cardinandum' (1, 389, 18–9 Hartmann). The permission is granted because the Church of Venafro is at present held by the enemy and has no bishop; therefore the bishop of Naples may employ him, 'habituro licentiam diaconem illum, nostra interveniente auctoritate, ecclesiae tuae, Deo propitio, constituere cardinalem' (389, 22–4 Hartmann).[55]

From the clause in the first of these letters: 'if he (Liberatus) was not made a cardinal by your predecessor, he must by no means be set over the deacons ordained by you,' it has been inferred by some writers that *diaconus cardinalis* is equivalent to 'principal deacon,' i.e. archdeacon.[56] But the true sense of the term is made quite clear by the concluding phrase: 'if you wish to make him a cardinal, remember to abstain from any incardination, unless he has obtained from his own bishop the formal permit of transfer (*cessio*).'[57] Consequently this case, too, is but one of incardination,[58] and the Pope's prohibition to place Liberatus ahead of the other deacons, unless he had been made a *cardinalis* by the predecessor of the addressee, refers to nothing but the principle of seniority:[59] if the former bishop had incardinated this deacon, he would precede in orders,

[55] This text passed on into Gratian: D. 71 c. 5. It was correctly understood by the *Correctores Romani* (ch. I note 6 *supra*); Tamagna, *Origini* I, 104; Phillips V, 462; Hinschius I, 315 n. 5.

[56] Panvini, *De orig. card.* 480; Thomassin, *Vet. et nova discipl.* 1, 2, 115, 4; Ewald, MGH *Epp.* 1, 99 n. 1; O'Donnell, *Vocabulary* (n. 3 *supra*) 2; 136.

[57] Cf. note 32 *supra*.

[58] Tamagna, *Origini* I, 93f.; Nardi, *Dei parrochi* II, 403; Hinschius, *Kirchenr.* I, 315 n. 5.

[59] This was already noticed by Joh. Diaconus, *Vita* 3, 21, who cited our letter as instance for the fact that St. Gregory 'antiquissimum ecclesiasticae consuetudinis ordinem . . . adeo studiosissime retinebat, ut nullum . . . anterioribus clericis in conventu, concessu, statione, sive subscriptione praeponeret' (PL 75, 142). Hinschius II, 184 and Amanieu, 'Archidiacre,' *Dict. de droit can.* 1 (1924) 950 wrongly deny that seniority was as a rule the selective principle for the archdeaconate.

and hence in rank, the deacons ordained by the present bishop. He then would be indeed the archdeacon—not, however, for his being a *cardinalis*, but for his seniority in orders.

4. *Etymology*

We have abstained so far from discussing our problem from the etymological angle which too often induced authors to force the texts of St. Gregory, St. Gelasius, and Pelagius into preconceived definitions. For there is no doubt that the 'Gregorian' usage of the word, *cardinalis*, is at variance with its derivation and meaning in classical language. Literally, the adjective *cardinalis* means something belonging to a *cardo*, first of all what belongs to the material pivot (or whatever tenon of a timber is inserted into the wedge of another): in this sense Vitruvius speaks of cardinal beams of the doors.[60] But *cardinalis* is also that which belongs to the imaginary 'hinges' of the world, and thus the ancients speak of cardinal winds or, as we do today, of the cardinal points in geography and astronomy.[61] In figurative speech, *cardo* and *cardinalis* stand for something central, essential, fundamental, principal, firmly established. Hence we read of the cardinal numbers in Priscianus; of the cardinal virtues in St. Ambrose; of cardinal causes and, again, of *cardinales Donatistae* in St. Augustine; of cardinal thoughts in Eustathius.[62] More or less in this sense, *cardinalis* seems also to be understood in some texts dealing with Roman public administration,[63] although the interpretation of these texts is by no means certain: it still remains puzzling, for instance, what the *officium cardinale* really meant which distinguished, in the military hierarchy of the East, the staff of two among the five imperial *magistri militum* from that of their colleagues.[64]

Be this as it may, the canonical usage of *cardinalis* in Gregorian language differs from all the others in that it is not associated with the notion of a *cardo*, but with the verb *cardinare, incardinare*, which—though itself derived from *cardo* —does not mean to make, or to use as, or to join with, a hinge. It is of importance to realize that the use of the verb in ancient speech was almost entirely restricted to, and thus shaped by, Canon law: apart from the Gregorian letters,

---

[60] *De architectura* 4, 4, 6 (ed. V. Rose, Leipzig 1899, p. 96).

[61] Copious references in Bannier's article, ThLL 3, 442f. s.v.

[62] Priscianus, *De figuris numerorum* 19 (ed H. Keill, *Grammatici latini* 3, Leipzig 1855–9, p. 412 line 27); St. Ambrose, *De excessu fratris Satyri* 1, 57 (ed. P. B. Albers, Florilegium patristicum 15, Bonn 1921, p. 44 line 17); St. Augustine, *De civitate Dei* 9, 22 (ed. E. Hoffmann, CSEL 40, 1, 440, 8); *De baptismo* 1, 6, 8 (ed. M. Petschenig, CSEL 51, 153, 8–9); Eusthatius Afer, *Versio hexaemeri S. Basilii* 3, 2 (PL 53, 892A). Cf. ThLL *loc. cit.*

[63] *Notitia dignitatum Orientis* 6, 70; 7, 59 (ed. E. Böcking, Bonn 1839, pp. 24, 28; ed. O. Seeck, Berlin 1876, pp. 18, 22); Cassiodorus, *Variae* 7, 31 (ed. Th. Mommsen, MGH *Auct. antiquiss.* 12, Berlin 1894, p. 218). For discussion of these two texts see Appendix B *infra*. Cf. also Joh. Cassianus, *Conlationes* 1, 20, 6: '. . . (nomismata) non sunt a legitimis monetariis . . . nec de cardinali ac publica . . . prodeunt officina' (ed. M. Petschenig, CSEL 13, 31, 25–32, 1).

[64] Cf. Appendix B *infra*. It was with regard to the relative statements in the *Not. dign.* that Gothofr. *Comm. Cod. Th.* 12, 6, 7 made the complaint quoted at the beginning of the present study.

146

incardinare is not found at all,[65] and *cardinare* only in one passage of Vitruvius. Because *cardo* technically is any tenon used for wedging one timber into the cavity of another, he describes as *tignum cardinatum* a beam which is joined and fastened to a structure.[66] In this ἅπαξ λεγόμενον with its connotation of inserting or attaching (rather than that of 'providing with a *cardo*'),[67] the canonical usage of *(in)cardinare*, 'to insert into another title or diocese,' had its model and origin, and with it the peculiar usage of *cardinalis* as connoting incardination.

The fundamental difference between *cardinalis* in canonical language and the same term as used in other contexts is certainly a most striking phenomenon. It is not, however, entirely unparalleled in the history of canonical terminology. If we recall the semantic changes of common nouns such as *titulus, feria, ministerium*, etc. in their peculiar application by the ancient Church, *cardinalis* appears only as one more instance of the tendency of early Canon law to create a technical language of its own.

III. Origins of the Roman Cardinal Bishops and Priests

The name, *cardinalis*, is not given as an attribute to members of the Roman clergy, at least in genuine texts, before the second half of the eighth century.[1] By this time, however, the first signs of a decay of the Gregorian terminology are already at hand,[2] and perhaps for this reason even authors who are not unaware of the peculiar Gregorian usage of the word do not stop to ask whether the Roman cardinals may not owe, after all, their name to an element of incardination in their functions. In the following pages we are endeavoring to answer that question in the affirmative.

Since the early post-apostolic times, the Church of Rome was distinct from almost every bishopric of the οἰκουμένη[3] in that the pastoral and liturgical functions were not centered in a cathedral but distributed throughout the city among a number of churches, the *tituli*. For the Pope had no cathedral and no stable seat of his government before the end of the persecutions.[4] The *tituli*, at the

---

[65] Cf. ThLL 7, 848 s. v.

[66] Vitruv. *de archit.* 10, 15, 4: '. . . arrectaria duo compacta . . . coniuncta capitibus transversario cardinato tigno et altero mediano inter duos scapos cardinato et lamnis ferreis relegato' (275 Rose). There is one other passage (*ibid.* 10, 14, 2) using not *cardinare*, but *intercardinare*.

[67] Thus Bannier, ThLL s. v.: 'cardinatus, idem quod cardine praeditus.' But see Panvini, *De orig. card.* 472 and Muratori, *Antiq.* 5, 156 for the better interpretation, *cardinatus = insertus*.

[1] Thomassin, *Vet. et nova discipl.* 1, 2, 115, 11; Hinschius, *Kirchenr.* I, 313; 318; Klewitz, *Entstehung* 149.

[2] See ch. IV, 1 *infra* (Pope Zachary 747).

[3] The well known exception was Alexandria, perhaps also Constantinople. Cf. e.g. C. H. Turner, 'The Organisation of the Church,' CMH 1, 159f.; H. K. Schäfer, 'Frühmittelalterliche Pfarrkirchen und Pfarreinteilung in römisch-fränkischen und italienischen Bischofsstädten,' *Römische Quartalschrift für christliche Altertumskunde und für Kirchengeschichte* 19, 2 (1905) 26.

[4] Cf. A. von Harnack, 'Zur Geschichte der Anfänge der inneren Organisation der stadtrömischen Kirche,' *Sitzungsberichte der Preussischen Akademie der Wissenschaften* 1918, II, 957–9. This distinguished the Roman situation sharply from that at Alexandria or Constantinople.

outset private houses placed at the disposal of, and since the third century made over to, the Church by their pious owners,[5] became definitely reorganized as centers of parochial functions—*quasi dioeceses*, as the *Liber pontificalis* terms it— at the beginning of the fourth century.[6] While eighteen titles were of pre-Constantinian origin, they gradually attained the number of twenty-five after the end of the persecutions. This number was considered stable, at least since the early sixth century.[7]

At these *tituli*, the members of the Roman *presbyterium* were domiciled[8] and exercised their regular priestly duties which comprised chiefly the preparation of their flock for baptism and penance and the offering of the Holy Sacrifice.[9] There were always two or three priests permanently assigned to each title, the senior of whom came to be known as *presbyter prior*.[10]

The conditions by which the priests of the titles would eventually become *cardinales* were given by another peculiar feature of the divine service in the City. While the *tituli* remained the only churches with quasi-parochial functions—as St. Innocent I wrote in 416, they had *plebem sibi creditam*[11]— many other churches had arisen after the great persecutions over the tombs of the martyrs. These cemeterial churches originally were entrusted each to the care of a neighboring *titulus*.[12] But with the destruction wrought by the Gothic and the Lombard wars in the sixth and the seventh centuries, regular service in most of the cemetery churches was disrupted.[13] The priests of the *tituli* remained definitely in charge—apart from their titles—only of the three great basilicas built over the tombs of St. Peter, St. Paul, and St. Lawrence, where Pope Simplicius (468–83)

[5] J. P. Kirsch, *Die römischen Titelkirchen im Altertum* (Paderborn 1918) 133-7.

[6] LP I, 164, ascribing this reorganization to Pope Marcellus (308–9): 'Hic . . . et XXV titulos in urbe Roma constituit quasi diocesis, propter baptismum et paenitentiam multorum. . .'. It is unlikely, however, that it was accomplished during the persecutions; the confiscated churches of Rome were not restored before 311. Cf. Kirsch, *Titelkirchen* 137; J. Christ, *Title* 104.

[7] The *Liber pontificalis* delights in antedating this number into the earliest times (Cletus: I, 122; Urban: I, 143; Marcellus: I, 164), but archeological evidence shows the origin of seven *tituli* only after the end of the persecutions. Cf. Kirsch 6f. 117f. 127f.; Christ 110f.; Klewitz, *Entstehung* 148. The seemingly greater number of *tituli* represented in the Roman Synod of 499 is explained by the fact that several titles were known by more than one name, cf. Duchesne, LP I, 165 n. 5; Sägmüller, *Cardinäle* 6.

[8] Kirsch, *Titelkirchen* 175f.

[9] LP I, 164: '. . . propter baptismum et paenitentiam multorum.' The individual titles were fitted with baptismal fonts not before the fourth century, cf. Kirsch 186f. For the celebration of the Holy Eucharist in the titles see Kirsch 191f.: The *fermentum*, consecrated and sent by the Pope (Innocent I JK 311 c. 5: 'De fermento vero quod die dominica per titulos mittimus': Mansi 3, 1030 B), was mixed with the species consecrated by the priest, in token of the *communio* with the Pope.

[10] Kirsch, *Titelkirchen* 178; Klewitz, *Entstehung* 148f. Cf. Greg. *Reg.* 6, 12 (JE 1391): '. . . una cum tribus presbyteris prioribus' (1, 391, 27 Hartmann).

[11] JK 311 c. 5: '. . . quia die ipsa propter plebem sibi creditam nobiscum convenire non possunt' (Mansi *loc. cit.*).

[12] Kirsch, *Titelkirchen* 200f. 212f.: the *presbyteri per diversa coemeteria constituti* in JK 311 were priests detailed from the titles. Mabillon's theory (*Mus. ital.* II, xvi) that the cemeteries themselves were 'minor titles' cannot be upheld.

[13] Kirsch, *Titelkirchen* 217f.

148

had established a schedule of pastoral services in weekly turns (*hebdomadae*), to be observed by the title priests of the pertinent ecclesiastical districts (*regiones*) of the City, *propter penitentes et baptismum*.[14]

Between the end of the fifth and the beginning of the eighth century—the time cannot be more closely determined—two other great basilicas were integrated in this hebdomadary system, because both of them were not among the *tituli* and yet far more important as liturgical centers than any of the *tituli*: St. Mary Major[15] and the basilica of Our Saviour which had been constructed by Constantine in the Lateran palace and had soon come to be considered, on account of its connection with the *episcopium Lateranense*, as the Pope's cathedral.[16] True, there is no written evidence for an hebdomadal service of title priests at the Lateran basilica as antedating that of the seven neighboring bishops, who appear early in the eighth century as *episcopi hebdomadarii*.[17] But such an original inclusion of the Lateran in the hebdomadary schedule of the *tituli* has been convincingly deduced by modern research.[18] Suffice it to say that no numerically equal and no topographically reasonable distribution of the twenty-five *tituli* could have been devised for four patriarchal basilicas only. Nor would it be conceivable that the principal church of Rome had been left without regular priestly services[19] until the eighth century.

At that time, when the liturgical functions in the Lateran were turned over to the seven bishops of Ostia, Albano, Palestrina, Porto, Silva Candida, Gabii, and Velletri, a reorganization of the *tituli* in relation to the remaining four basilicas became necessary. It is therefore to the eighth century that we probably have to look for the increase of the *tituli* from twenty-five to twenty-eight,

[14] LP I, 249. The distribution was: 'regio III ad s. Laurentium, regio prima ad s. Paulum, regio VI vel septima ad s. Petrum.' For the individual *tituli* involved see the chart in Klewitz, *Entstehung* 156.

[15] As shown by the *Ordo Romanus I* (early 8th cent.) num. 3 (ed. Mabillon, *Mus. ital.* II, 5). Cf. Phillips, *Kirchenr.* VI, 122 n. 9; Klewitz, *Entstehung* 155.

[16] For *episcopium* (later *patriarchium*, then *palatium*) *Lateranense* as name of the papal residence see Klewitz, *Entstehung* 182 and his reference to E. Caspar, *Geschichte des Papsttums* II (Tübingen 1933) 625, 630. For the Lateran basilica as cathedral see e.g. LP I, 249, 15: 'Hic (Simplicius) fecit in ecclesia Romana scyphum aureum', quoted by Phillips VI, 120 n. 4.

[17] *Ordo I Rom.* num. 8; 13 (pp. 8, 11 Mabillon). Cf. Phillips VI, 171 n. 10; Hinschius, *Kirchenr.* I, 324 n. 1; Sägmüller, *Cardinäle* 12 n.

[18] The ingenious thesis, which solves so many difficulties left unexplained by older historians of the Sacred College, was developed with an array of convincing arguments by Klewitz, *Entstehung* 151-8, pursuant to a brief and tentative remark by Harnack, *Die Mission und Ausbreitung des Christentums* (4th ed. Leipzig 1924) 857 n. 4. For a reconstruction of the resulting assignment, five by five, of the *tituli* to the great basilicas see Klewitz' chart p. 156.

[19] Not to be confused with the singing of the daily Office, which was entrusted since olden times to the monks of the three monasteries of St. Pancras, St. Stephen, and Pope Honorius; a custom renewed by Gregory III (731–41). A fourth monastery, Sts. Sergius and Bachus was included in this schedule by Paschal I (817–24). Cf. LP I, 419, 506; II, 58; Kehr, IP 1, 33–4.

and for that redistribution at a ratio of seven for each basilica the result of which is recorded in a list of the eleventh century.[20] By now it should be evident for what reason the senior priests of the titles and the bishops of seven suffragan sees acquired the appellative of *cardinales*. Significantly enough, the name appears for the first time in papal documents[21] under the pontificate of Stephen III (768–72),[22] whom the *Liber pontificalis* praises as a faithful guardian of ecclesiastical tradition and as having restored the old rites of the Church *in diversis clericatus honoribus*.[23]   Pope Stephen decreed in the Roman Synod of 769 that henceforward only deacons or priests of the Church of Rome might be elected to the See of Peter, in order to make impossible for the future such a scandalous event as the elevation of the lay intruder Constantine (768) to the pontificate.   On this occasion, he termed the title priests *presbyteri cardinales*.[24]   Likewise, when he ordered that the seven hebdomadary bishops be obliged on Sundays to celebrate Mass and to sing *Gloria in excelsis* at the altar of St. Peter in the Lateran cathedral, he spoke of them as the *septem episcopi cardinales ebdomadarii qui in ecclesia Salvatoris observant*.[25]

[20] Klewitz, *Entstehung* 120, 151, 156f. (against the theory of Sägmüller, *Cardinäle* 6, who dated the increase of the *tituli* as late as the 12th century). For the list mentioned above, the so-called *Descriptio sanctuarii Lateranensis ecclesiae*, see at n. 38 *infra*.

[21] For one possibly earlier occurrence in a liturgical text see *infra* at n. 30.

[22] Sometimes considered as Stephen IV (e.g. in the *Annuario Pontificio*); the designation depends upon whether or not the *papa quatriduanus* Stephen (752), who died before his consecration, is counted as Stephen II.

[23] LP I, 478: 'Erat enim hisdem praefatus beatissimus praesul ecclesiae traditionis observator, unde et pristinum ecclesiae in diversis honoribus renovavit ritum.'

[24] *Conc. Rom.* 769 actio 4: 'Si quis ex episcopis vel presbiteris vel monachis aut ex laicis contra canonum et sanctorum patrum statuta proprumpens in gradus clericorum (*al.* gradum maiorum) sanctae Romanae aecclesiae, id est presbiterorum cardinalium et diaconorum, ire praesumpserit et hanc apostolicam sedem invadere quilibet ex supradictis temptaverit et ad summum pontificalem honorem ascendere voluerit . . .' (ed. A. Werminghoff, MGH *Conc.* 2,Hannover 1906–8, p. 88 lines 4–8 [revised ed. of pp. 85–8]); act. 3: 'Oportebat ut . . . in apostolatus culmen unus de cardinalibus presbiteris aut diaconibus consecraretur' (86, 21–3 Werminghoff): both texts as transmitted by Deusdedit 2, 163 and 161 (269, 21–6 and 268, 11–4 Wolf von Glanvell). A parallel tradition, generally ascribed to Anselm of Lucca, was first printed by L. Holstenius, *Collectio Romana bipartita veterum . . . monumentorum* (Rome 1662) I, 259–64; repeated in Labbe, Hardouin, Coleti, Mansi 12, 719f. and used for collation by Werminghoff *loc. cit.* In fact, this text is not part of Anselm's original collection (A, as edited by Thaner), but of the posthumous recension B (MSS *Vatic. lat.* 1364 and 6381: lib. 6 c. 25; cf. P. Fournier, 'Observations sur les diverses recensions de la collection canonique d'Anselme de Lucques,' *Annales de l'Université de Grenoble* 13 [1901] 438, 441; A. Mai, *Spicilegium Romanum* 6, Rome 1841, p. 346 = PL 149, 505).—Another testimony (overlooked by Klewitz, *Entstehung* 159 n. 1; 165 n. 5) is contained in LP I, 476, 2–3: '. . . nullus umquam praesumi laicorum neque ex alio ordine, nisi per distinctos gradus ascendens, diaconus aut presbyter cardinalis factus fuerit, ad sacrum pontificatus honorem promoveri.' For a tenth-century abstract from this passage see Werminghoff 79, 5–6; a later abstract in Ans. Luc. 7, 27 (375 Thaner) and Deusd. 1, 255 (146, 8–11 Wolf von Glanvell).—The three texts quoted passed on into Gratian: D. 79 cc. 5, 3, 4. From the first of them it is clear that the attribute, *cardinalis*, was meant only for the presbyters, not for the deacons, see ch. V at n. 70 *infra*.

[25] LP I, 478: 'Hic statuit, ut omni dominico die a septem episcopis cardinalibus ebdoma-

150

We may take it for granted that Stephen III, the *ecclesiae traditionis observator*, would not have applied in these two instances the term, *cardinalis*, were it not in accordance with the canonical tradition of the Church. Little does it matter whether he himself coined this nomenclature for the title priests and the Lateran bishops or found it already in use, though the latter seems more likely.[26] What matters, is the obvious connection between the hebdomadal service of the bishops and their designation as cardinals: it was for this liturgical function permanently entrusted to them in a church outside of their own bishoprics that they became *cardinales*. And as for the priests of the *tituli*, they had nothing in common with the cardinal bishops save a corresponding liturgical service in churches not their own—the four remaining basilicas—and the name, *cardinales*. The canonical meaning of that name thus proves to be in perfect harmony with the Gregorian usage: the Roman cardinal priests and bishops were 'incardinated' for permanent (though limited) purposes into the patriarchal basilicas while remaining bound nonetheless to the churches of their original ordination.

Not from any 'cardinal' importance of the suburbicarian sees or the title churches,[27] nor from any eminent rank (*cardinalis-principalis*) of their incumbents, did the Roman cardinalate take its origin. Equally mistaken is the assumption that the cardinals' name originally had to do with a quality of the patriarchal basilicas as *cardines*, main churches, of the papal see.[28] The figurative appellation of *cardo* for a principal church, and for the Roman Church in particular, would come into use only much later.[29]

Denoting at the outset but a canonical status of incardination, the attributive name of the Roman cardinal priests and bishops was bound, however, to develop into a dignity. Whereas in ancient times incardinations had been known only as isolated facts prompted by particular circumstances, the 'cardinal' relations of the title priests and the seven bishops to the patriarchal basilicas were in the nature of an institution permanently connected *ex officio* with the holding of

---

dariis, qui in ecclesia Salvatoris observant, missarum sollemnia super altare beati Petri celebraretur et Gloria in excelsis ediceretur.' Cf. Hinschius, *Kirchenr*. I, 323; Phillips, *Kirchenr*. VI, 171f.; Sägmüller, *Cardinäle* 12; Klewitz, *Entstehung* 127f.

[26] As suggested by the phrase, 'pristinum ecclesiae in diversis honoribus renovavit ritum' (note 23 *supra*), and by the possibility that the mention of cardinal priests in the second supplement of the first *Ordo Romanus* (note 30 *infra*) is older than Pope Stephen's decree.

[27] It is only in a much later text that the *Liber pontificalis* speaks of *cardinales tituli* (LP II, 196 on Stephen V, 885–91). Moreover, the expression is here probably a mere ellipsis for 'titles whose incumbents are cardinals'.

[28] For these alternative explanations see Sägmüller, *Cardinäle* 6f. 13; Hinschius, *Kirchenr*. I, 319f. They have been accepted in one or the other combination by current textbooks and reference works, e.g. those cited ch. I note 10 *supra*. Even Klewitz, who has recognized better than any other writer the fundamental connection of the Roman cardinalate with the hebdomadary service, misses the point and falls back on the common doctrine by deriving the name from the outstanding rank of the hebdomadaries in the chief basilicas (*Entstehung* 149f.). The correct view was hinted at briefly by Tamagna, *Origini* I, 111 (for the cardinal bishops) and by J. Christ, *Title* 116.

[29] See ch. IV at nn. 9ff. 38f. 106f. *infra*.

certain parochial and episcopal churches. As a consequence, the qualification as *cardinales* began to outgrow the hebdomadary functions for which the name had been given, and to obtain the connotation of a specific, exalted rank. This trend was all the more natural because the cardinal priests had, beyond their ordinary service in the basilicas, the unique and probably very old privilege of sacramental concelebration with the Pope in the pontifical Masses of Christmas, Easter, Pentecost, and the feast of St. Peter.[30] And of the cardinal bishops it has been noted that from the eighth century onwards they always stood out as a definite group—the *septem* as contrasted with the *forenses episcopi*[31]—in the Roman synods.[32]

But the development of the cardinalate into a distinctive dignity was rather slow. This is shown by the fact that only at the end of the tenth century the title priests began to change the style of their official signature from *Ego N. presbyter tituli N.*[33] into *Ego N. presbyter et cardinalis tituli N.*[34] (Note the incorrect position of the attribute.) And even then, the true canonical meaning of the term was occasionally recalled to memory. St. Peter Damian for instance, Cardinal Bishop of Ostia (1057-72), addressed his confrères as *Lateranensis*

---

[30] *Ordo I Rom.* suppl. II (num. 48): 'In diebus festis, id est Paschae, Pentecostes, s. Petri, Nativitatis Domini, per has quattuor sollemnitates habent colligendas presbyteri cardinales unusquisque tenens corporalem in manu sua . . .' etc. (29 Mabillon); cf. also Anselm of Lucca 6, 166 (345f. Thaner); Deusdedit 2, 114 (241f. Wolf von Glanvell); Martène, *De antiq. eccl. rit.* 1, 3, 8, 2 (I, 329f. Antw.; I, 120 Ven.). On the transmission of the 'second supplement' see Andrieu, *Ordines* 4, 472, 474, 486f. 520, 533, 540, 543 (his *Ordo III*); for a similar text mentioning the concelebration of the Roman priests, but not qualifying them as *cardinales*, see the *Ordo of St. Amand* (Andrieu's *Ordo IV*; ed. Duchesne, *Origines du culte chrétien*, 3rd ed. Paris 1902, p. 460; 5th ed. 1920, p. 480). The liturgical institution here described might be as old as the sixth century, cf. Duchesne, *LP* I, 139 n. 3; 246 n. 9; *Origines* (5th ed.) 185 n. 2; P. de Puniet, 'Concélébration liturgique,' *DACL* 3 (1914) 2473; *contra*, however, I. M. Hanssens, 'De concelebratione eucharistica,' *Periodica de re morali, canonica, liturgica* 17 (1928) 107ff. At any rate, the text of the *Ordo 'In diebus festis'* belongs to the eighth century, perhaps to its first half, and may thus be slightly older than Pope Stephen III's decrees. But there is no reason to assume with Dom D. Buenner, *L'ancienne liturgie romaine: le rite lyonnais* (Lyon-Paris 1934) 270 that the name, *cardinalis*, originated because of the concelebration. The pseudo-etymology, *cardinalis <ad cardines (cornua) altaris*, is of very late origin. Cf. ch. IV at n. 76 *infra*.

[31] *Invectiva in Romam pro Formoso papa* (ed. E. Dümmler, *Gesta Berengarii*, Halle 1871) 145. Cf. Hinschius, *Kirchenr.* I, 326 n. 9; Klewitz, *Entstehung* 131.

[32] Cf. (for the Roman Synod of 732) Duchesne, *LP* I, 423; Sägmüller, *Cardinäle* 12f. On the much discussed continuity of the seven sees see now Klewitz, *Entstehung* 128-33.

[33] Cf. e.g. St. Gregory's Roman Synods of 595 and 600, *Reg.* 5, 57a and 11, 15 (MGH *Epp.* 1, 366-7; 2, 275); or the Roman Synods of 745 and 761 (MGH *Conc.* 2, 44; 70f.); Gregory III JE 2234 (ed. W. Gundlach, MGH *Epp.* 3, Berlin 1892, p. 706f.); Roman Synod of 853 (Mansi 14, 1021). An earlier form of subscription—*Ego ille misericordia Dei presbyter S.R.E.*; *Ille humilis presbyter S.R.E.*—is recorded in LD 58, 82 (107, 173 Rozière; 48, 90 Sickel). Cf. Hinschius, *Kirchenr.* I, 313 n. 2.

[34] Cf. Roman Synod of 993 (JL 3848): 'Bonizo archipresbyter et cardinalis s. Luciae consensi; Benedictus presbyter et cardinalis s. Stephani consensi' etc. (Mansi 19, 172). The letter JL 3802 (dated A.D. 980), where similar subscriptions occur, is not genuine: cf. Kehr, *IP* 5, 133 num. 1.

152

ecclesiae cardinales;[35] Pope Alexander II (1061–73) issued a statute for the cardinal priests with the address, *septem cardinalibus s. Petri atque cunctis aliis;*[36] and we find in the same century some references made to individual cardinals not by their *tituli* but by the basilica of their incardination.[37] Finally, the anonymous author of the *Descriptio sanctuarii Lateranensis ecclesiae* (c. 1073–1100), who of course was chiefly interested in the liturgical functions of the Sacred College, listed the seven bishops and the twenty-eight *tituli* quite correctly under the rubrics: *septem cardinales episcopi hii sunt primae sedis* (i.e. St. John Lateran)—*cardinales s. Petri*—*cardinales s. Pauli*—*cardinales s. Mariae maioris*—*cardinales s. Laurentii.*[38]

Nevertheless, the detachment of a 'cardinal' rank from the congenital notion of an incardinated status was destined to prevail. This development, which eventually would lead to the inclusion of the Roman deacons in the class of *cardinales*, must be viewed in its connection with three important historical factors: (1) the general transformation of ancient canonical concepts in the early Middle Ages, especially with regard to the organization of bishoprics; (2) the communication of some of the Roman cardinals' liturgical privileges to the clergy of foreign churches; (3) the accretion of jurisdictional and political powers to the Roman cardinals during the great Reform of the eleventh century. The impact of these phenomena on the concept of the cardinalate will be next considered.

IV. SEMANTIC CHANGES

1. *'Clerici cardinis' of the Early Middle Ages*

We know to what extent the fundamental differences, in social and political structure, between the Germanic and the Roman world, have left their mark on

[35] *Epistola* 2, 1: 'Venerabilibus in Christo sanctis episcopis, Lateranensis ecclesiae cardinalibus' (PL 144, 253). Cf. Hinschius, I, 324 n. 3; Molien, *Dict. de droit can.* 2, 1317.—Klewitz, *Entstehung* 128 incorrectly speaks of Peter Damian as using the expression, 'Lateran bishops'.

[36] JL 4736; Kehr, IP 1, 7 num. 9. Sägmüller's doubts, *Cardinäle* 155, as to the authenticity are not justified.

[37] Abbot Desiderius of Montecassino, cardinal priest of the title of St. Cecilia (1058–86) and later Pope (Victor III, d. 1187), subscribes the acts of the Roman Synod of 1065 as 'cardinalis s. Petri et abbas s. Benedicti' (JL 4565). Gregory VII addresses him, *Reg.* 9, 11: 'Venerabili cardinali s. Petri et abbati Casinensi' (ed. E. Caspar, *Das Register Gregors VII.*, MGH *Epp. sel.* 2, 2, Berlin 1923, p. 598).—Cardinal Albert, priest of the title of St. Sabina, appears in 1098 as *cardinalis s. Pauli* (Kehr, IP 8, 355 num. 36). Cf. Klewitz, *Entstehung* 160 n. 1.—As late as 1154 we find in Anastasius IV (JL 9793) the expression: '. . . cardinalium episcoporum, qui sunt ad principalis altaris servitium deputati' (Mansi 21, 779E), and about the same time, the *Ordo Romanus XI* num. 38 speaks of 'unus de cardinalibus s. Laurentii basilicae' (135 Mabillon); cf. Phillips, *Kirchenr.* VI, 175 n. 35; 125 n. 18.

[38] MS *Vatic Reg.* 712, fol. 88v (ed. D. Giorgi, *De liturgia Romani pontificis* III, Rome 1744, p. 553; better in Kehr, IP 1, 3f.; Klewitz, *Entstehung* 119f.). On the approximate date of the *Descriptio* see Klewitz 123–6. Its survey of cardinals was taken over in 1160 by Johannes, deacon and canon of St. John Lateran, in his *Liber de ecclesia Lateranensi* c. 16 (ed. Mabillon, *Mus. ital.* II, 574; Ph. Lauer, *Le palais de Latran*, Paris 1911, p. 404), cf. Klewitz 118 n. 2.—Phillips VI, 124f. and Hinschius I, 335f. knew only this later list.

the institutions of the medieval Church, and how much the ancient canons were disregarded, overgrown as it were by new customs and concepts, in the formative period of the Frankish kingdom. In particular, the centralized organism of the bishoprics, so typical of Christian Antiquity, gave way to utter decentralization under the impact of a new parochial system, by which the innumerable proprietary churches (*ecclesiae propriae*) on the estates of the king and the nobility became endowed with parish rights and almost entirely withdrawn from the bishop's control. An overwhelming number of churches in private hands, on the countryside, thus stood apart from the few churches that were left to the bishop, besides his cathedral, in and around the cities. Here alone, the clergy remained fully subject to the bishop's diocesan government, distinct as a group from the rural priests and their quasi-feudal dependance upon the manorial lords.[1]

For expressing the essential difference between the bishop's clergy and that of the proprietary churches, the name, *cardinalis*, offered itself. To the medieval mind, the term 'cardinal priest' could not possibly have—apart from the peculiar situation of the Roman *tituli*—its old canonical sense: by the growing system of ecclesiastical benefices for the livelihood of the clergy, the ancient meaning of *titulus ordinationis* as the church of a cleric's first ordination faded away,[2] and with it, the reason for distinguishing between intitulated and incardinated priests. Reading the Gregorian texts without being conscious any longer of the ancient rigor in matters concerning the change of one's *titulus*, the medieval canonist could only notice what was merely accidental: the connection of *presbyteri cardinales* with cathedral and baptismal churches.[3] This seemed all the more legitimate since it agreed with the common, the uncanonical etymology and usage of the word 'cardinal.'

The equivocation appears for the first time in the famous instruction on some points of Canon law which Pope Zachary in 747 sent to Pippin the Short. One chapter of this instruction repeats the traditional Roman formulary for the conse-

---

[1] These fundamental aspects and effects of the proprietary church system are firmly established results of the researches conducted by U. Stutz and his school (of his numerous studies on the subject, see in particular *Benefizialwesen* [ch. II note 41 *supra*]; *Die Eigenkirche als Element des mittelalterlich germanischen Kirchenrechts*, Berlin 1895 [transl. G. Barraclough, in *Medieval Germany, Essays by German Historians*, Oxford 1938, II, 35–70]; the articles 'Pfarre, Pfarrer,' in Herzog-Hauck, *Realencyklopädie für protestantische Theologie und Kirche* 15 [1904] 239 ff. esp. 242–7; 'Eigenkirche, Eigenkloster,' *ibid.* 23 [1913] 364–77, with further bibliography)—regardless of the position one takes in the controversy (cf. ch. II note 42 *supra*) on the purely Germanic (Stutz) or nationally indifferent roots of the *Eigenkirchen*.

[2] Cf. Fuchs, *Ordinationstitel* 179–81. For tendencies in Carolingian times to reinstate the ancient law, see the Councils of Reims 813 c. 20 and Tours 813 c. 14 (ed. Werminghoff, MGH *Conc.* 2, 255; 288); the *Capitula a sacerdotibus proposita* 802 c. 13 (ed. A. Boretius, MGH *Cap.* 1, Hannover 1883, p. 107); Benedictus Levita, *Capit.* 1, 175 and 3, 393 (ed. H. Pertz, MGH *Leg.* 2, 2, Hannover 1837, pp. 55, 126; for Benedict's sources in these chapters see E. Seckel, 'Studien zu Benedictus Levita,' NA 31 [1905] 87; 41, 1 [1917] 194). Cf. Fuchs 97; 181 n. 6; also 185 n. 24; J. Christ, *Title* 121.

[3] The last who took cognizance of the true concept was Hincmar of Reims, cf. ch. II notes 27–8 *supra*.

154

cration of newly founded private oratories, with its characteristic prohibition to raise it to a baptismal church and to install a *presbyter cardinalis* at the place.[4] But in another chapter, Pope Zachary uses the Latin, *presbyteri cardinales*, for rendering the Greek, πρεσβύτεροι πόλεως, of the thirteenth canon of Neocaesarea, as contrasted with the πρεσβύτεροι ἐπιχώριοι of the same canon.[5] Here, the priests of the episcopal city,[6] that is, chiefly the priests of the cathedral,[7] are termed cardinals, as also in a third chapter in which the proper use of liturgical garments is inculcated upon the bishop and the *presbyteri cardinales*.[8]

Hereafter, the use of *cardinalis* for denoting the clergy of a cathedral was rapidly spreading. From the ninth to the twelfth century we find in a good many bishoprics, mostly of Italy, the cathedral clergy styled as *presbyteri* (*diacones, subdiacones, canonici, clerici*) *cardinales*, or *presbyteri* (etc.) *cardinis, de cardine*.[9] The words *cardinalis* and *de cardine* had thus become interchangeable, and this is characteristic of the new meaning given to the term: the bishop's church was now metaphorically called the *cardo* of the diocese in order to derive from it, by an *ex post* etymology entirely at variance with ancient canonical language, the 'cardinal' rank of the bishop's clergy. No particular function or dignity was originally meant by this qualification. When in some of the documents in question not all, but only a few of the subscribing cathedral clerics signed their names as *cardinales*, this apparent differentiation has no deeper

---

[4] Zachary JE 2277 c. 15 (ed. W. Gundlach, MGH *Epp.* 3, 484), in conformity with LD 11, JK 959, etc. (ch. II notes 38–40 *supra*); cf. Stutz, *Benefizialwesen* 218f.—Hinschius and Schäfer (ch. II n. 44 *supra*) give to this text the inadequate interpretation: cardinal priest = parish priest.

[5] JE 2277 c. 4: 'de presbiteris agrorum quam obedienciam debent exhibere episcopis et presbiteris cardinalibus. Ex concilio Neocesar. c. xiii. ita continetur . . .' (481, 34–6 Gundlach); cf. Phillips, *Kirchenr.* VI, 55; Hinschius, *Kirchenr.* I, 315 n. 7.

[6] Dionysius Exiguus translates: (I) *presbyteri eiusdem urbis*, (II) *presbyteri urbis ipsius*; both the *Versio prisca* and the *Hispana* translate: *presbyteri civitatis* (cf. Turner, *Monum.* 2, 1, 136–7). Cf. also Deusdedit 2, 14 (198 Wolf von Glanvell); Bonizo, *Vita chr.* 5, 15 (180 Perels).—Gratian D. 95 c. 12 uses the version of Dion. II.

[7] Pope Urban II (1088–99) refers to this canon with the words (Kehr, IP 1, 7 num. 11): '. . . iuxta concilium Neocaesariense in quo de cathedralibus presbyteris agitur' (ed. P. Kehr, 'Nachträge zu den Papsturkunden Italiens,' *Nachrichten von der Königl. Gesellschaft der Wissenschaften zu Göttingen*, phil.-hist. Kl. 1908, p. 228 num. 3; cf. Klewitz, *Entstehung* 161 n. 1).

[8] JE 2277 c. 1: '. . . ut episcopus iuxta dignitatem suam indumentis utatur, simili modo et presbyteri cardinales' (480, 40–481, 1 Gundlach). Cf. Phillips, *Kirchenr.* VI, 55 n. 68, who rightly understands this passage as treating of the cathedral canons, while Hinschius, *Kirchenr.* I, 317 n. 2 refers it to rectors of parishes because the text goes on to speak of *plebs sibi subiecta*. But as the priests of the cathedral chapter were exercising the bishop's pastoral functions in the city, they also had *plebem sibi subiectam*.

[9] Nearly all instances quoted in the ensuing note have been recorded, in varying selections, by Du Cange s. vv. *canonici cardinales, presbyteri cardinales*; Muratori, *Antiq.* 5, 158ff.; Tamagna, *Origini* I, 113–9; Nardi, *Dei parrochi* II, 408ff.; Phillips VI, 42f.; Hinschius I, 318f. Further research may well yield additional evidence.

(i) Italian bishoprics in alphabetical order: *Asti*, document of Bishop Alericus or Oldricus (924): '. . . consensu et consilio presbyterorum, diaconorum, seu reliquorum clericorum nostrae ecclesiae cardinalium' (Ughelli, *Italia sacra* 4, 352D).—*Bergamo*, document

significance than that of showing how little weight the attribute carried.[10]   It could be arbitrarily added or omitted, and there are even instances of charters which refer to members of the cathedral clergy as *cardinales* in the text, but bear their signatures without that qualification.[11]

---

of Bishop Adalbert (908): '. . . praenominatae s. Pergamensis ecclesiae cardinalibus canonicis, presbyteris, diaconibus, subdiaconibus quoque atque custodibus' (Ughelli 4, 426A); Bishop Reginfred (1000): '. . . Abel eiusdem ecclesiae car⟨di⟩nis presbytero' (Ughelli 4, 438B; cf. Tamagna I, 114).—*Como*, charters of Emperors Lothar (950), Otto III (996), Arduin (1002), Henry II (1004), Konrad II (1026): '. . . s. Cumanae ecclesiae gregi tam de cardine quamque omnium sacerdotum' (ed. L. Schiaparelli, *I diplomi di Ugo e di Lotario* . . ., Fonti per la storia d'Italia 38, Rome 1924, p. 284 lines 11–2; cf. MGH *Dipl.* 2, 618, 19–20; *Dipl.* 3, 95; 702f.; *Dipl.* 4, 60).—*Cremona*, judgment of King Berengar I (910): '. . . Leo archipresbyter, Petrus, Lampertus et Rapertus presbyteri, Lupus archidiaconus, Aldo, Oldepertus diacones cardinis ipsius episcopii' (Muratori, *Antiq.* 1, 125C); charters of Emperors Konrad II (c. 1037) and Henry III (c. 1040): '. . . quendam diaconem Henricum nomine, s. Cremonensis ecclesiae cardinalem et utilimum famulum' (ed. H. Bresslau, MGH *Dipl.* 4, Hannover-Leipzig 1909, p. 348 lines 20–1; cf. MGH *Dipl.* 5, 35).—*Florence*, document of Bishop Sichelmus (967), with an inserted document subscribed by several priests who are styled 'presbyter canonicus et cardinalis', 'presbyter et cardinalis' (Ughelli 3, 30 C).—*Ivrea*, document of Bishop Ogerius (1075): '. . . donamus etiam domino Taurino ibidem abbati et omnibus successoribus eius canonicas duas de ordine XII presbyterorum, ut tam ipse quam successores sui sint de ordine et officio nostrorum cardinalium' (*Historiae Patriae Monumenta* 1, Turin 1836, p. 649).—*Lodi*, document of Bishop Aldegrausus (c. 951–62): '. . . quo tantummodo cardinales sacerdotes, presbyteri scil. ac diaconi, subdiaconi ad comedendum conveniant; . . . Radbertus presbyter de cardine s. Laudensis ecclesiae' (ed. C. Vignati, *Codice diplomatico laudense*, Bibliotheca historica italiana 2, Milan 1879, num. 13 p. 19; cf. Tamagna, *Origini* I, 113, 119; wrongly referred to Laon by Phillips VI, 43 and Hinschius I, 318); document of 972: '. . . Landevertum nostrae ecclesiae cardinalem sacerdotem' (Vignati p. 26).—*Lucca*, document of Bishop Peter (904): '. . . Ego Viventius archipresbyter cardines et vicedomino . . . Ego Sichardus presbyter et chardinalis et primicerius . . . Ego Guntripaldus presbyter et cardinalis' etc. (Muratori, *Antiq.* 6, 407C–D); document of Bishop Peter (923): '. . . Andreas presbyter et cardinalis . . . Benedictus presbyter et cardinalis' etc. (*ibid.* 5, 162D; both documents and several others from 907 to 925 also in D. Barsocchini, *Memorie e documenti per servire all'istoria di Lucca* 5⁌ 3, Lucca 1841, pp. 27, 43, 108, 110, 115 etc.).—*Milan*: see notes 13ff. *infra.*—*Naples*, document of Archbishop Peter (1100): '. . . Sergius archipresbyter et cardenalis s. sedis Neapolitanae subscripsi' (Muratori, *Antiq.* 5, 161D); cf. also documents of 1177 subscribed by two *presbyteri cardinales*, 1183 by three *presbyteri cardinales*, 1213 by one *archipresbyter* and one *presbyter cardinalis* (Ughelli 6, 99D; 101C; 105B–C).—*Padua*, diocesan synod of Bishop Hildebert (962): '. . . convocata sacerdotum, levitarum, reliquorumque caterva tam ex cardine urbis eiusdem quamque ex singulis plebibus vel oraculis' (Ughelli 5, 430A); repeated in the synod of Bishop Gauslinus, 978 (Muratori, *Antiq.* 1, 549D).—*Pavia*, charter of Emperor Otto I (972): '. . . que actenus Iohannis cuiusdam presbyteri fuit de cardine s. Ticinensis aecclesiae' (ed. Sickel, MGH *Dipl.* 1, Hannover 1879–84, p. 567 lines 18–9).—*Piacenza*, election of Bishop Guido (904): '. . . Ego Andreas diaconus cardinis s. Placentinae ecclesiae' (P. M. Campi, *Dell'historia ecclesiastica di Piacenza* I, Piacenza 1651, p. 430); charter of King Charles III (883): '. . . qualiter inter diaconibus et presbyteris viginti et novem nostram adierunt celsitudinem, cardinales etiam s. Iustinae virginis et martyris' (Campi I, 468).—*Ravenna*: see note 12 *infra.*—*Salerno*, document of Judge Guaferius (1163): '. . . existentibus in eadem praesentia . . . Urso et Paschasio, primiceriis et cardinalibus, Matthaeo cardinali et archipresbytero, Constantino presbytero et cardinali et pluribus aliis eiusdem ecclesiae' (Ughelli 7, 401C); cf. also documents of 1176, 1178, 1187 (Ughelli 7, 403B; 404B; 415D).—*Siena*, document of

156

However, during the twelfth century we meet in some places with a tendency to reserve the name, as connoting a dignity, to a restricted group among the bishop's clergy, in obvious imitation of the Roman cardinalate. This trend may be best observed in Ravenna, where nothing but the inveterate spirit of rivalry with the see of Peter led to an assignment of definite *tituli* to the metropolitan cardinal priests.[12]—In Milan, the qualification of 'cardinal' originally served to distinguish the clergy of the Ambrosian *cardo* from the clergy of the city churches:

---

the cathedral chapter (1000): '. . . Johannes clericus & (*leg.* de?) cardine et prepostus . . . Sigizo presbyter & cardine, Petrus clericus & cardine, Martinus diaconus & cardine' etc. (Muratori, *Antiq.* 5, 609A; paleographical confusion of & and *de* is very likely).—*Vercelli*, Bishop Atto (924–c. 950; cf. F. Bonnard, 'Atton évêque de Verceil,' *Dictionnaire d'histoire et de géographie ecclésiastiques* 5 [1931] 191) in his *Capitulare* c. 90: '. . . Quodsi defuerit, cardinalibus primae sedis interim suggeratur' (PL 134, 46A).—*Verona*, Bishop Ratherius (d. 974) in his *Itinerarium* c. 7: 'Ad quod cum titulares (= city pastors) omnes et illos de plebibus (= rural pastors) paratos, Deo gratias, invenissem; vos cardinales . . . hinc manere adhuc cerno rebelles' (*Opera* edd. P. et H. Ballerini, Verona 1765, p. 447 with note 31 = PL 136, 589 with n. 1046).—Further references made by Du Cange s.v. *canonici cardinales* to cardinals in Aquileia, Benevento, Capua, Pisa can not be verified.

(ii) Much less evidence has been collected from non-Italian dioceses: *Nevers*, document of Bishop Franco (903): '. . . per consilium nostrorum fidelium canonicorum, scil. cardinalium et archipresbyterorum atque forensium sacerdotum' (*Gallia christiana* 13, instr. 18 col. 313E–314A).—*Orléans*, Bishop Walter's *Capitulare* (871) c. 2: 'Ut per archidiaconos vita, intellectus et doctrina cardinalium presbyterorum investigetur' (Mansi 15, 505).—On the particular feature of *cardinales archidiaconi* in Autun, Besançon, etc. see notes 23–6 *infra*. Also the 'liturgical' cardinals found in several other bishoprics outside of Italy are to be treated separately from the mere cardinals *de cardine*.—Finally, we have to eliminate some erroneous references to non-existing cardinals: i.e. to the *Lex Baiwariorum* 1, 10 (9?) 1 (Du Cange s.v. *diaconus cardinalis*; but see ed. E. von Schwind, MGH *Leg. nat. germ.* 5, Hannover 1926, p. 279f.); to the *Capitulare* of Bishop Haito of Basel 'c. 90' (Du Cange s.v. *cardinalis*; in fact Atto of Vercelli c. 90, see *supra*); to Laon (Phillips, Hinschius; in fact Lodi, see *supra*).

[10] The contrary was asserted by Muratori, *Antiq.* 5, 155; 162B; 163A, C; 164f. (also 1, 552): on the strength of the 'parochialist' theory he assumed that in medieval cathedral chapters only those clerics were *cardinales* who at the same time held parochial churches in benefice. See *infra* at nn. 35–6.

[11] Tamagna, *Origini* I, 116–8; examples may be found e.g. in the documents of Asti, Bergamo, Milan.

[12] For cardinal priests, deacons, etc. in general, see Synod of Ravenna (998): '. . . et subscribentes confirmaverunt . . . presbyteri cardinales ecclesiae Ravennatis' (Mansi 19, 221B); document of Archbishop Walter (1141): '. . . assidentibus Johanne quoque Ravennatis ecclesiae archipresbytero cardinale et presbytero Fantulino cardinale . . . Henrico diacono cardinale et Buniolo subdiacono cardinale' (Muratori, *Antiq.* 5, 159A). The *tituli* occur in Archbishop Walter's charter of 1122 for Bishop Dodo of Modena, which characteristically begins by aping the style of the Pope: 'Gualterius servus servorum Dei, divina gratia archiepiscopus' and creates Bishop Dodo and his successors cardinal priests of the 'title' of St. Agnes in Ravenna. It is subscribed, among others, by 'Ego Johannes archipresbyter s. Ravennatis ecclesiae et cardinalis s. Petri maioris tituli subscripsi; Ego Johannes presbyter et cardinalis s. Salvatoris manu mea subscripsi' etc. (Muratori, *Antiq.* 5, 178A). Hinschius I, 321 n. 4 correctly points to the obvious imitation of Roman institutions. I was not able, however, to verify his further reference to cardinals with *tituli* as occurring also in Naples.

it was applied to the twenty-four members of the bishop's *presbyterium* as set over against the *sacerdotes urbani;*[13] furthermore to the deacons, subdeacons[14] and, quite generally, the *ordinarii* of the Church of Milan.[15] The latter term included, in the early Middle Ages, the several orders of clerics peculiar to the organization of the Ambrosian cathedral,[16] even as elsewhere it was occasionally

[13] Landulfus senior, *Historia Mediolanensis* (c. 1100) 1, 3: '... Quin etiam locum in quo omnes convenirent, insignivit ... ubi omnes sacerdotes urbani in sexta feria vel kalendis convenientes ...' (ed. L. Bethmann and W. Wattenbach, MGH *Script.* 8, Leipzig 1848, p. 39 lines 31–2; ed. H. Bianchi in Muratori, *Rer. ital. script.* 4, 62); *ibid.* c. 4: 'At cum beatus Ambrosius supradictos sacerdotes Deo disponente ordinavit, visum est sibi ceteris cum fratribus viginti quatuor sacerdotes, qui quasi cardinales essent, debere constitui; ... sic misterium ecclesiae Ambrosianae per viginti quatuor cardinales aperiretur et regeretur' (39, 57–40, 5 Bethmann-Wattenbach; 63f. Bianchi). The *sacerdotes urbani* were also called *decumani,* cf. the synodal testament of Atto of Vercelli (946): '... Item iudico et lego Aldemano consanguineo meo, archipresbytero s. Mediolanensis ecclesiae et cardinalibus et presbyteris decumanis ...; et cardinales presbyteri cum primicerio decumanorum tantum habeant per unumquemque quam duo presbyteri decumani; ... archipresbyter et cardinales, primicerius et decumani, qui pro tempore erunt' etc. (ed. A. Mai, *Scriptorum veterum nova collectio* 6, 2, Rome 1832, pp. 5–6). For other texts referring to *decumani* see notes 14, 16 *infra.*

[14] Document of 905: '... Petrus diaconus de cardine s. eiusdem ecclesiae Mediolanensis' (Muratori, *Antiq.* 1, 773B; *Hist. Patr. Monum.* 13, Turin 1873, col. 699b); Atto's testament: '... et diaconi cardinales et subdiaconi (tantum habeant) quam unus presbyter decumanus' (Mai, *loc. cit.* 5); see also his shorter testament of 948: '... ut valles illae ... deveniant in iure et potestate s. Mediolanensis ecclesiae et presbyterorum seu diaconorum cardinalium atque sacerdotum decumanorum' (PL 134, 20C); document of Archbishop Aribert (1032): '... adhibitis sibi senioribus suae ecclesiae cardinalibus presbyteris et diaconibus' (quoted by Muratori, *Antiq.* 5, 158 from J. P. Puricelli, *Ambrosianae Mediolani basilicae ac monasterii ... monumenta,* Milan 1645, num. 222); Aribert's testament (1034): '... faciant presbyteri, diaconi et subdiaconi cardinales de ordine s. Mediolanensis ecclesiae' (Ughelli, *Italia sacra* 4, 105A).

[15] Archbishop Arnulph, *Gesta archiepiscoporum Mediolanensium* (c. 1085) 1, 3: '... ut decedente metropolitano unus ex praecipuis cardinalibus, quos vocant ordinarios, succedere debeat' (ed. Bethmann-Wattenbach, MGH *Script.* 8, 7, 26; ed. Muratori, *Rer. ital. script.* 4, 8A). The *praecipui* are the priests and deacons, since the entire passage is contingent upon Pope John VIII's mandate to elect the archbishop *de cardinalibus presbyteris et diaconibus* (JE 3294, see *infra* at n. 40). The clause, *quos vocant ordinarios,* refers however to *cardinalibus,* not to *praecipuis,* for the (grammatically possible) interpretation that only the highest ranking cardinals were *ordinarii* is contradicted by the sources; see the following notes.—Landulfus de s. Paulo (Landulfus iunior, c. 1136), *Hist. Mediol.* num. 34, document of 1105: 'Ordinarii cardinales s. Mediolanensis ecclesiae necnon et primicerius cum universo sacerdotio et clero Mediolanensi ...' (ed. Bethmann and Jaffé, MGH *Script.* 20, Hannover 1868, p. 34 lines 9–10; Muratori, *Antiq.* 5, 158). Cf. also the synonymous expression, *cardinales de ordine* in the document of 1034, note 14 *supra.*

[16] There exists unfortunately no adequate study of the composition of the Ambrosian clergy with its remarkable differences, in the minor orders, from the Roman scale of ordination. (M. Magistretti, *La liturgia della chiesa milanese nel secolo IV* [Milan 1899] I, 33–41 made an uncritical attempt to harmonize the two sets of orders.) Landulfus senior, *Hist. Mediol.* 2, 35 (71 Bethmann-Wattenbach; 93 Bianchi) and the *Ordo* of Beroldus (ed. Magistretti, *Beroldus sive ecclesiae Ambrosianae Mediolanensis kalendarium et ordines,* Milan 1894, p. 35f.; ed. Muratori, *Antiq.* 4, 861f.) give the following picture: 24 priests; 7 deacons; 7 subdeacons; the *primicerius presbyterorum* (only in B, cf. note 20 *infra*); the *notarii* without

158

applied to cathedral canons and prebendaries as such.[17] But by the twelfth century, *ordinarius* became in Milan a distinctive denomination of the four leading orders only—priests, deacons, subdeacons, and notaries—and moreover the cardinal's rank was now reserved to the twenty-four *sacerdotes cardinales* and seven *diaconi cardinales* alone, as can be seen from that outstanding document of the medieval Ambrosian rite, the *Ordo* of Beroldus (after 1125).[18] Among the

definite number, under their *primicerius*; the *primicerius lectorum* and 16 *lectores* (i.e. the *secundicerius*, 4 *clavicularii*, and 11 *terminarii*; L has 18 *lectores*); 4 *magistri scholarum*; 12 *sacerdotes decumani* (cf. note 13 *supra*; only in L); the *cimeliarcha* and 16 *custodes* (8 *maiores*, i.e. 4 *cicendelarii* and 4 *ostiarii*; 8 *minores*); the *schola* of 20 *vetuli*. Cf. also P. Lejay, 'Ambrosien (rit)' DACL 1 (1907) 1392f.—With the exception of the *decumani* (the city priests) all these ranks were *ordinarii*, cf. document of 1053: '. . . Domini ordinarii eiusdem s. Mediolanensis ecclesiae, presbyteri, diacones, subdiacones, notarii, lectores, cum primiceriis, . . . magistri scholarum seu (= et) custodes' as distinct from 'et presbyteri de ordine decumanorum s. Mediolanensis ecclesiae' (Ughelli 4, 107D). Also in the document of 1105 (note 15 *supra*) the *ordinarii cardinales* include the entire clergy of the cathedral as set over against the 'primicerius cum universo sacerdotio et clero Mediolanensi'. Cf. also Atto of Vercelli's shorter testament (948) in PL 134, 20D. Muratori's suggestion (*Antiq.* 5, 168) that the *ordinarii* might have been the hebdomadaries of the cathedral is entirely gratuitous.

[17] Ratherius of Verona, *Itinerarium* c. 6: 'Recolitis . . . me praecepisse, ut duobus diebus archipresbyter et archidiaconus me absente adventantes cum ordinariis omnibus pariter residentibus discuterent' (445 Ballerini; PL 136, 587); these *ordinarii* of Verona are evidently identical with the cardinals mentioned *Itin.* c. 7 (cf. note 9 *supra*). For Novara, see the compromise between the 'Novarienses ordinarios s. Marie' and the 'ordinarios s. Iulii' before Bishop Riprandus (1040) in Ughelli 4, 703B. For eleventh-century canonical opinion see Bonizo, *Vita chr.* (c.1090–9) 5, 77, who speaks of clerics 'qui . . . in quibusdam ecclesiis canonici, in quibusdam vero ordinarii, in quibusdam vero, ut Rome, cardinales nominantur' (204, 14–7 Perels), much as seven centuries after him the Ballerini, in their note 27 to Ratherius *loc. cit.* (PL 136, 587 n. 1042) point to the identity between *ordinarii*, *cardinales*, and *canonici*; cf. also G. Forchielli, 'Collegialità di chierici nel Veronese dall' VIII secolo all'età comunale,' *Archivio Veneto* 58 (1928) 81f. and Gaudenzi, *Nonantola* 401 (with reference to the expression *computari in ordine* in the anonymous tract on ecclesiastical offices, quoted n. 30 *infra*). On the 'minor clergy' of Verona cathedral, i.e. those without capitular prebends (as e.g. the *presbyteri cappellani*) see the Ballerini's prologue to their edition, pp. cxxiii–viii (PL 136, 103–6); Forchielli 82. They were probably not *ordinarii*.—Du Cange s.v. believes that *ordinarii* sometimes refers to 'dignitates quibus competit aliqua iurisdictio' (?) and sometimes to 'canonici ecclesiarum collegialium'.

[18] 'In primis sunt sacerdotes cardinales, prior quorum archipresbyter cum ferula sua et primatu suo praefertur in choro. Deinde septem diaconi cardinales subsequuntur, prior tamen archidiaconus cum ferula sua et primatu suo praedicto archipresbytero coniungitur' (35, 9–13 Magistretti; 861 Muratori); the subdeacons and all the subsequent orders are enumerated without qualification as *cardinales*.—For the *ordinarii* as set over against the lectors etc. see Beroldus: '. . . Item illis descendentibus, dum lectores cantant antiphonam, descendunt omnes ordinarii absque archiepiscopo usque ad medium pulpiti, et ibi ordinantur ex una parte presbyteri et notarii, idest a septemtrione; alii, scil. diaconi et subdiaconi ab austro' (41, 13–7 Magistretti; 865C Muratori); '. . . et lectores canunt antiphonam, et ordinarii paululum ascendunt, et finita antiphona a lectoribus, ordinarii incipiunt eandem' (41, 28–30 Magistretti; 865D Muratori. Cf. also 41, 36–7; 43, 8–35 Mag.; 865E, 866E–867A Mur.); 'In vigilia festivitatum . . . vadunt ad festum ordinarii et lectores et custodes et schola s. Ambrosii et mares et feminae' (63, 35–64,.1 Magistretti; 880D Muratori).—Magistretti, *Beroldus* 149 n. 3 overlooks the *notarii* among the *ordinarii*, and in his

subsequent ranks we find there, for instance, the *primicerius sacerdotum*, originally chorbishop and overseer of the city priests,[19] now himself a member of the *cardo*, but not a cardinal.[20]   Here too, it seems that the Roman usage influenced a terminology which some time before had been applied to the clergy *de cardine* in general.

In the framework of a medieval bishopric there existed, on the other hand, dignities and offices which by their very nature were always connected with rank and seat in the cathedral chapter and therefore needed no express qualification as *cardinales*.   This is especially true of the archdeaconate, the most important office, next to the bishop's, in the early medieval Church.   As long as there was but one archdeacon in the diocese, it would have been a tautology to call him a cardinal.[21]   Only when in the course of time—first in France (ninth century), later in Germany and England—diocesan territories became divided into several archdeaconries, with a plurality of archdeacons both in and outside the bishop's chapter,[22] did the term *archidiaconus cardinalis* find its way into ecclesiastical documents:[23] among the various archdeacons of a diocese it would now designate

---

Liturgia della chiesa milanese 40 n. 3 he even contends that the subdeacons were *ordinarii* only after the thirteenth century.   The term is also misunderstood by A. Pöschl, *Bischofsgut und Mensa episcopalis* I (Bonn 1908) 74f.

[19] Landulfus sen. *Hist. Mediol.* 1, 3: . . . qui primicerius vocaretur, . . . qui quasi co⟨r⟩episcopus circa omnes in crimine laborantes potestatem a s. Ambrosio magistro accepit, ut quod episcopus implere per se non posset, co⟨r⟩episcopus qui primicerius vocabatur circa illos implere curiose studeret.   Quin et iam locum in quo omnes convenirent, insignivit . . . (etc.: cf. note 13 *supra*); deinde subepiscopus qui co⟨r⟩episcopus usque modo et primicerius vocatur . . .' (8, 28–34 Bethmann-Wattenbach; 62 Bianchi).   No mention of the Milanese chorbishop is made in Th. Gottlob, *Der abendländische Chorepiskopat* (Kanonistische Studien und Texte ed. Koeniger 1, Bonn 1928), where other instances of chorbishops called *coepiscopi* (p. 61f.) or *subepiscopi* (p. 35) may be found.

[20] Beroldus, after enumerating the first three orders (cardinal priests and deacons, cf. note 18 *supra*; and subdeacons): '. . . Quarto loco ponitur primicerius presbyterorum, non minor ceteris dignitate, sed minor loco; . . . vice archiepiscopi poenitentes solvit et ligat; . . . et si contigerit quod pretium aut denarii dantur pro pastu, similiter partem suam recipit, quantum presbyter cardinalis' (35, 14–22 Magistretti; 861 Muratori), and *passim*. (Note that the *primicerius* has ordinary vicarious jurisdiction in the internal forum.)

[21] Note e.g. that Beroldus, while enumerating the archpriest among the *sacerdotes cardinales*, and the archdeacon among the *diaconi cardinales* (note 18 *supra*), never uses the term, cardinal, when speaking in the course of his treatise of the archpriest or archdeacon alone.   See also the testament of Atto of Vercelli (note 13 *supra*).

[22] On this development, see the copious literature cited by A. Amanieu, 'Archidiacre,' *Dictionn. de droit can.* 1 (1924) 962ff.; A. Koeniger, 'Archidiakon,' LThK 1 (1930) 616; Kurtscheid, *Hist. iur. can.* 257–61.

[23] *Autun*, document of 972: '. . . Gerardus humilis Eduorum episcopus; Rodulfus cardinalis archidiaconus . . .' (*Gallia christiana* 4, instr. 35 col. 73D); document of 1034: '. . . S(ignum) Helmoini episcopi, Widonis abbatis, Valterii cardinati archidiaconi, Gaufredi abbatis et archidiaconi . . .' (*ibid.* instr. 42 col. 79A); document of 929: '. . . Adso kardinalis archidiaconus subscripsit' (ed. A. Bernard and A. Bruel, *Recueil des chartes de l'abbaye de Cluny* I, Paris 1876, p. 269 num. 274; cf. A. Schröder, *Entwicklung des Archidiakonats bis zum elften Jahrhundert*, Augsburg 1890, p. 58 n. 17).—*Besançon*, document of Archbishop Hugo (1041): '. . . S(ignum) Gibuini cantoris et archidiaconi cardinalis.   S. Roberti archi-

160

the *archidiaconus maior*, i.e. the one whose jurisdictional district was the episcopal city, the *cardo* itself.[24] But instances of this nomenclature seem to be very rare,[25] and still more so is the use of *archipresbyter cardinalis* in an analogous sense.[26] So much for the 'cardinal' clergy in the medieval diocese. Now, the etymology *cardinalis* < *de cardine* led quite logically to a classification also of certain

diaconi et archiclavi' and several other archdeacons (ed. E. Martène and U. Durand, *Thesaurus novus anecdotorum* 1, Paris 1717, col. 166; cf. Schröder *loc. cit.*).—*Toul*, privilege of Bishop Udo for the collegiate church of St. Gengoul (c. 1065): '. . . constituimus etiam cardinalem archidiacon(at)um huius urbis ad eam pertinere, ut prepositus huius loci eum perpetuo in beneficium possideat' (quoted by Du Cange s.v. *archidiaconus cardinalis*, from *Probationes historiae Tullensis*); confirmed by Pope Alexander II in 1069 (JL 4665): '. . . constituimus etiam ut (*add.* sit?) archidiaconus ipsius civitatis secundum idem tuum decretum, ut cardinalem archidiaconatum (*leg.* cardinalis archidiaconatus?) illius civitatis ad eandem ecclesiam pertineat. Quatinus prepositus ipsius loci . . .' (ed. P. Ewald, 'Acht päpstliche Privilegien,' NA 2 [1877] 209; cf. his remarks p. 210 on the difficult reading of the original). Cf. also Emperor Henry IV: '. . . confirmamus etiam cardinalem archidiaconatum eiusdem urbis ad ipsum cenobium pertinere, ut prepositus . . .' etc. and Bishop Poppo (1105): '. . . ut cardinalem archidiaconatum obtineat' (both quoted by Ewald 209 n. 10). On the restoration of St. Gengoul by Bishop Udo and the privileges granted to the collegiate chapter see also *Gesta episcoporum Tullensium* c. 43 (ed. G. Waitz, MGH *Script.* 8, 645f.) and *Gallia christ.* 13, 990D. Du Cange *loc. cit.* quotes also a document, not to be verified at present, in which the *prepositus ecclesiae s. Gengulfi* signs as *archidiaconus cardinalis ecclesiae Tullensis*.

[24] Cf. the expressions, *cardinalem archidiaconatum huius urbis*, *archidiaconus ipsius civitatis* in the privileges for St. Gengoul. That this was only one of several archdeaconries in the diocese of Toul, is shown by the number of archdeacons signing e.g. the documents *Gallia christ.* 13, instr. 23 col. 470A (a. 1054); instr. 25, 26 col. 472A, E (a. 1076). Cf. also, for the major archdeacon in general, Schröder, *op. cit.* 58f.; Hinschius, *Kirchenr.* II, 192 n. 2; E. Baumgartner, *Geschichte und Recht des Archidiakonates der oberrheinischen Bistümer* (Kirchenrechtliche Abhandlungen ed. Stutz 39, Stuttgart 1907) 150ff.

[25] Du Cange s.v. *archidiaconus cardinalis* cites one more: 'Marbodus cardinalis archidiaconus ecclesiae Andegavensis'. On Marbod (Marbeuf), scholastic (1076) and archdeacon (1090–6) of Angers, later bishop of Rennes (1096–1123), author of didactic poems, lives of local saints, and very interesting letters (PL 171, 1463–1782), see Ch.Urseau, *Cartulaire noir de la cathédrale d'Angers* (Paris-Angers 1908) p. xlivf.; E. Amann, 'Marbode,' DThC 9, 2 (1927) 1939; M. Manitius, *Geschichte der lateinischen Literatur des Mittelalters* III (Munich 1931) 719–30. His signature, *Marbodus archidiaconus*, occurs frequently in the *Cartulaire noir* and in other cartularies published for the diocese of Angers (e.g. for the abbeys of St. Aubin and Ronceray, for St. John's hospital, and St. Sergius' church), but I was not able to find the form of subscription quoted by Du Cange.

[26] Among the documents of Autun, there is an undated charter of Bishop Agano with the signatures of four archdeacons and '. . . signum Ramerii archipresbyteri cardinalis, signum Rotberti archipresbyteri' etc. (*Gallia christ.* 4, instr. 45 col. 83). Since one passage of the document reads: '. . . auctoritate . . . domini Gregorii papae, domini quoque Hugonis Lugdunensis archipraesulis et apostolicae sedis legati, et nostra' (*ibid.* 82), it can be dated as of 1082–5: Hugo of Die became Archbishop of Lyons in 1082 (cf. E. Caspar, *Das Register Gregors VII.* [ch. III note 37 *supra*] II, 592 n. 1) and Gregory VII died in 1085.—Also in this case the multiplication of archpriests was the reason for designating one of them as cardinal; as to archpriests holding archdeaconries, in particular the city archdeaconate, see Baumgartner, *op. cit.* pp. 60 n. 1, 75, 118f. 140, 151f.

churches as *cardinales*, namely of those lesser churches which immediately belonged to the bishopric or depended upon the *cardo*-cathedral, as distinct from private oratories and proprietary churches. Thus, a royal statute for Lombardy (813) spoke of *praepositi cardinalium ecclesiarum*,[27] and the Council of Meaux (845), of *tituli*[28] *cardinales in urbibus et suburbibus constituti*.[29] Both texts refer to diocesan churches under the bishop's immediate jurisdiction. In the same sense, *ecclesiae* and *cappellae cardinales* are found in other documents down to the twelfth century.[30] The cathedral itself, being the *cardo* of the diocese, was

[27] *Capitulare Mantuanum* 1, 8: 'Ut prepositi cardinalium aecclesiarum obedientes sint episcopis suis' (ed. Boretius, MGH *Cap.* 1, 195). For the correct date see F. Patetta, 'Sull'introduzione in Italia della collezione d'Ansegiso e sulla data del così detto capitulare Mantuanum duplex,' *Atti della R. Accademia delle Scienze di Torino* 25 (1889–90) 87; Carlo De Clercq, *La législation religieuse franque de Clovis à Charlemagne* (Louvain-Paris 1936) 229 n. 1.—This text and the greater part of those quoted in the following notes were already known and commented upon by Thomassin, Du Cange, Muratori, etc. Cf. also Schäfer, *Pfarrkirche und Stift* (ch. II n. 44 *supra*) 124 n. 5.

[28] On *titulus* as a term used in the Middle Ages for churches, in particular for churches with parochial rights depending upon the cathedral, see Muratori, *Antiq.* 5, 1003; the Ballerini in their note to Ratherius, *Itin.* c. 7 (*Opp.* 447 n. 31 = PL 136, 589 n. 1046; cf. note 9 *supra* s.v. Verona); J. Christ, *Title* 119 n. 73. Especially on *tituli* as city parishes see Schäfer, *Frühmittelalterliche Pfarrkirchen* (ch. III n. 3 *supra*) 36 n. 3; 46; 51 n. 3.

[29] *Conc. Meld.* c. 54: 'Ut titulos cardinales in urbibus et suburbibus constitutos episopi canonice . . . ordinent et disponant' (ed. A. Boretius and V. Krause, MGH *Cap.* 2, Hannover 1897, p. 411). The text is correctly understood by Phillips, *Kirchenr.* VI, 48f. while Hinschius attempts to construe *cardinales* as denoting the contrast between city churches and rural churches (*Kirchenr.* I, 317 n. 3).

[30] *Aquileia*, charter of King Karloman (879): '. . . cum ecclesiis baptismalibus atque cardinalibus sive cum cellulis' (ed. P. Kehr, MGH *Urkunden der deutschen Karolinger* 1, Berlin 1932–4, p. 317 lines 10–1).—*Bergamo*, royal and imperial charters by Charles III (883), Henry II (c. 1023), Konrad II (1027): '. . . in monasteriis, xenodochiis, vel ecclesiis baptismalibus aut cardinalibus seu oraculis vel cunctis possessionibus' (Ughelli, *Italia sacra* 4, 417B; cf. MGH *Dipl.* 3, 632, 3–4; *Dipl.* 4, 122).—*Florence*, document of Bishop Raynerius (1023): '. . . ecclesiam s. Iohannis Baptistae cardinalem' (Muratori, *Antiq.* 5, 164B).— *Novara*, royal charters by Louis II (854), Karloman (877), Louis III (905): '. . . in monasteriis videlicet, xenodochiis, abbatiis, ecclesiis cardinalibus seu reliquis possessionibus' (ed. L. Schiaparelli, *I diplomi italiani di Lodovico III e di Rodolfo II*, Fonti per la storia d'Italia 37, Rome 1910, p. 60 lines 13–4).—*Pavia*, charter of Kings Hugo and Lothar (943): '. . . omnesque cardinales capellas tam extra quam infra urbem' (Muratori 5, 169B; Schiaparelli, *I diplomi di Ugo e di Lotario*, Rome 1924, p. 217, 17–8).—*Piacenza*, charter of Charles III (881): '. . . cum monasteriis et cellis vel ecclesiis baptismalibus quae intra civitatem praedictam cardinales habentur sive quae extra civitatem existunt' (Campi, *op. cit.* [n. 9 *supra* s.v. Piacenza] I, 467 num. 19).—*Siena*, document of Bishop Raynerius (1108): '. . . ecclesiam s. Martini cardinalem iuxta burgum Senensis civitatis positam' (Ughelli 3, 544B). —See also c. 6 of a little anonymous tract on ecclesiastical offices (11th–12th cent.; purporting to be extracted *Ex libro ordinis Romani*, as discovered in some Italian MSS, edited, and discussed by Gaudenzi, *Nonantola* 395–404: 'Ut hi computentur in ordine qui cardinales ecclesias habuerint. Hi debent facere processionem cum episcopo . . .' (p. 397). Gaudenzi's assumption however (p. 404) that the tract actually represents fragments of a lost *Ordo Romanus* composed under Nicholas I is to be rejected; not even an Italian origin of the text is sufficiently proved.

162

almost never considered *ecclesia cardinalis*,[31] but baptismal churches (parishes) sometimes were: royal charters for Piacenza, Aquileia, and Bergamo describe *ecclesiae baptismales* as *cardinales*[32]—for in Italy, otherwise than in France, the baptismal churches had withstood appropriation by private land owners and remained integral parts of the dioceses.[33]

The clergy of these lesser 'cardinal' churches was, however, as a rule not considered to be *cardinalis*, since such clergy could not be said to be *de cardine*.[34] This point must be stressed against the Gallicanists of the seventeenth and eighteenth centuries, who held—as did also to a certain extent Muratori—that on the contrary the name of cardinal always designated in the early Middle Ages a parish rector, or a cathedral cleric with parochial functions.[35] This 'parochialist' theory of the cardinalate is based, partly on a misinterpretation of the Roman formulary for the foundation of oratories (as if *cardinalis presbyter* in these form letters meant 'pastor'); partly on a misunderstanding of the cardinalate of the Roman title priests (as if they were cardinals of their *tituli*); and, above all, upon a fallacious inference from the twofold medieval usage of *cardinalis* for

[31] The distinction between the *cardo* and the other churches is expressly stated, e.g. in the documents quoted n. 9 *supra* for Como and Padua. There exists one single exception to the rule stated above: deed of foundation of an hospital by Deacon Dagobert in Verona (932): '. . . ut sit sub potestate et cura archipresbyteri et diaconi seu et sacerdotum diaconorumque s. cardinalis Veronensis ecclesiae qui pro tempore fuerint' (ed. G. B. Biancolini, *Notizie storiche delle chiese di Verona* I–II, Verona 1749, p. 697); '. . . sacerdotes et clerici universi s. cardinalis ecclesiae; . . . deveniant in potestatem archipresbyteri et archidiaconi et sacerdotum seu et diaconorum s. cardinalis ecclesiae' (*ibid.* 698). Cf. the Ballerini in their note cited n. 28 *supra* (a truncated reference to this piece in Phillips, *Kirchenr.* VI, 48 n. 48).—Hinschius, *Kirchenr.* I, 315 n. 1 quotes also Hincmar, *De iure metrop.* c. 20 on the *sedes cardinalis* of St. Boniface in this context, but this expression in fact means 'see of incardination', see ch. II n. 28 *supra*.

[32] See the charters n. 30 *supra*, rightly understood by Du Cange s.v. *ecclesiae cardinales* as referring to parochial churches. *Contra* Phillips VI, 49 n. 50, who understands *aut* disjunctively in the charter for Bergamo ('ecclesiis baptismalibus aut cardinalibus'); correctly Hinschius I, 317 n. 2: *aut = et*. There can be no doubt that *aut* (Bergamo), *atque* (Aquileia), and *quae cardinales habentur* (Piacenza) mean all three the same.—Cf. also Gaudenzi, *Nonantola* 400.

[33] On the resistance of Italian baptismal churches to the proprietary-church policy see Stutz, *Benefizialwesen* (ch. II, n. 41 *supra*) 112f.; G. Forchielli, *La pieve rurale* (Rome 1931).

[34] Tamagna, *Origini* I, 112ff. Nardi, *Dei parrochi* II, 395, 403ff. The distinction between *cardo* on the one, and *tituli* and *plebes* on the other hand appears very clearly in Ratherius of Verona, *Itin.* c. 7 (quoted n. 9 *supra*). The assumption of E. Mayer, *Die angeblichen Fälschungen des Dragoni*, Leipzig 1905, p. 41f.; also 'Der Ursprung der Domkapitel,' ZRG Kan. Abt. 7 [1917] 24) that the term *cardo* designated the community of clerics in a given church is quite unfounded.—Only in one isolated case does it seem that also parish priests signed their names as *presbyteri de cardine*: document of Bishop Rudolph of Siena (1081): '. . . Ego Bonizo presbiter de cardine s. Laurentii subscripsi. Ego Petrus canonicus & cardine s. Petronilla ss. Cardine s. Donati et Ilariani presbiter Bonfilio ss.' etc. (Muratori, *Antiq.* 5, 175C; but for contrary evidence from Siena see n. 9 *supra*). The true medieval terminology for rectors of (collegiate) parish churches is studied in detail by Schäfer, *Pfarrkirche und Stift* 121ff. (*archipresbyter, rector ecclesiae, praelatus, praepositus*, even *abbas*; never *presbyter cardinalis*).

[35] References ch. I n. 5 *supra*. See also n. 10 *supra*.

both clerics and churches that are *de cardine* (as if the 'cardinal' nature of a baptismal church did entail a 'cardinal' quality of its clergy).[36]—

As for *presbyteri de cardine* and similar terms, Rome did not hesitate, since Pope Zachary had set the fashion, to adopt the new manner of speech.[37]   In the ninth century, Leo IV (847–55), Hadrian II (867–72), and John VIII (872–82) occasionally qualified Roman cardinals as *presbyteri cardinis nostri*—as if there were no basic canonical difference between these and any foreign cardinal cleric of the new type.[38]   The same disregard of the peculiar status of Roman cardinal priests is revealed when John VIII, in the famous letter to Emperor Basil I which restored the communion with Photius (879), warned the Greeks that in future the Patriarch of Constantinople must always be elected, not *de laicis vel curialibus*, but only *de cardinalibus presbyteris et diaconibus Constantinopolitanae sedis*;[39] and when in the same year he admonished the clergy of Milan, after the deposition of Archbishop Anspert, to proceed to a new election and to choose the worthiest candidate *de cardinalibus presbyteris aut diaconibus*.[40]   In both

---

[36] Even modern authors do not escape this faulty syllogism; e.g. Hinschius, *Kirchenr.* I, 317f. who concludes that cardinals were not always, but sometimes parish rectors (see also n. 8 *supra* on his interpretation of JE 2277). His further thesis that almost every church could be considered as *cardo* in comparison to the next lower church is an unjustified *quid pro quo*. He even cites the Capitulare of 813 which speaks of *prepositi cardinalium aecclesiarum* (n. 27 *supra*) as an instance for archpriest = cardinal priest! (*Kirchenr.* II, 266 n. 2).

[37] However, it seems that the notion of *ecclesiae cardinales* (i.e. *de cardine*) was not adopted in Rome.   The one instance usually cited (e.g. by Phillips, *Kirchenr.* VI, 48 n. 47; Hinschius I, 318 n. 1) is LP II, 196 on Stephen V (885–91): '. . . reliquias . . . per diversi cardinales titulos . . . largitus est' (probably an elliptic expression, cf. ch. III n. 27).   Or should there be one instance in Urban II JL 5351 (cf. ch. V n. 95 *infra*)?—Among the examples that follow in the text above for *presbyter cardinis* etc. we have omitted the pseudo-decretal *Ministerium archipresbyteri* (JE †1986), in which the archpriest appears as the superior of *cardinales sacerdotes*.   In the later decretal collections this forged text is ascribed to 'Leo papa' or Leo III (*Coll. II Parisiensis* 6, 2; *Coll. Lipsiensis* 33, 7; *1 Comp.* 1, 16, 2 = X. 1, 24, 2) while two MSS of Burchard's *Decretum* (Lucca, Cath. Chapter 124; Pistoia, Cath. Chapter 119 [*ol.* 140]) and one MS of Ivo's *Panormia* (Venice, Bibl. Marciana *lat.* IV. 51 [Valentinelli VIII. 12; wrong number given in Gaudenzi, *Nonantola* 395]) present it in their respective appendices or preliminary matter under the inscription: 'Privilegium archipresbyteri a s. Gregorio digestum (et constitutum *add. Marc.*); Ex libro institutionum s. Gregorii papae' (cf. Mansi 10, 444B; Gaudenzi 404; Valentinelli, *Catal.* II, 234).   For a clue to its possible origin see n. 75 *infra*.

[38] In the Roman Synod of 853, 'Anastasius presbyter cardinis nostri, quem nos in titulo b. Marcelli ordinavimus' is deposed by Leo IV (Mansi 14, 1017B, not in JE; see also the shorter forms of the sentence as reported in the *Annales Bertiniani* an. 868, ed. G. Waitz, MGH *Script. rer. germ.* Hannover 1883, pp. 92–3; Mansi 14, 1026–7; JE after n. 2606 and n. 2635).   In fact, Anastasius Bibliothecarius was, as title priest of St. Marcellus, cardinal of St. Paul's.   The *Liber pontificalis* has more correctly: 'Anastasius presbyter cardinalis, tituli b. Marcelli' (LP II, 129 = X. 3, 4, 2).—Hadrian II repeatedly speaks of one of his legates as *Petrus religiosus presbyter cardinis nostri* (JE 2926–31; ed. Perels, MGH *Epp.* 6, 726, 15; 727–32); likewise John VIII, of *Petrus cardinis ecclesiae nostrae* (or *cardinis nostri*) *presbyter* (JE 3139, 3141, 3273, 3275; ed. Caspar, MGH *Epp.* 7, 86, 3; 99, 8; 186, 11; 189, 3).

[39] JE 3271 (172, 30–4 Caspar), also in Deusdedit 4, 434 (614, 13–5 Wolf von Glanvell). Already Nicholas I had spoken in 862 (JE 2692) of '. . . ad honorem cardinis ipsius sanctae ecclesiae' (446, 3–4 Perels) with regard to Constantinople.

[40] JE 3294 (202, 32–3 Caspar).

164

cases, Pope John actually copied the terms from the decree of 769 on papal elections,[41] thus indiscriminately applying Stephen III's precise designation of the Roman title priests to the cathedral clergy of Milan and Constantinople. And yet we know that John VIII was a remarkable canonist and that on another occasion—when transferring Archbishop Frothar of Bordeaux to the see of Bourges—he used the word 'cardinal' in its very technical sense.[42] Considering such inconsistencies, we are not surprised to see the Pope's intimate friend, John the Deacon, betraying a similar vagueness about *cardinales* in his biography of Gregory the Great.[43]

Later, in the eleventh century, we find Pope Alexander II adopting the term *cardinalis archidiaconus* for the archdeacon of an episcopal city.[44] Still more astonishing is the peculiar use made by Urban II of *cardinalis* in dissolving certain unions of benefices. Thus in a series of letters (1092–5) concerning the restitution of the bishopric of Arras which for a long time had been united by subjection to the see of Cambrai,[45] and again in a letter (1097) confirming the separation of the previously united abbeys of Figeac and Conches:[46] in both cases the Pope intimates that from now on the restored benefices should again have each its *episcopus* (or *abbas*) *cardinalis*[47]—that is, its 'own and proper' bishop or abbot, as contrasted with the former administration by foreign prelates.[48] This was, of

---

[41] This fact has been generally overlooked, even by Caspar, MGH *Epp.* 7, 172 n. 2 and 202 n. 9.

[42] See ch. II n. 26 *supra*.

[43] While Johannes Diaconus correctly records some incardinations (*Vita* 3, 15–6; 18–20: PL 75, 139–42—including however incorrectly some cases of union in c. 15, viz. Greg. *Reg.* 2, 48 and 3, 20), his references to Roman priests under St. Gregory as *cardinales ecclesiae suae* (3, 7–8: PL 75, 133) and to *revocare in pristinum cardinem* (3, 11: see ch. II n. 36 *supra*) are anachronistic.—Cf. Nardi, *Dei parrochi* II, 403 n. 1.

[44] JL 4665, cf. n. 23 *supra*.

[45] This group of letters is reprinted in Mansi 20, 668–75. On the history of the preceding union see R. Rodière, 'Arras (diocèse),' *Dictionn. d'hist. et de géogr. ecclés.* 4 (1930) 699f. *Gallia christ.* 3, 321f. Urban II repeatedly stresses the point that the union is to be dissolved unless Cambrai can show papal letters authorizing the subjection.

[46] JL 5654, printed in Mabillon, *Acta sanctorum ordinis s. Benedicti*, saec. 3, 2 (Venice 1734) 406; *Gallia christ.* 1, instr. 38 p. 44f. The preceding union had been authorized by Gregory VII.

[47] JL 5472 to the clergy and people of Arras: '. . . volumus . . . cardinalem episcopum vobis et ecclesiae utilem eligere' (Mansi 20, 671D); JL 5500 to the Archbishop of Reims: '. . . ut utraque ecclesia cardinali non destituatur episcopo' (*ibid.* 672E); JL 5512 to Lambert, the new bishop of Arras: '. . . ut Atrebatensi ecclesiae cardinalis restitueretur antistes; . . . ut Atrebatensis ecclesia deinceps cardinalem semper episcopum sortiatur' (*ibid.* 669A, B); JL 5513 to the archdeacons, and JL 5514 to the religious superiors of the diocese: '. . . ut ei deinceps tanquam cardinali episcopo . . . subesse et oboedire curetis' (*ibid.* 674C); JL 5518 to the Count of Flanders: '. . . ecce enim civitas Atrebatensis, quae in comitatu tuo principalis est, ex apostolicae sedis dignitate cardinalem recepit episcopum' (*ibid.* 675A).— JL 5654 to the Abbots of Figeac and Conches: '. . . placuit . . . ut utrique loco, sicut ante fuerat, abbas cardinalis restitueretur' (*locc. citt.*).

[48] Cf. JL 5472: '. . . solet enim fieri ut ecclesiae persecutionis tempore suis ordinibus, suis populis, subsidiis etiam temporalibus destitutae, aliis temporaliter committantur ecclesiis, postquam vero his quibus imminutae fuerant, Deo donante, abundare coeperint, pristinam

course, a complete reversal of the Gregorian terminology. On this occasion, Pope Urban even applied the verb *incardinare* in the sense of installing the properly elected and consecrated bishop.[49]

2. *'Liturgical' Cardinals Outside of Rome*

With all the blurring of the original concept, the early Middle Ages retained a notion that there was some difference between the Roman cardinals and the more or less self-styled cardinal clergy of other churches. From the second half of the tenth century onwards, certain churches secured themselves papal privileges of having among their clergy a number of cardinals *more Romanae ecclesiae*. These cardinals by papal grant were found in Magdeburg (968),[50] Treves (975),[51] Aix-la-Chapelle (997),[52] Besançon (1051),[53] Cologne (1052),[54] and Compostella

---

recipiant dignitatem' (Mansi 20, 671D).—Phillips, *Kirchenr.* VI, 58f. interprets Pope Urban's manner of speech as indicating that the people of Arras received back, as it were, their *cardo*; but this explanation would not apply to the Figeac-Conches case, for monasteries neither are nor have a *cardo*. Du Cange s.v. *abbas cardinalis* translates, *abbé en chef*— an expression which does not convey Pope Urban's idea any better.

[49] JL 5472: '. . . et electum per manum metropolitani vestri consecrari et ecclesiae vestrae incardinari studeatis' (Mansi *loc. cit.*).

[50] John XIII (JL 3729): '. . . Ceterum more Romanae ecclesiae ecclesiam tuam XII presbyteros et VII diaconos et XXIV subdiaconos cardinales, qui sandaliis et lisinis utantur, habere volumus. Super hoc vero iisdem presbyteris et abbatibus ecclesiae Iohannis Baptistae in suburbio eiusdem civitatis constructae tunicis uti concedimus. Quibus exceptis et episcopis super altare in honorem b. Mauritii dedicatum missam celebrare aliquis nullo modo praesumat' (Mansi 19, 5 C). Cf. also the confirmations by Benedict VII in 981 (JL 3808) and Benedict VIII in 1012 (JL 3989). The authenticity of JL 3729, denied by some earlier authors, can no longer be doubted, cf. Klewitz, *Entstehung* 151 n. 6 On the other hand, Klewitz' assumption (p. 153) that the number of cardinal priests in Magdeburg was only seven and that the number XII in the extant text (*Liber privilegiorum s. Mauricii*, c. 1100) would be a copyist's mistake, is voided by the evidence of JL 3989 which speaks of the *numerus duodenarius* of the cardinal priests (cf. the text in Hinschius, *Kirchenr.* I, 319 n. 2).

[51] Benedict VII (JL 3783): '. . . cardinales quoque presbyteri, fratre nostro Theodorico archiepiscopo missam celebrante, dalmaticis, et diaconi una cum presbyteris schandaliis utantur; hebdomadariis quoque presbyteris ad s. Petrum missam celebrantibus suae dilectionis intuitu dalmaticis uti permittimus' (PL 137, 322B). Confirmed by Victor II in 1057 (JL 4365), but not for the hebdomadaries.

[52] Gregory V (JL 3875): '. . . decernimus in supradicta ecclesia septem cardinales diaconos et presbyteros cardinales septem huic ecclesiae deservire, ea videlicet ratione ut nullius dignitatis persona super sacrum altare Dei genetricis Mariae ibidem constitutum missam celebret, praeterquam supradicti septem cardinales presbyteri et archiepiscopus huius loci (i.e. Coloniensis) et episcopus Leodiensis qui huic dioecesi praesidet' (ed. Quix, *Codex diplomaticus Aquensis*, Aachen 1839, vol. I, 36). The *cardinales ecclesiae Aquisgranensis* are subsequently mentioned in charters of Emperor Otto III (1000, 1001), see MGH *Dipl.* 2 (ed. Th. von Sickel, Hannover 1888–93) 776, 29 and 841, 13.

[53] Leo IX (JL 4249): '. . . Statuimus denique ad honorem nostri protomartyris super sanctum praedictum altare non ministrari nisi semel in die, et nullus praesumat super id accedere ad sacrificandum nisi quem archiepiscopus huius loci ad hoc destinaverit cum consensu fratrum, scil. septem e fratribus illius congregationis qui melioris vitae eligantur et cardinales vocentur; quorum unus sit eiusdem ecclesiae decanus, et sicut est maior in

166

(1108).[55] They were clearly distinct from the rest of the respective cathedral clergy by their limited number—in general seven or twelve priests, seven deacons, sometimes also subdeacons—and by their liturgical privileges which usually included: the privilege of officiating in dalmatic and sandals on solemn occasions;[56] for the cardinal priests in particular the privilege of functioning as assistants at pontifical Mass,[57] or the privilege of hebdomadal service;[58] and finally the reservation of the cathedral's main altar to the cardinal priests for celebrating Mass, to the exclusion of anybody else except the bishop.[59] It is evident that all these provisions, even where the actual rescript did not refer expressly to the *mos Romanae ecclesiae*, reproduced the Roman title priests' prerogatives in the patriarchal basilicas:[60] their liturgical garb[61] and hebdomadary service was imitated, their right to celebrate was turned into altar privileges, and their eucharistic concelebration, into the functions of assistant priests.

The analogy of the Roman basilicas is even more stressed by the fact that such privileges were held by a few outstanding churches only; a corollary, as it were,

congregatione, ita prior polleat dignitate. Horum itaque quicumque ibi celebraverit missam, induat dalmaticam et tunc demum audeat celebrare cum omni reverentia et religione; sandaliis quoque utantur et mitra tam ipse sacerdos quam diaconus necnon subdiaconus in festivitatibus Domini et Salvatoris nostri et b. Dei genetricis' etc. (PL 143, 668D–669A).

[54] Leo IX (JL 4271): '. . . ut maius altare ecclesiae tuae matris virginis honori dedicatum et aliud ibidem apostolorum principi b. Petro addictum reverenter ministrando procurent septem idonei cardinales presbyteri dalmaticis induti, quibus etiam, cum totidem diaconibus ac subdiaconibus ad hoc ministerium prudenter electis, ut sandaliis utantur concedimus' (PL 143, 687D–688A).

[55] Paschal II (JL 6208): '. . . quod secundum Romanae ecclesiae consuetudinem septem cardinales presbyteri in ecclesia tua ordinaveris qui ad altare b. Iacobi missarum officia succedentibus sibi vicibus administrent; . . . statuentes ut nec per te nec per tuorum quemlibet successorum constitutus ille sacerdotum numerus imminui debeat aut immutari; nec per aliam quamlibet personam, nisi per praefatos presbyteros aut episcopos aut Romanae ecclesiae legatos, missarum super altare b. Iacobi statuimus solemnia celebrari' (PL 163, 247). The glossator Bernard of Compostella mentions this institution, c. 1205–6; cf. Kuttner, *Traditio* 1 (1943) 315.

[56] See the texts for Magdeburg, Treves, Besançon, Cologne.

[57] Treves.

[58] Aix-la-Chapelle (? Gregory V speaks of *deservire*), Compostella (*succedentibus sibi vicibus*), perhaps also Cologne, cf. Wibertus, *Vita Leonis IX*: '. . . concessit domnus papa hoc privilegium sedi ecclesiae Coloniensis, ut ad altare s. Petri VII presbyteri cardinales quotidie divinum celebrarent officium in sandaliis' (ed. I. M. Watterich, *Pontificum Romanorum . . . vitae*, Leipzig 1862, vol. I, 155).

[59] Magdeburg, Aix-la-Chapelle, Besançon, Compostella.

[60] Cf. Hinschius, *Kirchenr.* 321; Klewitz, *Entstehung* 151f. 162. The older authors all overlooked the fundamental difference between these privileged cardinals and the clergy *de cardine* of other cities.

[61] Occasionally the right to wear dalmatic and sandals was also granted to other prelates, e.g. to the Abbot of Fulda by John XV in 994 (JL 3853; repeated by Gregory V JL 3874 and John XIX JL 4090: revoked by Clement II in 1046, JL 4134; reconfirmed by many popes, from Leo IX in 1049 to Eugene III in 1151: JL 4170, 4364, 4557, 6972, 7462, 7631, 8244, 9439); to the Abbot of Montecassino by Leo IX in 1049 (JL 4164; repeated by Victor II JL 4368). Cf. Sägmüller, *Cardinäle* 162 n. 3; Kehr, IP 8, 135 num. 66; 138 num. 79; K. Lübeck, 'Der Kardinalsornat der Fuldaer Äbte,' AKKR 120 (1940) 33–49.

emphasizing the papal recognition of their exceptional dignity:[62] Magdeburg, Treves, and Cologne were metropolitan sees of primatial rank. To the shrine of St. James in Compostella countless pilgrims flocked from all over Europe, and its bishops were striving for metropolitan, even for primatial rights.[63] The metropolitan cathedral of Besançon treasured a precious relic of St. Stephen Protomartyr, and the Pope himself had consecrated over it the new altar which was to be reserved to seven cardinals.[64] The collegiate church of Aix-la-Chapelle finally, where Charlemagne lay buried, was considered a sanctuary of singular national pre-eminence.

However, the papal rescripts had created a new type of 'liturgical' cardinals which was likely to spread where similar liturgical situations existed. When Leo IX in 1049 consecrated the new church of the monastery of Saint-Remi in Reims, he decreed that Mass at its main altar, over the body of the Apostle of the Franks, be henceforth reserved *secundum morem Romanae ecclesiae* to seven priests selected among the congregation.[65] By an obvious analogy to Besançon, these seven privileged monks later became known as *cardinales*.[66]

A similar historical process is found—while no certain instances are known from Italy[67]—in many French cathedrals where it was customary that a select

[62] Cf. Klewitz, *Entstehung* 151.

[63] The first goal they attained under Callixtus II in 1120 (JL 6823), for the second they claimed a privilege by Anastasius IV (1153–4: JL 9808?) which later popes rejected repeatedly. Cf. Sägmüller, *Cardinäle* 59 n. 3; Klewitz 161.

[64] JL 4249: '. . . dum illud (*scil.* brachium s. Stephani) recondidimus infra altare quod consecravimus te praesente' etc. (PL 143, 668C).

[65] JL 4177: '. . . quatenus nulla ecclesiastici ordinis magna vel parva persona in hoc altari quod consecravimus missam celebrare praesumat, nisi Remorum archiepiscopus et huius loci abbas et cui licentiam concedat [permissa eadem licentia canonicis Remensis ecclesiae bis in anno, in Pascha scil. et in Rogationibus], septem presbyteris legitimis ad hoc officium deputatis, quos et scientia ornet, morum gravitas et vitae probitas commendet' (ed. Mabillon, *Acta sanctorum ord. s. Ben.* saec. 6, 1, Venice 1734, p. 637 = PL 143, 617). The passage in brackets is suspect of interpolation.—Anselmus monachus, *Historia dedicationis ecclesiae s. Remigii* c. 13: 'Constituit etiam quod ad altare quod . . . consecraverat, non indiscrete a quibusque sicut hactenus sacrosancta mysteria agerentur, sed secundum morem Romanae ecclesiae septem tantummodo sacerdotes qui in illa congregatione digniores haberentur, ad hoc officium deputarentur' (ed. Mabillon, *ibid.* 632; Mansi 19, 736B). Cf. Martène, *De antiq. eccl. rit.* 1, 3, 8, 3 (I, 332E Antw.; I, 120 Ven.).

[66] *Chronicon s. Huberti Andaginensis* (after 1119): '. . .nec multo post (Lambertus) electus et constitutus unus ex septem cardinalibus maioris altaris (scil. s. Remigii). Dignitas huius ordinis firmata est privilegio Romano eidem ecclesiae a domno Leone papa quando eam dedicavit. . . . Septem vero cardinales ad hunc honorem assumpti publica electione praeminent in tota congregatione' (ed. Bethmann-Wattenbach, MGH *Script.* 8, 593, 17–23).

[67] The subject has not been investigated. Ughelli, *Italia sacra* 7, 390D writes of Bishop Alfanus of Salerno (d. 1085): '. . . hunc sanctissimum pontificem elegisse sibi . . . ad altaris ministerium viginti quatuor canonicos, quos et presbyteros cardinales nuncupasse, quatuorque diaconos, quos similiter diaconos cardinales vocasse tradunt Salernitani scriptores. Quibus per successores pontificis fuit in posterum concessa facultas gestandi mitras sericas quas vocant de damasco.' If Ughelli had substantiated his source, we could accept the statement of the *Salernitani scriptores* as evidence for a liturgical character of the cardinalate in Salerno. (On cardinals in subscriptions of documents from that city see note 9 *supra*).—A liturgical connotation is also possible in the admission of Abbot Taurinus into the *ordo* of the twelve cardinal priests at Ivrea (*ibid.*).

168

number of parish priests from the city assisted the bishop at pontifical Mass on certain high feast days, and especially at the blessing of the oils on Holy Thursday.[68] Their number varied in the different dioceses between six, seven, twelve, and thirteen.[69] This custom was rooted, partly in the ancient liturgy of sacramental concelebration,[70] partly in a canonical obligation, frequently stressed for the parish clergy of the Middle Ages, to attend on Sundays and feast days the bishop's functions at the cathedral instead of, or at least before, celebrating the parochial Mass.[71] In Lyons these priests, six in number, were called *symmistae*

[68] Our main sources on this subject are the informations collected in various French dioceses by Martène, *De antiq. eccl. rit.* 1, 3, 8, 2 (I, 331C–D Antw.; I, 120 Ven.) and by (Jean-Baptiste Lebrun Desmarets) Sieur de Moléon, *Voyages liturgiques de France* (Paris 1718) *passim.* Cf. also P. de Puniet, 'Concélébration liturgique,' DACL 3 (1914) 2476; F. Cimetier, 'Cardinaux,' *Dictionnaire pratique des connaissances religieuses* 1 (1925) 1090f.; L. C. Moille, 'The Liturgy of Lyons,' *The Month* 151 (1928) 402–8: Archdale A. King, *Notes on the Catholic Liturgies* (London-New York-Toronto 1930) 130; Dom Denys Buenner, *L'ancienne liturgie romaine: le rite lyonnais* (Lyon-Paris 1934) 246f. 260–71; A. Molien, 'Cardinal,' *Dictionn. de droit canonique* 2 (1937) 1314.

[69] *Angers*: thirteen parish rectors of the city assist the bishop on Easter, Christmas, the feast of St. Maurice (later: St. Maurice, St. Maurilius, St. Andrew) and the blessing of the holy oils (Moléon, *op. cit.* 93).—*Chalon-sur-Saône*: seven suburban parish rectors assist at the high feasts (Martène *loc. cit.*).—*Chartres*: six priests concelebrate and co-consecrate with the bishop on Holy Thursday (Moléon 231).—*Lyons*: six priests assist the archbishop on Easter, Pentecost, Christmas at the cathedral; two priests assist the dean on any *festum duplex I classis*; six priests assist the archbishop when he pontificates on one of the high feasts at the collegiate church of St. Paul (Martène *loc. cit.*; Moléon 45–7, 51–2, 73; Buenner, *op. cit.* 246f. 260f.).—*Orléans*: twelve parish rectors assist the bishop at his installation, on Holy Thursday, and the Exaltation of the Cross; later (15th cent.) they are in number of fourteen and assist at all pontifical Masses; six canons concelebrate on Holy Thursday (Moléon 181, 196).—*Paris*: thirteen priests (10 parish rectors, the Prior of Notre-Dame-des-champs, the Prior of Saint-Jacques, and the Abbot of Saint-Victor) are to be present at the cathedral on Christmas, Easter, and the Assumption (*Cartulaire de l'église de Notre-Dame de Paris* ed. Guérard [Collection de documents inédits sur l'histoire de France, 1st ser.: Collection des cartulaires de France 4–7, Paris 1850] 1, 3; cf. Cimetier *loc. cit.*).—*Sens*: twelve, later thirteen (out of sixteen?) parish rectors assist the Archbishop on the feasts of the Dedication, St. Stephen, and the blessing of the oils (Martène *loc. cit.*: Moléon 170, 173). These priests were organized in a confraternity, called *des treize prêtres*, the statutes of which were confirmed in 1220 by Archbishop Pierre de Corbeil, cf. *Gallia christ.* 12, instr. 7 col. 363; Abbé E. Chartraire, *Cartulaire du chapitre de Sens* (Société archéologique de Sens, Documents 3, Sens 1904) 168 note.—*Soissons*: twelve parish rectors assist the bishop on Christmas, Holy Thursday, Easter (Martène *loc. cit.*; *Rituale seu mandatum insignis ecclesiae Suessionensis, tempore episcopi Niveleonis* [i.e. 1175–1207] *exaratum*, Soissons 1856, pp. 40, 63, 69, 114, 305f.).—*Troyes*: thirteen (?) parish rectors assist the bishop on certain feasts (Moléon 24, 170).—*Vienne*: six suburban priests concelebrate with the archbishop in the third Mass on Christmas and on other high feasts (later only on Christmas, Easter, Pentecost); twelve parish rectors assist on Holy Saturday and bless with the archbishop the baptismal font (Martène *loc. cit.*; Moléon 11, 15–8, 22–4, 28, 32); see especially the *Ordinale* of 1524 quoted by Moléon 17: 'suburbani signa faciant durante missa ad modum episcopi et sic in omnibus aliis maioribus festivitatibus.'

[70] Cf. Martène *loc. cit.*; Moléon, *op. cit.* 17, 47, 172, 181, 196, 231; Puniet *loc. cit.*; Moille, *op. cit.* 408: Buenner, *op. cit.* 269f.

[71] On obligations of this kind see Schäfer, *Frühmittelalterliche Pfarrkirchen* (ch. III n. 3 *supra*), for Le Mans (p. 37), Verona, Ferrara (46), Arezzo, Mayence, Cologne, Florence (47).

(συμμύσται)—a name later distorted by popular etymology into *six muses*.[72] But in other places, as e.g. in Paris, Sens, Soissons, Angers, and Troyes, the old custom resulted in qualifying these rectors of parishes as *cardinales* with regard to their liturgical functions as *presbyteri assistentes* of the pontificating bishop.[73] It is unlikely, however, that the new name was adopted because of any 'incardination.' Although the service of parish rectors in the cathedral on given feast days could have been thus construed, medieval France had lost the Gregorian concept, as can be seen in those dioceses where priests from the parishes or neighboring abbeys had been given truly hebdomadal duties in the cathedral and yet were not considered *cardinales*.[74] The cardinals of Paris, Soissons, etc. had their name rather on account of their liturgical prerogatives, which recalled the concelebration of the Roman cardinals and the status of the above mentioned cardinals by papal privilege. It is characteristic of the vagueness of this 'liturgical' cardinalate[75] that a new etymology was sought: the assistant priests were

[72] Moléon, *op. cit.* 47; Buenner, *op. cit.* 247 n. 1, 260 n. 1.

[73] *Paris*: preliminary note in the *Chartularium episcopi* (13th cent.): 'Isti sunt presbyteri qui nominantur presbyteri cardinales qui debent interesse, per se vel per alios, dum episcopus celebrat in ecclesia Parisiensi, in festis nativitatis Domini, pasche et assumptionis' (ed. Guérard, *Cartul. de Notre-Dame* 1, 3); cf. also *Magnum pastorale* 19, 22 (c. 1080): '. . . Sacerdos qui parochiae (*scil.* s.Martini de campis) praeerit, curam animarum ab episcopo et archidiacono suscipiet, et quotiescumque diebus festis episcopus missam cantaverit, ipse duodecimus cardinalis ministerio assistet' (*ibid.* 2, 400). Cf. Du Cange s.v. *presbyter cardinalis*; Le Cointe, *Instit. et rang* 29 (who correctly points to the corresponding functions of the early Roman cardinals); Cimetier *loc. cit.* (n. 68 *supra*).—*Sens*: notice in the *Liber precentoris* (13th cent.): 'Et quocienscumque (archiepiscopus) missam celebrat in festis annualibus in ecclesia Senonensi, debent sibi assistere duodecim presbyteri cardinales induti sacerdotalibus' (ed. Chartraire, *Cartul. du chap. de Sens* 168).—*Soissons*: notice in the Ritual of c. 1175-1207, for Christmas: '. . . deinde sic redeunt, primum ceroferarii, thuribola, . . . diaconi tres, post hos XII cardinales indutis sacris vestibus' (*Rituale* ed. 1856, p. 40); '. . . in coena Domini XII presbyteri cardinales, similiter et VII diaconi et VII ypodiaconi cum totidem acolitis' (*ibid.* 63; cf. also pp. 69, 114).—For Angers and Troyes no other sources are available at present than the report in Moléon's *Voyages* (pp. 93, 170).

[74] For such hebdomadaries in Auxerre see the statute and *kalendarium* of Bishop Tetricus (695) in Mabillon, *Acta sanctorum ord. s. Ben.* saec. 3, 1 (Venice 1734) 90-2 and MGH *Conc.* 1, 223. For seventh-century Verdun a similar institution is hinted at in the *Vita s. Pauli episcopi Verodun.* (Mabillon, *Acta ss. Ben.* saec. 2, 262f.—cf. however, on the poor reliability of this *Vita*, B. Krusch's note in MGH *Script. rer. merov.* 4, Hannover-Leipzig 1902, p. 566 n. 1). See also Mabillon, *Mus. ital.* II, xxxi. Among the hebdomadaries in Tours there was, according to an ancient *Rituale*, besides six dignities of the chapter, one neighboring abbot, cf. Martène, *De antiq. eccl. rit.* 1, 3, 8, 3 (I, 332D Antw.; I, 120 Ven.).—An Italian (?) parallel is found in the tract on ecclesiastical offices (n. 30 *supra*) where the rectors of the city parishes (*qui cardinales ecclesias habuerint*) are *in ordine* of the cathedral and hebdomadaries (c. 6: '. . . hi debent facere processionem cum episcopo et per vices septimanas tenere in sancta matre ecclesia et assidue ibidem stare': 397 Gaudenzi)—but not cardinals.

[75] Perhaps the false decretal JE †1986 (X. 1, 24, 2; cf. note 37 *supra*) comes from circles acquainted with this institution, since it characterizes the functions of the cardinal priests who are under the supervision of the archpriest as follows: '. . . ministerium sacerdotum cardinalium, quod (*al.* qui) solemnissimum debent peragere officium in communicatione corporis et sanguinis Domini nostri Jesu Christi, ita ut (archipresbyter) vicissim eos sibimet succedere faciat' (Mansi 10, 444B).

now arbitrarily said to be *cardinales* because they officiated *ad cardines*, i.e. *ad cornua altaris*.[76]

3. The 'cardinales chori' of London

As a curious corollary to the liturgical cardinalate, we may mention here the twin dignities of one senior and one junior cardinal existing in the college of the twelve 'minor canons' at St. Paul's Cathedral in London. Originally, the minor or petty canons were a class of beneficiaries, clerics of the choir who stood in rank between the canons proper, i.e. the members of the chapter, and the mere *vicarii*.[77] Their name,[78] number, rights, and duties became fixed during the thirteenth century. By this time, they all had to be priests, and towards the close of the century we find the first of these twelve benefices coupled with the dignity of subdean in the chapter.[79] In the fourteenth century, however, also the second and the third of the minor canonries were raised to regular dignities, with the title of *cardinalis senior* and *junior* respectively. The functions of the two cardinals included chiefly: celebration of the funeral, anniversary, and capitular Masses; administration of the sacraments to the sick; and supervision of the choir discipline. Both received the double of the distributions due to their confrères.[80]

Anglican authors are inclined to date this quaint institution—which persists

[76] Exactly where and when this etymology originated, needs further investigation. It is first mentioned by Moléon, *Voyages* 170 (from oral tradition in Sens? from a medieval source?); repeated by the editors of the *Rituale eccl. Suession.* 305f.; by Puniet, King, Buenner, and Molien, as cited n. 68 *supra*.

[77] Cf. W. Sparrow Simpson, 'Charters and Statutes of the College of the Minor Canons in St. Paul's Cathedral,' *Archaeologia* 43 (1871) 165–200; id. *Registrum statutorum et consuetudinum ecclesiae cathedralis s. Pauli Londinensis* (London 1873) xxxiiiff. Marion Gibbs, *Early Charters of the Cathedral Church of St. Paul, London* (Camden Third Series 58, London 1939) xxvif.

[78] In the twelfth century, the name was simply *clerici prebendarii de choro* (cf. Gibbs xxi n. 2); still in 1231–7 a charter sets the *canonici residentes* over against the *reliqui clerici chori medii* (i.e. vicars and chaplains) *et superioris* (i.e. minor canons) *gradus* (ed. Gibbs 86 num. 114). The first references to 'alicui paruo canonico in ecclesia b. Pauli residenti' and 'alicui de minoribus canonicis beneficiatis' are found in 1202–12 and 1231–4 respectively, cf. Gibbs pp. xxvii, 95 (num. 128), 162 (num. 206).

[79] Cf. Simpson *locc. citt.* and Gibbs xxviif. (with n. 8). See Dean Baldock's (1294–1305) *Statutes and Customs* 5, 1ff. (ed. Simpson, *Registrum* 66ff.).

[80] Dean Lisieux's (1441–56) *Statutes* 6, 18 (102–3 Simpson, *ex* 1289 with interpolations, cf. n. 85 *infra*). Pope Urban VI, confirming on October 22, 1378 Bishop Simon Sudbury's statute of May 11, 1374: '. . . De istis autem minoribus canonicis sunt duo delegati ab antiquo qui cardinales vocantur, et sunt perpetui. Qui etiam privatorum funerum et anniversariorum recipiunt proventus, et missas celebrant capitulares, ac egrotantibus ministrant ecclesiastica sacramenta, et quilibet ipsorum duorum duplum percipit omnium que superius uni minori canonico assignantur tam in pecunia quam in pane et in cervisia' (ed. D. Wilkins, *Concilia Magnae Britanniae* 3, London 1737, p. 135; cf. Simpson, *Registrum* 325–6). King Richard II, charter of incorporation of the minor canons' college, 1394 (ed. Simpson, *Archaeol.* 43, 183 = *Registrum* 327). *Statutes of the College* (1396) §35: 'De iuniore cardinale' (198 *Archaeol.* = 358–9 *Registrum*). Dean Colet's (1505–19) *Statutes* c. 7: 'Ex minoribus canonicis a decano et capitulo delegantur duo qui cardinales chori vocantur. Horum officium est circumspicere cotidie et notare omnia in choro delicta et peccata' etc.

to the present day at St. Paul's[81]—back to immemorial times.[82]   But it must be borne in mind that the charters and ordinances of the twelfth and thirteenth centuries are completely silent about these *cardinales*.[83]   Also Dean Ralph Baldock knew nothing about this nomenclature when he compiled, between 1294 and 1305, the first five books of the cathedral's old statutes and described therein the functions of the minor canons, and in particular of the *duo minores prebendati* who 'deputati sunt ab antiquo, qui privatorum funerum et anniversariorum recipiunt proventus et egrotantibus ministrant ecclesiastica sacramenta.'[84]   No authentic text before the fourteenth century calls these prebendaries *cardinales*.   To be sure, the term occurs in two 'earlier' documents: an *Iniunctio* of 1289, and a set of *Constitutiones et statuta et declarationes* allegedly dating from the time of Ralph de Diceto's deanship (1180–1202).   But these two pieces are transmitted only in a much later and obviously interpolated recension, to wit, in the sixth and the seventh book of the statutes, collected and appended to Baldock's compilation in the fifteenth century by Dean Thomas Lisieux (1441–56).[85]   The untrust-

---

(ed. W. Dugdale, *The History of St. Paul's Cathedral*, 3rd ed. London 1818, p. 345; cf. Simpson, *Registrum* 222; Du Cange s.v. *cardinales chori*).   For further texts mentioning the cardinals, from the fourteenth to the eighteenth century, see *Registrum* 147, 150, 282–3, 302, 305, 321, 477.

[81] Cf. the latest editions of the *London Diocese Book*.   Canon W. Sparrow Simpson, the zealous historian and editor of the statutes, was himself for some time junior cardinal, cf. his *Documents Illustrating the History of St. Paul's* (Camden Society, new ser. 26, London 1880) xxvi note *b* and title page.

[82] Thomas Gibbons (1720–85: cf. *Dictionary of National Biography* 21, 265), as quoted from MS *Harl.* 980, fol. 179r by Simpson, *Registrum* xxxvif.: 'The Church of St. Paule had, before the time of the Conquerour, two Cardinalls, which office still continues.   They are chosen by the Dean and Chapter out of the number of the twelve Petty Canons, and are called *Cardinales Chori*. . . .   Not any Cathedral Church in England hath Cardinalls besids this, nor are any beyond seas to be found to be dignified with this title, sauing the Churches of Rome, Rauenna, Aquileia, Millan,Pisa, Beneuent in Italy, and Compostella in Spayn.'— Cf. also (Maria Hackett,) *Correspondence and Evidence Respecting the Ancient Collegiate School Attached to St. Paul's Cathedral* (s. l. 1832) app. p. xi: 'This ancient and very important office is peculiar to St. Paul's throughout the Protestant World.'

[83] There is no mention of *cardinales* in the *Early Charters* ed. Gibbs, nor in such texts as *Constit. Henrici de Cornhill* (1243–54), *Stat. de residencia canonicorum* (13th cent.), *De oblacionibus ad episcopum pertin.* (c. 1218–27) of Simpson's *Registrum* (cf. pp. 181–90).

[84] *Stat.* 3, 34 (48 Simpson).   Parts of this text are repeated in Urban VI's bull of confirmation, but with the words 'qui cardinales vocantur' inserted, cf. n. 80 *supra*.—Also in the account for the year 1283 of the *custos bracini*,Thomas Coulyng, on the daily allotments in bread to the clergy of the cathedral, we find *tres parvi prebendarii de choro* set over against the other *novem parvi prebendarii* and as receiving double rations, without any qualification as subdean or cardinals (ed. W. H. Hale, *The Domesday of St. Paul's*, Camden Soc. 69, London 1858, p. 170; cf. Hale's introd. p. xlix).   See also the distributions in bread and beer for the year 1286 (pp. 172, 174) and Hale's chart for monetary distributions from the *Statuta maiora*: 'To the 30 vicars of the 30 canons—10*d* each; to the 3 minor canons and the *scriptor tabulae*—10*d* each; To nine minor canons—5*d* each' etc. (p. xlvii).   Simpson, *Registrum* 173 n. 1 inexactly reports some of these accounts and budgets, substituting 'the subdean and two cardinals' for the three minor canons.

[85] *Stat.* 6, 18, in the *Iniunctio* of 1289: '. . . Item volumus quod quatuor canonici minores [scil. duo cardinales et duo alii] diligenter chorum de die et de nocte custodiant, ita quod

worthiness of their textual shape has a parallel in the fact that at the same period several scribes felt bound to insert into Baldock's statute on the *duo minores prebendati* a clause that qualifies the two as cardinals.[86]

It is difficult to explain this peculiar 'cardinalate' which made its appearance so abnormally late, at an age when the common connotation of the term had long since become that of an exalted Roman dignity. In the fourteenth century, the introduction at St. Paul's of such a nomenclature for two priests, who did not even have the rank of full canons, could not be justified by the early medieval usage of *cardinalis* < *de cardine;* nor had the two petty canons any such outstanding liturgical privileges as concelebration with the bishop or the exclusive use of the main altar. But it is very likely that on account of their less solemn prerogatives with regard to funerals and their ministry of the sick; of their acting as overseers in the choir; and of their double allotments in bread, beer and money, the clergy of St. Paul's started to call the two in mockery 'our cardinals.' It would not be an un-English trait if what had begun as a nickname, finished by becoming a title of honor.

4. *Rise of the Roman Cardinals*

An involved process of transformation shifted, during the eleventh century, the main functions of the Roman cardinal priests and bishops from liturgical duties and prerogatives to prominent participation in the government of the Church universal. This development was intimately connected with the great Reform whose phases and struggles would mold the history of a century, beginning with the accession of Leo IX (1048–54).

If already before these times usually one or the other of the cardinal bishops headed the papal chancery as *bibliothecarius*,[87] he held such office not by virtue of his cardinalate[88] but in his capacity as a bishop of the Roman metropolitan province, even as the direction of royal chanceries was generally in the hands

---

defectus ministrantium in ecclesia scribant et . . . decano . . . referant' (103 Simpson). *Stat.* 7, 6, in the *Constituciones et statuta et declaraciones . . . edite tempore magistri Radulphi de Disceto decani s. Pauli*: '. . . set tamen prima die illius mensis quo absentare se voluerit, sit in prima, et decano et capitulo absenciam intimet, [et camerario vel cardinalibus]' (127 Simpson). The passages included by the present writer in brackets are in his opinion interpolated. In the first case, we have to do with a gloss, in the second, with an after-thought caused by the precept of the *Iniunctio*. Also apart from the words, *vel cardinalibus*, the entire *Constituciones* in *Stat.* 7, 6 reflect a language and factual situation of a much later period than that of Ralph de Diceto. Their authenticity was denied as early as 1399 by Bishop Braybrooke, cf. W. Stubbs, *Radulphi de Diceto decani Lundoniensis opera historica* (Rolls Series, London 1876) I, lxviif. The genuine statute on the canons' residence issued under Ralph's deanship in 1192 (ed. Stubbs, *op. cit.* II, lxix–lxxiii) is entirely different and does of course not mention any *cardinales*. Lisieux evidently delighted in attributing undatable ordinances of the past to Diceto, cf. *Stat.* 6, 28; 7, 3 (109, 124 Simpson) etc.—On Lisieux as continuator of Baldock see Simpson, *Registrum* xxi.

[86] See the variants to *Stat.* 3, 34: duo minores prebendati] qui cardinales appellantur *add. A*, cardinales *BF in marg.*—listed without comment by Simpson 48 n. 2.

[87] For details see Bresslau, *Urkundenlehre* I, 211ff.

[88] The contrary is suggested, though very cautiously, by Klewitz, *Entstehung* 132.

of a bishop of the realm. And while it is true that a certain distinction seems to have been made in Roman synods, ever since the eighth century, between the other bishops of the metropolitan province and the *septem*, one would go too far in ascribing to the latter for that early period a predominant role and position.[89] Also, if before the reform era cardinal priests were occasionally sent on diplomatic missions,[90] they were not, *qua* cardinals, different from any other papal envoy. Finally, too much stress should not be laid upon the corporate jurisdiction, both contentious and disciplinary, over the clergy and laity of Rome which allegedly had been vested in the cardinal priests by a decree of John VIII (872–82): for the authenticity of this generally unsuspected text (JE 3366) is not beyond doubt,[91] and even if it were genuine it would account for Roman local administration only.

That the political rise of the cardinals in church government was but part of the fundamental changes brought about by the great Reform is now commonly accepted.[92] When Leo IX, after the rigorous elimination of simonists from the Roman clergy, ordained among his cardinal bishops and priests a number of ardent champions of the reform ideals from abroad,[93] he took this bold and unprecedented step of calling foreigners to the service of the Roman Church hardly for the sake of the cardinals' hebdomadary functions. Such appointments were a first symptom of new and important tasks to be assigned to the cardinal clergy in the program of the Reform popes.[94]

The individual steps of the cardinals' ascent to a key position of paramount import are not to be discussed here.[95] We know that the development was slower for the cardinal priests than for the cardinal bishops—witness the leading role assigned to the latter in Nicholas II's decree of 1059 on papal elections.[96] But

[89] For the distinction between the *septem* and the *forenses* see ch. III at n. 31 *supra*. Klewitz 133 assumes that the Seven were a sort of standing committee of the provincial synods; but any special role of the cardinal bishops in synods is not warranted by the sources before the eleventh century, cf. the examples in Sägmüller, *Cardinäle* 40f. See also A. Dumas in Fliche-Martin, *Histoire de l'Église* 7 (1940) 156.

[90] Cf. note 38 *supra* for instances under Hadrian II and John VIII.

[91] Cf. ch. V at nn. 74ff. *infra*.

[92] See e.g. Z. N. Brooke, introduction to CMH 5 (1929) viii; J. P. Whitney, 'The Reform of the Church,' *ibid.* 30; Dumas, *op. cit.* 159.—Already Le Cointe, *Instit. et rang* 34, considered the Roman cardinalate since Leo IX an institution entirely different in its scope from the functions of earlier *cardinales*, in Rome or elsewhere.

[93] Bonizo, *Liber ad amicum* 5: 'Interea Romae episcopi et cardinales et abbates, per simoniacam haeresim ordinati, deponebantur. Et ibi ex diversis provinciis alii ordinabantur' etc. (ed. E. Dümmler, MGH *Libelli de lite* 1, Hannover 1891, p. 588 lines 18–20). Cf. Sägmüller, *Cardinäle* 25; Brooke *loc. cit.*

[94] Cf. Klewitz, *Entstehung* 117.

[95] See the studies of Sägmüller and Klewitz, *passim*. The embittered controversy between K. Wenck and Sägmüller is more concerned with the later evolution, especially of the thirteenth century. See the various criticisms, rebuttals and rejoinders: Wenck, in *Theologische Literaturzeitung* 23 (1898) 113–6; 205; *Götttingische gelehrte Anzeigen* 1900, pp. 139–75; Sägmüller, in *Theol. Literaturzeit.* 23, 204–5; *Theologische Quartalschrift* 80 (1898) 596–614; 83 (1901) 45–93; 88 (1906) 595–615.

[96] Lateran Synod of 1059 (ed. L. Weiland, MGH *Const.* 1, Hannover 1893, pp. 539–41). The chief prerogatives of the cardinal bishops were: designation of the candidate (cc. 3–4);

174

in the second half of the eleventh century the differentiation tended to disappear: subscriptions to papal acts, advisory functions in matters of church government, participation in the judicial supremacy, were deemed essential privileges of the cardinal priests no less than of the bishops.[97] The schism of Guibert (Anti-pope Clement III, 1080–1100), who saw his chance in a large following among the cardinals and thus did everything to increase their constitutional position, hastened this development.[98] During the schism it became evident what an immense political asset the allegiance of the cardinals, both bishops and priests, was to the Pope. It is also significant that at this juncture even the most faithful adherents of the legitimate papacy did not recoil from circulating a counterfeit of Pope Nicholas' decrees such as to make the cardinal bishops' prerogatives appear common to all cardinals.[99]

They had truly grown in these turbulent times to be the Senators of the Church—*spirituales ecclesiae universalis senatores*, as St. Peter Damian first put it, perhaps under the influence of notions contained in the Donation of Constantine.[100] Even though reference was still occasionally made to their original

---

in cases of emergency, election of the Pope at any place outside of Rome, together with whatever number of Roman clerics and laymen they might be able to muster (c. 7). The old controversy as to whether the 'papal' or the 'royal' text (541–6 Weiland) of the decree is the genuine one has long since been settled in favor of the former. For a summary of arguments see A. Fliche, *La réforme grégorienne* I (Louvain-Paris 1924) 314–22; Whitney, CMH 5, 37. Other problems of textual criticism, as e.g. those discussed by A. Michel, *Papstwahl und Königsrecht* (Munich 1936); id. 'Zum Papstwahlpactum von 1059,' *Historisches Jahrbuch der Görresgesellschaft* 59 (1939) 290–351; R. Holtzmann, 'Zum Papstwahldekret von 1059,' ZRG Kan. Abt. 27 (1938) 135–53, may be passed over for the purposes of the present study.

[97] For the right of subscription see Sägmüller, *Cardinäle* 70f. 216f.; Bresslau, *Urkundenlehre* II, 52; 54; Klewitz, *Entstehung* 167. (An allegedly older example, JL 3802 [A.D. 980], cited by Sägmüller 46 n. 1 and Bresslau 52 n. 2, is however spurious: see Kehr, IP 5, 133 num. 1).—Advisory functions, esp. assent to alienation of church property: Sägmüller 74; Klewitz 139 n. 5; D. B. Zema, 'The Houses of Tuscany and of Pierleone in the Crisis of Rome,' *Traditio* 2 (1944) 160.—Judicial rights: see the *Descriptio sanctuar. Later. eccl.* as quoted at n. 111 *infra*.

[98] Cf. Sägmüller 41; 235f.; P. Kehr, 'Zur Geschichte Wiberts von Ravenna II,' *Sitzungsber. der Preuss. Akad. der Wiss.* 1921, II, 973–88; and in particular Klewitz 167–75.

[99] Anselm of Lucca, *Coll. can.* 6, 12–3 (272–3 Thaner); Deusdedit, *Coll. can.* 1, 168–9 (107 Wolf von Glanvell). Cf. Sägmüller 133f.; Klewitz 165 (with incorrect references in n. 3); Michel, *Papstwahlpactum* 336, 354. The alterations made by Anselm and Deusdedit do not affect the Lateran decree of 1059 (as Klewitz 165 and 175 seems to assume, confusing them with the 'royal' or Guibertine forgery), but a synodal letter sent out by Nicholas II after the council (*Synodica generalis* JL 4405–6) and the Lateran Synod of 1060 (JL 4431a). The significant variants in the two canonists are: *Syn. gen.* c. 1 (547, 9 Weiland): eorum (*sc.* cardinalium episcoporum)] cardinalium eiusdem *Ans. Deusd.*—*Conc. Lat.* 1060 c. 4 (551, 5 Weiland): cardinalium episcoporum] cardinalium *Ans. Deusd.* (see also Weiland's remarks, *ed. cit.* 546, 550). The texts as altered by Anselm were adopted by Bonizo, *Vita chr.* 4, 87 (156, 14–5 Perels) and Gratian D. 79 cc. 1 and 9, not however by Ivo, *Decretum* 5, 80 (PL 161, 352B).

[100] *Contra philargyriam* c. 7 (PL 145, 540B); see also *ep.* 1, 20 (PL 144, 258D). Cf. Sägmüller, *Cardinäle* 160.

functions in the Roman basilicas,[101] these liturgical duties of the cardinals had become quite secondary. When, for instance, during the second half of the eleventh century abbots of Montecassino, of Vendôme, and of St. Victor in Marseille were made cardinals,[102] it is obvious that these prelates who resided far from Rome were never able to fulfill the hebdomadal duties.[103]   Also the *tituli* of the cardinals had lost their old significance.   They were no longer the only parishes of the city, and the parochial services were no longer performed by the cardinals themselves: for all pastoral purposes, the title churches had now their archpriests like any other parish church,[104] while a statute of Alexander II

[101] See ch. III at nn. 35–9 *supra*.

[102] Montecassino: Abbot elect Frederic (the future Pope Stephen IX) is made cardinal priest with the title of St. Chrysogonus in 1057 (Kehr, IP 8, 138 num. 77); Abbot elect Desiderius (the future Victor III), cardinal priest with the title of St. Cecilia in 1058 (*ibid.* 141 num. 87); Abbot Oderisius, cardinal with the same title in 1088 (*ibid.* 151 num. 132). Abbot Odoric of Vendôme becomes cardinal priest with the title of St. Prisca in 1066 (JL 4594); and Cardinal Richard (title unknown) is made Abbot of St. Victor, Marseille, in 1079 (JL 5143–4).—Cf. Hinschius, *Kirchenr.* I, 333, 335; Gregory VII, *Reg.* 7, 7–8 (ed. Caspar, MGH *Epp. sel.* 2, 468–70); Klewitz, *Entstehung* 117, 162, 173, 213, 218.   Note however that the older opinion, according to which all abbots of Vendôme since the days of Odoric were 'born' cardinals of the Roman Church (thus e.g. Hinschius I, 334; Sägmüller 200), was based on the spurious privileges which Abbot Geoffrey had fabricated early in the twelfth century: cf. H. Meinert, 'Die Fälschungen Gottfrieds von Vendôme,' *Archiv für Urkundenforschung* 10 (1928) 232–325; Klewitz 205.   The arrogated 'inheritable' cardinalate became a reality only in 1205 under Innocent III who, deceived by the forged evidence presented to him, granted a privilege to this effect (Potthast, *Regesta pont. Rom.* Berlin 1874, num. 2628; cf. PL 215, 749A–B).

[103] Klewitz 117.—But genuine appointments of foreign bishops or archbishops as Roman cardinal priests did not occur before Alexander III, in 1165 (cf. Hinschius I, 335).   Allegedly earlier instances must be rejected.   When Benedict VIII in 1012 (JL 3989) granted to Archbishop Waltrad of Magdeburg the distinction to have 'inter cardinales episcopos nostre sedis consortium', this meant but equal rank with the cardinal bishops and precedence before any other bishop, not appointment to a suburbicarian see (Hinschius I, 332f.; *contra* Sägmüller, *Cardinäle* 200 n. 3).   When Leo IX appointed Archbishop Hermann of Cologne in 1052 (JL 4271) chancellor of the Roman Church—Hermann's predecessor, Archbishop Pilgrim, had held the same office, cf. Bresslau, *Urkundenlehre* I, 219—and gave him the church of St. John before the Latin Gate in benefice, this did not involve any cardinalate; the said church was not even among the twenty-eight *tituli* (Hinschius I, 333, Sägmüller 200. Moreover, JL 4271 is suspect of copious interpolations, cf. Bresslau I, 220 n. 2; 231f.).   Also the grant in benefice of the *cella* of *Ss. quatuor coronati* to Archbishop Theodoric of Treves in 975 (Benedict VII JL 3779: PL 137, 318C) did not make the archbishop a priest of this title nor a cardinal.   If any foreign bishop ever was cardinal before the time of Alexander III, this could only have been Bishop Stephen of Metz, cf. *Gesta episcoporum Metensium*, contin. I an. 1120: '. . . Hic Calixti (II) ex sorore nepos . . . in urbe Romana ab eodem pontifice summo consecratus est et tam pallii dignitate quam cardinalis titulo honoratus' (ed. Waitz, MGH *Script.* 10, Hannover 1852, p. 544 lines 14–7; cf. Hinschius I, 637).   But the reliability of the Continuator I of the *Gesta*, who wrote after 1180, is often marred 'sive negligentia sive nimio Metensis ecclesiae studio' (Waitz 532).

[104] Subscriptions etc. of archpriests of Roman (parish) churches from 1017 to 1160 are listed by Hinschius I, 378 n. 5.   Among these, we find e.g. (1081) 'Johannes archipresbyter de s. Caecilia'.   This was one of the *tituli* belonging to St. Peter's basilica.   For parishes which were not cardinal titles see also the documents of Urban II in Kehr, IP 1, 72 num. 3 (cf. Klewitz, *Entstehung* 122f.) and *ibid.* 7 num. 11: 'tituli et diaconiae et parrochiae' (ed. Kehr as cited n. 7 *supra*).

176

(1061–73) reserved instead to the cardinal priests rights of a quasi-episcopal jurisdiction in their titles.[105]

With all these developments the original meaning of the name, *cardinalis*, was definitely obliterated. The name was now understood as expressing the participation of its bearers in the primacy of Peter. Whereas the concept of *cardo* heretofore had been applied to any cathedral as indicating its pivotal function in the diocese, Pope Leo IX took up in 1054 a Pseudo-isidorian metaphor: the Apostolic See as *caput et cardo* of the Church universal.[106] 'Like the immovable hinge,' he wrote to the Patriarch of Constantinople, 'which sends the door forth and back, thus Peter and his successors have the sovereign judgment over the entire Church. . . . Therefore his clerics are named cardinals, for they belong more closely to the hinge by which everything else is moved.'[107]—Still more emphatic is the explanation which Deusdedit gave in his *Collectio canonum* (1087). In one of the rare passages in which the learned Cardinal of S. Pietro in Vincoli inserted his own thoughts among the collected texts,[108] he eloquently declared the *cardinales* themselves to be the *cardines* who rule and guide God's people.[109]

Coming from the pen of a canonist who always staunchly vindicated the prerogatives of the Roman cardinal clergy,[110] this proud definition has more than a

[105] JL 4736; Kehr, IP 1, 7 num. 9. Cf. ch. III n. 36 *supra*.

[106] Pseudo-Anacletus (JK †4): '. . . Haec vero apostolica sedes cardo et caput ut factum est a Domino et non ab alio constituta, et sicut cardine hostium regitur, sic huius sanctae sedis auctoritate omnes ecclesiae Domino disponente reguntur' (ed. Hinschius, *Decretales Pseudo-Isidorianae et capitula Angilramni*, Leipzig 1863, p. 84). Cf. Phillips, *Kirchenr.* VI, 45f. Hinschius, *Kirchenr.* I, 315 n. 2. The canon passed on into Gratian: D. 22 c. 2 §6.

[107] JL 4302 c. 32: '. . . Et sicut cardo immobilis permanens ducit et reducit ostium, sic Petrus et sui successores liberum de omni ecclesia habent iudicium . . .; unde clerici eius cardinales dicuntur, cardini utique illi quo cetera mouentur vicinius adhaerentes' (Mansi 19, 653B). Almost all authors who wrote on cardinals have quoted this passage.

[108] We do not mean to say that interpolations and alterations of texts are rare in Deusdedit. The contrary has been shown by P. Fournier, 'Les collections canoniques romaines de l'époque de Grégoire VII,' *Mémoires de l'Académie des inscriptions et belles-lettres* 41 (1920) 353 n. 2; 354–7. But if we look in Fournier's list for interpolations which have the nature of an author's personal *dicta*, the number is very low and the passage here quoted is the most conspicuous among them.

[109] Deusd. 2, 160: '. . . Vnde deriuatiue sacerdotes et leuite summi pontificis cardinales dicuntur eo, quod ipsi quasi forma facti gregi sacris predicationibus et preclaris operibus populum Dei regant atque adregant atque ad regni celestis auditum moueant et inuitent. Sicut a basibus, que sunt fulture columnarum a fundamento surgentes, basilei idest reges dicuntur, quia populum regunt: ita et cardinales deriuatiue dicuntur a cardinibus ianue, qui tam regunt et mouent, quod plebem Dei, ut superius diximus, doctrinis sanctis ad amorem Dei moueant . . .' (267–8 Wolf von Glanvell). This goes far beyond St. Peter Damian, who was wont to emphasize chiefly the pre-eminence of the cardinal bishops, cf. *epp.* 1, 20; 2, 1 (PL 144, 258D–259B; 253–5). The signal difference of Deusdedit's from Pope Leo's definition was pointed out by Sägmüller, *Cardinäle* 124; E. Hirsch, 'Die rechtliche Stellung des Papstes und der römischen Kirche nach Kardinal Deusdedit,' AKKR 88 (1908) 621; H. Grauert, 'Magister Heinrich der Poet,' *Abhandlungen der Bayerischen Akad. der Wiss.* phil.-hist. Klasse 27 (1912) 235–42.

[110] Some instances of this attitude are cited by Sägmüller 114, 133f. 185, 227, 239; Hirsch, *op. cit.* 596, 621f. Here follows a more complete list: In the prologue, Deusdedit points to the significance of the correspondence between St. Cyprian and the Roman priests and

rhetorical value. At about the same time, the anonymous author of the *Descriptio sanctuarii Lateransis ecclesiae* asserted that the cardinal bishops and priests have the power to pass judgment over all bishops of the Empire.[111] With the further development of the cardinals' right of assent to papal acts; with the eventual substitution of the Consistory for the papal synod; finally with the reservation of papal elections to the Sacred College,[112] the next century would see such high strung claims come true.

deacons during the vacancy of the Roman See (p. 2 lines 3–12 Wolf von Glanvell; the texts of the letters in *Coll.* 2 cc. 121–4; 126–9). Many programmatic theses are found in the *capitula* preceding the collection proper: 'Eosdem esse presbiteros quos episcopos, testimonii Petri et Pauli et Iohannis; . . . Quod episcopi magis consuetudine quam dominica dispensatione presbiteris sint maiores; . . . Quod apostoli presbiterorum usi sint consilio; . . . Quod presbiteri, qui presunt, habeant ligandi et soluendi potestatem' (p. 16 lines 9–13; 16 Wolf von Glanvell; cf. *Coll.* 2, 138–43, quoting the well known texts of St. Jerome); 'Quod Romani pontifices presbiteros suos fratres et compresbiteros appellant' (p. 16, 26–7; cf. *Coll.* 2, 46 from Pseudo-Isidore); 'Quod Sardicense concilium Romane ecclesie presbiteros appellet laterales iudices' (p. 16, 30–1; in fact, the Council of Serdica c. 3b [*al.* 6 or 7] has only: 'mouerit episcopum Romanum ut e latere suo praesbyterum mittat' ʌed. Turner, *Monum.* 1, 2, iii, p. 461, 16–7; cf. Deusd. *Coll.* 1, 27); 'Quod Romani pontifices tantum cum concilio cleri sui damnauerunt sepe quos oportuit' (p. 16, 32–3; cf. *Coll.* 2, 49; 106); 'Quod absente Romano pontifice clerus eius quorumlibet causas diiudicet' (p. 17, 1–2; referring to St. Cyprian, see *supra*); 'Quod in principalibus festis cum Romano pontifice cardinales presbiteri missam celebrent' (p. 17, 20–1; cf. *Coll.* 2, 114 on concelebration: see ch. III at n. 30 *supra*); 'Inde Romani clerici locum antiquorum habent patriciorum' (p. 17, 27; cf. *Coll.* 4, 1: Donation of Constantine); 'De presbiteris qui non sunt cardinales; . . . Quod hi qui non sunt presbiteri cardinis in sinodo cathedrales sedes non habeant; . . . Quod cardinalibus non debeat preponi non cardinalis' (p. 17, 36–9; cf. *Coll.* 2, 14: *Conc. Neocaes.* c. 13, see nn. 5–7 *supra*); 'Quod absque episcoporum concilio cardinalis urbis Rome remoueri non debet' (p. 19, 10–1; as contrasted with the thesis: 'Quod [Romanus pontifex] absque sinodo episcoporum damnauerit episcopos,' p. 10, 10 [cf. *Coll.* 1, 126; 2, 60; 106; 155]).—In the collection itself, we note: the alteration of Nicholas II's decrees on elections, in favor of the entire cardinal clergy (*Coll.* 1, 168–9; see n. 99 *supra*); the rubric of *Coll.* 2, 41: 'Quod singule Romane ecclesie singulis cardinalibus ab initio commisse sint' (p. 205); the inclusion of the spurious *Constitutum Silvestri* on trials of cardinals (*Coll.* 2, 43–4; cf. Appendix D *infra*); a signal interpolation in the papal profession of faith, LD 83 (p. 181 Rozière, 92 Sickel): '. . . Si qua uero emiserint contra canonicam disciplinam, [filiorum meorum consilio] emendare . . .' (*Coll.* 2, 110; interpolation not noticed by Wolf von Glanvell 236, 21); the definition of the cardinalate as quoted above (*Coll.* 2, 160); the revival of Stephen III's decree on elections (*Coll.* 2, 161–3; see ch. III n. 24 *supra*).

[111] MS *Vatic. Reg.* 712, fol. 87v: '. . . praedicti VII episcopi debent assistere cum XXVIII cardinalibus totidem ecclesiis infra muros urbis Romae praesidentibus, qui potestatem obtinent iudicium faciendi super omnes episcopos totius Romani imperii in omnibus conciliis vel synodis quibuscunque accersiti vel praesentes fuerint' (ed. Klewitz, *Entstehung* 123 n. 1; cf. 186).

[112] For the gradually developing requirement of consent to papal acts see Sägmüller, *Cardinäle* 216f.; Bresslau, *Urkundenlehre* II, 55–61; for the beginnings of the Consistory, Sägmüller 46–58, 97f. (the earliest example under Paschal II: Klewitz, *Entstehung* 202f.). The right of papal election became reserved to the cardinals by Alexander III in 1179, *Conc. III Later.* c. 1.

V. The Roman Cardinal Deacons

The last score of years of the eleventh century was also the time in which the deacons of the Roman Church became definitely included among the cardinals. Deusdedit coined his definition of *cardinalis* for the *sacerdotes et levitae summi pontificis*, and from the pontificate of Urban II (1088–99) onwards, subscriptions of cardinal deacons make their appearance in papal documents.[1] Until recently, historians in general did not realize that the cardinal dignity of the Roman deacons dates from this relatively late time.[2] Yet it is evident that the deacons could become *cardinales* only at an epoch which was no longer conscious of the basic canonical connotation of the term, for there was no incardination involved in their functions in the Church of Rome.[3] The rise of the deacons to the cardinalate thus reflects and illustrates the semantic changes of that concept itself.

1. *Original Number of the Roman Deacons*

In the Ancient Church, as is well known, the college of deacons everywhere held a position of highest importance. Besides their liturgical functions, they had the ministry of the poor, which in turn led to their assisting the bishop in the administration of his church's temporalities. Additional vicarious power in matters of jurisdiction and clerical discipline often fell to the senior deacon in his capacity as the bishop's secretary (*diaconus episcopi*). Thus we find as early as the time of the last persecutions a clearly marked separation of pastoral and administrative-jurisdictional duties in the diocese, the former being entrusted to the *presbyterium*, the latter, the domain of the deacons' college. In further development of this pattern, the manifold extraordinary assignments of the first deacon began to crystallize during the fourth century in the permanent and powerful office of the archdeaconate.[4]

While small bishoprics frequently had not more than two or three deacons, we find in Rome and in other great Churches their number established since the earliest times at seven, by analogy with the seven 'deacons' of the Apostolic

---

[1] Cf. the list of signatories in JL I, 657; Klewitz, *Entstehung* 184. For details see at nn. 100–1 *infra*.

[2] Only few authors can be cited as exceptions from the rule: Buenner, *L'ancienne liturgie rom.* (ch. IV n. 68 *supra*) 270, who however puts the origin of the deacons' cardinalate too late; V. Martin, *Les cardinaux et la curie* (ch. I n. 10 *supra*) 15; A. Molien, 'Cardinal,' *Dictionn. de droit can.* 2, 1312; Klewitz 183f.

[3] Incorrect are the reasons advanced by Buenner *loc. cit.* (the deacons lacked the right of liturgical concelebration) and Klewitz *loc. cit.* (the deacons did not belong to any of the main basilicas of Rome). These opinions are connected with the two authors' respective explanations of the term *cardinalis*, cf. ch. III, nn. 28, 30.

[4] See the summaries of the early history of the diaconate and archdeaconate, with bibliographical references, in J. Forget, 'Diacres,' DThC 4, 703–31; H. Thurston, 'Deacons,' *Cath. Encycl.* 4, 647–53; A. Amanieu, 'Archidiacre,' *Dictionn. de droit can.* 1, 948ff. Kurtscheid, *Hist. iur. can.* 53–6; 160–4. On the ancient *diaconus episcopi* in particular, A. Leder, *Die Diakonen der Bischöfe und Presbyter* (Kirchenrechtliche Abhandlungen, ed. Stutz 23–4, Stuttgart 1905).

community in Jerusalem.[5] In the third century, Pope Fabian divided the city of Rome into seven *regiones* for the discharge of the deacons' basic ministry—the care of the poor, the widows and orphans—assigning to each deacon one of these districts.[6] In early synodal subscriptions, the Roman deacons therefore sometimes signed their names with the number of their respective *regio* added,[7] and for the same reason the first *Ordo Romanus* in the eighth century qualified them as *diaconi regionarii*.[8] But this does not mean that the *regiones*—mere topographic units of ecclesiastical administration—corresponded in any way to titles of ordination, for the Seven were deacons of the Church of Rome, not of any particular church or title in the city.[9] As liturgical ministers of the Pope by virtue of their orders, and as his ministers in government by virtue of their office, they were properly termed in the official style *Diacones (-ni) Romanae ecclesiae*, which distinguished them sharply from the priests and clergy serving in the twenty-five (later twenty-eight) parochial *tituli*. Residence and *titulus* of the seven deacons, therefore, can only have been the church of the Roman Bishop himself, that is, since the fourth century, the Lateran basilica, although this title of ordination is never expressly mentioned in the ancient sources.[10]

It has been occasionally suggested that the Roman deacons might have been ordained and permanently attached to the cemeterial churches of the individual regions;[11] or that they might have belonged, each in his respective *regio*, to the clergy of one of the title churches.[12] Both theses lack any substantial proof. The first, moreover, reverses the true relation between deaconship and cemeterial administration: if the Seven had to do at all with the supervision of the ceme-

---

[5] *Act.* 6, 2–3. The ἑπτὰ πλήρεις πνεύματος καὶ σοφίας are not expressly called deacons in the Acts, but already by the early Fathers, with regard to *Act.* 6, 1; 2: ἐν τῇ διακονίᾳ τῇ καθημερινῇ . . . , διακινεῖν τραπέζαις. The earliest canonical statute limiting the deacons' number to seven for each diocese is *Conc. Neocaes.* c. 14.—Cf. J. Zeiller, in Fliche-Martin, *Hist. de l'Égl.* 1, 379; 2, 392.

[6] LP I, 148.—The often advanced opinion that Pope Fabian's seven *regiones* comprised each two of the fourteen Augustan (civil) *regiones* does not agree with the topographical facts; cf. Duchesne, LP I, 148 n. 3; L. Halphen, *Études sur l'administration de Rome au moyen âge, 751–1252* (Bibliothèque de l'École des Hautes Études 166, Paris 1907) 7f.; R. L. Poole, *Lectures on the Papal Chancery* (Cambridge 1915) 8; Harnack, *Anfänge der inneren Organis.* (ch. III n. 4 *supra*) 963f. 967–9. Cf. also Leder, *op. cit.* 178.

[7] Cf. the often cited *Conc. Rom.* 499: 'Cyprianus diaconus ecclesiae s. Romanae regionis VII his subscripsi' etc. (653f. Thiel; Mansi 8, 237C).

[8] *Ordo I Rom.* num. 1: 'Primo omnium observandum est septem esse regiones ecclesiastici ordinis urbis Romae; et unaquaeque regio singulos habet diaconos regionarios' (3 Mabillon). Cf. Hinschius, *Kirchenr.* I, 322 n. 4; Klewitz, *Entstehung* 179.

[9] Duchesne, LP I, 364 n. 7; Zeiller, *op. cit.* 2, 392; Harnack, *op. cit.* 967f.

[10] See the convincing deductions of Duchesne, 'Les titres presbytéraux et les diaconies,' *Mélanges d'archéologie et d'histoire* 7 (École française de Rome 1887) 218. Cf. H. Leclercq, 'Diaconies,' DACL 4, 1 (1920) 735. Klewitz, *Entstehung* 183 missed this fundamental point (cf. n. 3 *supra*).—If not ancient, at least medieval testimonies exist to the *intitulatio* of the seven deacons in the Lateran, e.g. the *Descriptio sanctuar. Later. eccl.* and Benedict VIII JL 4024 (notes 40, 91 *infra*).

[11] Leder, *Die Diakonen der Bischöfe* 179f. 196 n. 1.

[12] U. Stutz, 'Die römischen Titelkirchen und die Verfassung der stadtrömischen Kirche unter Papst Fabian,' ZRG *Kan. Abt.* 9 (1919) 310.

180

teries[12a] it was because of their diaconal office, but this office was by no means rooted in an appointment to the cemeteries.—As to the second hypothesis, it is based on a misapprehension of the Roman deacons' supra-parochial position. It would place the immediate assistants of the Pope under the command of a title priest, on an equal footing with the lower parochial clergy; and it would involve their eventual promotion to priesthood in the titles. Both implications are equally untenable. We know that in Antiquity the diocesan college of deacons was never considered subordinated to parochial presbyters: on the contrary, the priests had often reason to complain about their being eclipsed by the all-powerful deacons.[13] Also, the great number of popes elected from the ranks of the Roman deacons in ancient history forbids the assumption that the latter's career was normally mingled with that of the title clergy; any *diaconus Romanae ecclesiae* could legitimately have resisted promotion to priesthood in a title, even as it was uncanonical everywhere and a great offense in the Ancient Church to ordain an archdeacon priest and thus to remove him from his high office.[14]

It is quite another thing to ask whether the twenty-five title churches did not include among their clergy also a number of deacons[15]—deacons of the *titulus*, not of the Roman Church as such—for the reason that every title priest must have received at some time before his last ordination the order of deaconship. Harnack's assumption that priests of the titles were promoted directly from the order of acolythes, with but a nominal conferral of subdiaconate and diaconate, is highly improbable.[16] In fact the so-called Gelasian Sacramentary of the seventh or eighth century includes an *Ordo qualiter in Romana apostolicae sedis ecclesia diaconi, subdiaconi vel presbyteri eligendi sunt*, which begins with a formula for announcing the names of candidates elected for promotion:[17]

[12a] But Kirsch, *Titelkirchen* (ch. III n. 5 *supra*) 204ff. has shown that the cemeterial administration was rather in the hands of the presbyterate of the titles.

[13] Cf. the Councils of Arles 314 c. 15; I Nicaea c. 18; Laodicaea c. 20; the *Statuta ecclesiae antiqua* cc. 37–41 (1, 145 Bruns); Gelasius I JK 636 c. 7 (366 Thiel); the well-known complaints of St. Jerome, e.g. *ep.* 146 (ed. R. Hilberg, CSEL 56 [1918] 308–10); and Pseudo-Augustine, *Quaest. vet. et novi testam.* c. 101 (ed. A. Souter, CSEL 50 [1908] 193–8).—Harnack, *op. cit.* 972 tries to use some of these texts as arguments for his and E. Hatch's theory of the two types of constitution (diaconal-episcopal as against presbyteral) in the Ancient Church.

[14] See e.g. St. Jerome, *Comm. in Ezech.* 14, 48: '. . . Certe qui primus fuerit ministrorum . . . iniuriam putat si presbyter ordinetur' (PL 54, 484B); Leo the Great JK 487 c. 2; 489 c. 1; 493 c. 4; 509 c. 2; Greg. *Reg.* 2, 20–2 (JE 1173–5).—On the case of the archdeacon Aetius of Constantinople in the correspondence of Leo the Great see C. Silva-Tarouca, 'Nuovi studi sulle antiche lettere dei Papi,' *Gregorianum* 12 (1931) 583–90 who advances serious arguments against the authenticity of JK 487–9 (= *epp.* 111–3 Ballerini).

[15] This was affirmed in passing by Mabillon, *Mus. ital.* II, xvii; cf. also H. Achelis, 'Diakonen,' *Realencyklopädie für protestantische Theologie und Kirche* 4 (1897) 602; Forget, 'Diacres,' DThC 4, 711; J. Bilz, 'Diakon,' LThK 3, 274; Kurtscheid, *Hist. iur. can.* 54.— Forget (followed by Bilz and Kurtscheid) claims that these deacons were called *stationarii* and that about the year 520 their total number was one hundred (source? the reference to Mabillon *loc. cit.* is not to the point).

[16] Harnack, *Anfänge der inneren Organis.* 987. For criticism see Stutz, *op. cit.* 303f.

[17] *Sacram. Gelas.* 1, 20 (ed. H. A. Wilson, *The Gelasian Sacramentary, Liber sacramentorum Romanae ecclesiae*, Oxford 1894, p. 22); cf. Muratori, *Liturgia Romana vetus* (Venice 1748) I, 512.

Mensis primi, quarti, septimi et decimi, sabbatorum die in XII lectiones ad s. Petrum ubi missas celebrantur, postquam antiphonam ad introitum dixerint, data oratione annuntiat pontifex in populo dicens: 'Auxiliante Domino Deo et salvatore nostro Iesu Christo.' Iterum iterum (sic) dicit: 'Auxiliante Domino Deo et salvatore nostro Iesu Christo eligimus in ordine diaconii sive presbyterii illum subdiaconum sive diaconum de titulum illum. Si quis autem habeat aliquid contra hos viros....'

With varying alterations and interpolations this text passed on into many similar *Ordines* of the early Middle Ages.[18]   Now, whatever the Gallo-Frankish elements of the *Sacramentarium Gelasianum* may be (e.g. in the ordination prayers immediately following upon the *annuntiatio*),[19] this particular portion positively belongs to an old Roman liturgy of ordination[20] and proves that the title priests were recruited from among the deacons of the titles.   In view of this (generally overlooked) piece of evidence, even the spurious *Constitutum Silvestri* may be trusted, in this respect at least, as correctly describing the Roman situation of the early sixth century—the time of its fabrication—when it states: 'Et diaconi non essent plus nec amplius per paroeciarum examen nisi duo' and distinguishes these 'parochial' deacons from the seven deacons of the Roman Church.[21]

2. The Deacons and the 'diaconiae'

Toward the end of the seventh century, the historical picture becomes blurred by the appearance of a new type of churches in the city: the *diaconiae* which are for the first time mentioned as *monasteria diaconiae* under the pontificate of Benedict II (684–5).[22]   It seems that they were sixteen in number during the

---

[18] E.g. those edited by Martène, *De antiq. eccl. rit.* 1, 8, 11, nos. 2, 3, 4, 7, 11 (II, 92, 108, 118, 140, 176 Antw.; II, 33, 38, 42, 50, 63 Ven.); Muratori, *op. cit.* II, 408; M. Gerbert, *Monumenta veteris liturgiae Alemannicae* (S. Blasii 1777–9) II, 40f. (= PL 138, 1004); also in the *Codex s. Eligii* and the related MSS, on which Dom Ménard based his edition (Paris 1642) of the Gregorian Sacramentary (= PL 78, 220f.—see also Ménard's annotations nn. 737–9). Variants from Gerbert and from Martène's *Ordines* 2–4 are given by Wilson, *Gelasian Sacr.* 24f.   It may be regretted that M. Andrieu has excluded the 'Gelasian' *Ordo* of ordination and its offsprings from his investigations on the early medieval *Ordines Romani*, with the exception of Gerbert's text and of Martène's *Ordo VIII* (cf. Andrieu, *Ordines* 21, 104, 180, and the numerous MSS referred to in the *Index initiorum* s.v. 'Mensis primi, quarti, septimi'). But in the latter, the entire *annuntiatio* is missing (cf. Martène, *op. cit.* II, 142 Antw.; II, 51 Ven.).   A critical appreciation of the various forms of the *annuntiatio* must therefore await further research; the reprint of Ménard's text and the synoptic table of the Gelasian and some other texts in P. de Puniet, *Le Pontifical Romain* I (Louvain-Paris 1930) 282–5, 286–90, are no sufficient substitute for a critical discussion.

[19] These prayers are derived from the so-called *Missale Francorum* (ed. Muratori, *Lit. Rom. vet.* II, 667), cf. Wilson, *op. cit.* 22, 24f.   For Gallican elements in general see Wilson's introduction and all modern writers on the *Sacr. Gelas.*

[20] Its historical and chronological relation to the considerably different *Ordo* of Saint-Amand (ed. Duchesne, *Origines du culte chrétien* app. vii: a *recueil excentrique* in the words of Andrieu, *Ordines* 492) cannot be studied here.

[21] *Const. Silv.* c. 6 (ed. P. Coustant, *Epistolae Romanorum pontificum*, Paris 1721, app. col. 48; Mansi 2, 625). For details see at nn. 57ff. *infra*. Baronius, *Annales ecclesiastici* an. 112 num. 9, though mistaken about the authenticity of the canon, gives a correct interpretation of its meaning.

[22] LP I, 364.   Cf. Duchesne *ibid.* n. 7; id. *Les titres presbytéraux et les diaconies* (n. 10 *supra*) 236; Sägmüller, *Cardinäle* 10.—Outside of Rome, *diaconiae* are found as early as the

182

eighth century; Hadrian I (772–95) added two more *diaconiae* in the city proper, and three in the suburb of St. Peter.[23] Under Leo III (795–816), nineteen are mentioned in the city, and four *iuxta b. Petrum*, but afterwards only eighteen *diaconiae* altogether remained throughout the Middle Ages.[24]

This simultaneous existence of seven Roman deacons and eighteen diaconal churches is very puzzling. Most authors have been seduced by the term, *diaconiae*, to take a relationship between the deacons, the regions, and these churches—in analogy to the priests and their titles—for granted from the outset, and consequently to assume an increase in number of the regional deacons from the seventh or eighth century onward, so as to match the number of the *diaconiae*.[25] But in truth the organization of the *diaconiae* was, until the late eleventh century, entirely distinct from that of the college of the *diaconi Romanae ecclesiae*.[26] Duchesne showed that the diaconal churches and monasteries had nothing to do with the regional division of the city: we have e.g. as many as eight *diaconiae* in *regio II*, and none in *regio VII*.[27] From the first *Ordo Romanus* as well as from the *Liber diurnus* we have positive evidence that the titular of a diaconal establishment was the so-called *dispensator* or *pater diaconiae*;[28] that is, the office was not connected with a determinate sacred order.[29] To be sure, occasionally one or the other Roman deacon might have been given a *diaconia* in benefice, but such cases were exceptional.[30] As late as the eleventh century, we find other persons, even cardinal priests, as *rectores, augmentatores, dispensa-*

time of Gregory the Great, cf. *Reg.* 5, 25 for Pesaro (JE 1338); 10, 8 for Naples (JE 1775); 11, 17 for Ravenna (JE 1806). See J. Lestocquoi, 'Administration de Rome et diaconies du VIe au IXe siècle,' *Rivista di archeologia cristiana* 7 (1930) 265f.

[23] LP I, 504 lines 18–9; 505, 27–506, 6; 509, 29–30; cf. Duchesne's commentary I, 364 n. 7; 519 n. 70; 520 nn. 79–81; 522 n. 110; Sägmüller *loc. cit.* and Lestocquoi *op. cit.* 262, 284–8.

[24] LP II, 18ff. Cf. Duchesne's commentary II, 42 n. 74 and 43 n. 79; *Les titres* 237ff. Lestocquoi 288.

[25] Thus the earlier writers and Phillips, *Kirchenr.* VI, 67–72; Hinschius,`Kirchenr.` I, 322f.; Sägmüller, *Cardinäle* 10 and *Cath. Encycl.* 3, 334.

[26] This was Duchesne's fundamental discovery, cf. LP I, 364 n. 7; 'Les régions de Rome au moyen-âge,' *Mélanges d'archéol. et d'hist.* 10 (1890) 144. It has been adopted since by Lestocquoi, *op. cit.* 267, 273; Klewitz, *Entstehung* 180f. 185f.; A. Dumas in Fliche-Martin, *Hist. de l'Égl.* 7, 158.

[27] Duchesne, LP I, 364 n. 7 (a topographical survey is found in *Les titres* 237ff.).

[28] *Ordo I Rom.* num. 4 (6 Mabillon); LD 95 (231 Rozière; 123 Sickel). Cf. Duchesne *loc. cit.*; Lestocquoi, *op. cit.* 276f. Klewitz, *Entstehung* 180. Earlier writers usually held that the *pater* or *dispensator* was only an assistant of the deacon in charge of the *diaconia*, cf. e.g. Mabillon, *Mus. ital.* I, 150; II, xvii; Phillips VI, 68f.; Hinschius I, 322. But the *Ordo I Rom.* clearly speaks of the *pater diaconiae cum subdito sibi presbytero et mansionario.*

[29] Lestocquoi, *op. cit.* 281–3 goes too far, however, in deducing from certain inscriptions that the *dispensatores* or *patres* were originally laymen: their liturgical functions are unmistakably described in the *Ordo I Rom. cit.* See also the objections of Klewitz, 'Montecassino in Rom,' *Quellen und Forschungen aus italienischen Archiven und Bibliotheken* 28 (1937–8) 43 n. 2.

[30] The only instance is found in a short list of the Popes from John X to John XV, by Archbishop Sigeric of Canterbury (c. 990): '. . . Item Iohannes tituli (*sic*) s. Mariae qui vocatur in Domnico (*sic*) sedit annos VIIII m. I d. V' (John XII: 955–64); '. . . Item Benedictus diaconiae s. Theodori sedit annos I et dimidium, dies XII' (Benedict VI: 972–4), published by Duchesne, LP II, xv; cf. also Dumas *loc. cit.* (n. 26 *supra*).

tores of diaconal churches,[31] and still later, Urban II speaks of 'clerici diaconiarum quibus diaconi non praefuerint.'[32] The name of *diaconia*, misleading as it may be, is therefore to be explained otherwise: it indicates only that these institutions, created in the seventh century to succeed the dispensaries (*annonae*) of imperial Rome,[33] were destined to carry on the charitable activities which in the early Church had been the foremost function of the diaconal college, but of which the Roman deacons eventually had to be relieved with the increase of their duties as ministers of the Pope. Suffice it to recall how often deacons were absent from Rome for years, on permanent missions as apocrisiaries or as rectors of patrimonies of the Roman Church.

The preceding observations are corroborated by the fundamental fact that throughout the early Middle Ages there appear never more than seven *diaconi S.R.E.* in synodal or papal documents,[34] and that also the literary sources—with one specious exception—know but seven deacons of the Roman Church.[35] It was only toward the end of the eleventh century that the deacons became connected with, and their number determined by, the *diaconiae*.[36] In describing the Mass of the Pope at St. John Lateran, the anonymous author of the *Descriptio sanctuarii Lateranensis ecclesiae* mentions the 'archidiaconus Romae cum VI diaconibus palatinis ... et alii XII diacones regionarii.'[37] He gives however the total of these (19) deacons only as eighteen, and in listing later their eighteen *diaconiae*, he adds at the first of them, S. Maria in Domnica, the words: 'ubi est archidiaconatus.'[38] This shows that by this time the Roman archdeaconate was about to become permanently united with one of the deaconries, and in fact the archdeacon has disappeared, since the pontificate of Paschal II (1099–1118), from all documentary sources.[39]

---

[31] Examples in Klewitz, *Entstehung* 186f.; also *Quellen und Forsch.* 28, 42f. Note also a document of 1017 in Hinschius, *Kirchenr.* I, 378 n. 5.: 'Petrus archipresbyter de diaconia s. Christi martyris Eustachii. ...'

[32] Kehr, IP 1, 7 num. 11; text quoted from ed. Kehr (cf. ch. IV n. 7 *supra*) by Klewitz 187.

[33] Cf. Lestocquoi, *op. cit.* 262f. 267, 270.

[34] Klewitz, *Entstehung* 181 (with references in n. 2); 185 n. 3 (for the time of Gregory VII).

[35] Cf. Nicetas Paphlago, *Vita s. Ignatii Constantinop.*: Στέφανος μὲν καὶ Δονᾶτος ἐπίσκοποι τοῦ πάπα 'Ρώμης, καὶ Μαρῖνος εἰς τῶν ἐπτὰ διακόνων σὺν αὐτοῖς (Mansi 16, 261E); Photius, *Erotemata* 6: Σύμμαχον ὡς ἔνα τῶν ἐπτὰ διακόνων ὄντα (PG 104, 1225B)—both quoted by Phillips, *Kirchenr.* VI, 72 nn. 34–5; Hinschius I, 323 n. 4.

[36] Duchesne, *Les régions de Rome* (n. 26* supra) 144. Klewitz, *Entstehung* 182f. tentatively suggests that this development may have begun at the time of Stephen III (but admits p. 185f. that this remains uncertain). Lestocquoi, *op. cit.* 273 puts the decisive period too late, at the twelfth century.

[37] See the text from MS *Vat. Reg.* 712, fol. 87v in Klewitz, *Entstehung* 176.

[38] 'Isti XVIII diaconi totidem ecclesias habent infra muros civitatis' (*ibid.*); fol. 88v: 'Diacones sunt X et VIII. S. Mariae in Domnica, ubi est archidiaconatus ...' (120 Klewitz; Kehr, IP 1, 4).

[39] Cf. Klewitz 176, 189f.—Consequently, the *Descriptio* fol. 88v classifies only five deaconries as palatine (*palatii*), the sixth being merged with the archdeaconate; the five are St. Lucia in Septisolio, Sts. Cosmas and Damian, St. Hadrian, St. George in Velabro, St. Mary in Cosmedin (*in schola Graeca*). The emendation 'S. Theodori palatii', made by Kehr, IP I, 4 and Klewitz 120 (for the faulty reading 'S. Theodorici' in the MS) in order to bring up the number to six, is not warranted.

In the new system as recorded by the *Descriptio*, the six *palatini* with the archdeacon obviously represent the original college of the Roman deacons, the new name being easily explained by their traditional administrative and liturgical service in the Lateran palace.[40] On the other hand, the twelve new *diacones regionarii* must have been substituted for an equal number of *dispensatores* in the respective diaconal churches.[41] Yet, prior to the recent researches of Dr. Klewitz, textbooks usually taught the contrary, namely that the original college was somehow increased in the early Middle Ages to a number of twelve *regionarii*, and that subsequently seven *palatini* were added.[42] For origin and appearance of the latter this theory could, however, offer no explanation, even as it disregarded the counter-evidence: the archdeacon's inclusion among the *palatini*, and the constant number of seven deacons proper before the time of the *Descriptio*. The misleading factor which accounts for the older theory is the name *diacones regionarii*: for in the eighth century (*Ordo I Romanus*) it designated the Seven, and in the eleventh century, the Twelve. But the regional functions of the original *diacones Romanae ecclesiae* had ceased long before, with the establishment of the *diaconiae;* and name and number of the twelve new *regionarii* are probably connected with the then relatively recent division of the city, for purposes of military-municipal administration, into twelve *regiones*, the first traces of which appear in the second half of the tenth century and which has nothing to do with the old ecclesiastical seven regions.[43]

While everything thus points to the end of the eleventh century as the time in which the number of Roman deacons was brought up to nineteen (eighteen), our reconstruction of the historical process seems to be contradicted by Johannes Diaconus (d. before 882), who in his biography of Gregory the Great speaks of the *diacones apostolicae sedis* as 'quorum . . . decem et novem plenitudine redundaret.'[44] Taken at its face value, this testimony would indicate that the set-up which we know from the *Descriptio* was already complete at the end of the sixth century.[45] But this cannot be true, for the *diaconiae* did not exist at this early

---

[40] *Descriptio* fol. 87v: '. . . qui in palatio legere debent evangelium et in ecclesia Lateranensi' (176 Klewitz). The attempt of P. Fabre, *Étude sur le Liber censuum de l'Église romaine* (Paris 1892) 153 n. 1, to identify the palatine deacons with the seven *iudices palatini* is unfounded. Cf. Sägmüller, *Cardinäle* 27 n. 1.

[41] Klewitz 178–81; Dumas *loc. cit.* (n. 26 *supra*).

[42] See e.g. Phillips VI, 71f.; Hinschius I, 323; Sägmüller, *Cardinäle* 10; *Cath. Encycl.* 3, 334. All these writers start from the incorrect assumption that originally there had been one *diaconia* in each of the seven *regiones* (see also Phillips VI, 67; Hinschius I, 312). Entirely gratuitous is an assertion by Panvini, *De episcopatibus* (ch. I n. 2 *supra*) 63; Victorelli in A. Chacon's *Vitae et gesta summorum pontificum* (ed. Ughelli, Rome 1630) I, 46; Tamagna, *Origini* I, 145, and others, to the effect that there had been fourteen (!) regional deacons and that Gregory III (731–41) had added four (!) palatine deacons.

[43] On these twelve new *regiones* and their probable origin in the *scholae militum* of the Byzantine era see Duchesne, *Les régions de Rome* 126–34; LP II, 253 n. 7; Poole, *Papal Chancery* (n. 6 *supra*) 173–5; Halphen, *Etudes sur l'admin. de Rome* (n. 6 *supra*) 10–5. On the other hand, the addition of twelve *regionarii* might be simply the result of a policy of filling up the remaining *diaconiae* after six of them had been assigned to the *diaconi palatini*.

[44] *Vita s. Greg.* 3, 7 (PL 75, 133).

[45] Thus e.g. Hinschius, *Kirchenr.* I, 312, 323; Kurtscheid, *Hist. iur. can.* 244.

time, nor would their incumbents have been *diacones apostolicae sedis*. Likewise, the number of nineteen cannot be explained by adding to the seven deacons proper the deacons of the *tituli*:[46] these too could not have been termed deacons of the Apostolic See; besides, their number cannot have been as low as twelve.

It has been repeatedly suggested that John the Deacon may simply have dated back the diaconal organization of his own time by three centuries, ascribing it to the pontificate of Gregory the Great.[47] This theory seems to be supported by good evidence, namely by the existence of nineteen *diaconiae* in the ninth century. But even so the difficulties remain unsolved. According to this theory, we should have to admit that the original Seven, plus twelve other 'regional' deacons, were as early as the ninth century in charge of the *diaconiae*, and that the Twelve were as much *diacones apostolicae sedis* as the old college of seven Roman deacons. Both assumptions are incompatible with all the other historical evidence concerning the *numerus clausus* of the Roman deacons proper and the administration of the diaconal establishments by *dispensatores* or *patres* in the early Middle Ages. Certainly John cannot have confused the college of the *diacones Romanae ecclesiae*, of which he himself was a member, with the local *dispensatores*.

The critical passage therefore should be given quite another interpretation. When Johannes Diaconus states:

Solis diaconibus apostolicae sedis super hac quodammodo parte (i.e. promotions to bishoprics) parcebat. Quorum cum decem et novem plenitudine redundaret, ipse Bonifacium, Florentium et Epiphanium consecravit,

he did not mean to speak at all of nineteen diaconal offices but meant to say that nineteen different personalities successively belonged, during the fourteen years of St. Gregory's pontificate, to the college of the (seven) *diacones apostolicae sedis*, and that three of them had been ordained deacons by that Pope himself.[48]—

[46] As suggested by Achelis, *Realencykl.* (n. 15 *supra*) 4, 602. E. Caspar, *Geschichte des Papsttums* II (Tübingen 1933) 404 n. 8 wrongly refers this remark to *diacones regionarii*.

[47] Kleiner, *De orig. et antiq. card.* (ch. I, n. 2 *supra*) §19 (p. 454 Schmidt); Nardi, *Dei parrochi* II (Pesaro 1830) 403 n. 1; Caspar, *Papsttum* II, 777; Klewitz, *Entstehung* 183.

[48] The phrase 'quorum cum decem . . . consecravit' is awkward Latinity, to say the least. Grammatically, the translation 'of whom he ordained, while he had as many (*redundaret*) as nineteen if taken all together (*plenitudine*) . . .' cannot be challenged. The entire passage, however, is badly composed and invites misinterpretation: in the preceding paragraphs, John the Deacon speaks of various Roman priests, subdeacons and monks whom St. Gregory promoted to the episcopate, adding that in this respect the Pope spared his deacons 'somewhat' (*quodammodo*). Now, if no full stop is made after that statement—the Maurist edition has a colon—the reader is invited to believe that the words 'ipse Bonifacium . . . consecravit' likewise refer to episcopal consecrations and modify the *quodammodo* (in this way they are understood by Sägmüller, *Cardinäle* 194). But if that were true, the sentence 'solis diaconibus . . . parcebat' would lose its sense, because also for each of the other classes of clerics promoted to bishoprics not more than three or four names are mentioned (three priests, four subdeacons, three monks). Besides, there are no historical records of a bishop Florentius or a bishop Epiphanius under St. Gregory, and the deacon Boniface became Pope in 607 (see the following chart, num. 11). Therefore, either the entire passage of the *Vita* on the deacons has to be discarded as untrustworthy, or it must

186

How far can this statement be trusted? The Register of St. Gregory's letters yields information only about the following members, eleven or twelve, of the diaconal college during his pontificate (see table on the next page):[49]

1. Honoratus the deacon was apocrisiary to the court of Constantinople (*Reg.* 1, 6), presumably already before the accession of St. Gregory (cf. Ewald, MGH *Epp.* 1, 8 n. 6; on Gregory's apocrisiaries in general see Caspar, *Papsttum* II, 404 n. 5). He is first mentioned in 584, as notary under Pelagius II (JK 1052 ed. Hartmann, MGH *Epp.* 2, 441, 10). His identity with the Honoratus who was made archdeacon in September 591 (*Reg.* 2, 1) can be neither proved nor disproved. Ewald 101 n. 2 adduces against the identity the fact that in letters of the second and third years (*Reg.* 2, 36; 3, 7) the *apocrisiarius* is never styled *archidiaconus*. On the other hand, it is quite possible that Honoratus was nominally appointed archdeacon in 591 and returned temporarily to his diplomatic post but never began his archdeaconal functions: for the death of Honoratus (or of both of them, if there were two) must have occurred between *Reg.* 3, 7 and *Reg.* 3, 55, i.e. before the first mention of Cyprianus as deacon. Otherwise we would arrive at a college of eight deacons for that date. A successor for Honoratus in Constantinople was named in *Reg.* 3, 51–2: Sabinianus (nr. 7).

1a(2). Even if this Honoratus was not the apocrisiary serving as early as the accession of St. Gregory, he must have been an old member of the college, according to the principle of seniority governing the appointment of archdeacons in the Ancient Church; cf. ch. II at n. 59 *supra* and, for the Roman archdeacons in particular, Caspar, *Papsttum* II, 792; Klewitz, *Entstehung* 179.

2(3). Anatolius succeeded Sabinianus (nr. 7) as apocrisiary in Constantinople (*Reg.* 7, 27). He is mentioned as deceased in *Reg.* 12, 6: 'dilectissimae memoriae Anatolius diaconus' (352, 32 Hartmann).

3(4). The death of Servusdei is recorded in *Reg.* 9, 8: 'dilectissimum quondam filium nostrum Servumdei diaconum' (46, 16–7 Hartmann). He had served under St. Gregory's predecessor, cf. *Reg.* 13, 22: 'sanctae memoriae decessoris mei temporibus per Servumdei diaconem, qui tunc ecclesiastici patrimonii curam gessit' (388, 30–1 Hartmann).

4(5). On the difference between the two Bonifaces see Hartmann, MGH *Epp.* 1, 287 n. 2 (to *Reg.* 5, 6, as against Ewald, *ibid.* 39 n. 3), also the *Index nominum* s.v. (2, 478); Caspar, *Papsttum* II, 404 n. 6. The first Boniface is mentioned in St. Gregory's *Dialogi* 3, 20: 'huius nostri Bonefati (*sic*) diaconi adque dispensatoris aecclesiae', as having relatives in the province of Valeria (ed. U. Moricca, Fonti per la storia d'Italia 57, Rome 1924, p. 187 lines 8–10; on the meaning of *dispensator ecclesiae* see Caspar II, 776). He became St. Gregory's third successor as Boniface IV (LP I, 317: 'natione Marsorum de civitate Valeria'). H. K. Mann, *The Lives of the Popes in the Middle Ages* 1, 1 (London-St. Louis 1902) 269 remains uncertain. There is some confusion on the two Bonifaces in Mann 263 n. 2 and Moricca 187 n. 1.

5(6). Laurentius was deposed in September 591 'propter superbiam et mala sua quae tacenda duximus' (*Reg.* 2, 1: 101 Ewald).

6(7). In the letters the promotion of Epiphanius, who came from the province of Isauria, is not spoken of before *Reg.* 5, 35. But in his *Homiliae in Evangelium* 39, 10, St. Gregory mentions the presence of his deacon Epiphanius (PL 76, 1300B; cf. Hartmann, MGH *Epp.* 1,

---

be read as referring to the promotions of the three said clerics to deaconship (as is done by Peitz, *Lib. diurn.* 61; Caspar, *Papsttum* II, 404 n. 8). This interpretation is borne out in fact by St. Gregory's register; see the following chart.

[49] The figures in the chart indicate the first and the last mention of the several deacons in the letters, with year and number. The period during which any one belonged with certainty to the college of deacons is indicated by a straight line; dots (. . .) are used where the duration of a diaconate after its last (or before its first) mention in the Register remains unascertainable.

Name	Evidence from St. Gregory's register	Pope
1 Honoratus apocrisiarius	1, 6——3, 7...	
1a (2) Honoratus archidiaconus	...2, 1...	
2 (3) Anatolius	1, 11————————————11, 29 (d. bef. 12, 6)	
3 (4) Servusdei	1, 42————4, 34... (d. bef. 9, 8)	
4 (5) Bonifatius (i)	1, 50————————9, 72	Bonif. IV (608–15)
5 (6) Laurentius archidiaconus	——2, 1	
6 (7) Epiphanius	(subdiac. 3, 1–2) diac. (bef. 3, 39)——5, 35————————14, 3...	
7 (8) Sabinianus	3, 51——————8, 6	Sabinianus (604–6)
8 (9) Petrus	(subdiac. 1, 1——3, 39) diac. 3, 54——6, 24... (9, 11?)...	
9 (10) Cyprianus	3, 55——9, 65...	
10 (11) Florentius	(subdiac. 3, 15...) 9, 8...	
11 (12) Bonifatius (ii)	(defensor 1, 25——11, 58...) 13, 41——14, 8——	Bonif. III (607)

316 n. 2). Now, the last of the forty homilies was delivered the second Sunday after Pentecost, i.e. May 31, 593 (cf. Ewald 251, note to *Reg.* 4, 17a; also B. Steidle, *Patrologia*, Freiburg 1937, p. 231f.). The ordination of Epiphanius to the diaconate and *Hom.* 39 must have preceded that date and, therefore, the first letter (*Reg.* 3, 39) of June 593. (Incidentally, the career of Epiphanius is additional proof against the date of 592, found in most textbooks for the completion of the *Homiliae*: since he was still subdeacon in September 592 [*Reg.* 3, 2], *Hom.* 40 cannot have been delivered in that year on the second Sunday after Pentecost.)

7(8). Upon St. Gregory's election—he had been Roman deacon himself—there can have been no more than six deacons left. Sabinianus, his future successor, whose old age is occasionally emphasized (cf. Caspar, *Papsttum* II, 405), may have been one of them—if Honoratus is but one person. Otherwise, he may have been made deacon in Gregory's first year, to fill up the college. In the third year (*Reg.* 3, 51–2), he succeeded Honoratus as apocrisiary in Constantinople, which post he held until *Reg.* 7, 25.

8(9). Petrus (MGH *Epp.* 2, 503: *Index nominum* nr. 16 s.v.), known as St. Gregory's interlocutor in the *Dialogi*, held during his subdeaconship important posts as *rector patrimonii* of Sicily (590–2: *Reg.* 1, 1–2, 38) and of Campania (592: *Reg.* 3, 1–39). Before St. Gregory's pontificate, he had been Roman *defensor* in Ravenna (*Reg.* 3, 54 and 6, 24: 213, 2–4 Ewald and 402, 11 Hartmann; cf. Hartmann 308 n. 2 to *Reg.* 5, 28 and Caspar, *Papsttum* II, 395 n. 2; 404 n. 8). His identity with the 'dilectus filius noster' Petrus in *Reg.* 9, 11 is but an attractive conjecture of Hartmann 2, 49 n. 5. According to a pious legend reported by Johannes Diaconus, *Vita* 4, 69 (PL 75, 222A), but already rejected by Baronius, *Annal. eccl.* an. 604 num. 22, he would have died shortly after St. Gregory, in 604.

9(10). Cyprianus succeeded Petrus as *rector patrimonii* in Sicily: *Reg.* 3, 55; 4, 6–8, 7. His return is mentioned in *Reg.* 9, 15. Cf. Ewald 214 note to *Reg.* 3, 55.

10(11). Of Florentius no more is known than one mention as subdeacon and one as deacon.

11(12). For this Bonifatius the *defensor* (and *primicerius defensorum* since *Reg.* 8, 16) see Hartmann 1, 287 n. 2; Caspar, *Papsttum* II, 449; 464. His ordination to the diaconate and diplomatic mission as apocrisiary followed upon the death of Anatolius. Boniface III's pontificate lasted only a few months, from February 19th to November 12, 607.

Now it is arithmetically possible that eight or seven more deacons—the number would depend upon whether Honoratus the archdeacon and Honoratus the apocrisiary were or were not the same person—appeared and disappeared again during these fourteen years.[50] But such an assumption is highly improbable in the absence of any record, and we have no basis for assuming that John the Deacon had at his disposal source materials on the Gregorian administration other than those contained in the *registrum*.[51] For he did not even fully avail

[50] As the diagram shows, the presence of seven deacons is not documented by written evidence for the years 1–2, 5–8 (9?), 10–14. Thus there would be room, theoretically speaking, for many more—under the fanciful supposition that none of those mentioned in the Register was a deacon before his first appearance in the letters, and that every one died immediately after his last mention in a letter.

[51] The contrary, *viz.* that John possessed such information from archival sources lost to us, was held—not only with regard to the deacons but for every point on which the *Vita* is at variance with the Register—by Peitz, *Lib. diurn.* 58ff. esp. 60, 61 n. 2, 62 n. 3; id. *Das Register Gregors I.* (Ergänzungshefte zu den Stimmen der Zeit, 2nd ser. 2, Freiburg 1917). This hypothesis has been rightly rejected by most writers, cf. e.g. E. Posner, 'Das Register Gregors I.' NA 43, 2 (1921) 288–93; Caspar, *Papsttum* II, 329 n. 3 (with further bibliography); 404 n. 8.—If the differences between Johannes Diaconus and the Register (which, after all, is avowedly his chief source) consisted only of a surplus of information in the *Vita*, Peitz'

himself of the information obtainable from this source: witness his failure to mention the deacon Peter among those ordained by St. Gregory himself. We therefore have to conclude either than John made an uncontrollable mistake in his statement about the nineteen deacons—and this would not be the only blunder in his biography[52]—or that the text of the passage is faulty in the archetype of the manuscripts on which the extant editions of the *Vita* are based.[53] John might for instance originally have written *decem vel novem*. Since he overlooked Peter, he might as well have overlooked one more, or confused the two Bonifaces; and he might have been doubtful about the identity of Honoratus as we still are nowadays. This would account for 'ten or nine' instead of 'twelve or eleven'; and a copyist's error *(decem et novem* for *decem vel novem)* has much transcriptional probability, especially if his mind was distracted by the number of the Roman *diaconiae*. Future critical examination of the manuscript tradition may support or destroy such a conjecture, but it is certain that John the Deacon's text as it now stands makes no historical sense.

3. *The Deacons as Cardinals*

As long as the genuine canonical concept of *cardinalis* remained alive and undisturbed by extraneaous etymologies, the Roman deacons could not be qualified as *cardinales diaconi*: they were not incardinated in any other church different from their title of ordination, the Lateran basilica. It is therefore significant that the oldest document attributing to the Roman deacons the name of cardinals—and paradoxically the very first text to connect that name with any class of Roman clerics at all—should be a notorious forgery: the so-called *Constitutum Silvestri*.[54] Purporting to be the decree of a Roman Synod presided over by Pope St. Sylvester and Emperor Constantine in 324, the *Constitutum* belongs to a group of spurious documents known as the Symmachian forgeries, all of which

---

theory could be defended. But John not only gives at times less than the Register (e.g. on the deacon Peter, see the text above) but sometimes manifestly blunders: he names e.g. *(Vita* 3, 7) among the Roman priests whom Gregory ordained bishops, *Bonifacium Rhegii*. Now, Bishop Boniface of Reggio appears in the letters from 592 on *(Reg.* 3, 4) and 'Bonifatius presbyter titulo s. Xisti' subscribes as late as 600 the acts of a Roman synod *(Reg.* 11, 15 275, 17 Hartmann)!

[52] See the preceding note, also ch. II n. 36; IV n. 43 *supra*.

[53] For the various editions see the Bollandists' *Bibliotheca hagiographica latina* I (Brussels 1898-9) num. 3641; A. Potthast, *Bibliotheca medii aevi* (2nd ed. Berlin 1896) II, 1349, where also some MSS are mentioned. For collations made of some MSS see the Bollandists' *Acta Sanctorum* mart. II (3rd ed. Paris-Rome 1865) 121; the Maurists' *praefatio generalis* to the Works of St. Gregory (= PL 75, 17-20: criticism of Goussainville's edition, Paris 1675) and their preface to the *Vita* (num. 12 = PL 75, 39: on MSS collated and consulted).

[54] The classical proof of the spurious nature of the *Constitutum* remains the dissertation of P. Coustant, *Epistolae Romanorum pontificum* (Paris 1721) app. cols. 37-44 (reprinted PL 8, 841-5); see also his *praefatio generalis* pp. lxxxvf. (num. 97-9) and, of modern authors, in particular F. Maassen, *Geschichte der Quellen und der Literatur des canonischen Rechts im Abendlande* (Graz 1870) 411ff.; Duchesne, LP I, cxxxiii–v. The first to deny the authenticity of the decree, at least in its Pseudo-Isidorian form (n. 63 *infra*) was Hincmar of Reims, *De presbyteris criminosis* cc. 21-4 (PL 125, 1103-6). Cf. Coustant 39-40; Mansi 2, 615 n. 1.

190

were fabricated and circulated during the first years of the sixth century[55] by overzealous followers of Pope Symmachus (498–514), to strengthen his position which had been so greatly compromised during the schism of Laurentius. Among canonical collections, the *Constitutum Silvestri* appears for the first time in the *Collectio Sanblasiana*, the collection of MS *Vatic. lat.* 1342, and, in abridged form, in the *Theatina*—all dating from the sixth century.[56] As far as we can judge from the printed texts, the pertinent canons read:[57]

(c.3) Postea autem fecit gradus in gremio synodi, ut non presbyter adversus episcopum, non diaconus adversus presbyterum, non subdiaconus adversus diaconum, non acolythus adversus subdiaconum, non exorxista adversus acolythum, non lector adversus exorcistam, non ostiarius adversus lectorem det accusationem aliquam. Et non damnabitur praesul nisi in LXXII. Neque praesul summus a quoquam iudicabitur; quoniam scriptum est: 'Non est discipulus super magistrum.' Presbyter autem nisi in XLIV testimonia non damnabitur. *Diaconus autem cardine constructus urbis Romae nisi in XXXVI non condemnabitur.* Subdiaconus, acolythus, exorcista, lector, nisi, sicut scriptum est, in septem testimonia filios et uxores habentes, et omnino Christum praedicantes. Sic datur mystica veritas (47–8 Coustant; 623–4 Mansi).

---

[55] Cf. Duchesne *loc. cit.*; id. *L'église au VI* *siècle* (Paris 1925) 124; G. Pfeilschifter, *Der Ostgotenkönig Theoderich der Grosse und die katholische Kirche* (Kirchengeschichtliche Studien 3, 1–2, Münster 1896) 65; K. Silva-Tarouca, 'Beiträge zur Überlieferungsgeschichte der Papstbriefe des 4.–6. Jahrhunderts,' *Zeitschrift für katholische Theologie* 43 (1919) 665. The suggestion of a later date, seventh or eighth century, made by A. Gaudenzi, *Nonantola* 335, 337f. 353f. 359f. was rightly rejected by W. Levison, 'Konstantinische Schenkung und Silvester-Legende,' *Miscellanea Francesco Ehrle* (Studi e Testi 38, Rome 1924) II, 181 n. 4.

[56] For these collections and the MSS by which they are represented, see Maassen, *Geschichte* 411ff. 504ff. (506); 512ff. (515); 526ff. (530); Duchesne, LP I, cxxxiv-vii (with a stemma of later MSS: p. cxxxv and n. 1); Mommsen, MGH *Gesta Rom. pont.* 1 (Berlin 1898) xxii; Gaudenzi, *op. cit. passim*; Turner, *Monum.* 1, 2, i, p. viii; id. 'Chapters in the History of Latin MSS of Canons: VI,' *Journal of Theological Studies* 31 (1931) 9–20; Silva-Tarouca, *op. cit.* 664f.; L. Schiaparelli, *Il codice 490 della Biblioteca capitolare di Lucca e la scuola scrittoria lucchese* (Studi e Testi 36, Rome 1924) 15; Schwartz, *Acta conc. oecum.* 2, 2, ii, p. vi ff. and xv; id. book review, ZRG *Kan. Abt.* 20 (1931) 599f.; id. 'Die Kanonessammlungen der alten Reichskirche,' ZRG *Kan. Abt.* 25 (1936) 53ff.; E. Lowe, *Codices latini antiquiores* I (Oxford 1934) 34 and 44; H. Wurm, *Studien und Texte zur Dekretalensammlung des Dionysius Exiguus* (Kanonistische Studien und Texte ed. Koeniger 16, Bonn 1939) 87–9; 265; id. 'Decretales selectae ex antiquissimis Romanorum Pontificum epistulis decretalibus,' *Apollinaris* 12 (1939) 44; 47.

[57] A critical edition does not exist. The parallel edition from two slightly different MSS by P. Crabbe (Cologne 1538) is reprinted in Labbe, Hardouin, etc. and in Mansi 2, 217ff. The latter adds variant readings from a *Codex Lucensis*, probably MS Lucca 490 of the *Coll. Sanblasiana*. The best edition is that by Coustant, *Epp. Rom. pont.* app. 43–52, from MS Paris, B.N. *lat.* 3836 (*ol.* Colbert 784; cf. Coustant p. lxxix, app. 37–8). Eusebius Amort, *Elementa juris canonici veteris et moderni* (Ulm 1757; used ed. Ferrara 1763) I, 378–85 printed the *Constitutum* as part of his (generally overlooked) edition of the *Coll. Diessensis* (8th–9th cent.; MS Munich *lat.* 5508). Coustant's text is given above; of the variants recorded by him, or resulting from Mansi and Amort, only the following may be noted as they bear on the 'cardinal' passages:—(c. 3) cardine constructus] cardine constrictus *Mansi 1*, in cardine constitutus *Amort*, cardinalis *Mansi Luc.*—(c. 11) diaconus cardinalis] subdiaconus cardinalis *var. Coust. Mansi 2.*—The *Coll. Theatina* omits in c. 3 the critical words and reads: '. . . diaconus autem (nisi) in XXXVII non condemnabitur' (ed. Duchesne, LP I, cxxxiv, col. 2 n. 1).

(c.6) Et diaconi non essent plus nec amplius per paroeciarum examen nisi duo, et *diacones cardinales* urbis Romae septem (48 Coustant; 625–6 Mansi).

(c.7) Ita tamen Silvester clara voce dicebat ad coepiscopos, ut a subdiacono usque ad lectorem omnes subditi essent *diacono cardinali urbis Romae*, in ecclesia honorem repraesentantes tantum; pontifici vero presbyteri, diaconi, subdiacones, acolythi, exorcistae, lectores in omni loco repraesentent obsequium, sive in publico, sive in gremio ecclesiae, tamquam pontifici (*ibid.*).

(c.11) Ut nullus ex laica persona ad honorem acolythus usque ad episcopatum sublevaretur, nisi prius fuisset lector annis XXX, deinde . . . et in subdiaconatu esset annos quinque; deinde ad diaconatus honorem pertingeret fixus, rogantibus XXX presbyteris examen, ut esset *diaconus cardinalis*, quia a prima sede erat constitutum ut serviret annos septem . . . (50 Coustant; 627–8 Mansi).[58]

The four canons show all the barbarous Latinity of the fake, all its notorious ignorance in matters canonical, let alone the fantastic rule on the number of witnesses required for the trials of ecclesiastics.[59] This also accounts for the forger's untechnical and wavering use of the terms *diaconus cardine constructus*, *diaconus cardinalis*: untechnical, because at that time the canonical concept *cardinalis* < *incardinatus* was as yet unmistakably distinct from the everyday meaning of the word; wavering, because the *Constitutum* uses it to designate, now the deacons of the pope's cathedral (cc. 3, 6, 11), now the archdeacon alone (c. 7).[60]

Nevertheless, the clumsy forgery contributed to spread the uncanonical usage of the term 'cardinal.' The Symmachians resorted to it again in the so-called *Gesta Polychronii* which they presented as acts of a Roman Synod of 433.[61] In the ninth century, Pseudo-Isidore took over the third canon of the *Constitutum Silvestri*[62] and dressed it up with several interpolations, among which the most conspicuous is the insertion of *cardinalis* also in the passage concerning the trials of presbyters.[63] From now on the text was bound to appear to the uncritical mind of later generations[64] as proof for a very early existence—at least as old

---

[58] For the relation of c. 11 to c. 6 of the pseudo-Sylvestrian 'Synod of the 275 (*al.* 270) Bishops' (ed. Ch. Poisnel, 'Un concile apocryphe du pape saint Sylvestre,' *Mélanges d'archéol. et d'hist.* 6 [1886] 5; cf. Mansi 2, 1083A) and to LP I, 171, 15ff. (on St. Sylvester's decree concerning interstices) see Duchesne, LP I, pp. cxxxix and 190 n. 25 (counting *Syn.* c. 6 as c. 5).

[59] See Appendix C *infra*.

[30] On the latter canon (c. 7) Panvini, *De episcopatibus* etc. (ch. I n. 2 *supra*) 63 based his conviction that originally the archdeacon alone among the Roman deacons had been cardinal.

[61] *Gesta Polychronii* c. 2 = *Gesta de Xysti purgatione* c. 8: 'Et subscripserunt . . . episcopi vero LXXVI et duo diacones cardinales Romani et tres presbyteri . . .' (Coustant, *Epp. Rom. pont.* app. col. 122; Mansi 5, 1073A).

[62] *Excerpta ex synodalibus gestis s. Silvestri* cc. 2–4 (449 Hinschius).—Duchesne, LP I, cxxxv n. 1 and H. Grisar, *History of Rome and the Popes in the Middle Ages* (author. engl. trans. London 1911–2) III, 218 erroneously deny a transmission of the *Const. Silv.* in Pseudo-Isidore.

[63] *Excerpta* c. 3: 'Presbyter autem cardinalis nisi quadraginta quatuor testibus non damnabitur, diaconus cardinarius constructus urbis Romae nisi in XXXVI non condempnabitur. . . .' For details see Appendix D *infra*.

[64] Not only to the glossators and the authors of the sixteenth century, but even to some modern writers: e.g. McBride, *Incard. and Excard.* (ch. I n. 12 *supra*) 5; P. Pisano, 'Cardinale,' *Enciclopedia Italiana* 8 (1930) 989.

as the time of St. Sylvester—of the Roman cardinal deacons and priests. Chiefly instrumental in spreading such a notion were the canonical collections which transmitted the *Constitutum*—mostly in the Pseudo-Isidorian recension—from the ninth century down to Gratian.[65] But also apart from the canonists, the effects of the Pseudo-Sylvestrine-Isidorian terminology can be seen: e.g. in the *Annales Fuldenses* (late ninth century)[66] or in the pompous eulogist of Emperor Otto I, Liudprand of Cremona (d. 972).[67]

Still, officially the Roman deacons remained but *diacones ecclesiae Romanae* until the eleventh century. 'Ego N. diaconus Romanae ecclesiae' was the style of their synodal signatures,[68] and simply as deacons, not as cardinals, were they referred to in papal letters and by Roman writers.[69] When Stephen III in the Roman Synod of 769 spoke of 'unus de cardinalibus presbiteris aut diaconibus,' he certainly did not mean to extend—although the construction would be grammatically possible—the attribute, *cardinalis*, to the Roman deacons: witness another passage of the synodal acts where the pertinent text reads: '. . . in gradus clericorum sanctae Romanae aecclesiae, id est presbiterorum cardinalium et

---

[65] C. 2 q. 7 cc. 2, 10 + C. 2 q. 4 c. 2 (= *Const. Silv.* c. 3); D. 93 c. 5 (= *Const. Silv.* c. 7). The complex textual history of these canons is by no means clarified in the apparatus of Friedberg's edition. For *Const. Silv.* c. 3, the Pseudo-Isidorian tradition is represented by at least five different families of texts, the archetypes of which are the *Coll. Anselmo dedicata*, Burchard's *Decretum*, Ivo's *Tripartita*, the *Coll. V librorum*, and the *Coll. LXXIV titulorum* respectively (Gratian belongs to the last mentioned group); there are further three traditions independent from Pseudo-Isidore (Angilramnus, Cardinal Atto, and the Frankish capitularies). For *Const. Silv.* c. 7, three families of texts are found, headed by the *Coll. Ans. dedicata*, Burchard, and Anselm of Lucca respectively (the latter being the ancestor of Gratian's text). *Const. Silv.* c. 6 is only transmitted by Deusdedit 2, 43. See appendix D *infra*.

[66] *Ann. Fuld.* an. 885: '. . . et omnium presbyterorum et diaconorum cardinalium . . . scripta destinavit' (ed. F. Kurze, MGH *Script. rer. germ.* Hannover 1891, p. 104; cf. Pertz, MGH *Script.* 1, Hannover 1826, p. 402, 48–50). The pertinent portion of the Annals was written before 888 by Meginhardus, cf. Kurze p. vii.

[67] Liudprand, *Historia Ottonis* c. 1: '. . . nuntios s. Romanae ecclesiae, Iohannem videlicet cardinalem diaconem et Azonem scriniarium . . . regi . . . destinavit' (ed. J. Becker, *Die Werke Liudprands von Cremona*, 3rd ed. MGH *Script. rer. germ.* Hannover-Leipzig 1915, p. 159 lines 7–11; cf. ed. Pertz, MGH *Script.* 3, Hannover 1839, p. 340, 6–8; repeated in E. Dümmler, MGH *Script. rer. germ.* Hannover 1877). And so forth, we read of Roman cardinal deacons in cc. 6, 10, 20, 21, 22 (pp. 163, 1 and 13–4; 166, 26–8; 167, 5–11 and 20–1; 173, 24–5; 174, 5–7 and 23 Becker) and even in the inserted 'original' documents: the imperial synod of November 963 (c. 9: 166, 3–5 Becker), the speech of the Emperor (c. 11: 168, 1 Becker), his letter to Pope John XII (c. 12: 168, 33–4 Becker), and the synodal message to the Pope (c. 14: 171, 1 Becker). But we must remember that the 'originals' are all studded with interpolations in Liudprand's customary, flowery style; see Becker's notes, *passim*, and his introduction, p. xxi.

[68] References to sources are found in Klewitz, *Entstehung* 181 n. 2.

[69] It is impossible to list here every reference or address to a Roman deacon in the papal letters of the early Middle Ages. They may be easily checked in the Indices of the several volumes of *Epistolae* in the MGH (but it should be noted that these Indices sometimes use the incorrect lemma *cardinalis diaconus*). As for Roman writers, see in particular Johannes Diaconus, *Vita s. Greg.* 3, 7 (discussed in sect. 2 *supra*); see also the Greek writers quoted n. 35 *supra*.

diaconorum.'[70] Nor can it be argued that the somewhat younger *Ordo IX Romanus*[71] in its paragraph on the consecration of the Pope comprises the Roman deacons among the cardinals:

> (c.5) Summus namque pontifex quando benedicitur, eligitur unus de cardinalibus, de qualicumque titulo fuerit, tantum ut a praecessore sit pontifice ordinatus aut presbyter aut diaconus, nam episcopus esse non poterit . . . (92 Mabillon).

For, the construction of the passage is logically defective.   The clause 'tantum ut' *rell.* envisages the election of a priest or deacon ordained by a previous Pope, in reminiscence of Stephen III's decree and in particular of the lay intruder Constantine who had been ordained deacon and priest within two days by the Bishop of Palestrina.   But the preceding clause, 'eligitur unus' *rell.*, with its correlation of cardinals and *tituli*, can of necessity apply only to a title priest.   The sentence thus suffers from a change of subject and cannot be adduced as an instance for *diaconus cardinalis.*[72]   And so wherever the higher ranks of the Roman clergy are named together, the added qualification of the presbyters or the Lateran bishops as cardinals cannot be referred to the deacons.[73]

There is only one isolated document, allegedly of the ninth century, which seems to prove the contrary: the fragment discovered by Baronius of a so-called *Constitutio de iure cardinalium* by Pope John VIII (872–82).[74]   This text

[70] Texts ch. III n. 24 *supra.*

[71] Ed. Mabillon, *Mus. ital.* II, 89–94; Martène, *De antiq. eccl. rit.* 1, 8, 11, 9 (II, 151–3 Antw.; II, 54–5 Ven.).—The chronological problems connected with *Ordo IX* (Andrieu's no. XXXVI) are unsolved.   Most authors attribute it to the early ninth century; cf. the references in Klewitz, 'Die Krönung des Papstes,' ZRG *Kan. Abt.* 30 (1941) 111 n. 50.   The assumption of J. Kösters, *Studien zu Mabillons römischen Ordines* (Münster 1905) 2f. that its section on the papal consecration and inthronization had been inserted only at the time of Leo IX (1048–54) has been rightly rejected by most writers.   The thesis is disavowed by the MSS; and particularly the clause 'nam episcopus esse non poterit' would hardly have been written under a Pope who formerly had been bishop of Toul.   If the passage is genuine—as we must assume until the contrary be proved from the earliest MS, St. Gall 614 (9th cent. second half: Andrieu, *Ordines* 487)—one would be inclined to assign the text to the agitated times after the pontificate of Formosus (891–6).   For the reasons which induced the later canonists, Anselm of Lucca 6, 43 (289 Thaner) and Deusdedit 2, 113 (240, 20 Wolf von Glanvell) to suppress this passage, see F. Wasner, 'De consecratione, inthronizatione, coronatione Summi Pontificis,' *Apollinaris* 8 (1935) 100 n. 59; 250 n. 251.

[72] As is done by Buenner, *L'ancienne liturgie rom.* (ch. IV n. 68 *supra*) 270 n. 3.

[73] Besides *Conc. Rom.* 769 and *Ordo IX* the following instances are found: LD 118 (app. IV), dating of the tenth century (cf. Garnier's note and Hinschius, *Kirchenr.* I, 318 n. 3): 'Ego N. s. Romanae ecclesiae diaconus vel presbyter vel episcopus cardinalis electus' (261 Rozière; not in Sickel).   In this form of papal profession of faith the addition of the word *cardinalis* became necessary because a suburbicarian bishop cannot be simply called *S.R.E. episcopus*; in earlier forms, which do not envisage the election (transfer) of a bishop to the Holy See, the adjective is lacking (see e.g. LD 83).—Clement II JL 4134 (an. 1046): 'Totus pene mundus noverit quod specialissimas dignitates nostri episcopi ac cardinales presbyteri atque diacones habeant' (PL 142, 580D).

[74] JE 3366; ed. Baronius, *Annal. eccl.* an. 882 num. 8f. whence Mansi 17, 247–8 and all other editions are derived (cf. Kehr, IP 1, 6 num. 8).—The *Constitutio* should have been discussed by Klewitz, since it represents the most serious objection against his (basically correct) view, *Entstehung* 183: 'Der Terminus diaconus cardinalis ist vor dem 9. Jahrzehnt

194

sanctions, among other prerogatives of the title priests, their hebdomadal service and a relative share in the offerings at the great basilicas, adding the restrictive clause: 'salva semper cardinalium diaconorum prisca consuetudine.'[75] Absolutely speaking, such a terminology at variance with the strict canonical concept of cardinal would not be astonishing in John VIII.[76] But for several reasons the authenticity of the statute, although never challenged heretofore, is more than doubtful. The only extant MS (Rome, Biblioteca Vallicelliana C. 24) dates from the sixteenth century; according to Baronius it was transcribed from a Vatican MS which however can no longer be traced.[77] In the eleventh century, both Alexander II and Urban II in their important decrees dealing with the rights of cardinal priests made no mention of such an earlier statute and of the sweeping jurisdictional privileges it contains.[78] Nor did Deusdedit, that most solicitous advocate of the cardinals' prerogatives,[79] have any information about this text, notwithstanding the systematic researches which were conducted during the Gregorian reform in the archives, in order to unearth older papal documents showing the rights of the Roman Church and its clergy.[80]

The *Constitutio* cannot withstand internal criticism any better. It gives the title priests as a body unlimited right of disciplinary jurisdiction over the Roman clergy, and of contentious jurisdiction over suits between the clergy and the laity.[81] As early as the ninth century such an infringement upon the traditional disciplinary and judicial powers of the archdeacon and the deacons' college—let alone the then flourishing civil jurisdiction of the palatine judges[82]—is hardly

---

des 11. Jahrhunderts aus Originalen päpstlicher Urkunden nicht zu belegen.' If JE 3366 were genuine, it would not matter whether or not the original is lost.

[75] 'Item sancimus de parochiis nostris, quantumque pontifici competit, pontificali beneficio vos in perpetuum possidere et in principalibus ecclesiis iuxta primatum vestrae consecrationis vicissim officia divina peragere et earum oblationibus, salva semper cardinalium diaconorum prisca consuetudine, aequaliter participare. . . .'. Mann, *Lives of the Popes* III (London-St. Louis 1906) 347 is mistaken in holding that this section of the statute 'seemingly' refers to the cardinal bishops. For the correct interpretation see Hinschius, *Kirchenr.* I, 321 with n. 1.

[76] Cf. ch. IV at nn. 38–41 *supra*.

[77] See Kehr, IP 1, 5 (before num. 1). Baronius' footnote *loc. cit.* is unfortunately defective: '. . . reperitur in Vaticanae bibliothecae monumentis: Liber canonum inscriptus num.'

[78] Alexander II: JL 4736 (cf. ch. III at n. 36; IV at n. 105 *supra*); Urban II: Kehr, IP 1, 7 num. 11 (ed. Kehr, *Gött. Nachr.* 1908, p. 228 num. 3; cf. Klewitz, *Entstehung* 161 n. 1). It is therefore not correct when Klewitz 160 speaks of these Popes as having further developed (*weitergebildet*) the statute of John VIII.

[79] Cf. ch. IV nn. 109–10 *supra*.

[80] On these researches see P. Fournier and G. Le Bras, *Histoire des collections canoniques en occident* II (Paris 1932) 7–14; 31f. 46.

[81] 'Itemque . . . vos convenire mandamus (cf. n. 83) et ob vestram et inferiorum clericorum vitam et mores et qualitates et habitus vestium perscrutando, et qualiter quilibet praepositi se erga subditos habeant, vel quod subditi suis praepositis non obediant, et ad quaeque illicita amputanda, clericorum quoque et laicorum querimonias quae ad nostrum iudicium pertinent, quantum fieri potest, definiendas.'

[82] On the *iudices palatini* see Sägmüller, *Cardinäle* 18–24; S. Keller, *Die sieben römischen Pfalzrichter im byzantinischen Zeitalter* (Kirchenrechtliche Abhandlungen ed. Stutz 12, Stuttgart 1904); Halphen, *Etudes sur l'administr.* (n. 6 *supra*) 37–48; Th. Hirschfeld, 'Das

conceivable.   Still more suspect is the fact that, for the discharge of the judicial functions, one passage of the statute prescribes semi-monthly meetings of the presbyters at one or the other title, *diaconia*, or any church whatsoever; while another passage prescribes meetings for the same purpose twice a week at the Lateran palace.[83]   The latter passage further includes a reference: 'iuxta decreta praedecessoris nostri Leonis quarti,' but the only extant decree of Leo IV which could be cited here contains nothing of the kind.[84]   In fact, there is no instance known under or after John VIII which would show the cardinal priests acting as a court of justice.[85]

Other clauses of the *Constitutio* equally arouse suspicion: it says that those among the title priests who are professed religious should take care of Roman monasteries destitute of their abbots and even appoint new abbots.[86]   Yet, monks as priests of the Roman *tituli* are not found at that early date.   It further says that the priests shall be possessed in the parishes, by papal grant, of all that is due to the Pontiff.[87]   But as far as the *tituli* are concerned the priests held all such rights and revenues already by common law, and there existed no other parishes in Rome at that time.   Finally, the clause which describes the hebdomadal service in the major basilicas as following the order of seniority among the

Gerichtswesen der Stadt Rom vom 8. bis 12. Jahrhundert,' *Archiv für Urkundenforschung* 4 (1912) 419–562.—Halphen's assumption (p. 45 n. 6) that at times a Roman deacon might have been also *primicerius notariorum*, i.e. one of the palatine judges, is unfounded; cf. Bresslau, *Urkundenlehre* I, 199 n. 6; Becker, *Liudprand* (n. 67 *supra*) 166 n. 1.

[83] 'Itemque ex nostra praesenti constitutione bis in mense vel eo amplius vel apud illum vel illum titulum, sive apud illam vel illam diaconiam, sive apud alias quaslibet ecclesias vos convenire mandamus et ob vestram et inferiorum . . . (*rell.* n. 81) definiendas.'   And then: '. . . Propter sollicitudinem autem ecclesiarum et eorum clericorum, earumdem disciplinam sive laicorum querimonias definiendas bis in hebdomada ad sacrosanctum palatium, iuxta decreta praedecessoris nostri Leonis quarti, vos convenire mandamus.'

[84] Leo IV JE 2633: 'Precipimus ut in nostra absentia nec ecclesiasticus nec palatinus ordo deficiat.   Sed recurrentibus diebus, tamquam si nos hic fuissemus, omnes nobiles ad Lateranense palatium recurrant et quaerentibus ac petentibus legem ac iustitiam faciant' (ed. A. de Hirsch-Gereuth, MGH *Epp.* 5, 599).   Sägmüller, *Cardinäle* 23 and Hirschfeld, *Gerichtswesen* 450 consider *nobiles* a collective noun for *ordo ecclesiasticus* and *ordo palatinus*, and therefore would have it include also the cardinals.   This interpretation is untenable. Even Sägmüller must admit that a reference to JE 2633 in the *Constitutio* is not more than a slight possibility (pp. 23, 36 n. 3).   In fact, JE 3366 regards the cardinal priests, but JE 2633, the palatine judges.

[85] Among the judicial documents gathered by Hirschfeld, *Gerichtswesen* 456ff. there is none coming from the cardinals before the twelfth century (compare p. 456 n. 4 with 458 n. 3: *iudices palatini*; see also 493ff.).   Nonetheless Hirschfeld 449–51 upholds judicial functions of the cardinals, even of the deacons and bishops (!), on the strength of the *Constitutio*.   The examples given by Sägmüller 30 n. 5 for cardinals as judges side by side with the *iudices palatini* in the eleventh century (JL 4075; Kehr, IP 2, 66 num. 40) are not to the point, because these were judgments rendered by the Popes themselves with the several cardinals and curial officers only assisting.

[86] 'Item monasteria abbatibus viduata et abbatum nostra praecedente conscientia substitutionem his qui sunt inter vos vel fuerint monasticae professionis disponenda committimus.'

[87] Text in n. 75 *supra*.   For the interpretation see Hinschius, *Kirchenr.* I, 320 n. 3.

196

title priests[88] is at variance with the established assignment of determinate *tituli* to determinate basilicas.

All this evidence speaks against the genuineness of the *Constitutio de iure cardinalium* and for its being fabricated at a later time, when the original functions of the *tituli* and their presbyterate were waning, but when, on the other hand, the jurisdictional powers of the cardinal priests had been greatly increased and extremist tendencies were rampant to push these powers still farther. That would bring us down at least to the time of Guibert's schism (1080–1100) and to a schismatic cardinal as the possible author of the *Constitutio*.[89] By this time, the qualification of the Roman deacons as *cardinales* was no longer a startling manner of speech, as it would have been three centuries before, under John VIII.

In the course of these centuries we have witnessed the decay of the canonical terminology regarding cardinals. Outside of Rome, *cardinales diaconi* were nothing unusual among the self-styled cardinal clergy of Italian cathedrals, and even among the 'liturgical' cardinals created abroad by papal privileges since the late tenth century.[90] With the original meaning of the term obliterated, it was to be expected that it should become applied to the deacons of the Church of Rome, too.

The first authentic papal document to do so dates from 1018. It is a privilege made out by Benedict VIII for the Cardinal bishop of Porto, granting to him and his successors the island of St. Bartholomew in the Tiber, with all its churches, houses and appurtenances in perpetual freehold, together with full powers of ordination extending over all the Trastevere, with the sole exception that there shall be no power of ordaining any one to be 'cardinalis presbyter, vel cardinalis diaconus vel subdiaconus vel acolythus sacri palatii Lateranensis.'[91] This charter, in that it surrenders a considerable part of the Pope's episcopal jurisdiction in his own diocese, is typical of the alarming disintegration of diocesan unity in the very city of Rome during that period. Even more sweeping rights, for instance, were granted a few years later (1026) by John XIX to the Bishop of Silva-Candida for St. Peter and its suburb[92]—which eventually led to a clash

---

[88] Text in n. 75 *supra*.

[89] Perhaps even later: one clause of the statute compares the cardinal priests to the seventy elders in *Num*. 11, 16; otherwise this simile is not applied before St. Bernard of Clairvaux, *De consideratione* 4, 4 (PL 182, 778B).

[90] Cf. ch. IV nn. 9ff. and for the liturgical cardinals, *ibid*. nn. 50 (Magdeburg), 52 (Aachen); no cardinal deacons were created, however, for Treves, Besançon, Cologne, Compostella.

[91] JL 4024 (cf. the text in PL 139, 1621B; some editions—e.g. *Bullarium Taurinense* 1, 527—omit the words 'cardinalis presbyter vel'). The privilege was later confirmed by John XIX and Leo IX (JL 4067, 4163). Klewitz, *Entstehung* 183 (cf. n. 74 *supra*) overlooks this text; but even if the original is lost, we have the authenticated transcript made from it under Gregory IX (Auvray, *Les registres de Grégoire IX*, Paris 1890ff. num. 3553), cf. Kehr, IP 2, 20 n. 10.

[92] JL 4076, including the possession of monasteries and churches; ordaining powers for St. Peter and the *civitas Leonina*; the right to pontificate in Holy Week and to baptize on Holy Saturday in St. Peter's; jurisdiction and judicial powers in all these churches, etc. (see Hinschius, *Kirchenr*. I, 330f.). Later confirmed by Benedict IX and, to a limited

between the sees of Silva-Candida and Porto.[93]

On the background of such abnormal conveyances we cannot expect much canonical precision as to the nomenclature for members of the Roman clergy. Still, Pope Benedict VIII's mention of *cardinalis diaconus s. palatii Lateranensis* remains an *obiter dictum*. For the greater part of the eleventh century, the official style, *diacones s. Romanae ecclesiae*, continued unchanged.[94] Even Gregory VII who in his earlier career occasionally had signed his name as 'Hildebrandus S.R.E. cardinalis subdiaconus'—one of the very rare instances of a Roman cardinal sub-deacon[95]—did not qualify, during his pontificate, the Roman deacons as cardinals.[96] Also the author of the *Descriptio* avoided the term for the deacons: a signal precision in full accord with his correctness in relating the cardinalate of the bishops and priests to their respective basilicas of incardination.[97] Only when *cardinalis* had definitely become, toward the end of the century, a dignity connoting participation in the supreme government of the Church, were name and dignity extended almost by intrinsic necessity to that class of Roman clerics who had formed a body of ministers to the Pope since the earliest times.[98]

It is significant for the political reasons connected with this development that the deacons of Anti-pope Clement III (Guibert) were the first to change their official signature into *diaconus cardinalis*.[99] As for the legitimate papacy, the

---

extent, by Victor II (JL 4110, 4366).

[93] The controversy broke out about the *insula Lycaonia*, which was mentioned in both privileges. Leo IX in 1049 decided in favor of Porto (JL 4163; cf. Kehr, IP 2, 20f. num. 12–3). However, some seventy years later (c. 1120–4) Silva-Candida, which had been vacant since 1074 because of the depopulation resulting from malaria (cf. Klewitz, *Entstehung* 138ff.), was united by Calixtus II to Porto (Kehr, IP 2, 21 n. 14).

[94] See e.g. John XIX JL 4076 to the Cardinal bishop of Silva-Candida: '. . . aliquem diaconorum nostrorum ministrare' (PL 141, 1130B); references to synodal subscriptions are found in Klewitz, *Entstehung* 181 n. 2.

[95] See Klewitz 190f. (references in n. 3) who also shows that Sägmüller, *Cardinäle* 11 nn. 1–2, is wrong in assuming that the appellative, *cardinalis*, was occasionally used by Roman acolytes, and by the *mansionarii* of St. Peter's. Klewitz fails however to discuss the following isolated instances of cardinal subdeacons: Urban II in 1088 to Lanfranc of Canterbury (JL 5351): '. . . dilectissimus filius noster Rogerus cardinalis ecclesiae nostrae sub-diaconus' (PL 151, 287A; cf. Hinschius I, 320 n. 1—although *cardinalis* may here belong to *ecclesiae*) and Calixtus II in 1123 (JL 7045): 'Data per manum Hugonis S.R.E. subdiaconi cardinalis' (PL 163, 1280C; cf. Sägmüller 11 n. 1; on the subdeacon Hugo see Bresslau, *Urkundenlehre* I, 246). Note also that among the liturgical cardinals created in other metropoles by papal privilege there were twenty-four cardinal subdeacons in Magdeburg (ch. IV n. 50 *supra*).

[96] References in Klewitz 183 n. 5. It may be added that the letters JL 5079 ('Data per manum Johannis S.R.E. diaconi cardinalis') and 5256 ('Data p.m. Cartan' S.R.E. diaconi cardinalis et cancellarii') are not genuine, cf. Bresslau, *Urkundenlehre* I, 239 n. 6.

[97] Cf. nn. 37–8 and ch. III n. 38 *supra*. Klewitz, *Entstehung* 183, 186.

[98] This may also be connected with, and was at least supported by, the revival of the *Constitutum Silvestri* in the canonical collections (*Coll. LXXIV tit.*; Anselm; Deusdedit) of the Gregorian era. Deusdedit was the first to speak of the *levitae summi pontificis* as cardinals, ch. IV n. 109 *supra*.

[99] Kehr, *Zur Geschichte Wiberts* (ch. IV n. 98 *supra*) 987; Klewitz, *Entstehung* 184.

198

new style was introduced, first for the seven deacons proper, by Urban II (1088–99).[100] Under his successor Paschal II (1099–1118) we find the cardinalate extended to all eighteen papal deacons; that is, the twelve 'regionals' of comparatively recent origin advanced to equal rank with the old palatine college. Moreover, in the same pontificate the new cardinals began to add to their signatures, each the name of his *diaconia:* 'Ego N. diaconus cardinalis sancti (-ae) N.'[101]—as if the newly acquired diaconal churches could simply be likened to the presbyteral *tituli* and the episcopal sees of the other cardinals. The full assimilation of the cardinal deacons to their senior colleagues was thus accomplished. The original meaning of the term *cardinalis* was definitely extinct.

The later history of the Sacred College lies beyond the range of this study, for the concept of a cardinal underwent no further change. To be sure, the clerics of some metropolitan cathedrals continued to style themselves as *cardinales* until the sixteenth century,[102] but this anachronism had no longer any canonical significance. Compared with the Senate of the Roman Church, their cardinalate—as the glossators have put it[103]—was worth as much as the royal dignity of the king of chess.

APPENDIX A (cf. ch. II nn. 9, 43, 47)

THE DIOCESE OF TERAMO (APRUTIUM, INTERAMNA)

The origins of the diocese of Teramo are shrouded in darkness. Of the place itself, *castrum Aprutii*, we hear for the first time in St. Gregory's letter *Reg.* 9, 71 (JE 1596):

[100] Cf. the list of subscriptions in JL I, 657; Klewitz *loc. cit.* and p. 185 n. 3.—In announcing his election to the Archbishop of Salzburg, Urban II still contrasts *omnes cardinales* with *omnes diaconi* (JL 5348, cf. Klewitz 184); but in the simultaneous letter to Abbot Hugo of Cluny (JL 5349) he already mentions among his electors: 'S.R.E. episcopi et cardinales, . . . abbas vero Casinensis cardinalis diaconus ceterorum diaconorum, P. (*leg.* R.) quoque cardinalis tituli s. Clementis omnium cardinalium' (PL 151, 285A).

[101] Also for this step the fashion had been set by Guibert, cf. Kehr *loc. cit.*; Klewitz 184, 189. Subscriptions of cardinal deacons with the *diaconia* appear in Paschal II's letters from the beginning of his pontificate (cf. the list in Klewitz 218–21 nos. 2, 3, 4, 14, also JL I, 702f.), not only in 1116 (thus Hinschius, *Kirchenr.* I, 322 n. 2). But the new style was not yet firmly established: subscriptions reading simply *diaconus cardinalis* are numerous as well under Pope Paschal (see JL *loc. cit.*; also Klewitz 187 for the deacon Theobald). The deacon Johannes of St. Mary in Cosmedin (the future Gelasius II) occasionally used even to sign as 'Johannes diaconus de titulo (!) Cosmidin' (1107, February 24–September 1: JL I, 702).

[102] E.g. Ravenna, Naples (Hinschius I, 319 n. 7); the cardinals of Compostella even after the statute *Non mediocri* of Pius V (February 17, 1567) which reserved the name of cardinal to the Sacred College: Gonzalez Tellez, *Commentaria . . . decretalium Greg. IX* (Lyons 1673) 1, 24, 2 ad v. *sacerdotum cardinalium* treats the dignity as still persisting. For the noncatholic cardinals of London see ch. IV n. 81 *supra.*

[103] Johannes Teutonicus, *Glossa ordinaria* on C. 32 q. 2 c. 1 ad v. *principem mundi:* '. . . vel ad derisionem dicitur (diabolus scil.) princeps talium, sicut dicitur rex schacorum, vel cardinalis Ravennas, non tamen simpliciter est rex vel cardinalis . . .'; frequently repeated, e.g. by Prospero Fagnani, *Commentaria in libros decretalium* (Rome 1661) 1, 5, 3 num. 14: '. . . dicuntur cardinales sicut dicitur rex scaccorum, ut inquit glos. in c. Pudorem in ver. Principem mundi, 32 q. 2' (I, 277).

Bishop Passivus of Fermo was ordered by the Pope in November or December, 598, to consecrate an oratory built in honor of St. Peter by 'Anio comes castri Aprutiensis Firmensis' at his castle or village (*castrum*) if, says the Pope, 'in tuae dioceseos, in qua visitationis impendis officium, memorata constructio iure consistit' (2, 90, 11–6 Hartmann). The bishop was also to install a cardinal priest at the oratory,[1] but evidently he did not find a worthy candidate. For, three years later (October or November, 601), St. Gregory writes to Passivus (*Reg.* 12, 4; JE 1855) that Aprutium has been for a long time destitute of pastoral care; 'ubi diu quaesivimus quis ordinari debuisset, et nequaquam potuimus invenire' (350, 9–11 Hartmann). The bishop now shall call upon a certain Oportunus and, if he sees fit, ordain him subdeacon, 'et post aliquantum tempus, si Deo tum placuerit, ipse ad pastoralem curam debeat promoveri' (350, 15–7 Hartmann).

Historians have gone far astray in interpreting these two letters as dealing with a visitation by the bishop of Fermo in the diocese of Teramo.[2] In fact, St. Gregory expressly speaks of the oratory as situated *in tua diocesi*, and of Count Anio as *comes castri Aprutiensis Firmensis*; that is, the place was at that time known as *Aprutium Firmense*: Teramo in the diocese or territory of Fermo. (The reading '. . . Aprutiensis Firmensis territorii' in the Maurist edition is interpolated, but substantially more to the point than Hartmann's impossible construction[3] of *Firmensis* as referring to the person of Anio, 'a native of Fermo').—Also in *Reg.* 12, 4 the Pope does not speak of *ecclesia Aprutina*[4]— which indeed would mean 'the bishopric of Teramo'—but only of *Aprutium*; see also *Reg.* 12, 5 (JE 1856), addressed: 'Oportuno de Aprutio'. Nor does St. Gregory contemplate Oportunus as prospective bishop, but only as a future choice for *pastoralis cura*; a qualification which applies to bishops as well as to rectors of baptismal churches. In fact, *Reg.* 9, 71 shows that Count Anio's oratory was soon to obtain parochial functions.[5]

In Pope Hilary's Roman Synod of 465 a Bishop Praetextatus *Interamnanus* was present (160 Thiel), and among the signatories of Pope Symmachus' Synods of 501 and 502, Felix *episcopus Interamnensis* is found (667, 693 Thiel). Mommsen, in the valuable *Index locorum* appended to his edition of Cassiodorus' *Variae*, declined a decision as to which of the three ancient *Interamnae* (*-nia*)—namely *Int. Lirenas Sucasena* in Campania; *Int. Praetuttianorum Piceni* (= Teramo); *Int. Nahars Umbriae* (= Terni)—would be meant in these texts.[6] Lanzoni, without giving his reasons, decided for Terni.[7] Indeed this seems the only possible solution. The obscure place in Campania was never a bishopric; Teramo was not yet a bishopric a hundred years after Symmachus as we must conclude from St. Gregory's correspondence; but for the early origins of Terni (founded by St. Peregrinus?) there exists an old literary tradition.[8] It must have been the Bishops of Terni who sat in the Roman synods of the fifth and sixth centuries.

---

[1] Cf. ch. II n. 43 *supra*.

[2] To name only the more recent representatives of the *opinio communis*: Phillips, *Kirchenr.* V, 459 n. 8; 462 n. 15; also VI, 57; Hinschius, *Kirchenr.* I, 313 n. 4; Ewald in his summaries (JE 1596, 1855); Hartmann, MGH *Epp.* 2, 90 n. 2; Peitz, *Lib. diurn.* 76; Kehr, IP 4, 311 num. 1–2; F. Lanzoni, *Le origini delle antiche diocesi d'Italia* (Studi e Testi 35, Rome 1923) 257.

[3] MGH *Epp.* 2, 90 n. 2.

[4] JE 1855, Hartmann 2, 350 and Kehr incorrectly use this form in calendaring the letter.

[5] Cf. ch. II n. 43 *supra*.

[6] MGH *Auct. antiquiss.* 12, 505: 'parum liquet. . . .'

[7] *Op. cit.* 261, wrongly ascribing in note 4 his own opinion to Mommsen.

[8] Cf. Gams, *Series episcop.* 730; Kehr, IP 4, 18.

At the present state of research, there exists no historical evidence for Teramo as a diocese before the ninth century; i.e. before a letter written by Pope John VIII to John, the *reverendus Aprutiensis antistes*.[9]

APPENDIX B (cf. ch. II n. 63)

OFFICIUM CARDINALE, PRINCEPS CARDINALIS

It might be permissible to ask whether the abundant evidence for *cardinalis* <*(in)-cardinare* in ecclesiastical administration should not induce the student of late Roman history to reconsider the current interpretations of the scanty texts in which the crucial term is found with reference to secular administrative institutions. From the *Notitia dignitatum* we learn that in the military hierarchy of the East two of the five imperial *magistri militum*—to wit, the second *magister militum praesentalis* (Master in Presence, scil. of the Emperor) and the *magister militum per Orientem*—have each a bureau (*officium*) which is termed *cardinale*;[10] while each of the respective staffs of the three other *magistri* 'in numeris militat et in officio deputatur.'[11] As the five Masters were equal in rank and command,[12] the reason for this discrimination remains unexplained to the present day.[13] But ever since Gothofredus the text itself has been understood as referring to *officia cardinalia* in the sense of bureaus consisting of a proper, permanent and ordinary personnel of their own, and as set over against those which are merely composed of soldiers detailed for office work from the troops.[14] This common explanation, however, appears to be contradicted by the fact that the *cardinale officium* obtained its chief subordinate official, the foreman or *princeps*, from another agency: like the *principes* serving on the staffs of prefects, governors, and other high ranking dignitaries, the head of the bureau of a *magister militum* was sent from the *schola agentium in rebus*, i.e. from the body of officials that stood under the jurisdiction of the *magister officiorum*.[15] The *princeps* of a 'cardinal' office therefore was, strictly speaking, outside the *officium*,[16] and thus it could be well argued that the *Notitia* speaks of a *cardinale officium*, in contradistinction to an office entirely manned by career soldiers from the ranks, with a meaning exactly opposite

---

[9] The lost letter (Kehr, IP 4, 311 num. 4) is mentioned in the same Pope's letter JE 3310 (Kehr 312 num. 5); ed. Caspar, MGH *Epp.* 7, 204, 13.

[10] *Not. dign. Or.* 6, 70; 7, 59 (24 and 28 Böcking; 18 and 22 Seeck).

[11] *Not. dign. Or.* 5, 67 (first Master in Presence: 20 Böcking; 14 Seeck); 8, 54 (*magister mil. per Thracias*: 32 Böcking; 25 Seeck); 9, 49 (*magister mil. per Illyricum*: 35 Böcking; 30 Seeck).

[12] E. Stein, *Geschichte des spätrömischen Reiches* I (Wien 1928) 367; *contra* R. Grosse, *Römische Militärgeschichte* (Berlin 1920) 186f. See also Stein's review in *Byzantinische Zeitschrift* 25 (1925) 386f.

[13] Gothofr. *Comm. Cod. Th.* 12, 6, 7; and, more recently, A. E. R. Boak, 'Officium,' PWK 17, 2 (1937) 2049.

[14] Gothofr. *loc. cit.*; Böcking, *Not. dign.* I, 205 n. 50; Mommsen, 'Ostgothische Studien,' NA 14 (1888–9) 472; O. Karlowa, *Römische Rechtsgeschichte* I (Leipzig 1885) 877; Boak *loc. cit.*

[15] Karlowa, *op. cit.* 881; J. B. Bury, *History of the Later Roman Empire* (London 1923) I, 31f.; Boak, 'The Master of the Offices in the Later Roman and Byzantine Empires,' in *Two Studies in Later Roman and Byzantine Administration* (University of Michigan Studies, Humanistic Series 14, New York 1924) 72; id. PWK 17, 2054; and in particular Stein, *Geschichte* I, 367, citing Marchi, in *Studi giuridici in onore di C. Fadda* 5 (1906) 381f. 393f. See also Stein, 'Untersuchungen zum Staatsrecht des Bas-Empire,' ZRG *Rom. Abt.* 41 (1920) 195ff. 212.

[16] Bury, *op. cit.* 32. It is not correct when Mommsen *loc. cit.* asserts that the two *magistri militum* in question had 'einen eigenen Princeps'.

to that assumed by the common opinion: namely with reference to the 'civil servants'[17] incardinated from the *magisterium officiorum* into the bureau staffs of certain military officials.

Another instance is found in the State Papers of Cassiodorus (c. 537). Among the various formulae of the Ostrogothic royal chancery he records a form letter dealing with the *comitiacum officium*, i.e. the constabulary force or agency established for dispatching, serving, and executing royal orders. The letter in question (*Var*. 7, 31) states that not only at the king's residence in Ravenna but also in Rome 'necesse sit partem ibi esse comitiaci officii' and continues by commissioning a subordinate official, 'ut quia principem cardinalem obsequiis nostris deesse non patimur, tu eius locum vicarii nomine in urbe Roma sollemniter debeas continere.'[18] Why is the foreman of the *comitiaci*—the chief provost marshal[19]—styled in this text as *princeps cardinalis*? Mommsen, who considered the *comitiaci* a Gothic variety of the *agentes in rebus*, consequently held that their *princeps* was none but the foreman of the *schola agentium* (that is, ultimately, the head of the bureau of the *magister officiorum*) and that he was *cardinalis* because he essentially and properly belonged to this *officium*, in contradistinction to officials detached to it from other departments.[20] Professor Stein, who accepts Mommsen's premise as to the nature of the *comitiaci*, but who moreover holds that the *principes* of the *schola agentium* were at the same time *principes* of the bureaus of the several praetorian prefectures in the Empire, prefers to explain *princeps cardinalis* as the office chief of the central prefecture (*praefectura praetorio in comitatu*), in contrast with the *principes* of any *pars officii* outside the residence.[21] However, if Seeck be right, the *comitiaci* were not *agentes in rebus* but originally officials of the *comes* or *magister militum*, and as such immediately subject to the king.[22] In this case, one could assume that the chief of the staff of *comitiaci* was called *cardinalis* for the simple reason that the Ostrogothic king, since Theodoric, held himself the dignity of an imperial *magister militum praesentalis*[23] and was therefore entitled to an *officium cardinale*, whatever that meant, under the *Notitia dignitatum*.

But the text admits also of another explanation. We know that the seat of many high ranking officials had been transferred, along with the center of administration, from Rome to Ravenna, while deputies (*vices gerentes*) were appointed in the old capital.[24] Thus the chief provost marshal who now appeared as *princeps cardinalis* of the constabulary at the court of Ravenna may originally have been *princeps comitiaci officii* in Rome:

---

[17] For the civil nature of the service rendered by a *princeps officii*, even of a military official, see Stein, ZRG 41, 198 ('Die Stellung . . . ist . . . durchaus die eines friedlichen Kanzleibeamten'); for parallel instances in which military-administrative positions were filled, not by officers from the ranks, but by members of the *schola agentium*, see *ibid*. 213f.

[18] Ed. Mommsen, MGH *Auct. antiquiss*. 12, 218, 23–6.

[19] Hinschius, *Kirchenr*. I, 319 n. 9 speaks of him as *praefectus urbis*.

[20] Mommsen, *Ostgothische Studien* 470f. Cf. also Gothofr. *loc. cit*. and Muratori, *Antiq*. 5, 156 (he understands the 'cardinal' principate as *stabilis dignitas* and *ordinaria auctoritas*, contrasted with mere vicarious power). Mommsen's view on the *comitiaci* is shared by Bury, *op. cit*. I, 458 n. 2 and by Stein, cf. the following note.

[21] Stein, ZRG 41, 219f. 226; 232–4; id. *Untersuchungen zum Officium der Prätorianerpräfektur seit Diokletian* (Wien 1922).

[22] O. Seeck, 'Comitiaci,' PWK 4, 1 (1900) 715–6; Boak, *Master of the Offices* 73. *Contra* Stein, book review, *Byzant. Zeitschr*. 25 (1925) 174.

[23] Cf. Bury, *op. cit*. I, 413; 457f. Assunta Nagl, 'Theoderich,' PWK 2nd ser. 5, 2 (1934) 1749.

[24] Cassiod. *Var*. 11, 4–5; 12, 25. Cf. Mommsen, *Ostgoth. Stud*. 463; Boak, *Master of the Offices* 43.

for the addressee of Cassiod. *Var.* 7, 31 is told to take 'eius locum vicarii nomine'. With the transfer of the *principatus in urbe Roma* (the term is used in the rubric of the formula) the *princeps* had become incardinated in the royal residence, and therefore *cardinalis*.

The tentative interpretations presented here of the two crucial texts are, to be sure, of a purely hypothetical nature. But it may be said in favor of this hypothesis that it is not less well founded than the current explanations. On the contrary, it has the advantage of linking the term *cardinalis*, in the rare instances where it is found with texts treating of state administration, with the established usage in the, at least, somewhat related field of church government, rather than with cosmographical, arithmetical, or theological locutions.[25]

APPENDIX C (cf. ch. V n. 59)

THE PSEUDO-SYLVESTRIAN RULE OF SEVENTY-TWO WITNESSES FOR A BISHOP'S TRIAL

The Symmachian forgers resorted to the rule that a bishop could be tried only on the testimony of seventy-two witnesses in *Const. Silv.* c. 3 and again in another of their productions, the *Gesta Marcellini papae* (or 'Synod of Sinuessa'):[26]

(c. 6) ... ut intra hos LXXII testimonia ipse iudex, ipse reus, ipse semetipsum praesentia eorum innocentem se servaret et infidelem se damnaret: quoniam in LXXII libra occidua[27] reparationem resurgit annus (31 Coustant; 1253E–4A Mansi).

(c. 12) ... quoniam duodecim unciae in libra probabitur sensus, et in LXXII comparatus damnabitur praesul (34 Coustant; 1256C Mansi).

Both the *Const. Silv.* and the *Gesta Marcell.* may or may not have been influenced by the fact that Bishop Macedonius of Constantinople had been deposed, in 360, παρουσίᾳ ἐπισκόπων οβ' ('praesentibus episcopis LXXII'), according to the *Chronicon Paschale*;[28] and that a certain ex-bishop Chronopius is spoken of in *Cod. Theod.* 11, 36, 20 (an. 369) as having been first condemned by seventy bishops: 'Quoniam Chronopius ex antistite idem fuit in tuo, qui fuerat in septuaginta episcoporum ante iudicio, et eam sententiam provocatione suspendit ...'.[29] Also St. Augustine's *Breviculus collationis cum Donatistis* 2, 14, 26 may be quoted in this connection: '... et recitatum est a Donatistis concilium ferme septuaginta episcoporum contra Caecilianum apud Carthaginem factum, ubi eum absentem condemnaverunt.'[30] But it is not correct when these texts, which mention seventy or more bishops sitting as judges in synodal trials, are adduced as instances of a procedure

---

[25] For these locutions see ch. II nn. 61–2 *supra*.

[26] On these *Gesta* see Coustant, *Epp. Rom. pont.* p. lxxxiv f.; app. col. 27f. Duchesne, LP I, cxxxiii f. The text given above is Coustant's, app. col. 31ff. Chief variants from Mansi 1, 1253ff. (cf. also Coustant 34 note *i*):—(c. 6) hos] horum.—praesentia] in praesentia. —et] aut.—reparationem] in reparationem.—(c. 12) unciae] unciis.—sensus] census.— comparatus] comparentibus.

[27] On *libra occidua* cf. Gothofr. *Comm. Cod. Th.* 11, 36, 20 (V, 308 Lugd.; IV, 322 Lips.); Binius' note *d* in Mansi 1, 1260; Coustant 30 note *b*. See also *Gesta Marcell.* c. 3: 'Hi omnes electi sunt viri libra occidua qui testimonium perhibent videntes eum (se vidisse eundem *Mansi*) Marcellinum thurificasse' (30 Coustant; 1252D Mansi).

[28] *Chron. Pasch.* Olymp. 285 (ed. Dindorf, Corpus Script. Histor. Byzant. Bonn 1832, p. 294 = PG 92, 736).

[29] Ed. Mommsen-Meyer (Berlin 1905) I, 651. Cf. Gothofr. *loc. cit.*; Hinschius, *Kirchenr.* IV, 794, n. 6.

[30] Ed. M. Petschenig, CSEL 53 (1910) 75. Cf. Gothofr. *loc. cit.*

with so many witnesses, i.e. as furnishing a factual basis to the claims of the Symmachian forgers.[31]

From the ninth century onwards, however, the Roman Church considered the 'Sylvestrian' number of seventy-two witnesses against bishops as canonical. Evidence of this are the following papal letters: (1) Leo IV (JE 2599, an. 847–8) to the bishops of Brittany;[32] (2) a lost letter of Benedict III (JE 2671*, an. 855–8), quoted along with JE 2599 by: (3) Nicholas I in 862 (JE 2708) to King Solomon of Brittany;[33] (4) Nicholas I's great epistle to Emperor Michael on the Photian affair, in 865 (JE 2796), where not only *Const. Silv.* c. 3 ('Fecit gradus *rell.* . . . super magistrum') but also several other texts from the Symmachian forgeries are quoted.[34] Cf. also the papal legates in the first Photian Synod (861), act. 4: 'Item apocrisiarii dixerunt: "Canon s. Siluestri docet ut episcopus non condemnetur nisi in LXXII testibus" . . .'.[35]

APPENDIX D (cf. ch. V n. 65)

NOTES ON THE MEDIEVAL TRANSMISSION OF THE CONSTITUTUM SILVESTRI

The literary and textual history of the *Constitutum Silvestri* (= CS) cannot be written before the countless MSS of unprinted, or uncritically printed, canonical collections preceding Gratian[36] are again accessible. The following notes have the much more limited purpose of showing, as far as printed information allows, the diversified forms of transmission of those three canons which perpetuated the 'Sylvestrian' usage of *cardinalis*: CS cc. 3, 6, 7. The fourth pertinent canon (c. 11) may be left aside since it had no influence to speak of. For the parallel text on interstices in the pseudo-'Synod of the 270 Bishops' (c. 6 *al.* 5) does not contain the term *diaconus cardinalis*, and it was this latter text, not CS, which served as model to the note in LP I, 171, 15ff.[37]—which in turn was paraphrased in Pseudo-Isidore's *Excerpta ex synodalibus gestis s. Silvestri* (= PsI) c. 7.[38]

In describing the medieval tradition of CS cc. 3, 6, 7, the early collections (6th–8th cent.) which reproduce the integral form of the *Constitutum* are not considered. They have been studied by Maassen, Duchesne, Turner, and others.[39] The complications of

---

[31] Thus Wolf von Glanvell, *Deusdedit* 609 n. 27, confusing moreover Chronopius with the notorious Chromatius, and the *Conc. Cp.* of 360 (on which see Hefele-Leclercq, *Histoire des conciles* I, 2, Paris 1907, pp. 956–9) with the Ecumenical Synod of 381.

[32] Ed. Dümmler, MGH *Epp.* 5, 2 (Berlin 1899) 593, 34–594, 5. Cf. Gratian, C. 2 q. 4 c. 3.

[33] Ed. Perels, MGH *Epp.* 6, 2, i (1912) 621, 1–6.

[34] 466, 24–9 Perels and *passim*; cf. Coustant, app. cols. 37–8; Perels 464 n. 3, 465 nn. 1–3 etc.

[35] Deusd. 4, 431 (609, 14–5 Wolf von Glanvell).

[36] Reference is made once for all to P. Fournier and G. Le Bras, *Histoire des collections canoniques en occident depuis les fausses décrétales jusqu'au Décret de Gratien* (Paris 1931–2).

[37] Duchesne, LP I, cxxxix; 190 n. 25.

[38] Hinschius, *Decretales Pseudo-Isidorianae* 450.

[39] Cf. ch. V n. 56 *supra*.—Still less can we enter here upon a discussion of the peculiar, abridged form which the Collection of Chieti (6th cent.) gave to the pseudo-Sylvestrian statutes (ed. Duchesne, LP I, cxxxiv col. 2 n. 1; for one signal variant, the omission of 'cardine constructus' in CS c. 3, see ch. V n. 57 *supra*). The text of the *Theatina* had a medieval tradition of its own which is largely unexplored. It influenced a passage of the LP (see n. 42 *infra*) and c. 51 of the so-called *Poenitentiale II Vallicellianum* (cf. E. Seckel, 'Studien zu Benedictus Levita: VII,' NA 35 [1909] 139 n. 5); it even reappeared, transmitted

source history begin only when we first meet with selections and transformations. On the other hand, CS cc. 14–16 are included in the analysis[40] because we shall find them frequently contaminated or combined with c. 3.

I. *The Fourfold Tradition of CS c. 3*

A. The Frankish Capitularies

1. *Capitula excerpta de canone* (c. 806): 'Fecit hos gradus in gremio synodi—mystica veritas' (ed. Boretius, MGH *Cap.* 1, 133, 41–134, 8).—Source: *Collectio Andegavensis*, according to C. De Clercq, *Législation religieuse franque* (ch. IV n. 27 *supra*) 156 n. 1.
2. Ansegisus, *Capitularia regum Francorum* (827) 1, 133: 'Fecit hos gradus—mystica veritas' (411, 29–38 Boretius).—Source: *Cap. exc. de can.*
3. Benedictus Levita, *Capitularia* (after 847) 1, 302: 'Fecit hos gradus—mystica veritas' (ed. Pertz, MGH *Leg.* 2, 2, 63).—Source: Ansegisus. Cf. E. Seckel, 'Studien zu Benedictus Levita: VI,' NA 31 (1905) 103 and n. 2.

Leading variants:

(*CS c.3*) Postea autem fecit gradus] Fecit hos gradus *Cap. Ansg. Ben.*
testimonia] testimoniis *Ansg.* testibus *Ben.*
constructus] constitutus *Cap.* (*var.*) *Ansg. Ben.*
urbis Romae] in urbe Roma *Cap. Ansg. Ben.*
in XXXVI] triginta septem *Cap. Ansg.*
testimonia] testimoniis *Ansg. Ben.*

B. Cardinal Atto and Deusdedit 4, 329

1. Atto, *Capitulare* (c. 1073–6) rubr. *Ex decretis Silvestri* c. 1: 'Non presbyter adversus —det accusationem aliquam.' c. 2: 'Non dampnabitur episcopus—exorcista, lector, in duobus vel tribus testimoniis.' c. 5: 'Nulli omnino clerico licere causam in publico examinare, nec ullum clericum ante iudicem laicum stare placet.' c. 8: 'Testimonium— recipiat' (ed. A. Mai, *Scriptorum veterum nova collectio* 6, 2, Rome 1832, p. 70).—Sources: (c. 1) CS c. 3, first sentence; (c. 2) *id.* rest abridged; (c. 5) *Syn. 270 episc.* c. 5 (ed. Poisnel, *Mélanges d'archéol. et d'hist.* 6 [1886] 5; cf. Mansi 2, 1082D; Duchesne, LP I, cxxxix [c. 4]); (c. 8) CS c. 14.
2. Deusdedit, *Coll. can.* (1087) 4, 329: (a) 'Nulli omnino—stare placet.' (b) 'Testimonium—recipiat.' (c) 'Clericus inferioris ordinis non det aliquam accusationem adversus potiorem' (567 Wolf von Glanvell).—Sources: (a–b) Atto cc. 5, 8; (c) free summary of CS c. 3, probably indirectly, as found in Atto c. 1.

Leading variants (only Atto collated for CS c. 3):

by channels unknown, in a southern French law book of the early twelfth century, i.e. in the respective appendices of the London and Cambridge MSS of the *Liber Tubingensis* (cf. H. Kantorowicz, *Studies in the Glossators of the Roman Law*, Cambridge 1938, p. 120f. with bibliography; ed. p. 270). Unfortunately, both Kantorowicz's discussion and edition of this piece suffer from his failure to take cognizance of the full text of the canon in *Coll. Theat.* as published by Duchesne.

[40] CS c. 14: 'Testimonium clerici adversus laicum nemo recipiat.' c. 15: 'Nemo enim clericum quemlibet in publico examinet, nisi in ecclesia.' c. 16: 'Nemo enim clericus vel diaconus aut presbyter propter causam suam quamlibet intret in curiam, quoniam omnis curia a cruore dicitur et immolatio simulacrorum est: quoniam si quis clericus in curiam introierit, anathema suscipiat, nunquam rediens ad matrem ecclesiam. A communione autem non privetur propter tempus turbidum' (50f. Coustant; 629–30 Mansi).

(CS c. 3) Postea autem—ut non] Non *At.*
Et non damnabitur praesul] Non damnabitur episcopus *At.*
LXXII] testibus *add. At.*
quoniam scriptum—super magistrum] *om. At.*
Presbyter autem *rell.*] presbyter urbis Romae nisi quadraginta quattuor, diaconus
   cardinalis nisi triginta sex, subdiaconus, acolythus, exorcista, lector, in duobus vel
   tribus testimoniis *paraphr. At.*
(Syn. 270 episc. c. 5) causam quamlibet] causam *At. Deusd.*
examinare nisi in aecclesia] examinare *At. Deusd.*
stare] placet *add. At. Deusd.*

The combination of passages from CS and *Syn. 270 episc.* is a peculiar feature of Atto's
abstract. Of the eight chapters composing his rubric *Ex decr. Silv.*, four (cc. 1–3, 8)
are taken from CS (cc. 3, 4, 14); and three (cc. 4–6) from the Synod (cc. 3, 5, 7 Poisnel;
cc. 2, 4, 7 Duchesne). One canon in Atto (c. 7 'Nullo schemate monachus . . .') remains
uncertain.—Deusdedit's adherence to Atto is unusual, since in other portions of his work
he follows the PsI tradition for CS (see D*a infra*).

C. The Angilramnus Tradition

1. Pseudo-Angilramnus, *Capitula* (after 846), first series c. 51 §2: 'Neque praesul
summus—super magistrum' (ed. Hinschius, *Decr. Pseudo-Isid.* 766). 2nd ser. c. 13:
'Presbyter non adversus—Christum praedicantes.' c. 14: 'Testimonium—suscipiat.'
c. 15: 'Nemo enim clericum—nisi in ecclesia et reliqua' (768 Hinschius).—Sources: (1st
ser. c. 51) CS c. 3, third sentence; (2nd ser. c. 13) CS c. 3; (cc. 14–5) CS cc. 14–5.

2. Council of Mayence (888) c. 12: 'Presbyter non adversus—uxores et filios habentes'
(Mansi 18, 67f.).—Source: Angilr. 2nd ser. c. 13.

3. Pseudo-Theodore of Canterbury, *Capitula* (early 10th cent.) c. 39: 'Presbyter non
adversus—Christum praedicantes' (ed. J. Petit, *Opp. Theod.* I, Paris 1677 = PL 99,
947D).[41]—Source: perhaps *Conc. Mog.* according to E. Seckel, 'Zu den Akten der Triburer Synode 895: II,' NA 20 (1895) 329 and n. 4; but Angilr. (not mentioned by Seckel)
may be as likely.

4. Anselm of Lucca, *Coll. can.* (c. 1083) 3, 88–9 incorporates Angilramnus' *Capitula*
in their entirety; the canons here discussed are printed in Thaner 165; 167.

Leading variants (Anselm's readings not listed):
(CS c. 3) quoniam scriptum est] quia dicente Domino *Ang. c. 51*
(CS c. 3) Postea autem—ut non presbyter] Presbyter non *Ang. 2, 13. Conc. Th.*
non subdiaconus adversus diaconum] *om. Ang. (ed. tantum?)*
damnabitur praesul] dampnetur pr. *Ang.* condemnabitur pr. *Conc. Th.*
in LXXII] LXXII testibus *Ang.* in triginta duo *Th. (ed. tantum?)*
praesul summus a quoquam iudicabitur] summus iudicab. a quoq. *Th. (ed. tantum?)*
Presbyter autem] in cardine constitutus *add. Ang. Conc. Th.*
nisi in XLIV testimonia non] nonnisi in XLIV (quadr. duobus *Conc.*) testibus *Ang.*
   Conc. nisi in quadr. et quatuor testibus (non?) *Th.*

---

[41] Further reprints from Petit's spurious publication: F. Kunstmann, *Die lateinischen
Pönitentialbücher der Angelsachsen* (Mainz 1844) 121; Royal Record Commision, *Ancient
Laws and Institutions of England* (London 1840) 311. The true origin of the forgery, composed on Frankish soil more than two centuries after Theodore's death, has been demonstrated by F. W. H. Wasserschleben, *Die Bussordnungen der abendländischen Kirche* (Halle
1851) 16f. and, with a detailed analysis, by Seckel as cited above, NA 20, 296–301; 328–51.
See also P. Fournier, 'De l'influence de la collection irlandaise . . .,' *Nouv. Revue histor. de
droit français et étr.* 23 (1899) 46.

206

Diaconus—condemnabitur] *om. Th. (ed. tantum?)*
autem cardine constructus] cardinarius constitutus *Ang. Conc.*
XXXVI] XXVI *Ang. Conc.*
nisi . . . non] nonnisi *Conc.*
lector] ostiarius *add. Conc. Th.*
in septem testimonia filios et uxores habentes] in VII testes (testibus *Conc. Th.*) non
    condemnabitur. Testes autem sine aliqua sint infamia ux. et fil. hab. *Ang.*
    Conc. Th.
et omnino Christum praedicantes] *om. Conc.*
Sic—veritas] *om. Ang. Conc. Th.*
(*CS c. 14*) recipiat] suscipiat *Ang.*
(*CS c. 15*) examinet] examinare praesumat *Ang.*
nisi in ecclesia] et reliqua *add. Ang.*

The most signal variants of this tradition are its interpolations, especially the attribution of the title 'cardinal' to the *presbyter* and the lengthy insertion concerning the qualification of the seven witnesses. With both these novelties Angilr. became a model for PsI (see *infra*). On the other hand, the insertion of *ostiarius* in *Conc. Mog.* may be derived in turn from PsI; it is also the only reading which would support Seckel's otherwise doubtful assumption that *Conc. Mog.* is the source of Pseudo-Theod.—Many of the omissions in the latter text are probably due only to Petit's carelessness, especially those of a homoeographic nature. Also the one startling omission in Angilr. may be caused by homoeography on the part of Hinschius because this clause is not missing in the texts derived from Angilr.—Note that Angilr. evidently planned further abstracts ('. . . et reliqua') from CS.

D. The Pseudo-Isidorian Families

PsI (c. 847–52), *Excerpta quaedam ex synodalibus gestis s. Silvestri papae* c. 2: (a) 'In qua et consensus—audeat inferre,' (b) 'et ut presbyter non adversus—super magistrum.' c. 3: 'Presbyter autem cardinalis—in septem testibus non condempnabitur.' c. 4: 'Testes autem—Christum praedicantes.' c. 5 (a) 'Testimonium—nemo recipiat.' (b) 'Nemo enim clericum—nisi in ecclesia.' (c) Nemo enim clericus—in curiam,' (d) 'nec ante iudicem—dicere praesumat,' (e) 'quoniam omnis curia—anathema suscipiat' (449–50 Hinschius).—Sources: (c. 2, a) LP I, 171, 10–11; (b) CS c. 3, as from Angilr. 2nd ser. c. 13; (cc. 3–4) *id.*; (c. 5, a–b) CS cc. 14–5, probably as from Angilr. 2nd ser. cc. 14–5; (c) CS c. 16, first clause; (d) LP I, 171, 12–3; (e) CS c. 16 continued.

Leading variants:

(*CS c. 3*) Postea—in gremio synodi] In qua et consensus (*var.* etiam consensu et) subscriptione omnium constitutum est, ut nullus laicus crimen clerico audeat inferre
    (*cf. LP*: Hic constituit ut nullus laicus—inferre)
ut non presbyter] et ut presb. non
damnabitur praesul] dampnetur pr. (*cum Angilr.*)
LXXII] testibus *add.* (*cum Angilr.*)
iudicabitur] iudicetur
Presbyter autem] cardinalis *add.* (*cf.* in cardine constitutus *add. Angilr.*)
in XLIV testimonia] quadr. quatuor testibus (*cf. Angilr.*)
autem cardine constructus] cardinarius constructus (*var.* constitutus, *cf. Angilr.*)
lector] hostiarius *add.*
in septem testimonia filios et uxores habentes] in septem testibus non condempnabitur.
    Testes autem et accusatores sine aliqua sint infamia ux. et fil. hab. (*cum Angilr.*)
Sic—veritas] *om.* (*cum Angilr.*)

(*CS c. 15*) examinet] examinare praesumat (*cum Angilr.*)
(*CS c. 16*) causam suam] causam
intret in curiam] nec ante iudicem cinctum causam dicere praesumat *add.* (*cf. LP*:
    Hic constituit ut nullus clericus . . . in curia introiret nec ante iudicem cinctum
    causam diceret nisi in ecclesia)
immolatio simulacrorum est] immolatione simulacrorum
quoniam si quis clericus] Et si quis cler. accusans clericum
nunquam rediens—turbidum] *om.*

The skilful composition made from CS, Angilr. and LP is a good specimen of the
Pseudo-isidorian method. The dependence on the interpolations of Angilr. in CS c. 3—
and, we may presume, on his combination of CS cc. 3, 14, 15—betrays the well known
origin of the Frankish forgeries of the ninth century in a common workshop. PsI ex-
pands one of these interpolations ('Testes autem *et accusatores* sine aliqua . . .'), continues
the excerpts from CS (as planned by Angilr. c. 15: '. . . et reliqua') with CS c. 16, and
refines the whole composition by inserting two passages from LP.[42]—In the following,
five distinct families of texts derived from PsI are described.

    a. Class Headed by the *Collectio Anselmo dedicata*

    1. *Coll. Ans. ded.* (c. 882–96) 3, 143 (137?): 'Ut autem cardinalis presbyter—in septem
testibus non condempnabitur' (cf. Friedberg, *Corp. iur. can.* I, 465–6 nn. 25–42; Wolf
von Glanvell, *Deusd.* 206 note to c. 43). 4, 150: 'Testes autem . . .' (? cf. Wolf von
Glanvell *loc. cit.* who does not specify the contents of this canon).—Sources: (3, 143 or 137)
PsI c. 3; (4, 150) PsI c. 4?

    2. Deusdedit, *Coll. can.* 1, 89: 'Neque praesul summus—super magistrum' (74 Wolf
von Glanvell). 2, 43: (a) 'Presbyter cardinalis—condempnabitur.' (b) 'Testes autem—
praedicantes.' (c) 'Et constituit ut diaconi non essent amplius—Rome VII' (206 Wolf
von Glanvell).—Sources: (1, 89) PsI c. 2, last sentence; (2, 43, a) *Ans. ded.* 3, 143; (b)
PsI c. 4 (*Ans. ded.* 4, 150?); (c) CS c. 6.

    3. Bonizo, *Vita christ.* (c. 1090–9) 4, 68: 'Neque presul summus—super magistrum'
(141 Perels).—Source: PsI c. 2, last sentence or Deusd. 1, 89.[43]

Leading variants (for *Coll. Ans. ded.* as far as ascertainable from Friedberg's notes to
Gratian):

    (*PsI c. 2*) quoniam scriptum est] quoniam sicut scr. est *Deusd.*
    (*PsI c. 3*) Presbyter autem cardinalis] Ut autem cardinalis presbyter *Ans. ded.* Presb.
    card. urbis Rome *Deusd.* (*cf. Atto*)

---

    [42] For the sources which in turn were used in LP, see Duchesne I, 189 n. 20 (for 'Hic
constituit ut nullus laicus—audeat inferre'): *Coll. Theatina*: 'Placuit eis et ad omnem Christianorum populum Romanorum ut nullus laicus audeat clerico crimen ingerere . . .'; and
ibid. 190 n. 23 (for 'Hic constituit ut nullus clericus—causam diceret nisi in ecclesia'):
CS c. 16 and *Syn.* 270 *episc.* c. 4 (c. 5 Poisnel).—Incidentally, we observe that the note on
Pope Julius I in LP I, 205, 5: 'Hic constitutum fecit ut nullus clericus causam quamlibet in
publico ageret (*al.* diceret) nisi in ecclesia' is also composed on the same basis (CS cc. 15–6;
Syn. c. 5; LP *Silv.*).

    [43] No specific source can be assigned to another passage in Bonizo, in the course of his
catalogue of Roman Pontiffs (4, 33): '. . . hic constituit ut Romanus presul a nullo iudicetur,
et ut presbiter non condempnetur nisi sub quadraginta (*sic*) testium certa comprobatione,
et ut minoris ordinis aliquis maiorem se non possit accusare, et ut clericus ante laicos non
iudicetur . . .' (124, 16–9 Perels), which may be a free summary of CS cc. 3, 15, or (as Perels
124 n. 3 suggests) of PsI cc. 2, 3, 5.

quadraginta quatuor testibus] in quadr. quat. test. *Deusd.*
cardinarius constructus] cardinarius constitutus *Ans. ded. Deusd. (cf. var. PsI)*
XXXVI] XXVI *Ans. ded. Deusd. (cum Angilr. et nonnullis codd. PsI)*
(*CS c. 6*) Et diaconi non essent plus nec amplius] Et constituit ut diac. non essent ampl. *Deusd.*
diacones cardinales] diaconi card. *Deusd.*

It is peculiar to Deusdedit that he, alone among all medieval canonists, combines the PsI tradition (which he follows in 1, 89 and 2, 43, a–b) with a direct use of CS c. 6. For still other traditions of CS adopted by him elsewhere, see B *supra* and sec. III *infra.* Wolf von Glanvell, who fails to recognize the source of 2, 43, c, lets the canon begin with the words: 'Siluester papa in concilio CCLXXVII episcoporum dixit:'—but this is evidently only the inscription (the same as for 1, 89), not part of c. 43.—In singling out the sentence 'Neque praesul summus' *etc.* as a separate canon, Deusd. was preceded only by Angilr. c. 51. But the latter can not have been his source, as the readings of Deusd. come from PsI.

β. Class Headed by Burchard

1. Burchard, *Decretum* (c. 1008–12) 1, 151: 'In consensu et subscriptione—nisi in LXX duobus idoneis testibus' (PL 140, 593).—Source: PsI c. 2.

2. Ivo, *Decretum* (c. 1093–6) 5, 264: 'In consensu—idoneis testibus' (PL 161, 405).—Source: Burchard, cf. P. Fournier, 'Les collections attribuées à Yves de Chartres,' *Bibliothèque de l' École des chartes* 58 (1897) 31.

3. Ivo, *Panormia* (c. 1095–6) 4, 90: (a) 'In consensu—inferre' (PL 161, 1201). (b) see δ3C *infra.*—Source: (a) Ivo *Decr.* first sentence (= PsI c. 2, a).

Leading variants:

(*PsI c. 2*) in qua et consensus subscriptione] In consensu et (et *om. Ivo P.?*) subscriptione *Burch. Ivo D. P. (cf. var. PsI)*
crimen clerico audeat] episcopo vel alicui in ordinibus posito crimen aliquod possit *Burch. Ivo D.P.*
et ut presbyter non—LXXII testibus] *aliam ex alio fonte lectionem dat Ivo P. (cf. δ3C infra)*
testibus] idoneis testibus *Burch. Ivo D.*
Neque praesul summus—super magistrum] *om. Burch. Ivo D.P.*

Burchard changes PsI by a further interpolation (in the sentence: '. . . ut nullus laicus crimen clerico audeat inferre'); he omits, on the other hand, the last sentence forbidding a trial of the Pope. Ivo *Decr.* follows Burchard entirely, while *Pan.* is strangely conflated from two different traditions, tacking the second part of PsI c. 2 from Anselm of Lucca's text (δ) onto the β-tradition of the beginning.

γ. Class Headed by the *Tripartita*

1. Ivo, *Coll. tripart.* (c. 1093–4) pt. 1 c.?: 'Iam fatus papa—sepultum fuit' (cf. Fournier, 'Les collections . . . ,' *Bibl. Éc. ch.* 57 [1896] 654).—Source: PsI c. 1 (449 line 7 Hinschius: '. . . Iam factus papa') –c. 6 (450, 5 Hinschius).

2. Ivo, *Decr.* 6, 334: 'Presbyter autem cardinalis—anathema suscipiat' (PL 161, 513–4).—Source: *Tripart.* (cf. Fournier, *Bibl. Éc. ch.* 58, 44) = PsI cc. 3–5 *in toto.*

Leading variants (Ivo *Decr.* only):

(*PsI c. 3*) quadraginta quatuor] in quadr. quat.
cardinarius constructus] cardinalis constitutus
(*PsI c. 4*) praedicantes] timentes [praedicantes] *(sic ed.)*

δ. Class Headed by the *Collectio LXXIV titulorum*

The great variety of selections and combinations of portions from PsI in this class makes a separate treatment of three series of texts, headed by *Coll. LXXIV tit.* (= *Csqt*) cc. 60, 61, and 69 respectively, advisable. The series will be numbered 1A, 2A etc.; 1B, 2B etc.; 1C, 2C etc.

1A. *Csqt* (c. 1050) c. 60: (a) 'Nullus laicus—inferre.' (b) 'Testimonium—nisi in ecclesia' (cf. Fournier, 'Le premier manuel canonique de la réforme du XI⁰ siècle,' *Mélanges d'archéol. et d'hist.* 14 [1894] 161–2; Thaner, *Ans. Luc.* 128, notes [speaking of 'Coll. minor'] to c. 23).—Sources: (a) PsI c. 2, a; (b) PsI c. 5, a–b; cf. Thaner *loc. cit.* (Fournier's observation, 'Ps. Silv. c. 2 à c. 5' is not correct).

2A. Anselm of Lucca, *Coll. can.* (c. 1083) 3, 23: 'Nullus laicus—nisi in ecclesia' (128 Thaner).—Source: *Csqt.*

3A. Ivo, *Pan.* 4, 89: 'Nullus laicus—nisi in ecclesia' (PL 161, 1201).—Source: *Csqt* or Ans. Luc. (Fournier, *Bibl. Éc. ch.* 58, 304 mentions *Csqt* c. 68 [*sic*] only and believes that the canon is lacking in Ans.).

4A. *Collectio XIII partium* (c. 1090–1100) 9, 171, according to Friedberg, *Corp. iur. can.* I, 627–8 n. 66 (without details).

5A. Gratian (c. 1140) C. 2 q. 7 c. 2: 'Nullus laicus—inferre' (483 Friedberg).   11 q. 1 c. 9: 'Testimonium—nisi in ecclesia (628 Friedberg).—Sources: (2 q. 7 c. 2) probably Ivo *Pan.* 4, 89, a; (11 q. 1 c. 9) *id.* b.

Leading variants (without *Coll. XIII part.*):

> (*PsI c. 2*) In qua—constitutum est] Silvester papa in generali residens synodo dixit
>   *inscr. Csqt. Aᵤs. Ivo P.*   Item Silv. pp. *inscr. Grat.*
> ut nullus] Nullus *Csqt. Ans. Ivo P. Grat.*
> crimen clerico audeat inferre] crim. aud. cler. inf. *Csqt. Ans. Grat.* aud. inf. crim.
>   cler. *Ivo P.*
> (*PsI c. 5*) Testimonium] autem *add. Csqt. Ans. Ivo P.*
> recipiat] suscipiat *Csqt. Ans. Ivo P.* (*cf. Angilr.*)
> Nemo enim clericum quemlibet in publico] Clericum vero queml. nemo in publ. (in
>   publ. nemo *Ivo P.*) *Csqt. Ans. Ivo P.* Nemo cler. queml. in publ. *Grat.*

The use of different sources for PsI c. 2 in Ivo *Pan.* (see β3 *supra*) leads to a duplication of the rule 'Nullus laicus crimen clerico audeat inferre,' which appears in 4, 89 as taken from Ans. Luc. and in 4, 90, as from Burch. and Ivo *Decr.*—Friedberg's notes on the sources of Gratian go far astray. For 2 q. 7 c. 2 he cites (483–4 n .9) Burch. and Ivo *Decr.* both of which belong in their readings to a different class (see β *supra*). For 11 q. 1 c. 9 he cites (627–8 n. 66) Burch. 2, 204; Ivo, *Decr.* 6, 278; Ivo, *Pan.* 4, 89; *Coll. XIII part.* 9, 171.   The first two references are not at all to the point: Burch. 2, 204 and Ivo, *Decr.* 6, 278 ('Ex concilio Triburiensi: Testimonium laici adversus clericum nemo suscipiat') express the reverse of the Pseudo-sylvestrian rule ('Test. clerici adv. laicum . . .'), purportedly from another source.[44]—On the other hand, Friedberg wrongly denies ('. . . immerito citatur') the presence of our canon in Ans. Luc. 3, 23 and contends (627–8 n. 70 v. *nemo clericum*) that a part of it (i.e. PsI c. 5, b) is found in the non-existing canon 'Ans. Luc. 8, 171'.   Here as elsewhere (cf. Kuttner, in *Studia et documenta historiae et iuris* 6 [1940] 290 n. 22) Friedberg fell victim to his belief in a spurious seventeenth-century compilation posing as Anselm's text.—Note that Gratian's readings in some

---

[44] *Ex conc. Trib.* is a pseudepigraph of Burchard's invention, cf. V. Krause, 'Die Akten der Triburer Synode von 895,' NA 17 (1892) 82; Seckel, 'Zu den Akten der Trib. Syn. 895: I,' NA 18 (1893) 408.   The canon itself is inspired by Angilr. or PsI.

210

points are closer to PsI than to the intermediary collections (vv. *Testimonium, recipiat, nemo enim clericum*).—Friedberg's reference to *Coll. XIII part.* cannot be verified at present.

1B. *Csqt* c. 61: 'Nemo clericus—anathema suscipiat' (cf. Fournier, *Mél.* 14, 162; Thaner, *Ans. Luc.* 424–5 notes to c. 149).—Source: PsI c. 5, c–e.

2B. Ans. Luc. 7, 149: 'Nemo—suscipiat' (424–5 Thaner).—Source: *Csqt*.

3B. Ivo, *Pan.* 4, 30: 'Nemo—suscipiat' (PL 161, 1189).—Source: *Csqt* or Ans. Luc.; cf Fournier, *Bibl. Éc. ch.* 58, 304.

4B. Gratian C. 11 q. 1 c. 33: 'Nullus clericus—dicere presumat' (635 Friedberg). c. 10: 'Si quis clericus accusans—anathema sit' (629 Friedberg).—Source: probably Ivo *Pan.*

Leading variants:

> (*PsI c. 5*) Nemo enim] Nemo *Csqt. Ans. Ivo P.* Nullus *Grat.*
> aut] vel *Csqt. Ans. Ivo P. Grat.*
> cinctum] *om. Ans.* cinctus *Ivo P.* (*ed. tantum?*) civilem *Grat.*
> causam dicere] causam suam dicere *Csqt. Ans.* (*cum CS et nonnullis codd. PsI*) caus. dic. suam *Grat.*
> quoniam omnis curia—et immolatione simulacrorum] *om. Grat.*
> a cruore] quasi a cr. *Ivo P.*
> et immol. simulacr.] *om. Csqt. Ans. Ivo P.*
> Et si quis] Si quis *Grat.*
> anathema suscipiat] anath. sit *Grat.*

Gratian, even as in the preceding case (5A) splits the canon in two. In view of all the liberties he took with his text, as he was wont to do, it cannot be said with certainty whether Ans. or Ivo served him as model—though the latter is more likely, as will be seen from 5C *infra*. At any rate, there is no reason to assume with Friedberg (629–30 n. 91; 635–6 n. 320) that the two canons are based on different sources.

1C. *Csqt* c. 69: (a) 'Presbyter adversus—dare accusationem.' (b) 'Presul autem—LXXII testibus.' (c) 'Presbyter autem cardinalis—sint infamia' (cf. Fournier, *Mél.* 14, 162; Thaner, *Ans. Luc.* 136 notes to c. 43).—Sources: (a–b) PsI c. 2, b; (c) PsI cc. 3–4.

2C. Ans. Luc. 3, 43: 'Presbyter adversus—sint infamia' (136 Thaner).—Source: *Csqt*.

3C. Ivo *Pan.* 4, 90: (a) see β3 *supra*. (b) 'et ut presbyter adversus—dicere accusationem'. 4, 91: 'Praesul autem—sint infamia' (PL 161, 1201).—Sources: (4, 90, b) *Csqt* c. 69, a, or Ans. Luc. 3, 43, a; (4, 91) *ibid.* b–c.

4C. Cardinal Gregory, *Polycarpus* (c. 1109–13)[45] 5, 1, 28: 'Quot testibus—sint infamia' (? cf. Friedberg I, 465–6 nn. 19–42; 485–6 nn. 59–60; readings not always clear).—Source: Ans. Luc.?

5C. Gratian C. 2 q. 7 c. 10: 'Clericus adversus—ferre non valet' (485 Friedberg). 2 q. 4 c. 2: 'Presul non dampnetur—sint infamia' (466 Friedberg).—Sources: (q. 7 c. 10) uncertain, see below; (q. 4 c. 2) Ivo, *Pan.* 4, 91.

Leading variants (without Grat. 2 q. 7 c. 10; for *Polyc.* as far as ascertainable from Friedberg's notes):

> (*PsI c. 2*) et ut presbyter non adversus . . . det accusationem aliquam] Presbyter (et ut presb. *Ivo P.*) adversus . . . nullo modo aliquam presumat dare (dicere *Ivo P.* dare presumat *Polyc.*) accusationem *Csqt. Ans. Ivo P. Polyc.*

---

[45] Cf. Klewitz, *Entstehung* 165, who thus narrows the time limit, 1104–13, assumed by Fournier-Le Bras II, 170.

Et non dampnetur praesul] Presul autem non dampnetur (damnabitur *Ivo P.*) *Csqt.* *Ans. Ivo P. Polyc.* (?) Presul non dampn. *Grat.* in LXXII] cum LXXII *Grat.*

Neque praesul summus—super magistrum] *om. Csqt. Ans. Ivo P. Polyc. Grat.* (*cf.* *Burch. Ivo D.*)

(*PsI c. 3*) nisi XLIV] nisi in LXIIII *Ans. Polyc. Grat.* nisi in XL *Ivo P.* dampnabitur] deponatur *Grat.*

diaconus cardinarius constructus] diac. (autem *add. nonnulli codd. Ans. Ivo P.*) cardinalis *Csqt. Ans. Ivo P. Polyc. Grat.*

XXXVI] XXVI testibus *Csqt. Ans.* XXVII testibus *Ivo P. Polyc. Grat.* (*cf.* XXVI *Angilr. Ans. ded. Deusd. et nonnullos codd. PsI*)

condempnabitur] damnabitur *Ivo P.* sicut scriptum est] *om. Csqt. Ans. Ivo P. Polyc. Grat.* condempnabitur] condemnabuntur *Ivo P.* (*ed. tantum?*)

(*PsI c. 4*) uxores—praedicantes] *om. Csqt. Ans. Ivo P. Polyc.* (?) *Grat.*

Among the several omissions only that of the final sentence of PsI c. 2 ('Neque—magistrum') has a precedent: Burch. 1, 151 (*β supra*). In the δ-tradition, however, it may be rather explained by the fact that all the collections of this group transmit the very similar rule of CS c. 20: 'Nemo iudicabit primam sedem . . .' (52 Coustant); see *Csqt* c. 8; Ans. Luc. 1, 19 and 4, 40; Ivo, *Pan.* 4, 5; Grat. C. 9 q. 3 c. 13 (Friedberg I, 609–10 n. 189 cites also *Polyc.* 1, 16 [18] 5; *Coll. Caesaraugust.* 5, 2; and Deusd. 4, 41).—For the source of Gratian 2 q. 4 c. 2 nothing can be argued from common variants in numerals (Grat. has 64 witnesses for priests, instead of 44, in common with Ans.; but 27 for deacons, with Ivo *Pan.*). The decisive factor which determines his dependence upon Ivo is the choice of the peculiar segment 'Presul (autem) non dampnetur (damnabitur)—sint infamia' from PsI cc. 2–4, common to Grat. and *Pan.* 4, 91 alone. But Gratian does not follow the δ-tradition (*Csqt.* c. 69, a; Ans. Luc. 3, 43, a; Ivo, *Pan.* 4, 90, b), nor Burchard or the *Tripartita* (*β, γ*) for the portion 'et ut presbyter non adversus episcopum . . . non ostiarius adversus lectorem det accusationem aliquam' of PsI c. 2. Instead, he presents a strangely inverted text of his own in 2 q. 7 c. 10:

> Unde Silvester papa. Clericus adversus exorcistam, exorcista adversus acolitum, acolitus adversus subdiaconum, subdiaconus adversus diaconum, diaconus adversus presbiterum, presbiter adversus episcopum accusationem dare aut testimonium ferre non valet.

Friedberg's notes, as usual, are confusing rather than helpful. He cites (485–6 n. 59) as parallel texts: Burch. 1, 151 (to whom he wrongly imputes a false inscription: *Ex conc. Carthag.*—in fact, Burch. has *Ex decretis Sylv. pp.*); Ivo, *Decr.* 5, 264; and *Polyc.* 5, 1, 28. He does not indicate that Burch. and Ivo have a positively different text (*β*); and we must assume a different order of text also for *Polyc.* since it belongs to the *Csqt*-Anselm class, as shown by the one variant 'dare praesumat accusationem' which Friedberg cares to register (n. 60). Unfortunately we do not know the beginning of the canon in *Polyc.*: the words *Quot testibus* given by Friedberg are obviously only the first words of the rubric, for similar rubrics are found in PsI, Anselm, Ivo, and Gratian.[46] Unless, therefore,

---

[46] PsI c. 3 rubr.: 'Quot (Quod *Hinsch.*) testibus damnari possint singuli ordines ecclesiastici.' Ans. Luc. 3, 43 rubr.: 'Ut inferiores gradus superiores non accusent et in quot testibus episcopus, presb. diac. subdiac. et ceteri condempnandi sunt' (variant as recorded in Thaner 136 note b). Ivo, *Decr.* 6, 334 rubr.: 'Sub quot testibus cuiusque ordinis accusatio fieri debeat.' *Pan.* 4, 91 and Grat. 2 q. 4 c. 2 rubr.: 'Quot testibus episcopus vel presb. vel reliqui clerici sint convincendi (sunt communicandi *Pan. ed.*).)'

212

another source turns up for C. 2 q. 7 c. 10, we have to conclude that Gratian himself composed the singular wording of this canon—a procedure which is in line with his velleities in the handling of texts as known from other instances (cf. e.g. Seckel, NA 20, 317–8; Kuttner, *Studia et docum.* 6, 290–3).

ε. The Collection in Five Books

Coll. quinque libr. (c. 1080–6) 2, 10, 6: 'Silueri pape c. II: In consensu et subsceptione— super magistrum' (cf. Wolf von Glanvell, 'Die Canonessammlung des Cod. Vatic. lat. 1348,' *Sitzungsberichte der kaiserl. Akademie der Wissenschaften in Wien*, phil.-hist. Klasse 136, 2 [1897] 20).—Source: PsI c. 2; not Burch. 1, 151 (as Wolf von Glanvell assumes) where the concluding sentence is lacking (see *β supra*).

The preceding analysis of five classes of texts derived from PsI is graphically summarized in the table on the following page.

II. *The Tradition of CS c. 6*

Deusdedit, *Coll. can.* 2, 43, c: 'Et constituit ut diaconi—Rome VII' (206, 12–3 Wolf von Glanvell).—Source: CS c. 6, while Deusd. 2, 43, a–b are derived from PsI (for CS c. 3), see IDα2 *supra*.

III. *The Threefold Tradition of CS c. 7*

A. *Coll. Ans. ded.* 4, 160: 'Ita autem dicebat—tantum pontifici' (cf. Friedberg, *Corp. iur. can.* I, 321–2 nn. 51–65).—Source: CS.

B1. Burchard, *Decr.* 2, 224: 'Ita fratres iubet—in gremio ecclesiae' (PL 140, 662).— Source: CS.

B2. Ivo, *Decr.* 6, 299: 'Ita fratres—ecclesiae' (PL 161, 506).—Source: Burch.

C1. Ans. Luc. *Coll. can.* 7, 57: 'Ut a subdiacono—ecclesiae' (386–7 Thaner).— Source: CS.

C2. Deusd. *Coll. can.* 2, 44: 'Ut a subdiacono—ecclesiae' (206 Wolf von Glanvell).— Sources: Ans. and Burch.

C3. Gratian D. 93 c. 5: 'A subdiacono—ecclesiae' (321 Friedberg).—Source: Ans. Luc. Leading variants:

(*Cs c. 7*) Ita tamen Silvester—dicebat ad coepiscopos] *om. Ans. Deusd. Grat.* Ita autem dic. Silv.—coep. *Ans. ded.* Ita fratres iubet auctoritas divina et affirmat *Burch. Ivo*

ut] *om. Grat.*

lectorem] lectores *Grat.*

essent] sint *Burch. Ivo Ans. Deusd. Grat.*

urbis Romae] viro reverentissimo *Ans. Deusd. Grat.*

honorem repraesentantes tantum] repraes. hon. tm. *Ans. Deusd.* repraes. ei honorem *Grat.*

pontifici vero] porro pontifici *Ans. Deusd. Grat.*

presbyteri, diaconi—lectores] presbyter, diaconus—lector, abbas (abba *Deusd.*), monachus *Burch. Ivo Deusd.* presbyter, presbytero diaconus, diacono subdiaconus, subdiacono acolytus, acolyto exorcista, exorxistae lector, lectori ostiarius (hostiario abbas *add. Grat.!*), abbati monachi (monachus *Grat.*) *Ans. Grat.*

repraesentent] repaesentet *Burch. Grat.* praesentent *Deusd.*

tamquam pontifici] *om. Burch. Ivo Ans. Deusd. Grat.* tantum pontifici *Ans. ded.* (*cum nonnullis codd. CS*)

The three classes are clearly distinguished by their treatment of the beginning (Ita tamen Silvester . . .') which is replaced in the Burchard class by another introductory

PsI	α			β			γ		δ⁶					ε
	Ans. ded.	Deusd.	Bonizo	Burch.	Ivo D.	Ivo P.	Trip.	Ivo D.	74 tit.	Ans. Luc.	Ivo P.	Polyc.[7]	Grat.	5 lib.
2 In qua et consensus— constit. est ut						4, 90a								
nullus laicus—inferre									60a	3, 23a	4, 89a		2 q. 7 c. 2	
et ut presb. non adv. det accus. aliquam.		—[1]	—[4]	1, 151	5, 264				69a	3, 43a	4, 90b	5, 1, 28	(2 q. 7 c. 10)	2, 10, 6
Et non dampn. praesul in LXXII testibus.									69b	3, 43b	4, 91a		2 q. 4 c. 2a	
Neque praesul summus super magistrum.		1, 89	4, 68											—
3 Presbyter autem card. non condempnabitur.	3, 143 (137?)	2, 43[2]	—[4]				1, c. ?[5]		69c	3, 43c	4, 91b	5, 1, 28c	2 q. 4 c. 2b	—
4 Testes autem—sint inf. uxores—praedicantes.	4, 150?													—
5 Testimonium clerici— nisi in ecclesia.		(4, 329b)[3]	—[4]					6, 334	60b	3, 23b	4, 89b		11 q. 1 c. 9	—
Nemo enim clericus dicere praesumat,													11 q. 1 c. 33	—
quoniam omnis curia immol. simulacr.									61	7, 149	4, 30			—
Et si quis clericus—anath. suscipiat.													11 q. 1 c. 10	—

[1] But see the summary Deusd. 4, 329 (e): B2 supra. [2] Canon continues with CS c. 6. [3] Only first sentence (CS c. 14), not from PsI: cf. B2 supra.
[4] But see the summary Bonizo 4, 33: n. 43 supra. [5] PsI cc. 1-6. [6] Coll. XIII part. (84A) omitted. [7] Presence or absence of other canons uncertain.

214

phrase of free invention, but altogether omitted in the Anselm class. The most remarkable variants of the latter are: the qualification of the cardinal (arch-)deacon as *vir reverentissimus*, substituted for the original *urbis Romae*, and the interpolations (*presbytero* ... *diacono* ... etc.) in the final clause. Deusdedit, however, sides here with Burchard, and we thus have another piece of evidence for the variety of sources which he consulted for rendering CS (Atto, PsI-*Ans. ded.* and CS itself: see IB2; D*a*2; II *supra*; Ans. Luc. and Burch.). Gratian, as usual, introduces some peculiar changes of his own. Of all this, Friedberg's apparatus gives but a very blurred and incomplete account.

Tedious as details of textual criticism may sometimes appear, they are the only means of establishing the often complicated lineage of the early medieval collections of Canon law. They are in particular indispensable for determining—as far as it can be done without manuscript research—the sources of Gratian's all-important work. Friedberg's 'critical' edition has left this problem not only unsolved but even untouched. It will not be easy in every case to substitute for his indiscriminate listing of older collections a well-reasoned choice of those which really may have served Gratian; [47] it will be less difficult to record the variant readings with accuracy and completeness where Friedberg is disappointing in both. At any rate, the standard edition of the *Corpus iuris canonici* is a work that sooner or later will have to be done all over again.

The Catholic University of America.

---

[47] For an example of methodical criteria to be followed see also the study of E. Perels, 'Die Briefe Papst Nikolaus I.', NA 39 (1914) 43ff. esp. 125–30.

X

DAT GALIENUS OPES ET SANCTIO JUSTINIANA

Relations between men of letters and men of law have often been strained in the course of Western history. The antagonism seems to have been unknown to the ancient and the early medieval world; but with the spectacular rise of the law schools, beginning in the twelfth century, complaints about the preponderance of legal studies were to become a topic of European literature. It is often difficult to disentangle such complaints from popular distrust of the lawyer's craft, or from other targets of medieval satire such as the proverbial greed of the Roman Curia, where the poor Christian in search of justice is fleeced in costly, long-drawn litigation. Goliardic song and vernacular poetry are brimming with this type of invective in which venality and pride are castigated as the common vices of judges, lawyers, and the higher clergy alike.[1]

We must distinguish these railings from the wistful concern for the survival of the arts in a world in which all success and all material reward of study appeared to go to the trained lawyer, be he canonist or "civilian"—*decretista* or *legista*; a world in which the *familiae* of bishops and princes were preferably staffed by clerics who had obtained a degree in the laws, and in which the business of government, both of the Church and of secular society, required ever more legal proficiency and became more and more a preserve of the *magistri* who had acquired such proficiency in the schools. The twelfth century had discovered scientific jurisprudence as a new discipline of higher learning; and it was both the genuine enthusiasm for a new field of intellectual pioneering and the prospect of advancement which made students flock from all over Europe to the law schools, Bologna and Paris above all.[2]

It would be interesting to isolate the many strands of anti-legalism in medieval thought. Not only the humanists but theologians as well raised their voices against the encroachment of the law schools. The analysis of these

---

[1] Cf. texts discussed in M. Manitius, *Geschichte der lateinischen Literatur des Mittelalters*, III (Munich, 1931), 912, 929-935; E. Meynial, "Remarques sur la réaction populaire contre l'invasion du droit romain en France aux 12ᵉ et 13ᵉ siècles," *Mélanges Chabaneau* (Romanische Forschungen, XXIII; Erlangen, 1907), pp. 557-585; E. Genzmer, "Hugo von Trimberg und die Juristen," *L'Europa e il Diritto Romano: Studi in memoria di Paolo Koschaker* (Milan, 1953), I, 291-336; see also W. Holtzmann, "Propter Sion non tacebo: Zur Erklärung von Carmina Burana 41," *Deutsches Archiv für Erforschung des Mittelalters*, X (1953), 170-175.

[2] The importance of Paris in this respect is frequently overlooked, cf. the remarks in S. Kuttner and E. Rathbone, "Anglo-Norman Canonists of the Twelfth Century," *Traditio*, VII (1949-1951), at pp. 284-290.

phenomena becomes even more complex if one turns to the relations between the branches of learned jurisprudence itself, to find canonists disparaging civilian legists and *vice versa*—although much of this internal rivalry has to be taken as conventional academic banter.[3] Moreover, there was the rivalry between the gradually consolidating national laws and the imperial Roman law; and from there it was only one step to the issues of world politics, of national kingdoms *vs.* the Empire.[4]

The writer of these pages wishes to examine only one little thread in this great tapestry, the recurring motif of riches and material reward that beckoned to the student of law, but not to him alone. In this context, we often find medicine (*physica*) named together with the civil law (*leges*), as it was repeatedly done, with a view to preserving monastic discipline and fostering theological studies, in the legislation of the Church. Conciliar enactments and papal decrees of the twelfth and the thirteenth century repeatedly forbade monks and regulars to leave their houses for the study of *leges* or *physica* in search of worldly gain, "gratia lucri temporalis," as Innocent II first put it at the Council of Clermont (1130).[5] Let them go to the schools to study theology, for this should be their avocation "ex debito facte professionis," Celestine III wrote to the bishop of Sigüenza in 1197; and the neglect of the *scientia Domini* by clerics who run after the *scientiae lucrativae* was lamented by Honorius III in the arenga of his famous constitution *Super speculam* (1219), which he designed to stem the tide of the Catharist heresy and in which, among other measures, he decreed an extension of the earlier prohibitions from monks and regulars to certain classes of the secular clergy.[6]

---

[3] Cf. Kuttner, *Harmony from Dissonance: An Interpretation of Medieval Canon Law* (Wimmer Lecture, X; Latrobe, 1960), pp. 48-49, pp. 62-63, nn. 34-37.

[4] Cf. P. Koschaker, *Europa und das römische Recht* (Munich, 1947), pp. 212-223. There have been many studies on the origin and meaning of the maxim, "Rex est imperator in regno suo"; for a detailed discussion, see B. Tierney, "Some Recent Works on the Political Theories of the Medieval Canonists," *Traditio*, X (1954), at pp. 612-619.

[5] Council of Clermont, c.5, in J.D. Mansi, *Sacrorum conciliorum nova et amplissima collectio*, XXI (Venice, 1776), 438; repeated in 1131 at Reims (c. 6: *ibid.*, col. 459) and in 1139 at the Second Lateran Council (c.9: *ibid.*, col. 528). Cf. also Alexander III, Council of Tours (1163), c.8 and Third Lateran Council (1179), c. 12 (Mansi XXI, 1179; XXII, 225).

[6] The letter of Celestine III (*Significasti*, 7 June 1197) is printed in W. Holtzmann, "La 'Collectio Seguntina' ... ," *Revue d'Histoire ecclésiastique*, L (1955), 450 Nº. 117. — Honorius III, *Super speculam* (22 November 1219) is best accessible in H. Denifle's edition, *Chartularium Universitatis Parisiensis*, I (Paris, 1889), 90-93, Nº. 32 (with a different date, 16 November); its main provisions were eventually included in the *Decretals* of Gregory IX (1234): V. 5.5, securing stipends and benefices for masters and students of theology while absent from home; III. 50.10, extending the prohibition mentioned above; V. 33.28, closing the civil law school of Paris, "ut plenius sacrae paginae insistatur." Cf. Kuttner, "Papst Honorius III. und das Studium des Zivilrechts," *Festschrift für Martin Wolff* (Tübingen, 1952), pp. 79-101, with earlier bibliography cited.

The language of such papal pronouncements is paralleled by the taunting of law and medicine as the "lucrative sciences" in academic quarters. But song is more catching than the rhetoric of the legislator, and the heart of the matter would seem to be best expressed where it was expressed in verse. The hexameter quoted in the title of this paper had European currency from at least the early thirteenth century to the age of the *Epistolae obscurorum virorum*, as Karl Strecker noted in his edition of a poem from the school of Walter of Châtillon, where it forms the concluding line to clinch the poet's argument: all endeavors in the arts are futile as compared with the reward that awaits the *legista*.[7]

> Meum est propositum gentis imperite
> mentes frugi reddere melioris vite,

he begins, with an intended echo of the "Meum est propositum in taberna mori," which had originally been a stanza of the so-called Archpoet's *Confessio* and enjoyed wide circulation as a drinking song.[8] The poem consists of twenty-two stanzas, composed in the Goliardic measure *cum auctoritate* ("Vagantenstrophe mit Auctoritas"), i.e., four rhymed lines in which three Goliardic verses are followed by an hexameter or pentameter from a classical or contemporary "authority"—a form that was dear to Walter of Châtillon and which he seems to have invented.[9]

It would be hard to say for whom our poet has more contempt, the lawyer with his wealth or the student of logic, whose lot is wretched poverty. In a delightful simile borrowed from Peter of Blois[10] he compares the poor logician to the spider which spins its web out of its own intestines: its best prize will be—with luck—a fly (st. 20 v. 1-4). The logician is content with naked glory, but in truth he envies the rich (5.1-3); he sows his seed in the sand and will never earn fruit (10.1-2); you may have reached the summit of the arts, yet shortly youth will despise you (11.1-3). If the disciple of the arts has committed a fault, he must run to the *legista*: with all his learning of Greek he can not defend himself any better than one who is dumb (18.1-4). The halls of the noble are open to the legist, yet if Homer came himself in the company of the Muses, he would have to sit outside (19.1-4).[11] Thus again and again

---

[7] K. Strecker, "Quid dant artes nisi luctum!," *Studi medievali*, Nuova Serie, I (1928), 380-391; cf. his commentary on stanza 22, p. 391.

[8] Cf. Strecker, p. 383; Manitius, *Geschichte*, III, 933.

[9] Strecker, p. 382; F.J.E. Raby, *A History of Secular Latin Poetry in the Middle Ages*, 2nd ed. (Oxford, 1957), II, 196.

[10] *Epist.* 14 and 16, in Migne, *Patrologia latina* [=PL] 207, 46C and 60B; cf. Strecker, p. 382.

[11] The *auctoritas* is Ovid, *Ars amat.* II.280, frequently used by the poets; cf. Strecker, p. 390 *ad loc.*; Raby, *Secular Latin Poetry*, II, 197, 209, n.2.

the poem stresses the reward which the law holds for its followers,[12] and only in the last stanza, somewhat surprisingly, medicine[13] is brought in:

> Nature cognoscere si velis archana,
> stude circa phisicam, que dat membra sana,
> que dat quicquid postulat egestas humana:
> Dat Galienus opes et sanctio Justiniana. (22.1-4)

Obviously this was done only in order to prepare for the closing line on the riches which Galen and the law of Justinian hand out. And since this verse, in accordance with the whole structure of the poem, is quoted as an *auctoritas*, Strecker observed that it must already have circulated at the time the poem was written, presumably before 1250.[14] This assumption is correct, even though Strecker could marshal no earlier evidence than the fifteenth-century *Vocabularius utriusque iuris*,[15] where these verses are found s.v. *ars*:

> Esurit ars, decreta tument, lex lucra ministrat,
> pontificat Moyses, thalamos medicina subintrat,
> dat Galienus opes et sanctio Justiniana,
> ex aliis paleas, ex istis collige grana.

Here as well as in other instances from the fifteenth and the sixteenth century,[16] the hexameter "Dat Galienus ... " is always followed by the rhyming line in which law and medicine gather the grain and the other [sciences or arts] the chaff. It is indeed in this form—with the image of reaping echoing again Walter of Châtillon[17]—that the couplet had been quoted two centuries before the *Vocabularius* at Bologna, in the *Glossa ordinaria* of Accursius on the first part of Justinian's *Digest* (*ante* 1234)[18] and, still earlier, in Stephen Langton's biblical lectures given at Paris between 1180 and 1206, as Miss Beryl Smalley

---

[12] See also the verses 2.1-2, 12.3-4 ; and 14.1-4 ; quoted below.

[13] Manitius, III 933, strangely renders *phisicam* by physics ('Physik').

[14] Strecker, commentary on stanza 22, p. 391; the date, "eher vor als nach 1250," p. 383.

[15] Comm. on st. 22. — E. Seckel, *Beiträge zur Geschichte beider Rechte im Mittelalter*, I (Tübingen, 1898), established the authorship (pp. 17-23) and the date (pp. 30-36) of the *Vocabularius*: Jodocus, *doctor decretorum* in Erfurt, A.D. 1452. There exist at least 73 editions, from before 1475 to 1622 (Seckel, pp. 4-10, 502).

[16] References in Strecker, *loc.cit.* and H. Walther,*Initia carminum ac versuum medii aevi posterioris latinorum* (Göttingen, 1959), Nº. 4060. (I have not seen the article by H. Simon, in *Die medizinische Welt*, 1928, Nos. 23 and 26, referred to in both places.) For the quotation in the *Epistolae obscurorum virorum* (1515) see the edition by F.G. Stokes (London, 1925), p. 170.

[17] "Seminat grammatica, semper tamen indiget, / Lex autem et phisica manipulos colliget," quoted by Strecker, pp. 381, 391.

[18] So dated by E. Seckel, "Distinctiones Glossatorum," *Festschrift der Berliner Juristischen Fakultät für Ferdinand von Martitz* (Berlin, 1911; separately reprinted, Graz, 1956), p. 412, n.2. The passage is in *Gloss. ord.*, const. *Omnem*, v. *ditissimi*.

and the late Hermann Kantorowicz have shown.[19] Langton, of course, had
the encroachment of law and medicine on theology in mind, when in his gloss
on Osee 2.5 ("I will go after my lovers that give me my bread") he quotes the
couplet, with a different line of introduction:[20]

> Ita dicunt multi scolares:
> Vadam ad physicam, ad leges, et non ad vana,
> Dat Galienus opes . . . .

This leads us back, then, to the turn of the twelfth century, and it can actually be shown that Strecker's date "before 1250" for the *Meum est propositum*
is too conservative a guess. While he noted that all its models—Walter,
Peter of Blois, the Archpoet — belong to the second half of the twelfth century,
he overlooked an important clue which allows us to narrow down the search
for the time and the place of the poem:

> Propter leges merito labor est ferendus,
> ager reddens centuplum non est deserendus.
> Est libellus pauperum pauperi legendus,
> hic tibi precipue sit pura mente colendus. (14.1-4)

The book which the poor should read to become proficient in the law is the
Liber pauperum of Master Vacarius, the man whom Archbishop Theobald had
brought to Canterbury not long after 1139 and who introduced the formal
study of Roman law in England. The *Liber pauperum* contains in abridged
form the most important portions of Justinian's codification and became the
basic text for the teaching of Vacarius and his school—the *pauperistae*
as they were called in mockery—which flourished at Oxford in the second half
of the twelfth century but did not survive the early years of the thirteenth.[21]
It is very unlikely, then, that at any later period a reader or listener could
have understood the line, "Est libellus pauperum pauperi legendus," and it
is even more unlikely that at any time it would have been understood outside
of England—the country to which the manuscript tradition of the *Meum
est propositum* and its connection with Walter of Châtillon and Peter of Blois
would point in any case. The poem thus must have been composed at about
the same time as Stephen Langton's glosses on the Minor Prophets.

By a curious coincidence the distich on Galen and Justinian turns up again
in an early-thirteenth-century manuscript of English origin which has likewise
Vacarian connections. This is British Museum, Additional MS. 24659. Its
main interest lies in the canon law treatises it contains (fol. 22ᵛ-43ᵛ), partly

---

[19] "An English Theologian's View on Roman Law: Pepo, Irnerius, Ralph Niger," *Mediaeval and Renaissance Studies*, I (1941), 246.

[20] Kantorowicz and Smalley, p. 246, n.2.

[21] F. de Zulueta (ed.), *The Liber Pauperum of Vacarius* (Selden Society, XLIV; London,
1927), Introd. pp. xix, cxlviii.

coming from the school of Bologna, partly from the French and Anglo-Norman schools.[22] The first two folios were used for miscellaneous entries, among which Innocent III's great decretal *Pastoralis*, 19 December 1204, to the bishop of Ely (fol. 1)[23] and several short pieces — *distinctiones, quaestiones, summulae* — of civil law, mostly on actions (fol. 2ʳ); of these, a *quaestio* on *actiones negatoriae* must arrest our attention, because it contains one of the few references to an opinion of Master Vacarius[24] that can be found outside the glosses of the *Liber pauperum*.[25] This is followed by a *summula* analyzing the definition of *actio* in Justinian's *Institutes*;[26] and then we read, written in two columns, two stanzas of nine hexameters each, in praise of the study of law. Directly underneath each stanza the same hand has entered a number of mnemonics on legal subjects;[27] a third column contains, as a kind of afterthought (always in the same hand), five more hexameters in which the praise of "rewarding labors" is placed in conventional contrast with the sterile efforts of logic. More mnemonics follow.

In printing here the text from B.M. MS. Addit. 24659, I have omitted the mnemonics as being definitely extraneous matter; but I have added the five lines from col. 3 although in their artificial construction and allegorical conceits they sharply differ from the plain language of the preceding verses, to which in all likelihood they did not originally belong.

---

[22] Simon of Bisignano, *Summa decretorum* (Bolognese, fol. 3-26ᵛ, 28-41ʳ); anon. *Prologue* "*Sapientia edificauit*" (Anglo-Norman, fol. 2ᵛ); anon. *Distinctiones "Lex naturalis"* (Anglo-Norman, fol. 2ᵛ-4ᵛ, 10ʳ [marg. inf.]; fol. 43ᵛ); anon. *Summa "Permissio quedam"* (French, fol. 41ᵛ-42ᵛ, 27ʳ-27ᵛ, 43ʳ): cf. Kuttner, *Repertorium der Kanonistik 1140-1234* (Studi e Testi, LXXI; Città del Vaticano, 1937), pp. 148-149, 192, 227; "An Interim Checklist of Manuscripts," *Traditio*, XI (1955), 441, 448; "Notes on Manuscripts," *ibid.*, XVII (1961), 533.

[23] A. Potthast, *Regesta Pontificum Romanorum* (Berlin, 1874-75), N°. 2350.

[24] "De his enim actionibus in rem negatoriis queritur quis probare debeat ... Magister Vacar̄.: Quodsi actor est in possessione libertatis, reo incumbit probatio ... ; si reus est in possessione seruitutis, actor probare debet ... ; set si neutrum eorum apparet, reus probare debet ... " A full transcription and discussion lies outside the scope of the present paper. (In an *actio negatoria* the owner of a piece of property sues for having the land declared free from an easement (*servitus*) claimed by the defendant.)

[25] The other known references are listed in Kuttner and Rathbone, "Anglo-Norman Canonists ... " (n. 2 *supra*), pp. 287, 318, n. 7a. To these can be added: Oxford, Oriel College, MS. 53 (from St. Andrew's, Northampton), fol. 355ʳ, marginal addition to a Bolognese collection of *quaestiones*: "Quod contra leges factum est ... Set mag. va. soluit sic, et melius: ... "; this corresponds to the gloss in MS. *W* of *Lib. paup.* I.8, n. 45b (ed. de Zulueta, p. 19).

[26] Begins: "Actio sic describitur. Actio nichil aliud est quam ius persequendi .... [*Inst.* 4.6]"; ends: " ... ut in contractibus."

[27] Col. 1: three mnemonics, of 2, 2, and 3 lines respectively (beg. "Anno si debes, in fine teneberis anni"); col. 2: again three, of 4, 2, and 1 line(s); three more (2, 1, 1) at the end of col. 3 (ends: "Scissum in raptu fractum constat periisse").

[1] Dat Galienus opes et sanctio Justiniana,
Ex aliis paleas, ex istis collige grana.
Si quis forte cupit Juris consultus haberi,
Continuet studium, uelit a quocumque doceri,
5 Inuigilet, nec uincat eum tortura laboris,
Fortior insurgat cunctisque recentior horis.
Pandectam relegat, pandectam scire laboret,
Alte mentis opus colat, amplectatur, adoret.
Nec minus est codex opus imperiale legendus.

[2] Terminat hic leges, fit questio iuris in illis:
Hic iubet, illa docent, lex pendet ab hoc et ab illis.
Justicie duo templa patent responsa petenti,
Thesaurosque nouos aperit labor hic fodienti.
5 Dat nomen clarum, dat amicos, implet auarum,
Informat mores, animum regit, auget honores.
Ergo laboremus qui noscere Jura studemus:
Ergo malo mori quam uertere terga labori.
Sumptus atque labor licet instent, non superabor.

[3] Torquens tortorem superabo labore laborem.
Vsque modo sterili mandasti semen harene.
Quid Plato, quid Sortes, quid friuola gentis egene?
Preferrem uberes: luo sumptibus otia pene.
Pinguis aratur ager, spem messis concipe plene.

Notes on the Text:

1.1 Galienus] This form occurs in medieval literature also where no prosodic
reason (as here) would demand the quadrisyllabic, e.g., in John of Salisbury's *Policraticus*, ed. C.I. Webb (Oxford, 1909), II, 255.24, 256.13 (=Migne,
PL 199, 727B-C).
1.3 Juris consultus] The classical Roman term for designating a member of the
higher legal profession. In later forms of this verse (see note 28 *infra*) it
is replaced by the less technical 'in iure peritus.'
1.7 Pandectam] Justinian's *Digest*, i.e., the codification of tens of thousands
of excerpts from the writings of the classical jurists. According to the bilingual constitution *Tanta* (Δέδωκεν) of 16 December 533, prefixed to the work,
the official Latin title was *Digesta seu Pandectae* (" ... nomenque libris im-
posuimus digestorum seu pandectarum": *Tanta*, § 1; cf. §§ 12, 23), but
in Δέδωκεν the Greek word appears in the singular: ὅπερ βιβλίον digesta
εἴτε πανδέκτην προσηγορεύσαμεν (cf.also the Greek *Index librorum* of the
Florentine MS: ... τῶν Digeston ἤτοι τοῦ Πανδέκτου). On the whole,
the Greek name was used much less frequently in the Middle Ages

than *Digesta*, and then preferably in the plural. But the singular is found too, e.g. in Peter of Blois, *Epist.* 140: "... Vides ... quam immeabile pelagus sit Pandecta, in qua civile ius continetur" (Migne, *PL* 207, 416C). This recondite usage could hardly stem from $\Delta\acute{\epsilon}\delta\omega\varkappa\epsilon\nu$, since in the twelfth-century law schools "graeca non leguntur"; but one should remember that to the early Middle Ages—when the single surviving MS. of the *Digest* lay forgotten — the singular 'Pandecta' had long become familiar as a name for the Bible, especially through Alcuin's verses at the end of his revision of the Vulgate: "Nomine pandecten proprio vocitare memento/ Hoc corpus sacrum, lector in ore tuo/ ... " (ed. E. Dümmler, in *MGH*, Poetae aevi Karolini, I [Berlin, 1881], 283).

1.9 codex] Justinian's *Code*, the official collection of imperial constitutions, promulgated on 16 November 534.

2.1 hic] the *Codex*; in illis] the *Digesta*; note the implicit substitution of the Latin plural for the singular 'Pandecta'; also in the next line ('hic ... illa').

2.1-2 Terminat leges, questio iuris; iubet, docent] Different from the terminology of the earlier classical law, the word *leges* had come to designate in Justinian's time the imperial statutory legislation, and *ius*, the opinions of the classical jurists; the statute (in the *Code*) 'commands,' the jurists' opinions (in the *Digest*) 'instruct.' Both together form *lex* 'the Law' as a whole.

2.2 ab hoc] ab hac (h^a) MS.

2.3 Justicie duo templa] This again refers to the two books. On the 'temple of Justice' in medieval thought, see E.H. Kantorowicz, *The King's Two Bodies* (Princeton, 1957), pp. 107-115.

3.1 I take this leonine verse to be a kind of title for the next four lines. It resumes the theme and vocabulary of 1.5 and 2.9, thus serving as a transition to the verses that follow (new paragraph mark before line 2).

3.2 sterili mandasti semen harene] cf. *Meum est propositum* 10.1: "In arenam logicus frustra semen serit."

3.3 Plato, Sortes] On the stereotype use of the names of Plato and "Sortes" (Socrates) in medieval syllogistic exercises see Strecker's commentary on *Meum est propositum* 16.2 "discat capram facere de persona Sortis" (p. 389); Raby, *Secular Latin Poetry*, II, 229, n.6.

3.3 friuola] here as substantive, 'trifles'.

3.4 Preferrem uberes] The adjective is here used as an absolute: *uberes agros, artes, scientias,* or even *homines* (contrasting with "gentis egene") could be understood.

3.4 luo sumptibus otia pene] Interlacing word order, "I redeem [my] leisures with the cost of toil."

3.5 Pinguis ager; messis plene] For the conventional image of harvest and reaping, see above, at n. 17; also *Meum est propositum* 14.2: "ager reddens centuplum non est deserendus."

*
* *

The poem on legal studies (stanzas 1 and 2)—if such didactic versification deserves to be called poetry—apparently is made up of several clusters of verses that existed also elsewhere separately: the change in 2.5 from rhymed pairs of hexameters (*hexametri caudati*) to leonine verse should suffice to indicate this. Moreover, we find parts of the two stanzas used later on in similar school compositions: thus, e.g., in MS. Vat. lat. 5066 (late thirteenth century), where the lines 1.3-6, 2.7-8 appear with seven other intercalated lines in the same vein;[28] or in Henry of Susa's (Hostiensis) celebrated *Summa aurea* or *copiosa* on the Decretals, completed in 1253,[29] where the lines "Si quis forte cupit ... recentior horis" (1.3-6), capped by the Vergilian "Nam labor improbus omnia vincit" (cf. *Georg.* 1.145-146) are quoted in the prologue.[30] Probably from this source, they were incorporated by Jean de Jean (Johannes Johannis), abbot of Joncels, into his *Memoriale decreti*, a vast encyclopedia of references, definitions, and quotations,[31] which he completed in 1339:[32] the four verses with the added line from Vergil appear here in the section on mnemonics and similar *poetica metra*.[33] Only a few years earlier, a German Augustinian friar, Hermann von Schildesche, had cited the same verses from Hostiensis in the opening sentence—after the dedicatory epistle—of his *Introductorium*: "Si quis autem desiderat studio iuris operam dare, omnia obseruare debet ea que Hostiensis ponit in principio summe sue: 'Si quis forte cupit consultus iuris haberi. ... '"[34]

All this is only evidence *ex post*, but it would indicate that our versifier used to a large extent currency already coined. Thus we have no reason to credit him with the opening lines; but next to two other Englishmen, Stephen

---

[28] Vat. lat. 5066, fol. 52ᵛ (after Johannes de Deo, *Libellus dispensationum*): "Si quis forte cupit in iure peritus haberi/ ... "(= *L*[ondon] 1.3; for the variant see the commentary above, to 1.3 *Juris consultus*). Five hexameters after *L* 1.3-6; an elegiac distich after *L* 2.7-8; ends: "Hec duo iunta [*sic*] simul fructiferare solent."

[29] On the career and works of Henry of Susa, who died as cardinal bishop of Ostia (whence the traditional sobriquet, used also by Dante, *Parad.* 12.83) see now Ch. Lefebvre, "Hostiensis," *Dictionnaire de Droit canonique*, V (Paris, 1953), 1211-27; on the *Summa*: col. 1215-20.

[30] *Summa aurea*, prol. (ed. Lyons, 1568, fol. 2ᵛᵃ).

[31] The uncommon use by the author of *quota* 'quotation' should be noted; cf. "Dubito in quotis istis que sequuntur" (text in H. Gilles' article [cited n. 32, *infra*], p. 593, n. 72).

[32] H. Gilles, "Un canoniste oublié: l'Abbé de Joncels," *Revue historique de Droit français et étranger*, 4ᵉ sér., XXXVIII (1960), 578-602, at pp. 589-599. For other writings, overlooked by Gilles, see A.M. Stickler, "Decretistica Germanica adaucta," *Traditio*, XII (1956), 600; idem, "Iter helveticum," *ibid.*, XIV (1958), 464; for the Abbot's career, see also Kuttner, note on Gilles' article, *Traditio*, XVII (1961), 537.

[33] Cf. Gilles, p. 593, n. 74, where two emendations are needed (line 3 *vitat*] uincat *L*; 4 *retentior*] recentior *L*) and where neither the quotation from Vergil nor the borrowing from Hostiensis are recognized.

[34] Seckel, *Beiträge* (note 15 *supra*), p. 199. For the date—between 1328 and 1337, probably *c.* 1330-32—see *ibid.*, pp. 151-156; for the author and his other works, pp. 129-145 ("Nachträge": pp. 503-507), also A. Zumkeller, *Hermann v. Schildesche O.E.S.A.* (Cassiciacum XIV; Würzburg, 1957).

246

Langton and the writer of the *Meum est propositum*, our eager student of Roman law from the Vacarian school was certainly one of the first to make use of the couplet on Galen and Justinian which was to remain a familiar quotation down to the sixteenth century. Unless evidence to the contrary is found, it is perhaps not too much to presume that an English wit of the late twelfth century was the author of the felicitous ditty.

The Catholic University of America
Washington 17, D.C.

Plato in Gratian's *Decretum*
(MS Vat. lat. 1370, fo. 3v)
(Foto Biblioteca Vaticana)

[Facing p. 93

XI

GRATIAN AND PLATO

In the course of his often analysed discussion of natural law, Gratian tackles the problem of private ownership in the section the school designated as Distinction Eight. It has often been observed that one could describe the whole introductory part of the *Concordia discordantium canonum* as an expanded commentary on the chapter *de legibus* of Isidore of Seville's Etymologies;[1] thus Dist. 8 partly serves to illustrate the words 'communis omnium possessio' in Isidore's description of the *ius naturale*.[2]

Here, by way of introducing St Augustine's famous challenge of the right of the Donatists to own property,[3] Gratian presents the thesis that by the law of nature all things are common to all men ('omnia communia omnibus') and finds this vestigial communism not only practised by the early company of believers of whom we read in the Acts of the Apostles, but also prefigured in the pre-Christian philosophers:[4]

> Unde apud Platonem illa ciuitas iustissime ordinata traditur in qua quisque proprios nescit affectus.

The terse dictum on 'not knowing one's own attachments' remained a puzzle for most of the medieval glossators. Modern writers, for all their interest in Gratian's general doctrine of law, have all but bypassed it and certainly made no efforts at finding its source.[5] Only a few, by now

---

[1] See J. Gaudemet, 'La doctrine des sources dans le Décret de Gratien', *Revue de droit canonique*, I (1951), 5–31.　　　　[2] D.1 c.7: Isidore, *Etymologies*, v. 4.1.

[3] D.8 c.1: Augustine, *In evangelium Joannis* VI. 25. For the medieval discussion of common (public) and private ownership in relation to natural law, see R. Weigand, *Die Naturrechtslehre der Legisten und Dekretisten von Irnerius bis Accursius und von Gratian bis Johannes Teutonicus*, Münchener theologische Studien, Kanonistische Abteilung XXVI (Munich, 1967), 307–61.

[4] D.8 pr.: '...quod non solum inter eos seruatum creditur de quibus legitur,..."Multitudinis autem credentium erat cor unum et anima una" [Act. 4:32], uerum etiam ex precedenti tempore a philosophis traditum inuenitur. Unde...'

[5] Among the very few who even mention it, derivation of Gratian's dictum from the pseudo-Clementine passage on 'Grecorum quidam sapientissimus' in C.12 q.1 c.2 (see at nn. 44ff. below)

forgotten, twelfth-century decretists recognised *proprios nescire affectus* as a quotation. But it was a quotation out of context, and we may safely assume that Gratian himself was unaware of the contextual meaning of the phrase he quoted: or else he would have chosen a less embarrassing parallel to the communal property of the first Christians than the communal marriage bond and common offspring of the Guardians in Plato's ideal State.

For Gratian's phrase can be traced back to the book that occupied the central place in medieval Platonism: the *Timaeus* in its Latin version (*c.* A.D. 400) by Calcidius.[6] Some of the influence the dialogue exerted on legal thought of the twelfth century has been discussed elsewhere: it came chiefly from the opening pages, where Plato had Socrates recapitulate major points of 'yesterday's discourse', i.e., the *Republic*; it also came from Calcidius's commentary and the contemporary glosses of William of Conches and others.[7]

The Guardians of Plato's City, the *Timaeus* reminds us, have no property of their own. Their women must be moulded according to the same values and conventions as the men.[8] Regarding marriages and children, Socrates recalls, 'we ordained that all should have all in common, so that no one should ever recognise his own offspring (ὅπως μηδείς ποτε τὸ γεγενημένον αὐτῷ ἰδίᾳ γνώσοιτο) and all should regard all as their kinsmen'.[9] But Calcidius chose the Latin *affectus* (plural) in the extremely rare[10] meaning of 'the loved ones' for rendering Plato's τὸ γεγενημένον, 'the offspring':[11]

> de existimandis communibus nuptiis communique prole, *si suos quisque minime internoscat affectus* proptereaque omnes omnibus religionem consanguinitatis exhibeant...

has been baldly asserted by D. Composta, 'Il diritto naturale in Graziano', *Studia Gratiana*, II (1954), 151–210 at p. 179; Ch. Leitmeier, 'Das Privateigentum im gratianischen Dekret', *ibid.* 361–73 at p. 365. Weigand, *Naturrechtslehre*, p. 311 and n. 15, rightly expresses doubt but considers the source unknown.

[6] *Timaeus a Calcidio translatus commentarioque instructus,*...adiuncto P. J. Jensen ed. J. H. Waszink; Corpus Platonicum medii aevi, ed. R. Klibanski: Plato Latinus, IV (London–Leiden, 1962). This now replaces J. Wrobel's edition, *Platonis Timaeus Chalcidio interprete* (Leipzig, 1876).

[7] S. Kuttner, 'Sur les origines du terme "droit positif"', *Revue historique de droit français et étranger*, 4e série, XV (1936), 728–40; and 'A forgotten definition of Justice', in the forthcoming *Mélanges G. Fransen*; S. Gagnér, *Studien zur Ideengeschichte der Gesetzgebung*, Studia iuridica Uppsalensia, I (Stockholm–Uppsala, 1960), pp. 211–40.

[8] *Timaeus* 18 B-C.

[9] *Timaeus* 18 C-D (see R. G. Bury's translation in Loeb Classical Library, p. 21).

[10] Lucan, *Pharsalia*, VIII.132 and Julius Capitolinus, *Vita Maximini*, c.23, are the chief instances quoted in Lewis and Short's *Dictionary*, *s.v.*

[11] ed. Waszink, p. 9; ed. Wrobel, p. 7.

Gratian and Plato

Thus *affectus* became the key word for Gratian (*proprios nescit affectus*) and his interpreters. But very few, if any, could guess the original and rather recherché connotation of the term as indicating not emotions but persons.

Stephen of Tournai was the first of the Bolognese to comment upon the passage in Gratian, and he set the pattern for its traditional explication. In that great fictional republic of Plato's, he says, all things are common and no one must prefer affection (*affectus*) for one's own to that for others; that is, all must love all in equal measure.[12] This formula comes close to the ultimate goal in the Platonic scheme, and it was repeated in one way or another by many of the glossators.[13] Some also pointed to the parallel with St Paul's description of Charity 'which does not seek its own'.[14] But all these explanations remain unaware of the specific foundation, the *communes nuptiae*, on which the equal love for everyone's offspring was to be based in Plato's City.

The only twelfth-century comment on Gratian's Dist. 8 that shows a direct acquaintance with the context of the passage in the *Timaeus* is that of the *Summa Antiquitate et tempore*.[15] Its anonymous author belonged to the French school of the 1170s and probably taught for some time at Cologne.[16] He begins his discussion with a critique of the Master's *omnia omnibus communia* which, he says, cannot be called a characteristic of the natural law if we maintain (with Gratian) the

---

[12] Stephanus Tornacensis, *Summa*, D.8 pr.v. *nescit proprios affectus*: 'Sic enim dixerat Plato esse in illa maxima ciuitate cuius rem publicam fingebat omnia communia et neminem suorum affectus aliis preponere debere, idest omnes ab inuicem equaliter diligendos esse' (Vatican MS Borgh. 287, fo. 13va). The text in Schulte's selective edition (Giessen, 1891), p. 17, is marred by serious misreadings.

Hereafter, glosses and other material from manuscript sources will be printed with their full text only in appendix 1 below; in the footnotes, references to MS and folio will be given only for short texts not included in the appendix.

[13] Johannes Faventinus, *Summa*, Dist. 8 pr. (with only minor verbal variants); *Summa De iure canonico tractaturus* (Laon MS 371 bis); Alanus, *Glossa Ius naturale*; Johannes Teutonicus, *Glossa ordinaria*. For Laurentius and Huguccio see n. 36 and text at n. 84 below.

[14] *Glossa Ecce uicit leo* Dist. 8 pr. v. *nescit*: 'idest nescire debet, uel *nescit*, tantum. Similiter caritas nescit que sua sunt' etc. (see appendix 1 below for full text); cf. 1 Cor. 13:5. The gloss 'tantum' is derived from Huguccio's exegesis; cf. the text at n. 84 below.

[15] Göttingen MS 159, fo. 11ra/b; published only in part and without adequate explanation by H. Singer, 'Beiträge zur Würdigung der Decretistenlitteratur, 11', *Archiv für katholisches Kirchenrecht*, LXXIII (1895), 70–1; full text in appendix 1 below. The inferior MSS of the *Summa* omit this important piece together with several other passages in Dist. 4–10; see J. F. von Schulte, *Die Summa magistri Rufini* (Giessen, 1892), pp. l–lvii and Singer, 'Decretistenlitteratur', pp. 35–40; hence not discussed by Weigand, *Naturrechtslehre*, who only consulted one MS, Mainz 477 (52), cf. p. xv.

[16] S. Kuttner, *Repertorium der Kanonistik (1140–1234)*, Studi e testi, LXXI (Vatican City, 1937), 178f.; S. Kuttner and E. Rathbone, 'Anglo-Norman canonists of the twelfth century', *Traditio*, VII (1949–51), 279–358 at p. 299.

equation of natural and divine law.[17] Then, after citing scriptural proof from the Decalogue, the Old and the New Testament, for the right to own property, he goes on to say: 'We could pass over this text (*locus*) if he (Gratian) had not confused matters by appending examples to show that nothing is one's own', and refers to the quotations from Acts and from Plato.[18] In a somewhat sophistic argumentation, which echoes another work of the early French school, the *Summa Magister Gratianus in hoc opere* (*Summa Parisiensis*), our author charges Gratian with the blunder (*peccauit*) of having drawn a universal conclusion (*omnium omnia*) from limited examples: first, the common possessions of those early Christians 'with one heart and one soul' were not possessions of 'all', since they did not include unbelievers;[19] and the second blunder is 'obvious to all who understand Plato':

For only the Guardians (*milites*, φύλακες) of that City were to have their expenses in common, lest, being concerned with their own [affairs], they give less service to the common good of their guardianship.[20]

This is pure *Timaeus*, followed by the platitude that this does not mean common to 'all': at least the enemies are excluded.[21] After some more sententious remarks – on worthy Homer nodding, on property beginning with Adam's sons[22] – the author concludes that Gratian's examples were only meant to show what *ought* to follow from the natural law. They may be insufficient but remain useful: 'non sufficiunt

[17] *Antiquitate et tempore*, Dist. 8 pr.: 'Set quod iste non sit effectus iuris naturalis ex his innotescat: ius nature inferius appellat ius diuinum et illud dicit contineri in scripturis diuinis. Quod si scripturam diuinam appellat decalogum preceptorum, patet quoniam secundum illud aliqua sunt propria', etc.

[18] *Ibid.* 'Sic transiri posset locus iste, nisi rem turbaret exemplis suppositis. Duo enim subiungit exempla quibus conatur ostendere nulla esse propria, quorum unum sumptum est de actibus apostolorum...alterum a Platone, scilicet de ciuibus platonice ciuitatis', etc.

[19] *Ibid.* 'Set in utroque exemplo peccauit: in priori quia, etsi singulorum quorum erat cor unum et anima una non essent aliqua propria, tamen que eorum erant communia non erant "omnium" communia, quia infidelium non'; cf. *Summa Parisiensis*, Dist. 8 pr.: 'set laborat in positione exemplorum, et salua pace sua melius potuisset de his tacere, quia que erant apostolorum inter se erant communia, set non omnibus aliis' (ed. McLaughlin, p. 7, emended: see appendix I below).

[20] *Antiquit. et temp.*: 'Quod in secundo exemplo peccauerit palam est intelligentibus Platonem, quia tantum milites illius ciuitatis debebant expensam habere de communi, ne propriis intenti minus ad communem utilitatem milicie deseruirent.'

[21] *Ibid.* 'Nullatenus tamen "omnium" erant communia que possidebant ibi ciues, quia saltem non inimicorum.'

[22] *Ibid.* 'Ad hoc dicendum non esse mirum si quandoque bonus dormitat Homerus...quia modo non est iste effectus iuris naturalis, nec fuit forte ex quo Adam filios habere cepit, quia probabile est quod statim ceperint esse propria.'

Gratian and Plato

set proficiunt'.[23] Here again he follows in the steps of the *Summa Parisiensis*, which had called them 'non...exempla set quoquo modo uestigia exemplorum'.

When *Antiquitate et tempore* turns to the exegesis of Gratian's 'in qua quisque proprios nescit affectus', the author's familiarity with the Calcidian text – and, presumably, its twelfth-century commentaries – becomes once more apparent. The single manuscript, however, stands here in need of some emendation:[24]

quia 'quisque' minores se dilexit[a] ut filios, maiores ut parentes,[b] et sic non habuit 'proprios' uel speciales[c] circa unum 'affectus'...

   [a-b]dilexit inter filios maiores. ut parentes. MS   [c]spirituales (sp̄uales) MS

This renders the thought of a kinship pattern which Plato expressed at this point in the *Timaeus*:[25] to treat all one's elders as parents, all one's juniors as sons (the third Platonic relation, equals as brothers or sisters, is omitted). In his vocabulary, however, our author seems closer to the medieval glosses than to the Latin dialogue itself.[26] A brief speculative remark follows about the equal distribution of goods 'if there really were people who had no greater *affectus* for one than for another',[27] and only then, for the first time, the author of *Antiquitate et tempore* alludes to the specific context of all this, the communal marriages in Plato's City. He does so in a rather oblique fashion:

Nota quod quidam [quia MS] dicunt Platonem loqui ibi de nuptiis catarorum et eum sensisse illas esse celebrandas.

The marriages of the Cathari – this indeed leads us far afield into a Manichean world where the absolute rejection of the flesh made all monogamous unions as 'evil' as any fornication or sexual perversity. Not only in popular Catholic belief but also in learned opinion, the

---

[23] *Ibid.* 'Verumtamen ostendit hic M. G. qualis deberet esse effectus iuris naturalis....Si ergo M. G. non ponit exemplum usquequaque sufficiens, est tamen quod dicit in parte proficiens: ista enim exempla non sufficiunt set proficiunt.' Cf. *Summa Paris. ad loc*: 'dici potest quod hec non sunt exempla set quoquo modo uestigia exemplorum' etc.

[24] The following is one of the passages omitted by Singer, 'Beiträge', p. 71.

[25] *Timaeus*, 18 D.

[26] Compare William of Conches, *ad loc.*: '...maioritas ut pater, mater, minoritas ut filius, equalitas ut frater, soror,...docuit Plato ut maiores etate diligeremus ut maiores sanguine', etc. in the edition by E. Jeauneau, *Guillaume de Conches: Glosae super Platonem*, Textes philosophiques du moyen âge, XIII (Paris, 1965), 78. The *Timaeus*, on the other hand, goes into greater detail, specifying *religio* not only *parentum* but also *auorum atque atauorum*; and it calls the juniors *infraque filii* and *nepotes*, but not *minores*: ed. Waszink, p. 9.

[27] *Antiquit. et temp.*: 'Et forte si aliqui essent qui non maiorem ad unum quam ad alium affectum haberent et illi omnibus equaliter cuperent ⟨dare?⟩, et talium bona omnibus essent communia.'

Catharist rejection of marriage was tantamount to a licence for promiscuous intercourse;[28] and there is reason to believe that within the Catharist establishment not a few *credentes* shared this view, leaving the suppression of the body to the *perfecti*.

To arrive at this equation between the 'unlimited' marriages of the Cathari and the community of wives and children among the Guardians of Plato's State was an intellectual feat which testifies to the sophistication of the unknown French or Rhenish canonist who wrote *Antiquitate et tempore*. It belongs in the same intellectual climate as Alan of Lille's observation concerning the Cathari's promiscuity (which he took for granted in his *Contra hereticos*): 'They say that marriage is contrary to the Law of Nature, because Natural Law prescribes that all should be common to all.'[29]

With a final remark, 'But we are accustomed to excuse Plato when we read his book', our author follows the lead of William of Conches and other glossators of the *Timaeus*, all of whom defended the philosopher against the imputation of lewdness (*turpitudo*) and tried to get around a literal understanding of the *communes nuptiae et communis proles*.[30] We shall have to return to this exegesis in discussing the second Platonic text of the Decretum.

The thoughtful commentary of *Antiquitate et tempore* left disappointingly little trace among the glossators of Gratian's Dist. 8. There is a brief passage in the *Summa Tractaturus magister* repeating the criticism of the Master's 'insufficient but useful' example;[31] and we have a remarkable gloss by an academic (i.e., non-scribal) hand in the Biberach manuscript of Gratian, to Dist. 8 pr. v. *nescit*:[32]

idest non internoscit. maiores enim minores ut filios diligebant et hii illis ut patribus obsequebantur.

[28] See e.g., Alan of Lille, *Contra haereticos*, I. 63: 'Dicunt enim quidam eorum quod omnibus modis se homo debet purgare ab eo quod habet a principe tenebrarum, idest a corpore, et ideo passim et qualitercumque fornicandum esse, ut citius liberentur a mala natura', in Migne, *PL*, CCX, 365–6. Further references and discussion in A. Borst, *Die Katharer*, MGH Schriften, XII (Stuttgart, 1953), 2, 179, 182; J. T. Noonan, *Contraception: A history of its treatment by the Catholic theologians and canonists* (Cambridge, Mass., 1966), pp. 183–8. See also G. Couvreur, *Les pauvres ont-ils des droits?*, Analecta Gregoriana, CXI (Rome, 1961), p. 128 and n. 398.

[29] *Contra haeret.* I. 63: 'Dicunt etiam coniugium obuiari legi naturae, quia lex naturalis dictat omnia esse communia', col. 366B.

[30] *Antiquit. et temp.*: 'Set nos eum excusare solemus in legendo librum ipsius'; cf. William of Conches: 'Hic quidam...Platonem turpitudinis arguunt,...Nos uero dicimus Platonem non imperasse turpitudinem sed affectum', ed. Jeauneau, p. 78.   [31] Text in appendix I below.

[32] Biberach MS B 3515 fo. 12ra. On the MS and its several layers of glosses see R. Weigand, 'Die Dekrethandschrift des Spitalarchivs Biberach an der Riss', *Bulletin of medieval canon law*, N.S., II (1972), 76–81; on its decretals also S. Kuttner, *ibid.* III (1973), 61–71.

Gratian and Plato

The use of *internoscere* even suggests a direct knowledge of Calcidius's text; all the same, a relation also exists between this layer of glosses and *Antiquitate*: a little earlier on the same page, the glossator of the Biberach manuscript mentions the existence of a copy of the *Codex Theodosianus* in Chartres – an assertion that has its only known parallel in our *Summa*;[33] and this in turn is related to a similar remark of the *Summa Parisiensis* on copies of the Theodosian Code in Orléans and in St Denis.[34]

No other texts have come to light to indicate an influence of the *Summa Antiquitate et tempore*. Among the later Bolognese glossators, Alanus Anglicus had read the *Timaeus*, though at Dist. 8 he limited himself to a mere mention of the dialogue.[35] But in the early thirteenth century, some must still have had a notion of the original meaning of Calcidius's vocabulary: they were rebuked by Laurentius Hispanus when he glossed (*c.* 1210–14) the words *quisque nescit proprios affectus* in Dist. 8 pr.: 'Do not understand this as if everyone ought not to know his own sons, or were permitted to sleep with his own daughter' – and then followed instead the conventional exegesis: those words mean, to accept strangers like one's children.[36] The rejected interpretation may, in its second part (*coire cum filia*), easily have been made up for polemical purposes, perhaps by Laurentius himself, as a *reductio ad absurdum*. But its first part (*ut nesciat filios suos*) renders of course Plato's true sense. It may, together with its negation, somehow be derived from the gloss of William of Conches on the passage *de communi prole* in the *Timaeus*[37] – though by what channels, we could at present not say.

---

33 The Biberach gloss to Dist. 7 c.2 v. *Theodosianum* is partly hidden in the fold of the volume and hence not fully legible on the microfilm: '///dicem carnotenses ///cut dicitur ut (?) quedam scripta ///decretis habentur'; cf. *Summa Antiquit. et temp. ad loc*: 'Hunc codicem adhuc habent Carnotenses, unde in decretis Iuonis multa ab hoc codice excepta inueniuntur' etc.; Göttingen MS 159, fo. 10vb.

34 *Sum. Par.* C.2 q.6 c.24: 'Sed cum Theodosianus codex non sit in Lombardia, est enim [*leg.* tamen?] Aurelianis et apud sanctum Dionysium' etc.; ed. McLaughlin, p. 109. The testimonies of the two *Summae* have been frequently discussed and variously evaluated, ever since Maassen first published the text from *Sum. Par.* in 1858; see *inter al.* Th. Mommsen in the *Prolegomena* of his edition of the Theodosianus I.1 (Berlin, 1905), lxxviii, cv; and A. von Wretschko, 'De usu Breviarii Alariciani...', *ibid.* p. cccxlix, with bibliography in nn. 3–5. (Note that the word 'excepta' in *Antiquit. et temp.* [n. 33] is always misquoted 'excerpta'.)

35 *Glossa Ius naturale*, Dist. 8 v. *Platonem*: 'in Thimeo. *proprios*: idest tanta affectione' etc. (More at n. 47 below).

36 *Glossa Palatina*, Dist. 8 pr. v. *nescit*: 'Non ita intelligas ut nesciat filios suos et ut ei liceat cum filia sua coire, set ita: idest eodem affectu suscipit extraneos quo et filios proprios' etc.

37 According to William of Conches some believe that Socrates and Plato ordained 'quod... cum aliquis coire uellet, prefectus quam uellet tenebris supponeret, ignorante utroque cui commisceretur et ita nec proprium filium cognosceret'; but we take Plato's meaning 'ac si diceret: unusquisque uxorem et filios alterius in bono diligat ac si sui essent', ed. Jeauneau, p. 78; and see at n. 81 below.

Even further remote is the chance that the opinion Laurentius rejected was a late echo of Abaelard's teaching. Peter Abaelard in his *Theologia christiana* appears to have been the only major writer of the twelfth century who held that Plato here meant what he said. The interpretation of the passage from the *Timaeus* is part of Abaelard's exposition of the 'harmony of evangelical and philosophical doctrine' in respect of the active life.[38] But in placing – as Gratian would do after him – the Acts of Apostles and Plato next to each other, Abaelard for one left no doubt that 'illud decretum Socratis in Timaeo Platonis inductum' really meant community of wives, so that 'nullus proprios recognoscat liberos'.[39] This led him to a rhetorical question on *turpitudo* and *abominabilis obscoenitas* in so great a moral philosopher and hence to a digression quoting Jerome's harsh censure of passion and ardour in the act of marriage ('nihil est fedius quam uxorem amare quasi adulteram').[40] He concluded that the marital communism decreed by Socrates was not intended for the delight of sexual unions but for their fruits – thus ending in a sombre, utilitarian kind of *caritas* in which the individual possesses anything he has, children and all, for the sake of the common weal alone.[41] And as if to clinch his point, Abaelard related the story from Valerius Maximus how Aulus Fulvius, when his son went over to Catilina, had the lad seized and put to death, proclaiming, 'I did not sire my son for Catilina against my country (*patria*) but for the country against Catilina'.[42]

---

[38] Abaelard, *Theologia christiana*, II. 45–8, ed. E. M. Buytaert, Corpus Christianorum, Continuatio mediaeualis, XII (Turnhout, 1969), 150–1; Migne, *PL.* CLXXVIII, 1180A–81A. (The term 'euangelicae ac philosophicae doctrinae concordia' is from c. 44, ed. Buytaert, p. 150, lines 619–20.) See also his *Dialogus inter Philosophum, Iudaeum et Christianum*, Migne, *PL.* CLXXVIII, 1653B–C. Both texts briefly mentioned by Couvreur, *Les pauvres* (n. 28 above), p. 171.

[39] *Theol. christ.*, II. 46 (lines 648–51).

[40] *Ibid.* c. 47, from Jerome, *Adversus Iovinianum*, I. 49: Migne, *PL.* XXIII, 281. On this text and its use in Gratian, C.32 q.4 c.5, see Noonan, *Contraception* (n. 28 above), pp. 79–80, 196–7; and authors cited in P. Weimar's 'Addenda and corrigenda' to the reprint of H. Kantorowicz, *Studies in the glossators of the Roman law* (Cambridge, 1938; repr. Aalen, 1969), no. 20, pp. 328–9.

[41] *Theol. christ.*, II. 48: 'Vxores itaque uult communes esse secundum fructum, non secundum usum, hoc est ad utilitatem ex eis percipiendam, non ad uoluptatem in eis explendam, ut uidelicet tanta sit in omnibus caritas propagata, ut unusquisque omnia quae habet, tam filios quam quaecumque alia, nonnisi ad communem utilitatem possidere appetat'; ed. Buytaert, p. 151, lines 673–9.

[42] *Ibid.* lines 679–85. After the present pages were written Professor John Benton kindly called my attention to the recent paper by T. Gregory, 'Abélard et Platon', in *Peter Abelard: Proceedings of the International Conference, Louvain May 10–12, 1971*, Mediaevalia Lovaniensia, ser. I, Studia II (Louvain–The Hague, 1974), 38–64. Professor Gregory discusses *Theol. christ.*, II. 45–8 on p. 59 and apparently finds no great difference between Abaelard's exegesis and that of William of Conches ('un commentaire analogue'). Yet it was one of William's chief concerns to shield Plato from a literal understanding of the *communes nuptiae*; see nn. 30, 37 above and 81 below.

Gratian and Plato

This austere reading of the *Timaeus* seems to have found no followers in the Middle Ages.

With the exception of the few authors thus far mentioned, all canonists took their information on the sharing of wives in Plato's State from another text in the Decretum. This was the Pseudo-Isidorian Letter Five of Pope Clement I, to St James and the brethren in Jerusalem, on having all things in common. Gratian presented this text as one of his authorities (c.2) in discussing the first question of *Causa* 12: whether clerics may have any possessions of their own.[43] 'Clement' backed his counsel on *communis vita* and *communis usus omnium* with various maxims, scriptural proofs, and the affirmation that 'one of the wisest of the Greeks said that friends must have all in common: but "all" includes without doubt the wives' ('in omnibus autem sunt sine dubio coniuges').[44]

It was, on the whole, a troublesome text. The glossators found it difficult, for instance, to explain a passage which preceded this one and declared that iniquity was at the root of all private ownership.[45] It was even harder to admit that St Clement should have followed a pagan philosopher and recommended the sharing of wives. They knew that the *sapientissimus* was Plato, reporting in the *Timaeus* on his imaginary republic;[46] a gloss by Alanus even cited the exact paragraph of the Latin text.[47] (The glossators could not know, of course, that the source behind the pseudo-Clementine reference was the *Republic* itself: for only there all things are said to be 'common to friends', κοινὰ τὰ φίλων, while in the *Timaeus* it reads 'common to all', κοινὰ τὰ ... πᾶσιν.[48]) What is more important, however, is that several canonists refused to

---

[43] Clemens, *ep.* 5 in *Decretales Pseudo-Isidorianae et capitula Angilrammi*, ed. P. Hinschius (Leipzig, 1863), pp. 65–6; Gratian, C.12 q.1 c.2.

[44] *Ibid.* 'Denique Grecorum quidam sapientissimus, hec ita esse sciens, communia debere ait esse amicorum omnia: in omnibus autem' etc.

[45] Cf. Weigand, *Naturrechtslehre* (n. 3 above), pp. 310–60; Couvreur, *Les pauvres*, pp. 121–54.

[46] Rufinus, *Summa* C.12 q.1 c.2 v. *Grecorum quidam*: 'scilicet Plato in Timeo'; ed. H. Singer (Paderborn, 1902), p. 321. Stephanus Tornacensis, *Summa, ad loc.* v. *coniuges*: '...ex uerbis Platonis...qui in re publica illa quam fingebat uxores et liberos communes esse dixit' etc. Cf. Johannes Faventinus and Huguccio *ad loc.*; also the *Summae Magister Gratianus in hoc opere*, *Omnis qui iuste*, *De iure canonico tractaturus*, and *Tractaturus magister*.

[47] Alanus, *Glossa Ius naturale* C.12 q.1 c.2 v. *coniuges*: 'supra di. viii. § Differt. In Platone c. de feminis; set intelligas' etc. See *Timaeus* 18C, tr. Calcidius: 'De feminis quoque opinor habitam mentionem...de existimandis communibus nuptiis' etc.; ed. Waszink, p. 9.

[48] *Republ.* 423E-424 on marriages and the procreation of children, κατὰ τὴν παροιμίαν πάντα ὅ τι μάλιστα κοινὰ τὰ φίλων ποιεῖσθαι, 'the proverbial goods of friends that are common' (P. Shorey's translation, Loeb Classical Library; and see his discussion of the proverb and Plato's use of it, I, p. 330 note *b*); 449C on wives and children, ὅτι κοινὰ τὰ φίλων ἔσται. The wording of *Tim.* 18C is given in the text at n. 9 above.

accept it. 'I do not believe', Stephen of Tournai said, 'that Clement placed this sentence of Plato's into the letter' ('non credo hoc apposuisse Clementem'), and others adopted or at least reported these doubts.[49] One gloss ascribes the passage to forgers, 'a falsatoribus dictum est',[50] while a French anonymous *Summa* observes that the words are Clement's but the meaning is Plato's.[51]

None of these writers was aware that a number of manuscripts of the (Pseudo-Isidorian) Decretals, especially of Hinschius's class A–2, indeed omitted the offensive words 'in omnibus autem' etc.[52] They were also omitted by one of the earliest major users of the Decretals in the A–2 form, the *Collectio Anselmo dedicata* of the late ninth century.[53] Two hundred years later, the canonical collection of Anselm of Lucca, in its recension B, presented this expurgated version of the letter as the first chapter of a cluster of texts on the *vita communis* at the beginning of Book VII (it is absent from the other recensions).[54] Hence Anselm cannot be the model of Gratian's text: the chapter is derived from another tradition, which has its fountainhead in the so-called *Collectio Tripartita* of Ivo of Chartres and has not been noted before.[55] This version cuts out some parts and reverses the order of others in the pseudo-Clemen-

---

[49] Stephanus, *Summa* C.12 q.1 c.2 v. *coniuges* (preceding the reference to the *uerba Platonis*, n. 46 above); 'non credo...' also in Johannes Faventinus, *Summa ad loc.*; the *Summae Omnis qui iuste* and *De iure can. tract.* merely have 'hoc non dicunt Clementem apposuisse' etc.

[50] Cues MS 223, gloss *ad loc.* v. *coniuges.*

[51] *Summa Tractaturus ad loc.* v. *in omnibus autem*: 'hec sunt uerba Clementis, tamen ex sensu uerborum Pla. sumpta' etc.

[52] See Hinschius, *Decretales Pseudo-Isid.* p. 65 n. 6; H. Fuhrmann, *Einfluss und Verbreitung der pseudoisidorischen Fälschungen*, MGH Schriften, XXIV (3 vols. Stuttgart, 1972–4), I, 55 n. 134 (at p. 56).

[53] *Coll. Ans. dedic.*, VI.1: Vercelli, Cathedral Chapter MS XV, fo. 141rb. For the collector's general dependence on the A–2 class of Pseudo-Isidore see P. Fournier–G. Le Bras, *Histoire des collections canoniques en Occident* (2 vols. Paris, 1931–2), I, 237; Fuhrmann, *Einfluss und Verbreitung*, II (1973), 429–30; for the distribution of parts of Clem. *ep.* 5 in the collection, see the tabulation in Fuhrmann, III (1974), 828.

[54] Ans. Lucensis, *Collectio* (rec. B) VII.1: MSS Vat. lat. 6381, fo. 161r; Vat. lat. 1364, fo. 161r. Already Antonio Agustín [Augustinus], *De emendatione Gratiani dialogorum libri duo* I.15 (in the posthumous edition, Tarragona, 1587, p. 151; *Opera omnia*, III (Lucca, 1767), 80) and the *Correctores Romani* commented upon the difference from Gratian's text; moreover Agustín recorded in the margin of his MS of Anselm (today Vat. lat. 6381) the absence of the chapter in another MS he had collated (today Venice, Marc. lat. IV.55; recension A). The chapter is also in recension C, VII. i: MS Vat. lat. 4983, fo. 331r. I have discussed some of Agustín's work on these three codices in 'Some Roman manuscripts of canonical collections', *Bulletin of medieval canon law*, N.S. 1 (1971), 16–20. For Anselm see further Fuhrmann, *Einfluss und Verbreitung*, II, 511–20; on Ans. B VII.1 also *ibid.* I, 56n.

[55] *Coll. Tripart.* I.1.23–4; also the chronological collection of decretal letters in MS Vat. lat. 3829 (on which see Fournier–Le Bras, *Histoire*, II, 210–18), fos. 14v–15r (11v–12r, old foliation). This should not have been overlooked since another fragment from the same pseudo-Clementine letter in Gratian Dist. 37 c.14 is correctly traced to *Tripart.* I.1.25 in Friedberg's edition, n. 137 *ad loc.* and Fuhrmann, III, 829 n. 303.

Gratian and Plato

tine letter and labels it as *epistola quarta*.[56] But Gratian, as Ivo before him, had no qualms about leaving the reference to Plato intact.

It is almost touching to see how similar the worries of sixteenth-century scholars about this passage were to those of the early glossators on Gratian. Until it was recognised and admitted that the decretals of Clement were all spurious, the only way to save the text of *ep.* 5 was to declare the passage on sharing the women to be interpolated. In 1551, Petrus Crabbe's collection of the *Concilia omnia* still left the letter unchanged[57] as it had been printed by Merlin, but from Surius on (Cologne 1567) all the great conciliar collections excised the words 'in omnibus autem...coniuges'.[58] The *Correctores Romani* of Gratian first addressed themselves to the problem in the meeting of 17 October 1570, as we learn from their (much too little-known) manuscript volumes of minutes and drafts in the Vatican Library.[59] The line the *doctores* took then was essentially the same as twelve years later when the edition went to press: the minutes record no discussion of the authenticity of the letter itself, but the incriminated passage, they say, should be branded as absent from the original and as added by some Nicolaite heretic. By right the words ought to be cancelled, if it were not for the editorial principle that all parts of the text commented upon in the *Glossa ordinaria* must be maintained.[60] Instead, there would have to be a note warning the reader that the words are *pessime addita*, as well as a theological refutation; also, the collection of Anselm of

---

56 Details in appendix II below.

57 *Conciliorum omnium tam generalium quam particularium* Tomus I (Cologne, 1551), p. 52b; see also his first edition, *Concilia omnia...*, I (Cologne, 1538), fo. xxvi r. In both printings, Crabbe's marginal note to *Grecorum...sapientissimus* reads: 'Pythagoras philosophus'. Cf. Diogenes Laertius, x.11, καθάπερ τὸν Πυθαγόραν κοινὰ τὰ φίλων λέγοντα.

58 Cf. Ph. Labbe and G. Cossart, *Sacrosancta concilia* I (Paris, 1672), 115 [= J. D. Mansi, *Sacrorum conciliorum nova et amplissima collectio*, I (Florence, 1759), 143], marginal note v. *sapientissimus*: 'Platonem intelligit'; *omnia*: 'In MS. atque editis Merlini et Crabbi pauca interseruntur, de quibus in notis. Ea Surius et post eum alii resecuerunt' etc. (The promised *notae* were not printed.) Cf. also J. Hardouin, *Acta conciliorum* I (Paris, 1715), 62 not. marg.

59 MSS Vat. lat 4889–94, 4913; cf. S. Kuttner, 'Brief notes', *Traditio*, XXIV (1968), 505; 'Some Roman manuscripts', pp. 13 n. 25, 14, 17 n.46, 21; A. Theiner, *Disquisitiones criticae* (Rome, 1836), pp. xi, xiii n. I (wrong reference); and for Vat. lat. 4913, Ae. L. Richter, *De emendatoribus Gratiani dissertatio historico-critica* (Leipzig, 1835), pp. 1, 39–45; K. Schellhass, 'Wissenschaftliche Forschungen unter Gregor XIII. für die Neuausgabe des Gratianischen Dekrets', in *Papsttum und Kaisertum: Forschungen...Paul Kehr zum 65. Geburtstag dargebracht*, ed. A. Brackmann (Munich, 1926), 674–90.

60 See the *Leges constitutae...in correctione Decreti*, no. v, published by Theiner, *Disquis*. Appendix I, pp. 4–5; cf. Friedberg's *prolegomena* to his edition, p. lxxvii; also the preface of the *Correctores*, ibid. p. lxxxv. H. von Schubert, *Der Kommunismus der Wiedertäufer in Münster und seine Quellen*, Sitzungsberichte der Heidelberger Akademie, philos.-hist. Klasse 1919, No. 11, p. 56, seems to believe that the *Correctores* eliminated the offensive passage.

Lucca was to be collated.[61] In the end this resulted in a long *notatio* of the printed text in which the *Correctores*, before quoting some patristic material to refute the offensive passage, reported that it was absent from Surius's edition of the Councils, from two old manuscripts (of the papal letters) and from Anselm's collection.[62]

Even a scholar of the stature of Antonio Agustín would not commit himself further than this, although briefly and cautiously ('ni fallor') he referred to the true source of the words which are read in Gratian but not in Anselm's collection (of which Agustín owned an important manuscript) nor 'in melioribus Clementis libris'.[63] This is quite in keeping with his well-known reluctance to arrive at a final conclusion on the Pseudo-Isidorian problem.[64]

Then came St Robert Bellarmine. The Jesuit controversialist has never been properly credited with his share in unmasking Isidorus Mercator, because his treatise entitled *Epistolas Summorum Pontificum quae in primo tomo Conciliorum habentur a sancto Clemente usque ad Siricium supposititias esse* remained unpublished until 1913.[65] Bellarmine probably wrote it about 1589 as an expert opinion for Cardinal Carafa's committee in charge of editing the decretal letters of the popes.[66] As a piece of historical erudition and critical sensitivity it leaves Dumoulin's invectives[67] and the embittered diatribes of the Magdeburg

---

61 Text in appendix III below.

62 *Notatio correctorum*, see ed. Friedb. col. 675 *ad loc.* and appendix III below for Michael Thomasius's draft. The *duo codices manuscripti* cited in the *notatio* – one *Vaticanus* and one *bibliothecae S. Marci Florentiae* – are probably Vat. lat. 3788 and Florence, Bibl. Naz. MS Conv. soppr. J.III.18 (Nos. 71 and 18 in S. Williams, *Codices Pseudo-Isidoriani*, Monumenta iuris canonici, Subsidia, III (New York, 1971)). Couvreur, *Les pauvres* (n. 28 above), p. 129 n. 400 misunderstands this note in assuming that there are variations in the Gratian MSS at this point.

63 *De emendatione Gratiani*, 1.15: 'In Anselmi veteri libro (*marg.* Ans. lib. 7 c.1) haec de coniugibus non sunt. Omittuntur etiam in melioribus Clementis libris, sed sumuntur, ni fallor, ex Recognitionibus Clementis'. (See also n. 54 above.)

64 See his *Hadriani papae capitula cum notis*, to which the Dialogue here refers but which was published only posthumously at Cologne in 1618 by S. Binius, *Concilia generalia et provincialia*, III.1.1 pp. 436–50 (whence Ant. Aug. *Opera omnia*, III, 349–69), *passim* on Angilramnus, cc. 7, 8, 22, 23, etc.; and especially at c.63 on the Pseudo-Clementines, ed. Binius, p. 449a; *Opp.* III, 367. Cf. F. Maassen, *Geschichte der Quellen und der Literatur des canonischen Rechts im Abendlande* (Graz, 1870), pp. xxxi–xxxiii.

65 *Auctarium Bellarminianum: Supplément aux oeuvres du Cardinal Bellarmin*, ed. X.-M. Le Bachelet (Paris, 1913), no. 50, pp. 490–3. Not mentioned in Fuhrmann, *Einfluss und Verbreitung*, I, 10 (on Bellarmine), but see I. A. Zeiger, *Historia iuris canonici* (2 vols. Rome, 1939), I, 49 and n. 48, quoting C. Silva Tarouca's comments in the *Liber Annualis* of the Gregorian University for 1931 [not seen].   66 Le Bachelet, *Auctarium Bellarminianum*, p. 490 n. 2.

67 *Decretum Divi Gratiani...resectis verò nothis, absurdis, difficilibus ijsdemque inutilibus...pseudographijs...* (Lyons, 1554). The anonymous editor – 'impius Carolus Molinaeus' to the Roman canonists, see Th. Manrique's *censura* of 1572 in Theiner, *Disquis.* p. xv, n. 3 – alludes to his name in the *praefatio* and signs the marginal notes, 'C.M.' These were republished by F. Pinsson in

Gratian and Plato

Centuriatores[68] far behind, and perhaps even surpasses the lawyer–humanist Antoine Le Conte's critique, or at least what is preserved of it.[69] But in the congregations of the Curia, it was Bellarmine's confrère Francisco Torres who won the day: 'propter aliquos canonistas' the false decretals were included in Carafa's 1591 edition, though set off from those of Siricius and later popes; '...neque Turrianus magnam laudem assecutus est ex defensione harum epistolarum', as Bellarmine laconically noted years later.[70] Had his views been accepted at the time – if we may indulge in some day-dreaming – there might have been no need for David Blondel's scathing classic, *Pseudo-Isidorus et Turrianus vapulantes* in 1628.

The fifth letter of St Clement was one of Bellarmine's main pieces of evidence. He showed that it was a forgery based to a considerable extent on the pseudo-Clementine *Recognitiones*,[71] the early Christian romance which survived in Rufinus of Aquileia's translation, and where *inter al.* the pagan philosopher Faustinus espouses the doctrine of 'Grecorum quidam sapientissimus' on the common possession among friends of all goods and women and is properly refuted by St Clement.[72] It goes beyond the limits of this paper to speculate why Bellarmine's

Caroli Molinaei *Opera omnia* (Paris, 1681), IV, 1–67. Cf. Richter, *De emendatoribus*, pp. 24–8. The historical value of Dumoulin's notes has been overrated. His remark on the letter of Anacletus at Dist. 22 c.2, 'ut sit manifestum hoc capitulum et alia pleraque multis postea seculis a monachis vel Papis conficta esse' (p. 66a; *Opp.* IV, 5b with Pinsson's note), has often been quoted; it is about his only contribution to the Pseudo-Isidorian question.

[68] *Ecclesiastica historia...congesta per aliquos studiosos...in urbe Magdeburgica* (Basle, 1560ff.), centuria II, 142–53; III, 177–85; IV, 575–82. Cf. Fuhrmann, *Einfluss und Verbreitung* I, 5–7, with bibliography in n. 2.

[69] *Decretorum canonicorum collectanea...* (Antwerp, Plantin 1570 and, with new title page, Paris, Du Puys 1570). The original edition, for which Du Puys had a *Priuilege du Roy* dated 23 October 1556, never appeared; as Le Conte himself tells in his *Lectiones subsecivae iuris civilis*, I.10 (Antonii Contii *Opera omnia* (Naples 1725), p. 15a), it was carried off to Antwerp, heavily censored, and printed 'tandem post longum exilium amputatis dedicatoriis epistolis et proprio titulo,...mancum et lacerum'. But a few comments on false decretals escaped the Spanish censor, thus to Dist. 16 c.13, C.30 q.5 c.18 (ed. 1570, pp. 47, 988); and a fragment of the original dedicatory epistle to the Chancellor Michel L'Hôpital, with its general critique of the papal letters prior to Siricius, was published by Pinsson in Dumoulin's *Opera omnia*, IV, pp. viij–x. See J. Doujat, *Praenotationum canonicarum libri quinque*, IV.13 (5th edn Venice, 1748) p. 397; Richter, *De emendatoribus*, pp. 28–36. Hence H. E. Troje, *Graeca leguntur*, Forschungen zur neueren Privatrechtsgeschichte, XVIII (Cologne–Vienna, 1971), p. 79 n.16, is mistaken in believing that the 1556 edition exists.

[70] *Auctarium Bellarminianum*, no. 111, 'Observatio ad secundam partem Antimornaei...', pp. 679–80.

[71] *Auctarium*, no. 50, sec. 4.2 (p. 491b). Cf. Antonio Agustín, *De emendatione Grat.*, 1.15 (quoted n. 63 above), whose hesitant statement Bellarmine may or may not have seen.

[72] Bellarmine, *Auctarium*, '...ad uerbum desumptus est ex libro 10 Recognitionum, ubi ista dicuntur a Faustiniano haeretico [al. ethnico] et a Clemente refelluntur'. See *Recogn.* x.5 and 7: Migne, *PG.* I, 1422C–D and 1423B–C; ed. B. Rehm and F. Paschke, *Die Pseudoklementinen*, II, in Die griechischen christlichen Schriftsteller, LI (Berlin, 1965), 327.12–19 and 328.8–23.

censura had to remain hidden; and also why in the fourth volume of his *Controversiae*, several years later, he resumed it only in a slightly softened manner which left the alternative of a genuine but interpolated epistle,[73] thus returning to the rather cautious approach he had taken before he came to write the treatise of 1589.[74] It remains to be investigated whether all this is connected with the troubles Bellarmine had during the pontificate of Sixtus V on account of his denial of a direct power of the pope *in temporalibus* – a doctrine for which he narrowly escaped being put on the Index, and which was to delay the process of his canonisation for centuries.[75] But it should also be recorded that his observations on this pseudo-Clementine *ep.* 5, even in the less outspoken formulation of the *Controversiae*, provided one of the very rare instances in which Blondel, the relentless critic of popish (*pontificii*) scholars, would exclaim, 'Quandoquidem Bellarmini iudicio per omnia subscribimus', before he proceeded to refute Torres.[76]

From this long digression let us retrace our steps to the medieval exegesis of the pseudo-Clementine letter (in C.12 q.1 c.2) by the glossators of Gratian. Since they could not throw out its *auctoritas*, they endeavoured to render it less embarrassing by giving the crucial passage a harmless interpretation. Thus we find 'in omnibus autem sunt sine dubio et coniuges' explained as if the words were an exercise in grammar: *in omnibus*, that is, in the word 'all', *sunt coniuges*, that is, there must be understood or included [the word] 'wives'.[77] The passage thus serves as an occasion for legal maxims such as 'general words must

---

73 Bellarmine, *Disputationum de controversiis christianae fidei*, Tomus IV (Venice, 1596), controv. 3, *De bonis operibus in particulari*, III.11: '...constat enim eam epistolam aut non esse Clementis aut ab aliquo valde corruptam ac depravatam' (p. 597a in ed. Venice, 1721, here used), as against the treatise of 1589, sec. 3: 'Epistolae istae videntur omnino compositae ab uno atque eodem auctore' (*Auctarium*, p. 491a).

74 *Disputationum*...Tomus I (Ingolstadt, 1586), controv. 3 *De summo pontifice*, II.14: 'at quamvis aliquos errores in eas [*sc.* epistolas] irrepsisse non negaverim, nec indubitatas esse affirmare audeam; certe tamen antiquissimas esse nihil dubito' etc. (p. 316a in the Venice, 1721 edition). Authors discussing Bellarmine on Pseudo-Isidore usually refer only to this passage.

75 The Index affair is summarised in P. Dudon's article 'Bellarmin', *Dictionnaire d'histoire et de géographie ecclésiastiques* VII (Paris, 1934), 798–824, at col. 806–7. E. A. Ryan, *The historical scholarship of St. Bellarmine*, Recueil de travaux...d'Histoire et de Philologie, 3e sér., XXXV (Univ. de Louvain, 1936), 151, sees the main reason for Bellarmine's caution in the *Controversiae* as stemming from the purpose of the work: he did not want to furnish weapons to the Protestants, since any concession made in this matter would be exaggerated.

76 David Blondellus (Blondel), *Pseudo-Isidorus et Turrianus vapulantes* (Geneva, 1628), p. 99.

77 Thus in the gloss composition *Ordinaturus magister* (e.g., MSS Cues 223, Vat. Ross. 595), incorporated in Huguccio's *Summa* C.12 q.1 c.2 v. *in omnibus*: 'idest in eo uocabulo, scil. "omnia", *sunt coniuges*: idest intelliguntur et comprehenduntur coniuges,' etc. See also *Glossa Animal est substantia*, *Glossa Palatina*.

Gratian and Plato

be taken with a general meaning', or 'words generally uttered include all particulars'.[78]

More significant than these commonplaces were the efforts to purify Plato's saying. From Rufinus onwards, all asserted that wives were to be held in common not as regards the flesh ('quo ad carnis usum', 'coniunctionem', 'amplexandi dilectionem'), but by common respect, affection, deference, courtesy ('honesta servicia', 'obsequium', etc.), and dutiful love.[79] This text, we are told, gives no licence to do anything sordid; and one temperamental glossator calls those stupid (*stulti*) who take the passage about the wives literally (it was the same glossator who proposed the alternative that it had been put in by forgers).[80]

All this is quite in line with the twelfth-century glosses on·the *Timaeus*. William of Conches, as mentioned before, defended Socrates and Plato against the *quidam indocti* who accused them of *turpitudo*, unaware perhaps that thereby he placed Tertullian and Lactantius and other early Fathers among the unlearned. By the words 'de existimandis communibus nuptiis et communi prole', William affirms, Plato had not commanded promiscuity but common affection: for he had not said that marriages and children 'are' common (*essent communes*) but 'should be considered' (*reputarentur*) common. This clears the way for an interpretation where all is reduced to the principle of showing the same love for strangers as for one's own[81] – and the canonists who

[78] Huguccio continues *loc. cit.*: 'et est arg. quod uerbum generale est generaliter intelligendum' etc. *Gl. Ordinaturus* in Vat. Ross. 595: 'et est arg. quod in uerbo generaliter prolato comprehenduntur particularia' etc. Thus also *Gl. Palat.*; the gloss of Alanus follows Huguccio's phrasing.

[79] Rufinus, *Summa* C.12 q.1 c.2 v. *coniuges*: 'non quo ad carnis usum sed quo ad dilectionis officium', ed. Singer, p. 321. Cf. Stephanus Tornacensis, Johannes Faventinus, the *Summae Omnis qui iuste* and *De iure can. tractaturus*: '...set quantum ad dilectionem et obsequium'; *Summa Tractaturus*: 'quantum ad honesta seruicia'. Similar formulations in the *Summa Parisiensis*, the glosses of the Biberach MS and Leipzig, Univ. MS Haenel 18; in Huguccio, Alanus, Bernard of Compostella, the *Glossa Animal est substantia*, and the *Gl. ordinaria*. Cf. also Couvreur, *Les pauvres* (n. 28 above), p. 129 n. 400.

[80] *Glossa Ecce uicit leo*, v. *coniuges*: '...quo ad effectum [*sic*] caritatis et seruitium licitum, non autem quo ad turpe aliquid committendum'. Cues MS 223, gl. v. *coniuges*: 'A falsatoribus dictum est, uel dictum est non quantum ad carnis usum ut stulti putant, set quantum ad dilectionem' (cf. at n. 50 above).

[81] William of Conches, *Glossae super Timaeum* 18C: 'Hic quidam indocti Socratem et Platonem turpitudinis arguunt, credentes eos precepisse omnes mulieres esse communes sic quod omnes ...ignorante utroque cui commisceretur;...Nos uero dicimus Platonem non imperasse turpitudinem sed affectum. Non enim dicit quod "essent" communes sed "reputarentur". Ac si diceret: Unusquisque uxorem et filios alterius in bono diligat ac si sui essent' (ed. Jeauneau, p. 78). Cf. nn. 30, 37 above. Similarly the glosses of Uppsala MS C.620, ed. T. Schmid, 'Ein Timaioskommentar in Sigtuna', *Classica et Mediaevalia*, X (1949), 220–66, at p. 230: '*De extimandis*: Hic quidam imponit Platoni quod uoluisset communes esse mulieres

adopted this formula for the text of 'Clement' in Gratian thus came around full circle to what had been their understanding of Gratian's dictum on Plato and the *nescire proprios affectus*.[82]

Now this might seem hardly worth saying if it were not for the fact that the first generations of Bolognese glossators remained as unaware as Gratian himself of the true context from which his observation on the Platonic City was derived. To be sure, the letter of Clement was placed by some early gloss compositions as a cross-reference in the margin of the opening dictum of Dist. 8: 'infra xii.q.i. Dilectissimis', so they write,[83] but this indicated no more than a parallel, a verbal concordance:

Gratian	C.12 q.1 c.2
iure nature sunt omnia communia omnibus...	communis enim usus omnium ...omnibus hominibus esse debet;... communia debere ait esse amicorum omnium...
unde apud Platonem...	Grecorum quidam sapientissimus...

Slow as the development may seem to us from hindsight, it took an Huguccio to make the connection between the two texts and to discover that the wives (from Plato in C.12 q.1) must be included in the *omnia* (from Plato in Dist. 8 pr.), of course with the proper understanding that this means equal affection for strangers as for one's own, etc.:[84]

Huguccio Dist. 8 pr.	Stephanus Dist. 8 pr.
nescit proprios affectus: idest tantum se ipsum diligere.	*nescit proprios affectus:*
Confinxit enim Plato quandam suam rem publicam, quam fingendo sic disposuit ut omnia omnibus essent communia, *etiam coniuges quo ad dilectionem et obsequium,*	Sic enim dixerat Plato esse in illa maxima ciuitate cuius rem publicam fingebat omnia communia

omnium, sed falso;...uoluit intelligi quod unusquisque pari dilectione suam et alterius mulierem et prolem diligeret: unde dixit "extimande", non "esse" communes.' On the problem of authorship for the Uppsala glosses see Jeauneau, p. 14.

[82] Stephanus Tornac. *Summa* C.12 q.1 c.2: 'ex uerbis Platonis...uxores et liberos communes esse dixit, idest affectum dilectionis communiter exhibendum ait suis et extraneis; non communes dixit uxores quantum ad carnis usum' etc. See also Johannes Faventinus and the *Summae Omnis qui iuste* and *De iure can. tractaturus* at C.12 q.1 c.2. Compare Stephanus (n. 12 above), Johannes and *De iure can. tractaturus* at Dist. 8 pr. Ph. Delhaye, 'Morale et droit canon dans la Summe d'Étienne de Tournai', *Studia Gratiana*, I (1953), 447–8, considers this interpretation 'assez proche de celle d'Abélard', but see nn. 41 and 42 above.

[83] Thus MSS Leipzig Haen. 18, fo. 3va; Vat. Ross. 595, fo. 16ra; Cues 223, fo. 3ra; also in the *Summa Tractaturus*.

[84] In the text of Huguccio that follows (Admont MS 7, fo. 9vb), from 'Confinxit enim' on, I have set off his expansion of the traditional gloss, which goes back to Stephen of Tournai (MS Vat. Borgh. 287, fo. 13va).

Gratian and Plato

et omnibus equaliter dilectionis affectus exiberetur, scilicet tam suis quam extraneis, *ut xii. q.i. Dilectissimis.*

et neminem suorum affectus aliis preponere debere, idest omnes ab inuicem equaliter diligendos esse.

From here on we can follow the few brief flashes of true insight. There was Alanus who combined, at C.12 q.1 c.2, his precise indication of the passage in the *Timaeus* with a telling cross-reference to Gratian's dictum at Dist. 8. There were those unnamed writers whose correct understanding of the Calcidian term *nescire affectus* was rejected by Laurentius.[85] But in the *Glossa ordinaria*, Johannes Teutonicus left all this by the wayside.[86] The few bits salvaged in Guido de Baysio's *Rosarium* from the pre-*ordinaria* glosses[87] were not enough to keep the interest in Gratian's use of Plato alive during the later Middle Ages. Guido Terreni, who read the Decretum very much with the eyes of a fourteenth-century schoolman, would comment upon the two passages[88] only to point out that Aristotle in the *Politics* had criticised the communism of Plato's State.

APPENDIX I

Texts from manuscripts: Summae and glosses on Gratian

Stephanus Tornacensis, *Summa decretorum* (Bolognese school; Orléans, after 1160)

(D.8 pr.) *nescit proprios affectus:* Sic enim dixerat...diligendos esse.
  Vatican Library, MS Borgh. 287, fo. 13va, printed above, note 12, to replace Schulte's faulty edition (Giessen, 1891), p. 17.

(C.12 q.1 c.2) *quidam Grecorum:* Plato in Thimeo.[1] *sunt et coniuges:* Non credo hoc apposuisse Clementem, cum tamen ex uerbis Platonis hoc haberi possit, qui in re publica illa quam fingebat uxores et liberos communes esse dixit, idest[2] affectum dilectionis communiter exhibendum ait[3] suis et extraneis. Non communes dixit

---

[85] See nn. 47 (Alanus) and 36 (Laurentius) above.

[86] *Glossa ord.* Dist. 8 pr. After the conventional remark on 'tantum diligit alium ut se', Johannes merely writes: 'Finxit enim Plato quandam rem publicam: in qua omnia enim sunt communia' (the Latin is rather rough).

[87] Guido de Baysio, *Rosarium* at Dist. 8 pr. first quotes Laurentius's gloss 'non ita intelligas' etc. ('dicit lau. sic...') and then Huguccio's 'idest tantum seipsum diligere' ('secundum hu.').

[88] I am grateful to Dr Kenneth Pennington for having called my attention to the pertinent passages in Guido Terreni's *Commentarium super Decretum* and for the copies he took from MS Vat. lat. 1453; see appendix I below. For this commentary see P. Fournier, 'Gui Terré (Guido Terreni), théologien', *Histoire littéraire de la France*, XXXVI (1927), 432–73, at pp. 464–8, 'Expositorium Decreti' (which appears as title in the Paris MS, B.N. lat. 3914). I have not consulted B. Xiberta, *Guiu Terrena, carmelita de Perpinyà* (Barcelona, 1932) nor I. Melsen, *Guido Terreni (1260?–1342) iurista* (Rome, 1939).

uxores quantum ad carnis usum set quantum ad dilectionem et obsequium.

MS Borgh. fo. 62vb, ed. Schulte, pp. 213–14.

[1] *gl. om. Sch.*   [2] ubi *Sch.*   [3] a *Borgh.*

Johannes Faventinus, *Summa decretorum* (Bologna, after 1171)

(D.8 pr.) *nescit proprios affectus:* Sic enim dixit[1] Plato…diligendos esse.
Reims MS 684, fo. 4vb (repeats Stephen's text).

[1] dixerat *Steph.*

(C.12 q.1 c.2) *quidam Grecorum:* Plato[1] scil. in Timeo.   *sunt et coniuges:* Non credo
hoc…et obsequium.
MS Rem. fo. 79ra (repeats Stephen's text).

[1] prelato *Rem.*

Summa Magister Gratianus in hoc opere (*Parisiensis*) (French School, *c.* 1170)
(D.8 pr.) *Differt:* Differentiam ostendit inter effectus iuris naturalis et constitutionis
siue consuetudinarii, set laborat in positione[1] exemplorum, et salua pace sua
melius potuisset de[2] his tacere, quia que erant apostolorum inter se erant communia,
set non omnibus aliis, et in illa ciuitate quam fingit Plato multi propria habebant,
set se debebant equaliter diligere. Ideo dici potest quod non sunt hec exempla set
quoquo modo uestigia exemplorum, scilicet ex quibus ⟨uidetur quod⟩ quoquo modo[3]
omnia sint communia iure nature. Verum quicquid dicat Gratianus enititur probare
auctoritate Augustini dicentis: *Quo iure.*[4]
Bamberg MS Can. 36, fo. 2vb; ed. T. McLaughlin (Toronto, 1952), p. 7.

[1] ĩ poñe *Bb,* imponere *McL*   [2] ab *Bb McL*   [3] uidetur quod *scripsi:* ex quibus quoquo
modo *Bb,* ex quibus, quo, quomodo *McL*   [4] D.8 c.1

(C.12 q.1 c.2) *sapientissimus:* forte Plato.   *et coniuges:* quia communes debent esse
non usu carnis set quantum ad exhibitionem caritatis.
Ed. McLaughlin, p. 156 (with MS readings).

Summa Antiquitate et tempore (French school, after 1170)
(D.8 pr.) *Differt autem ius nature:* Assignauit supra differentiam iuris naturalis ad
cetera iura, scil. ius consuetudinarium, quod est ius non scriptum, et ius constitutionis,
quod est ius scriptum, dicens ipsum inter omnia iura precellere et tempore et dignitate.
Consequenter eiusdem ad alia iura assignat differentiam secundum effectum, dicens
hunc esse effectum iuris naturalis quod omnia sint omnibus communia. Set secundum
ius consuetudinis uel constitutionis aliqua sunt propria, hoc meum, illud alterius. Set
quod iste non sit effectus iuris naturalis ex his innotescat: ius nature inferius appellat
ius diuinum et illud dicit contineri in scriptis diuinis. Quod si scripta diuina appellat
decalogum preceptorum, patet quoniam secundum illud aliqua sunt propria: ibi
enim continetur, 'non concupisces rem proximi tui';[1] ergo aliqua est res proximi.
Item ibi fit mentio furti, furtum autem non fit nisi ubi fit contrectatio[2] rei aliene
inuito domino;[3] quod si omnia essent omnibus communia, nulla essent aliquibus
aliena. Quod si diuinum ius appellat quod continetur in ueteri testamento, scil. in libris
Moisi, secundum illud etiam aliqua sunt propria, quia ibi promissa est Iudeis terra

Gratian and Plato

promissionis ut hereditario iure eam possiderent, et postea data est eis et possederunt eam.[4] Et item ibidem dicitur quod si attenuatus fuerit frater tuus et emeris eum, seruiet tibi vi. annis et vii°. liber erit etc.[5] Sin autem ius diuinum uocatur quod continetur in euangelio, secundum hoc etiam aliqua sunt propria, unde in euangelio: 'Reddite Cesari que sunt Cesaris et que Dei Deo'.[6] Item non negauit Cesari dandum tributum, set filium regis debere dare negauit.[7] Ex his palam est quod quicquid hic appelletur ius diuinum, secundum illud aliqua sunt propria. Nam quod dicit, 'iure diuino Domini[8] est terra et plenitudo eius',[9] uerum quidem est set minus pertinet ad rem dictam, quia omnia sunt Domini per creationem et hoc non prohibet aliqua esse propria. Ad hoc tandem post omnem disquisitionem dicendum est diuinum ius hic appellari primam illam equitatem que a prima creatione naturaliter mentibus hominum indita fuit, secundum quam unusquisque ita rem ad usum suum habere deberet ut et alius[10] ad suum usum eandem haberet dum ei esset necessaria.

Sic transiri posset locus iste nisi rem turbaret exemplis suppositis. Duo enim subiungit exempla quibus conatur ostendere nulla esse propria, quorum unum sumptum est de actibus apostolorum, hoc scil. 'multitudinis credentium erat cor unum et anima una',[11] alterum a Platone, scil. de ciuibus platonice ciuitatis, idest illius ciuitatis quam Plato iustissime ordinatam fuisse testatur. Set in utroque exemplo peccauit: in priori quia etsi singulorum quorum erat cor unum et anima una non essent aliqua propria, tamen que eorum erant communia non erant 'omnium' communia, quia infidelium non. Quod in secundo exemplo peccauerit palam est intelligentibus Platonem, quia tantum milites illius ciuitatis debebant expensam habere de communi, ne propriis intenti minus ad communem utilitatem milicie deseruirent. Nullatenus tamen 'omnium' erant communia que possidebant ibi ciues, quia saltem non inimicorum. Ad hoc dicendum non esse mirum si quandoque bonus dormitat Homerus.[12] Preterea M. Gra. competentia exempla habere non potuit, et ideo indulgendum est ei si ista posuit, quia modo non est iste effectus iuris naturalis nec fuit forte ex quo Adam filios habere cepit, quia probabile est quod statim ceperint esse propria. Verumtamen ostendit hic M. G. qualis deberet esse effectus iuris naturalis. Sicut enim illis omnia erant communia quorum erat cor unum et anima una, et sicut[13] milites platonici de communi uiuebant, ita iure naturali omnibus omnia deberent esse communia. Si ergo M. G. non ponit exemplum usquequaque sufficiens, est tamen quod dicit in parte proficiens: ista enim exempla non sufficiunt set proficiunt.

in qua quisque proprios nescit affectus: quia 'quisque' minores se dilexit ut filios, maiores ut parentes,[14] et sic non habuit 'proprios' uel speciales[15] circa unum 'affectus'. Et forte si aliqui essent qui non maiorem ad unum quam ad alium affectum haberent et illi omnibus equaliter cuperent ⟨dare⟩,[16] et talium bona omnibus essent communia. Nota quod quidam[17] dicunt Platonem loqui ibi de nuptiis catarorum et eum sensisse illas esse celebrandas. Set nos eum excusare solemus in legendo librum ipsius.

Göttingen MS 159, fo. 11ra/b.

---

[1] *Gen.* 20:17   [2] contrectio *Gt*   [3] cf. *Inst.* iv.1.6   [4] cf. *Exod.* 6:8; *Lev.* 20:24, 25:46; *Deut.* 1:21 etc.   [5] cf. *Lev.* 25:35, 39–40   [6] *Mt.* 22:21   [7] cf. *Mt.* 17:24–5   [8] dictum (dcm) *Gt*   [9] *Ps.* 23:1 *ap. Augustinum* (D.8 c.1)   [10] aliis *Gt*   [11] *Act.* 4:32   [12] *Horat.*

Ars poet. 359   [13] Sicut...sicut] Sic...sic *Gt*   [14] ut filios—parentes *scripsi*: inter filios maiores. ut parentes. *Gt*   [15] spirituales (sp̄uales) *Gt*   [16] *om. Gt*   [17] quia *Gt*

Summa Tractaturus magister (French school, *c.* 1181–5)

(D.8 pr.) *multitudinis credentium:* Non est exemplum sufficiens set proficiens, quia etsi inter eos omnia communia, quod non uidetur, non tamen extraneis.[1] *apud Platonem:* et c. xii. q.i. c.ij. *iustissimus ordo:* si talis possit inueniri.

Paris, B.N. lat. 15994, fo. 3vb.

[1] Non—extraneis *etiam apud Weigand, Naturrechtslehre (laud. supra n.* 3), *p.* 316.

(C.12 q.1 c.2) *Grecorum quidam:* Plato in Timeo. *in omnibus autem:* Hec sunt uerba Clementis, tamen ex sensu uerborum Platonis sumpta. *coniuges:* quantum ad honesta seruicia.

MS Par. fo. 53vb.

Summa Omnis qui iuste (Lipsiensis) (Anglo-Norman school, *c.* 1186)

(C.12 q.1 c.2) *sine dubio sunt coniuges:* Hoc non dicunt Clementem apposuisse, cum tamen ex uerbis Platonis hoc haberi possit, qui in re publica quam fingebat[1] uxores et liberos communes esse dixit, idest affectum dilectionis communiter exhibendum ut suis et extraneis. Non dixit uxores communes[2] quantum ad carnis usum set quantum ad dilectionem et obsequium.

Leipzig, Univ. MS 986, fo. 155rb; Rouen MS 743, fo. 76rb.

[1] figebant *Lp*   [2] communis *Lp*

Summa De iure canonico tractaturus (Anglo-Norman school, *c.* 1186)

(D.8 pr.) *apud Platonem:* Hoc in Timeo Platonis inuenitur, ubi Plato in illa maxima ciuitate cuius rem fingebat publicam omnia dixit esse communia debent, neminem suum affectum scire,[1] omnes equaliter inuicem diligendos.

Laon MS 371*bis*, fo. 84vb.

[1] effectum sen[i] *Ld*

(C.12 q.1 c.2) *quidam Grecorum:* idest Plato in Thimeo. *sine dubio sunt coniuges:* Hoc non dicunt Clementem set alium apposuisse,[1] cum tamen...et obsequium.[2]

MS Laud. fo. 131vb.

[1] et p̄posuisse *Ld*   [2] cum tamen...et obsequium *verbotenus ut in Sum. Omnis q.i. praeter:* haberi] fieri *Ld*   qui in re publica] quia in illa re publica *Ld*

Gloss composition Ordinaturus magister (Bologna, *c.* 1180)

(D.8 pr.) printed above at n. 83. (The gloss from MS Biberach printed above at n. 32 is not part of this composition.)

(C.12 q.1 c.2) *sapientissimus:*[1] subaudi Plato. *in omnibus:*[2] idest in eo[3] uocabulo, 'omnia',[4] *sunt coniuges:*[5] intelliguntur et comprehenduntur coniuges, et est argumentum quod in uerbo generaliter prolato omnia comprehenduntur particularia, arg. di. xviiii. Si Romanorum.[6] *coniuges:*[7] (i) quantum ad affectum non ad usum. (ii) quantum ad obsequium non ad coniunctionem. (iii) A falsatoribus dictum est, uel

Gratian and Plato

dictum est ⟨non⟩[8] quantum ad carnis usum ut stulti putant, set quantum ad dilectionem.

Biberach MS B 3515, fo. 160rb; Cues MS 223, fo. 122va; Leipzig, Univ. MS Haen. 18, fo. 132rb; Vatican MS Ross. 595, fo. 144ra. Cf. gl. interlin. in Paris, B.N. lat. 15398.

[1] *Ross (al.m.)*, scil. Plato *Par*, om. *cett.*   [2] *Cus Ross (cf. gl. interl.* in hoc uocabulo omnia./(sunt) idest continentur *Par*), om. *cett.*   [3] idest in m̄o *Ross*   [4] scil. praem. *Ross*   [5] sunt ho. *Cus*   [6] D.19 c.1   [7] gl (i) *Bib*, (ii) *Haen*, (iii) *Cus*   [8] *illegib. Cus*

Huguccio, *Summa decretorum* (Bologna, c. 1188–90)

(D.8 pr.) *inter eos:* scil. apostolos et alios tunc temporis credentes, ut xii. q.i.Dilectissimis. Scimus.[1] *nescit proprios affectus:* idest tantum…Dilectissimis.

Admont MS 7, fo. 9vb. The second gloss is printed above, at n. 84.

[1] C.12 q.1 cc.2, 9.

(C.12 q.1 c.2) *quidam*: scil. Plato in Timeo. *in omnibus sunt coniuges:* Coniuges debent esse communes non quo ad usum carnis set quo ad alterius officii obsequium et quo ad dilectionem etcet. *in omnibus:* idest in eo uocabulo, scil. 'omnia', *sunt coniuges:* idest intelliguntur et comprehenduntur coniuges, et est argumentum quod uerbum generale est generaliter intelligendum, ar. di. xviiii. Si Romanorum.[1]

MS Adm. fo. 235vb.

[1] D.19 c.1.

Alanus, *Glossa Ius naturale* (Bologna, c. 1192, second recension c. 1205)

(D.8 pr.) [*Platonem:*[1] in Thimeo.] [*proprios:* idest tanta affectione amplectitur extraneos et proprios.] *affectus:*[2] idest in qua quisque sic diligebat alienos ut proprios consanguineos.

Paris, B.N. lat. 3909 (= Pr), fo. 1vb; lat. 15393 (= Ps), fo. 5rb; Bibl. Mazarine MS 1318, fo. 5rb; Vatican MS Ross. 595, fo. 16ra (second layer); Seo de Urgel, MS 113 (2009), folios unnumbered.—*Pr Urg:* first recension; *Ps Maz:* second rec.; *Ross:* selected glosses. Passages and glosses not found in the first recension will be printed here within brackets.

[1] gl. om. *Ross*   [2] gl. in Pr tantum, om. *cett.*

(C.12 q.1 c.2) *Grecorum:* supra d. xxxvii. Si quid ueri. arg.[1] *in omnibus:* [arg. generaliter dictum generaliter intelligendum.] supra d. xix. Si Romanorum. arg.[2] *et coniuges:* supra di. viii. § Differt.[3] In Platone c. de feminis.[4] [set intelligas non quo ad usum set quo ad affectionem.]

Pr fo. 35rb, Ps fo. 139rb, Maz fo. 202rb, Urg (n.n.). No glosses in Ross.

[1] D.37 c.13. arg.] contra add. et del. *Urg*   [2] D.19 c.1   [3] D.8 pr.   [4] *Tim.* 18C

Glossa Ecce uicit leo (French school, after 1202)

(D.8 pr.) *nescit:* idest nescire debet. ⟨uel⟩ *nescit*, tantum. Similiter[1] caritas nescit que sua sunt,[2] ⟨tan⟩tum, quia ita diligit proximum ⟨s⟩icut[3] se, et xii. q.i. Scimus.[4]

Paris, B.N. MS nouv. acq. lat. 1576, fo. 24ra; not in the St Florian MS mentioned below. Pointed brackets enclose letters hidden in the fold of the volume and hence not legible on the microfilm.

[1] Simile *Par*   [2] *1 Cor.* 13:5   [3] *||ſic Par*   [4] C.12 q.1 c.9

(C.12 q.1 c.2) *coniuges:* quia[1] et coniuges debent esse communes, et hoc uerum est quo ad affectum[2] caritatis et seruitium licitum,[3] non autem quo ad turpe aliquid committendum.

MS Par. fo. 196ra; St Florian MS XI.605, fo. 61va.

[1] *om. Fl.*   [2] effectum *Par Fl*   [3] licentium *Fl*

Glossa Animal est substantia (French school, *c.* 1206–10)

(C.12 q.1 c.2) *in omnibus:* idest in uniuersitate.[1] *sunt coniuges:* non quantum ad usum carnis[2] set quantum ad obsequium honestatis.

Bamberg MS Can. 42, fo. 83va; Cues MS 223 (second layer), fo. 122va; Liège, Univ. MS 127E, fo. 148rb.

[1] idest in v^{co} (uocabulo?) n̄o *Bb*, idest inuni^{to} *Cus*   [2] castitatis *Leod*

Bernardus Compostellanus, *Apparatus glossarum* (Bologna, *c.* 1202–6)

(C.12 q.1 c.2) *coniuges:* quantum ad obsequii exhibitionem, non amplexandi dilectionem. b.

Gniezno MS 28 (folio numbers illegible on film).

Laurentius, *Glossa Palatina* (Bologna, *c.* 1210–15).

(D.8 pr.) *nescit:* non ita intelligas ut nesciat filios suos et ut[1] ei liceat cum filia sua coire, set ita: idest eodem affectu suscipit extraneos quo et filios proprios.[2] xii. q.ii. Dilectissimis,[3] ff. de nundinis l.ii. in fine.[4]

Vatican MSS Pal. lat. 658, fo. 2rb; Reg. lat. 977, fo. 3ra; also MS Vat. lat. 1367 (second layer), fo. 3rb.

[1] *om. Vl*   [2] la(urentius). *add. et reliqua om. Vl*   [3] C.12 q.1 c.2   [4] *Dig.* 50.11.2 (*ubi laud.* 'Plato cum institueret quemadmodum ciuitas bene habitari possit', *de negotiatoribus, Rep.* 371A, C); *allegatur etiam al. m. in Par. lat. 15393 post primam gl. Alani*

(C.12 q.1 c.2) *in omnibus:* in hoc uocabulo 'omnia'. *coniuges:* idest intelliguntur et comprehenduntur coniuges, et est argumentum quod in uerbo generaliter prolato[1] omnia comprehenduntur particularia, arg. xix. Si Romanorum.[2]

Pal. fo. 49rb, Reg. fo. 139rb (no gloss in Vl).

[1] probato *Reg*   [2] D.19 c.1

Johannes Teutonicus, *Glossa ordinaria* (Bologna, *c.* 1217)

(D.8 pr.) *nescit:* Quisque[1] tantum diligit alium ut se. Finxit enim Plato quandam rem publicam: in qua omnia enim[2] sunt[3] communia.[4]

Bamberg MSS Can. 13, fo. 3ra; Can. 14, fo. 5va; Vatican MSS Vat. lat. 1367, fo. 3ra; Pal. lat. 624, fo. 3va; Pal. lat. 625, fo. 5vb.

Gratian and Plato

Preliminary note. Even with the punctuation here proposed the Latin remains awkward with its redundant second 'enim', which the consensus of MSS does not allow to cancel. In Bartholomaeus Brixiensis's recension, the text remained at first unchanged (= *Barth. I*, e.g. Vat. lat. 1365); but in the fourteenth century, MSS will prefer 'in qua omnia sunt communia' (= *Barth. II*, e.g. Vat. lat. 1368, 1371, 1372, 1373). The printed text of this version (= *ed.*) is slightly expanded and remains constant, from the incunabula I have examined (Hain-Cop. *7882, *7912, *7913) to the official Roman text (1582) and its successors.

[1] enim *add. ed.*　　[2] enim *Vl Pal. 625 Barth. I et (ante omnia) Pal. 624:* eī *Bb. 13,* eis *(al.m.? seqr. rasura) Bb. 14, om. Barth. II et ed.*　　[3] fuerunt *Pal. 625,* essent *Bb. 14*　　[4] xii. q.i c.ii *add. ed.*

(C.12 q.1 c.2) *coniuges:* non quo ad usum carnis sed quo ad usum obsequii, uel quo ad dilectionem.[1] Et est argumentum quod uerbum generale generaliter intelligendum est. xix. di. Si Romanorum.[2] Jo.[3]

MSS Bamb. 13, fo. 117ra; Vat. lat. 1367, fo. 136ra; Pal. 624, fo. 148vb; Pal. 625, fo. 123va (not in Bamb. 14).

[1] xxxi. dist. Omnino (c.11) *add. ed.*　　[2] D.19 c.1　　[3] Jo. *add. Bb Pal. 624*

Guido de Baysio, *Rosarium* (Bologna, A.D. 1300)

(D.8 pr.) *affectus:* dicit lau. sic, 'nescit' non ita intelligas...ff. de nundi. l. ii. lau.[1] Vnde dic *nescit,* idest *affectus,* idest tantum seipsum diligere, secundum hu.[2]

Vatican MS Vat. lat. 1447, fo. 8ra; ed. Lugd. 1549, fo. 9ra.

[1] *vide gl. Laurentii, supra*　　[2] *vide gl. Huguccionis in textu prope adn. 84 supra*

(C.12 q.1 c.2) *sapientissimus:* Plato in timeo. h.[1] *in omnibus:* materialiter tenetur, et in hoc uocabulo 'omnia' 'sunt', idest[2] intelliguntur et comprehenduntur, coniuges,[3] et facit viij. dist. § i. et c. seq.[4] [et repete et uideas quod dixi j. di. Ius autem. ij. in glos.j. res etc.][5]

MS Vat. fo. 204ra; ed. Lugd. fo. 218rb.

[1] prelato intraneo. h. *ed.; vide gl. Huguccionis, supra*　　[2] ei *ed.*　　[3] *vide gl. Hug.*　　[4] D.8 pr et c.1　　[5] et repete...etc. *om. Vl; glossam laud. in ed. ad loc. (D.1 c.7) non inveni*

Guido Terreni, *Commentarium super decretum* (Elne [Perpignan], 1339).

(D.8 pr.) *Differt autem.* Gratianus insistit[1] circa differentiam iuris naturalis et aliorum iurium...set erant eis omnia communia. Set et a philosophis legitur traditum, inter quos Plato hoc posuit obseruandum in ciuitate bene ordinata. In hoc tamen Aristotiles Platonem reprobat ii°. pol.[2] Iure autem consuetudinis...

Vatican MS Vat. lat. 1453, fo. 5va (ex apogr. K. Pennington).

[1] incistit *Vl*　　[2] *Polit.* 1261b, 1262b–1264b

(C.12 q.1 c.2) *coniuges:* Hoc reprobat philosophus 2° pol. quo ad usum carnalis copule, quia ex hoc sequeretur prolis incertitudo et honor parentum tolleretur propter incertitudinem quis genuerit;[1] sequitur minor dilectio ad filios, inde oriretur odium inter ciues.[2] Nec est lex bona quod coniuges sint communes quo ad obsequium,[3] ne obsequendo committatur adulterium et obsequendo impediatur matrimonii[4] debitum reddendum.

MS Vat. fo. 100ra.

[1] genuit *Vl*   [2] *cf. Arist. Polit.* 1262a 25–33   [3] *cf. Glos. ord.*   [4] matrimonium *Vl*

APPENDIX II
The text of Pseudo-Clement, ep. 5 in Gratian (cf. at note 56 above)

Abbreviations:
  Fr = Gratian, ed. Friedberg
  H = Pseudo-Isidore, ed. Hinschius
  Tr = Ivo, Tripartita, from Paris, B.N. MSS lat. 3858, fo. 5r/v and lat. 3858B, fo. 3v–4r
  Or = Collection of MS Vat. lat. 3829 (prov. Niccolò Ormaneto)

C.12 q.1 c.2

Dilectissimis—sunt ambo (pr.–§5 at n.37 *Fr*): *H* p. 65 pr.–*ante* n.9.
  Tr 1.1.23; *Or* part (i), beginning.
  inscr. Item Clemens in epist. IV *Grat.* Clemens in quarta epistola (epistola iiij.) *Tr, sine inscr. Or*
  rubr. Omnibus clericis communis est uita seruanda *Grat.* Communem uitam omnibus necessariam *Tr,* De bono uite communis *Or*

[Cetera que—digna sunt] (cf. n.37 0 *Fr*): *H* 65 at n.9–*ante* c.83.
  Not in Friedberg's codd. ABCDF but in EGH and the editions, also in at least four MSS saec.xii/xiii I inspected. Not in *Tr* and *Or;* perhaps indication of an early revision of Gratian's text. The variant in *Fr* n.38 (sunt] uidentur EGH) is nowhere confirmed.

Quapropter—predicanda sunt (§5 concluded): *H* 65 at c.83–*ante* n.15.
  Tr 1.1.24 (i); *Or* part (i) continued.
  rubr. Apostolorum exempla imitanda *Tr, cf.* Obediendum esse doctrinis et exemplis apostolorum *H* c.83

Vnde consilium—adimplere satagatis (§6): *H* 66 *post* n.11–*ante* n.14.
  Tr 1.1.24 (ii); *Or* part (i) concluded.

D.37 c.14

Relatum est—competenter asserere (pr.–at n.157 *Fr*): *H* 65 at n.15–66 *post* n.5
  Tr 1.1.25; *Or* part (ii), with large initial.
  inscr. Item Clemens *Grat.*
  rubr. Ad intelligentiam sacrarum scripturarum secularium peritia est necessaria *Grat.*

Gratian and Plato

Scripturas ex proprio ingenio non esse legendas *Tr*, De his qui non recte docent *Or* (*marg*)

Cum enim ex diuinis—simulata declinet (*post* n.157 *Fr*–end): H 66 *post* n.5–*post* n.7. Not in *Tr* and *Or*.

Summary

H 65 pr.–*post* n.14	*Grat.* 12 q.1 c.2 pr–§5	*Tr.* 1.1.23–24(i)	*Or.* (i) beg.
65 at n.15–66 *post* n.5	D.37 c.14 (i)	1.1.25	(ii)
66 *post* n.5–*post* n.7	D.37 c.14 (ii)	—	—
66 *post* n.7–*post* n.11	—	—	—
66 *post* n.11–*ante* n.14	12 q.1 c.2 §6	1.1.24 (ii)	(i) concl.
66 at n.14–end			

APPENDIX III

From the papers of the Correctores Romani (cf. at nn.59–62 above)

(i) From the book of minutes, MS Vat. lat. 4891, fo. 118r/v:

Die xvii Octob. MD.LXX. Congregatio apud Illust^{mum} Cardinal. Alciatum. Interfuerunt doctores R. P. Cornelius V(triusque) S(ignaturae) S^{mi} D.N. Refer(endarius). Doc. Thomas, Doc. Latinus, Doc. Parisetus, Doc. I. Marsa Sec(retarius). (*marg.:*) Episcopus Segninus S. D.N. Sacrista Vrbe aberat ad visitandum suum Episcopatum. Videatur an in superioribus aliquid habeat quod non sit annotatum.

(*fo. verso*) can. ij. dilectissimis

. . . In omnibus autem sunt sine dubio et coniuges.] Desunt hec in or(iginali) et pessime sunt addita ab aliquo Nicolaita. Viderentur* quidem delenda sed propter commentarios sustinentur. notetur tamen in marg. pessime esse addita et remittatur lector ad notationem in qua rationibus impugnetur hereticorum opinio et demonstretur quam aliena sit a religione christiana et ab vnitate coniugalj. Et referatur in congregatione generali.

(*marg.*) *Videatur Ans(elmus) siue Authentica an habeat haec verba [Note that the *Correctores* in the beginning of their work used the name 'Authentica canonum' for the (lost) MS of Anselm from which the present MS Vat. lat. 4983 is copied; see *Bulletin of medieval canon law* N.S. 1 (1971), 13–14.]

(*marg. sin.*) Con(gregatio Gen(eralis). In notatione monstretur haec verba deesse in antiquis original. et sapere haeresim Nicolaitarum, de qua Epiphanius contra Epiphani [?] haereticum fo. 100.

(ii) From the draft by Michael Thomasius (Miguel Tomás Taxaquet) for the *Notationes*, MS Vat. lat. 4890, fo. 88r/v.

Causa xij q. p^a 2 c. Dilectissimis No. 1103

In uer. in omnibus autem sunt sine dubio et coniuges] uerba hec non sunt in concilijs Coloniae quatuor tomis impressis neque in duobus uetustis exemplaribus huius epistolae, altero Vaticanae, alterò bibliothecae S^{ti} Marcj Florentiae, neque in Anselmo. quam opinionem a Platone acceptam haeretici quidam uolebant ad religionem christianam transferre, ut testatur Epiphanius haeresi 32 his uerbis: Primum quidem... perficiens. Verùm quod apud ueteres christianos haec uxorum communio vehementer damnaretur, Tertullianus in Apologetico c.39 expressè ait [et testatur his uerbis *add. marg. autogr.*] omnia indiscreta...communicauerunt.

[The quotations (here indicated by suspension points) are the same as in the printed text of the *Notationes.*]

RETRACTATIONES

I. Harmony from Dissonance

p. 3 n. 6: Add now G. Le Bras, Ch. Lefebvre, J. Rambaud, *L'Age classique 1140-1378: Sources et théorie du droit* (Hist. du Droit et des institutions de l'Église en occident 7; Paris 1965).

p. 5 n. 14: For the source of the *Poenitentiale Gregorii III* (Ebo of Reims to Halitgar, PL 105.652) and for instances of the musical metaphor in Alger of Liège see S. Kuttner, 'Urban II and the doctrine of interpretation', *Studia Gratiana* 15 (1972) 76 n. 78; add Burchard of Worms in the genuine prologue of his *Libri decretorum*, on *dissonantia* of the *canonum iura et iudicia poenitentium*, reprinted from the Ballerinis' text in PL 140.499-502, at col. 499D; a passage that was mutilated in the doctored prologue of the 1549 edition (= PL 140.537); cf. G. Fransen, 'Les sources de la préface du Décret de Burchard de Worms', *Bull. Med. Can. Law*, n.s. 3 (1973) 1-7, at p. 4.

p. 8 n. 21: For a survey of this and later research see J. Rambaud, in *L'Age classique* 119-28.

p. 13 n. 27: From among the great number of studies after Vatican II the volume of J. Zeliauskas, *De excommunicatione vitiata apud glossatores* (Instit. historicum Iuris Can. 4; Zurich 1967), should be especially mentioned.

p. 14 n. 29: Johannes Andreae as quoted here actually resumed a *quaestio* by Gerard of Siena O.S.A. (d. 1336), see G. Fransen, 'De analogia legis apud canonistas', *Periodica de re morali et canonica liturgica* 66 (1977) 535-47, at p. 541f. A strong statement on the spiritual and pastoral nature of canon law by Humbert of Romans O.P. (d. 1277) is quoted from his *De eruditione praedicatorum* by J.H. Boehmer, *Corpus iuris canonici* (Halle 1747) I p. xxix, note *a*. To the modern writers add Pope Paul VI, who quoted the words of Panormitanus in his allocution of 19 February 1977, see *Acta Apost. Sedis* 65 (1977) 211 and *Periodica...* 66 (1977) 387n.

p. 15 n. 34: A similar thought on the dignity of man was expressed in the twelfth century by Placentinus, *Summa Codicis* 2.12 (ed. Mogunt. 1536 p. 54).

p. 15 n. 36: Paul VI in his allocution (*loc. cit. ad* n. 29 *supra*) also quoted from this text.

II. Liber Canonicus: A Note on Dictatus Papae c. 17

Among the numerous publications concerned with the reform movement of the eleventh century in its relation to the history of canon law, H. Fuhrmann, 'Das Reformpapsttum und die Rechtswissenschaft', *Investiturstreit und Reichsverfassung*, ed. J. Fleckenstein (Vorträge und Forschungen 17; Sigmaringen 1973) 175-203, is particularly important for the topics discussed in this paper. Many pertinent observations on the ecclesiological context are found in several articles of O. Capitani; see especially his book, *Immunità vescovile ed ecclesiologia in età 'pregregoriana' e 'gregoriana'* (Biblioteca degli Studi medievali 3; Torino 1966), revised from two articles published in *Studi medievali,* 1962 and 1965.

p. 388 n. 4: Add R. Morghen, 'Richerche sulla formazione del registro di Gregorio VII', *Annali di Storia del diritto* 3/4 (1959/60), 40, 45, on DP 17.

p. 389: Authorship of Humbert of Silva-Candida for the Coll. 74T can no longer be maintained. The question of its date—pre-Gregorian or after 1070—remains *sub iudice;* see H. Fuhrmann, *Einfluss und Verbreitung der pseudoisidorischen Fälschungen* II (Stuttgart 1973) 487-92, with bibliography, and J.T. Gilchrist, *Diuersorum patrum sententie* (Monum. Iur. Can. ser. B vol. 1; Città del Vaticano 1973) xxi-xxxi.

p. 391: The opposite of the Pseudo-Isidorian principle had been held in Carolingian times by Agobard of Lyons (d. 840) against the 'Roman innovators' (*neuterici Romani*); cf. Fournier-Le Bras I 124f.; Fuhrmann, *Einfluss und Verbreitung* I (1972) 235, II 245f.

p. 392 n. 19: See also Bernold, *de excomm. vit.* §58 (p. 140.36) on the pope as *auctor canonum.*

p. 392 n. 20: Aurelius of Carthage to Innocent I: rather the African bishops assembled at Carthage in 416 to Innocent I. Earliest canonical tradition in *Coll. Quesn.* 6.2 (PL 56.455f.); also printed as *ep.* 175 of St. Augustine. Cf. Munier, *Concilia Africae* (CCL 149; Turnhout 1974) p. xxix, with references.

p. 393 n. 24: Here Bernold of Constance actually took up an argument already used in Carolingian times in the preface of the *Coll. Dacheriana,* cf. Fournier-Le Bras I 104.

p. 393 n. 27: The authenticity of Nantes has recently been defended by D. Aupest-Conduché, 'De l'existence du concile de Nantes', *Bulletin philologique et historique* (1973-76) 29-59.

p. 394: For the same teaching on non-contradiction in Peter Damiani see J.J. Ryan, *St. Peter Damiani and his canonical sources* (Pont. Institute of Mediaeval Studies, Studies and texts 2; Toronto 1956) 140-48. The oldest expression of this doctrine is found in the preface to the fifth-century *Epitome* of the Sardican canons, in *Coll. Frisingensis*, ed. Turner, *Eccl. occident. monum. iuris antiquiss.* I 2.3 (1930) 540: 'si quid in his rationabile reppererit, quod tamen a sancta atque apostolica ecclesia Romana non discrepet, sequi debebit' (repeated p. 542; cf. p. 535 for earlier editions).

p. 396: Concerning the topic of papal power to alter the law 'if need be', see now 'Urban II and the doctrine of interpretation' (No. IV in the present collection).

p. 398 n. 51: There is one early instance of *ius canonum* as 'Law': Celestine I, *ep.* 5.2 (JK 371) admonishes the 'fratres karissimi, qui iuris nostri idest canonum gubernacula custodimus', on the uncanonical promotion of laymen. The relative clause was (accidentally ?) omitted in Coll. 74T c. 114 (see *app. crit.* to line 7 in Gilchrist's edition p. 76), whence also in Ans. Luc. 7.28 and Gratian, D.61 c.7. Thus a passage which could have furnished a strong proof-text to the Reformers for the pope as the guardian of the law (cf. p. 396 supra) disappeared from the canonical tradition   after Pseudo-Isidore.

p. 399 n. 54: Add the so-called Dictatus of Avranches (*Proprie auctoritatis s. sedis*) c.5: 'Nulla scriptura est autentica sine auctoritate eius', for which see now H. Mordek's critical text, *Deutsches Archiv* 28 (1972) 105-32 at p. 115.

p. 399 n. 55: The earliest clear reference to the *canon s. Scripturae* as the object of DP 17 is by Christianus Lupus O.S.A. (Christian Wolf, d. 1681), 'S. Gregorii VII pontificis Dictatus', *Opera* (Venice 1725) 5.248.

p. 400: On the kinship between DP and contemporary *capitulationes* I should have referred to the study by E. Sackur, 'Der Dictatus papae und die Canonessammmlung des Deusdedit', *Neues Archiv* 18 (1893) 135-53, which remains fundamental; for DP 17 see p. 151 n. 4.

Don Borino's thesis has recently been questioned by H. Fuhrmann, 'Quod catholicus non habeatur qui non concordat Romanae ecclesiae: Randnotizen zum Dictatus papae', *Festschrift für Helmut Beumann zum 65. Geburtstag* (Sigmaringen 1977) 263-77.

III. Sur les origines du terme 'droit positif'

After the appearance of this article and the corresponding pages 175-77 in my *Repertorium der Kanonistik* (Città del Vaticano 1937; the date 1936 was given here, p. 728 n. 1 *avant la lettre* from the page proofs) investigation of the name and concept of 'positive' law was pushed much farther, especially by D. Van den Eynde, 'The terms "ius positivum" and "signum positivum",' *Franciscan Studies* 9 (1949) 41-49 and S. Gagnér, *Studien zur Ideengeschichte der Gesetzgebung* (Studia iuridica Uppsalensia 1; Stockholm-Uppsala 1960) 210-48; cf. also S. Kuttner, 'A forgotten definition of Justice', *Studia Gratiana* 20 (1976 = Mélanges G. Fransen II) 87f. and n. 49 [reprinted here, No. V]. For M. Radin's paper see *infra,* ad p. 738f.

p. 730: For Abaelard's *Dialogus,* the text in Migne remains preferable to the new edition by R. Thomas (Stuttgart-Bad Cannstadt 1970), cf. the notice by G. S(ilagi), *Deutsches Archiv* 31 (1975) 260. Dom Lottin's remark in *Le droit naturel...* p. 28 should have been quoted correctly as calling Abaelard's distinction a 'conception entièrement intemporelle'. The influential texts of Hugh of St. Victor, *Didascalicon* 6.5 and 3.2 (see Van den Eynde 43f. and Gagnér 213, 238f.) and of Petrus Cantor, *Verbum abbreviatum* c.51 (PL 205.162-65) should have been added to the dossier of French theologians.

'Maître Odon de Doura': the toponym should be read as 'Dovra' = Dover, see Kuttner and Rathbone, 'Anglo-Norman Canonists', *Traditio* 7 (1949/51) 293.

p. 732 n. 2: For Laborans, add his *De iustitia et iusto* 2.7, ed. Landgraf p. 30.

p. 732: The text of the *Introductio In prima parte agitur* seems to be derived from Hugh of St. Victor, as is probably that of the *Summa Inperatorie maiestati (Monacensis,* here not mentioned), see 'A forgotten definition of justice', *loc. cit. supra.*

p. 733: Other French or French-educated canonists operating with the concept of 'ius positivum' are the author of the fragment 'Inter cetera' (cf. Singer, 'Beiträge...', *Archiv für kath. Kirchenrecht* 69 [1893] 447), the English master Honorius, *Summa questionum* 3.2 §'Item cum dicitur' (Douai MS 640, fol. 29rb), and Sicard of Cremona as quoted by F. Gillmann, *Zur Inventarisierung der kanonistischen Handschriften...* (appendix to the offprint of his 'Des Johannes Galensis Apparat zur Compilatio III', from *Archiv kath. Kirchenr.* 118; Mainz 1938) p. 66f.

Before the end of the twelfth century, Alanus Anglicus in the first recension (*c.* 1192) of his *Apparatus* began the gloss on D.10 pr.: 'Ostenso ius positiuum cedere iuri naturali...', see A.M. Stickler, 'Alanus Anglicus als Verteidiger des monarchischen Papsttums', *Salesianum* 21 (1959) 351; this was repeated in the Anglo-Norman *Summa Induent sancti (Duacensis),* see R. Fraher, 'Alanus and the Summa "Induent sancti",' *Bull. of Medieval Canon Law* 6 (1976) 51.

p. 734: Further texts by glossators of the *Compilationes antiquae* are cited by F. Gillmann, *Zur Inventarisierung* p. 67. See also the prologue to the *Glossa Palatina* in Douai MS 590 and (separately) in Bamberg, MS Can. 13, fol. 272v: 'Ex ore sedentis in throno...gladius iste bis acutus [Apoc. 1.16; 19.15] est ius bipartitum, naturale scil. et positiuum'.

p. 735: What has here been called '*Casus* du décret' (cf. also *Repertorium* p. 231) is not one but two writings: (1) the *Summa brevis* of Ricardus Anglicus in the London MS (and three others), on which see Anglo-Norman Canonists' p. 330f., also *Dict. de droit canonique* 7.678; and (2) an anonymous *Summa brevis* in the Berlin and Trier MSS, compiled much later from the *Casus decretorum* of Bartholomaeus Brixiensis.

p. 736: Calcidius's translation of the *Timaeus* and his commentary were much more closely analyzed in the present context by Gagnér, *Studien* 221ff., who also showed the particular importance of the glosses on the *Timaeus* by William of Conches as a source for theologians and canonists, *ibid.* 225ff. Cf. Kuttner, 'A forgotten definition...' p. 98; and 'Gratian and Plato...' (No. XI in the present volume) *passim*.

p. 738f.: On classical models, both Greek and Latin, for Calcidius see Gagnér p. 240ff. M. Radin, 'Early statutory interpretation in England', *Illinois Law Review* 38 (1943) 16-40 at 25f. has pointed out the importance of the Stoic dichotomy of *physis* and *thesis,* and its full development in Philo of Alexandria (references p. 26 n. 45 to several passages in the *Opera,* ed. Cohn and Wendland I 70.2, II 177.2, 185.6 etc.), 'who ranked in medieval and Renaissance times as a Church father'. But Philo remained untranslated in the Middle Ages and no bridge leads from his writing to the medieval *naturalis* and *positiuus.*

IV. Urban II and the Doctrine of Interpretation

p. 56f.: Daimbert's case and the intransigent attitude of the Vallombrosans are discussed at length by Sofia Boesch-Gajano, 'Storia e tradizione vallombrosana', *Bullettino dell' Istit. Storico Ital. per il Medio Evo* 76 (1964) 98-215, at pp. 118-33; on Urban II's action see esp. p. 122 and the long note p. 123 n. 1 (-126).

p. 65 and n. 35: On the adulterated version of John VIII's letter JE 3271 see also D. Stiernon, *Constantinople IV* (Hist. des conciles oecumeniques 5; Paris 1967) 186-90, 213, 309. Joannou's text and notes are nonetheless unchanged in the 3rd edition of *Conciliorum oecum. decreta* (1972) 157-58.

p. 65 and n. 36: The collection of Turin MS E.v.44 served E. Caspar in the edition of fragments from John VIII's letters, see MGH *Epp.* 7 (1928) 273ff. and 330ff.

p. 66f.: For Gregory VII's sense of balancing dispensation (*tolerare con-siderata ratione*) and *concordia canonice traditionis* his letter to King San-cho of Aragon, *Reg.* 2.56 (JL 4927), ed. Caspar 190f. is likewise very instructive.

p. 67f.: For a radical critique of the Gregorian and post-Gregorian doctrine see the Philosopher in Abaelard's *Dialogus inter philosophum, Judaeum et Christianum:*

> ...Romani quoque pontifices uel synodales conuentus quotidie noua condunt decreta uel dispensationes aliquas indulgent, quibus licita iam prius illicita uel e conuerso fieri autumatis, quasi in eorum potestate Deus posuerit uel permissionibus ut bona uel mala esse faciant quae prius non erant...(PL 178.1656-57).

p. 69: There is, however, an *obiter dictum* on the parallel between Urban's letter and Ivo's prologue in Sofia Boesch-Gajano (cited ad p. 56 *supra*) p. 126 n. 3.

p. 72 n. 61: See also John IX, Roman synod of 898 c. 10, '...cui Deo auctore presidemus', quoted as 'Stephanus papa' in Ivo, *Pan.* 3.2 (= 3.1§ii in the edition), Grat. D.63 c.28.

p. 74: Further doubts have been cast on the reliability of the *Coll. Britan-nica* by J.L. Nelson, 'The problem of King Alfred's royal anointing', *Journal of Eccl. Hist.* 18 (1967) 145-63 at p. 147, 153, with regard to the fragment JL 2645 (Leo IV). Cf. W. Ullmann, *Law and Politics in the Middle Ages* (London 1975) 138 n. 1.

p. 75 and n. 73: On Urban's second letter (JL 5451) concerning Daimbert see S. Boesch-Gajano 129ff.

p. 76 n. 79: The attribution to 'Gregorius' of D. 29 c. 2 apparently comes from the Collection in Three Books, 2.34.22.

p. 78ff.: Further twelfth-century examples of 'cessante causa cessat lex' were given by H. Van de Wouw, *Notae Atrebatenses* (Diss. Leiden 1969; offset printing) pp. xxxviii-xl, from glosses of Gratian D. 48 pr. See also Ricardus Anglicus, *Generalia,* Vatican MS Chis. E.vii.218, fol. 74vd, and the *Brocardica* of Vatican MS Borgh. lat. 287, fol. 5rc.

For early patristic antecedents of Innocent I's ruling, the text of Tertul-lian, *Adversus Marcionem* 4.34.5 (ed. Kroymann, CCL 1. 635-36),

> et quod non prohibuit in totum [Christus] permisit alias, ubi causa cessat ob quam prohibuit,

deserves quotation and invites further study.

V. A Forgotten Definition of Justice.

p. 98: The *Derivationes* of Huguccio ought to be dated earlier than *c.*1191, since he cited the work in his *Agiographia,* which in turn is quoted in his *Summa decretorum,* see A.M. Stickler on Huguccio in LThK² 5 (1960) 522 and *Dict. de droit can.* 7 (1967) 1357. But this does not make the work a 'travail de jeunesse', especially if we consider that the quotation of the *Agiorgraphia* (at *De cons.* D.3 c.19) occurs in one of the latest-written parts of the *Summa.*

For William de Conches as a source for other material in the *Derivationes* see e.g. R.W. Hunt, 'Hugutio and Petrus Helias', *Mediaeval and Renaissance Studies* 2 (1950) 174.

p. 109 n. 136: The authorship of the *Moralium dogma philosophorum* remains controverted; see M.Th. d'Alvery, *Alain de Lille* (Études de philos. médiévale 52; Paris 1965) 65.

VI. La réserve papale du droit de canonisation

Important criticism of my interpretation came from E.W. Kemp, who in his 'Pope Alexander III and the canonization of Saints', *Transactions of the Royal Historical Society⁵* 27 (1943) 13-28, collected impressive hagiographic material I should have considered in presenting the twelfth-century trends moving towards an exclusive papal right of canonization; he concluded that Alexander III himself believed this right to exist, even before any definite canonical enactment. In reviewing Kemp for the *Analecta Bollandiana* 63 (1945) 273-75, P. Grosjean concurred; Kemp himself used his earlier study in a broader historical framework for his book, *Canonization and authority in the western Church* (Oxford 1948), especially at pp. 99-104. Cf. W. Ullmann's paper on DP 23, in *Studi Gregoriani* 6 (1959/61) at pp. 261f.

Today, I would myself place greater emphasis than I did in 1938 (cf. pp. 182-87) on the growing conviction in many quarters, during the twelfth century, that for canonization to have its full effect some measure of *auctoritas apostolica* is needed. But I would still hesitate to decide whether this was seen as a measure of validity or of canonical propriety (*Romanae sedis obseruantia,* as Archbishop Eskil of Lund put it in the case of St. Canute, *c.* 1197; MGH *Script.* 29.18). I also believe that on the whole my argument stands that Innocent III was the central figure in the history of the *réserve papale.* I would agree that Alexander III firmly believed in his right to intervene in any case of veneration of a new saint. But he never formulated this authority as an exclusive right, nor did he assume its existence as a sort of customary law. (The parallel with the doctrine on the pope as 'universal ordinary' comes to mind: his having direct, ordinary power anywhere in the Church never excludes the local ordinary's jurisdiction until the pope 'lays his hands' on a specific matter.)

As for another general point E.W. Kemp raised in the concluding pages of his 1943 essay: I remain convinced that evidence such as I assembled from decretal collections and the glossators of canon law is historical evidence also in such fields as the veneration of saints. Canonists were not merely concerned with tithes, marriages, and litigation. At an epoch in which reading the *De consecratione* of Gratian's Decretum was considered an integral part of the canonist's training, it could not have been otherwise.

The following studies should be added to the general bibliography: R. Klauser, 'Zur Entwicklung des Heiligsprechungsverfahrens bis zum 13. Jahrhundert', ZRG Kan. Abt. 40 (1954) 85-101; J. Schlafke, *De competentia in causis sanctorum decernendis... usque ad annum 1234* (Diss. Angelicum; Rome 1961).

p. 183 n. 3: For canonization by legates, earlier bibliography is now superseded by J. Petersohn's detailed study, 'Die päpstliche Kanonisationsdelegation des 11. und 12. Jahrhunderts und die Heiligsprechung Karls des Grossen', *Proceedings of the Fourth International Congress of Medieval Canon Law, Toronto...* (Mon. Iur. Can. ser. C vol. 5, Città del Vaticano 1976) 163-206. The case of St. Anno of Cologne (see A. Brackmann, 'Zur Kanonisation des Erzbischofs Anno', *Neues Archiv* 32 (1907) 151-65) remains instructive for the emphasis the papal legates in the 1180's placed on the need for a special mandate to canonize, over and above the general legatine powers; cf. Kemp, 'Alexander III...' p. 24f., Petersohn p. 180f. The case is also instructive for what I have called (p. 185) the *affaiblissement* of the old practice of canonization: the abbots of Siegburg, the legate was told, found it too cumbersome, but apparently necessary, to treat the matter at the Apostolic See, while the rights of the Archbishop of Cologne are not even mentioned.

p. 187: The double canonization of St. Rosendo of Dumio by Celestine III, first as cardinal legate in 1172, then as pope in 1196 (JL 17287) belongs in the same context. Cf. Kemp p. 21f. and the original documents published by A. Garcia y Garcia from the archives of the Hispanic Society, New York, 'A propos de la canonisation des saints au XIIe siècle', RDC 17 (1968) 3-15.

p. 192f.: 'Aeterna et incommutabilis' was addressed to King Kol of the Stenkel dynasty, not to Canute, and should be dated 1171 or 1172. The case reported of the 'drunken saint' may well be a propaganda piece of the Stenkel party in the struggle against St. Eric's descendants; the latter finally succeeded to the throne only in the thirteenth century. See S. Tunberg, 'Erik den helige, Sveriges helgenkonung', *Fornvännen, Meddelanden fran K. Vitterhets Historie och Antikvitets Akademien* 36 (1941) 257-78, as reviewed by P. Grosjean, *Analecta Bollandiana* 60 (1942) 267-70; cf. *ibid.* 63 (1945) 273-75; Petersohn p. 165 n. 11.

p. 194: In even stronger terms than John of Salisbury, Thomas Becket's old secretary, Herbert of Bosham challenged any papal prerogative:

> ...nullo expectato superiore mandato martyris palmam martyris gloria mox subsequi debuisset...Nec enim arbitror exemplum extare uel scriptum quo debeat ad tuae auctoritatis, quae omni praeminet, consultationem referri gloria martyris...(ed. J.B. Sheppard, *Materials...Becket* 7 [R.S. 1885] 532).

This is diametrically opposed to the vision of the monk reported in William's *Miracula s. Thomae* (ed. Robertson, *Mat. Becket* 1.150) and quoted in Kemp's 'Pope Alexander III...' p. 19f. as evidence for a definite opinion on canonization as a papal prerogative; but this text might indicate no more than the (correct) attitude that, once the Holy See has begun the informative process, one cannot go ahead before the final act, when the saint will be 'ex apostolica auctoritate catalogo martyrum ascriptus'. For this informative process, cf. also the new letter of Alexander III to the papal legates, 'Dilecti filii', discussed by Ch. Duggan, 'Bishop John and Archdeacon Richard...', *Thomas Becket: Actes du Congrès international de Sédières,* ed. R. Foreville (Paris 1975), at p. 78f. and to be published in Chodorow and Duggan, *Decretales ineditae saec. XII* (Mon. Iur. Can. ser. B vol. 4; Città del Vaticano 1980).

p. 196f.: For the collections here cited as *Cottoniana I, Cottoniana II,* and *Bodleiana,* the names *Claudiana, Cottoniana,* and *Tanneriana* are now commonly used; see C.R. Cheney and M.G. Cheney, *Studies in the collections of twelfth-century decretals,* from the papers of the late W. Holtzmann... (Mon. Iur. Can. ser. B vol. 3; Città del Vat. 1979) p. xxiiff.

p. 198: the encyclical 'Redolet Anglia' is also found in the collections *1 Par.* c. 39, *1 Dert.* c. 58, *Aureavall.* c. 14, *Brug.* (MS Ottob.) app. 3.

p. 202: The comment by Benencasa on De cons. D. 1 c. 37 passed into the *Apparatus Ius naturale* of Alanus (whence also the excerpts in MS Vat. Ross. 595, cf. note 2): Paris B.N. lat. 3909 fol. 54rb and lat. 15393 (set i) fol. 275ra.

p. 202f.: The glossator *b.* quoted by Laurentius (*Glossa Palatina*) and Johannes Teutonicus was more probably Bernard of Compostella, cf. S. Kuttner, 'Bernardus Compostellanus antiquus', *Traditio* 1 (1943) 277ff. at p. 203 n. 6.

Another gloss by Laurentius (*c.* 1210-1215), only found in Paris B.N. lat. 15393 (set ii) fol. 275ra, is probably the earliest unequivocal statement of the exclusive papal right:

> De cons. D.3 c.1 v. *festiuitates:* 'Loquitur de canonizatis sanctis, quia de non canonizatis non posset intelligi, cum hoc soli pape competat. la(urentius). arg. extra. ii. de uenera. sancto. Audiuimus.'

As the position of the siglum *la.* shows, the reference to 'Audiuimus' was an addition.

p. 206ff.: On Innocent III's outstanding place in the history of canonization more light was shed by Raymonde Foreville's book, *Un procès de canonisation à l'aube du XIIIe siècle: Le livre de saint Gilbert de Sempringham* (Paris 1943), in which for the first time the whole record of a process of information has become available; it shows how Innocent conceived of, and developed the steps leading to the act of canonization, as a strict and formal procedure. See also Foreville's historical introduction, pp. xxii-xxxi, xxxi-xxxv, and the fine pages on Innocent, the canonists, and the English canonization cases in C.R. Cheney, *Pope Innocent III and England* (Stuttgart 1976) 51-59.

p. 208: The canonization of the Empress Cunegunda *ex plenitudine potestatis,* and expressly styled as a judgment of the Vicar of Christ, marks also the end of the alternative of delegating canonizations, cf. Cheney p. 52.

The importance of Innocent's pronouncement on the empress is not impaired by the observation (Schlafke, *De competentia* 88f. and Petersohn p. 116 n. 4) that the pope probably took the clause 'cum hoc sublime iudicium ad eum tantum pertinet' etc. from the petitioners' text. I may rather have understated its high importance when I qualified it as a mere definition of the pope's universal power and not a *réserve papale.* Still, it is significant that the clause was not used in the case of St. Gilbert where Innocent III ordered celebration of his feast not universally, but only for the provinces of Canterbury and York, although otherwise the form, '(Cum secundum euangelicam...) Licet enim ad hoc—sequentibus signis', from St. Cunegunda's case (= *La réserve* p. 225-6) served as model; see the text in Foreville pp. 32-36; Cheney and Semple, *Selected letters of Innocent III* (London etc. 1953) pp. 26-32.

p. 209 n. 2: The *autre travail* alluded to appeared as 'Johannes Teutonicus, das vierte Laterankonzil und die Compilatio quarta', *Miscellanea Giovanni Mercati* V (Studi e Testi 125; Città del Vaticano 1946) 608-34.

p. 210f.: Today I would no longer contrast as sharply *Compilatio secunda* and the Gregorian Decretals. The canonical value of *Audiuimus* was no doubt enhanced by its inclusion into Gregory IX's compilation, but the precedent was not thereby turned into a legislative command. Recent opinion no longer classifies the *Gregoriana* as a piece of codification like that of Justinian; see e.g. S. Kuttner, 'Quelques observations sur l'autorité des collections canoniques dans le droit classique de l'Église', *Actes du Congrès de Droit canonique...22-26 Avril 1947* (Paris 1950) 305- 12; K.W. Nörr, 'Päpstliche Dekretalen und römisch-kanonischer Zivilprozess', *Studien zur europäischen Rechtsgeschichte,* ed. W. Wilhelm (Frankfurt 1972) 53-65.

p. 211: For continuing local 'canonizations' without papal authority in the later Middle Ages see Kemp, *Canonization* pp. 137-40; J. Lenzenweger, *Berthold, Abt von Garsten* (Forsch. zur Gesch. Oberösterreichs 5, Graz - Köln 1958) pp. 69ff.

VII. Pope Lucius III and the Bigamous Archbishop of Palermo

p. 410: It is uncertain when the hybrid Latin term *bigamus* replaced the older *digamus*, taken from the Greek. Turner, *Eccl. occident. monum. iur. antiquiss.* 1.2 p. 17 (sec. 4), says that Innocent I (414) and Zosimus (418) were the first to use it, but his examples were unfortunately taken from inferior editions in Mansi or the preceding conciliar collections. Inn. I, *ep.* 17 (22 in Mansi), JK 303 c.3 has 'Deinde ponitur non dici oportere digamum eum qui...' in Coustant's edition, *Epistolae Rom. pont.* (Paris 1721) col. 831, in Justel's text of the *Dionysiana* (PL 67.258), in the Ballerinis' text from the *Quesnelliana* (PL 56.507), and in the *Hispana* (see e.g. the facsimile edition of the eighth-century Vienna MS 411 [Graz 1974] fol. 253 v). Zosimus, *ep.* 9 (*ep.* 1 in Mansi), JK 339 c.2 §5 likewise reads 'digamus' in all these texts: Coustant 971, *Dion.* (PL 67.264), *Quesn.* (PL 56.573), *Hisp.* (see cod. Vindob. fol. 258r). On the other hand, Turner, *Eccl. monum.* 2.2 p.viii, doubts that the editions of the Council of Elvira (*c.* 300/305), c.38 '...nec sit bigamus' can be trusted; 'veram lectionem suspicor esse "digamus",' but at least the cod. Vigilianus (ed. J. Vives, *Concilios Visigóticos e Hispano-Romanos* [Barcelona-Madrid 1963] p. 8) and the cod. Vindob. (fol. 89v) of the *Hispana* do not bear out this suspicion.

p. 411 n. 12: The source remains to be established from which Innocent I quoted as biblical (*scriptum est*) the words 'Sacerdotes mei semel nubant' and '...non nubent amplius' in JK 286 c.6 §9, and again in JK 292 c.6 §10: 'quia scriptum est in veteri testamento, "Uxorem virginem accipiat sacerdos" et alibi, "Sacerdotes mei semel nubant"...' (ed. Coustant [1721] cols. 750-51, 770-71); cf. later (842) Pope Zachary to St. Boniface, JE 2264 (MGH *Epp.* 3.303.18-20). Coustant pointed to similar statements by Tertullian, invoking OT authority, *De exhort. castit.* 7.1 and *De monog.* 7.7 (=CCL 2.1024.5 and 1238.48-9). Levit. 21.13, to which modern editions usually refer, has only the injunction for the high priest to marry a virgin (followed by the exclusion of widows etc.) and was so quoted by Innocent I in JK 292; but the '...semel nubant' he expressly quoted as 'elsewhere'. Cf. also the Collection in 74 Titles c.145 (and the editor's note) in *Diuersorum patrum sententie* (Mon. Iur. Can. ser. B vol. 1; Città del Vaticano 1973) p. 97. As Professor Judah Goldin has kindly pointed out to me, an exegesis which forbids the high priest to have two wives exists in the Talmudic tradition; some of this is earlier than the Maimonides text referred to *inter al.* by L. Ginzberg, *The legends of the Jews* VI (Philadelphia 1968) 354.

p. 412 n. 15: For these Councils see now Ch. Munier's edition, *Concilia Galliae, a.314-a.506* (CCL 148; Tournhout 1965) pp. 84, 123, 138, 144; add Valence (374) c.1, Agde (506) c.1, *ibid.* 28, 193; and for the stricter rule, as in Tours 461, the *epist. Lupi et Euforii* (= Dekkers, *Clavis* no. 988), *ibid.* 140.

p. 417 n. 31: For additional texts and discussion on 'general welfare' of the Church see G. Post, 'Ratio publicae utilitatis, ratio status und "Staatsraison",' *Welt als Geschichte* 21 (1961) 8ff. at p. 24f. and n. 46 = *Studies in medieval legal thought* (Princeton 1964) p. 264 and n. 49; J.H. Hackett, 'State of the Church: A concept of the medieval canonists', *The Jurist* 23 (1963) 259-90; Y.M. Congar, 'Status ecclesiae', *Studia Gratiana* 15 (1972 = *Post Scripta*) 1-31.

p. 420 n. 47: In 1063, Pope Alexander II had actually issued a prohibition to his successors (JL 4501), see S. Kuttner, 'Urban II and the doctrine of interpretation', *Stud. Grat.* 15 (1972) 66 (No. IV of the studies in the present volume).

p. 422 n. 54: Add the text published from an appendix of several MSS of Robert of Flamborough's *Poenitentiale* by F. Firth, 'The Poenitentiale...', *Traditio* 16 (1960) 554, lines 1-9.

p. 424 n. 62: On the history of this conception in which Christ *gestabat cuiuslibet ordinis officium,* see now the fumdamental book of R.E. Reynolds, *The ordinals of Christ from their origins to the twelfth century* (Beiträge zur Gesch. und Quellenkunde des MA 7; Berlin-New York 1978).

p. 424 n. 63: 'hoc is inquirat quem mundi labor exagitat' seems to have been a set phrase; Simon used it also in C.16 q.7 c.26; and see the *Summa Inter cetera* on natural law as law governing the universe; quoted by R. Weigand, *Die Naturrechtslehre der Legisten und Dekretisten* (Münchener theol. Studien, Kan. Abt. 26, München 1967) p. 167 §282.

p. 425: The source of Innocent III's dictum is Dig. 4.8.4; cf. *Glos. ord.* Dig. 36.1.13.4, v. *imperium.*

p. 425 n. 71: Richard cited the same passage from Nov. 10 (Auth. 2.5) in his *Summa brevis super Decreto* C.25; printed in Kuttner and Rathbone, 'Anglo-Norman canonists', *Traditio* 7 (1949/51) 334.

p. 426 n. 73: On Laurentius see 'Addendum' p. 453.

p. 428f.: M. Bertram, 'Kirchenrechtliche Vorlesungen aus Orléans (1285/7)', *Francia* 2 (1974) 213-33, publishes at p. 230 an amusing story told with gusto by one of the masters in his *lectura* on X 1.29.40 (Paris, B.N. lat. 14328, fol. 101vb): 'I was together with another cleric (he wrote) in a church where a priest celebrated of whom it was said that he was *bigamus*. The other man did not want to stay at Mass,

> et dicebat quod ille non poterat conficere nec in ordine receperat caracterem, et plus dicebat quia papa non poterat dispensare cum bigamo cum esset sacerdos. Ego dixi sibi contra et adhuc dico...

Then the story is spun out: our master is denounced as a heretic by the other cleric for having declared valid the papal dispensation of a bigamist; three bishops and a famous master of theology become involved in the argument etc. Now, apart from showing how hotly debated the issue still was in the 1280's at Orléans, the story has a humorous twist: the writer calls his opponent repeatedly a jackass ('quidam magnus asinus', 'ille asinus'). He could be sure that his students would understand the cleverness of hurling back at a follower of Nicolaus Furiosus's doctrine the famous insult which its originator had coined for ordained bigamists.

p. 429: The *Glossa Palatina* also cites Nicolaus Furiosus in another context, as holding the opinion 'quod imperator semper debeat esse subdiaconus', D.63 c.3 v. *ordinem* (MSS Vat. Pal. lat. 658, fol. 17ra, Reg. lat. 977 fol. 47ra).

p. 431 n. 92: On *disputare de facto regis* more material was pointed out by G. Post, 'Vincentius Hispanus, "Pro ratione voluntas", and medieval and early modern theories of Sovereignty', *Traditio* 28 (1970) 159ff. at pp. 180-82 (see *ibid.* on *facta* = royal written acts such as grants, appointments, etc.). On the problems of transmission concerning the passage in Bracton fol. 34 see now S.E. Thorne's translation, II (1968) p.109, note 18. There is an interesting gloss in cod. W of Vacarius, *Lib. paup.* 9.21.2 (3) (ed. de Zulueta p. 296). The canonistic texts remain to be studied more closely, e.g. glosses on D.40 c.1; the canonists' handling of Cod. Just. 9.29.2(3) as quoted by Gratian in C.17 q.4 p.c.29; and Petrus Blesensis, *Spec.* c.23 (for which Singer 'Beiträge...', *Archiv f. kath. Kirchenr.* 69 [1893] 388 n.41, unconvincingly suggested Petrus Cantor, *Verb. abbr.* [PL 105.139D] as source). Intrusion of an early gloss 'uel facto' in certain MSS of Cod. 9.29.2 'disputari de principali iudicio...' or in Gratian's dictum is not impossible.

p. 433: This was not the only time that Huguccio reported an unusual action of Lucius III in matters concerning ordination. Thus on C.9 q.1 pr., after recording that Alexander III did not reordain those ordained in the schism of Octavian (Victor IV):

> Papa tamen Lucius, ut audiui, fecit reordinari ordinatos ab illis qui ultimam manus impositionem acceperant extra ecclesiam, et fuit mirum qualiter consenserint cardinales' (MS Vat. Arch. S. Petr. C.114, fol. 176va).

p. 436: On Matthew of Salerno see also C.A. Garufi, *Ryccardi de S. Germano Chronicon* (Rer. ital. script. nuova ediz. 7.2; Rome 1937/38) p. 5 n. 3; the day of death is given there (p. 6) as 18 July.

p. 438 *prece uel precio*: This is an old play on words, see C.1 q.1 c.113 and D.83 c.1 (Gregory VII); Cod. 1.3.30.4.

p. 453: Laurentius's commentary on *Lector* appears in another form in Arras MS 592 (500); see text in A.M. Stickler, 'Il decretista Laurentius Hispanus', *Studia Gratiana* 11 (1967) 524-25; again differently in Charleville MS 269, fol. 22ra; cf. also the reference 'prout notaui xxxiiii. di. Lector' in the *Apparatus Servus appellatur*, gloss on 3 Comp. 1.14.2 v.*sacramenti defectum*, printed by F. Gillmann in what he called *Des Laurentius Hispanus Apparat zur Compilatio III...* (Mainz 1939) p. 115.

Over the years I have collected more texts which could be added to these pages, e.g. glosses on D.34 in Paris B.N. lat. 3905B, fol. 21ra; Cambridge, Caius College MS 676, fol. 21vb (Anglo-Norman school); Cues MS 223, p. 35a/b (enlarged version of *App. Ordinaturus* and recension of *Animal est substantia*); Grenoble MS 62 (482), fol. 27ra (Willelmus Vasco), and in the *Lectura* of Reims MS 686, fol. 28ra (Johannes de Fintona?); also on X.1.21.2 in the *Apparatus* of Goffredus de Trano (Vienna MS 2197, fol. 20ra). But it would lead too far afield to print and comment on all these glosses here.

IX. Cardinalis: The history of a canonical concept

Of all the papers assembled in the present volume, this one could not be taken in hand again (*retractari*) by the mere addition of a set of notes, in order to absorb all that has been written since 1945, or all that I overlooked in the first place. It is a lengthy paper, a paper with a thesis; a paper going over a vast amount of canonical and factual evidence concerning semantics, doctrines, and institutions. Short of writing additional notes to almost every page of an essay which already contains 'eine ungewöhnlich grosse Menge von Material..., das leider in Hunderten von Anmerkungen untergebracht ist' (R. Elze, *art. cit. infra*, p. 42 n. 74), no substantial *retractatio* could be done. But then, one might as well sit down and write the whole essay again. *Quod absit.*

Writing at Washington before the end of World War II, I had no opportunity to consult B. Fischer, 'Der niedere Klerus bei Gregor dem Grossen', *Zeitschrift für kathol. Theologie* 62 (1938) 37-75, and L. Santifaller, *Saggio di un'Elenco dei funzionari, impiegati e scrittori della Cancellaria Apostolica dall'inizio all'anno 1099* (Bullettino dell'Istituto per il Medio Evo e Archivio Muratoriano 56; Rome 1940). Two important papers by Michel Andrieu appeared in Europe shortly after mine, without either of us knowing that we were covering substantially the same ground, arriving at largely similar results: 'L'Origine du titre de cardinal dans l'église romaine', *Miscellanea Giovanni Mercati* V (Studi e testi 125; Città del Vaticano 1946) 113-44, and 'La carrière ecclésiastique des papes et les documents liturgiques du môyen age', *Revue des sciences religieuses* 21 (1947) 90-120. A thorough reworking of the chapter on the Roman *diaconiae* and the deacons as cardinals (pp. 178-98) would be necessary to absorb the results of important studies by O. Bertolini, 'Per la storia delle diaconie romane dell'alto medio evo sino alla fine del secolo VIII', *Archivio della Società Romana di Storia patria* 70 (1947) 1-145; by A.P. Frutaz, 'Diaconia', *Enciclopedia Cattolica* 4 (1950) 1521-35, and now especially by R. Hüls, at pp. 14-44 of his *Kardinäle, Klerus, und Kirchen Roms...* (1977; cited below). Much relevant source material was competently analyzed by R. Elze, 'Das "Sacrum Palatium Lateranense" im 10. und 11. Jahrhundert', *Studi Gregoriani* 4 (1952) 27-54.

C.G. Fürst's important book, *Cardinalis: Prolegomena zu einer Rechtsgeschichte des römischen Kardinalskollegiums* (Munich 1967) represents the foremost challenge to the basic assumptions and interpretations of my article. But it also offers a more thorough study than ever undertaken before of the 'cardinal' clergy in churches outside of Rome: this alone (pp. 74-86, 119-200) would make it necessary for me to go over much of the material again which I discussed pp. 152-72, and make the needed corrections and additions of detail. As for Fürst's critique of my interpretations and above all of my main thesis on the original meaning of 'cardinalis' in canonical parlance—a critique which is also directed at the work of Klewitz and Andrieu—this cannot possibly be discussed and answered in these pages. Objections to Fürst's position have been raised by some of his reviewers, thus F. Kempf in *Archivum historiae pontificiae* 6 (1968) 452-57, and K. Ganzer in ZRG Kan. Abt. 56 (1970) 132-37. I have learned much from the book, but I still believe that on the whole my interpretation stands.

For the history and prosopography of the Roman cardinalate in the eleventh century (pp. 172-77) the following recent studies are of major importance: E. Pásztor, 'San Pier Damiani, il cardinalato e la formazione della Curia romana', *Studi Gregoriani* 10 (1975) 317-39, and 'Riforma della Chiesa nel secolo XI e l'origine del collegio dei cardinali: Problemi e ricerche', *Studi sul Medioevo Cristiano offerti a Raffaelo Morghen...* (Istit. Storico per il Medio Evo, Studi storici 88-92; Roma 1974) II 609-25; R. Hüls, *Kardinäle, Klerus und Kirchen Roms 1049-1130* (Bibl. des Deutschen Histor. Instituts in Rom 48; Tübingen 1977). See also L. Spätling, 'De mutatione Cardinalatus romani saeculo undecimo', *Antonianum* 42 (1967) 3-24. In the notes that follow I have only singled out a some points of the original article for additions or corrections.

p. 134 n. 7: The comparison by Pope Siricius of a bishop's transfer with adultery should not have been cited as a canon of a Roman synod; it is a section (c. 5 §16, *al.* c. 13) of his decretal 'Dominus inter cetera', to which the Collection of St. Maur (see Maassen, *Geschichte* p. 620) prefixed the rubric 'Incipiunt canones synodum (*sic*) Romanorum ad Gallos episcopos...'. Sirmond's and Labbe's attribution to Innocent I (=

JK *post* 285) has long been abandoned; but the attribution by E.Ch. Babut to Pope Damasus (*La plus ancienne décrétale,* Paris 1904) is still accepted by J.R. Palanque in Fliche-Martin, *Histoire de l'Église* III (Paris 1945) 482-83, and by Dekkers, *Clavis* no. 1632. For recent bibliography see P. Kottje, 'Das Aufkommen der täglichen Eucharistiefeier...', *Zeitschr. für Kirchengesch.* 82 (1971) 225 n. 44.

p. 152 n. 36: On JL 4736 see R. Hüls, 'Cardinales sancti Petri und Cardinales sancti Pauli', *Quellen und Forschungen aus ital. Archiven...* 57 (1977) 332-38.

pp. 152, 177, 183 *Descriptio sanctuarii Lateranensis ecclesiae*: A later recension is edited in R. Valentini and G. Zucchetti, *Codice topografico della Città di Roma* 3 (Fonti per la storia d'Italia 90; Roma 1946) 326ff. See further C. Vogel, 'La "Descriptio ecclesiae Lateranensis" du diacre Jean', *Meélanges en l'honneur de Mgr. Michel Andrieu* (Strasbourg 1956) 456ff.; Hüls, *Kardinäle* pp. 22, 38ff. For the date (cf. p. 177) see now Hüls p. 42: after 1099. My conjecture (p. 183 n. 39) on only five (instead of six) deaconries being qualified as palatine (*palatii*) in the *Descriptio* was based on a misreading of Kehr's emendation *loc. cit.* : the MS (Vat. Reg. lat. 712 fol. 87v) has 's. Theodorici palatii', cf. Elze, 'Das Sacrum Palatium...' p. 42 n. 78, Fürst, *Cardinalis* 109-10. For 'S. Maria in Domenica ubi est archidiaconatus' see Hüls p. 42f.

pp. 156, 198 n. 102: My observations on Ravenna are obsolete; the origins of these cardinals, their college, their *tituli* and privileges were studied by Angelo Duranti in an unpublished doctoral thesis, *I 'Cardinales' della Chiesa di Ravenna* with an appendix of archival documents (205 typewritten pages, Bologna 1955/56), and by Fürst, *Cardinalis* 164-72; 206-11 (documents). On 17 February 1568, Pope Pius V united the chapters of canon-cardinals and canon-cantors in the cathedral and abolished the two titulatures, see Fürst pp. 83-86, and the text of the papal brief 'Superni dispositione' *ibid.* 209-11 (also discussed and copied in Duranti's unpublished dissertation, pp. 89-92, 198-205). I have not seen the text published by A. Codronchi, *Constitutiones capitulares s. Ravennatensis ecclesiae* (Ravenna 1790) pp. 53-63, which Duranti cites p. 198. A general statute of Pius V which suppressed all local cardinalates and reserved the name to the Roman cardinals never existed: Fürst pp. 83-86 has shown how the bibliographical legend of a constitution 'Non mediocri', 17 February 1567 originated and was repeated, down to Hinschius and my p. 198 n. 102.

p. 165 n. 50: On John XIII's privilege JL 3729 as a forgery, see Fürst, *Cardinalis 146ff.,* H. Zimmermann, *Papstregesten 911-1024* (J.F. Böhmer, Regesta Imperii 2.5; Wien-Köln-Graz 1969) No. †451.

p. 170f.: On the cardinals of St. Paul's, London, add K. Edwards, *The English secular cathedrals* (Manchester 1949) 178, 268, 298.

p. 175 n. 103: On foreign bishops as cardinals see K. Ganzer, *Die Entwick-*
lung des auswärtigen Kardinalats im hohen Mittelalter (Bibl. des Deutschen
Hist. Inst. in Rom 26; Tübingen 1963) 173-204: prior to Alexander III,
cardinal priests consecrated as bishops had to leave the College, and
bishops appointed cardinals had to resign their bishoprics. There were,
however, exceptions: see R. Volpini, 'Additiones Kehriannae (II)', *Riv.*
di storia della Chiesa in Italia 23 (1969) 337 n. 88, 341(-343) n. 96.

p. 189 n. 53: Of the early MSS of John the Deacon listed by Manitius,
Geschichte der lateinischen Literatur des Mittelalters I (Munich 1911) 695, I
have collated Vatican, Arch. S.Petri B.43 (saec. X), which does not bear
out my conjecture (fol. 74v: 'decem & nouem').

p. 192 n. 69: My statement on the proper style of the Roman deacons is
confirmed by an examination of all the references to names of deacons
which Santifaller, *Saggio di un'Elenco* cited *supra*) pp. 684ff. gave in the
index s.v. 'Cardinali della S. Chiesa Romana': none of these sources,
when they are genuine documents, show the style 'cardinalis diaconus'.
In the case of the deacon Gemmulus, for instance (*c.* 738-753),
pp. 240-42, the designation is merely based on a conjecture of M. Tangl,
in his edition of St. Boniface's correspondence (MGH Epp. sel. 1, index
s.v.; also his 'Studien zur Neuausgabe...', *Neues Archiv* 40 [1916] 746f.).

p. 193f.: The authenticity of John VIII's *constitutio de iure cardinalium* (JE
3366) was challenged already by Guillaume Du Peyrat in the seventeenth
century, cf. Fürst, *Cardinalis* p. 72. The 'liber canonum' of the Vatican
Library from which Baronius published the text without giving the shelf-
mark still remains to be found; its copy among the miscellaneous papers
from the circle of the *Correctores Romani* that are bound together in MS
C.24 of the Bibl. Vallicelliana (from the library of Antonio Agustin) has
much deteriorated by acidic action of the ink; it is now partly illegible.
But another text, this time from the thirteenth century, has come to
light: it is one of the many interpolations of the Gratian MS Rouen E.21
(707), see J. Rambaud-Buhot, 'Manuscrits canoniques ques du fonds de
Jumièges: Décret de Gratian', *Jumièges: Congrès scientifique du XIIIe cen-*
tenaire (Rouen 1955) 669-79, at p. 677 n. 21. From the more detailed
information I owe to Mme. Rambaud, it can be concluded that the two
copies of JE 3366 in the 'liber canonum' represented by the Vallicelli-
anus (V) and the Rouen MS from Jumièges (J) are derived from the
same source: both are part of a little twelfth-century collection on cardinals and the clergy of their *tituli,* ten chapters in V, of which cc. 1-6 are
inserted in J after Grat. C.13 q.1 c.1 (fol. 117r). Sequence, inscriptions,
rubrics, incipits, and explicits are identical. This interesting composition
'verdient noch eine genauere Untersuchung', as Paul Kehr remarked
long ago when he edited Urban II's decree 'Quia ut decessor noster' (IP
1 p. 7 no. 11; JL -) from V in 'Nachträge zu den Papsturkunden
Italiens, II', *Nachrichten Ges. der Wiss. Göttingen* 1908 p. 288 (repr. in
Papsturkunden in Italien [Città del Vaticano 1977] V 66). But that

Untersuchung would go beyond the purpose of these pages. We should merely note here that JE 3366 is sectioned in four parts (cc. 2-5 VJ), of which the first is inscribed 'Item (Idem V *ante corr.*) Joannes Octauus (VIIII. J) omnibus cardinalibus cap. iiij.', thereby confirming what could already be guessed from the opening words, 'Itemque ex nostra presenti constitutione...', of the known text: whether genuine or forged, it is not a complete *constitutio.*

p. 198 n. 102: see *supra,* to p. 156.

p. 198 n. 103: The jest of *Gloss. ord.* C.32 q.2 c.1, comparing the Ravenna cardinals to the king of chess, comes from Huguccio *ad loc.*

p. 199: Against my interpretation of *pastoralis cura* in Greg. M. *Reg.* 12.4 as applicable to rectors of baptismal churches as well as bishops, see J.A. Eidenschink, *The election of bishops in the letters of Gregory the Great* (Catholic Univ. of America Canon Law Studies 215; Washington D.C. 1945) 39, who observed that such usage would not correspond to Gregory's vocabulary.

p. 203ff.: On the medieval transmission of the *Constitutum Silvestri:* I should have included the printed texts of the *Regula* of Chrodegang of Metz (for editions and bibliography on the text see Dekkers, *Clavis* no. 1876) c.85, and Alger of Liège, *De misericordia et iustitia* 2.16 (PL 180.93B; cf. Ivo, *Pan.* 4.90a at p. 208). But any revisions or additions to my textual investigation should now have to be made by way of manuscript research, which was not possible when this article was first published in 1945.

X. Dat Galienus opes et sanctio Justiniana

p. 237: An important addition to the vernacular poetry inveighing against the vices of judges, lawyers, and prelates was made by the eminent medievalist who published the poem 'Nouus regnat Salomon in diebus malis: Une satire contre Innocent III', *Festschrift Bernhard Bischoff* (Munich 1971) 372-90, and whose anonymity we shall respect. See especially pp. 379-82 and stanzas 22-31 with commentary. (One may note in passing that stanza 30, after naming several civilian jurists from Bulgarus to Azo, contains in verse 3 'Per hos mundus regitur iure non diuino' an allusion to the opening lines of Gratian, 'Humanum genus duobus regitur, naturali uidelicet iure et moribus'.)

p. 239: The comparison of the student of the arts with a spider that makes its web out of its own entrails is also found in Stephen of Tournai, *ep.* 251 (PL 211.517D; Denifle-Chatelain, *Chartular Univ. Par.*1.48) and, as J.W. Baldwin has pointed out to me, in Gerald of Wales, *Gemma eccles.* 2.37 (*Opera* II 356).

p. 241: The common opinion on Vacarius's having introduced the study of
Roman law in England (Oxford) is now being challenged by R.W.
Southern, 'Master Vacarius and the beginning of an English academic
tradition', *Medieval learning and literature: Essays presented to R.W. Hunt*
(Cambridge 1976) 257-86. This does not affect, however, the importance
of the *Liber pauperum* (of which Karl Wenck's long-lost MS [=W] was
recently rediscovered by P. Stein in Leningrad, see his 'Vacarius and the
civil law', *Church and government in the Middle Ages: Essays presented to
C.R. Cheney [Cambridge 1976] 119-37 at p. 120f.).*

The number of manuscripts containing references to glosses or opinions
of Vacarius could be increased beyond those mentioned p. 242 notes 24
and 25: Vienna MS 2436 fol. 1r/v and London, B.L. Harley 4967, fol. 3v
(see P. Legendre, in *Tijdschrift voor Rechtsgeschiedenis* 29 [1961] 335 n.
17; 33 [1965] 362 n. 49); glosses on the *Ordo Olim edebatur* in Paris B.N.
lat. 3922A (Legendre in *Traditio* 15 [1959] 491 n. 2); the *Summa de dila-
toriis* in Cambridge, Trinity College B.I.29 (P. Weimar in *Ius commune* 1
[1967] 64f.). More work on Vacarius and his place in English legal learning is to be expected in coming years.

General Index

Three special indices follow below. Index 2: Councils and Synods, Index 3: Papal letters, Index 4: Manuscripts. All items in the *Retractationes*, printed here after the last article, are indexed by the number of the article and the page(s) to which they refer, followed by the symbol R (thus III 730R = article No. III, *retractatio* to p. 730.

Aachen: see Aix-la-Chapelle.

Abaelard: I 8; III 729, 730R, 731, 738; IV 67f R; XI 100.

Accursius: VI 76, 96, 98; X 240.

Adalbert of Hamburg-Bremen: VIII 367.

Agobard of Lyons: II 392n R.

Agustín, Antonio: I 1; 102n, 104.

Aix-la-Chapelle: IX 165, 166n, 167, 196n.

Alan of Lille: V 90n; XI 98.

Alanus Anglicus: III 733R; VI 202R, 210; VII 415n, 417n, 419n, 420n, 422n, 424n, 429n, 434-435, 443; see also *Collectio Alani.*

Albertus (canonist):VI 203n, 221.

Albert (St.):VII 432n.

Aleria: IX 133.

Alessio: IX 133.

Alexander II, pope: IV 66; VII 420n R; IX 152, 160n, 164, 175-176, 194.

Alexander III, pope: VI 177-178, 183n, 193-195, 204; VII 418, 433R, 438; IX 175n, 177n.

Alexandria: IX 146n.

Alger of Liège: I 5n R; IV 76, 79-80; IX 203ff .

Ambrose of Milan (St.): VII 411, 416.

Ambrosius (canonist): VI 207n, 227; VII 422n, 448.

Anacletus (Pseudo-): IX 176n.

Anastasius IV, pope: IX 152.

Anastasius Bibliothecarius: II 394; IX 163n.

Anatolius (diaconus): IX 186-188.

Angilramnus: IX 192n, 205-208, 209n.

'Animal est substantia': see *Apparatus Animal est substantia.*

Annales Bertiniani: IX 163n.

Annales Fuldenses: IX 192.

Anno of Cologne (St.): IV 67; VI 183n R.

Ansegisus (*Capitularia regum francorum*): IX 204.

Anselm of Lucca: II 330n, 391, 399n; IV 73-84, 81; IX 149n, 174n, 205, 208-214; XI 102, 104.

Apostolic Canons: II 395; VII 411, 413, 418.

Apparatus Animal est substantia: III 733-734; VII 416n, 425n, 433n, 434, 445.

Apparatus Ecce vicit leo: VI 6 202, 218, 220; VII 415n, 419n, 422n, 425-428nn, 444.

Apparatus Ius naturale: see Alanus Anglicus.

Apparatus Materia auctoris: VII 419n, 447.

Apparatus Ordinaturus magister: VII 433n; XI 112-113.

Apparatus Seruus appellatur: VII 453R.

Appendix Concilii Lateranensis: VI 197; VII 431n.

Aquileia: IX 154n, 161n, 162.

Arngrímur Jónsson: VIII 371.

Arras: IX 164.

Asti: IX 154n.

Athanasius (Pseudo-): II 399, 401.

Atto , Cardinal: II 394; IX 192n, 204-206, 214.

Index 2 : Councils and Synods

Index 3: Papal Letters

JE 1191: IX 133, 135n.
JE 1197: IX 136n.
JE 1202: IX 136n.
JE 1217: IX 133, 136n.
JE 1228: IX 136n.
JE 1229: IX 136n.
JE 1240: IX 134n.
JE 1285: IX 144.
JE 1311: IX 143n.
JE 1365: IX 141n.
JE 1389: IX 136n.
JE 1390: IX 144.
JE 1391: IX 147n.
JE 1420: IX 134n, 143n.
JE 1513: IX 139n.
JE 1596: IX 134n, 198-199n.
JE 1920: IX 134.
JE †1986: IX 169n.
JE 2264: VII 411n R.
JE 2277: IX 154n.
JE 2633: IX 195n.
JE 2650: IV 66n.
JE 2692: IX 163n.
JE 2723: IV 82.
JE 2764: IV 68n.
JE 2796: IV 81.
JE 2903: IX 137n.
JE 2904: IX 137n.
JE 2945: IX 137n.
JE 3049: IX 137n.
JE 3054: IX 137n.
JE 3271: IV 56f R, 65n, 65n R;
    IX 163n.
JE 3366: IX 173, 193n, 193f R.
JE 3522: II 395n.
JE 4501: IV 66n.
JL 2645: IV 74R.
JL 3729: IX 165n, 165n R.
JL 3783: IX 165n.
JL 3848: IX 151n.
JL 3875: IX 165n.
JL 4177: IX 167n.
JL 4249: IX 165n, 167n.

JL 4271: IX 166n.
JL 4302: IX 176n.
JL 4501: VII 420n R.
JL 4575: VII 418n.
JL 4736: IX 152n R.
JL 4925: IV 66f R.
JL 5208: IV 67n.
JL 5349: IX 198n.
JL 5362: IV 78.
JL 5383: IV 76, 78.
JL 5386: IV 81.
JL 5393: IV 77.
JL 5394: IV 77.
JL 5442: IV 84-85.
JL 5451: IV 75n R.
JL 5472: IX 164n, 165n.
JL 5500: IX 164n.
JL 5512: IX 164n.
JL 5513: IX 164n.
JL 5514: IX 164n.
JL 5518: IX 164n.
JL 5760: V 86n.
JL 5775: IV 78.
JL 5776: IV 78.
JL 6208: IX 166n.
JL †6613a: IV 74.
JL 8882: VI 184n.
JL 9793: IX 152n.
JL 10653: VI 184-185nn.
JL 10886: VI 184n.
JL 11646: VI 185n.
JL 11690: VII 418n.
JL 12201: VI 185n.
JL 12329: VI 185n.
JL 13546: VI 178n, 188, 190,
    210-212.
JL 16395: VI 206n, 224-226.
JL 16411: VI 184n.
JL 16514: VI206n, 224-226.
Po. 126: VII 425n.
Po. 425: VII 425n.
Po. 573: VI 207n.
Po. 1000: VI 207n.

Index 4 : Manuscripts

Durham

Cathedral Library
C.II.1: V 82.

El Escorial

Biblioteca real de San Lorenzo
M.III.3: V 101-102.

Erfurt

Wissenschaftliche Bibliothek
der Stadt
Amplon. quart. 117: III 733; VII 416n.

Florence

Biblioteca Medicea-Laurenziana
S. Croce , Plut. III sin.6: VI 209n.

— Biblioteca Nazionale Centrale
Conv. soppr. G.IV.1736: V 81n.
Conv. soppr. J.III.18: XI: 104n.

Fulda

Hessische Landesbibliothek
D.14: VI 198n, 213f.

Gniezno

Biblioteka Kapitulna
28: XI 114.

Göttingen

Universitätsbibliothek
159: XI 95n, 97, 111.

Grenoble

Bibliothèque Municipale
62 (482): VII 453R.

Halle

Universitätsbibliothek

Ye. 80: VII 446.

Laon

Bibliothèque Municipale
371bis: VII 442; XI 95n, 112.

Leipzig

Universitätsbibliothek
983: VII 422n.
986: VI 216; VII 441; XI 112.
Haenel 14: V 78n.
Haenel 18: XI 107-108nn, 113.

Liège

Bibliothèque universitaire
127E: VII 425n, 445; XI 114.

London

British Museum (now British Library)
Cotton Claudius A.IV: VI 196, 213.
Cotton Vitellius A.III: III 730.
Cotton Vitellius E.XIII: VI 196, 197n, 213f.
Harleian 980: IX 171n.
Harleian 4967: X 241R.
Royal 11.A.II: III 735.
Addit. 24569: VII 440; X 241-242.

— Lambeth Palace
105: VII 446.

Lucca

Biblioteca Capitolare Feliniana
124: IX 163n.
490: IX 190n.

Metz

Bibliothèque Municipale
250 (destroyed): V 80n.

Vienna

Oesterreichische Nationalbibliothek
lat. 212: V 78n.
lat. 411: VII 410R.
lat. 575: V 102.
lat. 2121: V 92-93.
lat. 2125: III 731; V 85-87.
lat. 2176: V 94n.
lat. 2197: VII 453R.
lat. 2436: X 241R.

Wroclaw

Biblioteka Uniwersytecka
IV.39: V 104.

Zwettl

Stiftsbibliothek
162: VII 418n, 447.